Overlanders'
HANDBOOK

A ROUTE & PLANNING GUIDE – ASIA, AFRICA, LATIN AMERICA

CHRIS SCOTT

TRAILBLAZER PUBLICATIONS

The Overland Zone
Selected highlights

ARCTIC

Greenland

Alaska

Iceland

Canada

NORTH
ATLANTIC OCEAN

Norway

Denmark

USA

Ireland UK

France

Germ.

Switz.

Shipping the Darien Gap
The 30,000-mile-long Pan-Am
Highway stops in Panama and
resumes in Colombia. Ship the
vehicle between the two.
Pages 445–447

Morocco and the Sahara
Morocco is a great destination in
its own right – or you can carry
on south over the Sahara and
into West Africa. *Page 407*

Portugal

Spain

Mexico

Cuba

Haiti Dom.
Rep.

Morocco

Algeria

Belize

Western
Sahara

Guatemala Honduras

Mauritania

Mali

Ni

El Salvador Nicaragua

Costa Rica

Panama

Venezuela

Suriname

French Guiana

Senegal

Burkina
Faso

Gambia

Guinea

Guinea
Bissau

Sierra
Leone

Ivory
Coast

Ghana

Togo

Benin

Nige

Colombia

Guyana

Liberia

Galapagos
Islands

Ecuador

Equatorial
Guinea

Trans-Amazon
La Paz to Cayenne; from
the altiplano to the
Caribbean shore, it's downhill
all the way. *Pages 465, 469*

Ecuador and Peru
Get off the Pan-Am to
explore the many rugged
inland routes over the
cordillera and into the
jungle. *Pages 452–456*

Peru

Bolivia

Brazil

Paraguay

West Coast to the Cape
Once out of Nigeria the going
gets tough. The finale is
Angolan visa issues or the
abandoned 'road' through DRC
to Zambia. *Pages 412–419*

SOUTH
PACIFIC OCEAN

Argentina

Uruguay

Chile

Atlantic Cruise
Drive on a Ro-Ro freighter
and cruise from Europe
via West Africa to Uruguay
over a month. *Page 470*

Carretera Austral
Where glaciers and volcanoes
meet the Pacific. When you're
done, hop on a ferry to Puerto
Natales for Tierra del Fuego and
the t-shirt. *Pages 460, 463*

Falkland
Islands

SOUTH
ATLANTIC OCEAN

OCEAN

Caucasus
It's decision time: north,
trans-Caspian or Iran.
Proceed to *page 468*

Russia, Siberia and beyond
Russia and the long road to
Vladivostok, or even Magadan.
Just don't get strafed.
Pages 371-379

Mongolia
Still a raw wilderness of
nomadic grasslands,
mountain and desert
– in Mongolia you are
the road. *Page 402*

Belarus
Ukraine
Romania
Bulgaria   Georgia   Azer-
Greece   Turkey   Armenia baijan   Turkmenistan
Kazakhstan
Uzbekistan   Kyrgyzstan
Tajikistan
Mongolia
Russia
China
N Korea
S Korea   Japan

Syria   Iran   Afghanistan
Lebanon   Iraq
Israel   Jordan   Pakistan   Bhutan
Libya   Egypt   Kuwait   Qatar   Nepal
Saudi   UAE
Arabia   Oman   India
Chad   Sudan   Eritrea   Yemen
South   Djibouti
SAR   Sudan   Ethiopia   Somalia
Bangladesh   Myanmar   Laos
Thailand
Sri   Cam-   Vietnam
Lanka   bodia

Pakistan, India and Nepal
Drive the legendary KKH
and the world's highest roads,
and encounter a Buddhist
culture richer than present-
day Tibet. *Pages 387-397*

Myanmar transit
Thai-restrictions notwithstanding,
the overland route to Singapore
has reopened for business.
Page 401

Uganda
DRC   Kenya
Rwanda   Tanzania
Burundi
Malawi
Zambia   Mozambique
Zim-   Madagascar
babwe
Botswana   Swaziland
South Africa   Lesotho

Malaysia
Singapore
Indonesia
Papua
New
Guinea

Iran and Central Asia
Weave your own 'Silk Route'
through a tapestry rich in
history, landscapes and
hospitality. *Pages 379-388*

The Nile Route
From the Pyramids, across the
Nubian desert and Ethiopia's
Simien Mountains to the plains of
the Serengeti – this is the classic
African adventure. *Pages 420–429*

Australia

INDIAN OCEAN

trailblazer

Tasmania

New
Zealand

Among other things CHRIS SCOTT is an adventure travel writer for whom good transportation is just a means to an end. He's cycled in the Himalaya and Hindu Kush, kayaked off the West Australian coast, packrafted in Scotland, France and Utah, and motorcycled across the Sahara where he's also travelled by bush taxi, truck, 4x4 and camel caravan. Occasionally, he runs tours in the Sahara.

His other titles for Trailblazer are the *Adventure Motorcycling Handbook* and *Morocco Overland*. His other books include the original editions of *The Rough Guide to Australia*, as well as *Desert Travels* and *The Street Riding Years*.

Overlanders'
HANDBOOK

A ROUTE & PLANNING GUIDE
ASIA, AFRICA, LATIN AMERICA
CAR – 4WD – VAN – TRUCK

CHRIS SCOTT

WITH
**Lorraine Chittock, Claire Davies, Doug Hackney
Mark Harfenist, John Higham, Charlie Weatherill**

AND
**Richard Clafton, Bill Eakins, Russ Humphreys
Graham Jackson, Chris Lockwood
John Marano, Jan Rutters, Nick Taylor**

ADDITIONAL MATERIAL BY
**Hugh Bergin, John Bernstein, Mick & Mo Newing
Richard Q, Matt Savage, Toby Savage, James Stephenson**

AND TRIP REPORTS BY
**Gerbert van der Aa, Keelan Bell, Haydon Bend
Tom Flynn & Natasa Dupalo, Dan Grec
Marc Heinzelmann, Gee CM Hurkmans
Fabian Plock & Jasmine Kempe
Pablo Rey & Anna Callau
Roy Rudnick & Michelle Weiss, Emile Waite-Taylor**

TRAILBLAZER PUBLICATIONS

Overlanders' Handbook

Second edition: 2017

Publisher
Trailblazer Publications – The Old Manse, Tower Rd, Hindhead, Surrey, GU26 6SU, UK
info@trailblazer-guides.com www.trailblazer-guides.com

British Library Cataloguing in Publication Data
A catalogue record for this book is available from the British Library

ISBN 978-1-905864-87-4

© Chris Scott 2011, 2017
Text, maps and photographs (unless otherwise credited)
The right of Chris Scott to be identified as the author of this work has been asserted
by him in accordance with the Copyright, Designs and Patents Act 1988

Editor: Clare Weldon
Series Editor: Bryn Thomas
Typesetting: Chris Scott
Layout: Chris Scott
Proofreading: Anna Jacomb-Hood
Cartography: Nick Hill
Graphics: Richard Kemplay & Nick Hill
Index: Patrick D. Hummingbird

Acknowledgements

Along with the production team at Trailblazer, above all I would like to thank the many
contributors of words, pictures and know-how. Without them *OLH2* would be a pretty thin book.

A request

Every effort has been made by the author and the publisher to ensure that the information contained in this book is as up to date and accurate as possible. Nevertheless things are certain to
change; even before the ink is dry. If you notice any changes or omissions that you think should
be included in the second edition of this book or have any other feedback, please email the
author at the website below or via Trailblazer (address on p2).

Warning

Global travel in cars, trucks and vans is unpredictable and can be dangerous.
Every effort has been made by the author, contributors and the publisher to ensure that
the information contained herein is as accurate as possible. However, they are unable
to accept responsibility for any inconvenience, loss or injury sustained by anyone
as a result of the advice and information given in this guide.

overlanders-handbook.com

Photos Front cover: In Cameroon © Marc Heinzelmann
Back cover – Left: © Matthew Kelham. **Right**: © Chris Scott

Printed in China; print production by D'Print (☎ +65-6581 3832), Singapore

CONTENTS

INTRODUCTION   **8**

PART 1: PLANNING AND PREPARATION   **9**
A plan 10 – Which continent 10 – Seasons and Climate 11 – Time and Money 12 – Fuel prices 14 – **Getting information** 15 – Overlanding: what are the alternatives? 16 – Travel documents 18 – Visas 19 – Insurance 21 **Vehicle documents** 22 – Carnet 24 – **Money and currencies** 26 Sponsorship 27 – Credit and debit cards 28

PART 2: CHOOSING A VEHICLE   **29**
What car, van or truck? 30 – Vehicle budget 31 – Regional differences 32 Daily travelling budget 32 – Size of group 32 – Itinerary and duration 33 Space and comfort 33 – Payload 33 – Manual or Auto 36 – Mechanical simplicity 37 – Availability of parts and know-how en route 37 – Build quality 38 – Ground clearance 39 – Shipping limitations 41 – ECUS and CAN bus technology 42 – **Which fuel?** 44 – Diesel engines 44 – Petrol 50 Buying and equipping a vehicle far from home 51 – **Two-wheel drive** 52 Road cars 52 – Vans and people carriers (MPVs) 54 – Cab-over flatbeds 59 Dual-wheel rear axles 61 – Towing trailers 62 – **Recreational vehicles** 64 Motorhomes 65 – Campervans 66 – Demountable cabins 69

PART 3: 4x4s   **73**
The mechanics and electronics of 4WD 75 – 4WD systems 76 Limited-slip differentials 77 – ETCs 78 – **Choosing a 4x4** 79 Wheelbase 80 – Hardtop or station wagon 80 – Tailgates and doors 81 Pickups 81 – **Toyota Land Cruisers** 82 – **Land Rover Defenders** 93 **Trans-Africa with a Puma** *Jan Rutters* 104 – **Land Rover Discovery** 109 Mercedes G-wagens 112 – **Nissan Patrol** 114 – **Double-cab pickups** 115 **AWD trucks** 116 – Ex-NATO trucks 119 – Mercedes Unimog 124 – Iveco Daily and WM/VM90 *Richard Clafton* 127 – Mitsubishi Fuso and Isuzu NPS *John Marano* 129

PART 4: MODIFYING YOUR VEHICLE   **133**
Overland, not overload 134 – Redundancy 134 – **Mechanical assessment** 135 – Engine 136 – Transmission 141 – Undercarriage protection 141 – Suspension 143 – **Tyres and wheels** 147 – Tyre brands 148 Tyre dimensions 148 – Upsizing 151 – Tread 153 – Pumps and compressors 154 – Wheel rims 156 – Spare wheels 157 – **Road-car specific modifications** 158

PART 5: CONVERTING A VEHICLE   **161**
Sleeping, eating, washing 162 – Access and storage 163 – Where to start 163 **Long-range fuel and water** 164 – Fuel range and capacity 164 – Jerricans 165 Long-range fuel tanks 167 – Water tanks 172 – **Where to sleep** 176

PART 5: CONVERTING A VEHICLE (*cont'd*)

Ground tents 178 – Roof tents 179 – Sleeping inside the vehicle 182 Raising or lifting roofs 183 – Mattresses and bedding 184 – Awnings 185 **Packing and storage** 186 – Packing systems 187 – Roof racks and roof bars 192 – **Elementary electrics for overlanders** 195 – Alternators 196 Batteries 197 – Solar power 201 – Calculating electrical consumption 204 Inverters and generators 205 – Camp lighting 207 – **Cooking on the road** 207 – Stoves 209 – Ovens, microwaves and kettles 212 Fridge-freezers 214 – Cooking utensils 216

PART 6: BUILDING A CABIN   218

Grand designs for the open road 219 – **Self-build strategy** 221 – Chassis torsion 224 – The layout 229 – Electrical power supply 230 – Water 230 Heating and ventilation 230 – Shower and toilet 231 – Roof 235 – Storage 236 **Building and mounting a cabin** 237 – Interior layouts 238 – Fabricating the box 238 – Mounting the cabin shell 242 – Insulation and lining 244 Electrics 247 – Plumbing 247 – **Hot and cold running water** *Graham Jackson* 249 – **Cabin cooling and heating** 253

PART 7: LIFE ON THE ROAD   255

Shakedown trip 255 – Culture shock 256 – **Driving abroad** 258 – Women driving alone, *Lorraine Chittock* 262 – **Borders and checkpoints** 264 **Changing money and bargaining** 267 – **Keeping in touch** *Nick Taylor* 269 **Maps and route finding** 271 – GPS & Satnav 274 – Navigation 275 – **Wild Camping** 277 – **Vehicle maintenance and troubleshooting** 279 – Fault diagnosis 280 – Spares list 288 – **Tyre repairs** 289 – **Dirt-road driving** 293 Off-road driving 298 – **Off-road recovery: equipment and techniques** 306 **Single vehicle shipping** *Doug Hackney* 317 – **Health for overlanders** *Claire Davies* 330 – First-aid kit 333 – Accessing healthcare overseas 335 Accidents 336 – Stomach ailments 337 – Heat-related illness 338 – Bites and stings 339 – Malaria 340 – Other common health problems 340 – **When things go wrong** 345 – Road accidents 346 – Robbery 348 – Survival situations 351 – **Honey let's take the kids** *John Higham* 352 – **Taking the dog** *Lorraine Chittock* 358

PART 8: ASIA: ROUTE OUTLINES   364

Planning 364 – **Turkey** 365 – (**Map**: Main overland routes across West Asia 366) – Carnets in Asia 366 – **Middle East** 368 – **Caucasus and the Caspian** 368 – **Russia** 371 (**Map**: Main overland routes across the Russian Far East 378) – **Central Asia** 379 – **Iran** 384 – **Pakistan** 387 (Karakoram Highway 388, Xinjiang transit, western China 391) – **India** 391 – (**Map**: Main overland routes across India and western China 393) – Kashmir and Ladakh 394) – **Nepal and into Tibet** 397 – **China** 398 – **Southeast Asia** 399 (**Map**: Main overland routes across Southeast Asia 400) – **Myanmar** 401, **Mongolia** 402

PART 9: AFRICA: ROUTE OUTLINES 404

Planning 404 – Carnets in Africa 406 – Trans-Africa routes 406 – **North Africa and across the Sahara** 407 – **Morocco to Mauritania** 408 **West Africa** 409 (Senegal, Mali and Burkina Faso 410 – East for Chad or Nigeria 411) – **Western route via DRC** 412 – (**Map**: main overland routes across North Africa 414) – DRC: the congo ferry to Kinshasa 417 **Angola** 418 – **The Nile route** 420 (**Egypt** 420 – **Sudan** 422 – **Ethiopia** 423 Into **Kenya** via Marsabit 424) – **East and Southern Africa** 424 (Into **Kenya** 425 – **Kenya to Tanzania** 426 – **Map**: Main overland routes across Southern Africa 427 – West to **Uganda** and the Rwenzori Mountains 428 South of Tanzania 429 – **Rwanda** and **Burundi** 429 – Tanzania to Zambia 430 – **Zambia** 430 – Tanzania to Malawi 430 – **Malawi** 431 – Zambia to **Botswana** 431 – **Zimbabwe** 431 – Zambia to Zimbabwe via Victoria Falls 432 – Zambia to Zimbabwe via Chirundu 432 – **Mozambique** 433 Zimbabwe to South Africa via Beitbridge 434)

PART 10: LATIN AMERICA: ROUTE OUTLINES 435

Planning 435 – **Mexico and Central America** 436 – (**Map**: Main overland routes across Central & South America 438) – **Belize** 441 – **Guatemala** 441 **Honduras** 442 – **El Salvador** 443 – **Nicaragua** 443 – **Costa Rica** 444 Panama 444) **Shipping around the Darien** 445 – Vehicle release in Cartagena 446 – (**Map**: Main overland routes across South America 448) **South America** with *Mark Harfenist* 449 – Routes in South America 449 **Colombia** 449 **Ecuador** 452 – Ecuador–Peru border 453 – **Peru** 454 – Over the border into Bolivia 456 – **Bolivia** 457 – Descent into Chile 458 **Chile** 459 – **Argentina** 461 – **Uruguay** and **Paraguay** 463 **Venezuela, the Guianas and Brazil** 464 – **The Guianas** 465 (Guyana 465 – Suriname 465 French Guiana 466 – On to northeast Brazil 466) – **Brazil** 467) **Trans-Amazon** north to south 469

APPENDIX

A Short History of Roads   471

ABOUT *THE OVERLANDERS' HANDBOOK* CONTRIBUTORS   475

INDEX   476

INTRODUCTION

Many of us recall the thrill of getting our first cars and the new freedom they gave us. Vehicle-dependent overlanding might be said to recreate that adventurous epiphany, opening up an entire world of new experiences and encounters. It's one that won't require following a tour guide's raised umbrella, or surrendering yourself to the schedules and discomfort of public-transport services as you may have done as a backpacker.

The decision to pack it all in and take off for months or even years in your car, van or truck across the highways of Asia, Africa or Latin America can mark a major turning point in your life. It will also require a daunting amount of research and preparation, not least in the vehicle you choose.

The *Overlanders' Handbook* is the only manual to cover the entire undertaking, from the moment of inspiration through vehicle selection and preparation right up to the practicalities of living on the road.

As the miles roll by, the tyres wear down and the passport fills up, you can be sure that the challenges which initially seemed so daunting will become just another eventful day in your own unfolding road movie.

Enjoy the adventure!

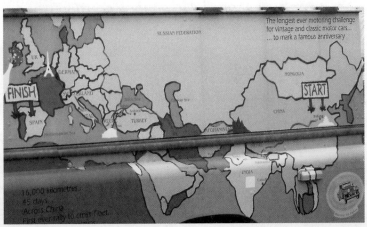

PLANNING & PREPARATION

1

The decision to undertake a long overland journey in a vehicle can germinate from a moment's inspiration, a decision to take on 'the Big Trip' after a successful series of lesser journeys, or just the plain old desire to cut loose from the regimented lives many of us lead and have a big adventure.

Within a few pages you'll discover the mushroom effect of taking on such a venture. Choosing and preparing a vehicle might take up the lion's share of your time and the budget, but realigning your dream itinerary with the reality of visas, borders and regional security issues also takes a huge amount of research. And the situation won't stop once you're on the road, so the planning is never really over until the journey is complete. The more you learn the more there is to consider until you get to a magical point where, however briefly, you're ahead of the game. If you're very lucky, that moment of overlanding nirvana will coincide with your departure.

The extent of preparation varies between individuals. Some will want a waypoint for every fuel station and booked accommodation. Others will be satisfied with a good map, some guidebooks and a loose schedule for any visa applications that must be made en route. You need to find a level of preparation that satisfies you and gives you enough confidence in a venture that'll always have elements of unpredictability.

Getting the right **paperwork and visas** and sorting out your **money** are tedious but vital. It's common to worry about carrying masses of cash and acquiring visas or motor insurance on the road. Without just one of the several documents listed in this section, your trip will eventually grind to a halt, but the two key items are and always will be a passport and the ownership documents for your vehicle.

Do yourself a favour and set off knowing that, whatever happens, you've done all the preparation you hoped to do. The more effort you put into planning, the smoother your trip is likely to be.

You need to find a level of preparation that satisfies you and gives you enough confidence in a venture that'll always have elements of unpredictability.

PLANNING & PREPARATION

A plan

Before the preparation comes **a plan**, an outline of the regions and destinations you'd like to visit. It's not uncommon initially to come up with a certain romantic flow or theme: following the Silk Road to Beijing, tracking the Pan American Highway to Cape Horn or setting off in an old Land Rover as your parents may have done before you came along. Then you discover there's no single 'Silk Road', the Pan-Am is impassable between Panama and Colombia, and these days modern 4WDs, including Land Rovers, are a lot more comfortable than they used to be.

Compared to the life you've been leading up to now, life on the road will be unpredictable and requires flexibility.

This is just the start. If you make it to p363 your expertise in the whole project will have multiplied exponentially. A few edges may have been knocked off your starry dream too, but you'll be in much better shape to take on what lies ahead.

Once you've got over that possible disappointment there comes another shock that can be paraphrased from the Prussian military strategist Helmuth von Moltke's famous quote: 'no plan survives contact with the road'. It's hard to imagine not having some sort of outline before you leave, if only to avoid undesirable interruptions and expenses. But sooner or later that original **schedule** gets derailed. It's rare to leave on your original departure date, so don't set this in stone. Compared to the life you've been leading up to now, life on the road will be unpredictable and requires flexibility.

Above all be wary of **over-ambitious goals**, or anticipate them and be happy to return home having done much less than you planned but still satisfied. Even in the right season (see opposite) most first-time overlanders greatly **underestimate** the time it takes to cover ground in parts of Asia and Africa, let alone the much under-rated value of simply slowing down.

To want to try and see it all is understandable when you consider the cost and effort you're making to get this far, but once you're inching out of a Far East container depot into the chaos of the city, or rolling off the end of a sealed highway into a remote area of tracks, reality bites. Sitting at the sharp end of your adventure, it then runs around and jabs you in the butt and your trans-continental expedition, unparalleled since the sweeping hordes of Genghis Khan, crumples like a paper cup. The good thing is: you're there.

WHICH CONTINENT?

Assuming most of us come from affluent countries of the developed West – North America, Europe, Southern Africa and Australasia – certain **classic overland routes** present themselves. They're sketched in each of the three Route Outline maps for **Africa** (pp414-5 & p427), **Asia** (pp366-7) and **Latin America** (pp438-9 & p448), with an overview map in the colour section.

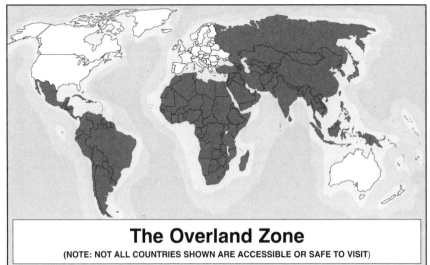

The Overland Zone
(NOTE: NOT ALL COUNTRIES SHOWN ARE ACCESSIBLE OR SAFE TO VISIT)

PLANNING & PREPARATION

It's worth comparing these three big continents in terms of difficulty. Assuming you live there, **European departures** offer the most overland options, with both Asia and Africa accessible without getting bogged down in shipping (the latter only by the Straits of Gibraltar at the moment). From Europe, the northern route across **Asia** reaches over to Far Eastern Russia. The southern route runs via India and now continues overland via Burma (with escorts) to Southeast Asia. China remains a special case – see p398. The southern route to India can be comfortably done in a normal car with as few as four visas.

Alternatively, departing from Europe you can head down the length of **Africa**, typically ending at the Cape of Good Hope. With the situations in Libya and Syria blocking overland access to Egypt, Africa still represents a challenge, a real adventure both in terms of riding conditions, visa acquisition, security and even expense.

Many overlanders not from North America choose to start their transit of **Latin America** above the Arctic Circle in Alaska to end it some 25,000km (15,000 miles) later in Tierra del Fuego, just 1000km (600 miles) from the Antarctic mainland. Assuming you follow the easiest route, Latin America is the least challenging of the three big continental routes in terms of paperwork, road infrastructure and languages, while offering as impressive scenic and cultural attractions as anywhere, particularly in the Andean countries.

If you're intent on **ringing the globe**, shipping across the oceans that separate these continents is easily done from certain key ports described on p325.

SEASONS AND CLIMATE
The season and expected weather at certain key stages of your route must be factored in; it's still a wild planet out there. Seasons and the climate can be anticipated (🖥 worldclimate.com); the actual weather on a given day cannot. In regions where the road infrastructure cannot deal with these extremities,

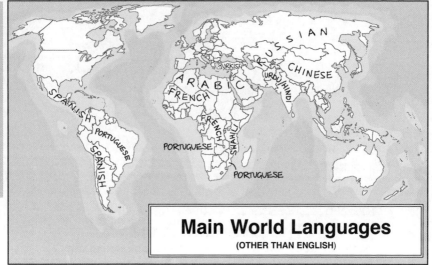

Main World Languages
(OTHER THAN ENGLISH)

progress may be slow or briefly impossible. At other times, even if the driving is straightforward, extreme temperatures can make simple survival a challenge. The Sahara is a good example; it's no hotter than the interior of Australia, Pakistan or Arizona in **summer**, but driving alone on anything other than the main trans-desert highways can become unnerving, even with the air-con on full blast.

To head blithely across northern Asia or into the Andes in **winter**, or the equatorial regions of the Amazon or Congo basin in the **wet season**, is also asking for trouble. Ironically, in Far Eastern Russia (as in northern Canada), some ice roads only exist in winter, following the courses of deeply frozen rivers able to support 20-ton trucks. Whether you're equipped to manage such conditions is another matter.

By and large Himalayan passes over 4000m (13,100ft) are closed from the end of October until late spring, while in the Congo Basin transportation takes to the rivers at the height of the rains and can be a fun interlude if there's room for a vehicle.

TIME AND MONEY

Once the spark has been lit, assuming you're beginning preparations while in full-time employment, organising a trans-continental journey for the first time requires up to **a year**. If you're just taking an exploratory nibble into one continent, six months will do. Preparing to explore a wilderness region within your own country may only require a few weeks of planning and, as you'll soon learn, doing so as a test-trip prior to the Big Day is a very good idea.

Ask yourself how much of a commitment you want to make to your overland adventure. Do you have an urge to see some distant part of the planet, but still like the idea of returning to a job and house? Or are you ready to throw the dice and take an entirely new direction in your life for several

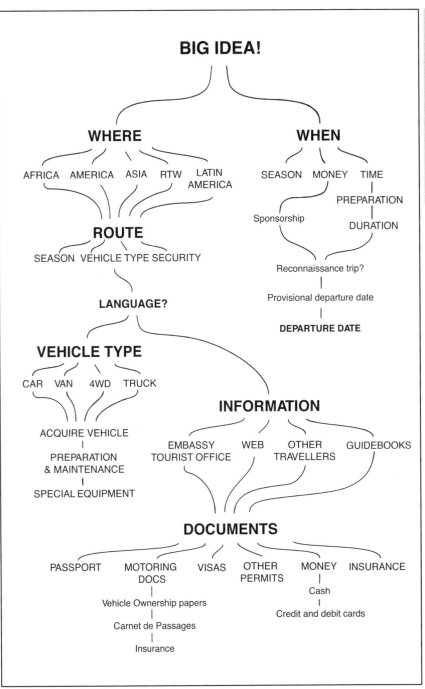

months or even years? If heading into an unknown future, having enough money (or the means to make some) will help in dealing with predictably unpredictable events. If you're organised you ought to be able to **calculate an average daily expenditure** fairly closely. How precisely you need to plan your budget will depend on whether you've cut loose from life back home, whether you'll still have some sort of income while on the road – like rent or a pension for example – or if you've given yourself a set amount of money or time to undertake the journey.

Assess carefully if you have the will and opportunity to put the money together in the time you've given yourself – let alone to be on the road for months. To cross Africa expect to **budget** on at least £4000 or US$5000, in addition to the cost of your vehicle. The expense of the carnet and some visas apart (see p20 and p24), Asia can be cheaper. You could probably drive from Europe to India for around £3000 or $4000. To cross the length of the Americas costs at least as much as Africa, and a genuine round-the-world (RTW) trip is going to set you back around £11,000 or $15,000, mostly in fuel and freighting your vehicle from one continent to the next. Some people will achieve the above for less, most will spend a lot more, but these estimates account for at least some of the unplanned expenses that most trips encounter.

FUEL PRICES AROUND THE WORLD

With the price of fuel in Europe being typically two to three times more expensive than in North America, the **cost of motoring** and with it vehicle choice is deeply ingrained in our regional mentality. In the US a diesel SUV doing 25mpg is pretty damn good; in Europe it's not something to celebrate. This has led to the development of small, fuel-efficient diesel engines that aren't even sold in the US, where readers might think 'Cost of fuel? Who cares!'. In Europe, on the other hand, we're obsessed with **fuel economy**.

Fuel prices vary staggeringly around the world, from a couple of cents a litre for diesel in Venezuela and Iran (a fraction of the price of the crude oil from which it is actually refined), to at least double the fuel's true value. Extreme subsidisation in a dozen or so countries and heavy taxation in many more is what explains this dramatic variation.

At around $2.30 a US gallon (or 77 US cents per litre), the **price of fuel in the US** (gasoline and diesel) can be considered average by international standards, neither amazingly cheap nor punitively expensive, including as it does a reasonable 15% in tax. Compared with the US, many countries in Africa with low GDPs tax fuel extremely highly, as do the UK, Ireland, Netherlands and Norway.

For overlanders this has the biggest impact when the size and what might be called the 'touristic desirability' of a given country in the overland zone are all taken into consideration. The **cost of fuel in a neighbouring country** has an impact too, especially where fuel is as much as eight times more expensive across the border. Filling up a lorry tank in Venezuela rather than Brazil, Iran rather than Turkey or Egypt before Israel could save a packet. Among others, the website 🖳 globalpetrolprices.com graphically displays the recent prices of diesel and petrol around the world.

Getting information

You may well have a lot to learn, particularly regarding information about routes and border regulations; this book was probably out of date long before the ink was dry so here are the most likely sources of up-to-date information.

ONLINE

Everything you need to know (including the contents of this book rearranged and repeated ad infinitum) is online. The trouble is it's spread all over cyberspace like the Milky Way; the task is to track down what you need sometime before the Milky Way implodes.

Though it's motorcycle based, the Horizons Unlimited Bulletin Board, aka the **HUBB** (🖥 horizonsunlimited.com/hubb) is a great place to start. Its dozen **regional forums** (North Asia, sub-Saharan Africa, etc) cover topics that relate to all wheeled travellers and a day or two browsing the HUBB will answer many questions as well as raise many you'd not thought of. Nothing else in English comes close to its truly global reach although the 🖥 **ioverlander.com** app seems to be catching on. Please contribute usefully to both.

Lonely Planet's **Thorn Tree** (🖥 thorntree.lonelyplanet.com) isn't vehicle-oriented, but has border and route details, and for a North American perspective the **Expedition Portal** (🖥 expeditionportal.com/forum) is a good source of Latin American reports, but remains more useful for opinions on locally sourced vehicles and equipment. A portal linking to overland travellers' websites (now from all over the globe, despite the name) is the **Africa Overland Network** (🖥 africa-overland.net). Although quite a few of the older linked websites have expired, wherever you're going and whatever you're planning, someone is probably doing something similar.

GOVERNMENT OVERSEAS DEPARTMENTS

More useful to you than a country's tourist office is the opinion of your country's foreign ministry. In the UK it's the Foreign & Commonwealth Office (FCO) Travel Advice Unit; in the US it's the Department of State; and the French Ministère des Affaires Étrangères is better than most for the Francophone countries of Africa.

In Britain at least, the lazier end of the travel media has a habit of taking the FCO's advice as gospel. The FCO has got much better at acknowledging that distant or outdated threats need not write off a whole country, but like all these agencies they're primarily concerned with avoiding international incidents involving their nationals, if not discouraging casual visits to countries with whom political relations may be strained. Take everything these advisories say with a pinch of salt and accept that politics and convenience inevitably colours their advice. At the same time be warned that many **travel insurance** providers (see p21) won't offer cover for countries deemed unsafe by the FCO or its equivalent. There is more on this subject in 'When Things Go Wrong' on p345.

VEHICLE-DEPENDENT OVERLANDING – WHAT ARE THE ALTERNATIVES?

For those intending to make an overland journey as described in this book, the **vehicle** is the key element, which is why so many pages are given over to choosing, preparing and using a vehicle. Other, more general, travel information is knee-deep in any good bookstore or online.

Although it's not fashionable to admit it, humans love driving cars. We may well enjoy rollerblading, horse riding and hiking too, but as a practical means of getting about and carrying stuff in all weathers, a motorised cart ticks most of the boxes. There are drawbacks of course and hidden costs both to ourselves and the **environment**. According to one website, driving from London to Sydney in a Land Cruiser Prado puts out as much CO_2 as flying there. Other costs include the **expense** of running a car across continents, the relatively passive and **insulated** experience of travelling the world in your own steel bubble, and the psychological burden of running a conspicuous vehicle that houses all you have. Vehicle-dependent overlanding is not for everyone and can at times be quite a millstone, but as a way of seeing the world what are the credible alternatives?

Joining an **organised overland tour** in a converted lorry is a great way of minimising costs and avoiding the more burdensome responsibilities of planning and executing a long trip; plus you'll be in the company of what will hopefully prove to be a like-minded gang. This is what many people understand as 'overlanding', rather than the somewhat clumsy but more precise 'vehicle-dependant overlanding' that we're on about in this book. Overland tours appeal particularly to those young women and older travellers who are nervous about doing a long journey alone but still want an adventure. At the cost of independence and spontaneity, you get the camaraderie, an experienced operator dealing with all the logistics and a guide and driver who knows the ropes. An overland tour may well bring you together with your future spouse, or it may generate a vow never to travel like that again!

Backpacking around the world gives you more independence than joining a truck tour, but without your own wheels you're still quite restricted. With a sarong and an LP in your pack, you can travel as most of the developing world does – in bush taxis, over-crowded buses, slow trains and on river boats. It's a great way to meet people, primarily other backpackers, and experience a foreign culture without spending a fortune. However, backpackers often find themselves in the same tramlines that every other backpacker is following, using the same guidebook, and this can get wearying. Moving on entails either negotiating chaotic bus stations or taking day tours offered by the local backpackers' haunt. It's difficult, expensive and maybe even risky to break away from the tramlines. When you're young and inexperi-

enced it can be fun to be part of the crowd for a few weeks. After a while you may want something more.

Disregarding walking the earth with a beast of burden (actually more complicated than it sounds in this post-medieval era) you're left with **motorcycling** and **cycling** (Trailblazer also produce guides to overlanding for this, see end of book). In most cases you won't consider either unless you're an enthusiast, but for those who don't ride there's a romance and coolness associated

with motorcycles that might be akin to a cowboy on his horse. Motos give you the satisfaction of being out in the breeze, but without the pedal-bashing effort of a bicycle. They also enable you to leave sealed highways which on a loaded cycle escalates the effort considerably. On a good day riding a motorcycle in the overland zone is more exhilarating than doing the same in a car; as bikers like to say 'you're in the movie, not watching it [through a windscreen]'.

The price for all this freedom is the **exposure** and **risk**. No two ways about it, crashing a motorcycle hurts more than crashing a Mercedes Sprinter with wrap-around

airbags. Most motorcyclists know a rider who's been killed, although holidaymakers who are inexperienced riders are much more at risk hiring a twist-and-go scooter in places like Greece or Thailand. Just as with driving, it's unlikely you'll set off overland without a few years' riding experience, and all those years will stand you in good stead dodging traffic in foreign lands not accustomed to the speed of big motorcycles.

Cyclists share with motorcyclists the thrill and the pain of being out there; you might smell the flowers and hear the birds, but you'll also get smacked in the face by the bees as well as sunburned and wind chilled. At the end of a hard day there's nowhere to crawl into and lie down until you've pitched a tent, by which time you can be too tired to cook.

In the right environment, cycling can be the ideal form of adventurous overland travel but some places like Kazakhstan, eastern Russia, the Sahara or Patagonia can be just too dull at 10mph into the wind. More

culturally or scenically diverse regions with a network of quiet roads, manageable infrastructure and a tolerable climate would be ideal: somewhere like southern Asia. Where motorised overlanding is restricted, such as China, a bike is the best way to see the country on your own terms. My brief travels in High Asia on a bicycle cost far less than getting there by car or on a motorbike – an inexpensive way of reconnoitring a place I'd like to go back to.

Not only are bikes mechanically simple and culturally unintrusive, they can also be flung on to the back of a passing lorry when you've had enough; cyclists are also happily immune from the tedious documentation that comes with any vehicle requiring a licence to operate it. There will be days when a driver dreams of that kind of freedom and unobtrusive profile.

So, despite all the headaches, a car or truck's advantages add up to **mobility and independence**, along with security – a little house on wheels. Sure you may miss out on the wind-in-your-hair thrill of two-wheeling, but a four-wheeler's payload means you can explore wilderness areas unhurriedly or even spend time there, an aspect of overlanding that's hard to achieve by other means.

Back home most of us own cars and vans for their practicality, and the same applies to overlanders. A mobile home requires less physical endurance than two-wheeling and offers a level of independence, comfort and range that you don't get when touring or backpacking. For most travellers in search of a long-term adventure, that's a good thing.

NATIONAL MOTORING ORGANISATIONS

Again not a lot of help for the aspiring overland adventurer, but sometimes useful on documentation and essential when it comes to coughing up for a Carnet de Passage (see p24). In the UK now, an International Driving Permit is all the **RAC** or **AA** can do for you, though, to be fair, overlanding is such a minority form of motoring, you can't expect them to devote too many resources to it.

TRAVEL GUIDEBOOKS

Although users often grumble about their inaccuracies or opinions, for what it costs, a guidebook will repay you in advice and recommendations many, many times over. Lonely Planet and Rough Guides are the two best-known series in English; the former covers just about every country on the planet, but both have their origins in the backpacker or independent traveller market, not overlanders. Because of this you'll find only the most general advice on driving, and accommodation offering secure parking is an example of a commonly overlooked detail.

In the place of guidebooks, be they used paper copies for a penny on Amazon, or more practical e-book versions, **Trip Advisor** (💻 tripadvisor .com/forums) has become the world's most visited travel website. For a traveller it'll be most useful in the users' accommodation recommendations when faced with too great a choice in a foreign city. Very often knowledgable expats also contribute to the website's forums.

ONCOMING TRAVELLERS

Don't overlook the likelihood and usefulness of running into travellers coming from where you're going. You couldn't ask for a more up-to-date source of information unless you're bitten by the horse's mouth itself. They'll be able to assuage your current anxieties about fuel prices, road conditions and the friendliness or otherwise of border officials, and, likely as not, will be as keen to hear your news too.

Travel documents

For any journey covering half a dozen countries or more, visas are something you need to address at the very start of your planning because they can take weeks and occasionally even months to arrange and so will have a vital impact on your departure date and maybe even your route. With some visas starting from the date they're issued or only available in your home country, this sort of planning ahead is easier said than done.

PASSPORT

If you don't yet own a passport, get onto it straight away. If you already own one, make sure it's **valid for at least six months** after your anticipated journey's end, better still a year. Many countries won't issue visas for passports that have less than six months left to run. As ever, by ensuring that your passport has plenty of use left in it (as well as actual pages), you're one step ahead of some awkward border official. Once you get your passport, check all the details. Discrepancies between it and your other vital documents, even just the misspelling of one word or date, can be all the excuse someone needs to bring your day to a premature stop.

Many countries issue so-called **'diplomatic' passports** with up to double the number of pages for frequent overseas travellers. Visas acquired in advance tend to fill a whole page and anyone who's travelled in Africa will know how officials love to 'mark their territory' by slapping a blurred triangular stamp bang in the middle of a blank page. Count on each country that requires **a visa taking up two pages** in your passport. At this rate the 23 usable pages of a standard British passport won't go so far on a round-the-world trip.

Although they don't exactly shout it from the rooftops, in Britain at least it's possible to get a **second passport**. The Passport Office will want a good reason; the most convincing is to explain you need to make protracted visa applications en route during which time you'll also need your other passport to cross borders. Better still is to somehow tie it in with your work. If your request is sound and you have documentary evidence, a second passport may be issued without a fuss. Dual nationality – passports in your name from two countries – isn't the same thing but can be as useful. It's better never to declare to an immigration official that you're travelling with two passports or under two nationalities, chances are it's not legal but as you'll soon learn, what is considered legal in one territory and what is actually useful or permitted don't always overlap.

VISAS

A visa is a temporary immigration permit allowing nationals of one country to visit another. Some countries (very often neighbouring) don't require a visa at all, others will issue one at the border allowing a stay up to a certain period, usually a month or 90 days. Some countries require visas to be secured **in advance** and it's these that'll make up the bulk of your bureaucratic headaches and can govern the pace and direction of your travels. Brits and Americans will have few visa hassles in Latin America, but across Africa or Central Asia anyone might end up paying hundreds in **visa fees**. Very often the onerous demands and associated delays are down to similar regulations imposed on that country by your country, or an antipathy towards your country that has its origins in colonial times; it's something that Brits and Americans experience more than, say, Canadians or Irish.

Applying for a visa

Some visas **start** from the day of issue, others require the exact date and place that you expect to arrive at a border – something hard to pinpoint when there's 950 miles of desert, jungle and yeti-infested mountains between you and that place. Still others have no set entry date, just a certain amount of time before their validity expires. You need to understand the difference between this **validity** – say three months before you must begin using the visa by entering the county– and the **duration** of a visa, typically 30 days. At some borders where a visa in advance is essential, just turning up may get one issued on the spot or a pass to get a visa in the nearest city.

Don't expect to get all your visas nicely sorted out before you go. Instead, work out as closely as you can where you'll pass a consulate for your next country. (Very often the websites of previous overlanders will spell out the routine.) On a trans-continental trek this need to **apply for visas as you go** will be a game of careful timing and anticipated arrival dates that'll mould your itinerary. You may find yourself racing across a country or taking a thousand-mile detour just to be sure you can gain entry to your next destination. Crossing Africa down the west side, for example, once out of Nigeria (and depending on your nationality), the need to acquire a succession of visas across the western Congo basin will dominate the journey and, for some, will culminate in what can be just a few days to get across Angola.

When applying back home, consider using a **visa agency**. Though pricey, these agencies earn their money by providing a speedy postal service as well as doing the queuing and applying for you. They can make getting visas from consulates not represented in your country much easier and they may also be clued up on tricks or procedures that can help facilitate a successful application. Even for relatively straightforward applications, an agency can save you valuable time if you're busy working or live far away from the capital, where consulates are usually located.

As a rule, avoid **business visas**: they're more expensive and risk awkward questions on arrival. Russia is known as an exception. Stick to simple, innocuous **tourist visas**.

Before applying for any visa find out:
- What other documentation apart from your passport must you present on application? Besides a handful of passport photos, this might also include bank statements or other evidence of funds, letters of introduction or onward travel tickets.
- How to pay? Many consulates are very specific about the currency.
- How long do you have before you need to use the visa (typically from one month to a year)?
- Is the visa easily renewable or extendable, and if so for how long?
- Can you easily get a **multiple-entry visa** (which often have longer validities), enabling you to make excursions to neighbouring countries?

Visa problems

All you can do is give yourself plenty of time do deal with **problems**, expect those problems to crop up and have a Plan B to Z. Without experience it's hard to know this in advance, but don't underestimate your ability to deal with problems en route; it's one of the key lessons learned from this sort of travelling. Remember that countless others have succeeded in traversing the same route; they've all worked it out – by using their wits, being flexible and, as a last resort, offering an 'incentive'. So can you.

It must be remembered that having a visa won't guarantee you entry into that country; if they don't like you for whatever reason, the rules have changed or something is wrong with your paperwork, you'll be turned away. And being sent back to a country that's just officially wished you *bon voyage* can be tricky.

Although what appears above might seem like a rigid set of **rules** created to discourage international travel, these rules can get usefully mushy once on the road: expired visas need not mean a firing squad at dawn (but could mean a big fine). Not nailing the aforementioned transit of Angola from DRC down to Namibia in record time can cost you $70 or just a scowl, but in Russia you'll be in the doghouse.

Take visas seriously but recognise that once on the road, the further you are off the beaten track anything goes; this is where the fluid interpretation of laws and regulations in the Overland Zone can work in your favour. If you happen to stumble into a country via an **unmanned border**, present yourself at the nearest police station unless you're leaving soon in the same clandestine manner.

A word of warning: most of the countries in the Overland Zone are paranoid about their security and very often have tense relationships with their neighbours. Accusations of being 'a spy' might seem absurd, but might well be taken very seriously, especially if you happen to turn up in a country without proper documentation.

LOCAL PERMITS

Once you're on the road, **additional documentation** will be gleefully issued by local officials for any number of reasons (mainly to get more money out of you, or 'fine' you for not having it). Typical examples include registering with the police within so many days of arrival, photography and filming permits (although a tiny modern camcorder is often immune to these), 'tourist registration cards', currency declaration forms, and permits to cross 'forbidden' areas such as China, Egypt's Western Desert or tribal homelands/reserves. As these are the sorts of places where police roadblocks are frequent, not getting one of the required permits may cost you more in the long run.

As much as following correct procedure, paperwork is a game of wits as well as an opportunity for corrupt officials to create difficulties that can only be solved with a **bribe**. By at least starting your journey with proper documentation you'll have a good chance of getting well underway without unnecessary hassles until you learn the ropes and find out what you can and can't get away with.

TRAVEL AND MEDICAL INSURANCE

For what it costs, travel insurance covering you to an adequate level can set your mind at ease. Ordinary travel insurance that can come free with your credit card may offer 'package holiday' cover but is unlikely to cover a fraction of the cost of an evacuation from Bolivian altiplano. While getting travel insurance for anything involving a car is much easier than for motorbikes, it's best to approach insurance companies who specialise in **adventurous activities**. A recent online quote from a UK specialist for a three-month trans-African trip including 'Level 1' activities came to £150. Including North America and the Caribbean would cost another £20.

Be sure your insurers understand the nature of your intended trip and where you're going. As well as covering you for robbery, cancellation and lost baggage, travel insurance also includes **medical cover and repatriation** – realistically the most vital component. The worst-case scenario is getting yourself evacuated by air from some remote spot and requiring intensive medical care.

Along with admitting to any previous **medical history**, which the insurers may dig up anyway, it's vital to obtain travel insurance that's compatible with your mode of travel and the regions you'll visit. In the UK, many insurers won't offer cover for countries that are on the FCO 'black list' – countries where your government advises against all travel – or if they do it won't be valid. Right now on the FCO website there is a short list of countries that you can guess from watching the news. There follows, however, a very long list advising against all travel *to parts of* nearly half the countries in the world, all but a few of which are covered in this book.

If you're a European in Africa, most medical emergencies involve **repatriation**, which is where the greater expense can lie. As a European or US national in Central or South America, the US might end up as your ultimate destination if you need urgent medical treatment. Anything involving repatriation to the US, even from neighbouring Mexico, could run in to six figures so it's vital that you have sufficient medical cover: £500,000 may sound like an astronomical sum but is just a starting point, £1m ($1.5m) is better. Make sure this figure covers *everything* to do with an accident, including medivac, ambulances, hospitalisation and possible surgery.

Remember too that to get an insurance claim underway you must first make that all-important phone call to the country where the policy was issued. When you receive your policy, find this **telephone number**, highlight it and write it clearly somewhere obvious and easy to get to; in your wallet or passport and behind the sun visor. This way you can direct someone to ring the number if you can't do so yourself. For more on what to do in a dire emergency see p345.

Vehicle documents

Travelling overland in your own vehicle might seem a fairly innocuous activity: you arrive, drive around for a bit and drive away. Unfortunately, just as with visas, a bureaucracy of **paperwork** developed early on in the history of the motor car and these days in some places it's easier to import a gun. The explanation might be that in many developing countries a vehicle is a highly prized commodity whose ownership is restricted by swingeing import taxes.

Of all the documentation required, the **carnet** presents the biggest burden in financial terms, while getting **third-party insurance** is simply not always possible and so not something to worry about until you have an accident.

You'll accumulate a whole lot of additional paperwork at various borders, mostly to do with temporary vehicle importation or driving permits. Keep it all until you're in the next country, even if you don't know what half of it's about. Now is the time to invest in a wallet that expands like an accordion.

With all the documentation listed below you need to establish early on:
- What papers you already have
- What additional items are needed before you leave
- What others you can get on the road

You also need to know:
- How long it'll take to get what you don't have
- How much it will all cost

VEHICLE OWNERSHIP DOCUMENT

Your **vehicle ownership document** is much more important than a driver's licence and will be used and inspected so many times you may want to laminate it. In the UK it's called a 'logbook' or, officially, a vehicle registration document (VRD); the US has a state registration document as well as a 'title' or ownership document. In French it's a *carte grise*, in Hispanic Latin America it's a *titular* and in Russian it's your *svidelstvo* or *registratsii avtomashiny*. The lingua franca is of course, 'Papers!', with or without a 'Halt!' beforehand.

Having a vehicle ownership document that's **not in your name** isn't always the problem. All you need is a good story and an official-looking letter from the owner in the local language(s) – official-looking stamps help too.

At many borders you'll need to present your passport and vehicle documents simultaneously. It's crucial that the details on the ownership/registration document, particularly **the chassis and engine numbers** (aka 'VIN'), match those on your vehicle and carnet, if applicable. Outside Latin America photocopies may not be good enough, but a duplicate is always handy. If your vehicle has had a replacement engine, check those numbers or risk losing all to some nit-picking official down the track.

The reason for these elaborate checks is to ensure you've not committed the cardinal crime against humanity of secretly selling your vehicle, or even part of it, in the country concerned. Even slightly damaged engine or chassis numerals may be grounds for raising complications. To you the very idea of selling your dream mobile home is absurd, but because of punitive import taxes, locals go to extreme lengths to fit a desirable foreign-registered model onto a local chassis with the right papers. It explains why you see so many clapped-out cars in some developing countries.

I also find that it helps to **highlight your Vehicle Identification Number** (VIN; usually the same as the chassis number) on your vehicle ownership document. This is what the Customs guy will be looking for amongst all the other details, so it helps speed things up. It also doesn't hurt to sign your ownership document somewhere, even if you don't need to.

DRIVING LICENCE, IDP AND ICMV

Like your passport, your **driving licence** ought to show correct (or, at least, consistent) information with other documentation and be valid long after your trip expires. In the UK your driving licence lasts till you're 70, elsewhere in the world they're valid for as little as a year. If you expect to be on the road for longer than that and renewing it is not possible by post, making a good facsimile is a way round it.

If your licence doesn't show your photograph, it should be supplemented with an **International Driving Permit** (IDP) which does. These multi-lingual translations of your domestic driving licence last a year or more and can be picked up by presenting your domestic licence plus a photo or two at your local motoring organisation's office. In the UK an IDP costs just £5.50 from selected post offices or a bit more from the RAC.

IDPs are not an 'international driving licence' and aren't usually mandatory, but in **Asia** they're especially useful and in Latin America officials will often ask to see your driving licence, something that's rarely demanded in Africa. You may never have to show your IDP, but **be on the safe side and get one**. With their official-looking stamps they can double-up as another important document with which to dazzle a semi-literate official.

There are **two main IDPs** covering different territories. The '1968 convention' (amended 2011) has been ratified by 72 states and the '1949 convention' was ratified by 96 states. A '1926' IDP covers Iraq and Somalia but as no one's going there the 1968 and 1949 IDPs will cover you for the whole planet; the latter will greatly ease entry into Thailand (see p401).

If your vehicle is rated at **over 3500kg gross vehicle weight** (GVW; more on p33), make sure your IDP vehicle-class categories indicate that you're entitled to drive vehicles above this weight (as well as any other entitlements that might be handy such as **motorcycles**). It should be 'C' on the 1949 version. Your regular driving licence may show it, but only the IDP's multi-lingual translations will make sense abroad. No upper GVW limit is indicated on IDPs.

An **International Certificate for Motor Vehicles** (ICMV) is to your vehicle registration document what an IDP is to your driving licence; a multilingual translation issued by motoring organisations (in the UK the AA and RAC do them for £5.50) for countries that don't recognise or can't read the original. It's especially useful in Russia and Mongolia.

CARNET DE PASSAGES EN DOUANE (CPD)

A carnet (or CPD) is an internationally recognised temporary importation document that allows you to bring your vehicle into participating countries without having to deposit duties or pay fees with customs officials. To get a CPD requires lodging a deposit related to the value of your vehicle with an issuing authority (as outlined below).

A carnet **lasts one year** and isn't transferable between other users or vehicles and if necessary it can be renewed or extended on the road. Which countries ask for a CPD varies, but most agree much of east and southern Africa plus Egypt, Iran, Pakistan and India demand them and a CPD will help in Australia too. Some visit these places without a CPD, but that requires either luck, persuasion or deposits/fees.

Carnets can be said to be an aberration, a relic from a bureaucratic heyday. Most countries are content to note your vehicle details in your passport or sell an inexpensive **temporary vehicle importation permit** (TVIP), which adds up to the same thing as a CPD. You can go right through the Americas, northwest Africa and across northern and southeast Asia without a carnet.

In 2016 there was a shake-up and what might be called a 'deregulation' of carnets, with issuing times tumbling and the possibility (or need) to use overseas issuing authorities. EU nationals apply with Germany's ADAC (🖳 adac .de) with a fee of €200-300 and a fast turn-around; in the UK it's 🖳 carseurope .net. Boomerang Carnets in Illinois (🖳 atacarnet.com) do the job for Canadians and Americans for around $800. In South Africa it's the AA of SA (🖳 aa.co.za) and in Australia the AAA in Canberra (🖳 aaa.asn.au).

Carnets guarantee covering the highest possible import duty on your vehicle if it's not re-exported properly; a way of controlling tax-dodging car importers. Egypt, Iran, Pakistan and India (plus Sri Lanka) have long been in the most costly zone – let's call it 'EIPI'. But where once having those countries listed on your CPD required depositing up to *eight times the value of your vehicle*, the ADAC currently asks no more than 100% and as little as 30% for non-EIPI places. So for example, a £15,000 Land Cruiser falls in the ADAC's €15,000–25,000 bracket which means a fixed deposit of €15,000 if visiting any of the EIPI countries. That drops to €7500 if not visiting the EIPI but passing through the South African Customs Union (SACU: SA, Swaziland, Lesotho, Namibia and Botswana), and only €5000 for anywhere else that requires a CPD but not including the EIPI or SACU. The problem is the classic overland routes of Cairo–Cape Town and Istanbul–Kathmandu both cross EIPI and/or SACU territories. Of course the **valuation** of your vehicle is open to interpretation – you'll want it as low as possible even if your adaptions have effectively cost as much again. But with the latest changes you now simply pay the deposit into the issuing authority's bank and with the ADAC at least it's returned in full when your carnet is discharged at the end of your travels.

How a carnet is used

Carnets come in a number of pages from five to twenty-five, each page is used for a country where this document is required. A page is divided into three perforated sections, or **vouchers** a bit like an old cheque book: an entry voucher (*volet d'entrée*), an exit voucher (*volet de sortie*), and a counterfoil (*souche*).

When you **enter a country that requires a carnet**, the Customs official will stamp your counterfoil and exit voucher and tear off and keep the entry voucher. When you leave that country, the counterfoil will be stamped again and then the exit voucher will be retained. When your travels are complete you return the carnet to the issuing authority for discharging. What they'll want to see is a bunch of double-stamped counterfoils or stubs and probably a few unused but intact pages.

Should you **sell your vehicle** and slip out of the country, your carnet will not be discharged and you may lose your deposit. Should you have **missed a stamp** for whatever reason, all is not lost. On arrival back home get the Customs in the port to inspect your vehicle's VIN and issue some sort of official notification that the vehicle as described in the carnet has been returned.

BACK-UP DOCUMENTS

With all these documents, keeping photocopies, duplicates, a list or even just photos of the vital details, makes replacement easier if they go missing. Stash paper **copies** somewhere secure or better still scan or photograph them and put the information onto an SD card or a USB stick plus a private webpage. You may also want to add travel insurance details, consular offices en route, your vehicle's main dealers in the countries you pass through – in fact your whole overlanding dossier. This way even if your rig gets burned to a crisp or sinks on the high seas, you'll be able to retrieve the details online.

Another good idea is to carry **duplicates** or 'spare' originals: ownership documents can be duplicated, either officially or by 'losing' the original and requesting a replacement (sometimes for a small fee).

THIRD-PARTY MOTOR INSURANCE

If you're boldly going where no one has gone before, don't expect to be able to get motor insurance from your domestic broker. In the UK you can get cover as far east as Turkey as well as Morocco and Tunisia at a push, although travellers on the Continent have long been able to get both motor insurance as well as vehicle recovery insurance to cover the Mediterranean rim, which potentially included countries like Algeria and Egypt.

Instead, **buy motor insurance as you go** but, again, don't expect to be able to buy it everywhere. You can often buy insurance at the border; if not, border officials may be able to advise where to get it. In the economic confederation of Francophone West Africa around $5 a day covers several countries; in Uzbekistan you pay a few dollars for two weeks' cover; in Colombia even less.

The dubious validity of motor insurance in the developing world or the impossibility of getting it at all underlines the fact that should you **cause an accident** such as killing someone's child or, worse still, a breadwinner, the complications may take years and large amounts of money to resolve. You may find yourself getting nailed for compensation even if you were not at fault.

Motor insurance is an unravellable quandary; rigorously enforced in Western countries, out in the world it may be unattainable or of little actual value but a necessary part of your papers to present at checkpoints. Make an effort to buy it and if you can't then drive carefully and avoid doing so at night when the risks are far greater (more on p258).

Money

Along with insurance, money and how to carry it is another thing that many overlanders worry about before they leave, although year by year it gets easier to get hold of **cash**, the most useful form of money. Any major trip is likely to cost you a few thousand pounds on the road and carrying that sort of money through the insecure parts of Asia, Africa and Latin America is enough to make anyone nervous. For advice on changing money and dealing with the black market, see p267.

Best currencies

Thanks in part to the pervasive tentacles of the Coca-Cola culture, the **US dollar** is well known in even the remotest corners of the world. Certainly, throughout **South America** and **most of Asia** this would be the most readily convertible hard foreign currency to carry. In **Africa**, especially the north, they're now more used to the **Euro**, though in East Africa it's still the US dollar. These two currencies are by far the best to carry; nothing else comes close any more. Avoid collecting too many US$100 or €100 notes. They may save space but are rarely seen abroad and are often thought to be fakes. The €500 note was withdrawn in May 2010 as it was seen as an overly compact way of smuggling cash. For the same reason don't accept street deals for $100 bills, especially anywhere too close to Nigeria, where they are printed by the roll.

SPONSORSHIP

Thank you for your enquiry. We regret to inform you that as we have allocated our annual marketing budget/due to current economic conditions, we are unable to support your venture.

For some travellers, sponsorship is part and parcel of their overlanding adventure. Some go out of their way to attract sponsorship or at least attention, often in the name of a good cause. It's an idea many overlanders toy with, ostensibly for the very tangible appeal of getting free stuff, but more profoundly, I suspect, as a means of validating or – when it involves charitable causes – justifying the journey.

Thirty years ago in Western countries it was fairly easy to get gear on a pretty thin premise. These days the field is much more competitive and while it's still possible to get free stuff for stickers, it takes a lot of nous and good connections to get actual **financial support** (unless you're famous).

Unless you're doing something truly extraordinary and original, there is a certain vanity in assuming your overland adventure deserves to attract sponsorship. Applicants often get resentful when they receive replies like the one quoted above, or when replies are not forthcoming or appear patronising, but you must remember that the most obvious targets are hit with scores of requests.

The big question that must be addressed is: **what's in it for them**? What have Land Rover got to gain by supplying you with a new Defender to drive to Cape Town, as thousands have already done? Even if a spirit of outdoor adventure helps sell the Land Rover brand, they'd rather loan their latest luxury saloon to a prominent sportsman who's likely to get photographed outside nightclubs at 2am with a starlet on each arm.

Getting some

Sponsorship can broadly be divided into three categories:
- Being funded to undertake the trip, usually in return for some form of promotion.
- Receiving products or services for promotion.
- Undertaking your trip in the name of a charity, involving both the above as well as donations from well-wishers.

The minimum you should offer a potential sponsor is exposure of their product or service in the form of prominently positioned **stickers**, just like on racing cars. If you can also promise to feature photos on a website, in magazines or on TV, a **local business** will likely be thrilled to support your big adventure in this way.

Sponsors are usually offered all this, but it's not uncommon for the sponsored to **lose interest** and fail to deliver. Oddly enough I've also found that sponsors or supporters also lose interest in acknowledging the rewards of any promotion or publicity put their way. Nevertheless, whether they appreciate it or not, it's good form to notify sponsors of any publicity you secure. Invite them to any presentations you may give or events you attend, and try to make them feel as if their contribution has been valued rather than grabbed.

My experience is that having a genuinely great proposal or an appropriate background is not enough. Rewards are far more likely if you have a certain **self-promotional acumen allied with thick-skinned persistence** – or of course are happy to accept trivial, low-value items in exchange for stickerage and website banners.

I know of many genuinely noteworthy expeditions that have put themselves hugely in debt, partly due to a lack of skill or even any desire to exploit their marketability, while other comparatively ordinary trips get much better results. It's who you know of course, but also your ability to sell yourself – something that's all too commonly confused with persistence.

Overlanders typically overestimate the appeal of their project to sponsors, but if approached in the right way or with good connections, sponsors can still be won over. I've found it's something much more easily done in countries where overlanding is little known or that are overshadowed by more conspicuous neighbours. Someone in Poland, Holland or Greece may find it much easier to attract the attention both of local sponsors and the media, who'll trumpet a plucky local hero, than another bunch of Brit students setting off for Cape Town in a Landy.

CREDIT AND DEBIT CARDS

Plastic cards are the best way of avoiding carrying rolls of cash and will great-ly simplify a long overland journey. **Take a few** because, despite reassuringly familiar logos, there's a good chance one won't work with a certain bank's ATM somewhere, although it's hard to know until you're actually there.

Some day, somewhere, you're going to bless your flexible friend for get-ting you out of a fix, most probably to cover shipping to the next place or just paying for a restful night in a plush hotel when you're out of cash. And across North America, Europe, Australasia and South Africa you need hardly ever use cash at all.

Contrary to the reasonable assumption that credit card companies stiff you for overseas purchases, they can actually offer the best rates of exchange for the day of your purchase (at least with Visa in Europe). Drawbacks include **service charges** when withdrawing from ATMs or banks abroad, and the pos-sibility of **fraud** when paying for a service or goods like a night in a hotel.

There are many stories of credit card accounts getting hung out to dry – in fact it's surprising it doesn't happen more often. For this reason it's best to **withdraw cash from ATMs only and pay for everything in cash**. Resist using your card as liberally as you might at home, even if it's possible. By doing so you greatly reduce the chance of someone cloning your card to make fraudu-lent withdrawals or purchases. Although there's a good chance any suspicious purchases will be refunded, before that's cleared up your card may get blocked until you contact the issuer and prove it hasn't been lost or stolen. Use cards to get cash, use cash to pay for things and check your online statements once in a while. Keep tabs on how much you're spending on the card, and at the very least, get your **minimum monthly payment** sorted out (arrange a direct debit with your bank before you go, or simply load up your card before you leave or use a pre-paid card like Caxton (🖥 caxtonfx.com).

Use cards to get cash and use cash to pay for things.

With the prevalence of credit card fraud, it's not uncommon to find your **account frozen** when you try and withdraw cash in places like Khabarovsk or Kampala. Some companies do this automatically, others might try and call you at home to confirm a purchase. If your contact number is a mobile that happens to be on, you're in the clear, but the way round this is to call your credit card company and bank before you leave and explain where you may be using your card. It may be worth confirming it in writing as some travellers still get their accounts blocked. As with insurance, have the magic phone number and any passwords or other security infor-mation handy so you can call them and set about unlocking your card.

A good travel guidebook should tell you which of the three main brands (Visa, American Express or MasterCard) are widely used in your destination, but with the negative connotation 'America' has in some places, the more anonymous Visa or MasterCard are more reliable.

CHOOSING A VEHICLE

2

Firstly, accept that your vehicle will be a **compromise**. Parked up for a week waiting for visas, you'll wish you were either back home or in a Winnebago Starship XXL with satellite TV. On a highway, in cities or when it comes to parking or shipping, an automatic hatchback with air and a good stereo will do nicely. For driving dirt tracks out in the wilderness, there'll be the odd occasion when the agility of a Land Rover Defender or even a Unimog will make short work of the obstacles. And when something breaks or wears out, you'll wish you were driving whatever the locals drive and can fix for a fiver and a packet of cigs.

Rest assured that the vehicle that fulfils most of your criteria most of the time will be the one you set off with, though it's unlikely you'll think the same way when you get back. Online chat on the pros and cons of vehicles spirals off into infinity as this is a subject that can be confidently discussed without actually having any experience. Even with some experience under the fanbelt, it's not unknown for overlanders to become somewhat evangelical on their return about what worked for them, especially in technical matters.

What car, van or truck?

With over a billion vehicles on the planet since the turn of the century (about a third of them in the US), the choice can be daunting. They all go, stop and turn so what's the difference? For overlanding, realistically most people will choose the type of vehicle similar to what's portrayed on the front cover of this book: a **4x4 station wagon** or van. For what these vehicles cost to buy, fit out and run, their versatility (let alone the all-terrain, fun factor) satisfies most overlanders most of the time. There's a box summing up 2WD versus 4WD on p71, and a whole section dedicated just to 4x4s starting on p73.

Because your vehicle is such an integral part of the trip, most will instinctively know what they want, be it a panel van, a Land Cruiser with a roof tent or a Pinzgauer with a periscope. These are some of the factors to consider:

• What's easily available in your market
• Your marque and image preferences
• How much do you want to spend?
• Daily travelling budget
• Size of the group
• Your itinerary
• The expected duration of your trip
• Space and comfort
• Carnet costs (go back to p24)
• Payload or manufacturer's GVW (gross vehicle weight)
• Fuel type
• Manual or auto
• Mechanical simplicity
• Availability of parts and know-how en route
• Build quality
• Ground clearance
• Shipping limitations

No single vehicle can tick all the boxes and as you agonise over your choice you'll flit from an off-roader to an ex-military truck mounted with a GRP cabin (see p118 & p218), to an RV with all mod-cons and heavy-duty suspension. In the end, after a lot of research and thought, you'll accept the compromise but it's still worth going through some of the above factors in more detail.

WHAT'S AVAILABLE?

It makes sense to settle on a machine that's widely if not globally available, is well supported in your territory and is commonly used for overlanding. Hankering in Estonia for an Australian-built OKA or in Portugal for a Sportsmobile is just making life hard for yourself. It's the same story in the States with Defenders or any decent, small turbo-diesel 4x4.

CHOOSING A VEHICLE

The limitations of right-hand drive (RHD) notwithstanding, the UK has the best of many worlds. Regular cars are cheap, often worth much less than the cost of insuring and taxing them for a year. Land Rover lore and know-how comes free with many breakfast cereals, while used Land Cruiser VXs and older Hiluxes can be the cheapest in Western Europe. Excepting Mitsubishi's and Iveco's desirable mid-sized 4x4 trucks (see p116), the choice of vans or AWD trucks is as wide as you like, with former airfields lined with seemingly bargain-priced ex-military trucks with tiny mileages (see p119).

In Australia the situation is broadly the same, but errs strongly towards the Japanese marques, while in the States the pickings seem comparatively leaner. Here, Jeep is the locally produced equivalent to the Land Rover, while modest payloads notwithstanding, the pickup trucks like Ford's F-series (the US's best-selling vehicle), Dodge RAM/GMC Sierra and Chevrolet Silverado and Toyota's Tundra make a viable overlanding platform to the older MANs or Mercedes trucks used in Europe.

IMAGE AND OTHER PREFERENCES

The vehicle you choose for your journey is central to the whole endeavour and our vanity has a lot to do with what we drive. A rugged-looking 4x4 like a Defender or a 40-series Land Cruiser, a panel van with a chimney and a flowery paint job, a converted school bus or a Unimog with bars on the windows – all send out signals about how you'd like to be perceived.

Remember, it's your adventure and you'll probably only do it once.

You want to feel inspired about your trip and what you'll drive for the months ahead is a big part of that adventure. Some choose to be ostentatious, possibly to assist self promotion, others – many experienced travellers among them – recognise the value of adopting a low profile while using a simpler but bigger machine.

Whatever you choose, remember it's your adventure and you'll probably only do it once. You may never use your 4x4's amazing off-road ability, but until you found that out for yourself it was nice to know it was there. While taking into account many of the other factors listed in this section, recognise the value in having a machine that even after months on the road still gives you a thrill just to look at it.

VEHICLE BUDGET

Unless you know better, spend as much as you can afford and expect to spend at least **half as much again** uprating, equipping and modifying the vehicle for the journey. At least £5000 or the local equivalent ought to get you a 4x4 in good shape, and maybe as little as half that for a van. These prices are a guide; you could spend a little less or a whole lot more. A regular car is the absolute budget option; aim to spend at least £1000 and even then be prepared to settle for a petrol engine. A good unmodified diesel van can be found for £2000.

From around £10,000, older ex-military 7.5-tonne (7500kg) trucks come within range in Europe, but require outfitting with a cabin. At least £10,000 is what you need for a plain U-series Unimog or MAN, or any of the above options in a better state of preparation for overlanding, but before you run away with yourself, remember the cost of a carnet (see p24).

REGIONAL DIFFERENCES

Vehicle types and the know-how and equipment found in North America differ from what's found in Europe, Australia and South Africa. Writing about vehicle choice for my *Adventure Motorcycling Handbook* is much less complicated as, broadly speaking, a KLR 650 is the same bike the world over and even the same range of equipment is available in the four territories listed above.

Although I try to offer a broad perspective, Europe is the background from which I'm writing and is the source of much overlanding lore and equipment (particularly in Germany), if not actual activity. In saying all this it's worth repeating what 'overlanding' is as defined by this book: vehicle-dependent journeys most commonly undertaken *from* Europe, North America or Australasia *to* Africa, Asia and Latin America.

Australia and South Africa have a long heritage of recreational domestic wilderness travel; spending a fortnight's holiday out in the bush with the family is not unusual. This know-how and equipment (as well as the related publications) equips travellers from these two countries well for long-haul overlanding. It also explains why, despite their relatively small combined population, you'll meet many Australians and South Africans on the road. It's in their blood as it has been among Western and lately Eastern **Europeans**, where 'gap-year travels' is just a newish name for what's long been an accepted institution. To judge by the available equipment and media, in North America overlanding is largely a domestic trend, although the vehicles commonly found there are no less capable (see below).

The vehicles used by overlanders from Europe, southern Africa and Australia are also broadly similar: the major Japanese or European brands of 4x4s, vans and trucks. But a 4.2-litre Land Cruiser – a 'big vehicle' by European standards – will seem modest to **North American drivers** accustomed to running a 7.3-litre petrol-engined pickup. At the same time a 120hp 2.5-litre turbo-diesel doing 40mpg would be regarded as quaint or fashionably right-on, even if diesel engines in non-commercial vehicles are less unusual in Canada. In the US expectations of physical size, acceptable economy, day-to-day comfort and levels of equipment diverge dramatically from what's acceptable to a Dutch or Brit overlander.

DAILY TRAVELLING BUDGET

Even if you don't have some sort of income supporting you back home, here are some factors to consider. Can you afford a truck's abominably high fuel consumption, £500 tyres and high shipping costs? Maybe you sold the house, got a substantial redundancy package and expect to save a whole lot on hotel bills by living in the vehicle? Or maybe you've only a few thousand to last you and are attracted to the economy of an old station wagon and avoiding places where a carnet is required. Would you rather spend less on an uneconomical banger, or spend more and get a vehicle that's thrifty and well equipped? There are more thoughts on how much it all costs on p12.

SIZE OF GROUP

Typically, most overlanding parties are composed of **two people**: a pair of young mates or a couple covering a greater age range right up to retirees. For such a configuration any vehicle will do, from the tiniest car to an all-terrain motorhome. Outside of continental Europe, **families** taking to the road are rare, but a group of more than two adults over an extended period will get crowded in a regular car or 4x4; kids especially will be frustrated by the inability to move around (see p352). Families do manage in the short term, but if it's a matter of taking them out of school, an extended-cab truck (see p126) or a converted bus will be much more acceptable to Social Services.

ITINERARY AND DURATION

How far and how long you plan to travel ought to have a major influence on your choice of wheels. The longer you plan to travel and the more variable the climate en route, the more you'll appreciate a house on wheels rather than a car you can live out of. But remember that what can enable you to roam far and wide across Latin America and Asia (in the less extreme seasons) may struggle or limit your options in **Africa**. Even with a roof tent, many travellers who undertake trips of more than a few months in regular 4x4s return in a bigger vehicle, usually because they encountered others doing it this way and saw the clear advantages.

Despite Africa being a perennially warm continent, tent camping or crawling around in the back of a car with a few inches of headroom will get to you, and takes a lot of organisation to keep things in order and relations cordial. The longer you go for, especially if you envision parking up for extended periods, the better off you'll be with a large living space without feeling the need for a night in a hotel once a week just so you can have a proper break.

SPACE AND COMFORT

No matter how much you may like the idea of roughing it to the extreme ends of the earth, you're possibly going to be driving your vehicle for months. Wouldn't you rather it was **a quiet, temperate and comfortable experience**? Probably not if you're a certain type of Brit or German who equates 'expeditions' with a little suffering and self-denial. It's one reason the much-admired Land Rover Defender still rolls into the arms of willing customers.

Comfort and space are something that you'll only truly appreciate after some time on the road and is one reason why some travellers consider an AWD truck **conversion** with a cabin you can stand up in, a long wheelbase van or even a motorhome. The ability to park up, switch off and simply lie back on a bed or sit at a table makes a big impact on day-to-day living. It may be overlanding but it's not all about driving. There will be challenges enough waiting for you out in the world. Too hot or cold, cramped, deafened, shaken about, fighting heavy controls: all these things will tire you prematurely and are what modern SUVs have succeeded in eliminating but is what you may get in spades driving a Cold War-era truck.

In the right vehicle you'll feel a lot better if the **suspension** is supple, the **driving position** is relaxed, the **steering** is light, the **engine noise** minimal, and your **surroundings** are at a pleasant temperature. If you also have somewhere amenable to spend the night then so much the better.

PAYLOAD, OR GROSS VEHICLE WEIGHT RATING (GVWR)

A vehicle's **gross vehicle weight rating** (**GVWR**; in the UK called MAM or maximum authorised mass, elsewhere gross load rating) is usually printed in the registration document as well as stamped on an alloy plate riveted inside the vehicle's door frame or the back of the engine bay.

It adds up to the **maximum permitted total weight of a vehicle including its payload**, not the vehicle's actual weight, which is often opaque, overlooked or inaccurate but can sometimes be divined from a brochure. Other jargon on the same theme includes: GVTW (maximum 'train' weight when towing)

CHOOSING A VEHICLE

The VIN plate on this Mazda pickup shows the GVW of nearly 3 tonnes, the GVTW when towing, the payload when not towing and the unladen vehicle weight.

'tare' or 'UVW', which is unladen weight with fluids but no driver; and 'kerb weight': with a full tank and a nominal 75kg driver in blue overalls.

Leaving aside manufacturers' technical design limitations, in many countries a vehicle's GVW is a critical **legal designation**, separating domestic cars from commercial vehicles. As many commercial drivers are well aware, this has ramifications for operator licensing, insurance, tax brackets, what roads it can drive and bridges it can cross, tolls and so on. All in all, a list of regulations you're probably wanting to escape from and the sorts of concerns that don't exist in many African countries, where a vehicle's payload is only limited by its 'APC' or absolute physical capacity.

Calculating the permitted payload

In an overland sense, the GVW is a way of calculating the permitted **payload**. Deduct the vehicle's unladen weight from the GVW and you have the payload. This is something typically overlooked by first-timers, just as their vehicles are also routinely overloaded. Long before settling on your final vehicle choice and layout, establish its payload: both in terms of chassis and tyre loads.

Manufacturers set GVWs on the conservative side (or so you'd hope; in certain light-commercial categories you can't help wondering if marketing has more to do with it). However, in an engineering and safety sense, they're closely tied to the **axles**, what the **tyres** can safely handle, the **braking** set-up and performance, and the **suspension** as fitted from the factory. In this regard

Pushing the 'APC' in the Sahara.

don't be surprised to find the standard suspension on a 4x4 squashed flat at its GVW limit. Uprating the tyres and suspension is almost mandatory for overlanding (see p147 and p143). Modifying the chassis and brakes is beyond the reach of normal overland preparation; in the States it's common to fit heavier-duty axles to 4x4s, though more to run huge tyres than improve payload.

Disregarding legal issues and the mistaken belief that 4x4s are immune to overloading, to ensure the safety of your vehicle and the longevity of its components, right down to the chassis, it's vital to recognise payload limits. Remember too that payloads can rise dramatically when fully loaded with fuel and water and can effectively be multiplied when driving off-road. Especially at the lighter end of the scale, always aspire to **stay well below maximum GVW values** – 70% is a good figure to aim for.

The limits of payload will also become the governing factor when making extensive modifications or full-on self builds. Suddenly bull bars, second spare wheels, huge roof tents and spare fuel tanks edge you swiftly towards the GVW limit. The sources of this information of course vary wildly, but when you see how modest the typical payload is in the list of 4x4s below you may be surprised.

In Europe the 3.5 tonne GVW limit (in the US it's around 10,000lbs) covers private vehicles which don't require special licensing or training. Motorhomes can be an exception.

Some 4x4 payloads

Jeep Wrangler V6	388kg (856lb)
Toyota FJ Cruiser V6	510kg (1124lb)
Subaru Forester 2.5i-L	536kg (1180lb)
Nissan X-Trail ST-L	537kg (1182lb)
Mercedes G-Wagen V6	588kg (1296lb)
Toyota Land Cruiser GXL	610kg 91345lb)
Land Cruiser Amazon	620kg (1367lb)
Land Cruiser 200 V8 diesel	650kg (1433lb)
Land Rover Discovery Td5	655kg (1444lb)
Land Rover Discovery 4	675kg (14884lb)
Toyota Prado 2.8D	750kg (1653lb)
Toyota Tundra 5.7 V8	943kg (2080lb)
Land Rover 110 Defender	1009kg (2224lb)
Ford F150 2.7 Eco Boost	1020kg (2250lb)
Mitsubishi L200 2.4D	1050kg (2315lb)
Ford Ranger	1190kg (2300lb)
LR 130 chassis cab	1200kg (2645lb)
Land Cruiser HZJ79	1410kg (3108lb)

Before you rush out and buy an HZJ79 Land Cruiser from a Somali warlord, remember that not all vehicles are created equal. An excess load that will break a Toyota Hilux in half will be shrugged off by a similarly over-

> ... always aspire to stay well below maximum GVW values – 70% is a good figure to aim for ...

loaded HZJ79. My old Mazda pickup had a claimed maximum payload of just over 1170kg (2560lb). I've loaded it to maybe 70% of that capacity while towing another 500kg, at which point the standard suspension would have been on its knees. But even with uprated suspension, running it for long at the claimed 1170kg limit would be hard on the tyres and the transmission, as well as the brakes on long downhills. Driven off-road in this state I'd fully expect something to break pretty soon. All the more reason then to treat the claimed payloads with a pinch of salt and **adopt broad safety margins**. If you expect to have a big payload, get a big vehicle.

MANUAL OR AUTO TRANSMISSION

In Europe, auto transmission has gained popularity among normal road users; in North America hardly anyone drives 'stick'. Traditionally manual transmission was considered better for overlanding, due to easier diagnosis and repairability by bush mechanics. A clutch is a different matter, but it's also rare for a manual gearbox to go suddenly – the signs and sounds of imminent failure can last for thousands of miles and it's usually possible to engage one gear to keep moving. Outside of the States (or places where old US cars end up), automatic gearboxes are uncommon. Taking an auto gearbox apart takes some nerve and auto specialists are comparatively rare in the overland zone.

Even though some **power and response** is lost, autos are effortless to drive and are nearly as fuel efficient as manuals. The lack of direct drive (or ham-fisted driving) reduces shocks on the transmission which makes them popular with fleet operators such as car rental agencies, where a stream of non-owner drivers might not always treat the transmission like a new-born baby.

The much-repeated adage that an auto can't be push-started with a flat battery has never been a significant issue unless you're heading solo across the Rub-al Khali; the same has become the case with many modern engines and is a problem easily solved with a pair of **jump leads** and a friendly wave. As the name implies, a manual gives you more **control**, but an auto can recover itself from mud and soft-sand with much less reliance on perfect technique.

On the road there's not much in it, but **driving an auto 4x4** up a steep, rocky track is so much easier than a manual; the box smoothes out the transmission in a way that's hard to do in a manual. The popularity of 'rock crawling' in the US wouldn't have developed as a form of recreation – or in some extreme cases wouldn't even be possible – with manual gearboxes. It's only in remote locales that the perceived mechanical simplicity of manual transmission – using tangible gears and shafts rather than a fluid at an optimal temperature – inspires confidence away from the beaten track.

Design flaws apart, **overheating** under heavy loads is the main problem with auto transmission, and driving a heavily loaded machine at low speeds in tropical or mountain areas (let alone towing) can expose this weakness. Automatic transmission fluid (ATF) works best at around 85°C (185°F) and in normal driving conditions needs changing at around 30,000 miles. For every 7°C (44°F) above that figure the oil's operational life is reduced by half and at only 95°C (203°F) or more it breaks down and resin forms on the plates, causing slippage. At over 110°C (230°F) the seals become brittle and drive can be lost – crawling up a rough Atlas Mountain track on a very hot windless day in Morocco with the gearbox bathed in the engine's heat, that figure is not so unattainable. The answer is an ATF **oil cooler**; some vehicles have one as standard and some will require up to three fan-assisted coolers in somewhere like Africa. If you decide to get an auto make sure that:

- The gearbox has been serviced by specialists before departure.
- It has the ability to manually lock lower gears (giving direct drive). Most off-road vehicles have this, which reduces the chances of overheating.
- It has an effective fluid cooler with a capacity for added fan cooling.
- You fit a temperature gauge to the auto box.
- You start off with synthetic ATF and carry some spare for your vehicle.

MECHANICAL SIMPLICITY

Perhaps the biggest quandary today's overlander faces is that vehicles have become less suited to the rigours of unsupported overland travel far from approved service centres. Engines are no longer recognisable as such and complicated networks of **electronics** govern entire systems, as successive governments introduce ever more stringent emissions regulations.

Cars have become cheaper over the years, but they've also become less robust and more complex. By the mid-1990s mechanically simple vehicles were dying out in the face of inexpensive electronic components, a clamour for improved emission controls and the introduction of the common rail diesel engine to domestic motoring. Many of the most suitable overlanding vehicles were made in the years leading up to this time. They weren't light or sophisticated and didn't automatically fold the wing mirrors in as you closed the door, but you'll find many of them still operating daily as workhorses in Africa and Asia.

The latest Land Rover or Toyota flagships will soon be able to drive themselves (actually this is no longer a joke!), some can already park themselves and are undoubtedly a pleasure to drive in a civilised environment. Load them to the hilt and hammer them for days on corrugated desert tracks, push them along the waterlogged trenches of the Amazon basin, or just add a hundred thousand miles on the clock and, among other things, **electronic failures** are bound to crop up. And don't expect all cars to come with a spare wheel.

At worst the **electronic control unit** (ECU; see box p42) can immobilise a vehicle with just a trivial fault. No great drama on the Ventura Highway with 0800-RECOVERY on a nearby billboard; not so good trying to get out of Ethiopia with the rainy season bearing down on you and two days left on your visa. Overlanding is one of the tiniest niches in motoring. This is partly why your choice will have to be a compromise and why, global and regional differences notwithstanding, that choice remains relatively narrow and conservative. Unless they know better, people use what works, because with slab-like plastic engine covers stamped with 'Keep Out – Service Personnel Only', **tinkering with modern vehicles** is severely discouraged and home maintenance has become a thing of the past. At the same time, fault diagnosis has become a new black art deciphering computer-generated error codes.

AVAILABILITY OF PARTS AND KNOW-HOW EN ROUTE

Perhaps the biggest anxiety overlanders face is the vehicle breaking down in some complicated or expensive way. Anything too obscure, exotic or with odd wheel-sizes may eventually raise complications. Again it's for this reason that older **Land Rovers, Toyotas and Mercedes** rank so highly on the list of overlanders' vehicles, particularly in Africa and Asia. A century ago nine out of ten of all cars were Fords. Today, Toyotas and Mercedes are sold in over 120 countries and Toyotas may be just about the most prolific vehicles on the planet.

Chances are your vehicle will take you far from the regimen of approved dealers' service stamps, roadside recovery networks and easy access to parts. You may want to explore the planet's extremes of climate and terrain, but are probably not a qualified mechanic (and even if you are there may not be much you can do when some things go wrong).

The worldwide reach of marques like Ford, Toyota and Mercedes (including their derivatives sometimes sold under other names) is one reason why their products remain popular. There may well only be one **dealer** in the distant capital of the banana republic where you motor has chosen to throw a fit, but that'll be a whole lot more comforting than trying to obtain a clutch slave cylinder seal for an '88 MAN in the Algerian oilfields.

The upside is that with internet and a mobile phone, solving a complex problem and **sourcing a part** can be done, just not necessarily by the roadside. As long as you don't mind hanging around a couple of weeks (something that can occur even back home for a seemingly common component), with the likes of DHL covering the globe, using a marque whose parts are guaranteed to be widely available is no longer so critical. However, although DHL may ship a new water pump to Tashkent in a couple of days, customs will have other ideas and can hold on to it for a lot longer and charge more than you'd expect. It's another reason for playing it safe and **avoiding obscure makes and models**, as well as of course having a vehicle in good shape and carrying a few obvious spares (see p288).

Within reason an **old car** need not be a risk; many bangers from Europe or North America end up south of the borders and survive on pattern parts and local know-how. **Tyre sizes** too should be considered in your chosen destination. Although the choice of rim sizes has multiplied for cars and trucks back home, out in the world the most common is 12–14" for cars, 15" or 16" rims for vans and 4x4s, and formerly 20" now 22.5" rims for trucks.

The need for **creative improvisation** or 'bodging' should also be considered when all else fails, which is why mechanical simplicity is so desirable. You'll be surprised at the ingenuity of local mechanics. To you it may be a mechanical disaster but they'll have seen it all before and may have a solution. There's more on improvised repairs and trouble-shooting on p279.

BUILD QUALITY

As with many products these days, to be competitive cars must tick the boxes of visual appeal, passenger safety, comfort and efficiency, while being built down to a price. Up to a point they're cunningly (if not deviously) designed to squeeze past government regulations, and to pay for all this research and development, cuts are made elsewhere. Among other things, this affects build quality and so **longevity**. What looks good and so attracts high sales can often be shoddily put together and start rusting after a couple of winters. Only a few marques, the more conservative among them, have good reputations in this category and they'll always cost more.

In your parents' day vehicles were technologically crude, noisy and inefficient but were built like tanks and could last a lifetime; not something you could say for some cars extruded off today's production lines. This is why overlanders err towards 4x4s; they're perceived to be tough in an old-fashioned way, without necessarily being a lorry.

While less glamorous to an overlander, **commercial vehicles** are sold on the desirable attributes of toughness, longevity and low running costs. Operated round the clock, they sell on their reputation rather than the ability to adjust all the seats into more configurations than a Rubik's Cube.

As mentioned above, with the benefit of a vehicle recovery policy and a mobile phone, a breakdown at home is only a nuisance. Out in distant lands it's a pain. Much depends on the early years of the vehicle's ownership as well as its service history, but today's vans and wagons are built to handle only social, domestic and occasional recreational activities, not sustained hard use with high payloads on rough roads because 99% of drivers (in the West at least) don't need this. All this means that some vehicles are more

A 1940s Packard still running in Syria. The only black box in that thing is the high-capacity ash tray.

suitable than others, though you may not know it to look at them – and certainly won't know it from the advertising.

GROUND CLEARANCE

On many dirt roads as well as some back-country ferry-boarding situations, your vehicle's ground clearance will be a much more useful feature than all-wheel drive (of which more on p75). Remember, by the time you're loaded up, the machine will be an inch or two lower and the momentum of that added mass working on the suspension may regularly cause it to bottom out, so transferring shock loads to the chassis. The characteristics of any vehicle's ground clearance can be summed up as four measurements:

• approach angle
• departure angle
• ramp breakover angle or belly clearance between the axles
• minimum ground clearance, usually lowest under the axles

On most 4x4s vehicles and trucks, the **approach angle** is usually better than the departure angle and so less problematic; the small town-delivery vans discussed on p54 can be the other way round, with overhanging noses but great back ends. Short or long, it's worth knowing **what will get hit** if you drive into a ditch one dark night; on a 4x4 it will be the solid bumper, on regular road cars the bottom edge of the radiator may be just behind a flimsy cowling.

Ideally the **departure angle** should match the approach angle, as it does on a Jeep Wrangler or a Land Rover 101, both purposeful 4x4s, or on a Smart car, which isn't. On your average station wagon, LWB 4x4 or C-class motorhome (see p65), there's usually a considerable rear overhang, sometimes made worse by low-slung exhaust pipes, spare wheels or tow hitches. You need to get the balance right between having a usefully long body and maintaining a manageably short wheelbase that aids vehicle manoeuvrability.

The **ramp breakover angle**, better understood as 'belly clearance', is the point when the undercarriage between the two axles grounds as you go over something like a speed hump or a fallen tree. The longer the wheelbase, the less good the belly clearance is likely to be, but in fact getting bellied out is much less common than getting hung up by a low departure angle or mashing the nose of a van.

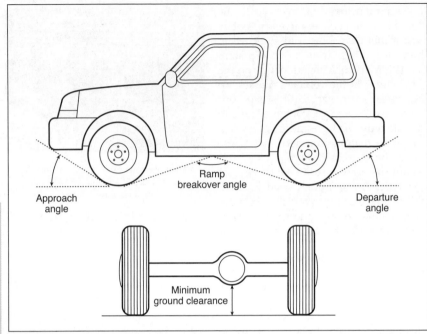

Finally, simple **ground clearance** is important when driving along an unconsolidated track that's been rutted by the passage of other vehicles, especially where mud hardens. On a traditional 4x4 the ground clearance is lowest at the diffs. With vehicles with independent suspension it's the shock mount by a wheel or a beam under the engine, but in ruts the centre line of the car – the engine's sump, exhaust system and gearbox – will be most vulnerable.

Improving ground clearance

Ground clearance can only be improved by fitting **taller tyres** along with possibly larger diameter wheels, although for stability, and therefore safety reasons, you only want to go so far. Marginally taller tyres can also help get a little more air under the floor, and with a higher load rating can also increase the vehicle's GVWR (see p33).

Unimog portal axles. How often will you need such clearance? © mattsavage.com.

The **portal axle** design of Unimogs and Pinzgauers radically improves axle clearance but is overkill for overlanders. Inexperienced off-roaders unused to the added height have tipped vehicles over. A couple of inches lift to regain compression from the payload is adequate.

On vehicles with independent suspension all round (most road cars and top of the range 4x4s) overall ground clearance can be improved by **raising the suspension** (as explained in part on p143) as well as removing running boards and other non-essential paraphernalia along the body's lower edge.

Permanently raising suspension (as opposed to height adjustment found on some 4x4s), as well as fitting taller tyres, raises a vehicle's **axle clearance** but also affects its **centre of gravity**. This reduces the stability of an already high but conventionally wide 4x4 from the likes of Toyota or Land Rover. (A heavily loaded roof rack or a badly packed load has the same effect on stability; more on that on p186.) Full-size American pickups have a wider track (axle width) and one reason the Hummer H1 was 2.5m (101 inches) wide was to enable it to race across a desert plain without flipping over as a Hilux might do.

The right balance must be struck between adequate ground clearance and a stable, loaded platform. Realistically, much bigger wheels are a bad idea as they cause complications with gearing as well as unplanned stresses on an axle half-shafts, CV joints and wheel bearings. It's one reason why it's common to talk about uprating an entire axle when building up a US off-roader, although this isn't the norm for overlanders.

Overall it's best to keep it simple: heavy-duty suspension giving a couple of inches lift is adequate for non-competitive overlanding. Messing around with tyre sizes isn't really necessary if you've chosen the right vehicle in the first place. There is more on suspension on p143; tyres are on p147.

SHIPPING LIMITATIONS

Beyond a certain height and width, vehicles won't fit in secure, standard-sized shipping containers. Depending on how you feel about this, it may govern your vehicle choice as well as the way you set it up or even your route. Especially if you start **from Europe you can see a lot of the world without having to get involved with container shipping**, but if you want to see it all, commercial container shipping, as opposed to ferries, will be a necessity.

The door aperture of a **standard 20ft shipping container** is 2.26m (7ft 5 inches) high, 2.28m (7ft 6 inches) wide and with 5.87m (19ft 3 inches) available inside. Forty-foot-long containers (11.9m or 39ft 3 inches internal) also exist, and some come as 'high cube', which are 2.56m (8ft 5 inches) high, but of course cost more. There is a little flexibility with height in that you can take stuff off the roof or let tyres down to gain a few more inches, and on some vehicles wheels can even be removed and vehicles rolled on their brake drums.

Anything taller or wider, which means most trucks, will have to be chained to a 2.44-metre- (8ft-) wide shipping pallet or extra wide **flat-rack**, with all the security issues and expense that entails. Up to a point, a truck with a driver's compartment separate or sealed from the accommodation cabin is less of a security risk and roll-on, roll-off (RoRo) ferries are even more risky if you're not present. On top of these real security concerns (pilfering at ports round the world is endemic) must be added the **cost** of transporting a large truck by sea. It's something you may only do a few times, but it will take a significant bite out of your budget, especially if it doesn't fit on a standard flat-rack.

CHOOSING A VEHICLE

ECUS AND CAN BUS TECHNOLOGY

But if I were in the middle of the Kalahari, I'd rather have two chunks of pig iron than some silicon chips that were designed and developed by four blokes in Banbury*.

Jeremy Clarkson

In all the time I drove my G-Wagen, the biggest problem I had was when the drive-by-wire throttle light came on. The vehicle went into limp-home mode. Driving it home from [southern Algeria] to Munich, Germany, in that mode was not fun. Three months of discussions pinned it on a random internal harness short. Sad to say, the ECU interprets a blown fuse as a global systems failure.

Tom Sheppard, writing on 🖥 trucktrend.com

These days all new cars, petrol or diesel, are managed by **ECUs** or **electronic control units**. It's a system sometimes called '**drive by wire**', only we're not talking the sort of push-and-pull wires that change the gears on your mountain bike. Electrical sensors report to a computer that calculates countless parameters several times a second in order to (among other things) optimise the efficiency, emissions or traction of your vehicle.

Having spent the best part of a century getting to understand the mechanics of engines, this complex digital technology featured on all common rail diesel engines can put some overlanders back in the Stone Age when it comes to self-diagnosis or repairs.

It's true that for decades we drove petrol-engined vehicles with capacitor discharge or electronic ignition, and electronic fuel injection (EFI) on diesels has been around for at least as long. The problem is that these days the main unit is connected on a network or 'bus' to many secondary ECUs – all part of a controller area network, or **CAN** – which monitor and react to everything. Although it's getting better, especially in a new model's early years, bugs in the programming, or just badly made connections, could immobilise a vehicle. Lately there's been a trend to make the critical power system a separate network from the less crucial body-control modules so if your electric window control fails your car will still run.

A typical overland journey will expose your vehicle to extreme levels of **dust, humidity, vibration and temperature**, all of which put these units and the sensors, let alone the mass of wires between them, under uncommon strain. Meanwhile the driver will be beyond the range of domestic roadside recovery services, and when faced with a malfunction indicator lamp (MIL) will quite possibly be unable to diagnose what's wrong or do anything about it. ECUs rarely have a 'reset to factory settings' feature and even if there's some sort of reset function – often something like turning the key on and off three times – it's not something you'll ever see in the handbook, but may unearth on vehicle owners' forums.

An OBD II reader

On-board diagnostics (OBD)

Since about 1996 most cars running ECUs have had to incorporate an **on-board diagnostics (OBD)** system that specifies what's malfunctioning in the vehicle. When the ECU registers something it's programmed not to like – such as poor fuel or the low oxygen levels found at high altitude, to give just two possible overlanding scenarios – the

*A small town in central England known for automotive research and development.

malfunction indicator lamp (MIL) lights up and one of 10,000 **diagnostic trouble codes (DTC)** may be displayed somewhere near the ECU or on the dash. Thankfully DTCs are largely analogous among all manufacturers; generally they're classified with prefixes relating to 'P' (powertrain), 'B' (body), 'C' (chassis) and 'U' (network).

If your vehicle doesn't identify DTCs visually (few do), buy an **OBD reader** from £20; these readers plug into the car's vehicle communications interface (VCI) via a 16-pin data-link connector (DLC) cable, enabling you to read off any DTCs (we're approaching an OLH acronyms-per-sentence record!). All 'OBD II'-compliant vehicles now have a VCI. (Modern Land Rovers are one notable exception, requiring their far more expensive TestBook system, but you can get round this with something like a iCarsoft TF930 for around £120).

Your enigmatic DTC must then be cross-referenced to a long list (available in your manual, on CDs or on websites like 💻 obd-codes.com and 💻 bba-reman.com, among others) to tell you where the problem is; or more accurately what the ECU thinks the problem is. Many of us won't remember exactly where we were when in May 2005 Toyota issued a service bulletin for the D-4D engine: 'If MIL warning light remains on and Fault Codes PO420 or P0430 can be read off ECU via OBD-II port then car needs an ECU software upgrade and a new catalytic converter with a modified cat matrix coating.' In other words, this wasn't an urgent fault and Toyota merely wanted to upgrade your ECU and change your exhaust pipe. Being able to *read and translate* the relevant DTC in the first place sure helps stave off panic.

A fault like the one described above won't stop your vehicle, it'll just make it **emit less cleanly**, something that you may not have even been aware of before the advent of ECU DTCs. After all, Mitsubishi Fuso dashboards are known to light up at an altitude of only 3800m (12,500ft), warning of insufficient oxygen (although oxygen masks won't drop from the cab roof). Again, all that will be happening is the vehicle has reached the lim-

its of what it thinks is normal and will run rich. More serious diagnoses may put your vehicle in limp-home/limited operation strategy (LOS), as Tom Sheppard describes. No doubt you'll have heard similar stories like a BMW that stopped after convincing itself one of the tyres was punctured when clearly all were fine. This is the downside of ECU technology; even if the 'black box' itself is well sealed and reliable (and not all are; look up the saga of 1998–2002 Td5 Land Rovers on the web), tracking down loose, worn, dirty or wet connections or sensors adds a new range of complications to conventional diagnosis and roadside repair.

Get used to it: it's here to stay

It may well be that in a few generations we won't bat an eyelid about setting off for the Cordillera Blanca in a hovercraft propelled by a telepathic plasma drive, but right now CAN bus technology can be a worry for most overlanding mortals, while finding pre-ECU vehicles in good shape is getting ever harder as governments encourage the scrapping of older vehicles.

At the very least, **track down the location of your vehicle's main ECU** and its VCI *before* you need to know where they are and what they look like (on some 4x4s they're positioned well below a vehicle's maximum wading depth…). At the very least get an **OBD reader** or a Multi-System Diagnostic Tool, and print out or download a list of DTCs for your vehicle. Then you'll be able to identify and either ignore a petty fault, or be a step closer to knowing which system or component may be causing a problem. Note that carrying a **spare ECU** (from around £250 for a Tdi Land Rover, for example) is not so simple, especially on newer vehicles where it has to be programmed to match your vehicle's security codes at the very least.

If you take this path, get your spare ECU matched to your vehicle and establish that such a swap can be done in the field (in some cases careful attention must be made to the earthing of the unit). Or just give up and put up with an HJ60 or a Peugeot 504.

CHOOSING A VEHICLE

Which fuel?

Most of us recognise **petrol** ('gasoline' in North America, *essence* in French, *gasolina* in Spanish, *nafta* in Russian) and **diesel** (the same in Spanish and Russian, and *gasoil* – pronounced 'gazwal' – in French).

Just about all big commercial vehicles run on diesel because, being an oil, it can be cheaper to refine, returns better fuel economy and motors are more durable. In Europe most cars are diesels too, these days with petrol-like performance and economy that's superior to many motorcycles. Only in North America and particularly the US are gasoline engines in cars and pickups the norm, with engine capacities and rates of fuel consumption unheard of in Europe. For overlanding diesel is the obvious choice , but not all diesel engines are tolerant of the varying quality of diesel available around the world.

DIESEL ENGINES
Although the tide is turning with regard to levels of toxic nitrogen oxide emissions and was exacerbated by the 2015 VW 'defeat device' scandal, in **Europe** diesels have been the engines of choice for years. Smaller and more efficient diesel engines now offer petrol-like performance while achieving fifty per cent better fuel economy. In France and the UK owning a large petrol-engined car as your main vehicle is eccentric.

In **Australia** diesel has long been a preference and **South Africa** has come round to diesels too in recent years as engines have become more sophisticated. Only **North America** is holding out. Fuel in North America is comparatively inexpensive and the market is accustomed to huge V8 petrol engines returning a mileage in the low teens. Since that time the so-called Big Three (Ford, GM, Dodge) have had proprietary diesel engines supplied by manufacturers or co-owners like Cummins, Detroit Diesel, Isuzu and Navistar (International).

Diesel injection
Before the advent of advanced diesel-injection technology for use in cars, **indirect injection** was seen as a crude but simple alternative to tall and noisy commercial direct injection engines. In the 1980s most compact diesel town cars used less bulky indirect injection engines; Toyota's 2H six was such an engine. The benefits used to be quicker starting and less noise at the cost of a relatively subdued throttle response and poorer fuel economy. Indirect diesel engines were also more tolerant of bad fuel and imperfect injectors – all desirable characteristics for real-world overlanding. The old 2.25 Land Rover diesel is another good example (although no excuse to rush out and buy one!). In recent years noise suppression as well as common rail diesel (CRD) technology, has advanced to the point where **direct injection** is now the norm in even the smallest diesel cars.

Common rail diesel injection (CRD)

Mechanical or hydraulic versions of 'common rail' diesel technology have been used since the 1940s in locomotives and ships, but in the late 1990s advanced electronics pioneered by Bosch enabled the same technology to be applied to cars. The diesel injector pump that formerly distributed bursts of fuel at relatively low pressures to each injector was replaced by a very high-pressure pump charging the 'common rail' linking all cylinders. Since around 2003, old-style injectors have been replaced by third generation, electronically operated piezo solenoid valves. These are used at phenomenally high pressures of up to 2000 bar (29,000psi!), resulting in far more accurate timing and much better atomisation of the fuel charge, so greatly improving efficiency, increasing power and reducing the diesel engine's notorious rattle. This has enabled smaller, lighter engines to do the work of one twice the capacity, while also reducing emissions.

Most of us drive in a controlled, domestic environment where clean fuel, regular servicing and, should you need it, recovery or repair are close at hand. But taking your super-efficient CRD-engined vehicle outside its comfort zone can cause problems. CRD engines are sensitive to **imperfect fuel** (see p46) and some don't respond well to running out of fuel (something to be avoided in any vehicle as muck and rust in the bottom of the tank can get sucked into the fuel lines). Any water or dirt contaminants are also propelled with enough force to damage injectors or valves and so filtration and water separation are all the more critical than on old-style 'low-pressure' engines. Fit a water separator or sedimentor and ensure you carry several spare **fuel filter cartridges**; very often the problem can be solved simply by changing them and, if necessary, re-priming the fuel system.

Injection pumps – critical and expensive components on all FI engines – are also sensitive to diesel fuel types. Old-fashioned inline **fuel injection pumps** are lubricated by engine oil but some rotary-type injection pumps are lubricated by the fuel. These rotary pumps built in the high-sulphur diesel era don't take well to running on **ultra low-sulphur diesel** (ULSD, more over the page), exhibiting increased wear in the pump and rubber o-ring failure right through the fuel system.

A clear-based sedimentor or fuel filter like this allows you to monitor gunge.

Turbo diesels and intercoolers

A **turbo-charger** uses the 'free' energy of exhaust gases being expelled from the combustion chamber to force more air into the engine. One side of the turbine is spun by the escaping exhaust gases like a water wheel, on the other side fresh air is sucked in and forced into the engine inlet. Like blowing on embers, more air improves combustion and more complete combustion creates more power.

CHOOSING A VEHICLE

Just about all diesel engines in the developed world are turbos, offering not only improved power, but also a marginal gain in fuel efficiency as well as reduced emissions. One notable exception is Toyota's enduring 1HZ 4.2-litre six, still fitted today in some 70-series Land Cruisers. A diesel engine without a turbo ('normally aspirated', NA, or just 'aspirated') is less complex and runs a little cooler, but makes less power and is less economical. I've run early Land Rover and Hilux 2.5 aspirated diesels in this low-performance category, as well as a 5.7-litre aspirated MAN truck. All would have trouble accelerating uphill through a wet paper bag, but well-thought-out gearing in both high and low range kept them moving along very nicely. Many ex-military MANs and Mercedes had big, low-tuned aspirated engines less sensitive to irregular engine oil changes and poor fuel.

But fitting an **after-market turbo** to an older, aspirated diesel engine is not a good idea just before a long overlanding trip. It's a bit like starting smoking – you won't drop dead after one puff, but you probably won't live as long. If you're buying used, stick with a **bog-standard diesel engine**, be it an aspirated old nail or a Tdi.

Intercoolers

Intercoolers look similar to radiators except they cool the air that's being driven from the very hot exhaust-driven turbo across the engine back into the inlet tract. Cooler air is denser and so contains more oxygen; better combustion or more power is the result. On a diesel you get around 25–30% more power with a turbo; an intercooler is good for at least another 10%, all with a negligible gain in weight or negative effect on the fuel economy.

Turbo-diesel engines often come from the factory with small intercoolers, but adding one, or fitting a bigger one is still a good way of broadly increasing the power range without stressing an engine. More under-bonnet heat will be generated with a bigger intercooler, which may find its way back into the cab but it's much less risky than adding a turbo. You'll need to **uprate the fuel mixture** to match the increased volume of incoming air, either manually or by replacing or reprogramming a computer chip. Intercoolers are maintenance free and at worst if one gets damaged just remove it, join up the pipes and carry on, if possible turning the fuel pump back to how it was before. There's more on Land Rover intercoolers on p72.

DIESEL QUALITY AND MODERN LOW-EMISSION ENGINES

The **problem for overlanders in diesel vehicles** is that the composition of diesel fuel, as well as the design of diesel engines, has diverged around the world as rich countries have adopted cleaner engines that must run on cleaner, low-sulphur fuel. Petrol, on the other hand, has become less of an issue; the process of reducing lead content began in the 1970s and leaded petrol has just about been eradicated in all but a half-a-dozen countries.

You don't have to be stuck behind a local bus crawling up an Andean pass to know that diesel exhaust can be bad for your health. That bus is probably running on **high-sulphur diesel** (HSD), just as much of the world was up to the 1990s. Compared to petrol, the high combustion pressure and lean mixture in diesels generates high temperatures and with it **particulate matter**, including black carbon – or 'soot' to you and me. Modern common rail diesel (CRD) engines go a long way in reducing this but, along with fuel filters, pumps and emissions equipment, they're more sensitive to fuel quality.

In the early 1990s **low-sulphur diesel (LSD)** was introduced in the US with sulphur levels reduced from 5000 to 500 parts per million (ppm). At that truck fleets across the nation experienced a rash of injector pump failures as o-ring seals shrivelled and subsequently leaked fuel. Much like the long-gone lead in petrol, sulphur has a lubricating and cooling effect on diesel fuel-injection components but was recognised as being similarly bad for human health. Engines have had to adapt, and new additives were introduced into LSD to get round lubrication deficiencies.

Sulphur is a natural component of diesel and at the start of this century sulphur levels of 2000ppm were considered acceptable. Since then strict laws have demanded as little as 10ppm: **ultra low-sulphur diesel** (ULSD) intro-duced around 2007. Since that time a range of additives such as the proven Opti-Lube XPD have become available to enable owners of old LSD diesel engines to cope with ULSD. Bio diesel (see p50) is said to work as well here.

In some poorer countries, reducing vehicle emissions isn't yet considered a priority and in two dozen or more HSD over 2000ppm is still sold. Just as truck fleets struggled to cope with the introduction of LSD in the nineties, now you may experience **problems running your ULSD engine on the HSD** found in parts of Africa, South America and parts of Asia.

Running on ULSD, a CRD engine emits about 10ppm, thanks partly to a **particulate filter** (DPF) in the exhaust system, a similar device to a catalyser ('cat'), which may also be present. Other emissions-reducing technology includes exhaust gas regeneration (EGR) valves, and intermittent burn-offs or 'regeneration' of the soot accu-mulating in the DPF once it reaches a pre-determined level. This **self-clean-ing cycle** greatly extends the life of the DPF by radically increasing exhaust

A diesel particulate filter.
© mattsavage.com

gas temperatures, changing the chemical composition of the exhaust gas to encourage soot burning, or injecting fuel directly in the chamber to burn at up to 600°C for over half an hour. As well as increasing fuel consumption, in tall, dry grass some of these methods are thought to be a fire risk (just as any hot exhaust can be) and, crucially, few DPFs can handle high-sulphur diesel for long. More recent regeneration technology involves a bank of less incendiary electrical elements in the filter (as in a toaster) that are said to operate with any grade of diesel. Especially **in the US**, it's well worth establishing exactly how your particulate filter is set up to remove accumulated soot.

Even with regeneration DPFs may require periodic **replacement**. Truck-engine estimates vary at around 150,000 miles, but this is when running and regenerating on ULSD. Filling up with diesel in rural Peru at ≤5000ppm (up to 500 times more than ULSD), you only need to divide a quarter of a million by 500 to work out how many miles a filter might be expected to last.

CHOOSING A VEHICLE

Whether the particulate filter just stops filtering but still allows the engine to run on HSD (much as a cat does once contaminated with leaded petrol) will depend on the manufacturer's intentions. Depending on the efficiency or ability of the regeneration, the DPF could clog up or emissions-monitoring sensors linked to the injection could trip the 'limp home mode' which requires heading straight for a garage with diagnostic equipment. Technology is evolving and the latest diesel engines are now said to recognise and deal with fuel quality, just as they do with other parameters such as varying elevations and ambient temperatures. This is because while there may be a huge market for vehicles, strict **emissions legislation** doesn't yet exist or may not be adhered to in parts of Africa, Asia or Latin America. A seemingly recognisable Asian-built sedan sold there may well be fitted with a cheaper, old-style 'Euro 2' engine (more on p50) that regulations in Europe or California outlawed nearly three decades ago.

This is the dilemma of running a modern diesel-engined road vehicle sold in 'green-conscious' markets but used in the overland zone, where crudely refined fuel can be cheaper than water to help keep the economy afloat.

DIESEL OR PETROL – THE PROS AND CONS

Out in the world just about everything runs on diesel or petrol/gasoline. Any other fuels such as LPG, hybrids or steam are eccentric choices for overlanding. Outside of the States, diesel is still the best option. If you still need persuading, read on.

DIESEL
For
- Usually cheaper than petrol/gasoline.
- At the same capacity and level of technological development, a modern turbo-diesel engine can be 50% more economical than petrol engine.
- Older diesel engines have few electrical and no electronic components so there's less to go wrong.
- Being an oil, diesel is less volatile and flammable than petrol: a major safety consideration.
- As long as you can start it, an old diesel will chug along happily almost forever, some even without a battery.
- Diesel engines are more reliable and last longer than petrol equivalents, especially old-style, large capacity, low-revving units. Truck engines can run for over a million kilometres without reconditioning.
- Diesels have superior engine braking characteristics to petrol engines, making steep off-road descents more controllable without having to resort to wheel braking

or electronic hill descent control gadgetry.
- Should you run out, diesel is easily available from passing trucks.
- Older (pre-CRD) indirect injection diesel engines are more tolerant of bad fuel than petrol engines from the same era.
- With no ignition electrics to speak of, older diesel engines are also less sensitive to deep wading and water spray.

Against
- Diesel fuel is messy and smelly and, unlike petrol, doesn't evaporate readily and without odour.
- Diesel-engined vehicles are more expensive than comparable petrol models.
- When something goes wrong with a diesel engine, particularly with injection, it can be hard to fix in the field and expensive to repair.
- Older diesel engines are incredibly noisy. Modern ones are much quieter.
- Because engine compression is typically double that of a car, push-starting a diesel requires a long run-up and good traction.
- At extreme altitude aspirated diesel engines without high-altitude compensation (HAC) can run potentially damaging high exhaust gas temperatures.
- Some older Japanese diesels sold in Europe have 24-volt electrical systems – good for winter starting but a pain when sourcing electrical components in the 12-volt world.

Which countries use HSD?

At ⌨ unep.org/Transport/New/PCFV you'll find maps showing **fuel quality data** country by country, including diesel sulphur levels. The good news is that since the last edition of this book VHSD appears to have followed leaded fuel. According to the 2016 UNEP maps, in **Latin America** HSD over 5000ppm has been eradicated, with 2000-5000ppm only found in Central America north of Costa Rica, Peru, Venezuela, Guyana and French Guiana. Most of South American runs on 500-2000ppm or less, with Chile and Panama running ULSD. In **Africa** Congo-Brazzaville, Tunisia and Egypt are said to run over 5000ppm, with much of West Africa as well as Cameroon, Zambia and Ethiopia using 2000-5000ppm. Southern and East Africa run 50-500ppm or much less. In **Asia** Turkey and Iran remain over 5000ppm while Mongolia, Bangladesh, Laos and Indonesia are on 2000-5000ppm.

It's possible that in the handful of >5000 countries in the Overland Zone – notably Egypt, and Iran – there may be two grades of diesel, and the UNEP data doesn't mean your DPF won't clog up in a country claiming to run on <500ppm. But at least you know for sure where it's way higher than that.

- Older turbo-diesels require relatively frequent changes of quality oil.
- Modern high-pressure-injection diesels with electronic engine management may not run well on the high sulphur diesel still sold in the poorer countries.

PETROL

For
- Can be cheaper to buy and easier to source (particularly in the States).
- Size-for-size, older petrol engines are lighter, quieter and more powerful than comparable diesels.
- Simple, carburettor-fed engines are easily understood and by bush mechanics.
- Wherever you live, if you're doing it on the cheap, a van or car with a petrol-engine broadens your options.

Against
- High flammability when stored.
- Potential problems with vapour lock (and so fuel starvation) in hot and slow conditions or at altitude.
- Combustion relies on an electrically generated spark (as opposed to spark-free compression with a diesel) and so the ignition components and electrical connections are prone to failures from dust, heat, vibration and moisture.
- Finally, there can be many reasons why a petrol engine may run poorly; with diesels these are comparatively few.

AUTOGAS

LPG (aka 'autogas' or 'auto propane') stands for liquefied petroleum gas, cheaper than petrol in Europe and North America, and a much cleaner-burning fuel. LPG is not the same as CNG (compressed natural gas – mostly methane). Along with India and even Iran, Brazil – which got into bio fuel way back – sells CNG as well as a petrol/ethanol blend.

In Europe and Australia many old V8 gas guzzlers get **converted** to LPG. You fit a bulky LPG tank alongside your conventional system and at the flick of a switch can run on gas or petrol. Although LPG has a high octane rating, it has less energy than petrol and so fuel consumption is a little higher, but is offset by the lower price.

In the UK today LPG is well under half the price of unleaded petrol, but for automotive rather than domestic cooking and heating uses it could be hard to find in developing countries. Turkey, with its extremely high fuel prices, and India are exceptions (Google for LPG stations in India) and so it'll be worth getting a filler adapter, which, being an LPG user, you'll know all about. Otherwise, an autogas conversion isn't recommended for overlanding.

Older diesel vehicles

Cleanliness, water contamination and sulphur levels apart, **diesel** is generally the same around the world. You won't get the detonation you can when low-octane petrol is used in a high-compression engine. Older, cruder diesel engines are more tolerant to all fuels, but as mentioned may benefit from additives when used in ULSD territories. For reasons other than the DPF, a CRD engine may not respond well to what comes out of the pumps in Uzbekistan.

And so, as with the whole ECU dilemma (see p42), err towards **more basic diesels** or attempt to divine from the manufacturer how a given engine will respond to extended if occasional operation on HSD. Your vehicle may smoke a little more (as it may do at altitude; it's relatively harmless) but it's definitely worth **changing your motor oil** more frequently, as sulphur breaks down motor oil more quickly. Simply removing particulate filters and cats and replacing them with a bit of pipe can be done (certainly with cats on motorcycles), but disconnecting any sensors down there may not agree with your ECU's parameters. At best a warning light or error code might blink annoyingly on the dash – at worst engine operation could be crippled.

Other diesel fuels

It sounds very green but **bio diesel** is nothing more than a few per cent of non-hydrocarbon-sourced oils and fats mixed in with regular diesel and you can almost certainly run it without concern in a ULSD engine. If anything, it's said as little as a 2% mix will lubricate injection mechanisms better than ULSD.

Older diesel engines can easily run on a 50% mix of cooking oil bought

from a supermarket, or heating oil (which is diesel without automotive additives). A while back in Europe, cooking oil was half the price of diesel and I ran an old Audi like that for a while. Now it costs about the same if not more, but in some countries may still be worth considering. Converting a diesel engine to run on waste cooking oil is another matter entirely and requires bulky filtration equipment as well as minor fuel line and injection modifications.

Causing a commotion while filling up at Safeways in Ankara. © Jurgen Stroo.

PETROL

After all that, you might think petrol is the way to go. Unleaded is now almost globally universal, but in remoter locations it may be hard to find a decent **95-octane** grade, which your modern engine may prefer. At times you'll have to rely on low-octane, regular, but modern EFI engines can adjust well to this.

With such an engine it's worth locating the oxygen-reading **lambda sensor** somewhere near the header pipe. Because it can be over-sensitive to certain fuels or conditions, consider disconnecting it or replacing it with a plug (you will be disowned by your vehicle's manufacturer, of course). It's commonly done with modern motorcycle engines running cats. The engine may run a little richer, which is no bad thing for longevity, if not for emissions.

BUYING AND EQUIPPING A VEHICLE FAR FROM HOME

For most of us, the buying and equipping of an overland vehicle is something that's best done from a secure base and with a steady income: usually at home.

However, depending on where you come from, where you want to start your journey and where you expect to end, it can make economic sense to **purchase a vehicle overseas**, avoiding the time, expense and bureaucracy involved in shipping. Just be aware you may find there's a problem then selling your vehicle at the end of the journey (more below).

For the sake of simplicity one can summarise the ideal places to buy overseas as the four 'Western' territories of North America, Western Europe, South Africa and Australia – which also happen to be the places where most overlanders and readers of this book will come from. Ex-pats or locals excepted, flying in and sourcing an overlanding vehicle elsewhere – in, for example, Borneo, Bolivia or Burundi – and setting off around the world will just get too complicated. Vehicle export and import regulations make this near impossible or very expensive.

For example it's extremely rare to see a vehicle from any North African country driving around Europe, even if we Europeans are free to visit and drive across Africa without too much hindrance. It's a similar story with Latin American vehicles in the US, or Chinese vehicles in Russia or India.

Travellers from Europe, South Africa or Australia wanting to explore **Latin America** may want to consider buying a vehicle in North America or possibly the more affluent countries of South America such as Argentina or Chile. Meanwhile, Canadians and Americans will have **Asia** and **Africa** at their feet if they buy in Western Europe or South Africa. As a non-resident, the problem of **vehicle registration** (and **carnets** where necessary) is not insurmountable. Neither is enough **motor insurance** to get you into the overland zone, after which you buy it where you can and as you go.

Buying an **overland-ready vehicle** from fellow travellers who are ending their journey can be ideal. Sure it may be worn and dusty, but it'll also be ready to go, requiring little in the way of time or expense to get it into shape. It's not uncommon for Brits and other Europeans to try and sell their vehicles in South Africa to overlanders heading back

up, especially as selling a foreign vehicle there is difficult or costly and invokes carnet issues.

Along with more isolated Australia, **South Africa** is a special case in that you have a great range of local, bush-ready overlanding vehicles that may have been used for recreational exploration of southern Africa and so will add up to what you need to cross continents. Doing the same in **Australia** will of course require shipping to somewhere like Kuala Lumpur or Vladivostok, but that's not so hard to do and, what's more, if you've always wanted to explore the outback now's your chance to put your new vehicle to the test for a couple of months before heading overseas. As mentioned on p83, Australia has about the best range of diesel Toyota 4x4s going, any number of Japanese minivans and campers, as well as bigger trucks like the Mitsubishi Fuso and N-series Isuzus (of which more on p129).

Selling abroad

There's something about foreign cars that state bureaucracies frown upon, and which for us otherwise lucky Westerners also affects **selling any car abroad**. In much of Africa, excepting South Africa, selling can turn into a clandestine operation where you're only in the clear once you're over the border with the cash, something best left to experienced car dealers. I know car sellers who've been set up in Africa. The buyer's 'brother' works in customs and when you rock up at the border he knows exactly how much cash you have on you. He takes half, pats you on the back and sends you on your way.

In **South Africa** don't bother trying to sell your vehicle unless you're a resident returning home after more than a year away; your vehicle must have been in your name for over a year, be right-hand drive and have been made after 2000. If trying to sell an old LHD you might be better off in Angola.

In most of **Asia** you won't even get that far, although in some **Latin American countries** it can be done entirely legitimately and without having to invoke Masonic privilege, as long as buyer or seller agrees to pay the customs duty. Remember too that some markets won't take to a vehicle with the steering wheel on the other side, and some countries won't even permit such vehicles to be imported.

Two-wheel drive: the road less travelled

Overlanding? Most people's thoughts turn immediately to a rugged 4x4. After all, the original steam engines of the early 19th century were all-wheel drive because a mule didn't use just two legs to get around so why would a traction engine? And why would you? Permanent four-wheel drive (4WD) was the norm between the wars and the original Land Rover of the late 1940s was full-time 4WD.

In fact you can see a whole lot of this planet in an inexpensive **two-wheel-drive** (2WD) car, van or truck, enjoying lower running costs and a profile to match. Excepting some trans-African routes and avoiding seasonal extremes, it's easy to follow all sorts of trans-continental highways and byways without recourse to all-terrain vehicles. Certainly, **good ground clearance** (see p40) will greatly increase your scope for exploration and adventure, as will an **extra-low first gear**; many commercial vans have this anyway. But, you might ask, where's the fun in that?

But, you might ask, where's the fun in that?

Apart from the perceived unadventurous **image** of overlanding in a repainted City Hoppa bus, a regular van or a converted tipper, the biggest day-to-day drawback is when roads and tracks turn bad (particularly after rain), and also in getting far enough off a road to bush camp in privacy. For some overlanders the prime motivation in going with a 4WD is to extend their off-roading skills, but really this is something you can do more safely – and in a more extreme fashion – near home. If you view overlanding more as a travel experience than an off-roading challenge you'll find you can get much further than you think in a 2WD. You'll recognise this when you get back. As you'll read on p293, successfully navigating off-road hazards is as much down to **driving skill** (judgement and experience) as the vehicle.

ROAD CARS

It's only a big road trip so why not take a regular road car? As long as it drives, brakes and turns, an old car can be the least expensive way of fulfilling your desire for an overland adventure.

Apart from the low cost of buying and running such a car, the main thing that separates it from a van is **space**, which adds up to comfort. But even in a genuine overland scenario – as opposed to a trans-America or round-Australia road trip – accommodation will be easier to find than you think (though on a budget, the sorts of hotels you can afford may make camping preferable).

When compared to a typical 4x4, a conventional vehicle also has advantages in **the way you're perceived**, observed and even received. Driving a regular vehicle that's seen and used locally, rather than some over-accessorised all-terrain special forces wagon, you're less likely to get turned over at borders, ripped off by mechanics or resented by the locals as a rich foreigner on holiday, even if that's what you actually are.

Road car mindset

By overlanding in a road car you're consciously putting yourself at a **disadvantage** in terms of both dealing with the less-than-perfect road conditions and the practicalities of roadside camping. Living basically out of the back of a car in all weathers will get tiresome. Typically it takes youth (inexperience matched with a devil-may-care enthusiasm and a lack of cash) or some level of eccentricity to regard the above limitations as trivial.

Much of the appeal of doing it this way is **keeping it simple** and cheap and taking each day as it comes. A trans-continental road car shouldn't cost you even half what it takes to buy and equip a decent 4x4. The whole point is road cars are easy to find and cheap to buy, prepare and run; in fact cheap enough to sell or abandon should a repair become non-viable. Therefore, an ethos worth cultivating with a cheap road car is one of existential optimism and ultimate disposability (this must be done responsibly, of course!).

These days purchasing an old hack can cost a lot less than running it for a year. Furthermore, the sort of solidly built, simply engineered (but now unacceptably inefficient) cars that fall within this price bracket happen to possess many of the qualities that makes them preferable for the overlanding life.

Look at such a car as something that owes you nothing. Equipped with the right attitude, the well-known line from that Kris Kristofferson song hits the mark: as long as your chosen machine runs well enough out of the coal mines of Kentucky to the altiplano sun you have **nothing to lose** and the consequent freedom from the anxiety a more precious machine engenders can be liberating. For most overlanders, more than borders, marauding bandits and showers of brimstone, the mechanical integrity and the security of their mobile home is a constant worry.

Just don't make the mistake of assuming that the developing world is full of 'they-don't-make-them-like-they-used-to' bangers. Sure, in the poorer countries you'll still find old Peugeots, Mercedes sedans, VW buses, Series Land Rovers and GMC pickups, but these are all running on a wing and a prayer, while around them run hordes of tinny, bland but efficient modern Korean and very often Chinese-Korean cars, vans and trucks. Resist falling into a nostalgic assumption that there'll be any **mechanical and parts support** for an old banger. The places answering your needs with be hole-in-the-wall garages with an oil-soaked sandy floor, a welder and a lathe.

Give yourself a good start by buying more than a rusted-out wreck and by servicing it, equipping it with essential **spares** and maybe making some of the **modifications** outlined below. Then equip it with used or cheap gear and travel light; light enough so that if your old dog barks at you one time too many, you can shoot it right there, hand someone the ownership documents and find another way of completing your journey.

CHOOSING A VEHICLE

Shedding no tears for a Mercedes 190 dumped in the Balkans.

Choosing a car

A **large estate** or station wagon with the rear seats removed gives two people the chance to sleep in the back should the weather or climate demand it. The benefits of an old, non-electronically managed engine and manual transmission have already been discussed, and coil suspension is much easier to modify reliably than torsion bars (see p143). All over the world, old diesel estates of two litres or more weren't around for too long before they evolved into smaller, more efficient units, but big old **petrol** engines (although often mated to an auto box) are still around and inexpensive.

Another old Merc going where it shouldn't.
© Jurgen Stroo.

Front- or rear-wheel drive?

Off the tarmac the jury is still out on which is better, but larger cars are usually rear-wheel drive (RWD) and tend to get stuck less. This could be a false impression as larger cars have bigger engines as well as more momentum, all of which helps off road. Certainly it contradicts the assumption that a front-wheel drive's (FWD) engine weight over the driven wheels is desirable for good traction.

All this only gets critical when the going gets rough and steep, but having one set of wheels steering while the others drive may have something to do with better performance off road. The complexities of driving and steering the same 'axle' can stress the **CV joints** of FWDs. Furthermore, on a steep, loose slope there's little weight over those front wheels to provide traction (only pertinent to a big, long van or motor home). If you take this route, get reconditioned CVs or a spare set, although don't expect DIY replacement to be as easy as changing a tyre.

If nothing else the traditional engine layout of a RWD car is easier to comprehend and work on as the engine and transmission are in line with the car. On a conventional FWD it's all packed in across the frame, and unless you know the vehicle well it can be hard to tell what's what, let alone get to it.

VANS AND PEOPLE CARRIERS (MPVs)

Any form of **light commercial load carrier**, be it for products or passengers, is far more suited to life on the road than a regular car, whose only real advantage is it's cheap and nippy. A van is built to carry loads so may cope better with what lies ahead, especially if you stay well below its GVW. A 3.5-tonne GVW is pretty small so a lightly built van won't be as tough as a 4x4, but it will cost less to run than bigger trucks and can be driven on a regular licence.

Unlike some unconverted 4x4s, you can easily **live and sleep** prone in a van, not be forced to live beside it most of the time. In the cold or wet, or when waiting for something like a border post to open or a ferry to arrive, this is something you'll appreciate. Vans and buses also have **tougher transmission** as well as **larger wheels** and firmer **suspension**; this is for carrying the load but also happens to achieve good ground clearance. What they won't offer, especially in older examples, is comfort and efficiency.

Which van?

In Europe at least the pick of the crop comes from Germany, such as Mercedes and VW, or from Japan, e.g. Mazdas, Mitsubishi L300s, Nissan Urvans, and various Toyotas; there's also Ford, Iveco and the French brands Peugeot and Renault. As with regular cars, rear-wheel drive is better, but less common in vans these days, as it enables a low and flat load bed. In the back, space and standing height, whether it's permanent, or temporary with a raising roof, are what you're after if planning on living in it for weeks or months.

Be warned that if you're planning to get your van professionally **converted into a campervan**, it's going to be expensive. A quality compact campervan conversion (especially on a VW) that won't fall apart after a few hundred miles of corrugations will easily double the cost of a plain van or add up to the price of a good 4x4. Full conversions with a sink, cooker and toilet start at around £4000 in the UK. Outlaying this amount on an old van is one reason why many overlanders try to do the job themselves or settle on a 4x4 instead, fitting a roof tent and adapting the interior to get a tough, go-anywhere machine that's not much more cramped than a kombi – or so it seems at the time. The other option is to buy an off-the-peg campervan: see p64.

RUNNING AN OLD VAN IN SOUTH AMERICA

For those reluctant to invest in a slick four-wheeler, buying a vehicle well past its scrap-by date may be just the solution.

Still, I was a little leery handing over $750 for an '82 Chevy 350 van. The number-one fear people have about travelling to distant lands is breaking down in the middle of nowhere. Stripped from your usual support networks, the thought of being stranded in an immobile hunk of metal can be daunting.

Breakdowns and repairs

One thing you'll find as a gringo/muzungu on the road is in the poorer, non-Anglo world people are less suspicious or indifferent to others in need. One time in Guatemala I hit a hole in the road and damaged the front end. The truck I'd passed speeding down the hill pulled over to help, even before he could see there was a woman driving. The man drove to town and returned with a friend who made a roadside repair. Three hours and $45 later I was on my way.

'South of the border' in the wider, global, sense, labour is cheap enough to invest in time-consuming repairs on an old crate like mine. Indeed the majority of drivers in the developing world will be running such a vehicle. Used parts and indeed vehicles are valued highly in poorer countries as the labour to keep them running is cheap. Part of the reason for cheaper labour is mechanical

jobs aren't charged on an extortionate hourly basis but by the job, an advantage with an older vehicle with rusted components that haven't been touched in years. And though an older vehicle might be an eyesore back home, or worse still stigmatise you as a poor or unstylish individual, in the overland zone you'll just blend in better and be less of a target for robbery.

Which old banger?

Try and match your marque with the destination. Chevrolets are common in Latin America, as are some other American brands. Francophone Africa will have plenty of aged French or German marques while Toyotas and lesser Japanese brands are built and found all over.

Buy from someone you trust or have it checked by a mechanic before buying. Sure, things went wrong but I could afford regular maintenance and things breaking occasionally. And I have to admit I'm a bit smug. At the bottom of South America, owners of flashier vehicles reeled at the cost of shipping a road-weary vehicle back home (let alone the risks involved in doing so). After thousands of miles of driving, I have the option of either ditching it or recouping my costs by selling it for parts – and maybe even coming out ahead.

LORRAINE CHITTOCK

Mercedes vans

The choice of travellers for decades, **Mercedes'** rear-wheel-drive **T1 series** (the 308/310 was built from 1989) followed the similar, widely used **TNs** dating from 1977, whose snub-nosed profile survives today as the Vario. Just about all TNs sold in Europe featured a diesel engine; earlier 2-litre versions were not surprisingly underpowered, but all easily outlived the body (as did many engines from that era).

The longer 407, 409 and 508s with the legendary five-cylinder, 3-litre **OM617 diesel engine** up to 1986 are a safe bet and a version of that engine is still made in India. From 1989 the TN became a T1. In a long-wheelbase (LWB) 406D, 408D or 508D high-roof version, the basic four-cylinder 4-litre engine

From top. **1**: Mercedes 508D resting in the shady overlanders' campsite in Islamabad. **2**: Spacious 406D; pretty good frontal angles too. **3**: Sprinter motorhome windjammer exploring the Middle East.

will never be too stressed and with payload to spare these make a great mobile home, although the higher GVW models have dual rear tyres and therefore certain limitations off road (see box p61).

Most run 16′ wheels and old camper versions can be found in the UK from under £2000. It's worth knowing that today Force Motors in India still make a van based on, although not a facsimile of the T1, so spares are available for everything except the locally modified engines.

These days it's the **Sprinter** that still leads Mercedes' van range. Common rail diesel 2.7- or even 3-litre engines are the norm, even in the US, with wheelbases up to 4.3m (170″) and payloads of a tonne or more. A factory four-wheel-drive version is even available bringing some extra clearance with it, and Sprinters are commonly used as the basis for smaller motorhomes (see opposite).

Just remember, **rust** will be a problem with anything from pre-2000s and any van with **twin rear doors**, particularly long-bodied versions, will flex enough and suck in **dust** past the seals on dry tracks. Even 4x4 wagons with stronger bodies that are rubber mounted on a stiff chassis are prone to dust suction like this and it's one reason why most larger campers have side doors.

VW Kombis

The classic rear-engined **T1 and T2 VW** Kombinationskraftwagen (hence 'kombi') popularised campervanning in the Sixties, but now are too old and valuable to take on the road unless you're a clued-up enthusiast. Fast forward to 1985 and a full-time 4WD '**Syncro' version of the T3** was most effective with a petrol engine or when converted to 1.9 Tdi. Although it often came with a viscous central diff and even axle diff locks, a Syncro T25 has no low range. Instead it features an extra-low 'cross-country' first gear for tricky situations; a great idea that would be a welcome feature on many 2WDs. T3s carried on being produced in South Africa with a 2.6 five-cylinder Audi unit until 2002.

With all Kombis and the like, the 'front row at the movies' **forward seating position** offers a great driving experience and simplifies precise manoeuvring and minimal overhangs make pretty good ground clearance thanks to **independent suspension**. As on a Citroen 2CV, this suspension provides a similar if far less extreme 'raised axle centre' effect to the much-vaunted portal axles of a Unimog and the like.

With age comes rust and wear, plus lame original engines and manual gearboxes are a weak point compared to the tougher Mercedes options of the same era. An old 1.6 turbo would need careful inspection, whereas a more modern and economical 1.9 Tdi conversion would be much nearer the mark.

In 1990 the **T4** ('Eurovan' in the US) dropped the much-loved Kombi shape to adopt a more conventional swept back front end positioned over a conventional forward-mounted engine. Despite front-wheel drive this made engine access much easier and created a more spacious rear at the cost of the 'front row' driving position. Using the 1.9-litre Tdi engines as fitted to T3s, performance and economy were much improved and the 2.4 five-cylinder engine had virtually no electronics. Later 1.9- and 2.5 Tdis were still pretty basic, but had electronically managed diesel pumps.

A **Syncro T4** was available at least in Europe and South Africa but with the front axle being primary. With some sort of raised roof a T4 could make a container-shippable camper with enough off-road ability.

From top. 1 Rear-engined T3 Syncro. 2: Forward engined T4 Transporter – good clearance. 3: A T5 camper. © Toby Savage.

People carriers (MPVs): minibuses and LCVs

People carriers or **multi-person vehicles (MPVs)** like Renault's trend-setting Espace (with variants now produced by all manufacturers) might come across as too suburban for an overland adventure, but they often have plenty of space, great access and are built for comfort. Almost all are FWD with transverse engines, which can make access tricky, but family ownership is no bad thing as it often comes with a full service history. A quick look at what's available shows angles and clearance are decent and wheel sizes are pretty good for unpaved roads. Access to the back tends to be a sliding side door and seats are often individual and can be taken out as necessary to make a living area.

Japanese minibuses and MPVs such as the Mazda Bongo also make great, competitively priced **compact campervan conversions**; see p66 for details. This roundup really only scratches the surface of some obvious options available in Europe. Mercedes are the best choice simply because of the perceived global reach of their parts network but you can't go too far wrong with any product from Japan, which once had the reach that Korean vehicles now have and Chinese vehicles soon will have over parts of Asia.

Minibuses

A long-wheelbase **15-seater minibus** such as a Toyota Hiace, or one of its many Japanese imitators from Mazda, Mitsubishi or Nissan and so on, is a short-range people carrier found all around the world, especially in Africa and the Middle East. With a near-continuous space of about five metres from the dashboard to the tailgate, they make a good conversion if you can live with the height limitations. With a big sliding door on one side and a lift-up tailgate, access is easy at the price of **narrowness and headroom**. Aim for the higher-roof models. Realistically you're looking at something like the **third-generation** Hiace produced from the late 1980s to 2005 in auto or manual and powered by anything up to a 3-litre turbo-diesel engine plus torsion bar independent front suspension (IFS) and leaves on the back. After that Hiaces followed the FWD semi-bonneted trend of modern vans.

The **drawbacks** are poor engine and transmission access, small, 14" wheels and modest ground clearance. A full length of windows might be considered an advantage, but think about security and cabin overheating issues. Apart from a lonesome camp out on the steppe, most of the time you'd prefer a lot less glass, for which you'll want a van.

Hands up, it's a Hiace with a fixed high roof!
© supercamper.co.uk

On the plus side: they're from the built-in-Japan era (not Japanese marques built elsewhere), the driving position is nice, and you'll probably find Toyotas hammering away as genuine people carriers, even as Hyundai and the like replace ageing fleets.

Pricier versions like VW's T5 Transporter not only have better angles, clearance and bigger wheels, but a solid build for which the marque has a name.

Light commercial vehicles (LCVs)

In Europe at least, car-like **high-cube vehicles (HCVs)** or **light commercial vehicles (LCVs)** and wagons are everywhere; some are commercial and spartan, others are trying to be mini MPVs like Citroën Berlingo/Peugeot Partner and the Renault Kangoo (Nissan Kubistar) or Ford's Transit Connect. The French models, in particular the Kangoo (there's an on-demand 4x4 'Trekka' as well as a heavy duty version) are based on the

Kangoo. Good angles and volume for a car.

'**farmer's car**' concept of the 2CV, with independent suspension, 15" wheels and good clearance, and with the Kangoo good angles at each end though it's said the rear torsion bars on a Kangoo can be a weak point when overloaded.

CAB-OVER FLATBED PICKUPS

In North America the wide-open prairies obviate the need for space-saving cab-over ('COE', or 'forward-control') vehicles, whether you're running a builder's ute or a freeway hauling truck. In more crowded Europe and parts of Asia it's another story, and to an overlander with a view to fabricating or mounting a cabin there are distinct advantages to choosing a **cab-over flatbed**.

Without getting bogged down in an ex-military truck that does 12mpg and has been sat on an airfield since the fall of the Berlin Wall, you get modern engineering and **comfort** levels with a **higher driving position** (and so visibility) than a regular van. You also get maximised load **space** for the vehicle length and so ferries and shipping can be cheaper and manoeuvring and parking easier. And if the **cab tilts** up, engine and gearbox access is better than some motorcycles. Ground clearance and angles are also good on these sorts of vehicles, and these two attributes are more useful more of the time than four-wheel drive. The presence of a proper flat bed with no wheel arches also greatly simplifies fitting a living module, with space below the bed alongside the chassis to mount extra tanks and so on.

Toyota's Dyna or **Nissan Cabstar** 'one tonners' (3.5 GVW) are examples at the smaller end of the range, with little more payload than a 4x4 wagon. The next jump typically goes from 3.5 to 7.5 tonnes, with something like the **Isuzu N-series** giving you at least four metres (13ft) of flat space to load or build on. With Mercedes trucks, the Vario has better angles than the 814 or 815s, but with less clearance all round.

These bigger examples are especially **adaptable** for overlanding because, as has been mentioned, their

A dinky Nissan Cabstar 3.5-tonner with a body that squeezes into a container. © Luke

Top: Saviem flatbed plus caravan. You can pay €500,000 for something like that. © Sue Shuttleworth. **Bottom**: Ex-Telecom body on back-to-front plus suitcases. © M. Edwards

chassis are over-engineered so once a load bed has been removed (gaining more potential payload), the typical 3–4 tonne payload available is surely more than enough. While not so easy to hop in and out of, cab-over pickups also improve on the off-road dynamics of a comparable van: without any bodywork in the way, at the back it's much easier to clear wheels and axles.

Drawbacks might be the **single cab** at the lower ends of the payload range. Even for two people it's worth getting the roomiest cab going. A family will of course need a **crew cab** as pictured on p70. Off road the ride will get bouncy as you're directly over the axle and perhaps the biggest drawback is the lack of a **crumple zone** in the event of a head-on crash.

On the back

For more on the practicalities of making an accommodation module see p218 but, in brief, what you can do here is give it the full treatment with a customised LAK body (see p120) or just attach something as humble as a caravan or whatever living-sized cabin you can get your hands on.

Perhaps the biggest negative is the **image**. Who'd want to be spotted on the Serengeti in a converted tipper or recovery wagon with a bank of flashing lights still on the roof plus a caravan on the back? Maybe only those who see how much further the thousands saved will take them.

CASE STUDY – A 7.5T CAB-OVER PICKUP

On my travels I came across this Chinese DFAG flatbed which exemplified many of the attributes of a nifty overlander's cab-over.

The **extended cab** makes your time in there more comfortable, the engine was a **4-litre Cummins** running **air brakes** which means good access to motor spares.

The loadbed was **4m long** by 1.8m wide and tyres were **700x16s LTs** duals. As mentioned opposite, they could be replaced with four slightly taller 750x16 ATs. The only question is could the wheel bearings hack the offset leverage.

As for overcoming **chassis torsion**, 'open' bolted up flat beds (and especially tippers) are fairly immune to it as regards to disintegration. A box cabin would require more so go to pp218-254.

DUAL-WHEEL REAR AXLES

Once inflated to the correct pressure, a tyre is designed to bear a limited weight, marked in a code on the side (see table p149). Big tyres or multiple tyres at higher pressures carry greater loads. **Dual rear wheels** (known as 'dualies' in the US) are a way of increasing the payload without resorting to either additional axles (a longer chassis, more weight and cost) or to a bigger, taller tyre, which raises a vehicle's load- or entry-height and the centre of gravity.

Most **road damage** is caused by heavy goods vehicles (HGVs) and studies have shown that dual tyres exacerbate this. In Europe many HGVs now run so-called **'wide-base single' tyres** (known as **'super singles'** in North America) on three axles instead of dual tyres on two axles. This is thought to produce less damage by spreading the load and also increasing stability.

Problems with 'dualies' can occur in off-highway overlanding scenarios. Dual set-ups use small tyres compared to the size of the vehicle, which certainly helps support a big payload but results in limited under-axle **clearance** and reduced 'suspension' flex inherent in tall tyre walls (desirable in the dirt, not on highways; for more see p148). Debris can also get jammed between the paired sidewalls (a tyre's most vulnerable area) and reducing pressures to improve traction (highly effective in soft sand,

see p295) causes the sagging paired tyres to rub each other and **overheat**. It's also hard to inspect the inner tyre at a glance.

This doesn't mean that if running duals you can't deflate them to extricate yourself, but running for days like this at low pressures across desert regions will wear them prematurely, or even ruin them.

Dual tyres also create more **drag** when driving through ruts typically cut by vehicles on single tyres (of course this has compensations elsewhere in more potential traction). And finally, the extreme **rim offset** required to make all six tyres interchangeable means relatively heavy rims are required.

These days, even the smallest AWD military trucks take the 'super single' approach, after which they resort to multiple axles. Unless you expect a fairly undemanding road trip, choose single rear tyres.

Running singles on a dual rear axle

Some cab-overs come with **smaller dual rear wheels** to ease manual loading of heavy objects and to lower the centre of gravity. Although this has the advantage of giving a low, flat load bed, allowing full use of the load area, for overlanding having two tyre sizes on one vehicle is a bad idea. Go for the models with **same size tyres** and, ideally, larger diameter singles.

Up to a point, dual wheels need not be a complete disaster on a mostly road-based trip (which covers most overlanders), but as long as the payload isn't pushed to the limit, **inner rear wheels can be removed** to improve performance all round (less weight, drag and power loss). Even then, running singles in this way may be **illegal** in your home country and can stress the axle and hub assemblies in a way they weren't designed to deal with.

You'll commonly see refuse and other commercial trucks with **lift axles** raised when there's no payload, although this isn't quite the same thing. In Africa you see old MAN and Mercedes trucks running singles on a dual rear axle, probably more down to the cost of six new tyres when four will do.

If considering this you could take the chance to **go up a tyre size** if there's room, as with the 700-to-750 example in the box opposite. As long as the engine is torquey enough to turn a larger diameter tyre and you don't have to meddle with the standard rims, you'll get a bit more clearance at the cost of slightly higher gearing. This isn't so desirable when pulling hard out of soft sand on a hot day with a full load so it's something best experimented with back home. There is more on tyres on p147.

CHOOSING A VEHICLE

TOWING TRAILERS

Sturdy off-road trailers suited to overland travel are made in South Africa, Australia and North America, places where they're widely used in domestic recreational off-roading. Applied to a genuine overlanding context, for a group greater than two a small trailer might seem like the answer to payload limitations or the expense of a larger, less agile vehicle, but overall they're rarely used, or used only once.

Setting aside the practical limitations in manoeuvrability, particularly the need to reverse from near-bogging situations or make a quick U-turn on a busy, narrow highway to get back on course, dramatic increases in fuel consumption can occur (especially at higher speeds or on soft terrain), and you'll also incur extra ferry and shipping costs. Along with this comes an additional strain on the transmission as well as frequently reported breakages of the trailer's chassis, axle or suspension (see opposite). Washboard tracks are hard enough on regular vehicles but they can pulverise the contents of a trailer and larger bumps will send it airborne.

If you decide to take this route, do the research and invest in a proven model able to take the beating and one that runs the same size wheels and tyres as the vehicle and has the same 'track', or axle width.

CHOOSING A VEHICLE

Lately you've got ultra-heavy, carry-and-do-it-all **camping trailers** that feature a kitchen, fridge, batteries and water tanks and that even fold out into a giant tent. As with pickup demountables mentioned later, it's a great idea for families going camping for a weekend. Friday night they can charge up the fridge and hitch up the trailer to an otherwise unmodified SUV that's used during the week as a regular car. But these are not the end-users who'll be fording rivers or negotiating rockfalls on the Karakoram Highway, two months and 4500 miles from home.

There's a temptation to think you can chuck all the heavy stuff into a trailer to spare your vehicle the stress and rattles. But just as you'd not **overload** a vehicle, don't plan overloading a trailer and expect to get away with it. As John Bernstein (right) knew before he made his decision, stories of trailer failures are common. Protective packing that allows no room for movement and thorough lashing down is essential.

This trailer literally weighs a tonne.
© mattsavage.com

If you decide to take this route, do the research and invest in a proven model able to take the beating and one that runs the same size wheels and tyres as the vehicle and has the same 'track', or axle width, between the wheels. Many models claim to be ready for off-road driving – maybe for a weekend – but few can sustain months of overland travel without regular maintenance and occasional repair.

ACROSS ASIA WITH A TRAILER

After reading several accounts of disasters with trailers I decided nevertheless to use one for our family's London to Beijing trip. The decision was made from necessity rather than choice – with four children there simply are no cars big enough for six people and their gear. We didn't want a truck since we were planning to follow some narrow roads into the remotest places we could find. I prefer the flexibility of a car and trailer.

We chose a 'built for off-road' Horizon Adventure Trailer, which came highly recommended by Frogs Island 4x4, who were doing up our 70-series Land Cruiser.

As you'd expect, the trailer was fine on tarmac, but as soon as we hit corrugations, things began to shake loose, starting with the latches holding the lid. We weren't worried until we headed out into Turkmenistan's Karakum Desert in the height of summer heat and onto some terrible surfaces. On low sand dunes the trailer acted as an anchor so we had to pick up speed or get stuck. That's to be expected with any trailer, but on uneven rock surfaces the rough treatment caused real issues. Some 90km from the nearest road, disaster struck. The plates holding the airbag suspension tore and punctured the air-bag and the lack of suspension broke the axle. And the wheel then fell off. In 50°C heat we tied it on with rope and inched our way out of the desert over many, many hours. When we finally reached the road the other wheel fell off, bouncing down the road. We were lucky to find a passing tractor driver who welded both wheels on again.

When we finally got to town, we replaced the airbags with metal springs, which kept us going, but the rough roads soon broke them too. For weeks we stopped for welding after every section of bad road – the axles cracked continuously, the springs broke, the bolts holding the A-frame to the trailer broke five or six times, and a shock absorber fell off. All this repeated welding melted the wires several times so we had no brake lights or power for the fridge. We ended up with a Heath-Robinson contraption of bits of bed frame and garden gate holding the broken springs together and various home-made reinforcements on the axle.

To their credit, Horizon took the matter seriously and did everything they could to help us out. They redesigned and upgraded the bolts holding the A-frame, the plates holding the air-bags and the axle joints, and shipped boxes of spare parts to Kyrgyzstan. The Horizon Mark 2 was much better and we only had minor problems from there on in.

So, pros include: lots of extra space, room for a kitchen and a fridge, easily accessible bags and, if the trailer is strong enough, water tanks. When we got stuck up narrow roads we could detach the trailer, hand turn it, and then turn the car. These situations would have been much more complicated in a larger vehicle. The drawbacks were initial reliability, manoeuvrability (difficult to reverse) and the drag in sand and mud. Would I do it again? Yes, but I'd go over every nut and bolt and get anything that didn't look like a tank part replaced.

JOHN BERNSTEIN

CHOOSING A VEHICLE

The crux is to have a **solid chassis** with repairable components and a simple design, not a flashy five-star mobile catering system with flood lighting and integral generators sat on a rail of welded girders.

And if you're thinking of towing a **caravan** (a 'trailer' in North America), you're reading the wrong book. Most examples aren't designed to take a hammering outside of holiday touring regions, though you may occasionally see them strapped down to the back of a flatbed truck, an inexpensive and ingenious way of making a motorhome and one that's bound to outlast a regular towed caravan.

OTHER THINGS TO THINK ABOUT WITH A TRAILER

• Ascertain the towing rating of your vehicle. It's one reason people choose 4x4s with a separate ladder chassis on which to securely fix the hitch and which are rated to tow up to 3.5 tonnes.

• If you acquire a vehicle with a hitch, don't assume that it's up to your needs. Disregarding the mounting and integrity of the vehicle chassis, the standard 50mm hitch is rated to tow up to 3.5 tonnes and take a nose weight of around 150kg, but only for normal towing on sealed roads. Off-road nose weight might double even when towing half the maximum rated payload.

• For this reason choose a lighter, uncomplicated trailer with a durable chassis and suspension. If the loaded trailer ends up weighing more than half of the towing vehicle you can be in for all sorts of stability and durability issues.

• Ideally the trailer's axle wants to be rated at twice the expected total weight. Two tonnes is a minimum, but recognise that trailer manufacturers may exaggerate claims, just as car makers do too. There's something to be said for making a trailer from the back end of a scrapped LWB 4x4, maybe even the same model of 4x4 that you're using.

• Can the brakes stop the extra mass without overheating? It's another good reason to keep it light. Beyond a certain payload (usually around 750kg), trailers must be fitted with over-run brakes, but these can be troublesome in dusty conditions.

• Carry spare springs, bearings and shocks.

• Proper loading is vital for stability and predictable handling, ideally balanced with a little weight on the hitch. Packing the trailer correctly in this way takes practice. Keep heavy weights low and directly over the axle.

• If your vehicle has one big rear door, make sure it can be opened with the trailer attached and jockey wheel up. And make sure a rear-door mounted spare wheel won't foul the trailer at steep off-roading angles.

• Leaf-spring suspension is easily repaired and doesn't require A-frames to locate the axle (see p218). Independent suspension may work better but is more complicated.

• If anticipating radical off-roading make sure your jockey wheel can be removed, not just wound up out of the way.

• Fit a light inside the trailer lid.

• On occasions the trailer will get pelted by flying stones, water spray and dust from the vehicle's rear wheels. Fit full-size mudflaps on the rear tyres. Some trailers have a huge 'bow plate' on the draw bar.

• Stainless steel looks nice and is durable and rust-free, but these are the only real advantages. It may work well on the trailer body, which takes less of a beating than the chassis, but, as with alloy or steel roof racks, regular mild steel can be galvanised, flexes more and is easily repairable on the road.

• A trailer might require registration.

Recreational vehicles

One of the things that separates the adventure that is overlanding from the recreational activity of touring or holidaymaking is the unpredictable nature of the **highway infrastructure** in the overland zone. The climate, a lack of maintenance or even a road-building programme, along with a much smaller volume of private traffic means a seamless network of well-signed highways is unknown out in the world. The Trans-Siberian Highway to Vladivostok and a road across the Sahara from Casablanca to Dakar were built soon after the millennium but still include unmade sections. The Pan-American Highway is separated by the Darien Gap either side of the Panama-Colombia border, which will never be sealed. And once you wander off the occasionally congested national trunk roads you'll be faced with rough, narrow backroads. This is one reason why robust vehicles (including 4x4s) are considered a natural choice for overlanding and why most 'RVs' or **recreational vehicles** are not.

A **motorhome** or **campervan** is the ideal tool for autonomous exploration in North America, Australia and Europe: comfortable to live in and often able to tow a small jeep as well as carrying your boat on the roof and your bike on the front bumper. But most RVs are too flimsy to travel in the overlanding zone. Not all cope with unsealed and ill-maintained roads or steep ferry ramps; they make it difficult to head off-road for a peaceful bush-camp; and their design doesn't lend itself to DIY repairs, maintenance and roadside improvisation. For all these reasons aspirant overlanders generally favour self-building their living quarters or commissioning a conversion on their own choice of base vehicle rather than go with an off-the-peg RV. (Guidelines for that whole monumental process start on p143.) However, *chacun à son goût*, so it's worth understanding how RVs are categorised because some classes are more suitable for overlanding than others.

A-CLASS MOTORHOMES

This is your 'coach-built' body fitted on a bus, van or truck chassis and engine unit. In the States they're an institution of which the Iowa-built **Winnebago** range is the best known. In Europe lavishly equipped, 12-metre (40ft) motorhomes with rear-mounted bus-like engines are rare. Smaller, front-engined A-classers of around six metres are more suited to local driving conditions.

An A-class motorhome appropriately stationed in Leadville, CO. There's a Harley on the back with a couple of MTBs and more bikes on the front. In between all your earthly desires are comfortably catered for.

Designed from the chassis up, the advantages of an A-class are clear: a spacious interior with no separation between the driving cab and the living area. They're a pleasure to cruise along the spacious highways of the American West or live out an Arizona winter, but the thought of navigating a full-size motorhome through the Delhi rush hour can induce panic attacks. If an A-class is for you, stick with the mid-sized examples with larger wheels and a departure angle that won't leave you high and dry.

C-CLASS MOTORHOMES

A C-class, also known as a 'motorcaravan', is a conversion based on a chassis-cab of a **commercial panel van**, called a 'cutaway' in North America. Along with retaining the front cab, the back end of the chassis is extended beyond the rear axle to add load space while maintaining short-wheelbase manoeuvrability. Once that's done, a **purpose-built 'caravan' body**, usually a few inches wider than the original cab, is grafted on. The wider body enables a permanent cross-body bed to be fitted, as well

Departure angles in single figures give some C-class vans an over-built appearance that's some way from the image of a purposeful overlander.

CHOOSING A VEHICLE

Top: Sportsmobiles – based on Ford 4x4 bodies and knows as 'day vans' in the US.
Bottom: A narrow boat on wheels; the ends of this bus are often in different time zones.

as a more user-friendly interior design. Some C-classers have over-cab extensions (known as a 'Luton body' in the UK) for storage or a bed, albeit with limited headroom.

The combination of small inset wheels supporting an **over-width** body and a rear extension with departure angles in single figures gives some traditional C-class vans an ungainly, over-built appearance that might be seen as some way from the image of a purposeful overlander. It's not all about looks, but in practical terms the driving dynamics of a C-class doesn't lend itself to the unpredictable and unsupported nature of overlanding.

Besides the high purchase price, the biggest drawback of A- and over-stretched C-classers is the inability of the heavier or less solidly built rigs to survive an overland beating or to maintain **traction** on less than perfect roads. Because the build is so closely integrated around the donor chassis and intended for undemanding domestic duties or even long periods of stationary living, there's often little consideration given to easy **access** to plumbing, electrics and other systems that may well require maintenance and repairs on the road. This seamless, integrated design also makes it hard to make important improvements such as all-season insulation, fuel and water capacity, tyre size, suspension and vehicle security (the latter being commonly not up to resisting even the lightest assault of a drunk with a cheese knife). All the slick provisions for electrical hook-ups and waste disposal will be of little use in the campsites commonly used by overlanders in Islamabad, Tamanrasset or Cusco, and the real-world payload for long-range travel will be minuscule.

Last and not least, because many C-class conversions are based on a 2WD van chassis and then elongated beyond the rear axle, the departure angle can mean that even on roads the trailing edge of the body drags as the front wheels ascend steep inclines. The biggest frustration is that you have a great vehicle to live in but a poor vehicle for exploration off the beaten track. 'Let's go up there!' 'Calm down honey, we'll get stuck for sure'.

B-CLASS: THE CAMPERVAN

As motorhomes go, a B-class can come closest to an affordable and functional overlander. Often called **campervans**, van motorhomes or just 'day-vans' in North America, these are generally straightforward conversions of commercial panel vans like a Ford Transit, VW Transporter or the

OVERLANDING IN A HYMER MOTORHOME

A few years ago we did a one-year tour of South America in our Hymer motorhome, based on a rear-wheel drive Mercedes Sprinter. Covering over 36,000km in a dozen countries, a very high percentage of the trip was on unmade roads and during that time we got stuck twice in deep sand and once in a river.

If you're considering taking your motorhome on a more adventurous overland trip, there are a number of things to consider. Plan and prepare your route and vehicle taking into consideration road conditions and weather patterns. What's passable in the dry may be impossible in the wet.

Provision for sufficient amounts of fuel and water. We increased our driving range to 1300kms by adding an **extra fuel tank**. We carried water for nine days, passing it through a Nature Pure filter system. **Electrical power** was provided by two 120amp batteries charged by the alternator, two solar panels, and when necessary, a generator.

The interior was standard apart from extra catches on drawers and cupboards. It stayed together as well if not better than some of the more expedition-oriented vehicles we met.

Gas supplies can be a problem depending on where you travel. We had an on-board tank but were only able to fill it twice, so **local bottles and regulators** are probably a better bet and were a lot cheaper than in the UK. We changed the gas heating to diesel. We found the standard **3-way fridge** even with extra fans was inefficient in hot climates. Compressor fridges seem to work better but require more power.

One of the biggest problems we found was our **departure angle**. Uprated springs can lift the rear and air suspension can help. We took two spare wheels, tow rope, tools and a spade and used all of these at some point!

Shipping is a big problem with a standard motorhome as you're unable to secure the inside of the van. Indeed we **lost some £5000** worth of gear in two shipping episodes. It seems hard to insure contents when the van is shipped unaccompanied.

On the plus side we enjoyed **more comfort, more space** and more windows for better views than other vehicles.

We were looking into a 4WD conversion but the mods we made to the rear chassis worked very well

Hymer on the altiplano. Has its limitations but more comfort and space and nicer to drive than a Mog.

on the next stage in Australia. Can you overland in an off the shelf motorhome? Yes you can!

MICK AND MO NEWING

CHOOSING A VEHICLE

Mercedes/Dodge Sprinter. The famous **VW Kombi conversions** by Westfalia and the American **Sportsmobile** 4WDs are well known B-classers. The lack of a purpose-built body makes them less expensive, but also less spacious and so frustrating to live in over extended periods or in inclement weather. In a way, even something as big as a **bus or coach** might be described as a home-made B-class conversion, as the entire original vehicle is retained. Compared to a VW Kombi, you have no issues with headroom or space, but plenty of issues with getting jammed in a Cambodian village.

The most common complaint about campervans is the seemingly trivial need to build up a bed every evening once the cooking is done – on smaller B-classers you can only do the former after the latter. Stoop-free standing

Above: Honda Element roof camper conversion. © thedarienplan.com
Below: The '93 GMC G20 Vandura by Tiara. © supercamper.co.uk

headroom in the back is another issue on a B-class, usually improved with an elevating roof of one design or another (see p70), or a fixed, high-roof moulding if original body shells don't come high enough. Doing so can make space for small children's bunks, but a fixed roof above the magical 2.2 metres has limitations in secure container **shipping** and, to a lesser extent, fuel economy. Some examples such as the Sprinter are available on a 4WD platform in certain markets, and US-built Sportsmobiles can come on a 4WD Ford or Mercedes van platform with an elevating roof. In Europe and Australia, capacious Toyota Troop Carriers are readily outfitted with a compact camper interior and an elevating wedge roof.

VWs are the best known and priciest of the compact campervan conversions, but many **Japanese minibus or MPV-based platforms** also make a great compact campervan for less money and with as good a reputation for reliability. From the Nineties Japanese manufacturers went through a phase of producing people carriers for their domestic market and, because of the expense of owning a vehicle over three years old in Japan, many get sold on as semi-official 'grey' imports to overseas right-hand-drive markets including South Africa, Australia and the UK. Despite goofy names these vehicles are usually **equipped** and accessorised to levels unheard of in Europe, with air-con, auto transmission, swivelling front seats (if the vehicle is not mid-engined), electric everything from mirrors to window blinds, and various styles of elevating roofs, which make them both good for living in and shipping-container friendly. Some have road-biased four-wheel drive (i.e. with no low range or significant ground clearance improvements). In the UK, and probably elsewhere, a whole new business developed in importing and converting these MPVs with elevating roofs into cute mini-campers.

Nissan Elgrand, Toyota Regius and Granvia will be some names you've never heard of and usually come with a 3-litre turbo-diesel engine. Perhaps the best known is the Mazda Bongo (Ford, who have a big stake in Mazda, call their version the Freda). As a diesel it comes with the 2.5 TD engine from the Ford Ranger/Mazda B2500 pickups. You get up to eight seats that flatten into a big bed, or it's set up as a basic factory-fitted campervan. All versions have the 'auto free top' rear hinged roof, which adds two small and chilled berths because these elevating roofs have fabric sides with poor insulation. For a cold environment you may want to improve this with lagging.

GROSS VEHICLE WEIGHT (GVW) AND LICENSING ISSUES

Before you get too excited about driving a big truck or motorhome, investigate licensing issues in your country or state. Usually they're based around **gross vehicle weight (GVW) limits** (as discussed on p33) or vehicle lengths. Anything greater than 3 or 4 tonnes GVW moves towards a commercial light- or heavy goods vehicle category, which can involve expensive training courses prior to 'commercial driver' testing, plus added issues with insurance and even tachographs.

Motorhomes are often exempt from commercial licensing, registration and taxing, and in the UK, for example, a lorry of up to **7.5 tonnes** can be driven on a regular car licence if the licence was obtained before 1997 and as long as the lorry has been reclassified as a motorhome.

In **Europe** the **maximum permissible size** of a motorhome is 12 metres (nearly 40ft) and 2.55 metres (8ft 4 inches) wide. Six metres is said to be the benchmark between medium and large motorhomes, but, incredibly, a 12-metre coach with all the seats removed and with motorhome fittings can also supposedly be driven on a regular car licence in the UK. It can be a little daunting to be let loose with no training in a 7.5 tonne

Driving a big vehicle you soon notice signs like this, as well as width and more especially height limits. The latter two may get you stuck, while exceeding a weight limit on a road or bridge may mean a fine if caught.

lorry, let alone a 40ft-long bus.

In **the States** 10,000lb (4.5 tonnes) GVW is said to be the limit of a regular car licence, beyond which **additional testing** is required, but here too, full-size motorhomes can be driven on a normal car licence, a common cause of complaint by everyone else on the Alcan Highway. Anything with a total train weight beyond 11.8 tonnes (26,000lb) requires a **commercial driver's licence (CDL)** and a sticker from the Department of Transportation, but again motorhomes are exempt and may be identified with 'Not for hire' (i.e. an RV) stencilled on the cab.

For big motorhomes there are all sorts of dodges to avoid the taxes, high insurance premiums, licensing and other restrictions associated with commercial use. In the UK it's possible to get a 10-tonne truck officially '**downplated**' to a 7.5 tonne rating, altering the truck's taxable weight and so enabling use with a regular, pre-1997 car licence.

As you can imagine in somewhere like Laos or Equatorial Guinea all these domestic licensing categories are much less of an issue; if local regulations are enforced at all, you'll probably be exempt, certainly at the less massive end of the scale.

D-CLASS: DEMOUNTABLE CABINS FOR 4X4 PICKUPS

There's another alphabetical category that, although not yet internationally mandated by the FIM Campervan Inspectorate, might be dubbed 'D-class'. **Demountables** are usually wide, fully-fitted camper cabins with over-cab extensions or elevating roofs that either slot onto on the load bed, or are bolted directly to the rear chassis of a 4x4 pickup once the load bed has been removed at which point they're less genuinely demountable. Bear in mind that removing the load bed will give significant weight savings; the tray on a Toyota HZJ79 weighs 180kg (nearly 400lb) and the equivalent off the back of a Ford F550 Super Duty will probably give you a hernia just looking at it.

From top. **1**: Dodge RAM with a huge demountable. © Chris Mcgovern. **2**: Tischer collapsible cabin was not so secure in the Hilux bed on Saharan tracks. **3**: A neat Defender pickup with a slide-in GRP cabin. Rounded edges make less wind noise. Both © Su Shuttleworth. **4**: Not a slot-on but an integrated Azalai 130 Defender.

For all this effort you don't get that much more room than a converted 4x4 station wagon or VW campervan with a flip-top tent. The appeal is **adaptability**: it's rather like hooking up a caravan, but without the turning issues or distress in watching it fall to pieces along the track in the Simien mountains. All you get for the weight and price is a little more space but if you already own a pickup that you trust, it's as easy as clamping on and driving off.

In North America, where pickups are put to use at work and at play, they're simply called '**campers**', but their weight can match the typically bigger pickups found there, while many locals suggest the **build quality** is not best suited to extended use on rugged roads.

In Europe and Australia these cabins have lately tended to be made from a glass-reinforced plastic (GRP) sandwich monoblock, a single-piece moulding, 25–30mm (1") thick, set in a plywood floor that's much more rigid and well sealed, but is expensive. North American 'campers' and the bulkier European cabins tend to be **quickly demountable** by deploying legs (as pictured top left) rather like Thunderbird II, cranking the cabin up and driving off back to work after a weekend's fishing. The question is, on a long overland journey how often are you going to need to do that?

Among the **European brands** are the huge cabins from Tischer and Nordstar with weights at around 600kg. When mounted over double cabs, rearward extensions on some German models can reach up to a metre beyond the load bed's original body in an attempt to add all possible volume within legal and GVW limits. It might be fair to assume

Grand Erg's chassis-mounted GRP cabin on a Land Cruiser pickup. © Grand Erg. It has to be stronger on a tough overland journey than a demountable cabin that clamps into a pickup bed, even if it does give you that 'Thunderbird 2' buzz.

these combinations are using a 4x4 as a strong, road-going platform not as an off-roader, because they don't look like something you'd like to drive down Ruta 3 from La Paz on a rainy night. Grand Erg in Italy make the slicker monoblock Gobi shell that keeps it all in proportion. The empty shell weighs 300kg; fitted out with fridge, toilet and water tanks it also comes up to 600kg.

If you're intending to head off road you need to be absolutely sure that the cabin will stay **securely mounted** to the vehicle through thick and thin, and that any flex won't see the over-cab portion hitting the cab roof. I once spoke to some D-classers whose daily task on the tracks of northern Mauritania was to tighten down their wobbling cabin; on another occasion I came across a Hilux that had broken its chassis midway while humping around a demountable.

CHOOSING A VEHICLE

2WD AND 4WD: SOME KEY DIFFERENCES

We're talking Land Rover-type 4x4s here, not Subaru and Quattros. More on p75.

• **Ground clearance**. This can often be adequate on 2WDs if you choose the right one and much more useful more of the time than 4x4.

• **Low-range gearbox**. Found in a proper 4x4, this enables slow-speed manoeuvring with control. It's the biggest drawback with 2WDs because without it you must use momentum and speed to get over an obstacle, risking damage, when you'd rather crawl carefully at 1mph.

• **Separate ladder chassis**. Usually makes for a stronger vehicle that can handle a bigger payload. Larger 2WD trucks have ladder chassis.

• **Larger wheels**. Found on 4x4s but also on commercial 2WD trucks and vans.

Vans and trucks are load carriers, albeit road based, but of all these qualities **ground clearance**, a strong body and then low range are most useful. Many European 2WDs, particularly French 'farmers'' cars, are still designed with great ground clearance.

LAND ROVER CARAWAGON – STANDING ROOM ONLY

Picture the scene. Your convoy, Cairo-bound in the depths of winter, has been on the road all day. It's been dark for hours, the rain's lashing down and it's blowing a hoolie. Knackered, you pull into a campsite, deserted of course, and prepare for the night. Your mate has to climb onto the roof of his 4x4, undo the stiff and cold cover off his roof tent, his fingers already numb and wet. Once erected it should, at least, be dry if cold, inside and the bed will probably be made up.

I have witnessed these pitiful scenes a few times through the windscreen of my 1970 Carawagon 110 hybrid, while the heater emits its welcome breath of warm air. If I can be bothered, I'll get out and pop the top, (eight over-centre clips and a bit of heave ho inside). If not, I can just slip into the back, probably banging my head on something, pull my warm sleeping bag out and fall asleep, stretched out on a very comfortable three quarter-width bed with room for two if you're close.

The one downside with a bed in the back that all camper vanners know too well is that it shares the precious space with the clobber. There are two options to consider. Take much less – which is best – or put up with having to remove stuff from the boudoir before settling down for the night. On a big desert run I usually have ten jerricans lashed down to the floor in the back. Hell to unload for the first few nights, but getting progressively lighter as the miles roll by, at which point they can be stashed empty on the cab's roof rack. This chore complete, I have a proper living space with cupboards full of crisp white linen, a fridge and cooker, all ergonomically placed to enable easy cooking either inside, or outside, the gas cooker being mounted inside the rear door. I can stand up too, a bonus when dressing for dinner. I can deal with any correspondence at a desk, or invite soggy, roof-tent refugees round for cocktails, all within the confines of the back of a Land Rover.

Cozy Carawagon interior, everything in arm's reach, even the steering wheel.

Party over, within ten minutes, it can be a regular 4x4 again with no extra weight, no extra wind resistance and therefore no adverse effect on fuel consumption.

In 13 years of ownership I have, like most overlanders, tailored the Carawagon to my own requirements. Along with all the usual off-road stuff, I have introduced a few luxuries to make life on the road more comfortable. I cannot bear to be cold, so have fitted 'oil-fired' central heating. Three rather nifty and compact radiators were liberated from an Arctic spec. military Land Rover, along with the Webasto water heater. The Webasto sits under the driver's seat and is plumbed into the engine water system, so pre-heating the engine as a bonus. This hot water is then pumped round the radiators in the back, just like in a house. Drain on the auxiliary battery is pretty alarming when the engine's off, but a half hour burst gives an all-enveloping warmth hard to replicate with other forms of heating. That and a small propane gas fire ensure it gets pretty toasty in the back, despite the aircraft hanger insulation properties of the Carawagon roof.

The bed doesn't have to be an off-the-shelf item either. If you're a dab hand at the old D.I.Y., it should be possible to rustle something up with a few bits of plywood and your granddad's old penknife. Any long-wheel base 4x4 would be a suitable starting point. Old caravan bits and bobs are plentiful on eBay, gas cookers are cheap, but as we know, a good fridge can empty the budget wallet. Standing room is a luxury, but various varieties of pop-top have been around for years. Some are even water tight!

Ambulance-bodied 4x4s are usually a good starting point as the rear body tends to be well insulated and the layout is conducive to lying flat, even if you don't need a drip. Headroom is better too, although few offer true standing room like my old Carawagon.

TOBY SAVAGE

4x4s

3

Time to stop beating around the bush and pretending that there's anything other on your mind than a chunky fourbie. Sure, it's a lifestyle phenomenon with an image of aspiring adventurousness and the desire to (literally) stand above the crowd, but you're not aspiring, you're actually taking your four-wheeler right to the places that feature so commonly in the ads.

Or so you think. Once on the move most overlanders find the thrill of a road-bound journey can be satisfying enough. Fun though it is to explore the limits of your vehicle you've read so much about, the sort of off roading where you really need 4WD is actually quite slow, noisy and tiring. You may have yearned to park up in the absolute remotest corner of the Sahara but you'll soon find just round the back of that dune will do.

It's easy to assume adventure = really hard off-roading but once out in the world, simply getting to Bolivia, Botswana or on the Baralacha Pass is an adventure.

It's your adventure and you'll probably only do it once

You'll spend more time drooling over gnarly tyres, raised air-intakes and radical clearance than you will actually using them. When you get back you may concede you might've managed in a Peugeot station wagon, but it's your adventure and you'll probably only do it once. If this is the one big trip you're planning before settling down, the vehicle is a big part of it.

Surely somebody's idea of a sick joke.

A distinction must be made between a 4x4* and an SUV. In case you've just got into the whole scene, the latter stands for **sports utility vehicle**, which, according to the all-knowing Wikipedia, means: '*a type of passenger vehicle that combines the load-hauling and passenger-carrying capacity of a large station wagon … with features designed for off-road driving. In more recent years, the term has also grown to encompass vehicles with similar size and style that are marketed as sports utility vehicles, but which do not actually incorporate substantial off-road features.*'

Other sources vary over the exact definition, but for the purposes of this book an SUV is classified as a 'soft roader'; examples include Land Rover's old Freelander, Honda's CRV, the Ford Explorer, Toyota RAV4 and Tiguans, Kadjars, X-Trails, Santa Fes, Sorentos, X5s, Q7, XC90s. There are scores of them that to a greater or lesser extent, all look the part.

Robustness and **simplicity** are two key attributes on the long road: vehicles built to take a hammering lugging heavy loads on rough roads without resorting to levels of complexity associated with promotional imagery featuring the forecourt of a Monte Carlo casino. Not all 4x4s can manage this for long and it's what used to separate something like a lighter-built RAV4 or a Toyota Hilux (Tacoma) from a Land Cruiser – or indeed the current ultra sophisticated all-terrain limousines. Making a vehicle strong, durable and field repairable doesn't always compliment economy, handling, crumple zones or clean emissions, but such a vehicle will last many years on rough, corrugated tracks that would quickly break up a regular SUV.

It's getting complicated

High-end 4x4s and SUVs all compete to offer an ever-increasing array of systems controlling traction, braking, suspension, power, security and safety, as well as some aspects you've never considered – like the idea of eliminating drivers altogether. Car designers are understandably infatuated with the possibilities of fast-moving technology and the glamourous flagship in the latest James Bond movie gets lapped up by the motoring media.

Not so glamorous are expensive visits to approved dealers to perform service checks with equipment that costs more than the vehicle itself. Taking something like a super-refined Discovery 4 away from that support requires a thorough understanding in managing on-board diagnostics to trace and eliminate faults which, in liability terms, err to the safe side by partially- or fully disabling a vehicle for its own good.

As old technology is superseded, this is the paradox you face. Things like Terrain Response are a marvel, and a certain level of electronics benefits all modern cars, not least in efficient fuel injection. But, just as with blindly following satnav instructions into a lake, when driving off-road or in remote areas, there's a need to stop, think and take responsibility of your decisions before ploughing into the unknown. Setting a console dial to the closest approximation of the terrain ahead, or trusting a wade depth graphic on a display screen are advertising fantasies. You will get stuck and your car will play up, so getting the job done with the least complexity, *even if it might lead to some operator discomfort*, is the best approach to all-terrain overlanding.

* In this book '4x4' refers to vehicles like Jeeps and Defenders, '2WD' occasionally signifies regular cars, and '4WD' or 'AWD' is 'four-wheel-' or 'all-wheel-drive' transmission systems.

The mechanics and electronics of 4WD

Regular road vehicles are two-wheel drive. In countries and urban areas where reliable, all-weather tarmac roads prevail, that's sufficient. Elsewhere, all-wheel drive machines provide drive to two or more axles in order to improve traction and, along with greater ground clearance, maintain mobility on unmade roads with loose or uneven surfaces, or where there are no roads at all. In human terms the difference is walking along a level path or scrambling up a rough hillside using your arms and legs.

True AWD? Only on Mars. © Nasa.

It may surprise some to learn that most 4x4s don't have continuous drive to all wheels at all times – that works best with a motor on each wheel. Continuous direct four-wheel drive from a *single* power source must address an inherent flaw of the **differential mechanism**. When a vehicle goes round a corner, the outside wheel travels a little further than the inner wheel, just like a runner in the outside lane of a race track has further to run. In a car it may only be a few inches but it's enough to make a difference. As power is fed from the engine to the wheels, they're expected to turn at the same rate, but because of the reality of bends and bumps, wheels on the same axle can't do this.

This was the quandary facing designers of horseless carriages in the 19th century. They got around it by adapting clock-making technology into the **axle differential** – the bulbous unit midway along the driven axle(s) of a conventional vehicle. Without a differential a car would be very hard to steer as the driven wheels resist turning through unequal arcs. Most go-karts have no diff and are an effort to steer around a twisty track. In a heavier vehicle on a grippy surface this tension in the driveline shows up as 'scrubbing', skidding tyres with the possibility of the transmission snapping at the weakest link.

With an ingenious arrangement of crown wheels and gears a differential allows torque to be transmitted continuously to both driven wheels while at the same time compensating for the slightly varying distances each wheel

A faulty locking diff from a 75 Toyota waits for the anaesthetic to kick in.
© Frederik & Josephine.

travels. The mechanism's operation is difficult to explain in words or even with graphics. Look for an animation online (and still end up none the wiser).

Clever as it is, most drivers will have experienced the frustrating lack of forward motion when just one powered wheel loses traction and spins uselessly, usually when you're half parked on mud, sand or ice or, less commonly, when stuck on very uneven ground with one wheel in the air. This immobility is due to an unwanted side effect of the differential mechanism, whereby most of the power is transmitted to the wheel with least traction – the wheel spinning on a slippery surface. Until you've stared at that online animation for a couple of hours, don't try and tax your brain too much as to what's happening; suffice to say diffs work brilliantly on grippy tarmac roads but show their limitations on loose, slick or uneven surfaces.

On a conventional 2WD car it only takes one spinning wheel of the driven axle to possibly immobilise it. On a 4x4 it only takes two **diagonally opposed spinning wheels** (front left and rear right, for example) to have the same effect. Your 4x4 isn't so 4WD after all. Over the years 4x4 manufacturers have come up with various mechanical and electronic solutions to reduce or eliminate this and keep the vehicle moving in all conditions.

4WD SYSTEMS

These days there are three ways of providing four-wheel drive. All try and address the fact that even commercial users don't need 4WD all the time and that many domestic users want a system that engages automatically. Disengaging four-wheel drive where possible also lightens steering, saves fuel and reduces transmission wear.

Manufacturers have also found that either permanent or on-demand four-wheel drive is one less thing to be misunderstood or applied incorrectly. Some auto makers offer all three systems in no less than nine formats.

Permanent

Permanent four-wheel drive is used in Land Rover Defenders and Discoverys, all Land Cruisers since the 80 series, most Mercedes G-Wagens and most non-Wrangler Jeeps. These are mostly 'serious' SUVs and 4x4s that also feature good ground clearance and a low-range gearbox.

Because the permanently driven front and rear axles would soon create inter-axle **transmission wind-up**, as described in the box on p305, an additional differential must be fitted between them. This **central diff**, incorporated in the gearbox enables the transmission of power to all wheels all the time without wind-up. It's a neat idea until you remember that, diffs being what they are, when just one wheel loses traction, all the power goes to that one wheel. When only **one** wheel loses traction on a full-time 4x4 you stop. So, to maintain all-terrain ability, the central diff must be **lockable**, either manually or automatically using something like a viscous coupling or electronics.

On-demand or 'intelligent'

This system is used by more road-focussed SUVs such as Freelanders, Honda HR-Vs, Toyota RAV4s, Volvo XC40s, Nissan Pathfinders and the Mitsubishi Outlander. The primary axle propels the car most of the time. When wheel spin on this axle is detected the secondary (usually rear) axle is brought into play by electronic or hydro-mechanical means. This automatic, 'on-demand' system is sometimes mistakenly called 'part-time' (see below).

It's a foolproof system whose default setting is 2WD to save fuel and wear with **4WD when you need it**, and can also be set up to run 4WD permanently. Because SUV owners' off-road needs are assumed to be limited to snow, wet grass and gravel, a low-range gearbox isn't usually present and on some models the permanent 4WD setting can't lock the central diff, all of which validates Wiki's 'soft roader' description of SUVs given earlier.

Part-time or selectable

This is an old-fashioned system in which the front axle can be engaged **manually** with a lever or **electronically** with a button; it's preferred by some traditionalists and is found on 'working' 4x4s like old Hiluxes, Patrols and current 70-series Land Cruisers, as well early Ford Ranger/Mazda B2500 pickups.

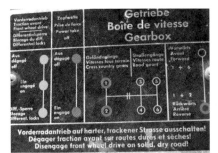

With this basic system there's no central diff; you're either in 2WD or locked into 4WD, which, depending on your vehicle, can be done on the move or at low speeds. This isn't so ideal on mixed surfaces because run-

Part-time? Selectable? It can get complicated. © mattsavage.com (and opposite)

ning in 4WD on grippy surfaces quickly leads to transmission wind-up. On something like an older Ranger for example you have to first stop and engage 4WD with a lever, after which you can disengage and re-engage the 'free-wheeling' front-axle diff with a dashboard button while on the move.

LIMITED-SLIP DIFFERENTIALS

In the late eighties many Japanese 4x4s featured **limited-slip differentials** (LSD) in the rear axle of their station wagons and they're still an option on some SUVs and even regular 2WD vans. LSDs work by limiting the differential effect so that *some* power is transmitted to an immobilised wheel when the opposite one loses traction and spins uselessly. A bit like auto-locking diffs, LSDs have their eccentricities on roads and in some situations need to be 'tricked' into action by applying the hand brake if it operates that axle's wheels. For this reason, as well as the advent of much cleverer electronic traction control (see next page), they're now not so common on newer vehicles. I've had vehicles which may or may not have had an LSD; I could never be sure. It's better in this instance, to simply fit a mechanical diff lock that you either know is engaged or not.

ELECTRONIC TRACTION CONTROL

Just about all modern 4x4s and high-performance cars now have ETC allied with an anti-lock braking system (ABS). Electronic **sensors** on each hub read when a wheel is spinning and momentarily brake that wheel. The differential effect then feeds power to the opposite wheel, which drives the vehicle forward. Should that wheel slip too, it's in turn braked and the opposite wheel picks up drive. ETC translates to continuous forward motion, especially on loose rocky ascents or where tyre traction or axle articulation are at the limit.

It's extremely effective but on soft sand slopes and creek banks I've found it swaps frantically from wheel to wheel and, if you don't apply some throttle finesse, each wheel is individually dug into the sand. This was on an old Discovery II; it's almost certain ETC technology has improved since then.

It must be remembered that with ETC at times only one wheel per axle is driving so you'll not get the fully locked-out traction of a pair of axle diff locks. Furthermore, braking one wheel makes the opposite one spin twice as fast, not at ground speed, so increasing the chance of digging that wheel in.

However, and this is the crux, ETC is a system that cannot be misused in the way diff locks can, so it's less easy to **damage the transmission** with careless or ignorant driving. ETC and systems like it ought not replace the need to think what you're doing and, if necessary, to find another route or get out and manually clear wheels or lower tyre pressures to improve traction.

SENSORS WORKING OVERTIME

Whatever modern vehicle you're driving you'll soon learn that it's often the sensors, be they for fuel or water, ABS or throttle-, suspension- or crank position, that can play up, whether you're overlanding, shopping or commuting.

Following reports of their vehicles suffering from 'sudden unintended acceleration' (some of them from a standstill with no foot pressure involved), Toyota's much publicised recall of some 10 million vehicles hit the headlines in February 2010. Officially and initially 'loose floor mats' were blamed. Other opinions suggested wear, corrosion and an intermittent malfunction, even including exterior electromagnetic interference in the electronic throttle control system.

This system had been gradually introduced into the entire range from 2002 and with it claims of unwanted acceleration increased five-fold in the US (still adding up to only a few dozen per year). If one accepts that neither the hinge mechanism, failing return spring or floor mats were to blame, then the Toyota fiasco proved how clever ECU technology could go wrong.

Usually relying on a small electrical current, **sensors** sometimes have to be positioned in parts of the vehicle that will inevitably get dirty or wet. Whether the problem the sensor recognises is genuine, or simply a corroded, weak or intermittent connection, it will register it on your dashboard as a warning light. This possibly puts the vehicle into a reduced-power, 'limp-home' mode or, as in the example of the Td5 crank sensor, immobilises the engine.

Eventually we'll all learn to get round these anomalies of **CAN bus technology** (there's an introduction to the subject on p42), which itself will improve, but these vagaries explain why an old Toyota 78 or a trusty 300 Tdi in a Land Rover are both still desirable for overlanding. Because generations have grown up learning to deal with them, **mechanical failures** are easily diagnosed, widely understood and repairable by humans in places without computers.

For older drivers used to traditional electrical and mechanical troubleshooting, this can all sound a bit daunting, but you'll have to get used to it. It demands a whole new way of diagnosing and, if necessary, repairing faults on modern vehicles, whose performance in most cases is much improved by complex electronic technology.

Choosing a 4x4

Of the vast range of vehicles with 4WD capability, only a few models are routinely used by overlanders. The following selection focuses on the limited range of older models most commonly used by overland travellers. These are established vehicles that have in most cases been around in one form or another for over half a century.

They're chosen because most intent on driving across Asia, Africa or Latin America aren't looking to make outlandish choices. They want something proven – what overlanders actually use. The vehicles include the sorts chosen by the military, NGOs and aid agencies, as well as commercial operators, for whom function and dependability are paramount.

Along with other manufacturers, Toyota, Land Rover and Nissan all produce SUVs with four-wheel drive systems, but these are merely capitalising on the luxury 4x4 or crossover trend. These popular vehicles all allude to, rather than directly confront a rugged, outdoorsy lifestyle with levels of refinement and complex systems that include adjustable suspension and four-wheel drive. Mind-bogglingly **advanced electronics** now enable cars to do amazing things, but would the aforementioned commercial operators actually choose to use them for their work, or are they just limited to the pampered CEO?

As you'll see, the selection focuses largely on **diesels**, which are thin on the ground in the US. In some cases the same base model is available there with the locally preferred large petrol engine. All the vehicles listed are assessed expressly for their potential as fully loaded long-range tourers and overlanders, focussing on the attributes of space, comfort and adaptability as well as reliability and durability. Drawbacks or strengths listed are unlikely to relate to driving to work or weekend off-roading. First there are a few variations in **body-types** to think about.

From a distance they all look the same so choice can involve the image you prefer.

WHEELBASE

Long story short: for an overlanding a long-wheelbase **(LWB)** 4x4 offers the best combination of space and stability. The limitations in a LWB's ground clearance (see p40) don't really impact on normal overland travel.

An old FJ40: great angles and nippy on the dirt but needs to be piled up high which can lead to instability.

Short-wheelbase (SWB, left) vehicles have a reputation for great off-road agility, but what makes a nippy urban runabout or an agile tool in muddy woodland can lose its composure when loaded up on fast tracks, and you'll be lucky to have more than a metre and a half of **load space** in the back. It can work if you're travelling alone or are a well organised duo but you probably won't be able to avoid having a load area piled high and a roof rack possibly with a roof tent, all of which can unsettle the **stability** of a short, high 4x4. And as explained on p186, you may get everything in, but can you **get to it easily**? Good accessibility is vital to happiness on the road.

SWB 4x4s also tend to pitch about on bumpy terrain and can **slide out** unexpectedly on fast washboard bends if your concentration drops. This can happen to all vehicles, but is less likely with a longer wheelbase with a low centre of gravity. Once a loaded 4x4 is sliding sideways, overturning is likely.

These shortcomings can be controlled with thoughtful packing and driving, but the superior stability of a LWB makes day-to-day driving more relaxing and so, less tiring. A SWB 4x4 would be in its element on an off-road focussed expedition with short, tough stages, and there may be times when a SWB's angles help you get through. But overall long wheelbase is best.

HARDTOP OR STATION WAGON

When your vehicle will be your home for months on end you want a bungalow not a bedsit. A bigger 4x4 is better and, for most overlanders, a three-door van or **hardtop** offers the best body format for up to two people. Any rear seating can be easily removed, leaving a large, uncluttered area in which to organise a living and storage space. The lack of rear passenger doors makes this simpler at a slight cost to access, but also means fewer windows and locks and so superior security and privacy. Along with their other widely recognised attributes, in mainland Europe at least, **Land Rover's 110 Defender** and Toyota's similarly roomy **HZJ78-series Troop Carrier** fit the bill.

Most 4x4s are **five-door station wagons** and are obviously more suited to parties of three or more – don't expect passengers, including kids, to be happy for long in the back of a three-door hardtop. With just two occupants, access presents no problems and there's rarely something that's hard to get to, but with an extra pair of doors and all that glass, **security and privacy** can be a worry. It's a good idea to blank out as many side and back windows as possible to keep out the sun and unwanted interest.

TAILGATES AND DOORS

Horizontally split tailgates feature on upmarket or non-commercial models such as Range Rovers, Jeep Cherokees and Land Cruiser station wagons. **Vertically split doors** range from one big door (Defender, early Discoverys, G-Wagens and some Pajeros), a 60/40 split (78 Land Cruisers and some Patrols) or a symmetrical 'ambulance door' (105-series Land Cruisers).

Whatever type it is, make sure the **rubber seals** are in good shape. Boxy rear bodies creates a low-pressure zone at the back, sucking in fine **dust** when driving fast on dry tracks. With an imperfect seal you can actually watch dust drifting forward through the cabin like a moorland mist. One solution is to keep the front-door windows or other vents open to generate some counter pressure, or run the ventilator fan on full if you're trailing other vehicles.

Tailgates

A **horizontally split tailgate** has two advantages: an instant table and handy shade from the upper section – assuming the rear window's blanked out or draped. Drawbacks include the lower section getting in the way when you want to reach deep into the interior, though with a station wagon rear passenger doors get round this. You may find yourself leaning over a lit stove and knocking over a pan. These are exactly the sorts of mundane accidents that cause most injuries on overland trips, not bandits, killer bees or rebel bullets.

Tailgates also make it difficult to mount a **roof-access ladder** onto the back of the vehicle. I copied some Land Cruiser ladder rings (p194) and fabricated some mini steps on a back corner. With a roof rack to grab on to, stepping from the bumper via the steps onto the roof rack was possible with just one hand.

Doors

Having **one big rear door** provides a great windbreak, less of a problem fixing ladders to a hardshell roof if there's no spare tyre in the way, and easy access deep into the rear load area. On a flat door, like on Defenders or G-Wagens, mounting a small fold-down table hinged inside the door is easy, although you're bound to need the extra surface of a camping table as well.

Two rear doors, equally divided or otherwise, offer good wind protection and an ideal frame over which to drape some shade. The insides of the doors make handy surfaces for mounting water filtration units or storage pockets and, again, access to the back is good. Even if one door carries a heavy spare wheel (more on p157), only one need be opened to sling something in.

PICKUPS

In single-cab form a 4x4 **pickup** is a versatile utility platform suited to farmers, ranchers and other commercial operators. For overland use it's only really practical when it is fitted with a hardshell canopy or, more commonly, a fully fitted-out camper body as mentioned on p70 and in more detail on p218. Double- or extended-cab pickups are on p115.

Toyota Land Cruisers

From the world's biggest motor manufacturer comes the world's best-selling 4x4 range. The reason for that popularity with tour operators, militias, outback ranchers, aid agencies, smugglers, mine contractors, the military, jihadis and overlanders is a consistent **build quality** and the reliability that comes with it, which adds up to **dependability**. These are the keys to successful mobility in remote locales or rugged environments far from a Toyota dealer.

You'll notice that list is composed of professionals and individuals who depend on their vehicles to do what they do, and less to express a kinship with a potentially adventurous lifestyle. Impressive performance figures and plush, gadget-laden interiors – which might be categorised as the 'urban' priorities of private owners – don't really come into it with Land Cruisers; they've never been fashionable in that way. If it's attention and admiration you're after, there are many flashier 4x4s to choose from.

Over the last forty years Toyota Land Cruisers have set the standards by which all other big working 4x4s are compared. As with Land Rover, the iconic and highly marketable name is now used to identify a range of models that differ greatly from market to market. Spartan load carriers, family SUVs and something the head of a UN delegation would expect to see waiting for them on a dusty African air strip – all now carry the Land Cruiser label.

WHICH LAND CRUISER?

It can all get very confusing, but you can start by dividing Land Cruisers into commercial workhorses with functional interiors – the 'J7' or 70 series – and station wagons: 60-, 80-, 100-, and now 200 series. The former mid-sized Prado (90-, 120- and now 150) adopted the Land Cruiser epithet, but its smaller four-cylinder engine separated it from the real thing's four-litre-plus sixes. A GX is a basic-spec vehicle; GXL is better and a VX is usually a top-spec auto.

What you settle on will depend on what's available in your market – there'll always be some sort of Toyota Land Cruiser – or how keen you are to go through the expense and hassle of importing your dream Cruiser.

Model history

Like Rover in the late 1940s, Toyota copied and improved on the wartime design of the Willys Jeep, but it took the success of the **40-series FJs** before Land Cruisers began to register on our radars. By the 1970s, when Land Rover's Series III was stretching its 20-year-old technology to breaking point, the FJ became established in many of Land Rover's former markets as well as the US. In recognition of the plucky FJ40, from 2006 the funky **FJ Cruiser** sold in North America and Australia for a few years, a flawed SUV responding to the retro/homage craze.

40-series on ferry duty.

Asia, South America and Africa took to the 40s, but Britain and much of Europe saw little of that series (Ireland and Germany were exceptions). The first Land Cruisers to appear here were the boxy **60-series** six-cylinder station wagons of the early 1980s which, in the UK at least, lagged far behind the Range Rover of the time in terms of comfort and style, if not long-term durability. Around the same time the utilitarian 40 series was replaced by the unstoppable **70 series** which survives today. The early 1990s saw the **80-series** bring Land Cruiser station wagons into the modern era with ABS, air bags and coil suspension, plus full-time 4WD on the VX models. The 80 became the even bigger 100-series in the late 90s, and since 2008 the broadly similar 200 series. Around this time the famed pre-CRD straight sixes, turbo or petrol, slipped quietly from Toyota's product lists in Europe, Canada and Australia.

Today **South Africa** and **Australia** have among the most complete range of Land Cruisers, while after a few years emissions caused the UK to drop the near-three-tonne 4.5 V8 twin-turbo. Currently only a 2-8-litre '150' Prado sells under the 'Land Cruiser' badge. Like the UK, the **US** never officially got the much-admired 70-series ute and hardtop. Instead, a 5.7-litre V8 petrol is unapologetically priced way above many locally built competitors.

Land Cruisers are a phenomenon, but are conservatively marketed and styled. As all-terrain limos, the high-tech flagships just can't compete with the best from Land Rover and Germany, but they survive on reputation and solid build, not looks or glamour. Apart from Australia, where the 70s are an

LAND CRUISER 60

Few would now choose to overland in a Land Cruiser wagon predating an 80, which in 1990 replaced the leaf-sprung 60s and was a leap forward in comfort and sophistication. But over twenty years after they stopped making them, passing through a remote oasis in Algeria one time, half the cars on the main street were 60s, many with well over half a million kilometres on the clock. These vehicles endure in places you've never heard of because, among other reasons, a 60's body is capable of surviving the overloading they typically suffer in developing countries.

In Europe good 60s have either long since rusted into parts, or been exported to markets where cheap labour can keep them running indefinitely. In the States FJ60s are now regarded as a classic restoration. If you're tempted go for the smooth, 4-litre sixes: the latest 3F petrol (EFI 155hp), a 1HZ aspirated 4.2 (from the 70-series) or the coveted, low-stressed 135hp 12H-T turbo of the HJ61. The still-surviving but sluggish 1HZ as well as 12H-T were pre-electronic pinnacles, all-mechanical nirvanas and the best TLC diesel they ever made. Because of this, a good HJ61 now goes for a lot more than an old 80. Later HJ62s or petrol-engined FJ62 have paired rectangular headlights.

I ran a 61 for 60,000km and the tractor-like grunt was well suited to chugging through dunes (see the *Desert Driving* dvd), if not necessarily rolling along a highway humming to the radio. Thirty mpg (10.5kpl) was attainable at a steady 100kph (62mph), with half that in the dunes.

As with many big, torquey manuals, the touchy throttle was difficult to manage on rough, rocky climbs. I used the hand throttle, a Stone Age equivalent of the electronic crawl assist on today's top-of-the-rangers.

All European six-cylinder diesels (and possibly Canadian too) came with 24-volt electrics making it hard to get parts in warmer, 12-volt Land Cruiser markets. With the diesels' lowly power outputs, gearboxes and axles rarely give trouble. Putting a 60's half shaft alongside a Land Rover of the same era tells the story, although with a very high-mileage vehicle it's worth checking the gearbox output shaft. Undo the rear prop-shaft from the transfer gearbox and with the car in gear, rotate the output flange. If play is excessive get it looked at.

Mercifully, the original springs and shocks will be long gone. I ended up with Old Man Emu on the back and something similarly heavy duty on the front. In this state, loaded up 800kg, the suspension was just right in the Sahara, but running around London was less relaxing – a common paradox with heavy-duty suspension. See p145 for more on that.

On most TLC wagons the spare is mounted, truck-style, under the body at the back: out of the way and easy to get to without hernia-inducing lifting. It's released on a chain winch that's prone to rust seizure and is operated by the crank rod you use to work the bottle jack. Make sure that rod is there.

Rust is what finishes off HJ60s in damp territories. Inspect the forward edge of the rear wheel arches (close to a body mount), the rear chassis channels behind the rear spring hangers, the cross tube on which the rear shocks mount, bubbling paintwork on the upper tailgate (not so serious) and the upper corners around the windscreen seal, which will leak (as they can do on 80s). And check the roof gutters if you're planning to mount heavy loads on a rack.

institution like Land Rovers are in the UK, the big sales have always been in Africa, the Middle East and now Russia and China. As a result, overlanding **know-how** in Europe and especially the UK is a niche compared to the Land Rover after-market industry. Only certain Land Cruiser models are detailed here, mostly diesels found everywhere except the US and the Middle East.

80 SERIES

In 1990 the all-new 80-series Land Cruisers arrived with their distinctive **rounded bodies** – more or less the same bland shape the Toyota 4x4 flagships retain today. With a much smarter interior, fit and finish, in Britain the 80 helped put Land Cruiser on the map, readily adopted like the similar Discovery, by well-heeled families as a 'bigger = safer' people carrier. It makes a great choice as an overlander. Even with very high mileages, a British 80 is unlikely to have seen the

80 – the first of the cushy TLC wagons.

sort of off-road use and possible neglect that taints some Land Rovers. The people that originally bought them weren't interested in winching out of a quarry, and at the same time could afford to maintain a full service history – critical in any vehicle's early years.

In the UK what you'd spend on a good, high-mileage 80 would buy you a pretty rough Defender. The 80's major failing is that it doesn't look the part the way a Defender or a Troop Carrier can. It was a situation unique to the UK. Over the Channel and probably throughout the world, 80-series Land Cruisers fetch much higher prices than their competitors.

Suspension sets an 80 apart from a 60 horse cart; **coil springs** were a long overdue admission that Range Rovers got it right twenty years earlier. This gives a smoother ride off road, though it's still necessary to fit heavier rear springs. Brakes and steering were greatly improved too, and the cabin was transformed.

European 80s were mostly turbo diesel VXs with **full-time 4WD** and two batteries. Starting used **24 volts** but, unlike the previous 24-volt 60s, the ancillaries like bulbs and wiper motors ran on 12 volts. Inexpensive **timing belts** replaced the noisy but low-maintenance timing gears of the 60s. But what plagued Land Rover 300Tdis engines for years, Toyota got right first time. A timing belt warning light comes on as you turn 100,000km to remind you to get it changed soon (not 'Timing belt about to shred, abandon ship!', as I thought halfway down a desolate track once!).

The **engines** in the earliest 80s models were hastily modified motors from the 60s, and for this reason you may want to steer clear of models built before 1992. The 80s manufactured **from 1993** received attention to the 1HD-T diesel engine, suspension, brakes (ABS) and gearbox (viscous coupling lockable in high range and automatically locked in low range). With **air-con** as standard, a vastly improved model emerged, although some turbo-diesel engines up to 1994 were prone to early main-bearing wear (see 🖳 lcool.org for the full story). By now they'll have all long passed the 100,000km mark and so ought to have been repaired, often under warranty. An injected 215hp 4.5 petrol engine (1FZ-FE) also appeared at this time to keep the traffickers, sheikhs and Americans happy, until it got too hot.

GX80 and VX80

An admiration for 80s is one thing North America and Europe have in common, except out west 80s are auto petrol V8s. Old style diesels may have benefits for overlanding, but in the US a petrol-engined 80 is inexpensive and a popular off roader.

GX80s have part-time four-wheel drive, free-wheeling hubs, vertical rear doors and usually had a 1HZ engine and axle diff locks. **VXs** have permanent four-wheel drive, tailgates rather than doors, carpets rather than vinyl, and other consumer-oriented interior features. With Land Cruiser models in Australia, 'GXL' is the same as VX in Europe.

Picking an old 80 depends on what's available in your market or how far you're prepared to look. Be more concerned by general neglect and rust than high mileage. The original 1HZ-based 158hp 1HD-T **engine** feels less grunty (or should that be 'truck-like'?) than the 12H-T it replaced. It's smoother, quieter and more powerful, though marginally less economical in manual form. It makes maximum torque at 1800rpm – just like the old Series III diesel, but there's two and a half times more of it.

Alternatively, if you can find the plain, part-time four-wheel-drive GX model, you'll spend less to get the aspirated IHZ power train of the legendary HZJ78/9, but with an 80-series suspension and body. Later, this model became known as the **105**, the workhorse 'GX' version of the 100-series Amazon, which sounds like the ideal '80' for overlanding until you look into it. By the mid-1990s the diesel six became more complex: the 24-valve 1HD-FTE engine with computer-controlled fuel injection produced 164hp and some say marked the end of the simple Toyota sixes suited to overland use.

In Europe at least a VX still came across as a big and ostentatious machine – a touch of the 'Range Rover syndrome' which can work against you in some overlanding situations. But of all the vehicles listed here, you get a genuine all-terrain machine that'll also run unobtrusively as a day-to-day people carrier back home. In the UK they go from £3000 with high mileages. No longer the bargain they once were, but as long as the car had a good start to life with a regular service history, there will be a trip left in it.

Problems I've heard of include broken coils (common to all coilers and no drama) and lighting relays. Petrol FZJ80s can overheat and blow head gaskets and 'pesky' heater hoses (search 'PHH'). Heavier springs, especially at the rear, are obligatory and at high mileages the original CV joints may be worn out; test them by turning slowly on full lock and listen out for clicking.

In the UK and probably much of Europe, most diesel VXs are **automatic**, a pleasure to drive and easily controllable over rocky terrain compared to a manual. On the road I've found they can be up to 20% more **economical** than a manual HJ61, which itself set a benchmark. One time an auto 80 achieved an incredible 14kpl (40mpg) on tarmac. My 61 managed around 11.5kpl (33mpg) – also a record – while a Tdi Defender delivered a slightly below average 8.75kpl (25mpg). A mysterious Toyotan simoon must have been behind us.

100 AND 200 SERIES

In 1998 the bigger 100-series replaced the 80s: heavier, wider, longer and more electronically complex than ever with, horror of horrors, independent front suspension (IFS; see p145) to produce car-like handling. In Europe it came with the same 24-valve 1HD-FTE engine now making 196hp with the help of an intercooler. The US and sheikhs got the 230hp 4.7-litre 2UZ-FE V8.

The Amazon, as it was called in the UK, also has hydraulic vehicle height adjustment to compensate for its lower road ride, plus traction control and other electronics that were now becoming commonplace. Many lamented the lack of a solid front axle, but only because it was perceived as a soft 4x4 limo. In my experience in Libya, an Amazon managed as well as the other 4x4s, although the owner reported various gremlins with the auto-retracting steering wheel. In the US post-2000 **UZJ100s** have stronger front diffs and brakes were notably better than the FZs. Fitting heavy-duty OME springs and shocks makes a reliable overland rig that's immune to all these HSD issues, and was described as 'one of the most reliable vehicles ever imported to the US'. In Colorado, Slee Offroad know their Land Cruiser 80s, 100s and LX 470s.

Along with all other 4x4 flagships, today's **200** TTD V8 takes this all a step further, which is why many overlanders now consider buying a 4x4 older than themselves or just get their head around the electronics.

Toyota didn't burn its bridges with the 80-series completely. The **105** took the Amazon shape but was fitted out as a GX-style workhorse with a front beam axle (non-IFS), part-time 4WD (but dispensing with FWHs), a 'hose-out' interior, wind-up windows, the aspirated 1HZ engine, but with an

A 200 series in Morocco. © Tim Gbedemah.

under-specified R151 gearbox (more on p90), and vertical back doors. Besides NGO use, the 105 was popular in Australia where it was chosen by many looking for 80-style comfort married to the no-nonsense 1HZ engine. Elsewhere, a 105 is harder to find or as expensive to import as a Troop Carrier. The 105 was supposedly replaced in 2006 by the five-door HZJ76 mentioned below.

70 SERIES: PICKUPS AND TROOP CARRIERS

Back in 1984 the 70-series replaced the 40 series as long- and short-wheelbase, no-frills workhorses, comparable with Land Rover's 90/110s of that era. Indeed it was the bigger 70s that drew on the export sales for Land Rover's utility models and helped drive that marque towards producing the refined and stylish SUVs with which it thrives today.

Designations from **70** to **74** were short- or mid-wheelbase 'jeeps' with smaller four-cylinder, 2.5-litre engines that offer limited practicality to overlanding. Though confusingly revived in 2006, **76** and **77** models from the 1990s were five-door slightly-less-long-wheelbase (SLLWB) station wagons. The original HZJ77 was made from 1990 and a 78-based HZJ76 from 1999. It was originally sold in Japan (RHD) as well as China, Thailand and Malaysia, and got grey exported from Japan to the UK and especially Australia. The current five-door 76 from the rounded-off, wider nosed generation of 70s still takes a 1HZ engine in 'emission-easy' markets, or comes with the Euro 5-compliant 4.5-litre V8 diesel.

No doubt you're completely baffled by now, so this is what you need to know about the bigger 70-series Land Cruisers. It's the original LWB **HZJ75** (pickup or hardtop) and current hardtop **HZJ78 Troop Carriers** ('Troopies') and **HZJ79 pickups** that retain the better qualities of the old 60s and add up to among the best bets in this category of vehicle for overlanding. They're little-known in the UK and the States, but were common in Canada and are as common as roadside beer cans in outback Australia, as well as being widely used as utility or military vehicles all over the developing world.

Toyota can take some credit that in 2010 their iconic Troopie, known as a 'Station' in Africa, was banned in Algeria without a special permit. Chad soon followed suit by severely restricting use of the HZJ79 pickup to all but the military and tribal chiefs. For the previous two decades, smugglers and other undesirables had done rather too well with 'Le Station' and its open-backed cousin. They were the only vehicles up to the job, and in 2015 an exasperated former U.S. Ambassador to the United Nations questioned Toyota Motor Company about how and why *the Toyota Land Cruiser and Hilux have effectively become [...] part of the ISIS brand.'*

A well-equipped HZJ75. Lifting roof conversions are popular in Europe.

75s

The 75s kicked off in 1984 and ran till about 1999 as a pickup, a three-door Troopie with vertical rear doors and, less commonly, with a second row of forward-facing seats (known as an 'RV' in Australia). So by now any 75 you manage to get will be well into its third decade but still holds its price annoyingly well. With a typical unladen weight of 2200kg, a loaded 75 with the aspirated 1HZ engine won't give you whiplash, but for overlanders nothing else comes close.

I've driven Troopies across the Libyan Desert with 600 litres of fuel stacked *on the roof* and half as much water plus six people and their gear in the back. In Mauritania we shared a pickup along with *twenty two* others including a couple on the cab roof, plus a few 50-kilo sacks of grain for ballast. It's taking this sort of abuse in their stride that's made the 70s peerless, even among other Toyotas 4x4s which I've seen crack under the strain.

Engines

Early 70-series diesel **engines** can be the BJ75 version with a 3.5-litre four, and the HJ75 with the 2H 4-litre six, which by the late 1980s became the legendary **128hp, 4.2 1HZ** still produced in its aspirated, particulate-disgorging form.

The main fly in the ointment is **mediocre fuel consumption** by modern European standards. The indirect 4-litre 1HZ derived from the preceding 2H was tuned for longevity and lacks a crisp response, while dropping to as little as 4kpl or 12mpg in deep sand. With the larger 4.2 1HZ motor the horsepower is the same as a 12H-T turbo, but with 80% of the torque. And torque counts for much more than horsepower, which is merely a factor of torque times rpm. With steady driving on normal surfaces expect 8kpl (23mpg). As with any old diesel engine, don't be tempted to fit an **after-market turbo** to a 1HZ.

1HZ: six of everything except known problems.

The 3.5-litre four-cylinder **BJ75** was sold in Europe but isn't the same as the 4.2 six once you're on a mission. Externally there's no easy way to tell so check for six of everything under the lid. The **1PZ** was a five-cylinder. Found in Japan, a few were built in South Africa, but the 4.2 six is the one you're after.

Running a 75

A Troopie has a **high roof** and masses of room in the back: around 4.5 cubic metres compared to 4.2 in a hardtop Defender 110. Drawbacks include the basic, cramped cabin and the **narrow track** (axle width) of around 1750mm which makes a Troopie on 7.50x16" tyres appear unstable next to a Nissan GR or a Humvee. Thirty-millimetre **spacers** can be fitted behind the hubs to broaden the track. In some markets Troopies come with twin tanks totalling up to 180 litres (47.5 US gallons), dual batteries, raised air-intakes and air-conditioning and front and rear axles diff locks all well suited to overlanding.

A 75 making a meal of a perfectly straightforward Congolese jungle track. © Frederik & Josephine.

Seventies are the Outback's workhorse. This high-roofed 1HZ 78 is a popular rental.

HZJ78 and 79

In 2000 the **HZJ78 hardtop** was released alongside an **HZJ79 pickup**. Last time I checked both were still available (see 🖥 toyota-gib.com). The classic profile was little changed but the new model had many improvements. The chassis was longer and wider, the wheelbase was 200mm longer at 2.98m (117") and had a 20mm wider track (a complaint with the 75), and the cab was roomier.

The front and rear **suspension** was radically revised. Solid axles were retained, but the front now used coil springs, while the rear featured longer, more supple leaves. The retention of leaves on the rear is a common feature on load carriers to this day: the inter-leaf friction limits the roll found on some all-coilers, which can be a liability or overwork the shocks. Drive shafts were also stronger and the brakes were beefed up so the 75's six-stud wheels would no longer fit. To make sure no one could try, 78s adopted five chunkier studs. Apart from spotting the front coils and lacking a tape measure, the **five stud wheels** are the easiest way to distinguish a 78 from a 75.

Like a Defender, it still drives and handles like a truck, but with part-time 4WD and comparatively low gearing it's noisy on the highway. Transplanted from the Prado and the diesel Hilux, the smaller front diffs and the R151 gearboxes on early 1HZs were said to be not so durable (output shafts were a warranty recall for a one-piece unit, and second and fifth gears played up). Chances are, as the owner you're not going to be hammering your 78 to get back at the boss for not paying overtime, and it's possible to run past 250,000km on an R151 without fault. The more powerful 1HD-FTE 4.2 turbo engine offered in the Troopie in Australia from 2002 had the tougher H151 gearbox from the wagons and petrol-engined 78s.

With its computer-controlled fuel injection the 1HD-FTE was more refined but not that more economical. Neither match a Troop Carrier's profile, just as similarly superior and sophisticated engines were seen by some as incompatible in Defenders. But that's what modern engines have become: electronics are a cheap way to make them conform with ever-stricter emission regulations.

In 2007 the classic Troopie profile had its sharp edges knocked off in a redesign and with it came the vehicle many had been waiting for (but which had in fact existed all along): a **five-door Troopie**, the HZJ76. It's still available in places like South Africa with the aspirated 1HZ engine, but has the shorter wheelbase of the old 60 series.

The five-door HZJ76. © TGS Ltd.

40,000 MILES WITH A TOYOTA PRADO 90

Prados are often referred to as Toyota's 'soft' Land Cruiser but don't let this put you off. Albeit smaller than the legendary 80s of the time, Prados held their own very well in the rugged 4x4 category. The older 70 series Prado is tougher but less comfortable than the 90 like ours.

As with so many 4x4s, the 120 series Prado (from 2002-09) fell into the luxury SUV category and although as capable as its predecessors, it had a higher degree of sophistication which we thought may work against us in demanding conditions or far from an approved service centre.

Our 90 series was a great middle-of-the-road choice: comfortable, reliable, tough, excellent off-road. As with most Toyotas, parts are straightforward to come across throughout Australia, Africa and Asia and we found every mechanic from Tblisi to Phnom Penh had seen one before. Like all vehicles, Prados have their drawbacks, some of which couldn't be easily remedied and in the course of our 40,000 mile trip across Asia in a 90 we became experts.

The **alloy cylinder head** was prone to cracking if it got too hot, so be vigilant with your coolant checks, especially in hotter countries. Don't even think about using a coolant/water mix; use pure undiluted Toyota coolant. Replacing a cracked cylinder head in a remote part of the world can be expensive, not to mention nerve-destroying as you watch a couple of local bush mechanics dismantling your engine on a dirt floor with care-free abandon.

Given this weakness (also found on some Toyota Surf engines), make sure the radiator and water pumps are in top condition before you leave. If you have any doubt about their history, replace them and bring the spares if you have the room. If the coolant isn't crystal clear, run a high quality coolant flush through the system, flush with fresh water until running totally clear and then refill with coolant. There are a couple of coolant passageways in the back of the cylinder head that can fur up leading to the head warping problems.

With **automatic gearboxes**, it's worth flushing the gearbox with fully synthetic automatic transmission fluid (ATF) before you set off. Additionally, if you anticipate driving through lots of mud and sand, fit an additional gearbox oil cooler.

A reinforced front **bashplate** is an essential bit of kit on a 90 as the sump and steering linkages are prone to damage on rocky terrain. The existing fuel tank protector won't help much in hard going, so consider replacing this too. Besides this, the **rear diff lock mechanism** is prone to seizing if not used for a while – in common with many similarly equipped 4x4s. Engage it on a regular basis even if you don't actually need it that often.

Overall, the **suspension system** isn't as tough as a Land Cruiser, but we managed at least 5000 miles off-road on our trip, and most things held up pretty well, so don't be put off by the doomsday predictions of 80-series enthusiasts. **Upgraded dampers** are a must, but the rear damper threads are prone to stripping, leaving your damper clanging around like a bell clapper. Make sure you use thread lock on the mounting threads and take a re-threading kit and some spare nuts with you.

Snorkels, diff breather kits, roof racks and other **overlanding gear** are all readily available for Prados. An **extended fuel tank** will only be necessary if you're planning on crossing the Sahara, but with the spare wheel mounted on the back door, fitting it is a relatively straightforward job. Otherwise, two jerricans on the roof give you a range of about 720km (450 miles) which was more than sufficient for anywhere in Asia, even Mongolia.

Alternatives include Discoverys (see p109), or Mitsubishi Pajeros, a cheaper option but less robust and without some of the off-road capability of a Land Cruiser or Prado. The older Hiluxes or Surfs are trusty beasts, again cheaper with less off-road capability but no less reliable.

Prado stats
Unladen weight 1900–2070kg.
Fuel capacity 90 litres (23.7 USg).
Max (safe) range 480km (300 miles).

We liked: Quiet and comfortable ride (90 and 120 series), strength and reliability, good off-road capability, relatively good fuel economy.
We didn't like: Alloy cylinder heads in the 90 series (1KZ engine) prone to cracking, chassis and suspension not as robust as the Land Cruiser.

CHARLIE WEATHERILL

Elsewhere it came with a 4.5 1VD-FTV twin-turbo Euro 5-compliant V8 diesel. Troopies have become a little easier to find or more common as special UK or EU imports, usually as LHDs. DPF kits are fitted to help them pass through emissions tests. For used examples try Germany, the Low Countries and France. Just remember you'll be paying a lot for comparatively crude vehicles.

PRADOS AND OTHER MODELS

The Prado (to use the most common name) is a shorter, mid-sized Land Cruiser station wagon featuring full-time 4WD, a coil-sprung beam axle on the back and IFS on the front. It's aimed right between the eyes of the family 4x4 estate brigade who'd taken to Discoverys and the like and are now spoilt for choice with SUVs from Mercedes, VW, BMW and probably Maserati. Like all those, it's never been that popular as an overlander, though there's no doubt it would be an able and very comfortable machine.

Although manufactured under this name from 1990 and deriving from the little-known 77 models of that era, the body of the Prado morphed when it became known as the **90 series**. In the UK it was briefly called a **Colorado**, elsewhere a **Challenger**, but finally they settled on the **Prado** name, except in the States where it was a **Lexus GX 470** with the obligatory V8 petrol engine. Lexus is the brand name for Toyota's luxury division outside of Europe and is often sold separately.

In 2002 a newer, sleeker **120 Prado** was introduced with the 3-litre 1KD-FTV, or the D-4D, but to their credit Prados stuck to their off-road origins with a separate chassis as well as lockable rear LSDs, and with the array of electronic traction, cornering, suspension and ear-warming aids that all vehicles of this type now feature. In 2009 it became the **150** with 4.0-litre petrol V6 or in the UK today the refined 2.8 1GD-FTV 'Land Cruiser' which if nothing else, came third behind Lexus in a recent reliability survey.

Less usefully, and like the big Amazons and 200s, they show their **road bias** with 17" wheel rims – not so good on the dirt or out in the world where 16s have been the norm. All in all it's hard to think why a prospective overlander would choose a Prado over a bigger six-cylinder Land Cruiser available for around the same price, but as with all these things, if you've owned one for a while and trust it, there's nothing stopping you. For Hilux pickups see p115.

Prado being dug out of Mongolian snow (see box p91). What ever happened to just taking the kids to school? © Charlie Weatherill.

A Lexus LX470 with a 270hp 4.7 V8 petrol engine. It's a similar shape to a 100 series. © sleeoffroad.com.

Land Rover Defender

There's something reassuring about the shape of the Defender. You see one coming and think everything's going to be alright.

Ray Mears, Land Rover Defender brochure

Google returns over 76 million hits for 'Land Rover' compared to just 28 million for 'Land Cruiser'. How's that for market research.

When many travellers, particularly Brits, first toy with the notion of over-landing in a 4x4, Land Rover's Defender is what springs to mind. Land Rover's **heritage** strikes a deep chord. Memories of rattling around in a Series III on a farm as a kid, 1960s adventure films and TV shows, and the Camel Trophies of the 1980s. All have helped the Land Rover brand earn such an iconic status that even today, whenever a TV celebrity sets off on some 'Around Britain' documentary that might involve the peril of muddy country lanes, they do so in a rugged Defender because, just like their North Face fleece, it's cool and looks the part. As Jan Rutters states on p104: *'There was never any doubt which vehicle we'd use for our adventure of a lifetime'*. In many cases it's simply the prospect of driving a Defender that accounts for much of the appeal of an overland adventure, such is the marque's association with tough, go-anywhere vehicles.

4 x 4 s

Since that reputation was earned Land Rover have diversified with great success and although the image of the classic Defender helped sell the brand, this venerable emblem only ever accounted for a fraction of sales. In part this is due to well-documented vagaries in production quality, but also because much more design and investment was lavished on the thoroughly modern and much better-selling Discoverys (LR4s) and Range Rovers.

The last of the classic hand-built Defenders rolled off the UK production line in January 2016, and at the time of writing there were no plans to move the old production line abroad. The Defender was a dinosaur that in terms of precision automated manufacturing and crash regulations, was an anachronism on a level with the Toyota 70 series. With both vehicles that's part of their appeal when set against the latest Range Rover with its heads-up windscreen displays, on-board cameras and the ability to be driven remotely from a smartphone. But take heart: the name is unlikely to die and some sort of 21st-century 'Defender' will be out shortly if not already, though probably more 'FJ Cruiser' capitalising on the name than farm yard workhorse.

Even with the final 2.2 TD, Defenders were so far behind the times that buyers convinced themselves its pedigree and **rugged simplicity** made it a good overlander. These are good attributes, but cabin noise and discomfort, fluid and rain leaks and a general lack of ergonomics can be traced back directly to the Series IIIs of the 1970s. Premature wear of core components as well as teething problems from new were incredibly frustrating, although this tendency is far from unique to Land Rovers. Complaints are commonly heard, but largely trouble-free ownership doesn't make headlines.

This suggests archaic design and what Overland Expo's co-founder Jonathan Hanson described as 'bipolar' **build quality**. Owning any kind of brand-new Land Rover product is still a lottery, something that even dyed-in-the-wool enthusiasts readily joke about. Once neglected, either by you or previous owners (a practice that the perceived 'toughness' of all 4x4s encourages), it can result in an endless string of minor faults. Used as a weekend runabout this is no drama, but out in the world, far from any recovery service or the huge support network in the UK, it can all get frustrating. Interestingly, it's an opinion shared by some US 4x4 fans about their no less iconic, Jeep.

This may all sound like a damning indictment, but the same criticisms can easily be levelled at any number of European, American and Asian marques. It's just that no one really cares if a Kia Cornetto or a Chevy Magnum Classic are crap cars. And anyway, even the worst automobiles these days are still 90% reliable.

The key is to approach **the Land Rover experience** with eyes wide open. Expecting the 'best 4x4xFar' (an advertising tag line from the 1980s) requires a positive attitude. As mentioned elsewhere, if you just want to get in, turn the key and drive off, get something else unless you know – or are prepared to get to know – your Defender well.

Many owners have come to do just that and even enjoy the challenge because, behind all the issues as illustrated with Jan Rudder's Puma on p104, there's no doubt that the Defender adds an expeditionary esprit to your overland adventure that no other vehicle can touch, and so it remains as popular as ever for overlanding.

BODY STYLES

The main market for Defenders is in the UK and Europe. One of the big advantages in the UK is that after-market accessories, parts, know-how and servicing are widely available and inexpensive, although for what it is, a Defender itself is comparatively expensive in the UK. It's hard to think why when an old Discovery (see p109) with near-identical technology and in a similar state can often be bought for half the price.

Defender 110s come in three body styles: pickups, including the high-capacity 'HiCap' version; three-door van bodies or 'hardtops'; and station wagons. The first two are regarded as the commercial models and so are basically equipped, but the five-door station wagons try to snare domestic SUVers so are better equipped and also have the largest interior volume once the back seats are ditched. Double-cab pickups and extra-long-wheelbase 130s are also available. With a great payload rating, the latter make more spacious platforms for campervan conversions.

With Defenders more than other vehicles, **age** isn't necessarily an indication of the condition. A renovated 20-year-old 110 on a new galvanised chassis may be in better shape than a rusty 300Tdi that was first registered a decade later. It's common, educational and fun to rebuild a Defender from the ground up if you have the means, and engine swaps are also common, but for overlanding you're much better off using an accessorised near-standard vehicle with few previous owners, ideally all of whom lavished lots of the right kind of attention on their Landie.

Finally, if you're concerned about Euro NCAP (New Car Assessment Programme) **accident safety ratings**, the antediluvian construction of a classic Defender makes it one of the worst cars to crash in or run someone over with. Other modern Land Rovers get near-perfect NCAP scores.

LIVING WITH A LANDIE

The Defender's cramped driving position jammed against the door has been a source of complaint since the second Ice Age and couldn't be fixed. But when it comes to **outfitting the vehicle**, the rectilinear interior is a definite plus, even if the wheel boxes on the hardtops waste a lot of space inside (you get most of it back by fitting lockers on the outside). Making your own customised containers fit without rattling is easy as there are no curves and few steps to complicate things. Outside, the flat surfaces make mounting extra gear straightforward too, and the flat front wings make an ideal small table on which to place a mug or engine parts. The steep glass angles (including the windscreen) means less sunlight penetrates the vehicle so keeping it cooler for longer; without air-con it's something you'll appreciate. **Payload** is very good for its class, with only a little less volume in the back than a capacious Troopie.

Aftermarket spare wheel carrier keeps the back door from falling off.

Spare wheels sit on the back door, where weak hinges and rust can cause problems; they frequently come loose or break on rough roads. An aftermarket spare-wheel carrier is essential; choose one that enables the door to be opened from the inside. Putting the spare on the bonnet may look cool but obscures forward vision and the bonnet weighs a ton. This might discourage regular engine inspections and isn't what you want crashing on your head while checking the coolant.

The modular aluminium **body** bolted to a steel frame can't be anywhere near as rigid as a monocoque body, which partly explains why doors must be slammed but still won't seal. (After driving a Defender you tend to slam *all* car doors, which can aggravate their owners). In particular the alloy roof gutters can officially only carry 75kg (163lb) and some gutter-mounted roof racks weigh up to half that. Support arms reaching down to bolt onto steel chassis members and the bulkhead double the rating. The relatively frail body of a Defender isn't something to overload or roll.

Rust

Don't assume that because Defenders bodies are aluminium they won't **rust**; there's plenty of steel underneath that rots like an old Toyota 60. Land Rover's alloy origins were down to a post-war surplus of aircraft aluminium alongside a deficit of steel, but nowadays if you're buying anything that's a few years old make sure you have a good poke around underneath with a screw driver and hammer. A solid chassis is vital for what you're taking on.

Despite being very rigid, holes in the thin-walled box-section chassis rails allow crud to get in and induce rust. Open, 'C'-channel chassis rails as found on other 4x4s and trucks use thicker metal to achieve similar rigidity (or design for the flex; see p224) so mud just dries up harmlessly and falls off.

Structural rust on a Defender is most common in the rear cross member (some owners say because it's too far from the 'preserving effects' of engine and gearbox oil leaks) – and the bulkhead, where water runs down the metal partition below the windscreen that separates the engine from the cab. However, until something falls off, the galvanic or electrolytic corrosion where aluminium meets steel (see p239) is merely unsightly.

The good thing is there are no rusting wheel arches, roof gutters or wind-screen edges to deal with, as there can be on older Toyotas or Discoverys for example, and new body panels and chassis outriggers to support the body mounts as well as rear cross members (if not a whole chassis), are all readily available to weld on once the rotten parts have been cut away. A vehicle with a new or zinc-plated chassis or wax oiled from new is worth the extra price.

THE FIRST COILERS
The bells finally tolled for the Series III Land Rover in 1983 – a model that had changed little since Land Rover's 1960s heyday, even though the rest of the world had moved on. In its place came the **One Ten**, followed by the **Ninety** a year later. Apart from a few early models (like the Stage 1 V8s), all Land Rovers from this time on used the proven transmission and suspension set-up of the original Range Rover released in the late-1960s: full-time four-wheel drive with a central-locking diff and beam axles with coil springs. For their time the One Ten and Ninety offered class-leading axle articulation, which helped maintain traction without resorting to diff locks or today's electronic marvels. Shocks sat out of harm's way behind the coils and for the 2.79m (110") wheelbase, ground clearance, approach and departure angles were excellent. Initially there were many reports from NGOs in Africa of the new coilers rolling, as was the case in Europe with the small Suzuki jeeps at the time. This 'instability' actually turned out to be local drivers driving way too fast on the much improved suspension and paying the price.

The first One Tens (as they were known) came with the old 2.24 engines or petrol V8s. You don't want either of those unless you know better and chances are if they're still around they've had a Tdi transplant. In 1984 the aspirated diesel grew to 2494cc (67hp); a 2.5 petrol four followed a year later making 83hp. These are startlingly low figures by today's standards, but many such Land Rovers have trundled staunchly round the world. As I've found with other 4x4s with similarly lame figures, off road it's all in the gearing, not being overloaded and, up to a point, technique. Overshadowed by the famed V8s, the 2.5 petrol slipped away unnoticed in 1994.

In 1986 the first turbo-diesel engine was introduced; the 85hp indirect injection 2.5 TD. Not to be confused with the Tdis that followed, it's common-ly accepted that early examples of this stop-gap engine were a time-bomb. **Avoid a 2.5 TD** unless you're sure it's the later sorted version, or is cheap enough to replace with a better motor. Go for the petrol four, the deafening and dog-slow 2.5 aspirated diesel if you must, or just plump for a Tdi.

Tdi ENGINES (1990–98)
The Tdi Land Rovers engines from the 1990s were the last of the pre-CRD injection examples and as such are very well suited to overlanding on diesel brimming with noxious sulphur. Production continued long after they were officially replaced with the electronically managed Td5.

In 1990 the 107-hp 2.5-litre **200Tdi** engine came in the renamed 'Defender' along with the new Discovery (see below). The quieter, more refined but slightly less economical **300Tdi** followed in 1994 with power up to 111hp (though some doubt this). Other differences between the original One Tens and the externally similar Defenders are negligible, apart from the

A much-adapted 300 Tdi engine.
© mattsavage.com (and right)

Plastic coolant air bleeding plug well worth
replacing with a more robust brass unit on top.

transmission and power steering as standard. The 'Defender' name and
110/90 were primarily marketing moves to help introduce the new engine.

On the road an inefficiently loaded 200Tdi Defender can be flat out at
60mph, but along with a marginally more powerful engine and a bigger intercooler, the higher-geared transmission from a Discovery is easily fitted to
improve cruising speeds at little cost to low-geared off-road utility, which a
Defender has to spare. The best thing with all Tdi engines, particularly the 200,
is that their **fuel economy** could easily reach the 9–10kpl (high-20s mpg).
Indeed, many Land Rover enthusiasts believe the 200Tdi was the **best diesel
engine** the Defender ever got.

With pre-CRD technology there's only so much power and torque you can
squeeze out of a 2.5-litre turbo, even with a bigger intercooler, and it's an
often-raised lament that Land Rover never saw fit to give their workhorse the
big diesel engine it deserved. For years all Land Rovers sold in Australia were
immediately fitted with a 3.9 Isuzu unit, although you do wonder what the
gearbox (more below) had to say to that.

Timing belts

Both engines themselves are strong, but **timing belt breakages** plagued the
300Tdi right up to the introduction of the Td5 engine, which reverted to a timing chain, partly to distance itself from the issue (something Honda did with
the VFR motorcycle in the 1980s following similar problems).

Many modern cars have rubber timing- or cambelts to keep the up-and-
down movement of the pistons synchronised with the in-and-out actions of
the valves, and they've been in Land Rovers since the aspirated 2.5 diesel of
the 1980s (which could also snap catastrophically in my experience). When a
cambelt breaks, it's not like a fanbelt: carrying a spare is of little use as the out-
of-sync pistons tend to mash some valves and a cylinder head rebuild is often
required. Assuming a 300Tdi's pulleys were correctly aligned at the time of
manufacture (some were, some weren't) and the original belt gets past 30,000
miles, you're in the clear. Officially, you then want to replace it every 60,000
miles, same as on many other engines fitted with timing belts. If you buy a 300
(or indeed any high-mileage diesel with a rubber belt) and the owner doesn't
know when the belt was last changed, fit a new one without hesitation; it's not
expensive or that difficult.

A good way of checking for cambelt wear in a 300Tdi is to inspect the drain hole at the base of the cover with a bit of hooked wire. Have a root around; any black fluffy matter is timing-belt shavings, indicating wear from misalignment and the need for a Land Rover **replacement kit**. Kit 1 includes modified pulleys with lips to hold the belt on; if this hasn't worked fit Kit 2, which includes more pulleys and a new front cover. A yellow mark on the timing cover should mean either kit has been fitted at some stage by a dealer.

The good news is that by now all 300s have been through their belt-breaking and factory-replacement-kit cycles. Other than that, on a long trip it's worth taking a spare water pump and alternator – useful items with any vehicle and cheap and easy to fit if the old ones pack up. See the full list on p288.

DEFENDERS IN THE USA

Defenders have long been **status symbols** in America, especially the 110, which was only imported and federalised for 1993. When I ran my green wagon I got my photo taken and a thumbs-up all the time. That's weird for a car that spent the first part of its life hauling sheep up and down the Derbyshire dales.

People here love them. Tacoma and Jeep guys regularly come and exclaim 'hey dude, I'd just love your D90, I'm gonna have one one day!' The Gen-X-ers think they're just so cool without knowing what they are, while people of my age who grew up watching Daktari long aspired to one. That's Land Rover magic for you.

Interestingly, I'm seeing more imports, though the overall number is tiny because to 'federalise' a vehicle it has to meet the safety standards mandated by the NHTSA, or be **over 25 years old** and meet emissions standards mandated by the EPA (Environmental Protection Agency). Land Rover 90s and 110s, have been easy to import, notwithstanding the state of a Land Rover that old.

The officially imported North American Specification (**NAS**) Defenders used to command a premium but are cheaper than they were. You'll still see occasional immaculate examples at dealers costing $30,000 plus for a 90, or $40k or more for a 110. Or pick up a 90

privately for as little as $20,000, although the cheaper ones will be rough. The 90s were officially imported for three years: 1994–95 and 1997, after which some law changed. The '94-'95s are 5-speed manuals, the '97 was the ZF auto. Square lights came on the '94s, the others had big round ones unique to NAS Defenders.

But time marches on and now the 25-year-rule means the much more desirable **200 Tdi Land Rovers** can come on in, and by 2019, the 300s too. A coiler with a half-decent diesel motor; now you're talking!

A word of warning. I know Defenders all look the same to a non-enthusiast. Just make sure you've paperwork to prove your Tdi is genuinely 25 years old *all over*. It's long been easy to muddy the waters with Defenders – metaphorically as well as literally with regards to provenance. That's part of their 'meccano' appeal. But US Customs and Border Protection are on it. In 2013 the salacious Brit tabloids ran stories of a 2005 Defender with a shonky VIN and plates getting brutally crushed by the wrecker's claw. "A favourite of the Royal family", it could have "fetched up to $100,000".

No need for that. Now you can legally import the first of the great Defender diesels from the pre-CRD and sensor era.

NICK TAYLOR

Transmission

The 200- and 300Tdi engines are less similar than the name suggests but it's said that the 200Tdi engine has the edge, being simpler, more economical and free of timing-belt issues. The weak point was its **LT77** gearbox. The transfer lever had a habit of jumping out under load or refusing to engage low range no matter what you did. One 200 owner I knew was on his third gearbox in 100,000 miles until the day he couldn't engage low to get round a small dune. It led to an accident that destroyed his vehicle and nearly killed him. Others I've met have literally got through an LT77 gearbox in one hard trip.

It's an old story with Land Rovers and transmission backlash was a common complaint to the very end. But one well-known problem with the LT77 was premature wear of the main shaft gear that transmitted drive into the transfer box. Due to a lack of splashed oil, the splines where the gear fits on the main shaft wore and eventually failed. The replacement gear on all the transfer boxes from about 1996 had holes drilled through it so the oil could get to the splines, solving the problem, but anyway in 1994 the better R380 box was introduced with the 300Tdi engine. It too wasn't without issues of premature wear, so seek out the stronger 'L' suffix unit. (In case you're wondering, fitting an R380 box to a 200Tdi engine can be done but isn't a bolt-on swap). The good thing is if a gearbox, any gearbox, is on the way out you'll have plenty of warning signs and sounds and usually manage to scrape together some sort of forward progress, even if it's in low-range reverse.

In the old Series days Land Rovers were notorious for snapping rear half shafts, the drive shaft between the axle differentials and the wheels. This became less common from the full-time four-wheel-drive One Ten era onwards, but from around 1994 300Tdi and later Td5 Defenders came with thinner axle hub flanges, the female splined counterpart bolted to the wheel into which the rear half shaft locates. The reason for this retrograde step may have been to allow thicker alloy rims to fit: an unnerving telling example of how form had taken precedence over function, even on a Defender.

Under a lot of transmission strain a worn **flange** can strip its splines; I've seen it happen merely pulling away in soft sand in low range. In this event, with drive lost to the back axle, you can lock the central diff and carry on in front-wheel drive, but you wouldn't want to drive like that for too long. Welding the flange to the half shaft is another get-you-home option. Better still, before you leave check the state of the flange splines: jack up each wheel, remove the flange nut with a big spanner and rock the wheel left and right in gear. Any wear or slack between the end of the half shaft and the flange will be evident; press your thumb over both and you may feel it. Performing the same type of visual check on the four **universal joints** (UJs) on each end of the main drive shafts is also a good idea; all UJs wear in time or if ungreased, but they're cheap and easy to replace.

A Land Rover factory replacement flange (#RUC105200; 24 splines) for the later Defenders costs £18 and is worth carrying as a spare. Alternatively you can buy heavy-duty flanges from UK specialists, but you'd better be sure the original half shafts aren't now the weak link. On any ageing vehicle these sort of piecemeal improvements can be a false economy, often exposing flaws further down the line, especially when it comes to transmission. The official line was that there's something to be said for the transmission's weak point being a readily accessible half shaft that can be swapped in five minutes.

In Europe at least, Defenders with **automatic transmission** are rare and were rarely matched with diesel engines, although the ZF auto box is said to be more reliable than the LT77 and early R380 manual gearboxes – not actually saying much. As far as **suspension and steering** go, any play in the linkages or clanking will most likely be down to worn bushes or ball joints which are normal wear items and easily replaced.

Td5 (1998–2007)

The five-cylinder, intercooled turbo-diesel **Td5** engine ran for around eight years until the then owners Ford slotted in their own Duratorq engine (more below) from the Transit van range. In Discovery specification the Td5 developed 136hp, or 122hp in a Defender, which adds up to a 9% increase in power and 13% more torque over the 300Tdi – a typical improvement when turbo-diesel engines of that time turned to common rail induction.

Td5: same old shape, whole new CRD motor.

Initially the impression of a lack of low-down torque was thought to be the price of a modest power increase at higher rpm, but now that 'chipping (reprogramming) the ECU' is the new way to tune electronically managed engines, it's possible to get a lot more power and torque out of Td5s. Oddly, fuel consumption was a little worse than the 300Tdi, but nothing too drastic. The notorious timing belt was abandoned in favour of a stronger **cam chain**, in part necessary to help turn the high-pressure common rail injectors on each cylinder. A superior filtration system meant oil-change intervals were raised to 12,000 miles, with primary filters lasting through three changes. While you may spend a little more on fuel, you'll save on oil and filters, although many owners wisely choose to play it safe and change oil sooner; good practice on any overlander.

Mechanically, Td5s seem as bombproof as their predecessors and while what's discussed below sounds like another long list of faults, these are all part of the preparation process and are well known and addressable issues. Many Td5s have managed as well as older Defenders over several tough trips.

ECUs and wiring harness

The Td5 was the first **electronically managed** CRD engine to be fitted to a Defender and for a while military and aid agencies thought it unsuitable for the remote operations. Before the CRD and ECU era, the great appeal of diesels was that compared to most petrol engines, they had few electrics and no electronics to go wrong.

Like so many new engines, the first Td5s got off to a bad start with an appetite for ECUs. Early examples with an 'MSB'-prefixed part number have been described as either 'too sensitive' or that they 'couldn't forget' (modern

ECUs 'learn and remember', though can be reprogrammed or 'chipped' to remember something else). A modified ECU (prefix: 'NNN') came out in 2002, but some of these didn't work on the older engines, or came up with irrelevant fault codes, even though part numbers suggested a direct replacement.

Worse still, on Td5s the engine immobiliser was closely matched with the ECU. An instructor from the Land Rover Experience admitted to me these used to become permanent engine-stoppers in wading situations. Disabling or resetting the **10AS alarm/immobiliser unit** is easily done with the well known diagnostic tools from Autologic, Testbook or Rovacom; these days as essential as feeler gauges once were.

The same cannot be said for the **injector wiring harness** inside the hot, oily rocker cover. Over time a misfire or loss of performance sets in as the insulation breaks down due to engine heat, contaminating the connections with oil. Get a spare (about £27; #AMR6103); they're pretty easy to replace.

Fuel pumps and water sensors

The other ongoing problem with Td5s more pertinent to overlanding was the primary **fuel pump** in the fuel tank. This isn't a normal, old-fashioned fuel pump that could be got around with a gravity feed from a roof-mounted jerrican, but a high-pressure, filtered two-stage unit needed to feed the CRD engine. Because this pressurisation sequence begins before the fuel has gone through the main fuel filter(s) in the engine bay, the pump has to process possibly contaminated fuel, which, not surprisingly, it doesn't always like and either packs up or loses pressure over time.

Early examples were notorious, but the modified replacements still wear out or fail over around 50,000 miles in normal conditions. When on the way out, a worn fuel pump may squeal and though an engine can still start, when it's gone the engine won't rev over 2500rpm or manage any incline. The lesson is to ensure your Td5 gets clean fuel, which can be a tall and tedious order on the road. What you can ensure is that you **never run out** or even get very low on fuel, and carry a spare pump assembly as well as fuel filters.

Knowing all this, clued-up Defender Td5 owners cut a hatch in the rear load bed right above the top of the fuel tank where the pump is positioned so they can get to it easily (this hatch is a standard feature on Discovery Td5s), and acquaint themselves with the re-priming technique. Doing so makes replacing the fuel pump from inside the back a much simpler job compared to the hours it takes to remove a Defender's fuel tank during a sweaty Indian monsoon.

Early on, **water sensors** in the fuel filter were also said to be unreliable and are best removed; later models didn't have a sensor. It's also said that a spare flywheel- or crankshaft position sensor (£30; #NSC100790) is worth carrying as its failure will stop the engine dead. The sensor is easily accessible under the vehicle, situated above the bell housing and held on with an M6 bolt.

Electronic traction control

Early Td5 Defenders came with **electronic traction control** (ETC), as described on p78. That may work brilliantly in mud, snow and on rocks, but in sand I've found old-fashioned brain-throttle control makes all the difference (along with tyre-pressure regulation, which requires stepping out of the car and crouching

HEATERS AND DRAUGHTS ON A Td5

Earlier models up to and including the Td5 had the older-style dashboard and owners of 90s and truck cabs find heating more effective than 110 owners as the former have a smaller internal volume. The general feeling is the older-style heater is fine but that many vehicles suffer from the following issues:

• Ducting hoses behind the dash separate from the windscreen vents resulting in a limited or no effect. Easily remedied by resecuring them.

• Poorly adjusted control cables running back to the airflow flaps on the ducting and heater matrix. Again, easily remedied by following instructions on many LR forums. If replacing control cables ensure the routing is correct. Internally lubricated ones have a smoother action.

• Water from rain or wading gets in and blocks the wing air-intake leading to the heater matrix. This is thought to be the cause behind the windows misting up when turning on the heater. Check the drain hole on the wing air-intake isn't blocked with mud and dead frogs.

• Long-term water build-up rusts the exterior of the heater matrix, resulting in limited or no heating. Replace the matrix with a standard or upgraded part. Most think the upgrade isn't necessary unless you're heading to very cold places, in which case an additional and more powerful heater and pre-heater may be worthwhile (see p78).

• Defender diesel engines run fairly cool unless there's a problem somewhere and so take a long time to warm up, which gives the impression the heater isn't much good. In winter some people use a radiator muff or cardboard to hasten the warm-up.

• The viscous cooling fan also delays warm-up; some replace it with an electric fan like a Kenlowe or Pacet. Both claim improved power and fuel consumption but not everyone is convinced. Overlanders seem to prefer the standard viscous fan, although I upgraded my radiator to improve cooling as my 130" camper (pictured) is heavy.

Draughts

You only start to notice draughts in Defenders when it's very cold or on those magical days when you're travelling at high speed. The main sources are:

• The bulkhead vents, where the foam seal is either failing or has fallen off. It's simply and cheaply remedied by replacing the foam seal.

• Many Defender doors are poorly adjusted making rubber seals ineffective. Adjust the slam latch so the door closes 'fully in'; that's to say far enough into the door frame to fully compress the rubber seal and so eliminate draughts.

• Missing or damaged rubber seals at the bottom of doors are often overlooked. A simple and cheap replacement is the solution.

JAMES STEPHENSON

down). My own experience with an early Td5 Discovery on the fringes of Australia's Simpson Desert proved that, in the end, short of momentum there's no substitute for airing down, though the ETC did help pull the car through a few marginal situations.

Electronic Traction Control technology evolves and when, a few years later, I tested a Td5 Defender 110 on an off-road training course, I was struck by how easily the Land Rover crawled up very steep, wet, chalky slopes (and down again with the help of ABS), far exceeding what you'd ever expect to drive over while overlanding. A pair of axle diff locks and reduced tyres pressures may have been as effective in skilled hands, but on any 4x4 the magic of ETC turns you into an all-terrain pro.

PUMA ENGINE (2007 – 2015)

Under Ford's ownership their more refined Duratorq 'Puma' **TDCi** engine replaced the Td5 unit in 2007, dropping from 2.4 to a 2.2 Euro V compliant unit in 2013 until production ended. By this time there was nothing wrong with the Td5 and many saw the Puma as a cost-saving exercise by Ford, who were in trouble at the time (they sold Land Rover to Tata a year later).

Used in Transit vans and London taxis, the four-cylinder 2.4 Puma used second-generation common-rail fuel-injection technology to deliver 120hp but more notably, nearly as much torque as a 2.8 TGVs Powerstroke. It was combined with a six-speed gearbox, with 1st configured as a 'crawler' gear, which can mean less dipping into low range and is useful when pulling away with heavy loads and trailers (1st is said to be 33% lower than a Td5 and 6th 25% higher than 5th on a Td5).

The front seats were improved and can be moved forward and backward, and after decades the **dashboard** was modernised. Heaters and air-con (where specified) are more effective, but the sum of doing so meant dropping one of the Defender's best-loved dry-weather features: the windscreen vent flaps.

On early models the **engine oil sump** hit the front propshaft when driving off road (a warranty modification and said to occur with TGVs too), which makes you wonder how much time they took over the whole project. **Fuel consumption** is thought to be a little worse than its predecessor.

Overall, owners' experiences seemed to cover the usual spectrum from frustration to delight, from reporting no problems and up to 34mpg, to selling on after both minor and major failures with clutches, gearboxes and vacuum pumps. The silent majority fall in between, with the traditional Defender litany of minor rattles, niggles and component failures, persistent leaks, misaligned doors and so on. Altogether though, you can't help thinking with the Puma you've heard it all before and it'll all come good in the end.

Trans Africa with a Puma

Jan Rutters

There was never any doubt which vehicle we'd use for our adventure of a lifetime, otherwise known to our friends as our mid-life crisis. The only decision was which one. Once the idea to transit Africa had germinated, we needed to decide on a Td5 110, an old 300Tdi, or the imminent Defender with the 2.4-litre TDCi. We set about establishing our major requirement. Speaking to other overlanders, **air-con** appears in their top five must-haves. The lack of legroom in a Td5 or 300Tdi when fitted with factory air-con immediately pushed the Puma to the top of our list.

In late 2007 we took a test drive and fell in love with 'Sully'. The electronics left us undeterred; we weren't leaving for two years so with additional time under the Puma's belt we felt by then the major cities en route would be able to provide support. This proved to be correct. Besides, as a safety net we bought the Diagnostic Box with FaultMate from Black Box Solutions to re-set faults on the EMU (engine management unit, aka ECU) and get out of 'limp-home' mode, which to us was the biggest drawback of the all-electronic Puma.

In our experience the mechanics in poor countries and far-off villages often find imported parts prohibitively expensive. Consequently they become adept at coming up with lateral solutions to keep vehicles running – something that proved to be valid even on our Puma. Our first problem occurred in Jordan after 5000 miles on the road. We approached a local mechanic and asked if we could use his pit so my husband could give the Landie a once over. All went well until he changed the fuel filter. Without pre-filling it with diesel, when he started up the engine ran for a few seconds before coughing and falling silent. So it went on for the next five hours whilst we cajoled and rocked her until her batteries finally went flat. By not pre-filling the filter we'd caused an air lock in the high-pressure CRD fuel system. Land Rover's response when we called them in UK was to ask us if we had the special tool needed to bleed air from the system (part #310-110 SPX). No we didn't, so a local mechanic manually pumped fuel through the system from beginning to end. In fact we later learned that this method is as good as the £170 Land Rover special tool, which some Puma owners make themselves anyway. But still nothing, so someone suggested we switch on the ignition and pump the accelerator, which in the Puma causes the fuel pump to operate. Still nothing.

We decided to call in a recovery vehicle to take us to the Land Rover dealer in Amman. As we turned Sully round out of the pit and her nose point-

WHICH LAND ROVER TO AVOID?

That would be the 1983 Range Rover with a 2.5 diesel Transit engine we drove from Ireland to Cape Town one time. We paid £328, changed the fluids, filters and stuck on a nice set of BFG tyres. These things broke:

UK: Gearbox – eBay replacement £80.
Switzerland: Front-wheel hub oil seals leaked.
Turkey: Various steering and suspension bushings.
Syria: Speedo cable snapped.
Sudan: Radiator mountings collapsed due to rust. Exhaust broke off, engine mount collapsed.
Ethiopia: Fuel-injection pump disintegrated.
Kenya: Clutch hydraulic pipe burst.
Tanzania: Rear-axle ball-joint mount broke. Rear chassis cracked right through.
Zambia: Overdrive gearbox bearing failed.
Namibia: Rear brake pipes cracked. Starter motor bushings wore out.
South Africa: Timing-belt tension pulley bearing failed (nearly killed engine).
Tanzania: No reverse gear, clutch slave cylinder failed.
Kenya: Fuel cut-off solenoid failed.

Those are the ones I remember – there were others. Obviously we had a lot of problems but I only needed a tow for the timing-belt incident, and that only cost £75 including the tow (most expensive repair of the trip). Had I paid attention to the screeching 500 miles earlier I'd probably have prevented it.

Needless to say, at the end of the trip, after covering 35,000 miles in 11 months, the Range Rover was in perfect working order and was parked up in Zambia. Unfortunately, a few months later the timing belt snapped and killed the Ford engine.

To be honest we didn't really expect the vehicle to complete the trip; our attitude was to drive as far as we could until she died. The up side is that repairs in Africa can be incredibly cheap and this is what kept us going. I reckon that on top of the bad roads and rusty vehicle, what caused a lot of our breakages was **overloading**.

When we started I had very little knowledge of mechanics; it's all about having the **right attitude** and telling yourself you can fix this (or pay someone else to). After this trip I know a Classic Range Rover inside out and bought two more.

I know this type of trip wouldn't be everyone's cup of tea but we found you meet the nicest people when trying to get your car fixed. Compared to our friends travelling in a Hilux, the Range Rover was very comfortable but was not a patch on reliability.

RICHARD Q (HUBB)

... crouched like a pair of bomb-disposal experts we nodded at each other silently, held our breath and unplugged the ABS/traction control unit

ed gently downwards, Trevor tried one last time to start her up. The engine roared into life and beaming faces surrounded the car, with much clapping and laughter. We can't pinpoint what sorted out the problem. Maybe the manual pumping helped or maybe the fuel system simply wasn't able to clear the air because over the pit the Land Rover was angled decidedly nose up. Anyway, we were on our way.

Three months later our next problem. We chose to bypass the Moyale–Marsabit road crossing from Ethiopia to Kenya in favour of the Omo Valley route (see p424). We left Addis Ababa with our friends Anja and Jörg in their Land Cruiser called Willi, and Ian on his motorbike with no name.

After five days of gravel roads, river crossings, boulder trails of boulders and deep sand, we headed for Loiyangalani. As we'd just completed 1000km of rough, off-highway driving, at a lunch stop Trevor decided to check under the bonnet to see if all was OK. To our utter dismay the engine was covered in oil! After trawling through the Puma workshop manual, we discovered that the telltale spray of hot oil on the inside of the bonnet had come from the vacuum pump. Luckily we were carrying a spare with seals as we'd been warned

LAND ROVER OR TOYOTA?

The vexed question of Land Rover versus Toyota only endures in **Europe**, where the two brands are both easily and widely available and admired to the exclusion of pretty much everything else. Australia is probably the biggest civilian Land Cruiser market in the developed world, and until recently South Africa had long been a fan of the Hilux built there. In the US, imports versus the big domestic brands is the big issue, with Land Rover only selling their luxury SUVs; Defenders have the exotic cachet of a Pinzgauer.

When people say 'Land Rover' they're usually referring to a Defender. For a Brit with little interest in cars, a **Land Rover Defender** will be the first 4x4 that springs to mind. Problem is in the UK Defenders were typically pitched against Toyota's VXs; a bit like putting a Toyota HZJ78 against a Range Rover, i.e: a tractor vs limousine.

Because of the enthusiastic following they inspire, Defenders are often tinkered with by hobbyists or bought by those curious to find out what the Land Rover aura is all about. To own a Defender is to be part of a community bound up in a much stronger relationship than most other vehicles, through thick and thin. Because of this and the higher than normal levels of care they require but sometimes don't get, it's a lot easier to buy a duff Defender than a rough Land Cruiser. That's partly because the latter is much more likely to have been originally used as a 'crash-proof' people carrier and school bus.

In most cases **problems** with Land Rovers are trivial glitches, not showstopping issues. Among other things, including a paucity of comfort and refinement, you'll find a Defender isn't as well put together or as reliable as a Toyota. But –

this was a Puma weak point. But us changing it in the blazing desert heat in the middle of nowhere? We did the next best thing and made a cup of tea, had a bite to eat, cleaned up the oil and decided to check it again in 50 kilometres. The oil leak stopped and since then we've done a further 30,000km without this having raised its head again. The vacuum pump fixed itself.

With a month of glorious Kenyan travel under our belts and 3000km further south, just as we were reversing over an innocuous-looking sand hump, we heard a loud crack. The aluminium stopper for the steering rod had sheared. It was a seemingly insignificant loss that was to come back and haunt us months later. This latest incident caused us to question Land Rover's thinking. Why manufacture an off-road-capable vehicle using such flimsy bits and pieces? Look at the stopper for the steering rod – a piece of soft aluminium four inches long used to stop the vulnerable steering rod from bending.

As we set out from Singida to Arusha in northern Kenya we were to ask this question again. About 30km along a corrugated dirt road, the ABS suddenly kicked in, applying the brakes and bringing us to an abrupt stop. Each time we started off, as we hit 20kph it engaged again, locking up the wheels. We stopped for a look and discovered the hammering of the track had caused both rear brake-disc dust protectors to shear off. They were both hanging off the axle and had in turn dislodged the ABS/traction control sensor on the back right wheel. Sounds obvious, but it took days for us to finally work this out.

excepting the huge 2010 recall which was down to dodgy electronics – what other car in the world is? Toyotas frequently top owners' reliability surveys.

Be aware that it's rare for Toyota owners to change to a Land Rover, while the hard-earned experience of overlanders and commercial users sees the opposite happen on a regular basis. Recognise too that it's rare that a Land Rover becomes utterly unrepairable. Dealing with minor faults and leaks can be a part of daily life, but short of a cambelt breaking, a decisive *coup de grâce* is as unusual, as with any vehicle.

Way back in *Sahara Overland* I suggested the characteristics of Land Cruisers made them the best choice for desert travelling, where **reliability** is paramount. I was surprised how little articulate flak the book received from partisan aficionados of the famed British marque, and suspect that even then the cat was already out of the bag.

Having weighed it all up (or in all probability made your mind up long ago), this is what you need to take away from this discussion: in the end the best machine is the one that inspires you to go overlanding, and both Land Cruisers and Land Rovers are rightly at the top of that list.

Some comments from the HUBB

FWIW I am culturally and temperamentally more of an LR person than an LC one, but when I did my trip I wanted to be sure something would happen every time I pushed a pedal or turned a key in foreign parts. But for some people emotion plays a bigger part and, provided you have access to the necessary support, the lesser reliability of LRs may be outweighed by the greater character.

IMHO the LR looks great and steals the hearts and minds of most Brits, however, once you have a bit of experience and some common sense it's got to be a Tojo product!

If only I had found HU [website] before we rushed out and bought our LR, we could have saved ourselves lots of cash... I am happy to say that at least we didn't continue throwing more hard-earned money away trying to keep the vehicle on the road and outfitting it with even more 'extras'.

Every time I turn the key, or jump on the roof I get an amazing sense of happiness. And to tell the truth, every time he breaks down (only twice!) I smile, pat him on the side and tell him I love him!

At the time we decided the best way around this one was to remove the protectors. The ABS/traction control system was a different story. Still limited to 20kph we had to come up with a solution ourselves. After consulting the well-thumbed manual, crouched like a pair of bomb-disposal experts we nodded at each other silently, held our breath and unplugged the ABS/traction control unit located under the driver's seat, so hopefully reverting to normal braking. Luckily the ECU took pity on us and didn't implement an all-systems shutdown while setting off a Code 9 Unauthorised Procedure Alert in Solihull. Impressed with our fault-finding skills, we were on the move.

In Dar es Salaam we bumped into a Land Rovering family heading back to the UK in a Td5. We were chatting about the Land Rover problems we'd had and, blow me down, if the driver hadn't had the same thing with dislodged protectors and unwanted sudden braking! We compared protectors and saw they'd broken at identical points. With that, Trevor was under our Land Rover like a ferret down a drainpipe. He carefully levered out the ABS/traction control sensors, wiped them clean and popped them back in. After reconnecting the system, with bated breath we started up and, bingo!, we had ABS! The trick worked fine and they remain intact today.

Another month passed and we entered Mozambique, where the curse of the missing steering rod stopper returned. On a particularly awful section of road we hit a deep hole with a shuddering crash. We inched out to find the steering rod bent so badly the wheels had taken on a distinctly cross-eyed look. We limped to our next stop and followed the well-honed procedure: cup of tea, slice of ginger cake and a consultation. Then Trevor attached the winch to the steering rod and slowly unbent it enough for us to carry on without too much bother – or so we thought. The next 800km to Durban wore down the insides of both front tyres, but with a new rod fitted and tracking redone, we rotated the tyres, got a new stopper welded on and learned a huge lesson.

Over a year into our trip we felt we'd come through relatively unscathed when you consider where we'd been. Our biggest problem hit us in Botswana when the Land Rover developed an oil leak from the transfer box. This time we knew it was serious. Topping it up, we set off slowly to Gaborone for diagnosis and repair. It turned out a breather pipe had got blocked, increasing the pressure in the box, which blew the seals. Not a minor job but not a major problem either and having imagined the worst, it was a huge weight off our shoulders.

Discounting the traction control problem, all the other issues were mechanical. We had no problems with the ECU and the Black Box Solutions Diagnostic Box still sits in its case.

So, travels with a Puma? To be highly recommended. And the solution to most problems? It's on page one of the workshop manual: put on the kettle, have a cuppa and a nourishing snack, mull it over, think laterally if necessary and have a safe journey.

Sullington's triumphant arrival at the Cape.

🖳 gapyear4x4.com

Land Rover Discovery

Introduced in 1989, the innovative Discovery very quickly became the best-selling SUV 4x4 in the UK. If you can find a good one, these models still have a lot going for them as dirt cheap overlanders. This is chiefly because until 2004, Discoverys closely matched Defenders under their skin: the same engine (but more powerful versions), the same transmission (but with higher gearing) and the same suspension, though with smaller tyres and less clearance.

If part of a Defender's appeal is its look, why get a Discovery and let yourself in for similar aggro without the charisma? The answer is it's an infinitely **more relaxing car to drive**. The Discovery had a conventional steel body shell, but unlike current monocoque (unibody) incarnations, it was clamped to a hefty ladder chassis. This adds up to a properly sealed, aerodynamic, car-like **cabin** that like an 80VX makes a Discovery something you can drive around at home *and* take overlanding without gritting your teeth. Indeed, since the very start and not least with current models, the design and layout of the Discovery **interior** has led the way for its competitors in the same category and is about as far removed from a Series III bunker as you can get.

Best of all, in the UK an old Discovery can cost a fraction of a similar aged Defender. Early Discovery 300Tdis go from under £1000 and high-mileage Td5s (below) from £1500. If you can live with the niggles and meltdowns, for normal overlanding a Discovery does nothing significantly worse than a Defender except not look the part, while offering SUV-like comfort.

Who says a Discovery can't go off road?

DISCOVERY TDi

In the original 200Tdi form the engine was considered crude: acceptable in a Defender, less so in a Discovery. Aim for a **300Tdi** which made a useful extra 10hp over the Defender. With **gearboxes** it's the same story as with Defenders, though Discoverys have a different transfer box with a ratio about 15% higher than a Defender. The 2.54m (100") wheelbase means overhangs are OK, though inside the curves inhibit optimum packing and load **space** is down compared to a Defender. For a big trip, removing all the rear seats is the first step, though it's unlikely you can genuinely stretch out and sleep in there, as you can in a Defender.

All that nice **glass** makes for a bright interior but also a hot and exposed one. Blocking out as much as possible will keep the inside cool and be less of an invitation to thieves. Larger tyres and fitting 16-inch **wheels** (some Discovery 2s came with road-biased 18-inch wheels) to carry heavier loads can be done, but requires uprated coils and possibly trimming the wheel arches; 245/75R16 tyres seems as big as you can go.

Something to look out for on older Discoverys is **rust**. Besides the usual wheel arches, rear door and front wings also commonly rot. And check that there's more than air under the carpet in the rear. Unlike the Defender, the spare tyre mounts on a well-supported rear door.

The 300Tdi Discoverys had an **immobiliser** with a secondary but effectively redundant 'spider' unit, which commonly malfunctions, stopping the engine from starting, running or turning off. Faulty soldering on a printed circuit board was thought to be the cause, but is easily neutralised by fitting a £12 official Land Rover bypass plug (#AMR4956) to the unit situated behind the radio. For the full story Google 'Immobiliser Spider Unit Bypass' or the part number. Other than that, with a 300 it's business as usual.

Td5 easing over some gnarly limestone.

DISCOVERY 2: Td5

In 1998 the Discovery got a makeover as well as the Td5 engine described on p101 and became the Discovery 2 (**LR2**). This could be a better choice than its predecessor and the later the better, particularly because ECU glitches ought to have been programmed out by now. With all Td5s – and indeed any vehicle of that age that's heavily reliant on an ECU and a while since its last official service – it's worth getting a diagnosis on the software to ensure you've the latest version, ideally from a specialist or a clued-up main dealer.

Reliability on the Discovery 2 was said to have been improved (the early issues mentioned above and leaky sun roofs notwithstanding). The second-generation Discoverys came with ABS (anti-lock braking) as well as ACE (active cornering enhancement), which reduced roll while cornering (a trait endemic to all tall 4x4s) with the aid of hydraulic pumps. At higher-trim levels came 18" wheels, which further improved road manners by having less sidewall height and so less flex. With ABS comes ETC (electronic traction control), but in snow and on rocks owners have found it rather unresponsive compared to the latest iterations. It was made worse by early D2s having no way to operate the installed central diff lock – and between 2001-03 removing it altogether as it was thought ETC was a cure-all for the intended soft-road users. From 2004 a locking central diff (see p305) became a factory option and so, along with the early issues, Discovery 2s from this date are a better choice.

SUBSEQUENT DISCOVERYS

In 2004 then Land Rover owners Ford spent a fortune hoping to revive the flagging sales of the Td5. The result was the all-new **Discovery 3** (**LR3** in North America) which took a significant step closer to sophisticated and complex Range Rovers, which themselves rose ever higher into the luxosphere. The only connection was the original name and the same airey, well thought out interior. Instead of beam axles car-like **fully independent suspension** (FIS) was fitted and at last a diesel engine with a bit of grunt: a 187-hp 2.7-litre TdV6 (3-litre in the D4) mated to a six-speed auto box. The US got a 4.4 V8.

The hybrid 'unibody' was clamped to the ladder chassis with front wings and bonnet in aluminium to address crush-zone compliancy. It's a way to reduce NVH ('noise, vibration, harshness') which owners now expect, even in a 4x4.

Dial-a-ride Terrain Response.

Coiled FIS can't manage the articulation of something like a Defender, so on all but the coiled base models, D3s came with height-adjustable, self-levelling electronic **air suspension** (EAS) cunningly cross-linked to mimic beam axles. Aided by the traction control, raising diagonally opposite wheels ensured grip on very uneven terrain. The engine, transmission and traction control/ABS were now all integrated to form the Terrain Response (TR) 'dial-a-ride' system. Set the console dial to what lies ahead and pre-set parameters (height; traction; gear) reduce the need for operator finesse or technique.

Early EAS compressors tended to overheat or pack up, and the 'computer said no' to raised suspension over 30kph. Other anomalies and EAS fault codes prompted owners to convert to coils, losing some height as well as the real benefits of height-adjustment. Have-your-cake-and-eat-it EAS has proved flaky on many 4x4s and unlike a coil, when it goes flat you've nothing. Nevertheless, especially in the US, the LR3 and similar 4s are seen as one of the best choices in this category for those unfazed by complex electronics.

MERCEDES G-WAGENS

The Mercedes G-Wagen was designed in the early 1970s by Steyr-Daimler-Puch in Graz, Austria and continues to be built there to this day using Mercedes parts. Said to have been a proposal by the former Shah of Iran (a major shareholder in Mercedes Benz) events outran him and the huge order was picked up by Argentina, who reneged following the Falklands War of 1982. In the end it was the failure of the military VW Iltis that saw West German and other north-European orders for the G, which in turn led to the civilian models. The 'G' by the way stands for gelände or 'cross-country'. The 'wagen' part you can probably guess.

460: the first G

The year 1979 saw the release of the original 460, including the 300GD with the five-cylinder OM617 3-litre diesel, making 88bhp; a 230GE petrol four; and the 280GE, a petrol six producing around 150bhp. All could be specified with manual (usually five speed), or four-speed automatic transmission. This pre-dated the SUV craze and as with the ageing Series Land Rovers and 40-series Land Cruisers of the time, 460s were basic. Most had hydraulically operated front and rear diff locks, coil suspension on solid axles with steering linkages out of the way behind the front axle; altogether a sophisticated offroading set-up for its time but now too old or rare to be a contender.

The 463

The 460 was replaced in 1990 with the 463 series. Although they retained the 460's boxy profile, a closer look reveals significant improvements. Matching the step up from 60- to 80-series Land Cruisers, the 463's interior was far plusher as Mercedes also attempted to cash in on the Range Rover's success. The drive train was now full-time 4WD with a lockable centre differential, but still fitted with chunky anti-roll bars to keep the car in shape on fast bends. The trademark three differential locks were now engaged with an electric/hydraulic set-up operated by buttons on the dash. Although more complex than a 460, it's pretty robust and foolproof.

Up to around 1997 all featured the OM603 six-cylinder 3-litre aspirated diesel, producing 113bhp (300GD), or a 177bhp petrol-six (300GE). Apart from ABS, the OM603 was devoid of any electronics and is regarded by G-lovers in the same way the 1HZ is admired by Toyota fans – both apogees of aspirated diesel technology in terms of longevity, if not power and refinement; to pull a hefty LWB G around, a 603 diesel has to work hard.

Depending on how it's packed and how you drive, the economy of a 300GD will be about 7–9kpl (mid-to-high 20s mpg) with fewer corrosion issues than the 460. Some people who've raised the suspension on 463s have experienced nagging vibration, usually remedied by fitting new UJs.

As an expedition vehicle the diesel 463 has a lot going for it, particularly in five-door LWB form. As long as you're not in a rush you'll get solid engineering, no show-stopping electronics and reasonable economy, comfort and space.

In 1991 the short-lived 350GD was introduced with the OM606.97, a 3.5-litre turbo diesel producing 136bhp. For overlanding it's best avoided unless you have solid evidence supporting the installation of a new engine or the required upgrades.

The G300DT

In 1996 Mercedes introduced the G300DT with a refined OM606 engine: a 3-litre diesel six with four-valves and an intercooler adding up to 177hp and, exclusively to this model, an electronic automatic five-speed gearbox. Some aficionados regard this as the ultimate G-Wagen, which is reflected in high resale values: up to £20,000 for an 18-year-old example. The engine and gearbox are electronically controlled and although having a good reliability record, will be a distraction when considering an expedition vehicle. The 300DT also has a low air-intake, which limits its wading depth – easily fixed with a snorkel. Overall, similar comments apply to the G500, a 300hp injected V8 that was introduced shortly after. From 1997 all G-Wagens, running whatever fuel, came with automatic gearboxes.

The utilitarian 461s

Intended for commercial use (i.e. good for overlanding), this series was introduced around 1997 with the range of engines initially limited to the 95hp 290GD aspirated diesel. In 1998 the five-cylinder DI intercooled 120hp OM602 was transplanted from the Sprinter van to make the **290GD Turbo Diesel**, coupled to a four-speed auto transmission. Although electronically controlled, it had a good reliability reputation.

The drive train is similar to the 460 series: front and rear diff locks with selectable 4WD. For an overlander they'd make an excellent choice. British desert explorer Tom Sheppard drove Land Rovers around the Sahara for years until he got a 461 for which he professed great admiration in his book, *Quiet for a Tuesday*.

G-Wagen summary

With a build quality matching Toyota, the limiting factor has long been the G-Wagen's **weight**: a LWB diesel checks in at 2800kg (6200lb), which can bite into the payload.

The full set of **diff locks** make off-road progress in mud and cross-axle situations (see p300) much easier once driving tactics are adapted. Misusing the axle lockers or misunderstanding how they work (see p305) could break something. Having said that, apart from competition off-roaders I don't know of anyone who's managed to break a half shaft or CV, which are clearly built to cope with diff locks. Mechanical engagement is always preferable to sensor-reliant ETC.

Limited axle articulation is only an issue when compared against a Defender and the like. When combined with the typically stiff anti-roll bar, fitting heavy-duty springs and shocks will reduce it further, but this is ameliorated by the diff locks.

With anything pre-1996, G-Wagens can be run on a budget as there's a range of pattern parts and good compatibility with other MB cars and vans. In particular the W124 (regarded by some as the last 'proper' Merc) shares a large number of parts with the 463 and it's said Mercedes Benz has an unparalleled world-wide spares network for older models. In Morocco, for example, you're never alone for long in a Mercedes.

The bad news is that from the late 1990s the whole marque, including the Austrian-manufactured G-Wagens, gained a reputation for poor reliability (the Chrysler influence, some say), and when combined with the added electronic complexity, it can all become an expensive nightmare as Tom Sheppard found with his 461. In common with others, later CRD-engined G-Wagens share a low tolerance of poor quality fuel. If I had to choose an overlanding G-Wagen on a budget I'd go for the 460 diesel with a full service history, or a LWB 463 300GD.

In a 4x4 world dominated by Land Cruisers, Land Rovers the G-Wagen is an unusual choice. Out of the box they'll perform as well as anything on the market. The down side is servicing can be extremely expensive. On the road G-Wagens may be exotic but the Mercedes brand is recognised and supported the world over.

For kit look up Off Road Exclusiv in Germany (⌨ orc.de). In the US early diesel Gs are as striking as a Defender. For the full story visit the G-Wagen-specific forum at ⌨expeditionportal.com.

RUSS HUMPHREYS

G-Wagen G320, among the most popular of the Gs.

Nissan Patrol

The old six-cylinder Nissan Patrols are the next best thing to a Land Cruiser, the same truck-like toughness without the build quality, popularity or indeed high prices. Used by parts of the UN, they never really caught on, as most utility operators progressed without thinking from Land Rovers to Land Cruisers.

Start with the classic **Y60-series Patrol GR** (aka **GQ**), which emerged in 1987, just before the Defender and 80-series Toyota hit the scene. In Japan they're known as the **Safari** and came with a usefully higher roof. In Australia the GQ was sold as a **Ford Maverick** until around 1994.

With its coil springs and wide, square-edged body, this was what most people associate with a 'Patrol'. The 115-hp RD28 2.8 TD six was a good engine for its time and over 150kg lighter than the huge 125hp 4.2-litre non-turbo TD42, which closely matched Toyota's IHZ. A TD42T is a 145-hp turbo version and a TB42 is a 152hp petrol six, but you probably knew that.

Unlike the early Toyota 80 series (or indeed later four-cylinder Nissan TD engines), they got these GR engines right first time. You need a big engine to haul 2300kg of Patrol around, but with its 16" wheels (exchangeable with drum-braked Toyota wheels) it's a tough overlander and for many years retained a part-time four-wheel drive option while others turned to foolproof full-time set-ups.

Patrols manage to look **big** and the widely spaced axles are nearly three metres apart. This makes for good angles at each end, but not such good belly clearance over creek banks or dune crests. The over-long tailgates found on some 2.8TDs were replaced by vertical doors on the big sixes, the larger of which carries the spare tyre. Better-equipped ST models came with rear axle diff-locks and a lever to disengage the anti-roll bar and release the axle's full articulation. Others had an LSD in the back axle.

In 1997 the **Y61** Patrols adopted a less angular look and in 2000 got a four-cylinder, 3-litre common rail ZD30 DDT engine. Initially these engines seem to have been a disaster, but from 2002 Nissan got on top of it, which is more than can be said for the D22 and D40 engines found in their Navara pick-ups.

The Y61 clung on right up to around 2010 after which the rebodied Y62 only came with a massive 5.6 V8 petrol as well as the now customary all-terrain conquering electronics and hydraulics. It does look like the demand for non-hybrid big diesels is on the wane in Western markets.

Your friends on the internet? ⌨ patrol4x4.com in Australia.

Old Patrol. Long, low and easy to live with.

Double-cab pickups

The LWB station wagons and hard-tops just described might sound like the obvious choice for an overlanding vehicle, but even if you don't clamp a camper cabin on the back (as described on p70), a **double-cabin pickup** can make a versatile and light-weight overlander with enough secure storage in the cabin but without the bulk of a station wagon and a handy open bed. And for once it's something that's true on both sides of the Atlantic, even if US versions are

Double cab pickup with rooftent on a frame.

half as big again as what's normal in little old Europe. Be it a huge V8 Toyota Tundra or a dinky D-4D Hilux, it can be all the vehicle you need, particularly with a roof tent set up over the back tray, as above.

In the UK, double-cab pickups in their various sizes became briefly popular as a tax dodge if chosen as a company vehicle, even if you weren't a builder or such like. Consumers were persuaded that a four- or five-seat cabin and a short load bed, usually with a hardshell canopy, exemplified a functional and vibrant lifestyle. Just as station wagons were transformed by the likes of Discoverys and coil-sprung Land Cruisers, so the forgotten ute gained a second row of seats and a modern interior straight from the aforementioned wagons to become a do-it-all transporter.

Top of the list is not surprisingly the **Toyota Hilux** (aka a V6 petrol-engined **Tacoma** in North America) – and largely for the same reasons as the Land Cruiser. Today it's the best selling SUV in Australia – so much so that hundreds have been stolen in Sydney, supposedly to end up in Syria and Iraq. In the UK, Toyota notably kept out of the race that Mitsubishi and Nissan pitched themselves into with their flashy L200 Warrior and Navara, respectively. Commonly blacked out, chromed up and fitted with 17" wheels, they looked great to some but the highly tuned 170hp 2.5- and 3-litre diesels were time bombs; the web will reveal all.

In Europe at least a Hilux might be called a light-duty Land Cruiser fitted with smaller engines and carrying lesser payloads. A vehicle like this can't be expected to take the prolonged beating of its bigger cousin, but with a light load will be less of a tank to drive and should return better mileage. Pick of the Hilux diesels are the basic, pre-CRD four-cylinder 2.8-litre '3L', and the 3-litre 1KZ-T turbo, which puts out 125hp, although both are rare in the UK at least. If you're not put off by CRD technology then the widely used D-4D is a safe bet; the 2.4 2L-TE turbo diesel found in the earlier Surfs is best avoided.

Various 4x4 formats for overlanding were discussed on p80.

AWD trucks

It's not unusual for overlanders who develop a taste for life on the road to get something bigger – if not a panel van then an **AWD truck** (that's 'truck' in the British 'lorry' sense of the word, meaning 4x4, 6x6, and so on, not a Ford F350). They're also the choice of some adventurous first-timers heading off for extended trips, who recognise that long term, and even with the higher running costs, the potential for roomy **living space** as well as the **overbuilt durability** of a commercial or ex-military truck is much more useful than all-terrain assist dials, motorway cruising speeds or nippy manoeuvrability.

Sure, there'll be times when you curse the ungainly bulk of your 4-metre-high, 8-metre-long colossus as you inadvertently reverse into a villager's hut, but away from the congestion and restrictions of Western Europe, or any capital city come to that, a truck needn't be a liability to own or a chore to drive. After all, it's the same rationale that makes motorhomes or recreational vehicles so popular, except that RVs are both expensive and not necessarily up to the prolonged rigours of overlanding.

Any sort of all-terrain camper is suited to a round-the-world trip where the climate can get miserable or where you don't want your itinerary governed by the seasons. You can have your go-anywhere-in-luxury cake and eat it (at a proper hardwood table), but this usually involves the hyper-expensive, purpose-built Unimog- or MAN-based conversions produced in Europe or the US and costing up to half a million euros. They're most commonly bought by early retirees who've seen the kids off, sold the company, rented out the house and who can now afford to explore the world in ostentatious style.

A round-nosed 911 Mercedes from the late-70s resting in Islamabad.

4WD TRUCKS

Pros
- Old examples can appear cheap to buy.
- On some, high GVWs and a large payload area make them difficult to overload.
- Plenty of room to fabricate a cabin or a caravan body.
- Over-engineered toughness makes them hard to break.
- Old trucks have simple diesel engines that are easy to understand and work on.
- Big wheels and clearance make underbody protection unnecessary.

Cons
- Although generally diesel powered, they still use a heap of fuel: don't expect more than 5kpl (15mpg), even on the road.
- The basic suspension and forward-mounted engine make some models hot and noisy.
- Don't overlook extra running costs such as higher ferry tariffs, shipping, hard-to-find spares and expensive tyres.
- No matter how big the engine, the weight of these vehicles makes them hard work off-road. They are slow.

Disregarding the not inconsiderable 'Tonka' fun factor of driving a truck, the potentially huge payload, overbuilt engineering and seemingly low purchase price of a big old truck it can initially be tempting. But don't kid yourself that the AWD element is any more essential than for any other overlanding vehicle. In this application it's all part of the tough package, though it also adds up to a cabin you can't simply step in to as well as a low cruising speed.

As mentioned on p34, local licensing regulations need to be addressed (at least while back home), as do shipping costs and the price of parts, especially new tyres.

TRUCKS: WHAT'S AVAILABLE

Since the fizzling out of the Cold War, surplus NATO (and former Warsaw Pact) hardware has poured into the civilian markets in **Europe**. You can get your hands on robust AWD troop carriers and cargo trucks of various shapes and sizes. While some, like the multi-axled Tatra or similar MAN missile launchers, look tough enough to drive through a house (indeed a video on YouTube shows a Tatra prototype doing just that), the driving experience in anything ex-military, especially vehicles from before the mid-1980s or anything Russian, is **crude, slow, noisy** and, in some less sophisticated older designs, very hot.

4 x 4 s

A spick and span Mercedes 1017 at Bad Kissingen (see p220) – and spotted a couple of years later in Africa searching for the car wash. A 1017 or something like it ticks all the boxes for most trucking overlanders; plenty of payload and decent power.

The **7.5-tonne limit** (which is a licensing threshold in the UK and probably much of Europe) typically adds up to something from around five metres long, which can include a rear cabin from 3.5m long. Flat load beds can be extended, but 3.5m (11.5ft) is as short as you'd want for a useful living area.

You'll find a few old **Bedfords** among the ex-NATO gear, which, while cheap, are these days the equivalent of the Land Rover Series III. In their time these trucks were the choice for UK overland tour operators until they moved on to Mercs. Easy to work on, old Bedfords are extremely slow and crude. Although many travellers have gone far and wide in an old Bedford, for a little more money you can have a lot more truck.

Mileages can often be tiny by truck standards. I bought an early '90s MAN (pronounced 'Em Ay En', short for 'Maschinenfabrik Augsburg Nürnberg') with less than 10,000km on the clock and such mileages for the age weren't unusual. Unlike cars, trucks are expected to last several hundred thousand miles so all the overlanding you can throw at them won't make much of an impression. In **North America** access to such trucks at similar prices seems to be much more limited, although up to a point the bigger civilian vehicles sold there nullify the need for small ex-military trucks.

Where to look

The German ⌨ padh.de and ⌨ aignertrucks.com **websites** have a good range of European trucks around €10,000. In the UK a good place to start looking online is ⌨ milweb.net, an advert-hosting website mostly of interest to military vehicle collectors, but with links to a few operations dealing in decommissioned military hardware vehicles from both sides of the former Iron Curtain, as well as private classifieds.

Among the big operations for **NATO gear** in the UK are Withams in Lincolnshire and Jacksons at the Rocket Site near Doncaster, who at the time of writing had no less than two hundred DAF YA4440 4x4 cargo trucks (similar to Mercedes 1017) from the late 1980s. It should be possible to have a wander around the huge sites to get an idea of what's what but, as a civilian looking for a single vehicle rather than two-dozen trucks and as many diggers to export to Malawi, don't expect these places to lay on a personal tour of the site or even to answer your enquiries too promptly.

No matter how cheap, don't be tempted by ancient air-cooled, multi-fuel spine grinders just because you had a toy one as a boy – nor by outlandish ex-missile launchers. You get horrendous fuel economy and 45 mph max. 'Noise-cooled' is how one owner described his MAN KAT (right).

The good thing with trucks: everything from the chassis to transmission and tyres is built to carry heavy loads while lasting much longer than a 4x4 – as long as you stay within weight limits which are usually generous. The payback: components are heavy and expensive. That wheel on the right is heavier than the guy next to it and a new tyre is £500.

Buying an ex-military truck

When considering buying any old truck it's worth knowing that many will have stood around on some lonely military base for most of their lives and their condition will be greatly dependent on **storage** circumstances and climate, rather than any use they may have been put to. Although it's hard to resist a 15-year-old lorry that's barely run in, at least a truck that's seen regular use over the years ought to have benefited from servicing and maintenance. With a decade or more of storage you never know.

Time spent at a standstill does no harm to mechanical longevity of course, but can be bad for **rubber components**. Tyres may have plenty of tread but may also have settled into a flat spot from being stood around. Once on the move they usually reform, but could soon start splitting with use, especially at lower off-road pressures which generate higher temperatures. It's the same story with other rubber items like radiator- and other hoses, drive belts and brittle o-ring seals in brake- and clutch master cylinders, fuel lines and so on.

Add some exposure to the mix and **rust** will prematurely age the body, let alone a myriad of other unseen components. As well as rubber and rust issues, trucks that have stood around for years often suffer from fuel blockage problems on delivery due to rust and water collecting in the fuel tanks. It's best to avoid anything that looks like it's been left out over a few too many European winters because your intended use won't simply amount to lovingly doing it up and trailering it around to shows.

After acquiring a vehicle like this from a dealer, give yourself at least **a year** and as much **money** as you spent on it to get it into shape. Alternatively, huge amounts can be saved by buying from someone who's bought and outfitted one for overland use. They'll never get a return on their investment and it's not uncommon for these vehicles to be done up but sold before anyone takes it anywhere.

EX-NATO TRUCKS IN EUROPE AND AMERICAN CAMPERS

I'm not qualified to go through the pros and cons of every model available since VE Day, but anything by **Mercedes, Iveco/Magirus, MAN or Leyland DAF** will do. If you're a Brit of a certain age, don't choke into your coffee at

From top. 1: This well-converted Leyland DAF GS did Africa and back. Full story at 🖥 over africa.org. © Steve Lorimer. **2**: Another Mercedes 1017 with what looks like a LAK body. **3**: Japanese Fuso 10-tonner from the US. **4**: A similarly modern, quiet, comfortable and economical MAN LE 10 220 – but probably twice the price of the Fuso.

the mention of the once-reviled 'L' word you just spotted next to DAF. A DAF YA4440 (4-tonne payload, 7 metres long, 153hp) is a post-British Leyland version and is comparable with a Mercedes 1017.

With German trucks of all brands, the **numerical naming** can be easily decoded as the payload plus horse-power, so a '1017' Mercedes is a 10-tonner (GVW is actually 12 tonnes) with 170hp, an Iveco 110-17 is about the same, and so on. These sort of horsepower figures would be a mini-mum at that size of machine; the 7-litre MAN 10.220 with an Allison auto box has been a popular choice for con-version to an expedition camper.

One thing to look out for is the presence of some sort of a **torsion-free subframe**. Being more or less in one plane, a 10-tonne flat-bed troop carri-er like a DAF with a canvas cover can twist on the chassis relatively harm-lessly off road; rubber mounts permit a little movement. A custom-made 'three dimensional' box won't survive that distortion unless it's as heavy as the truck. There's much more on the whole business below and on p218.

For an overland vehicle it's hard to see a need for more than **two axles** – i.e. a 4x4 – as the resultant payload of 3–5 tonnes is surely plenty. Fuel consumption on anything with three or more axles goes through the floor, plus manoeuvrability is compromised and there's premature tyre wear on the back tyres due to cornering scrub.

These NATO trucks will all be 24 volt with straight-six, aspirated or turbo **engines** of 6–8 litres making from 130–200 horsepower or more; all good numbers for overlanding as long as you're not expecting to lap the globe in eighty days. All follow the Western-European style of being '**for-ward control**' ('FC'; 'cab-over' or

'CoE' are terms used in North America, where this configuration is rare on articulated trucks). For overlanding purposes an FC means that none of the truck's length or wheelbase are wasted on a bonnet, and being perched high and forward gives you the best possible visibility, including easy front-wheel positioning which can be reassuring on the precipitous track to Skardu. You sit right over the front axle which in my experience can add up to uncomfortable bouncing when driving off tracks as you're launched constantly off the rebounding tyres. It's made worse with a suspension driver's seat where the seat belt is attached to the cab or floor; as you pogo up and down the belt binds up on you and becomes unusable, but we're talking off-piste here. If you've driving like this in mind, make sure the belt is attached to a suspension seat, not the floor.

Although a top-of-the-range stereo will be wasted once on the move, as long as you stick with the smaller, water-cooled units, **noise** needn't be too bad, with the engine below and behind you. The huge air-cooled V8s or bigger from Magirus or Tatra are another matter. Even if you find a handy 4x4 air-cooler (most of these are multi-axle), it wants to be a real bargain to outdo the water-cooled trucks listed here.

On a forward control there may be flaps on the front grill to access oil and coolant levels, but the engine is usually accessed by a **tilting cab**. With this set-up, if you're on the inner side of the wheel you can stand right by the engine and play it like a piano; all you need is a good tune. A tilting cab complicates 'crawl-through' access to a back cabin (see p223), but many such trucks often have a **spare tyre** mounted here on a winch.

From top. 1: Swiss Bucher Duro with a 4-tonne payload and a six-litre, 250-hp Cummins. **2**: From Italy, an older Bremach Xtreme with an Iveco engine. **3**: Their newer T-Tex model running various 3-litre CRD Fiat engines. **4**: An old 6WD Pinzgauer, probably with a 2.4 VW engine. All a bit narrow inside but this Pinz has an elevating roof.

Brakes and wheels

Most of these trucks will have **selectable four-wheel drive** with diff locks on all the axles. Brakes will typically be drum air brakes or air-assisted hydraulic (called 'air over hydraulic'), which can be much sharper in operation than regular car brakes. Trucks use drum **air brakes** because car-type discs would quickly overheat trying to slow the mass involved. Bigger trucks employ exhaust brakes as a way of controlling descents with huge loads without overloading the transmission or brakes. A truck with air brakes is literally a 'failsafe' system that requires air pressure to pull the brake shoes away from the drum. If you lose pressure the truck will be immobilised – all it takes is one pipe to break and you're locked up. Humidity in the air can also freeze any water in the brake system in very cold temperatures; track down exotic brake-tank antifreeze fluid.

With air brakes in an older truck it's not uncommon for some pressure to be lost overnight or if standing (either through small leaks or if temperatures plunge). In my MAN, on starting up an alarm would whine until the air compressor powered off the engine charged the air tanks with enough pressure to release the brakes; this never took more than a minute. The **handbrake** on trucks like this is extremely easy to use (especially after owning a Renault 4); a dinky little lever you flick into position once still and release with a toggle. For a big truck it makes hill-starts easier than many cars.

Wheel-rim sizes in this category will be either be 20", the old commercial standard, or 22.5s as on modern commercials. Twenty-inch tyres are still the norm on AWD trucks because they have higher sidewalls in relation to the

Cold war cabins. **Main picture**: a NATO alloy clad box is a popular conversion in the larger size.
Inset: Fully insulated East German glass fibre LAK body.

width and so provide more 'static suspension' to deal with rough surfaces. It can make a real difference off road because, unless you're running on parabolics (see p144), the actual truck springs are usually long leaves designed for carrying loads not nurturing dental fillings. With both these rim sizes it should be easy to find new tyres out in the world, and for probably a lot less than you'll have to pay back home.

Cabins and bodies

Double **cabins** ('Doka') are rare, but always get the biggest cabin you can find (deepest, front to back) – you'll always appreciate the extra space. Some cabins have a roof hatch or a roof rack with an access ladder; either are handy. The cabins or 'shelters' that sometimes come on the back of these military trucks (also available loose, see left) may be what you're after. 'Fall-out shelter' may be a better description, because as they come, these poorly insulated cells are about as accommodating to live in as a shipping container.

The camo-painted NATO versions come in two sizes: 4.25m long x 2.2m wide x 2.075m high (weighing 925kg/2400lb), or 2.9m x 2.05m x 1.89m (725kg/1600lb). Remember, you'll lose some interior width after fitting essential insulation; this is the appeal of the wider, fully-insulated LAK cabins, (left, inset). All you have to do is locate one that hasn't become a chicken coop.

With all the effort of tracking down one of these overweight shelters, it's easy to see why building one yourself from scratch might be a much better way of getting exactly what you want.

4 x 4 s

Selection of American campers, from the top. 1: Factory Mercedes 4WD Sprinter 316 CDI (2.7TD) **2**: The ideally-proportioned Sportsmobile now based on Chevy vans. **3**: EarthRoamer's luxurious XV-LT (Ford F550). **4**: Or just set off in your old man's gasoline dinosaur and spend your money on having a good time.

MERCEDES UNIMOG

Widely acknowledged as the ultimate all-terrain utility vehicle, **Mercedes Unimogs** are used by armed forces, forestry agencies and local authorities the world over. Few other vehicles come close for users who need a versatile platform to perform a variety of tasks. The guys at Mercedes thought of everything when they designed the Unimog back in the late 1940s: diff locks on each axle; a channel chassis designed to flex and body mounts to cope; coil-sprung suspension; portal axles offering huge ground clearance and reduced torque loads; oil-bath air filter (like old Series IIIs); up to eight gears plus low range.

Among off-road enthusiasts it's seen as just about the best thing on four wheels, although the not-so-widely-lauded agricultural-style three-point linkages and front and rear PTOs (power take-offs) belie the truth: for most users a Unimog (a German acronym for 'universal motorised device') is actually either a nippy **tractor**, or just another slow, noisy, fuel-guzzling 4WD truck. Indeed, a Unimog brochure compared the attributes of the SWB U216–530 'implement carriers' with a fast tractor. This means tractor-like low gearing designed for pulling buffalos out of mud holes and flat out at under 90kph while fuel consumption rarely exceeds 4kpl. Of course these attributes are common to many of the diesel trucks mentioned earlier.

Some overlanders, dazzled by the 'van-on-steroids' image manage to convince themselves that if Mercedes once made the best cars then this peerless all-terrain implement-carrier could be a great motorhome. The opportunity to act on such enthusiasm is made easier by the relatively **wide availability** of Unimogs in both Europe and North America, which means you don't need to deal with complex importing and re-registration hoops.

And that's not all. Many of the improvements (with associated time and expense) that a regular 4x4 requires for off-road overlanding, such as a raised air-intake, on-board compressor, suspension related to GVWRs, and copious ground clearance, are all standard on a Mog. But, unlike many of the trucks already discussed, which were designed to cover long mileages, Unimogs were always intended to be **short-range, high-maintenance machines**. They can take any distance thrown at them of course, but you do have to keep up with oil changes and lubing (and there's a lot of oil sloshing around in there).

It's also not coincidental that one reason a Unimog so readily fits the bill for some overlanders is that once your needs extend beyond a typical 3.5-tonne 4x4 wagon, the choice of suitable vehicles shrinks before you reach the **7.5-tonne GVW threshold** into which Unimogs slip. There are 130"-wheelbase Defenders (but which carry half the payload), Iveco Daily vans (see next page), even more pricey and rare Pinzgauers, as well as other examples of European exotica like Bremachs or Bucher Duros before you arrive at the best real-world compromise from Isuzu and Fuso (see p129).

If you have the cash and the nerve, buying a Unimog is easy. On eBay as I write: a usefully long 1981 U1700 flat bed with a 6.2 aspirated diesel and only 12,000 miles is going for £20,000.

Which Mog?
You'll be doing a lot of driving so for reasons of comfort and tinnitus you'd do well to avoid anything from before the mid-1970s. The recommended models are the longer, unencumbered flatbed versions often used by armed forces as troop carriers. Civilian examples will usually be mounted with wood-chippers, snow ploughs or cherry-picker platforms, because for a local authority a regular Transit van or Land Rover will do everything else and cost much less.

Although in North America some use Mogs as giant pickups, a cabin is what you want on the back. Just remember that by the time you have something you can stand up in without raising a roof, your vehicle may be **nearly 4m high** and may cause problems with trees, road bridges, migrating geese, entrance gates and even low-slung 'hot-wired' electricity cables in poor villages. As one couple in Morocco discovered, this raised centre of gravity allied with a short wheelbase and half a metre of ground clearance can make a Unimog (or anything else like it) unstable in inexperienced hands.

Old U1300 Unimogs (**left**) are still the overlander's choice, while later SWB models look like they got left in the oven too long – though are no doubt ten times better in all ways.

U1550L Hellgeth with a NATO shelter.

The very latest Unimogs are exorbitantly expensive so for overlanders on normal budgets the square-cabbed models built from the mid-1970s to the late 1980s are the pick of the crop. With a wheelbase of 3.25m (or sometimes 3.85m), the **U1250, 1300L and U1700** (also known as a '435') are the most popular choices for overlanders. Dimensions are 5.5m long and 2.6m high at the cab on standard tyres, with a width of 2.3m. This series represented a step up from the previous examples, with bigger and comparatively modern soundproofed cabs, power steering and disc brakes. They weigh about 4.5 tonnes and so easily fall within the 7.5-tonne GVWR, avoiding the need for HGV truck licensing. Avoid SWB (< 3-metres) Mogs for overlanding; they may be able to crawl up the side of the Grand Canyon but are too short for a usefully sized living module, without it hanging right far off the back.

Designation numbers correspond broadly to horsepower so if you drop a zero a U1300L (the 5.7 litre, OM352 six-cylinder aspirated diesel) gives you 130hp and a U1700L (an OM352A with a turbo) churns out 170hp and comes with heavier-duty axles. If considering fitting a camper body on the back, 130hp is the minimum figure to be looking at, but the good thing is this pre-electronically managed engine is still found all over the world.

Ways of increasing road speed or lowering engine rpm to reduce noise and improve fuel consumption include fitting 'high-speed' axles (actually just the differential) or, more commonly, fitting 14.50" tyres (standard tyres are 12.50 R20), which have a larger diameter. Using both tricks you can get just over 100kph (62mph) or more restful cruising speeds.

Finally, if you're taken by a Unimog-type vehicle consider an **MAN 8.136** or the rarer 150. Built for the military in the eighties and nineties to replace U1300s, the dimensions, capacity and engine are all similar but the set-up more conventional. An MAN can cost two-thirds of a similar mog.

If considering an old aspirated Unimog, take a look at an MAN 8.136 or 8.150 (right). Similar performance but a more conventional full-time 4WD package – and cheaper too. On the rare MAN 8.150 crew cab from the early 1990s. the box is held down by springs that allow it to lift away from the chassis as it flexes off road.

IVECO DAILY AND WM/VM90

RICHARD CLAFTON

Iveco is a subsidiary of the Italian car maker Fiat, formed in the late 1970s by grouping various European commercial truck manufacturers including Magirus. The Daily range was introduced in 1978, one of their earliest projects. Although an older, round-headlight version exists, this account describes examples built between **1990 and 2000**, not the modern Daily 4x4 introduced in 2007 and built for Iveco by Scam using Iveco engines, gearboxes and cabs.

Iveco 4x4s are chiefly available in **Europe** with production in Brazil and a presence in Argentina. A Canadian company produced a military variant under licence and they're also assembled in China. About the only thing with an Iveco badge in the US is the 5.9-litre, cab-over Eurocargo 4x4, pitched at quarry and mining operations and more akin to an MAN. Iveco also exist in Australia, all part of a **worldwide operation** with scores of sales and service points around the globe so spares shouldn't be too hard to find.

For an overlander the original Iveco-built Dailys fit well between 4x4 station wagons and 7.5 tonne trucks like Unimogs. **GVWs** range from 3.5 tonnes (the 35-10 model) and 4 tonnes (40-10) through to 4.45-tonne examples with uprated suspension, which all add up to actual **payloads** of 1000–2000kg. The only difference between the 3.5- and 4-tonne versions is the paperwork, a dodge probably based on weight-limit licensing issues.

The Daily **engine** from this era is either a 2.5- or 2.8-litre turbo diesel with a timing chain (2WD vans have a belt). Access is from the front, where you find essentially the same pre-CRD engine block found in Peugeot, Citroën and Fiat diesels, so spares can be obtained wherever these older vehicles are found. Many parts are also shared with the 2WD version. Stock motors produce **100hp**, not much for a small truck. Intercooling can add another 15–20hp and as Iveco offer an optional intercooler on the similar 2WD vans, you know the standard engine can take it.

Suspension is a chunky independent torsion-bar at the front, and a leafed beam at the rear. You get a five-speed **gearbox** (first being a crawler gear) and a Borg-Warner transfer box with high/low range. Drive is selectable 4WD with manual freewheeling hubs and a manual diff lock on the rear axle (optional front locker). The **WM/VM90** military versions come with **permanent 4WD** with diff locks all round. Brakes are disc at the front and drums on the back.

Bodies come as a chassis cab in 2.8-metre or 3.2-metre wheelbase (a bit less than a 130 Defender), or a separate box van, but only in the 2.8-metre wheelbase. There are a few coach-built campers around and you can find ambulances, box bodies and ex-police-bus-type bodies on the military version.

Tyres are 7.50x16s, standard Land Rover Defender items, which might be considered at the limit on a Daily that's set up as a self-contained camper so check the **load rating** (see p149); Michelin XZLs and XZYs cope well. Bigger 9.00x16s can be fitted with a bit of trimming to the bodywork; the military variants all run on 9.00x16, but they have stronger axles and wheel bearings, as well as gearing to suit. Wheels are two- or three-piece **split-rims** (see p156), the military rims being a little wider, but splits mean inner tubes.

On both models you also get **bash plates** as standard for the sump and transfer box, and the tubed steel front bumper is more of a bull bar. Front lights are protected by guards and **raised air-intakes** are an Iveco part, but as the regular intake is around 1.2m above the ground, they're not essential.

Daily on the road

Compare the **extras** like diff locks, bash plates and a lot of cab space against a standard Defender and you'll soon see the appeal. They're comfortable to drive and in the 1.9-metre-high panel van or a good camper conversion you can stand up quite easily in the back. Compared to a 101FC with a 300Tdi, my Daily was quiet. The ground clearance can't match a 101 but the angles are probably similar to other modern 4x4s. Off-road they work fine and can cruise at 85–100kph (50–60 mph).

Being short and with small tyres, Dailys also have a good turning circle and have a fuel economy similar to smaller 4x4 station wagons. Best of all, you get a bit more payload, so unlike a normal 4x4 you don't have to push it to the limit. Dailys make ideal compact and tough **4x4 camper conversions** while being small enough to be manoeuvrable off-road or in cities as well as affordable on ferries.

That's the good news. The bad news adds up to the four-letter word that is 'Fiat' and a notorious finish and electrics. Cabs and bodywork can be very **rusty** although the **chassis** is a 'C'-section so can't rot unseen from the inside. Chassis outriggers and cross members are bolted on so are easy to replace, if necessary. **Timing chains**, guides, gears and hydraulic tensioner/adjusters are all worth checking or replacing in a high-miler; it can all get pricey. Very occasionally, if the vehicle has stood for a while, the fluid can drain from the hydraulic tensioner, which means the loose timing chain slips a few teeth on start-up and the vehicle won't start until it's been re-timed; not a roadside job. Steering racks are difficult to get hold of but you can use the 2WD version, and **CV boots** are vulnerable and expensive so carry spares.

Many Dailys and W/VMs have been worked hard in forestry, farming, construction or military settings, although mileages are often low as it's no motorway cruiser. But there are also vehicles used by emergency services that have led pampered lives. The engines are long lived – mine was rebuilt by the previous owner at 200,000km but he was told he'd wasted his money as the insides were all fine.

SWB Daily 4x4 with a high roof and a C-class motorhome based around a 40-10.

MITSUBISHI FUSO AND ISUZU NPS

John Marano

Whilst there's a mass of small trucks to choose from, only a few are available in 4WD and by far the most common are Mitsubishi's **Fuso FG** and **Isuzu's NPS**. Both have a GVWR of up to **6 tonnes**, can be de-rated to 4.5 tonnes (to get around licensing or insurance restrictions) and, compared to a Unimog or a modern MAN, are very good value. New trucks can cost less than a Land Cruiser, but have the **payload** to mount an overland camper conversion.

Their main problem is that they're both only widely available in Australia, the US and South Africa. Neither is officially imported into most of Europe where Unimogs and other small AWD trucks dominate the field.

Although the 4WD models – available with old-school part-time four-wheel drive, manual FWHs and LSD rear axles – aren't sold as widely as the 2WDs, many of the driveline, mechanical and cab components are shared. Another useful feature is they both have a cab profile that allows them to slip into a high-cube **shipping container** (see p41), providing the camper body has been designed accordingly, normally with a pop-up roof. This allows them to be shipped securely.

Gearing, tyres and wheels

Initially both Isuzu and Mitsubishi trucks ran similar specifications. In the early 1990s both were **under geared** so benefited greatly from **larger tyres** and a single-rear-wheel (SRW) conversion from original dual rear wheels (see p61). This was simply achieved by removing the two inner rear wheels, which of course reduced load-carrying ability, but was compensated for by fitting larger and so higher-load-rated tyres (also mentioned on p147). It makes all the difference on and off road.

Running SRWs, **tyre sizes** were commonly increased from 750mm diameter to 930mm or more, although standard original **16" rims** used in this way could crack under heavier loads or when cornering hard. The use of military-style Michelin XZLs was common on these earlier SRW conversions, with the higher gearing resulting in comfortable highway speeds, a softer ride (due to

A Fuso and an Isuzu arrive at the Mask of Sorrows memorial near Magadan. © Kym Bolton.

taller tyre sidewalls), reduced fuel consumption and greatly improved off-road performance, particularly in soft sand.

Factory rims are now 17.5" on the Isuzus, but recent SRW conversions still go for stronger 19.5" heavy truck wheels running AT tread patterns for longer life and improved roadholding. If running back home, conversions should be approved as manufacturer's warranty or legal issues may arise.

Both models feature **exhaust brakes**, as found on heavy quarrying trucks engaged in long descents when fully loaded. This is just as well as with larger wheels the standard drum brakes are at the limit if you're near the GVW while descending the Camino del Muerte in Bolivia.

Suspension, chassis and body mounting

In virtually all Japanese trucks the original suspension provides limited travel and offers an extremely harsh ride off road. This is partially due to under-sized shock absorbers having to cope with the mass of the over-engineered diffs, as well as the short and over-sprung leaf springs, which were designed primarily for workhorse duties. Along with fitting heavy-duty shocks and low-profile suspension seats to an FG or NPS, fitting **longer leaf springs** specifically matched to the expected weight of a fully loaded conversion offers more travel and is a worthwhile if costly modification for anyone planning to spend months on the road.

Note that **mounting camper shells** (as opposed to heavy work bodies) requires special consideration with both the NPS and FG chassis. It's highly advisable to consult the manufacturer's body-building guides for best practices. Camper bodies must be well supported along the entire length of the chassis yet allow for articulation between the body and the flexing chassis when off road. The typical 3- or 4-point mounting systems (see p227) as used on Unimogs can crack the chassis, especially with the lighter-duty FG.

Fuso FG

Early FGs from the 1980s ran a four-cylinder, aspirated, 3.3-litre single overhead cam engine which grew to a capacity of 4.2 litres in the FG637 model towards the end of the 1990s. Like a lot of engines from that era, they were crude, noisy but simple to maintain and repair and, if serviced regularly, could be relied on to run for hundreds of thousands of kilometres.

Electrical systems with FGs were truck-standard 24 volt until 2003, when the **3.9-litre FG649** became 12 volt, received an even bigger LSD as well as intercooled turbo-charging and a new diesel injection system. This provided a great boost in mid-range power, but brought the added complexity of computer management. Fuel consumption on these and previous models was good, with many vehicles recording over 7kpl even at maximum payloads.

The next generation of FGs was introduced **between 2005 and 2008** across various markets and included many new design features, among them an all-new cab and an advanced double overhead cam, four-cylinder, 4.9-litre, CRD engine producing up to 470Nm of torque. In **Australia** this Fuso retained mechanical engagement of 4WD and low range, as well as wind-down windows and no ABS, all to suit rural bushfire-fighting applications. Other markets got Fusos with viscous couplings and more electronics, which are also more prevalent on NPSs.

In 2008 FGs sold in **North America** came fitted with an emission-reducing diesel particulate filter **(DPF)**, which added complexity to the engine management and when deep fording (if water runs into the exhaust). DPFs are programmed to make a 'control burn' every few hundred kilometres, at which time they reach over 600°C. Owners have learned to manage this 'burn' so it doesn't happen while winching or in long grass, where a fire may occur. Later models have engines running on ULSD (see p47) which can complicate travel in the overland zone. Because of this the pre-2008s FGs are the ones to look for, and as a result prices are hanging in there.

The **chassis** on FGs is extremely light for its potential payload and uses C-section rails only 4.5mm thick, modified from the 2WD version of the Fuso which is known as the FE. The FG chassis steps up alongside the transfer case to cater for the extra height of the cab over the front differential while maintaining a low load bed. This weight saving has the benefit of allowing an additional 200kg **payload** over a similarly rated Isuzu NPS. If a vehicle is down-rated to 4.5 tonnes GVW, this extra capacity is significant, but if the final, fully loaded camper weight is closer to the maximum of six tonnes (as always, it pays not to push it to the limit), then building on the tougher NPS chassis is a better option.

Model options vary from country to country but are generally available in three formats: a 2860mm SWB with 3.3 metres of exposed chassis to build on, a 3460mm MWB with a more useful 4.3 metres of chassis, and a mid-wheelbase seven-seat crew cab with about the same build space as the SWB.

Chassis-stretching can easily be undertaken by professionals, although ideally the wheelbase ought not to exceed four metres if you want to maintain a decent turning circle.

In recent years a limited number of significantly more powerful and faster **auto** models have appeared on the scene made available for the North American market (see ⌨ mitfuso.com) but as with all these things there's the drawback of ULSD motors running on HSD out in the world.

Isuzu NPS

Although Isuzu's NPS appear similar to FGs, they're generally a little heavier and stronger. Year for year, brakes (hydraulic drums all round), suspension and so on were all more suited to maximum loads off road. Likewise the engines were slightly bigger, and all ran 24-volts while being relatively detuned. That should mean longevity, an important factor beyond the black stump. The NPS also has continuous

Top: Three-litre Mitsubishi Canter at Cape York, northern Australia. **Below**: Open house day at this pop-top Isuzu.
© allterrainwarriors.com.au

MITSUBISHI FUSO, FG OR CANTER: WHAT'S THE DIFFERENCE?

'Fuso' is now the name for Mitsubishi's entire truck division, while the 4x4 Shoguns and L200s are still made by Mitsubishi.

'Canter' is the name given to Fuso small-trucks in some markets, but FG is the prefix for the three different **4WD models**. For example the SWB is a FG84DC, MWB is FG84DE and the MWB crewcab a FG84DEW.

The 649 models preceding the Australian '84's and American left-hand drive 140s were known as FG649DC and so on. In the US the 4WD is simply known as an FG, or Fuso FG140 if it's the newer truck. The similar 2WD is usually known as an FE or Fuso FE140, while the FH is a 2WD 8-tonner.

---

section, thicker **6mm chassis rails** developed for the 4WD set-up, rather than the three-piece bolted rail as on the 4.5mm FG. The downside? Isuzu **cabin interiors** were downright basic.

In 2008, Isuzu released a **new-generation NPS**. While it was equipped (some say 'plagued') with electronic gadgetry, it was a vast improvement. The only fly in the ointment was the now mandatory diesel particulate diffuser (**DPD**; p47) which may again deter overlanders. Some owners have success-fully removed the DPDs, but legal issues may arise in your home country with this kind of tampering (once on the overland road you'll doubtless still be the one of the cleanest emitting trucks on the highway).

The **variable geometry turbocharger (VGT)** offered amazing perfor-mance in soft sand and up long hills, and allowed the CRD engine to deliver peak torque all the way from 1600rpm right through to 2600rpm. Power could be easily raised with computer upgrades if required, as the same engine and much of the driveline featured in the 10-tonne Isuzu FSS 4WD, which was electronically tuned to produce 154kw (over 200hp) at 2600rpm and 637Nm at 1600–2600rpm. Therefore, much in this NPS was either overbuilt or, in the case of the engine, extremely detuned as standard – ideal for overlanding applica-tions. It also featured a new **chassis** with the straight 6mm C-section rails now 850mm apart instead of 750mm – well suited to mounting a camper body.

So, Fuso or NPS?

A new NPS is around 10–15% more expensive than an FG, but that clearly buys more truck. It's said that Fuso has a wider dealer network, but with all the current models reliance on **electronics** is a given and although many over-landers would prefer to travel without it, they're proving to be dependable.

If buying used, choose from the **mid-nineties or later**, checking for the usual issues and use. Cabs aren't normally known to rust but check the FG chassis where the stepped section is riveted in the lower chassis. Best used buys in Australia are ex-government vehicles as opposed to quarry, mining or beach trucks. With luck you'll find a **converted camper** which dodges a huge job and expense.

Whichever you choose, chances are you'll end up with one of the best overlanding rigs around. They may not be as rugged or agile as a Unimog, but how often will you need that? Instead, a Fuso or NPS offers great performance and economy in a fun, cab-over, easy-to-drive package that can handle just about all that the main overland routes will throw at you, while still having the payload and space to enable you to live comfortably.

MODIFYING YOUR VEHICLE

4

Prepare, take advice, read the books, then do it your way.

This section covers modifications that'll make your vehicle more suited to the terrain and conditions it may encounter. They should improve the vehicle's drivability on less than perfect roads and under maximum loads. *Modifying* the vehicle is about the **driving**, while *converting* is about stationary use as a camper – that's Part 5 which starts on p161.

How far you go depends on the money and time you want to throw at the project, but it's also about where you're going. As mentioned earlier, Latin America and Asia south of the Trans-Siberian Highway can be a road trip that can make minimal demands on a vehicle. For advice on enhancing regular cars see the 'Road-car modifications' p158.

One thing worth remembering is that it's possible to get so obsessed with the vehicle project that you soon find yourself jammed up your own exhaust pipe. The project becomes the adventure and the

> **The single biggest mistake first-timers make is over-equipping and overloading their vehicle.**

journey simply a validation of your sophisticated DIY or paypacket. Although it takes up the lion's share of the preparation in terms of time and money, the vehicle ought not to be more important than the journey, which is one reason why this book errs towards simplicity rather than a 24-hour *Gadget Show* special. When you have to grovel around looking for a leak or an electrical short, you'll know why that was worthwhile.

MODIFYING YOUR VEHICLE

Overland, not overload

You should aspire not to leave home looking like a wheeled blob. © Charlie Weatherill

There may only be one letter in it, but **the single biggest mistake first-timers make is over-equipping and over-loading their vehicle.** The ethos proposed here is this: implement essential modifications in a thoughtful manner while conserving resources, including your money and time. There is a presumption, on which consumerism itself is predicated, that more is always better; that the more you spend or take with you the better off you'll be. Many overlanders seem to be guided by the aphorism: 'it's better to have what you don't need than need what you don't have', and return home with long lists of what they didn't need or use rather than vice versa. Buying stuff seems easier than trying to find out and decide whether you'll actually need it.

In a way it's understandable, because you may not know what lies ahead. But the point is to concentrate more on what really counts and less on what looks good. Treat the vehicle as a means to an end, a tool for travelling, not an expression of your lifestyle. Less gear adds up to a more focused trip.

On the bright side, the whole vehicle preparation experience can be very satisfying. You're learning lots of new skills, enjoying seeing your machine take shape, and bit by bit can visualise the adventures ahead without yet getting bogged down in the nitty-gritty of life on the road. All this builds confidence in your endeavour, from your vehicle's practicality as a place to live in, to its suitability to dealing with the expected conditions.

REDUNDANCY

In its less commonly used engineering sense, **redundancy** is the duplication of critical components as a back up to a system or component should it fail. This concept can also be applied to overland travel, where the comparative absence of support make selective redundancy a good idea.

Some, like a spare tyre and a spare set of keys are obvious; others, expanded on elsewhere in the book, include batteries, lights, alternators and other electrical spares, stoves, wheel jacks, communications devices and so on. Many are clearly just spares, but others look to replicate a key function in the

event of failure: water pumps, cooking equipment or a small tent. Still others can be put to more than one use: a sand plate can be a bench or a table, a sand mat can be a shower mat or screen; a hi-lift jack has many uses. Thinking like this saves weight.

Get into the habit of adding redundancy to certain key systems while duplicating the use of certain items. Overlanding isn't like touring; you're out there on your own and a little forethought into what might go wrong as well as what need not be duplicated can save time and money without impinging too severely on the payload.

Mechanical assessment

A common fear among first-time vehicle-dependent overlanders is that only expert mechanics should dare venture out into the world. It certainly helps to have an understanding of mechanics, and these days electronics too, but you don't have to know how to strip an engine. More useful is a **logical, systematic approach to fault diagnosis** and sometimes a lateral or improvisational approach to solving problems.

... a logical, systematic approach to fault diagnosis and sometimes a lateral approach to solving problems.

Intimate familiarity with an old vehicle will pay off much more on a long trip than brief ownership of something much newer, even though some might hope the newer vehicle would be less fault-prone. The aim here is to give a clueless beginner an idea of what is important and what is not.

When checking over your vehicle, focus your efforts on what counts: the basics of **engine, transmission and suspension**. A leaking sunroof won't stop you reaching the gates of Persepolis. Make sure these three primary systems – the lungs, heart and limbs of your overlander – are in good order before you start buying out the catalogue. At the very least the vehicle should be **serviced** well in advance of your departure with fresh oil, coolant and air-, oil- and fuel filters. Doing this yourself isn't difficult and will help familiarise you with your machine. Some overland outfitters even run courses on distinguishing a fuel filter from a filler cap.

Workshop manual and vehicle maintenance log

Before you get too carried away, get a **workshop manual** for your vehicle, either as a book or in digital form on your laptop, and gather together any other snippets you may have copied from **online owners forums**, which cover just about every marque these days. Very often the manufacturer will produce an expensive official version, but these are usually for trained mechanics. The 'civilian' versions produced by Haynes and Gregorys (among others) will be much less expensive. You may well be better off with a bootleg pdf, which for popular models are often available online for free. A workshop manual might make your eyes glaze over, but down the road a clued-up bystander or a mechanic will make sense of it.

It's also a good idea to keep a **vehicle maintenance log**, beginning from the day you acquired the vehicle. It can be as simple as three columns: what you did, when you did it, and the mileage. It's good to keep tabs of oil and filter changes and, if you can be bothered, rotation and wear of tyres and so on.

'Yes mate, what can I do you for?'

Another handy item to have is a **parts number list** for your vehicle. As you'll know, to the guy behind the counter or on the end of the phone, an object is not a corporeal entity unless it's associated with a manufacturer's part number. That's what they want to hear when you finally manage to get through from the post office in Rio Diablo, not 'the round thing with two wires coming out of it near the battery'. By identifying the correct part number there should be no room for error. Bear in mind that, unlike a workshop manual, such lists may not be available over the counter, or they may require obtaining the vehicle manufacturer's proprietary and possibly restricted software.

'Fit new – keep spare'

To get familiar with the inner workings of your vehicle, it pays to start by fitting good-quality new **consumable items** like tyres, fanbelts, ignition components (for petrol engines), radiator hoses, brakes, batteries and even an alternator, exhaust system and radiator, then keep the part-used-but-still-serviceable items as spares. Taking new spares isn't the same because anyone who's worked on their own vehicle will be familiar with the discovery that the replacement fanbelt or oil filter you've just spent half the morning tracking down is the wrong one. It's something better found out on a quiet Sunday morning at home, than by the roadside on the outskirts of Istanbul. Fit new, keep the used item as a backup so you'll know for sure it fits.

ENGINE

In just about all cases the original engine in standard tune is best. Land Rovers in particular are often fitted with alternative engines to improve or replace worn-out originals, and in the US off-road scene it's possible to change everything but the body and chassis in a search for arachnid-like performance. Unless you know better, such experimentation is best left for domestic use, when there's a trailer nearby. On the road, problems with overheating, broken engine mounts or over-stressed transmissions due to increased torque are common with non-original engines. Be under no illusion that at times your engine will be working hard in hot, demanding conditions, on crap fuel and while carrying a heavy load; altogether something it's probably never done before. Unless you're on top of it, any serious leaks, noises, poor performance or intermittent problems ought to be fixed before you leave home, where dealing with the whole business will be a lot less stressful. There'll be enough other occasions when you need to trust in the skills of a roadside mechanic.

Cooling systems

If you don't live in a hot country it's hard to know just how your loaded vehicle might respond in the heat of an Indian summer. If there's any doubt about the original, fit a new or reconditioned **radiator** (especially if it's ever been repaired), along with new hoses and belts, keeping the old ones as spares as mentioned. When driving off road or on corrugated tracks, the engine rocks around much more on its rubber mounts, which can translate to an added strain on old radiator hoses.

Big engines are usually fitted with huge radiators and powerful fans that rarely overheat. Smaller or older engines must work harder and may benefit from a 'tropical' **fan** with extra blades (available for Land Rovers, although a well-running 200 or 300Tdi is a notably cool engine). Alternatively, on any vehicle consider supplementary (as opposed to replacement) electric fans such as those made in the UK by Kenlowe or Pacet. Not built for off-road driving, the frames of these fans can work loose on corrugations and spin into the radiator, so make sure the mounting is solid and that the retaining bolts are secured with locking compounds. Some brands use zip ties through the radiator core as mountings: a cheap idea that is bound to come loose on the dirt. Clearly they've never driven on Patagonian *ripio*.

Engine oil

New or old, the best thing you can do for your engine is **change the oil frequently**. Oil degrades as it works to reduce mechanical friction and dissipate the heat generated by combustion. It's also degraded by the chemicals released by burning fuel, and high-sulphur diesel degrades oil sooner than other fuels.

Chemically engineered **synthetic oil** is widely regarded as superior to conventional mineral oil, and today many new cars run on it. Although it costs at least double, it takes much longer before it turns thin and black and will often officially require changing at typically twice the mileage, up to 12,000 miles (19,000km) on modern engines. Covering that distance at home while running on low sulphur or unleaded fuel is possible, but out on the road, 12,000 miles over mountain and desert on carcinogenic diesel or low-octane petrol is asking a bit much of the oil and even if synthetic is available, an oil change at half that distance is better.

Wherever there are vehicles there's motor oil for sale. Run expensive, long lasting synthetic, or change frequently.

Most drivers will happily settle for the moderate price and still noticeable benefits of **semi-synthetic oil** (usually 30%) as chances are you'll not always find synthetic motor oil in the wilds, and may have to accept a change back to mineral oil. If you're forced to use it, change back to something better as soon as you can. Despite the bulk, for this reason it's worth carrying an engine's worth of oil on board.

Running **thicker engine oil** is a way of cooling and so, protecting a hot engine. If things get desperate, straight 40W or more can be used, but let the engine warm up fully on cold mornings and, unless there's an obvious reason, like Sudan in August, ascertain why the engine is running hot. Modern vehicles run **viscous fans**, which only start spinning when the fluid in the housing gets warm. They can pack up so check under the bonnet to see if the fan is actually spinning.

Air filters

Along with clean fuel and motor oil, your engine's longevity, like your own, will be extended by breathing clean air. In an urban setting it's not so vital, but driving on dusty tracks or in arid and windy conditions for weeks at a time will clog up the filter. With a diesel, black exhaust smoke can mean the engine is **running rich** (that is, not enough air in the air/fuel mixture), which can be down to a blocked air filter.

MODIFYING YOUR VEHICLE

Loose or split induction hoses, as well as a damaged or incorrectly fitted filter, are worse than a blocked filter, which merely reduces performance. You may need to inspect the filter daily in very dusty or sandstorm conditions. Many 4x4s have a warning light when the air filter is clogged, but it takes a lot of neglect to get this bad. Far better to clean the filter before that happens.

Work out where your vehicle **draws its air**; on a 4x4 or a car it's usually somewhere in the front wing. Some 4x4s have a 'cyclone' pre-cleaner arrange-

In arid, dusty regions such as deserts, greasing the inside of the airbox can help catch dust before it clogs a filter.

ment before the airbox, which spins out heavier particles by centrifugal force before they reach the filter; it works better on some vehicles than others. Older Land Rovers, Toyotas and Unimogs used to draw air through an oil bath: a very effective system for dusty conditions.

Air filters are usually **disposable**, but corrugated paper elements can be cleaned by carefully tapping out the dust from the exterior crevices or by blowing compressed air outwards. Make sure no dust gets on the inner surfaces. I also find greasing the inside surfaces of the airbox catches dust and sand and so keeps a paper element cleaner for longer, but eventually it'll need replacing and the inside of the air box cleaning.

Foam filter maintenance

Alternatives to bulky paper elements include similar-looking fabric water-washable items, which are available for Land Cruisers, but which are said to filter less well than paper and so require washing more regularly. More widely available are after-market, oiled, **open-cell foam filters** for 4x4s. Again these must be cleaned and re-oiled with a special air-filter oil more frequently than a proprietary paper filter, but with this sort of maintenance will last much longer than a standard paper filter.

The better ones like Uni Filter feature an outer sleeve that catches just about all the dust before it gets to the inner foam core. By carrying just a spare,

The inner core (right) stays clean while the oiled outer sleeve (left) catches all the muck.

pre-oiled sleeve, you can quickly replace a dirty sleeve to clean later on, and so never have to meddle with the inner core. Use the correct tacky **foam-filter oil** (available in aerosols and from dirt-bike shops), which doesn't seep down and dry out as engine oil can do (though clean engine oil is better than nothing). Rinse the sleeve in fuel, let it dry, oil it and squeeze out the excess – a messy job made less so with gloves or by oiling the foam inside a plastic bag.

Raised air-intakes or snorkels

Commercial trucks, especially those involved in dusty site operations, have raised air-intakes high up behind the cab. Fans of 4x4s also fit 'snorkels' to their vehicles, and Land Cruisers sold to NGOs and the like often come with snorkels topped with a bulky cyclone pre-cleaner and which is designed to work on the move as opposed to the bowl-like cyclones found on slow moving tractors and static engines).

The idea behind a raised air-intake it that it draws air a little higher than normal and away from dust kicked up by front wheels. In **dusty conditions** even just a couple of extra feet of elevation are enough to draw in substantially cleaner air, but all a raised intake does is save your air-filter element from getting dirty too quickly; in a full-on dust-storm it'll be no great advantage.

However, if properly fitted and sealed, a raised air-intake greatly increases the vehicle's **wading depth**,

Above: Safari snorkel is more effective for wading than taking in clean air.
Below: This cyclone pre-filter spins out grit as it sucks but is more suited to slow tractors.

to the point where you might be drowning but the engine will still be churning onward. While crossing a flash-flooded creek on the Pamir Highway or somewhere like the Congo Basin, where it's possible to misjudge the depth of a waterlogged trench, having a snorkel could make the difference between sucking water into your engine or merely soaking the electrics and insides of your vehicle. Electrics and your gear will dry out eventually, but when uncompressable water is sucked into a combustion chamber (particularly a diesel, which typically has nearly double the compression ratio of a petrol engine) the pistons hit a wall and a con-rod or crankshaft snaps. Assuming a red-hot turbo survives a sudden dousing like this, with a common rail diesel you can probably add a ruined induction system to that list. Of course driving into water deeper than your engine is foolhardy; most 4x4s have a factory-approved wading height that's typically no higher than the top of the tyre. There's more on river crossings on p304.

Unless you're really into your off-roading, so long as you undertake regular filter inspection and maintenance, a snorkel or raised air-intake isn't an essential fitment, although of course it sure **looks the business** on your fourbie! My old Mazda's pre-cleaning was pretty poor and the relatively small paper element needed attention every few thousand desert miles, but for the cost of fitting a snorkel I could have bought twenty new elements, enough for a quarter of a million miles.

Fuel filters

Filling from any garage with a fuel pump is usually reliable as any debris or water ought to have settled to the bottom of the storage tank. If filling from oil drums, as you may do in out-of-the-way places, any water or sludge will be at the bottom of the drum so consider leaving the last few litres in there. On all older vehicles, or those that have done many miles in dusty areas, draining and **flushing the fuel tank** in the preparation stage won't do any harm, though it's a messy job. As mentioned below, it's when you run low on fuel that sludge or rust from the base of a fuel tank can get sucked up into the fuel lines and cause problems.

Diesel engines should have at least two **fuel filters** between the fuel tank and the injector pump, and these should all be cleaned or renewed before departure. Some vehicles have a tap on the filter body in the engine bay,

A clear-based sedimentor or fuel filter fitted between the tank and injection system allows you to monitor gunge, but may not be compatible with some CRD engines.

which allows you to drain water in the event of a warning light coming on, and some off-road vehicles have a drainable draw-through **sedimentor** or water trap (left) usually located inside a chassis rail or at the back of the engine compartment. Fuel enters the small chamber and is drawn out from the top, leaving any water and particles to collect in the bottom. Their position means they can get neglected as well as blocked with rust flakes or sludge, especially if you've run the fuel tank dry. With the older glass bowl types you can see if any water is present just by looking at it, but these

days the collector bowl is made of metal, which is worth removing and cleaning out once in a while. Any jelly-like matter in the base are microbes that can survive in water-contaminated diesel. Otherwise, loosen the drain plug on the sedimentor and drain off any sludge until clear diesel trickles through.

The **disposable cartridge fuel filter** near the injector pump in the engine bay is less easy to miss and is usually good for up to 20,000km (12,500 miles), depending on what you put in your tank; replacing at half that figure may be a better idea. Set off with a new cartridge and take a spare or two. Replacing a filter cartridge is a good way of learning how to **prime or bleed air** from a diesel system – something you may need to do should you run out of fuel. As already mentioned, running out of fuel is a good way of clogging up these filters so don't do it. This is when you may need that spare cartridge and why a spare container of fuel is worth carrying.

Carburetted petrol engines are less sensitive to dirty fuel and carburettors are easily dismantled and cleaned – something that should be part of a pre-departure service. A **translucent inline paper fuel filter** is well worth fitting into the fuel line between the fuel tank and the carb, where it can be easily monitored and cleaned or replaced if necessary.

TRANSMISSION

The complex **manual transmission** system – from the clutch right through to the wheel hubs – responds well to a driving style that seeks to preserve this system from excessive strain and shock loads; broadly speaking the opposite of how we might treat a rental car while in a rush to catch the plane. Automatic transmission gets around most of these shock loads, but in Europe at least is still treated with suspicion for overland travel.

Because of the weight you'll be carrying and the rough roads you may encounter, on anything less than a heavy commercial van or a truck your transmission will be put to a greater test than your engine. Trucks, especially the ex-military examples mentioned, are so overbuilt that the better ones can be considered immune to failure when used for docile overlanding.

One way of **testing your clutch** is to drive the vehicle right up against a solid wall, put it in top gear, rev to 2000rpm and let out the clutch. If the clutch is worn it will slip; if it's in good shape the vehicle will stall immediately. Or the wall gets pushed over. Another method is to drop the revs uphill in third, and then accelerate hard to try and induce slippage. On any vehicle with a high mileage and an unknown history, **renewing the clutch friction plate** and the bearing, and keeping the old one as a spare, is the way to go, especially if the journey ahead includes hard driving.

If there's any undue slack in the drive train, track it down. Most commonly it'll be worn propshafts or **UJs** (universal joints) on a 4x4, or suspension arm bushes on coil-sprung vehicles – all of which are easily replaced. See that there's grease in the telescoping section of the propshaft(s), fit a gaiter to keep out dust, and check the UJs for play as they can wear unnoticed or lose retaining bolts. Especially on a 4x4, with its greater axle movement, UJs need greasing every few thousand miles. You can get this done for pennies in any roadside garage that has a pit, or carry a grease gun and overalls. Take spare UJs; they're cheap, small and prone to wear.

If gears jump out into neutral or are hard to engage (including low range on a 4x4) this suggests a problem that you can be sure won't be solved by driving overland from Cardiff to Cape Town via Bishkek. Having a **gearbox** rebuilt on the road will be a headache so a reconditioned gearbox may be the answer. Gearboxes rarely blow up and usually give early and audible warning before the insides turn into swarf.

UNDERCARRIAGE PROTECTION

Whatever you're driving, have a look underneath and try to visualise where damage might occur if the vehicle grounds out, both at each end as you approach and leave a slope, and in between when driving in ruts. For reasons of access it's impractical to completely protect the many underside components, but on a 2WD the **radiator** can be vulnerable, while on any vehicle the engine sump, gearbox and fuel tank may benefit from **thick alloy plates** protecting their casings. There's more on modifications specific to road cars in the box on p158.

You may never need these items until, when tired and lost one night, you accidentally run over something hard. At this point they make the difference between minor damage and a possibly ruined transmission. I'd sooner forget the night I drove my Land Cruiser over a milk-crate-sized boulder. The front prop, one gearbox bash plate and a rear shock were all destroyed, but when I cornered the boulder next morning I was amazed the car was even drivable.

In standard form, even some 4x4s are badly designed or deficient in this area and Defenders in particular have exposed track-rod **steering bars** in front of the axle whereas G-Wagens have them behind. Land Rover offers an accessory bar and several after-market manufacturers provide a range of far superior protection plates from bumper to bumper. Bent steering arms can easily be fixed by hooking over the bent bar with a rope tied to a tree and reversing (or using a winch), or taking them off and hammering them straight, heated over a fire if necessary. In a vehicle like this, diff guards aren't necessary unless you plan to be racing over rocks.

On a truck or a 4x4 that has a ladder chassis, **fuel and brake lines** are usually high up and well out of the way along the inside or top of chassis rails, but on a 2WD they can run along the floor plan, though ideally in a recessed groove. In this case a light plate or even grill welded over this recess can deflect an unwanted rock from crushing a line.

Rear fuel tanks are also vulnerable, a good reason to fit heavy-duty rear springs. An exhaust system is difficult to protect, especially in a 2WD, because it needs good airflow to cool it. Ageing **exhaust systems** regularly fall victim to corrugations and rough roads, so if yours has seen better days install a completely new system (ideally not a cheap pattern copy from a quick-fit outlet), along with new rubber mounts. Depending on where and how it breaks, a fractured exhaust system isn't a show-stopper though; at worst all you'll have to deal with is more noise. Some sort of bodge with coat-hanger wire or a tin can opened out and wrapped like a splint with jubilee clips will get you going.

EXTRA LIGHTING

Spot lamps and driving lamps

If you're racing or rallying you really need to see up to a kilometre ahead because you'll be there in 20 seconds. For this you need **spot lamps** producing a powerful but narrow beam pointed directly ahead. If you're doing some tricky nocturnal manoeuvres or driving along a narrow mountain track, you'll want a wide spread of light to see to either side, not the other side of the valley. For this you need **driving or flood lamps**, focused to point slightly outwards.

The best option is to have a pair of spots to see a long way ahead, and a pair of driving lamps for seeing to the sides. Driving lamps are most effective when mounted on the front corners of the roof rack so you can see what's next to the front wheels, but this also illuminates the bonnet, which is distracting.

High wattage and HID bulbs

HID (high intensity discharge) bulbs are an alternative to the halogen and use a special, 35w Xenon bulb and a ballast unit to ignite the bulb. The ballast unit puts out about 20,000 volts to initially start the bulb, after which it goes down to about 85 volts. Xenon bulbs are about 300 times more powerful than halogen and because the light is whiter it looks more like daylight. At 35w they also draw less from the battery so the bulb will last longer and the kits, though expensive, are easy to wire up. Rack-mounted lighting is fine, but consider a matt black bonnet or shade on the lamp to avoid lighting it up.

Otherwise, if your newer vehicle comes with HIDs, it's all the lighting you need, distinguishable by the bluish tinge.

MATT SAVAGE

SUSPENSION

Whatever you drive **uprated suspension** can get you to more places or just mean getting stuck less although it doesn't require the lifts some recreational North American 4x4 owners go to. The **correct amount** of modified suspension puts the vehicle a little over normal height when fully loaded and even 4x4s with high GVWRs will need uprated suspension to cope with an overlanding payload. This is most easily achieved by pre-tensioning the suspension or fitting heavy-duty springs. It gives a less comfortable ride when empty, but will have the vehicle responding correctly with a load on board. Again, anything from a 7.5-tonne truck upwards, especially ex-military examples, is unlikely to need any modification to the suspension.

Retaining **standard suspension** can mean continuous bottoming out against the axle rubbers or bump stops (make sure these are still attached) and having to keep slowing down for mild bumps. It's harder on the tyres too, which get compressed when the car bottoms out, and of course it reduces your ground clearance, which leads to other problems.

SUSPENSION SYSTEMS

Coil springs

Pro	Con
• Easy and cheap to uprate or replace.	• Can pitch, bounce, especially on SWBs.
• Compact and light to carry as spare.	• Body roll can be unnerving.
• Superior travel to all other systems.	• Shocks work harder. Failures are common.

Torsion bars

Pro	Con
• More supple than beam axles.	• Long, progressive travel hard to achieve.
• Durable, they rarely break.	• Replacement not as easy as leaves.

Leaf springs

Pro	Con
• Cheap to replace and easy to uprate.	• Mounting under the axle makes shock mounts vulnerable to damage.
• Less roll means better for load-carrying.	• Limited wheel travel and articulation.
• Secure location; few bushes to wear out.	• Short leaves give a harsh ride; longer leaves (as on Toyota 78s) are more supple.
• The inherent damping of closely-packed leaf springs puts less stress on shocks.	

Beam axles

Pro	Con
• Stronger and fewer moving parts.	• Vehicle body moves with the axle , which causes excessive pitching, a trait minimised by independent suspension.
• The axle moves up over bumps, maintaining clearance (good for off-road.	

Independent suspension

Pro	Con
• Less body pitching as you go over bumps and round bends. Much more comfortable and can result in better traction.	• Clearance lost when spring compresses.
	• Vulnerable to damage and not always designed for an off-road hammering.

MODIFYING YOUR VEHICLE

Leaves, coils, bars and air

Most vehicles rely on an inexpensive **steel spring** in the form of several leaves, a coil or a torsion bar. **Air suspension** is found on some commercial load carriers, and high-end cars and 4x4s. Its main advantage is the glide-like ride quality and height adjustability: low for fast motorways, high for rough tracks. It can also self-level to enable powerful 4x4s to corner faster – some vehicles use **hydraulics** to achieve similar effects. As with a lot of these things, when it works well it's amazing, but for overlanding air suspension has yet to achieve the reliability and easy repairability of cruder metal springs, if for no other reason than the only air-sprung vehicle out in the Overland Zone will be the president's bulletproof limo. It seems the materials used in the air bags or struts just isn't as durable as good old-fashioned sprung steel and if the engine-driven compressor fails (most often burning out due to a leak) or the ECU plays up the vehicle sinks on no suspension.

For passenger vehicles, semi-elliptic cart springs or leaves are considered old-fashioned technology because they're not compatible with independent suspension which works with coils, air or torsion bars. On trucks and commercial 4x4s with solid rear axles, leaves are still favoured, with vans and trucks often adopting parabolic leaf springs (two or three separated leaves which taper from the axle outwards at a 'parabolic' or progressive rate).

Conventional leaf spring with airbag support.

Some think the lateral rigidity of regular leaf springs makes them superior load-carriers and my experience is that, contrary to the impression that they're crude 'cart springs', a good leaf set-up that's not too short can match a coil system and shouldn't wear out dampers so often.

Their action can be greatly improved by squirting in some waste engine oil between the leaves (to get right in there jack the wheel up to de-tension the leaves). Other advantages of leaves are the secure axle-mounting points and repair or replacement of broken leaves can easily be done, even with a cut-down leaf off a wreck if necessary. Also, if a shock packs up, as they can do, handling isn't too badly affected as the rubbing leaves still manage to damp the bouncing.

But because they have to both suspend *and* locate the axle, what standard leaves can't do so well is articulate outlandishly all across the front cover of *Red Hot 4x4 Action* magazine. Leaves are best at going up and down. Once you start twisting a leaf to extremes it will break.

Coils on beam axles are now much more popular as the spring can flex in all directions to account for axle swing. Without inter-leaf friction, coils respond better to small bumps, are lighter and can be compressed and stretched without too much complaint. Removal and repair or replacement is also much easier than with leaves.

Although they articulate much better, the problem with a coil spring is it needs pivoting bars or 'radius' arms to locate the axle to the chassis. These arms require rubber or plastic bushes on the hard-working pivots and when they wear out (as they will) steering precision can suffer. Worn bushes on leaf-spring set-ups are less noticeable.

Uprating and replacing

Whatever you have, resist the urge to go over the top with **raising suspension**; a vehicle's stability is greatly compromised by just an extra couple of inches above standard. Use the 'looks near normal and level when fully loaded' rule as a guide. Don't forget that fitting high-walled tyres will

A shiny new heavy duty coil and shock – sorry, damper – on a 110. © Rob & Ally Ford

also gain clearance. This applies particularly to 2WDs.

If not available off the shelf, uprated **coil springs** are easily made by a spring manufacturer. All you need to do is give them a percentage rise in the spring rate or stiffness, as well as a greater height (length), if desired. On my old 190 Mercedes I guessed 20 per cent and half an inch which worked out well.

Semi-elliptic leaf springs can also be uprated, but are more expensive to replace than easily engineered coils. Adding a leaf or two to the pack or re-bending the current set (not as much of a bodge as it sounds) are some things you can do with leaves. A good leaf-spring manufacturer will theoretically be able to dial in exactly how much lift you want or the desired height when loaded. The secondary leaves on any 4x4 (i.e. the ones not clamped to the chassis) have a habit of cracking, but this is no drama compared to a main leaf breakage and is easily fixed by a bush mechanic.

Independent suspension

Another problem with **solid or beam axles**, whether coil or leaf sprung, is that when one wheel goes over a bump, the whole body is lifted. This is great for underbody clearance but it's not so good for occupant comfort, especially for passengers without a steering wheel to hold on to. For this reason **independent suspension** using either coils or torsion bars (see below) is found on just about all road cars and increasingly features on the front suspension ('IFS') of many 4x4s if not the back of luxury SUVs seeking car-like comfort. It improves road manners at a

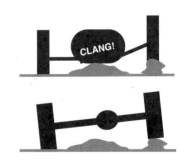

When a solid-axled 4x4 (bottom) drives over a bump the entire axle and body lift. Not great for the ride quality but ground clearance is maintained.

cost to clearance and extreme articulation but for overlanding needn't put you off. On some roads it may not be durable, but what's found on something like a 4x4 is up to the job. Indeed the multi-axle Tatra or MAN trucks owe their off-road mobility to independent suspension pioneered over a century ago.

Torsion bars

A **torsion bar** is a long bar with splined ends, often a component of IFS, or even used in all four corners of a car. One end of the bar is solidly clamped to a chassis cross member, the other attaches to a lever by the wheel. As the wheel gets lifted up and down the bar effectively twists and returns along its length.

It may not seem a very sophisticated system, but it works surprisingly well. Over a typical metre-long length, the bar needs to twist only a few degrees to translate to useful suspension movement at the wheel, though it will never articulate like a coil. Torsion bars are often adjustable at the fixed end, or you can try and remove the bar and replace it on the next spline to effectively raise the chassis, though chances are this will be too much. Heavy duty bars may be available and spares are easy to carry and fit.

Dampers and bushes

What most call a shock absorber is more correctly described as a **damper**, in that it subdues a spring's tendency to react to compression by bouncing, like a dropped tennis ball. The spring is actually the shock absorber but without dampers a car would pogo around uncontrollably.

Dampers play a vital role in controlling your vehicle's ride. They do so by pushing oil through valves in the body as they telescope in and out with each bounce of the spring. This action also creates heat which reduces the damper's effectiveness, so gas or external oil reservoirs are used to try and cool things. **Gas-pressurised dampers** still use some kind of fluid, but they run cooler and so last longer than old-style oil dampers.

Eventually a damper will wear out and before that happens it might leak, seize, burst, get crushed or break off at the fitting points. Such failures commonly occur when driving too fast on rough tracks or bad roads. You can still drive without dampers but the ride will be bouncy to the point where it'll limit your speed.

When it comes to uprating dampers owners are commonly torn between quality and price. What you're looking for is the middle ground from a reputable brand like OME, Koni or Bilstein. Dampers are a consumable item that can get damaged and will wear out sooner than you think in hot, overloaded, off-road conditions, so consider **spares**; they take up little space lashed out of the way on a chassis rail. Some off-roaders fit **twin dampers**, but this is usually a rally-racing modification and shouldn't be needed on an overlander.

When solid axles articulate over extreme terrain, one damper is compressed and the other can get fully extended, but dampers aren't designed for such loads; that's what the **rubber bump stops** and **axle straps** are for. The former cushions upward movement of the axle before the damper reaches full compression; the latter, not always needed on some suspension systems, limits the downward arc of the axle before the damper gets pulled apart. Too stiff bushings (see below) can also damage a damper. Unfortunately it's not uncommon for garages to make these mistakes and is one good reason to stick with standard, or tried-and-tested set-ups.

The worst terrain dampers have to endure is a washboard or corrugated track, when they're being pumped up and down several times a second. This creates very high temperatures that can lead to premature wear and seizure.

Bushes

If you're upgrading your suspension on a solid-axle 4x4, take the opportunity to fit new **bushes**. Worn rubber bushes give vague steering and clunky suspension and transmission, especially on the radius arms that hold coil-sprung axles in place. Hard plastic **polybushes** take longer to wear out and come in a variety of densities, but aren't necessarily better than rubber. Because they're firmer, they lack the flexibility of rubber and can transmit

Rubber and plastic bushes. There's a difference.

rather than absorb stresses to metallic components like bolts and mounts. I once travelled with an early model Discovery that snapped a rear radius arm using red polybushes. To be fair we'd just come down a pass in the Hoggar Mountains that broke something on all our cars, but our feeling was that the rigid polybush exacerbated the Discovery's failure.

There's nothing wrong with **rubber bushes** other than that they need to be replaced more often and they don't come in a sexy range of colours; factors which make them unsuited to most consumers. While they last, they actually work better and a new set is typically half the price of plastic polybushes.

Tyres and wheels

In a typical overlanding scenario your tyres are required to support a heavy payload while coping with migraine-inducing Indian highways, Andean hairpins, sidewall-shredding detours into the Atlas mountains, speeding along intercity motorways to catch an embassy before it shuts for Lent, and pummelling over Namibian washboard. All this while possibly suffering neglect and enduring monsoons, heatwaves, unseasonal blizzards and dirt-road diversions for months on end until your budget, your vehicle or the tyre is well and truly finished. You wouldn't want to be a tyre.

For overlanding, tyre priorities centre around **strength, reliability and longevity**. A sports car tyre will grip brilliantly but wear quickly because, driving styles notwithstanding, softer rubber compounds are used to provide better grip at the cost of longevity. At the other extreme, an all-out mud tyre with an aggressive tread pattern is great in its element, but hopeless or even dangerous on the highway, where the chunky blocks can fling off at speed. As always, it's a compromise.

For the sake of the transmission's longevity, keep tyre sizes near standard, while recognising that, for example, on a 4x4 changing from 19-inch rims to far more **internationally common 16-inch rims** will make finding replacements out in the world much easier.

TYRE BRANDS

Car, van or 4x4, overlanders' needs are largely analogous with commercial or **light truck** use (such tyres are suffixed with an '**LT**'). The best tyre may not be light, cheap or something to draw admiring glances, but it's something you'll be able to drive for long distances without worrying about punctures.

Start off with up to six good tyres that you're sure will last the duration of your trip. Don't cut corners just because your tyres will wear out anyway. Punctures can be the most frequent breakdown (tyre repairs are on p289) so, depending on the duration and expected conditions of your journey, departing with **new tyres** from one of the recognised brands will help ensure a trouble-free trip; those brands include BF Goodrich, Bridgestone, Continental, Dunlop, Goodyear, Michelin, Pirelli and Yokohama – the ones that come on new vehicles. Certainly they cost more than some Asian brands, but they'll have the reserves of strength and integrity of construction to keep performing in less than ideal conditions until completely worn out – and long after a 235/70 Golden Fang Gravel Gnasher has thrown off its tread.

For the rigours of overland use, what matters is the **quality of construction**, something that's hard to distinguish by looking at a tyre, but is something you can divine from research and buying one of the brands mentioned above. Factors like the load index rating and ply rating (see opposite) add up to more than the tread pattern and high-speed cornering performance.

TYRE DIMENSIONS

A tyre's dimensions are moulded on the sidewall in two to four measurements, and in what might be described as either Imperial, Metric or American formats. These numbers include the **tyre width** given in millimetres or inches; a forward slash followed by the **aspect ratio** or profile, given as a percentage of the width; then the tyre's **diameter** in inches; and, finally, following an 'R' designating radial construction and the wheel rim size in inches. Not all these measurements appear and the tyre width is typically 20% more than the actual tread width between the shoulders. Some examples include:

7.50x16 – A basic Imperial measurement describing a 7.5-inch-wide tread to fit a 16-inch rim. This was your traditional Land Rover Defender size, still fitted to NGO vehicles but regarded as unfashionably narrow by some 4x4 enthusiasts.

A BF Goodrich All Terrain tyre. This, or something like it from the recommended manufacturers will be fine for most 4x4s. Much of your driving will be on normal roads.

235/85R16 – The Metric equivalent of the above, where the width is 235mm, the sidewall height is a near maximal 85% of the width, or about 200mm, and the R16 again denoting rim size and radial construction. Another example is 365/85R20, a Unimog tyre equivalent to 13.00x20 in Imperial. The 365/80R20 looks like a smaller tyre but is actually the equivalent of a 14.5x20, a typical 'high speed' option for a Unimog.

31x10.50R15 – This is the American format for a typically 'fat' Jeep tyre. What you see is what you get: a tyre 31 inches high and 10.5 inches wide that fits a 15-inch rim. Once you frequent American 4x4 forums you'll see a lot of talk about fitting '33s' and the like because big is thought to be better.

One problem with reading tyre dimensions at face value is that they **vary from brand to brand**; it's one reason not to mix brands (or indeed unequally worn tyres) on the same axle. I once measured a 20mm or 2.5% variation on a new 7.50x16 Michelin XS sand tyre and Yokohama's equivalent; the difference between a new and totally bald XS.

The actual **height** of a tyre isn't moulded on metric-sized tyres (manufacturers' websites may have this information), but if upsizing (see below) it'll be something you'll want to ascertain accurately. Often the only way to find out for sure is to compare two mounted and inflated different tyres side by side.

Load and speed ratings

In addition to dimensions, the tyre's sidewall will identify a **load index** number followed by a **speed index** letter; both are categorised in the table below. For example the Bridgestone Duelers on my old pickup were rated as '110 S', which, according to the table, adds up to a maximum permitted load of 1060kg (2337lb) and a top speed rating of 180kph (112mph). On my 2-tonne 4x4, with its optimistic 1-tonne payload, this left a good safety margin because these rat-

TYRE SPEED RATINGS (LETTERS) AND LOAD INDEX CODES (NUMBERS)

Speed symbol	K	L	M	N	P	Q	R	S	T	U	H
Speed (kph)	110	120	130	140	150	160	170	180	190	200	210
Speed (mph)	68	75	81	87	93	99	106	112	118	124	130

Index	lbs	kg	Index	lbs	kg	Index	lbs	kg
36	181.7	125	50	276.2	190	64	407	280
37	186.1	128	51	283.5	195	65	421.5	290
38	191.9	132	52	290.7	200	66	436.1	300
39	197.7	136	53	299.4	206	67	446.3	307
40	203.5	140	54	308.2	212	68	457.9	315
41	210.8	145	55	316.9	218	69	472.4	325
42	218	150	56	325.6	224	70	487	335
43	225.3	155	57	334.3	230	71	501.5	345
44	232.6	160	58	343	236	72	516	355
45	239.8	165	59	353.2	243	73	530.6	365
46	247.1	170	60	363.4	250	74	545.1	375
47	254.4	175	61	373.6	257	75	562.5	387
48	261.6	180	62	385.2	265	76	581.4	400
49	268.9	185	63	395.4	272	77	598.9	412

MODIFYING YOUR VEHICLE

FITTING AN ILL-MATCHED TYRE

A time may come when you run out of tyres and have to take whatever is available locally, which may not even be exactly the right height. With a regular car or a 4x4 with part-time 4WD, the ill-matched tyre can go on the unpowered axle; with a full-time 4x4 a wrong-size tyre can complicate matters and get the diffs in a spin.

---

ings relate to optimal conditions. Driving the pickup at 110mph on a 40°C day with a maximum payload and a slow leak in one tyre could well be a recipe for a disastrous blow-out or overheating and delamination. As emphasised elsewhere, endeavour to keep a long way below all maximum ratings: top speed, your vehicle's GVW, and the tyre manufacturer's unverifiable load and speed ratings.

Modern radial tyres are constructed with several **plies** made of fabrics such as polyester running radially across the tread like tape wrapped round a steering wheel, as well as steel-wire belts and additional polyester plies running round the circumference of the tread to resist punctures. More plies make a tyre more resistant to damage and usually adds up to a higher load rating. However, just as with tyre sizes, the number of plies is not comparable across brands and doesn't give any real indication of the load-carrying capacity of the tyre. The quantity and quality of rubber as well as the plies themselves are what counts and only some tyres identify the number and type of plies. At the very least you should look for four in the tread (two being steel) and two in the sidewall. Only the load rating ought to be a good judge, but even then this could be optimised for marketing purposes; a Golden Fang Mud Muncher rated at 110 S is unlikely to last as long or perform as well as a 104 P-rated Michelin XPC, but it'll help get an old banger through a roadworthiness test at a third of the price.

Originally designed for use on building sites, **Michelin's XZY** is a heavy and rugged 12-ply tyre and has long been a popular choice among 4x4 over-

Michelin XZY truck tyre. © Michelin.

landers, with reports of tyres lasting over 100,000 miles. Though expensive, they can still be bought unused from ex-military disposals in the UK for under £100. It might be argued that on a regular 4x4 station wagon weighing only about three tonnes, an XZY is over the top. Certainly, you're unlikely to get any punctures and they'll last until the next Ice Age.

However, grip on wet tarmac or mud is not so good, nor can a thick-walled 12-ply tyre 'sag' effectively on deflation to elongate its footprint for effective driving in soft sand. Having four-wheel drive reduces this limitation of course, so if you just want to fit and forget a tyre, an XZY fitting to a 4x4 right up to any 10-tonne AWD truck could be for you.

TUBELESS VS TUBED TYRES

Most vehicles today run tubeless tyres, including many motorcycles and now even some bicycles. With no tube rubbing against the tyre interior as it flexes with each rotation, tubeless tyres generate less heat and so last longer. They're located in a groove in the well of the rim, which keeps the tyre mounted in the event of lost pressure, and when they do puncture the air escapes slowly through the puncture rather than all at once (as happens when a tube splits apart, with dangerous consequences).

For off-roading it's traditionally thought that tubes are required, because of the occasional need for low tyre pressures. The tube's sealed air chamber inside the tyre can run at the very low pressures sometimes necessary for maximum traction, and avoids the perceived risk of total air loss should a deflated tubeless tyre get pulled off the rim. It's also thought the relative ease of removing tubed tyres from a wheel to repair or replace tubes is preferable to getting a tubeless tyre properly repaired. In my experience in the desert, running with other tubeless-shod 4x4s for hours at one bar (14psi), this has not proved to be a problem with appropriate driving.

Nowadays most overlanders in all but old, ex-military trucks run tubeless tyres for all the right reasons. Breaking the bead off the rim to change a tubeless tyre can be done with the tools and techniques described on p290, and remounting – getting the bead back over the lip – can be done by the roadside with the aid of a bicycle tube and a decent compressor (also described later on).

The best thing with tubeless tyres is that normal punctures in the tread are very easy to fix. With a compact kit you just ram a soft, glue-covered rubber plug into the puncture with the special tool. You'll need to jack the wheel up to locate the puncture, but it may not be necessary to remove the wheel. Compared to the process of removing a tubed tyre off a rim and replacing a tube, it's effortless. Tubeless, ram-plug repairs are illegal in many Western countries, where tyre removal and patching from the inside is the approved method that keeps Fit-u-Like in business. Repairable sidewall damage would certainly require vulcanisation where a tube-type tyre might be successfully patched on the inside or even sewn up.

The ability to repair tubeless tyres in minutes, even temporarily, holds significant advantages and with the right tools, and with a spare inner tube in the correct size as a back-up, you need never be stranded.

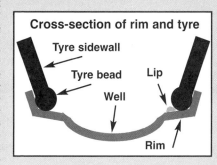

Cross-section of rim and tyre

Tyre sidewall

Tyre bead

Well

Lip

Rim

UPSIZING: TALLER BEFORE WIDER

Alternative tyres are commonly fitted to enhance the appearance of a car and bigger tyres are commonly fitted by 4x4 enthusiasts, ostensibly in the name of better traction. But car, van or truck, for overlanding what you want is **better not bigger tyres** because you'll be permanently loaded up, far from the nearest Fit-u-Like, and possibly traversing remote and rugged terrain. As with the vehicle itself, keeping close to the manufacturer's original specifications is always best, although a slightly bigger tyre or an alternative tread can improve your vehicle's dynamics without adversely affecting other aspects.

For overlanding that may include rough tracks, err towards alternative tyres with a **high aspect ratio**, in other words a tall sidewall. Not only does

Low profile tyre on an SUV.
Not suited to real off-roading.

this correspond to added ground clearance, it also effectively adds 'suspension' for a smoother ride on uneven surfaces and so better traction. Functional off-roaders such as Troop Carriers, Wranglers and Defenders have plenty of room in the wheel arches for taller tyres. Raising the suspension an inch or two gives more room for taller tyres, but make sure they can turn lock to lock unimpeded and on compression too.

High sidewall tyres are considered undesirable for performance-oriented vehicles as, among other factors, they flex under cornering forces. **Low-profile tyres** have become a trend, even on otherwise very capable SUVs like Discoverys. With large-diameter alloy rims of 20 inches or more, the sidewall is reduced to as little as a couple of inches in height. Such a lighter, low-profile tyre deforms less and so is more responsive to steering and braking on the road, and helps deliver impressive 0–60 times in motoring reviews. Nippy on-road performance is what you expect on a VW Touareg and other luxury SUVs that aren't pitched as serious off roaders, but a low-profile tyre is the last thing you want in the Ethiopian highlands while transporting a local farmer's sick ox to the day clinic.

With tall tyres your vehicle, especially a 4x4, won't feel so planted in bends (thoughtful packing makes a big difference here), but on pot-holed roads and tracks, and especially at ultra-low 'recovery' pressures, they'll still maintain good **ground clearance** and will always provide more **cushioning** to protect the wheel rim from damage. Particularly with alloy rims (more below), this is an important consideration.

Bigger tyres will have a larger contact area and so grip better on hard, dry surfaces but a substantially larger contact area for the same mass actually reduces ground pressure. This **'flotation' effect** can improve things on soft, low-traction terrain such as dunes and swamp, but is less effective in snow, shallow mud or on wet roads as the tread doesn't cut through to the harder surface so well and may aquaplane more readily. The point here is that an overland vehicle with a bigger tyre will be heavily loaded most of the time, so negating any theoretically reduced ground pressures from bigger tyres while benefiting from added ground clearance as well as higher load ratings.

Taller rather than wider tyres also work better in the **hyper-deflated state** necessary for recovery from soft sand or dune driving. In this condition, running as little as 8psi or .55 bar, the long contact patch extends still further to replicate a bulldozer's caterpillar track. More surface area gives better floatation and traction, but not at the cost of added rolling resistance. Think of a traditional tractor tyre: it's very tall but not very wide. At very low pressures the width of the contact patch barely increases, despite the 'sagged out' appearance; it's the less obvious long **footprint** that dramatically improves traction and reduces the chance of wheel spin.

Increasing **width** before height may have looked good twenty years ago but isn't the way to go for overland travel. On all surfaces they have a greater rolling resistance and in mud, and especially soft sand, they tend to push up a wall in front of them, which eventually they can't drive over. Traction is lost, the wheel spins and the vehicle starts going downwards instead of forward. Wider tyres may also compromise steering lock by rubbing on the wheel arches or suspension hardware.

Potential tyre problems

Disregarding the finer points of flotation and traction, which on most overland journeys will barely register in terms of distance (if not the time and effort involved in occasionally getting unstuck), **increasing tyre sizes** by much more than 10% above standard can lead to all sorts of other problems. Remember, the manufacturer designed the components of the car to run on a certain tyre size, and these days to save weight and cost the margin for overload is probably narrower than ever.

As a tyre's diameter increases, the leverage or 'moment' required to turn it increases too, and will be exacerbated by the inertia of the greater mass, let alone heavy payloads. Acceleration from a standstill is reduced and overtaking and braking takes more effort. In overlanding these drawbacks aren't that critical, but a substantially bigger tyre puts a greater strain on the standard transmission components. When running a 9.00xR16 in place of a standard 7.50, **hubs and wheel bearings** are certain to fail prematurely. At the same time the inertia of such a big tyre will exceed the load capacities of everything up to the clutch and is something that a more powerful engine merely exacerbates. Once you start meddling with the power train you have to be sure that the entire system can cope.

Clumsy gear changing while you're in a rush or bogged down – something that can happen to any tired, sick, hot or anxious overlander and not just a recreational off-roader showing off – could well break what's become the weakest link in your transmission.

TREAD

With tyres much attention is devoted by buyers, and indeed the tyre design and marketing people, to the appearance of the tread, but in all but specialist all-terrain use, it's not that significant. The fact is that the more conventional your tread the **quieter and cooler** it will run, the more predictably it will behave in the wet and the longer it will last.

As we know from F1, in dry conditions the most effective tyre had no tread at all; a tread's main function is to clear water from wet roads and reduce road noise with its irregular pattern. Aggressive **mud tyres** like a Michelin XCL have widely spaced blocks to claw at and fling off mud. On a true **sand tyre**, the less aggressive the better; it's low pressures that make all the difference, helped by a pliable sidewall, a feature of Michelin's near-obsolete XS.

Unless you're intent on tracking down the blue-ringed Amazonian puma, stick with a **conventional road pattern** on a road car; on a 4x4 go for an **all-terrain (AT) or mud-terrain (MT) pattern**, if that's on your itinerary. For unavoidably muddy itineraries an aggressive-tread-patterned mud tyre with distinct shoulder blocks will claw at the sides of muddy ruts to drive the car

On the once notorious muddy track near Ekok between Nigeria and Cameroon, a more aggressive mud terrain (MT) tread may be better. © Frederik & Josephine

forward, but will wear relatively quickly, whine on the highway and be unpredictable on wet tarmac.

Ex-military **trucks** often come with their original 20-year-old off-road tyres like XCLs. Chances are they'll be cracking so take the opportunity to replace them with something with a plainer, zigzag tread, such as the one found on an XZY. If a tyre is available in a **reinforced (RF)** or **extra load (XL)** version, so much the better.

In my experience, tread only becomes critical when the going gets muddy, but even then, reducing tyre pressures as well as employing other techniques (more on p296) can make all the difference. In a 2WD soon enough you'll run out of ground clearance and the tread pattern becomes immaterial.

There are no absolute rules or recommendations; much depends on what's available, rim types, driving style, payload and engine power characteristics. It's common for drivers to claim their tyres are the best if they got them at a good price and they've lasted for ages with no problems, but spend some time on vehicle owners' internet forums and you'll soon find that what lasted one guy 50,000 trouble-free miles is slated by the next poster.

PUMPS AND COMPRESSORS

Punctures are a certainty, so some sort of **air compressor** is an essential tool for overlanders, enabling you to make your own repairs (see p289). Wherever you are, be it with a slow puncture, having just fixed a flat, or after having deflated your tyres to improve traction on a stretch of sandy terrain, the ability to re-inflate your tyres without sweating over a manual pump or waiting for help is a real bonus. Compressors can also be used to inflate air-suspension bags, blast air to clean out air filters, or even help the less well-equipped.

Choosing a compressor

Stand-alone air compressors use an electric motor to turn a small piston that pumps air past a one-way valve into a tyre. The electrical **power** drawn, as well as the size of the piston and its ability to keep cool, all determine the efficiency. In the UK prices range from £4.99 to over £600, the more expensive engine-driven examples effortlessly pumping large volumes of air, irrespective of pressure and without overheating.

Forget the cheap compressors found in supermarkets that plug into the dashboard's cigarette lighter PTO. Many make highly dubious claims of '200psi'; what really counts is how many **cubic feet per minute** (cfm) or litres per hour they can pump, especially as pressure builds up in the tyre. This is something cheapies will rarely mention because it would be easier measured in cubic microns. They may last a while on smaller volume motorcycle tyres, but if used frequently on cars they'll overheat and burn out after as little as ten minutes' use.

Forget hand- or footpumps; you've got a car with an engine that produces electricity. Use it to power a compressor (optionally mounted out of the way in the engine), you won't regret it.

Along with the tell-tale cigarette plug, be suspicious of anything cased in black plastic with a short air hose, a cheap gauge and a built-in torch that can flash in three colours to the tune of Nancy Sinatra's greatest hits. These toys are fine forgotten in the boot until needed one dark night, but aren't designed for the heavy demands and large volume tyres used for overlanding.

Instead, aim to spend at least £100 for a **'recreational 4WD' compressor** that clips directly to the battery terminals, not your dashboard socket. Designed for off-roaders in the US, South Africa and Australia, these units pump out a useful **2–4cfm**. Viair is a well-known brand (beware of the T-Max clone), along with ARB and Warn (of winch fame). Viair makes several models; go for the 200-series or above. A 'P' on a Viair designates 'portable': a full kit in a bag. Others are just the pump, designed for permanent mounting and wiring up, out of the way in the engine bay for example (as pictured above) with a female coupling ready to receive the air line. For more on tyre pressures, see p294.

To **avoid flattening the battery**, keep the engine running if re-inflating all four tyres and, if you're working a portable compressor hard, keep it out of the sun and in a breeze. On all compressors, especially those mounted in the engine bay, check their **air filters** (where fitted and accessible) once in a while.

In-built compressors and air tanks

It's possible to modify a car's **engine-driven air-conditioning compressor** to pump air for the tyres. You'll have to give up your air-con so it's the sort of modification that suits an older car where the air-con has packed up. Just remember there'll be no freon gas to lubricate the mechanism.

Any truck with air brakes will have a compressor like this running full time off the engine, charging the air tanks at up to 10cfm, and an ex-military truck will doubtless have an air line for pumping up tyres too.

Although it's an off-roaders' forum favourite, having an **air reservoir** or tank doesn't save much time unless it's really huge, in which case it takes up space and will take ages to recharge. For tyre duties spend your money on a reliable and fast compressor with a good cfm rating that will reinflate a tyre in a couple of minutes. Some claim a tank is useful for running air tools, but that's better left to F1 pit crews or mechanics working on cars all day, not the once-in-a-blue moon use you'll put it to.

MODIFYING YOUR VEHICLE

WHEEL RIMS

Wheels come as heavy inexpensive steel or more commonly flashier and lighter alloy. Ex-military trucks and even some 70-series Land Cruisers sold new into Africa come with even heavier steel split rims to supposedly make tyre changing easier (more on that below).

Chances are your vehicle will have alloys and they'll be fine for the job as long as you drive and maintain tyre pressures accordingly. As has already been mentioned, you may want to consider changing **unusual rim sizes** (typically 17" and above as found on undesirable low-profile tyres) for something in the more utilitarian 13–16-inch range for cars and 4x4s if you have a long way to go.

Steel or alloy rims?

Steel rims are said to be better for overlanding because if dented, they can be beaten back into shape, so preserving a tubeless tyre's seal. The fact is, if you manage to dent a rim, steel or alloy, chances are you've either got very cheap rims, have just had a pretty serious accident and are in intensive care where a bent rim will be the least of your problems, or were driving too fast for the conditions. Steel, alloy or magnesium carbide, better to slow down, avoid driving at night and drive every mile of the trip with an unceasing goal of vehicle preservation. This also means keeping tyre pressures high enough to protect the rim, which is where a good compressor comes in.

Split rims

Split rims are two-part rims that come apart so a tyre can be lifted off without levering for a tube to be repaired (older splits usually need inner tubes). Some utility and military 4x4s have rims where the two halves simply bolt together, because 4x4 lore states that the alternative method – using a **locating ring** like a giant circlip – can spring off with deadly force on re-inflation. So much so that for health-and-safety reasons your local Fit-u-Like operative back home will suck through his teeth and not go near a split rim. Out in the world, they just get on with the job

Such accidents must have occasionally happened but, having worked on MAN and Toyota split rims over the years, I can't see how as long as the ring is observed to have located correctly and re-inflation is progressive. If you don't feel safe, wrap a chunky ratchet strap around the wheel as you re-inflate.

There is a knack to prising apart split rims.

A far bigger danger with truck split rims is putting your back out while working on a truck tyre that's heavier than a small adult.

I've watched African truck drivers pry off a split rim on a 14.50x20 truck wheel, pull the tyre off, patch a tube and remount it all in 20 minutes, without even removing the wheel from the axle or breaking into a sweat. The first time I tried, it took two of us on a similar truck a couple of hours. Split rims or plain, until you have the knack, both involve heavy work, even on a regular 4x4 station wagon, which is another reason why tubeless is better. Levering the locking rig up on Land Cruiser splits can take a lot of hammering, but once that's done you're on the way. With the repair done the key is to kick down in heavy boots to make sure the ring is correctly repositioned before re-inflation. Out in the world, local tyre repair shacks will have seen it all before and will do the job in their flip-flops while rolling a cigarette.

It's a good idea before you leave with old split-rim truck wheels to check that the locating rings have not **rusted into place** over the years. It could make a roadside tyre repair very awkward and, in my experience, even sand-blasted and repainted, rusty split rims are a recipe for regular punctures when running tubes.

On a Land Cruiser, for example, a set of replacement tubeless steel rims can cost just £200 and are well worth the effort if giving up on splits and getting new tyres. If you bought an MAN or a Mercedes truck and don't like the idea of its **heavy split rims**, which may be rusty, and are junking the old tyres they came with, getting tubeless rims and tyres would be the way to go, but at some considerable expense.

Spare wheels

Incredibly, the current trend with modern cars sold to mostly urban markets is to have no spare tyre at all. Instead, so-called run-flat tyres can deliver you to a garage at a reduced speed, where a professional repair can be made. The reason is presumably to save weight and make class-leading space in the back as that wins group road-test comparisons. Before this, undersized and speed-limited 'space saver' tyres were fitted. It ought not

come as a shock that you want a normal, full-size spare tyre. Indeed, if you've a long way to go and are in any doubt that correctly sized replacements (if not necessarily the same brand) can be bought on the way, a **second spare** gives added peace of mind. Even a loose, unmounted sixth tyre will do.

On a road car spares usually sit under the floor of the boot, along with a cheap jack and wheel brace. If it's a space saver there may not even be room for a full-sized spare. Most 4x4s have them on the back door or under the back body, as do many vans. If you fit bigger tyres you can expect the new spare not to fit on the rear carrier, or to protrude vulnerably from below the rear body. In this case the best position on all but a pickup is on the roof or on a spare tyre carrier on the back.

These after-market carriers are a better alternative to the rear-door mounting on a Defender, especially if the vehicle is past its prime. Mounting the spare on a Defender's bonnet looks the part, but reduces visibility and makes the bonnet incredibly heavy. With a spare in this position I've known drivers misjudge the terrain and end up in a ditch.

Road-car specific modifications

Apart from the lack of space to make an overland journey comfortable, the biggest drawback on **road cars** is the **limited ground clearance**. The good thing is that, because road cars feature independent suspension, the underneath is generally smooth, with no protruding 4x4 differential axle-casings. They therefore lend themselves well to the fitting of a large **engine guard**, as pictured below.

The parts that really need protecting are the sump or oil pan of the engine, along with maybe the gearbox, steering and suspension apparatus, exhaust pipe, and in some cases fuel and brake lines and an exposed fuel tank. Consider the bottom edge of the **radiator** too. Will it get mashed and pushed into the fan in the event of a low frontal impact or driving into a ditch?

The simplest way to make a guard is to fix on a flat sheet of steel or alloy. This **bash plate** only needs to work once to earn its keep, so it needs to be fixed on well as bash plates often come adrift on rough roads. Leave a small gap above the plate and stuff it with some thick, shock-absorbing material such as rubber so a severe impact is not transmitted directly through the plate to what it's supposed to be protecting.

Saloons/sedans and estates or station wagons invariably have long **rear overhangs** (the distance from the middle of the rear axle to the back bumper) and some have overhanging fronts too. Tailpipes, some fuel tanks and, on more modern cars, front spoilers with radiators positioned close behind, are all vulnerable to damage. Try to anticipate what will ground out and whether it matters. Shortening the end of the **tailpipe** might be convenient to stop it grounding, but the fumes need to clear the body so re-bending it or adding a flexible end is a better idea. Shorter cars such as hatchbacks have much better approach and departure angles (see p40), which means they won't ground out so easily going in and out of ditches, but of course they have much less capacity and almost all are front-wheel drive.

Left: A thin steel bashplate off a Mercedes 300 estate © Jurgen Stroo.
Right: For sustained off-roading a thicker bashplate running back past the gearbox is better.
This one on a Mercedes 190 came back full of dents and outlasted the car.

MODIFYING YOUR VEHICLE

Wheel and tyre size

Larger wheels roll over rough ground more smoothly than smaller wheels, while increasing clearance on suspension components. They also produce a marginally longer footprint, which when deflated helps traction in soft conditions (more on p294).

A 'tall' **tyre** – that is one with a high sidewall – is desirable for imperfect roads. You can tell the sidewall height just by looking at a tyre. Its aspect ratio (the second number in the tyre size moulded on the side, e.g. 185/**75** 15″) means how tall it is as a percentage of its width, which is the first number (in this example '185' in millimetres). A **high aspect ratio** of 75 or more is desirable for rough roads because it increases ground clearance, provides added cushioning as the tyre wall flexes over bumps, and gives enough scope to deflate the tyre without dangerously flattening it against the rim. Fitting much bigger wheels or taller tyres is not so ideal as it raises overall gearing on a vehicle which, unlike a proper 4x4, lacks a low-range gearbox. With bigger wheels, first gear becomes closer to second and so crawling up steep inclines and driving out of a heavy bogging becomes harder on the clutch, a vital transmission component whose welfare should be a priority, even if you do carry a spare.

Taller tyres will help raise the vehicle off the deck, but with standard suspension there'll be only so much room in the wheel arches to do so before the tyres contact the bodywork under suspension compression. Taller tyres will usually be wider too, which will reduce steering lock or again cause the tyres to rub inside the wheel arch when turning sharply. The way round this is to fit heavy-duty or longer suspension.

Suspension

Road cars have **independent suspension**, which is part of what makes them nicer to drive through bumpy tarmac bends than a beam-axled 4x4 or truck. On rough ground independent suspension displays the limitations described on p145, which is why it rarely features on traditional 4WDs (even though many top-of-the-range 4x4s have now adopted it). Typically, each corner of a car will be held up by a **coil spring** or a **torsion bar**. It's easy and inexpensive to get an uprated set of coil springs made. I paid £150 for an overlength set for an old Mercedes whose original springs had already effectively been round the planet ten times. Standard Mercedes springs would have cost £100.

On 4x4s it usually goes without saying that you need to replace the original factory suspension for something tougher; on a car it's not so usual. **Fitting heavy-duty coils** of the *same length* on a car ought not to cause a problem other than a firmer ride, but *longer* suspension (or repositioning the splines of a torsion bar so that it raises the car's body) is not so desirable when you factor in heavy payloads and rough roads. Doing so alters the

A 40-hp 2CV in the Atlas. © Frederik & Jo

factory-set geometry of the steering and final transmission components, putting a new range of stresses on the vehicle: the last thing you want when trying to cross Angola. Doing this will almost certainly reduce the life of the CV or universal joints, and any weakness brought on by rusting mounts will be exposed too. Significantly longer suspension will also require longer shocks.

The cheapest solution with coils is a **spacer** above or beneath a spring; the car instantly sits higher. Mercedes offer these 'spring pads' in a variety of thicknesses but anything will do. A body rise of around **two inches** or 50mm is probably the maximum, any more and something might snap. Don't forget the car will already be loaded to the hilt and heading for a hammering it was not really built for. Remember too that the coil sits more or less halfway between the wishbone pivot and the tyre, so a spacer or longer spring of 20mm will raise the gap in the wheel arch by 40mm, more or less.

On a rear-wheel-drive car it might be possible to **lower the differential** – usually bolted to the subframe or body – by an inch (this is now a commonly offered adaptation for 4x4s running independent front suspension, or IFS). This would mitigate the exacerbated geometry on final drive linkages to effectively one inch on a suspension rise of two inches, but you'd want to be sure the propshaft has the play to cope with such a modification.

Be aware that radically raising suspension on any vehicle like this undermines any normal **handling characteristics** and could be unsafe. It's worth reiterating then that, just as with 4x4s, the easiest way to get decent ground clearance (and reduce stresses overall) is to choose a car with good ground clearance in the first place and then to pack the vehicle correctly: don't **overload it**, and do keep any heavy weights positioned low and between the axles. Once you've made the best of your ground clearance and underbody protection, all that really remains is to ensure things like the exhaust pipe and fuel-tank fittings are in good shape (these items come loose or fall off on corrugated or washboard tracks). For other preparation guidelines, take your pick of what you find between p133 and p217.

Is it worth it?
In the end, with a car you have to add up the price of these modifications and wonder if you might be better off buying a decent panel van instead – giving you somewhere other than the driving seat to retreat to once the sun goes down – or opting for a 4x4, with its increased space and payload and/or rough-road durability. Realistically, few overlanders take on a big trip in ordinary road cars.

CONVERTING A VEHICLE

5

Converting a vehicle, be it car or truck, is about making the relatively small space into a comfortable and efficient place to use or spend time: a **home**. This may require no conversion at all: just sling your gear in the back, turn the key and hit the road. Or it can involve adapting the rear of a van or 4x4 right through to fabricating a motorhome-like cabin on the back of a flatbed truck and equipping it with running water, heating, auxiliary power, a permanent kitchen, shower and toilet, and a bed. Cabin fabrication is covered in the next section, which starts on p218; this bit focuses on less radical modifications that'll enhance your travel experience, specifically: how to increase your fuel and water storage capacity, designing a place to sleep, packing efficiently and facilitating easy cooking while on the road.

It might seem excessive to spend so much time and effort on making your vehicle more comfortable, but you'll soon change your mind after a long trip in a basically equipped vehicle where merely lying down for a rest or making a quick brew requires moving things around or getting them out. Sure, it all adds up to only a few minutes of effort, but as far as possible you want to imitate the convenience of home living.

Part of the pleasure of overlanding is being able to park up anywhere you can drive to and establish a temporary home in potentially spectacular surroundings. To do this you need to carry equipment for **sleeping, cooking, eating, drinking** and **washing**, all of which needs to be stored and organised so as to make access and use as hassle-free as possible.

Not every day will end in a grassy meadow alongside a stream with a warm breeze wafting birdsong from a nearby glade. You also need to anticipate driving late into the night because a hoped-for hotel was full, too rough or non-existent. You eventually stop by a busy roadside in the sleet, hungry, grubby and red-eyed, drive up a track in the dark and get bogged in a ditch. Your tiny stove requires you to siphon some petrol out of the tank; you've only a litre of water because the loose toolbox stabbed the water bag, which soaked your sleeping bag; and if you don't find a fuel station in the next 20 miles you'll be running on empty. Not every day on the road is a winner, but many more will end tolerably with a bit of forethought.

Outfitting an overland vehicle for months on the road compares with preparing a yacht for a long oceanic voyage. The mundane domestic necessities and cramped spaces are broadly the same, but be aware that some **marine equipment**, much of which can be commonly applied to vehicle-dependent overlanding, won't be designed for high altitude or sub-zero temperatures, or indeed the deadly hammering of a washboard track. Instead, investigate gear for the less glamorous worlds of **inshore boating** and **caravanning** (in the UK sense), which tends to be cheaper because it doesn't attract the 'expeditionary' mark-up added by overland and marine outfitters.

As with most aspects of overland travel, the goals here are securing reliable equipment that's convenient and accessible. I've heard of gullible overlanders being persuaded to spend tens of thousands of pounds equipping a 4x4 station wagon with every last gadget. This section is designed to help you become aware of such pitfalls and **spend your money and time wisely**. It's a mistake to think the more you spend the more successful your trip will be.

SLEEPING, EATING, WASHING

Banal though they sound, these three activities sum up your daily earthbound existence when not driving or indeed doing everything else. Being able to accomplish them with the same ease you do so at home is the key, and is clearly harder to achieve in the back of a Fiat 500 than an 8x8 land ship.

You may ask yourself whether you even need to go through all the hassle, time and expense of setting up your vehicle for sleeping, cooking and so on. After all, you're not the first to take the road to Kathmandu, Timbuktu or Machu Picchu: there'll be restaurants and hotels along the way. Theoretically, and with planning, being accommodated every night is possible, though less so in rural Asia or Africa. However, visas and other obligations notwithstanding, part of the appeal of a long journey is the spontaneity, in not being tied to a schedule of transporting yourself like a backpacker from town to town where lodgings and services are typically found. While there's no doubt you may choose to spend up to half of your overlanding nights out of the vehicle, in poorer regions some basic lodgings will feel many times worse than sleeping in a car.

Being autonomous is also the most **economical** option. A cheap and cheerful backstreet hotel may be a perfectly adequate place to sleep, but it probably won't be in a locale you'd want to leave your vehicle for too long. And staying at upmarket hotels with their own secure parking won't be possible, let alone financially sustainable for months on end.

Many overlanders will recognise that after an initial spell of agoraphobic acclimatisation, camping out in the wilds will provide some of the best

A secluded bush camp on the road in Angola.
© Rob & Ally Ford

memories of their travels. It's something that typically can't be done back in somewhere like crowded Europe without attracting unwanted local attention or a farmer's ire. Out on the steppes, in the desert or in the mountains you may meet honest and generous locals as opposed to men in hats or outstretched hands. You'll savour the space and freedom without risking a telling-off by a warden for straying off the trail, and you'll feel more than ever that you're out there having your adventure. Sleeping with your vehicle is secure, free, convenient, versatile and fun.

ACCESS AND STORAGE

Equipping and organising a vehicle for overland travel while **keeping the most frequently used items accessible** is a challenge that gets easier as volume increases or junk is reduced. It's why custom-built cabins and interiors designed in motorhome style work so well: they cleverly duplicate the multiple-use areas of the domestic setting in one small space.

Organisation is all the more important because your home will now be much smaller and mobile; you can't just chuck it under the sink or leave stuff lying around. People who've lived in one room or who frequently move around may adapt better than those who've lived for years in a big house or a farm where space – and so the need to be tidy or minimalist – is unimportant.

WHERE TO START

A good way to kick off the process is to first address how much **extra fuel and water** you want to carry; this will depend on your destination as well as your vehicle's economy and your own water set-up and management. Together, these two vital fluids add up to the biggest single element of your payload, but once stored out of the way can be forgotten about between replenishments.

Once you've worked out where the fluids go, think about how and where you want to sleep, because the large area required for, let's say, two intimate people to do this in comfort has a crucial bearing on the rest of your plans for adapting the interior of your vehicle. With that done you need to address the storage of other gear: clothing and camping gear, vehicle spares and tools, a secure place for valuables, cooking gear, provisions and so on. To summarise: calculate the position and quantities of extra fuel and water, then sleeping, and then storage which includes access and use.

Long-range fuel and water

When it comes to remote, long-range travel, 'water = time, fuel = distance'. In other words, your reserves of these two resources determine how far you can go and for how long. With enough water aboard or replenished locally you're able to spend extended periods parked up. A larger capacity increases your range but, taking the average weight of both including their containers to be around 1kg per litre (petrol actually weighs 74% of water and diesel from 82%), both will take a considerable bite out of your payload – something to consider before you start installing post-apocalyptic reserves.

You may see 4x4 outlets selling auxiliary roof rack tanks. There's no worse position for fuel or water, especially sloshing around in one big tank as opposed to jerries. If you're getting a fuel tank, fit it low and between the axles where it's out of the way and has a minimal effect on vehicle handling.

FUEL RANGE AND CAPACITY

Most normal road cars have a **typical range** of up to 300 miles or around 500km, which is perfectly adequate just about anywhere on the planet where there's a network of sealed roads. Nevertheless, an improved range has many benefits, even on the highway. Many of us get into the habit of not filling up until the last minute as it's so easily done back home, but out in rural or remote areas the expected fuel station may be closed, dry or not there. Just as you'd take a spare fuel can if going on a touring holiday, so a **full 20-litre jerrican** will one day pay off while overlanding. Anything like a can that requires the conscious effort of stopping, unloading and decanting and not just switching to a second tank ought to break your 'run it to the brink' habit.

A fuel range of about 500km (300 miles) is sufficient for most of the world.

If you're going remote, upgrading to a typical 1000km/620-mile range can give you peace of mind. Otherwise there are very few places in the world where you'd expect to cover that distance without fuel, although once off road or at very high altitude, **fuel consumption** can double. In dunes 4x4's range can halve, though you'd not expect to drive dunes any longer than necessary. It's also probable that the configuration of your vehicle, heavily loaded and possibly with a roof rack, will reduce optimal fuel consumption. Added fuel capacity can also mean big savings when crossing into neighbouring countries, where fuel can be many times more expensive. For all these reasons it's worth looking into.

JERRICANS

For travellers who don't expect to traverse the desert wastes or the Siberian outback, **steel jerricans** provide a simple and inexpensive solution. The standard steel jerrican is a German design from the late 1930s ('jerry' was British WWII slang for 'Germans') and has remained unchanged since that time.

A classic jerrican holds 20 litres (4.4 gallons or 5.3 US gallons) when correctly filled in the upright position. This leaves an air gap just below the three handles, which shouldn't be filled with fuel (by tipping the can backwards) unless you're really desperate. This air pocket, together with the X-shaped indentations on the sides, enables the can's sides to bulge as fuel expands under agitation and heat; especially the case with petrol, which is much more volatile than diesel. When a can has been warmed and shaken like this you need to open the cap slowly to avoid a dangerous, messy and wasteful spurt of fuel – the clamp's clever design makes this easy. A replaceable rubber seal fits into the cap and is pressed down onto the filler neck as the hinged clamp cranks down.

As well as being reliable and robust, jerricans can be used for other things. Shoved under an axle or driven onto, whether on its side or upright, a steel 20-litre jerry also makes a **good jack stand** when working under a light vehicle, as well as a handy step for working on an engine of a 4x4, or simply just something to sit on.

Jerricans can endure rough treatment for years: I've never seen a welded seam fail, though cap **seals do leak**. Carry spares or clamp a chopped-up inner tube or similar across the mouth; the clamp's cam action makes this easy to do. The insides should be painted red, but once rust or **flaking paint** begin to

CONVERTING A VEHICLE

About 360 litres or £200 of used jerries. Such an extreme capacity is rarely necessary for a diesel 4x4, but when fuel is cheap, filling up before crossing a border can cover that cost in one go.

CONVERTING A VEHICLE

Clones of the original German 'jerries' in 20, 10 and 5 litres. Inexpensive, even new.

come out, either make sure you use a fine pre-filter or junk it.

Jerries are available in Europe from military surplus outlets and sometimes still unused from **around £10**. Neat 10-litre versions are available with the same clamp, as well as nifty 5-litre models. For well under £100 in the UK you can therefore reliably double your vehicle's fuel capacity and most probably sell the jerricans on the road for what you bought them for. All you need is a place to store them.

Filling up with jerries

Like the Unimog, they got it right first time with the jerry. Grab a handle and indent in the base and pouring is as easy as the weight allows. The three-handle design also makes it easy to carry four empty cans in two hands, too.

A clamp-on spout (with integral gauze and breather) should make it easier still, but these spouts often leak and the gauze filter slows the flow, prolonging the effort required. A wide-bore funnel is quicker, but needs to be kept stored clean. Fold-flat vinyl fabric funnels store in a plastic bag or lunch box while cut-down PET bottles are the ubiquitous roadside funnel.

Or leave the can in situ and **siphon** the fuel with a hose or manual siphon-pump. People are leery of using the sucking method to get a siphon going. No need – just submerge a hose into a jerry, fold- or put your thumb over the end then draw out the hose full of fuel. Poke the end in the filler and the weight of the dropping fuel should create a siphon.

In certain dry atmospheric conditions there's a small risk from **static electricity** when refuelling vehicles, especially with petrol. If you feel static in the air (a rare phenomenon that sometimes precedes a storm) touch the vehicle before opening the cap or it may end like a scene from *Road Runner*.

Plastic fuel cans

Rotopax-style fuel can holds only 15 litres and costs $120. Looks cool, but.

Regular translucent plastic containers should never be used for long-term fuel storage. The soft slab sides and screw-on caps will swell before splitting, leaking or bursting, especially with petrol, which decays certain plastics. In Egypt driving with thirty plastic jerries on the roof, I was soon resorting to the wipers.

Harder plastic fuel cans sold in supermarkets up to 20-litres are fine. If you're taking just one back-up can, these are lighter and less rattly than a steel jerry, but of course don't have a steel can's 'jack-stand' benefits. In America where proper jerries are rare, Rotopax and similar cans have a clever expansion proof design but are poor value.

Plastic cans are lighter and less clanky and suit less effervescent diesel.

Low-profile, one-strap jerry frames; sold in Germany or easy to make.

Mounting jerries

If your vehicle has a nearly adequate fuel range and you're only using a single jerry, lashing it down securely inside the car simplifies things, so long as you don't mind the small risk of fuel odour. If the seal is good a jerry can safely be stored in any position, just make sure it won't budge. With more than a couple of jerries, they're much better **stored outside**. With a van or a 4x4, slinging them on a roof rack is a temptation. On the side they're easier to get to but involve drilling into the body which isn't for everyone.

In Britain and maybe elsewhere you'll find **steel 'baskets'** into which a jerrican can be locked. Fitting these baskets on the *sides* of a vehicle is rightly outlawed in Europe but they work better on back doors and can be used on their sides under the load bed of a truck. Bear in mind that petrol **expands** (diesel less so), so may well get jammed until the pressure is released or the contents stand and cool.

'Low-profile' 20-litre jerrican **mounting frames** work better on the sides of a hardtop, or even on the edge of a roof rack (picture above), where they're readily accessible. The weight is taken on the lower edge of the frame, a strap lashed through slots holds the can firmly in place and, on some, a tab on top of the frame also locates onto the jerry's inner handle in case it gets loose. Care must be taken to ensure the strap doesn't fray where it passes through the frame's slots; a ring of duct tape will do. They're sold in Germany in alloy or steel, or can be easily fabricated or bolted up from 1-inch angle.

LONG-RANGE FUEL TANKS

Extra fuel tanks, either used, home-made or for your vehicle in metal or lighter plastics, are the neatest way of adding fuel-range. They can be fitted low and out of the way into the otherwise unused spaces alongside any 4x4 or truck with a separate ladder chassis. Some Land Cruisers, particularly 70s, come with a second, 90-litre chassis-mounted tank plumbed to the same-sized main tank with a gauge and dashboard switch and gives up to 1500km range.

A tank like this is expensive, but its discreet position can have advantages at borders, both distant and local, where customs have been known to take offence to a rack of bulging jerries, even if the fuel is clearly for personal use. They'll be lucky ever to notice a chassis-mounted tank full of cheap fuel from the country you've just left, unless they're giving you the third degree.

CONVERTING A VEHICLE

Flat plastic tank in a Discovery. © J. Bignell

Interior tanks

The main benefit of a fuel tank inside a vehicle is it's easy to fit and can be mounted in a reasonably low and central position, while still relying on a simple, pump-free gravity feed. The ideal location is on the floor immediately **behind the front seats**, but anywhere between the axles is good. This works especially well on a hardtop 4x4 as this area is the least accessible and a permanently fitted tank can be positioned with minimal disruption.

With a tank in this location don't even think about having the filler cap inside the vehicle. You may always be careful but matey at some windblown, diesel-soaked Patagonian forecourt may not be so alert. Result: your vehicle reeks of diesel for weeks. Instead cut a filler cap into the vehicle's side and attach a wide-bore hose to the tank inlet. This means cutting into the body or replacing a window with Perspex and mounting the exterior filler into that.

If plumbing an interior tank permanently to the main fuel tank with a gravity feed you need to be sure the main tank's filler cap is above the level of the second tank, otherwise it could overflow once the lower tank is left connected. Better to have an accessible manual **tap** between the two tanks to top up. A thin-bore hose may take a while to refill the main tank, but it'll get there in the end and can be done on the move. The easiest place to splice low into the main tank's inlet or via a spare breather. Fitting **gauges** on a secondary tank isn't essential; it's better to get into the habit of completely emptying the second tank in one or two stages so you never forget how much is in there.

Used lorry tanks and oil drums

A rectilinear, 100-litre **lorry tank** can be picked up from a commercial truck breakers for less than the price of five jerries. But before you buy, save yourself some effort by making sure the tank comes complete with filler caps, breathers and senders, and isn't a rusted hulk. At twice that volume, huge lorry tanks become a real bargain, albeit an incredibly heavy one when full.

Two hundred litre drums can be free but make sure they're suited to fuel not molasses.

A home-made lorry tank of at least 250 litres. Chassis supports have to be very strong.

Because of this they're only really suited to fitting to another lorry – either replacing a smaller unit or adding range – as it'll have the space and chassis strength to support it.

As long as you have the space, a standard **oil drum** with a nominal volume of around 208 litres (55 gallons) can work well as a quick and easy way of hugely increasing fuel range, especially temporarily. They're most practical in an 'expedition' rather than an overland setting, where a group of

Five jerries and a drum for the long way round.

vehicles might have one truck designated to carry loads, including fuel. For overlanders they work best in the back of a pickup or fixed under a truck chassis, where the consequence of leakage is less messy.

Know as a '55-gallon drum' or barrel, it's still used as the unit of volume in the oil industry. A typical example weighs 15kg and, externally, measures around 890mm high by 590mm in diameter (33lb; 35"x 23"). All sorts of fluids come in oil drums and not all drums may be suited to carrying automotive fuel. The good news is that, even back home, used drums are easy to find or pick up for free from garages or farmers and, if your needs are temporary, can just as easily be disposed of down the road.

The **caps** are basic screw-on items with a rubber o-ring seal, which don't feel as secure as a jerry clamp, but then it's only one cap to worry about, not ten. It's worth carrying a spare or two. On the opposite side of the top there may be a smaller breather plug to enable pumping or pouring; you may want to ensure that this is plugged up for good. With no breather (see p170) this cap will be prone to pressure variations as altitude changes, but on oil drums it's not worth getting bogged down with breathers; the whole ethos is simplicity and low cost, so release the cap every 1000m of altitude change or keep it loose on a near-empty drum. Any full vessel is less affected by pressure.

Custom-made long-range tanks

An alternative to a get-what-you're-given used lorry tank or a cumbersome, oil drum is something made-to-measure. It's more costly but every inch of your interior space can be maximised, and mounting brackets can be positioned to use any existing fixtures. **Mild steel** of 1.5mm is the ideal material. Tanks in aluminium or stainless steel cost a fortune to manufacture or take hours to fabricate, and stainless steel in particular weighs a ton and isn't so easily welded.

Before you go too far down this route have a look at plastic fuel tanks over the page which now come in a huge variety of sizes and capacities and may cost less. You can also save money by getting the fabrication done en route, in a developing country where labour is cheap. Doing this is a gamble but the work can be undertaken while you enjoy the local sites on foot. You can also bask in the warm glow of supporting the local economy and not some accessory manufacturer who may get the work done in cheap countries anyway.

LONG-RANGE FUEL-CARRYING METHODS

	Jerrican	Inner tank	Under tank	Custom tank	Used tank	Oil drum
Inexpensive	Yes	No	No	No	Can be	Yes
Versatile	Yes	No	No	Can be	No	Can be
Out of the way	No	Can be	Yes	Can be	Can be	No
Functional	Yes	Can be	Yes	Can be	Can be	No
Good shape	Yes	Can be	Can be	Yes	Can be	No

In a custom tank, vertical **interior baffles** about a foot apart must be incorporated to add strength and reduce surging. In case you missed out on maths, with any box the height x width x depth measured in 10cm units will give the **volume** in litres (more or less). Therefore a tank that's 15cm high, 50cm wide and 120cm long adds up to 90 litres. There's something to be said for a huge, flat, floor-sized tank just a few inches high and so taking very little space. A 7cm x 1m x 1.8m slab tank like this would hold about 120 litres. The problem will always be fully refilling such a flat tank on less than perfectly level ground. To fill right up you'll need the vehicle tipping away from the filler and ideally a breather in the one or two corners furthest from the filler to avoid air locks. For this and other reasons, flat tanks like this are an idea many think of but few actually employ.

Have a breather

With any fuel tank (especially one plumbed into the fuel system) a **breather** is a good idea. A breather is simply a hose leading from the top of a tank to the outside air, enabling air pressure inside a tank to remain equal with its surroundings. A sealed jerrican or oil drum can usually take the pressure, but in a box tank the breather eliminates any strain on joints and fittings caused by thermal expansion or varying atmospheric pressure, and if plumbed to the fuel system allows fuel to be drawn by the pump. I had a 180-litre tank without a breather which was affected by even the mild altitude changes, causing it to flex with a loud clang when nearly empty. Imperfect welds and seals will leak under this sort of pressure.

A breather should rise above the tank and feature a loop to stop sloshed surging along it and out. During fabrication fix a splash plate in the tank below the breather outlet to limit this. Plug an inline fuel filter on the end of the hose for good measure and in a 4x4 station wagon run it off somewhere to a rear air-vent. If the loop is high enough the end can be below tank level.

It's vital that an interior tank is **securely mounted**; bolting to the body or chassis is best, and if it can butt up against a bulkhead or wheel arch, so much the better. Carpet tiles under the tank can reduce noise, chafing and vibration.

Plastic fuel tanks

Plastic rotomolding technology has advanced far enough to make lighter, rust-free and equally robust fuel tanks from high-density polyethylene (HDPE) at a much lower cost than metal tanks and with better noise suppression. Standard-sized tanks are typically used in boating applications, but adapt well to automotive use.

For an overlander they're ideal, if for no other reason than there's a much better chance of you finding a PE tank off the shelf in the capacity and shape to suit your needs and at a reasonable price.

Low tooling costs at low volumes is what makes all this possible and, among other places, Tek Tanks' (🖥 tek-tanks.com) range of box tanks come in many shapes and capacities from 33–140 litres, all including an inspection cap/filler and pick-up pipes. In Australia try Opposite Lock and in the US it's 🖥 grangerplastics.com.

A 55-litre plastic tank with a breather fitting near the cap. © Dolium pty

Underbody tanks for 4x4s and trucks

Purpose-built tanks are available to fit in the voids underneath various 4x4s and, though they cost a packet they can double or triple your range without you even knowing they're there.

With hardtop Defenders there's a lot of usable volume between the rear wheels and the front doors – a good position for an auxiliary tank that's outside the chassis rails but behind the sills, as with the Australian Long Ranger tank pictured below. A Land Rover 90's under-seat tank can fit in a LWB hardtop too, so increasing the capacity by at least 45 litres, but requires a filler to be fitted by the door. You can do the same under the other seat, but second batteries and other electrics more commonly use this space and the plumbing can get complicated. For much less effort there's a readily available 45-litre space at the back right-hand corner of a Defender (pictured below). A tank can be plumbed in behind the filler above the main tank. Essentially it's an 'upper reservoir' to the main tank, so there's no messing around with fuel lines, new fillers and so on.

Wider **Land Cruiser 60s and 80s** have masses of room between the chassis rails and still more between the rails and sills, as do many other 4x4s. A 60-series Cruiser can easily take a 70-litre tank between the rails without any

A 70-litre Long Ranger sill tank on a Defender. © thelongranger.com.au

And a 45-litre tank in the back corner of a Defender. © mattsavage.com

modification. You'll find a good range of underbody tanks from 40–200 litres downunder, and a lot of good 4x4 touring gear besides, mostly for Japanese 4x4s. These sorts of tanks are also available in Germany for G-Wagens and Land Rovers, but are eye-wateringly expensive compared to half a dozen jerries and can get complicated, requiring a new or split filler pipe, and taps, switches and pumps that may be best left to a fitter. But when fitted they enable you to save valuable space, keep the enormous weight of fuel low down and benefit from a vastly increased range.

Fabricating your own, or **fitting off-the-shelf HDPE underbody tanks** is not the simple gravity-feed/top-up operation of an interior tank, but the cost benefits over the made-to-fit items may inspire you to give it a go. If plumbed permanently into the main tank it requires an understanding of the function of **fuel return pipes** as well as careful routing to protect fuel lines from damage and support across the two chassis rails while keeping clear of the propshaft and the exhaust while adding protection against damage can all be a tall order. You can get round this plumbing complexity by keeping the auxiliary tank independent of the main tank, topping the main up with an electric fuel pump dipped in the other tank. The times when you need to run on both tanks without a roadside fuel stop will be few and, as with jerries, there's something to be said for **compartmentalising** your fuel storage. Should you fill up with bad fuel it's good to know you may have as much clean fuel in reserve.

When you think of having half-a-dozen jerries to stash somewhere, or the price you'd pay in Europe for as much added capacity, an HDPE tank is perhaps the best solution. It's not too expensive if the tank shape and filling system are kept simple, and if underneath has the advantage of keeping the vast bulk of extra fuel out of the vehicle, out of the way and as low as possible.

WATER TANKS

Your typical overland vehicle may well have an adequate fuel range that only needs supplementing with a plastic jerry for a rainy day, but chances are it won't have any water capacity beyond the windscreen wash reservoir. The choice comes down to inexpensive plastic containers, a permanently mounted tank with a filler and a tap, or a mixture of both. As with fuel, this all wants to be mounted low, centrally, securely and out of the way with an accessible means of refilling and decanting. You may also want to incorporate an inline pump as well as a water filter leading to a fixed tap.

How much water? Depending on the environment, the season and your route, a storage capacity of **20 litres per person** is a minimum, but having the option to carry easily two or three times that amount is better, not so much to stop you dying of thirst, but because it's one less thing to have to worry about for a few days.

Whichever water-storage system you choose, make it **simple and foolproof**. As with all systems and operations, try to visualise yourself working in adverse conditions: a sandstorm, a hurry, in the dark or under attack by vampire bats. The easier you make any repetitive but essential task, the less chance there'll be of making errors or having an accident because 'we couldn't be bothered to top up the water, it was such a hassle'.There's more on water pumping, filtration and more in **Part 6: Building a Cabin**, on p247.

Water storage

More so than with fuel, **compartmentalising** your water storage is worthwhile, so that you can separate potable water from water to be used for other purposes such as washing, showering or cooking. You may not always be able to fill right up with drinking water, but the latter can always be made drinkable (see p250). In desert areas, for example, it's not uncommon to take the precaution to fill up from a well that may have an unpalatable mineral content, or from a slimy waterhole that wouldn't make an award-winning Evian commercial. Knowing you have this water in reserve can be reassuring until you get to a better source where the slime water can be replaced or relegated to non-potable uses. Even with a built-in tank it's therefore always worth having a 20-litre water container or bag as a back-up.

Filling up such containers and using them as easily as in the kitchen back home can take some setting up. It helps to organise your placement in the vehicle without the need to remove or even move them at all. Aspire to fill rigid containers via a hose (carry your own) that you either attach to a mains tap or use to pump water in from another source, and then access that onboard water either by pumping it or by gravity drawing it from a single main tank with a tap that's mounted in a convenient position for daily use.

Plastic and steel water containers

The translucent **UPVC** or **PE water containers** in typical 20-litre 'jerrican' dimensions sold by most camping suppliers aren't always reliable: they can leak, and price doesn't always have much to do with it. A good test on a container like this is to see if you can easily keep screwing a cap in until it deforms over the threads and goes 'click'. This is a cap that'll probably leak.

Better alternatives to these cheaply made camping accessories are the stackable **square-profile containers** used for transporting catering or light-industrial fluids – it'll take some effort to get the cap on one of these to 'over-click'. Pictured over the page, they go new for a few pounds online, or are found round the backs of chip shops for nothing. When 'recycled' like this, much depends on what was in the container. Hand car washes are a good source of 20-litre soap containers which rinse out well; containers used for cooking oil are less reusable for water duties. Chemicals and other agents may come in thicker, tougher cans which are always preferable; just avoid anything from the back of a tannery with a skull and crossbones on the label.

Even though it's less easy to estimate how much water is inside, **non-translucent** examples inhibit the growth of the algae from cans exposed to even indirect sunlight. This algae is harmless but could host other organisms so is best discouraged.

Avoid anything with a moulded-in **tap** protruding from its base, even recessed; it looks handy but is more suited to static applications like a gar-

> Chemicals and other agents can come in thicker, tougher containers which are always preferable; just avoid anything from the back of a tannery or with a skull and crossbones on the label.

These 'commercial' 20L cans trounce camping shop cheapies and can be found free.

den shed. On the road it's certain to get bashed and leak. If you want a tap, go for the less vulnerable ones mounted on the filler cap. They may not have the seal of a Rolex Oyster, but as long as the can is upright, it won't drain completely. If these tapped containers (usually the camping ones rather than the light industrial examples) have a small breather cap to allow water to flow smoothly then so much the better. While stout enough to put in a few rounds with Henry Cooper, I've found the black ex-NATO jerricans with caps on small chains aren't so leakproof and are often overpriced.

Although some overlanding sources imply that only **stainless steel** jerricans should be used for water (the gullible can pay a staggering £180!), even a regular steel jerry is over the top for water. An equally robust and less clanky new red plastic fuel can would certainly make a tough water container. As a rule avoid anything over **20 litres** in capacity unless you don't ever expect to move it around. Anything above 25 litres is better regarded as a small in-built tank.

As with fuel jerries, rigid water cans need to be **lashed down** well; metal frames or baskets don't complement plastic – something like carpet-lined plywood is a better idea, with a board and a strap holding them all down to stop them jumping about like an old washing machine. If using a board over the top, make sure the filler caps remain accessible once it's all lashed into place so the cans can be refilled by simply spinning off the caps.

Water bags and flexible water tanks

For overlanding – long trans-continental journeys rather than adventure holidays of a few weeks – **PVC water bags or sacks** aren't such a good idea, even though they're light, are immune to vibration and take up little room when empty. While a rolled-up 20-litre water sack is certainly a handy back-up, larger bladders as big as you like could be vulnerable to damage and leaks.

Australian and South African outfitters sell **plastic bladders** with a tap on a hose which lie across the rear footwell of a station wagon, but these are more suited to family weekends out bush rather than months on the road. If you're set on this idea check out the water bladders from marine outfitters like Plastimo. In capacities up to 200 litres and costing around 50p a litre, the PVC bladder is protected in a nylon envelope, giving better resistance to abrasion and punctures.

An 18-litre Swiss army bag; about £15 and a handy back-up or day bag.

In-built water tanks

As with fuel, built-in water tanks provide a single water storage solution
that works best in conjunction with an
electric or manual pump rather than a
gravity feed. Unless such a **tap** is fitted over a sink inside, it's more common to have the outlet outside the
vehicle, where it can drip harmlessly,
even if it's less convenient and can be
prone to ice or gunge. Robust plastic
tanks in various sizes and capacities
are available from caravan or boating
outlets or from plastic-moulding
manufacturers (see the fuel tank ideas

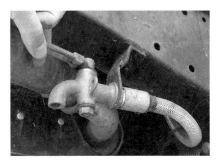

Outdoor tap; handy with a fixed bottle of
squirt soap nearby, too.

earlier). Don't forget a **breather** so that the pressure remains ambient.
Without it any pump will eventually have a heart attack trying to suck water
from the sealed container.

Your water tank will be taking on unfiltered water so choose one with a
plate-sized **inspection cover** for cleaning and flushing out. After a few months
you'll want to clean and disinfect it with bleach or something like Sanogene
(chlorine dioxide).

The back of a vehicle isn't an ideal place for this heavy weight, even if it's
most convenient. As with fuel, water is best positioned low and between the
axles, ideally on the floor **behind the front seats**. All water tanks are best
mounted inside away from damage and ambient temperatures, including heat
from the engine and exhaust, as well as pipe-damaging frost. A pressure-sensitive **electric pump** (which starts when a tap is opened) is easily plumbed in
but, as with fuel, think about breathers, ease of replenishment, pump maintenance as well as a secure, vibration-proof fixing. Ratchet tie-downs can be a
semi-permanent fitting to gain access to a gearbox or fuel-pump hatch.

Try and anticipate how you can most easily **fill the tank** without spillage
or transferring it laboriously from bucket to tank. Refilling can often be done
by hose from a garage, though you also need to be prepared to use a lake, river
or a well, where pumps can help. Use a big tank filler hose (6cm or 2.5") with
minimal curves so large volumes can easily and quickly be poured in from a
bucket or via some sort of funnel, if necessary.

With a tank mounted inside the vehicle, an exterior **filler cap** cut into the
body of the car works best, although, with
a five-door station wagon, refilling the
tank with a hose through a rear door
works too. Carry a spare filler cap if it's
unattached; it's easy to put it on the roof,
get distracted by what you could have
sworn was Penelope Cruz flying past on a
pterodactyl, and forget to refit the cap
until you notice water sloshing out down
the road.

**Carry a spare filler
cap, it's easy to get
distracted by what you
could have sworn was
Penelope Cruz flying
past on a pterodactyl,
and forget to refit it.**

Where to sleep

It may just be camping, but it's both worthwhile and possible to sleep as comfortably as you would at home. Overland travel is tiring and you're a lot more likely to make bad decisions or fall out with your companions if you're not sleeping well. Some of us like to rough it, but your set-up needs to be such that you *look forward* to going to bed. As with some days, not every night will be a winner; humidity, insects, barking dogs, fear of marauding dacoits or just a gaggle of inquisitive locals – all can undermine your much needed recharge.

The options include sleeping on the **ground** tent, in a **roof** tent, or **inside**. In, on or out, remember that not every single night will be by your vehicle. You're bound to crack and walk into a hotel room once in a while. To help narrow down your options, begin by considering the following points in no particular order.

Climate, seasons and altitude

Temperature varies between seasons but also with altitude. It's often easier to keep warm – even in a ground tent on snow – than to keep cool inside a vehicle, especially in the tropics and with all the doors open. Pop-top campers and roof tents with flimsy fabric sides can also get pretty cold.

Space

As many Japanese businessmen who've had one too many will know, it's possible to sleep in a capsule not much bigger than a coffin. You may think that a mattress on a board two feet below the roof of your van is all the space you need, but the limited headroom, if not the claustrophobia, may get to you after a while, and this includes the 'overcab' or Luton extensions that tend to accommodate beds. You'll want to do more than sleep on your bed, so try and provide sufficient space for that.

Comfort and convenience

Particularly if you're a couple, save the Thermarests and sleeping bags for a hiking expedition. It may take up space but a proper **foam mattress** plus domestic bedding, including a **duvet and pillows** are infinitely more homely. So are reading lights and storage space once tucked in and most importantly, **ventilation**. Inside a vehicle an overhead hatch that can open right out is best and small fans can be handy if it's really stifling.

Privacy

Rare will be the night spent all alone on the starry steppes with only the cries of distant wolves as a lullaby. Your rig will always attract attention. Inside and behind some curtains can feel a lot less exposed than in a tent. And no matter how much you enjoy the idea of adventure travel, there'll be days you want to shut out the world around you and not just zip up a flap.

Security

Dozing in its pyjamas, any animal can feel vulnerable and this often worries overlanders in the early days. It's one reason there's so much agonising over whether to sleep inside or outside, or with or without a walk-through from cabin to cab. In fact security has much more to do with common sense and luck, than whether you're in a ground tent or perched on a Unimog surrounded by tripwires. Your canniness in choosing good camp spots is also a factor.

Noise

A thickly insulated GRP box will be the quietest bedroom on wheels, if not always the coolest. And any worldly traveller knows the benefits of **ear plugs**, be it in a noisy jungle or in a downtown hotel with paper-thin walls.

Access and bed deployment

This is something that's easily underestimated. Overlanders are generally on the move most days, unlike weekenders, who park up in a campground and put their feet up by the esky. Clearing stuff out of the way and re-arranging seating to make a bed in your compact campervan, erecting a fiddly ground tent and even hauling out a roof tent and hanging the ladder can all get onerous at the end of a bad day. It's here that a fixed spacious bed has its blessings.

A back-up tent

If you plan on sleeping in or on the vehicle, a lightweight ground tent is still worth carrying. It can be used as a mozzie dome in a grim hotel room, while your car gets the head gasket fixed, and there may be hot nights out bush when a separate inner tent will certainly be cooler and offer better insect protection than the stuffy vehicle interior. A self standing tent can work as a roof tent too. You may never use it but it's worth the space.

A freestanding tent is easy to move with the shade and can even be pitched in a room.

CONVERTING A VEHICLE

A heavy canvas ground tent. Imagine hauling that thing out every day.

GROUND TENTS

There's no need to buy something that weighs just 1019g but is tough enough to survive an avalanche off the north face of Rakaposhi. About £50 will get you a decent two-person ground tent for occasional use and with a 2-metre-square floor area. Twice that price ought to be the limit as you're not looking for the weight savings and added quality that come as tent prices rise exponentially. You need to find a middle way between price, bulk, quality and weight. Some roof-tent manufacturers now offer small ground tents made from the same heavy canvas fabric that weigh nearly 30kg, like something Livingstone might have had portaged for him. On a roof tent that swings up effortlessly that's acceptable, not on a ground tent you have to pitch and repack every day.

If you know no better, choose a self-supporting, cross-pole geodesic tent that doesn't rely too much on guy ropes and tent pegs to stay up (but has them for windy conditions). A tent like this is spacious and can be picked up and moved around to make the most of any shade; it will stand up in soft sand and on a hard floor where pegs can't be used, such as in a ruined building or the aforementioned mozzie-infested hotel room.

Go for a tent with more **space** than you need; two people will appreciate the volume and height of at least a three-person tent. In a car the extra kilo won't break your Camel Trophy 110's back and will make camping altogether much less of a chore, especially in bad weather.

If you like the self-standing mozzie-net idea, choose a tent where the **inner tent** is made of airy gauze rather than merely unproofed fabric, and one where the inner clips onto the cross poles rather than has the poles slide into sleeves; it makes pitching so much simpler. Those cheap self-erecting 'flip-out' tents sold by Decathlon in Europe are fun, but the inner and outer cannot be separated and the bigger sizes need pegging down under tension to adopt the correct form. You can manage with rocks or jerricans, but these bigger flip tents lack any rigidity and will flop around in heavy winds like washing on a line even with the guy lines. Whatever tent you choose, you can greatly extend the life of the built-in ground sheet by using a **protector sheet** under it; it keeps the underside of the tent ground sheet cleaner too, which helps when packing up.

One good trick to making a ground tent work is to use a proper thick **mattress** (see p184). Get away from the backpacking mentality and buy yourself a length of open-cell foam up to four inches thick; cut it to fill the floor of your tent and fit it in a thick, washable cotton cover. Sure they're bulky but you'll use these mats much more than you think.

The chief drawback of sleeping on the ground is that ideally you'll want a **smooth, flat, dry area** which limits where you camp more than you think. And so it's something that's usually undertaken by travellers in a regular car packed to the gills.

ROOF TENTS

The idea of a quickly deployable tent securely mounted on the roof of a car goes back to the 1950s, when Autohome in Italy introduced their original models in both hardshell and later fabric (German Autocamp make similar claims). Today Autohome roof tents are much admired among recreationalists and adventurers, particularly in their **hardshell** Maggiolina and Columbus incarnations.

Roof tents: flip up and hop right in, although the desert is one environment where a tent is less essential.

Over the decades the idea was developed less expensively in South Africa by brands like Eezi-Awn Howling Moon, Hannibal and Technitop, and now Chinese knock-offs sell for half the price of the brands they imitate. These knock-offs reinvigorated the market because **prices** from £1000 for a fold-out fabric tent can baffle those who'd as happily sling a £20 cheapie on a roof-rack board. The appeal may not be initially obvious, but part of it lies in the instant transformation from anonymous box into ready-made bed, as well as the 'tree-house' aspect which satisfies our primal need for a secure nighttime shelter when away from home. Banging your head while rearranging the insides of your campervan into a mattress just isn't the same, because it sure is nice to get right out of the car once a day, even if it only means getting on top of it. The high cost and **weights** of over 70kg (150lb) don't seem to discourage buyers, and many owners go on to profess a deep attachment with their RTTs (roof-top tents).

Broadly speaking RTTs comes in **two styles**: smooth hardshells made of either GRP or ABS plastic and which look like a slick, aerodynamic roof box when closed. Or the bulkier fabric fold-outs which reach out over the back, side or less usefully, the bonnet of your vehicle (if it has one).

Whatever type of roof accommodation you opt for, you'll obviously need a strong **roof rack** or pair of roof bars capable of supporting the weight of two adults. Make sure the access **ladder** is stable, adjustable, easy to deploy and comfortable on bare feet. Also remember that you'll need to park the vehi-

> **It sure is nice to get right out of the car once a day, even if it only means getting on top of it.**

cle as **level** as possible; the slightest incline can upset your sleeping. Roof tents are well suited to African travel, but are less ideal in temperate or sub-arctic climates.

Hard or soft, roof tents are fun and many initially timid travellers are commonly appreciative of the feeling of security they offer. Now there are many cheapies on the market, it pays to do your **research carefully** and if you can, try and inspect one at an overlanding show for example (see p220). Be aware too of vehicle **height limits** if you're planning to ship via container in the course of your travels.

Autohome Columbus.

Hardshell roof tents

Hardshell roof tents have a full-length base attached to roof bars or a rack, and either a lid that lifts vertically with hand cranks or is assisted by gas-struts, or a taller, hinged wedge that springs up on gas struts, such as on Autohome's Columbus, Autocamp's Freelife and Hannibal's Impi.

The single-skin sides are made with inexpensive canvas or lighter synthetics like Dralon that claim to be waterproof and breathable. They're comparatively poor insulators in cold weather and, as with all tents, you'll want a secondary layer of **mosquito netting** over any doors and windows.

As crucial is the **insulation** in the plastic shell's two halves. During the night our bodies release water vapour as sweat and exhaled breath which can recondense as water droplets on cool, smooth surfaces – just as our warm breath condenses inside a car windscreen on a cold morning. The inside of a roof tent's plastic shell is prone to unseen condensation below the mattress and behind the ceiling lining, creating dampness and eventually mildew and musty odours. Ways round this include introducing thick laminates and air cavities into the shells, and raising the mattress off the base's plastic surface with an open-cell mesh or lattice to allow air to flow, rather like a futon-bed pallet (more on p184). Making a GRP moulding with a hinge is easy enough, making a condensation-minimising shell suitable for sleeping in something else and, along with build quality, is what separates near-identical roof tents as well as racking up the cost and weight.

Benefits of a hardshell roof tent add up to:
- The bed, complete with pillows, sheets is always made up.
- There can be some cargo space up there for other light items.
- Opening and closing can all be easily done from ground level.
- The shell creates far less drag and noise than a fold-over.
- In high winds they don't flap like some complex fold-out.

Drawbacks include:
- Hardshells typically take up the full roof length of a 4x4 wagon or van.
- Lack of a canopy over the entrance and windows on some models makes getting in and out during rain tricky.
- Lacks the overhangs of fold-out RTTs, which allow a bit more versatility in design (ground-level vestibules and the like).
- They're up to double the weight and often more than double the price of a fabric fold-out.
- In all three axes, hardshells can still be on the small side. Low-volume examples like a crank-up Maggiolina means a warmer tent, worth considering if you're staying north or going high.

Despite these drawbacks once you've 'gone hard' it's rare to return to the fold-out lifestyle, particularly when you've pinned down a good set-up inside the vehicle and have an awning that can be deployed with as little fuss.

Fold-out roof tents

These two-skin roof tents, originally made of heavy canvas with a steel frame unfolding from a plywood base, have been dubbed 'African' RTTs on account of their provenance as well as the 'safari' look, which suits a rugged 4x4 so much better than the slick, parmesian wedge of a Columbus. It's also no coincidence that they're at home in African conditions, which rarely get cold, so reducing the chances of dampness.

Of the several South African brands, Eezi-Awn seem to have the

An airy hardshell side flip roof tent; the shade element is always handy.

best reputation for build-quality and materials, although Italian manufacturer Autohome also produces three fold-out models and everyone, including the Taiwanese, are now on the bandwagon.

With all overlanding tents bigger is better as you may end up spending days living there waiting for something to pass. The best fold-outs want to be at least **1.4m (55″) wide** inside and hang off the vehicle's roof on a board supported by the ladder. Generally a **rear or side overhang** is more useful than over the front as the overhead projection protects you from sun or rain and creates a useful vehicle-side working area. As with an awning, a side overhang is best fitted to open over the passenger side of the vehicle.

Deploying a fold-out RTT isn't always as easy as with something like an AirTop. Once a cover is removed and any straps undone, you need to grab an attached ladder or strap to unfurl the tent. With the ladder adjusted and possibly fitting rods or guys to support canopies, you can climb in. These rods or poles are better made in bendable alloy rather than snap-prone fibreglass, while added tensioners should reduce the amount of flapping which can get quite annoying with some RTTs.

Having **bedding** as well as a fitted mattress can be a challenge as the whole deal is designed to be folded over onto itself with no room to spare and when packing up may require ungainly bouncing around on top, evoking Marilyn Monroe closing the overstuffed suitcase in a scene from *Some Like it Hot*. Room for bedding can be made by using a more squishy mattress, or self-inflating items from the likes of Thermarest or Exped – although topping these inflatables up is one more thing to do. There's more on this over the page.

Other **features to look out for on a fold-out** RTT include:
- Easy deployment and packing, ideally by one person.
- A marine-ply base: a good insulator which ought not warp for years.
- Solid roof attachment. Cheap racks can creep backwards on the move.
- Canvas inners breathe well but synthetic flys are lighter and dry fast.
- A full flysheet well separated from the inner to keep the inside cooler.
- Doors that zip from the top, better for venting and privacy.
- Doors at both ends for good ventilation and views.

CONVERTING A VEHICLE

SLEEPING INSIDE THE VEHICLE

Sleeping inside a 4x4 or van can get cramped and claustrophobic, but has the benefit of a lower profile, literally, and, short of finding yourself in a typhoon, gives you full protection from whatever the weather throws at you. Unless your vehicle is loaded to the roof (in which case it's overloaded, go back ten spaces), you should be able to squeeze in the back for the odd night. This is a useful option if you just can't be bothered with the tent for whatever reason.

If sleeping inside is the permanent plan, you'll need a strong, flat surface or a permanently fitted board or one that slides or swings down into position. A fixed **bed-board** enables you to stop and just crawl in the back for a rest or even lie there while being driven – always handy if one of you has come down with the *durchfall*. Boards that slide out must usually be in several parts, but on a hardtop can be stacked on top of each other or in a hinged 'accordion' pile behind the front seats to unfold or slide onto unobtrusive side supports.

On a relatively long and narrow Land Rover Defender or Troop Carrier this works well, but wider cars will need heavy, strong boards if they're not to collapse under your combined weight. The idea behind having **built-in storage systems** is that the strong containers or frame is designed to take the weight of sleeping adults, in some cases with just the addition of a couple of boards. For ideas on making a permanent bed in a bigger cabin see p229.

CONVERTING A VEHICLE

IS IT SAFE?

Snippets from a discussion on the HUBB.

I still don't get the safety thing? You wake up surrounded by an angry mob who want to rob (or worse) you... How difficult is it for them to ensure you cannot drive away? As I experienced (not that they wanted to rob me, they just wanted to ensure they got me immobilised enough to see what I was about), all it took was a few 30cm high logs! In more open terrain playing with the tyres would be equally effective.

If it is just a smash/grab/run-type confrontation then you are better in a rooftop tent anyway! After a day behind the wheel the last thing I want to do is sleep inside the car. Much as I love my Troopie there is a limit!!! If I was overlanding for weeks on end there is no way I could contemplate being inside the vehicle at night.

I think if you are inside a vehicle there is more of a psychological barrier to someone trying to rob you, or am I just kidding myself so I feel safer?! The time and noise for someone to break into a car and rob you allows you some degree of preparation (I always sleep with a handy implement when rough camping), whereas a tent can be slashed in virtual silence, as can you!

The reality is most robbers/muggers want a quiet life. They are opportunist thieves who want to get away with as little effort as possible and the threat of serious physical violence is likely to put them off, and you can only do that if you are awake! This of course wouldn't apply to a crazed crack-head in New York, who will take you on at the slightest provocation and kill you if you threaten any kind of resistance! So it's better to just hand everything over. Personally I would rather be awake to make those decisions rather than asleep while someone makes them for me.

Also, inside the vehicle you [can make] good your escape, unless they have fenced you in with large and inanimate objects as per the previous post, but at least it is an option, which you probably won't have if you are stuck up on the roof.

Having said all that, you will probably not have enough room in the vehicle to sleep anyhow. I have camped in tents and I don't really like it, I never feel completely secure. I don't in a vehicle either, but I do feel better than in a tent, although a girlfriend once stayed awake all night when we slept in the back of my 101, terrified something would happen. Needless to say the relationship didn't last long after that!

RAISED OR LIFTING ROOFS

Increasing headroom to suit a standing adult either requires a permanent **raised roof extension** – typically a professionally fitted GRP canopy – or some sort of hinged or articulated **lifting roof**. These latter have evolved over the years to become as effortless as possible but it can get tiresome spending much time in such a confined space. Cooped up during a rainy spring in Georgia waiting for an Iranian visa may bring out an epidemic of cabin fever.

Removing or cutting a hole in your vehicle's roof and adding an attic is not a job to be taken lightly, especially with something like an alloy-panel-bodied Land Rover Defender. Even in a steel-bodied vehicle some torsional rigidity will be lost and so a strengthening frame may need to be fitted around the aperture before the raised GRP roof and its own gutter frame are mounted and sealed. Overall, it's something best left to the professional **outfitters** who manufacture them.

As with tents on a regular roof, substantial **roof storage** is often lost, although the alloy checkerplate cappings or thick GRP ought to carry heavy loads, and are better off lifting with hydraulic assistance.

Fabric sides are very agreeable in tropical environments – much more so than a GRP cabin – but it's

From top: **1.** The famous Dormobile side lift on an old Land Rover. **2.** Wedge lift Kombi; another classic camping car. **3.** Heavy checkerplate wedge conversion on a Troop Carrier.

also important to recognise the **heat loss** and possible waterproofing issues during cold weather or storms. Without some sort of insulating jacket, any cabin heating would be wasted.

In this type of climate a **fixed raised roof** is better; it requires no deployment and offers a warmer and more secure interior. The big disadvantage is these don't fit in a shipping container or indeed in an underground car park, but as has already been mentioned, you can see a lot of the world without resorting to containering. It might be assumed that fuel consumption may be affected, but I suspect the smooth profile of a Britz-type camper as pictured on p82 has less drag than a regular 4x4 with a roof tent, a spare tyre and a Zarges box or two.

CONVERTING A VEHICLE

Mattresses in several parts make for easier storage and moving about. On this wedge roofed conversion, the three white slats below slide out to make a high bed platform.

MATTRESSES AND BEDDING

Wherever you decide to sleep – on the ground, in the vehicle or on the roof – you'll have fewer regrets doing so on a **high-density, deep-foam mattress**. At least 80mm or 3" thick and made of open-cell foam, they're bulky to store and, in the UK at least, are pricey but can be as comfortable as a proper bed.

Avoid foam mattresses in vinyl sleeves supplied with some roof tents; they're sweaty and suitable only for travellers still needing nappies. Instead, make a close-fitting case for the mattress from washable, comfortable but snag-proof material such as heavy-duty cotton or upholstery fabric.

Before you sew the sleeve, think about how you're going to store a mattress if it's not laid out full time. Finding a good place can be a problem. A full-length mattress of two metres can be cut into two unequal sections (the longer section matching the width of the car) and a fold sewn into the sleeve. This enables the two mattresses to stack on top of each other relatively compactly.

Even with a natural fabric sleeve, foam mattresses get clammy by the morning so, like all the bedding, are worth **airing**. Hang them out while making breakfast.

Air beds and lilos take up much less room but are also less comfortable and require daily inflation. Anything inflatable will also be sweaty and with double-sized air beds the lighter person will roll into the dip occupied by the heavier one – not always desirable, even with loving couples. **Individual airbeds** are better but overall on a long trip choose a covered foam mattress if you're planning to sleep in the vehicle frequently.

Like big air beds, **camp beds** are another blast from the past, even bulkier than mattresses and not that comfortable anyway. On dry ground they offer no particular advantage and allow cool air to pass underneath, which is desirable only in the heat of summer when hard packed earth retains its heat and actually warms you up – very unpleasant! If getting away from crawling insects is a priority, sleeping in a zipped-up tent, in the car or on the roof is one solution.

Make the most of sleeping comfort and go the whole hog with **bedding**: a duvet (eiderdown or quilt with pillows is so much nicer than a synthetic-skinned sleeping bag. The latter may be warmer and more compact, but limits leg movement which, depending on how you sleep, makes you ache in the mornings. Some brands zip out to make nearly a double duvet, or zip together into one large covering for two – a better way of keeping warm.

A duvet, sheet and pillows can be easily rolled up into a bundle, strapped up and thrown anywhere in the back or in a dustproof container on the roof.

While you're here don't forget to think about some well positioned and low draw lighting, ventilation as well as knick-knack storage.

CONVERTING A VEHICLE

AWNINGS

Although a roof tent's overhang can have the same effect at either end of the day, you won't regret getting an awning. Out in the wilds you'll always find you gravitate towards shade or shelter of some sort for a lunch break and so, for the occasions when nothing turns up, an awning can make stops or longer camps much more agreeable.

A quickly deployable awning will be used rain *and* shine.

To be fully useful a **3-metre**- or 12-ft-square surface area is best, giving enough shade for up to four people without having to shuffle around as the sun inches round or the rain lashes down.

I once made the mistake of using an old plastic tarpaulin I'd had lying around for years to make an awning; a **heavier natural fibre** would have been much less noisy and may have flapped less, as I found when spending a couple of days under an Eezi-Awn awning. Don't underestimate the effect of a daytime breeze outside of tropical areas: it'll make your awning flap and crack irritatingly as well as come adrift if not secured properly. The simplest **anchoring method** is a pair of poles in each corner, held in place by a guy line pegged or weighed down. Choose long, wide pegs for sand and bang them right in; in rocky terrain anything will do, including a rock.

Making your own awning has its benefits but here's an example where you'll be pleased you spent the money on a proper, quickly deployed awning. What counts is speed and ease of use, stability in winds and overall build quality which all adds up to the ability to be used daily and survive heavy winds day after day.

Choose an awning that **rolls out of a tube** like a shop front and drops two legs out; these support the weight without the need for guy lines. In most conditions short of a gale this should do. All around the sheet should be a **frame** to provide tension to the fabric and reduce flapping.

In the bigger sizes these are easily available and may be the best £200 you'll spend on your vehicle. Be wary of anything that **retracts automatically** on a spring; it's bound to break eventually. Better to spend the extra 30 seconds it takes to roll it up and clip it in.

The entirely free-standing awnings as pictured right are neat in that there are no poles or guylines in the way, but they need to be well built to take the strain or even the lightest gusts.

Clever, umbrella-like self supporting awning offers masses of shade providing the wind doesn't get up.

CONVERTING A VEHICLE

CONVERTING A VEHICLE

Packing and storage

Until you've tried it, it's difficult to visualise day-to-day life on the road, which is why a **test trip** is such a good idea. Just a single weekend's camping with a full 24-hour cycle of driving, stopping, eating, washing and sleeping can be long enough to assess your access, cooking and sleeping arrangements. Once the days on the road become weeks you can expect to refine further your systems. Try and visualise your **daily chores** in the order that they happen: getting up, having a wash, cooking and eating breakfast, putting it away, vehicle check or maintenance if necessary, breaking camp up and moving on, then a stop for lunch or to visit a market (where vehicle security might be an issue), and finally making camp for the next night.

The diagram below shows an ideal layout for distributing your gear, based on density and frequency of use. In a nutshell, heavy items should be packed low and between the axles, while regularly used items should be accessible without having to move anything out of the way. The principle is that nothing becomes too buried to discourage use when it's needed, be it a map, a jack, electrical spares or some medicine. As with all the ideas in this book, don't pull your hair out trying to duplicate this graphic exactly. For a start they don't make Ford Anglia's anymore and the diagram is just a guide to what works best, but may not always be easy or cost effective to put into practice on your vehicle.

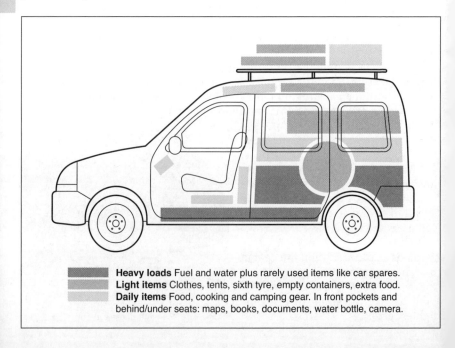

Heavy loads Fuel and water plus rarely used items like car spares.
Light items Clothes, tents, sixth tyre, empty containers, extra food.
Daily items Food, cooking and camping gear. In front pockets and behind/under seats: maps, books, documents, water bottle, camera.

One more important thing to consider is how all this gear will react **in the event of a crash**, particularly a head-on into a tree, ditch or another vehicle. A separate compartment is safer as with gear stacked loosely behind you, even a light shunt can end badly if a chopping board flies into the back of your head. Be very conscious of what loose items you have rolling around

behind you. A **cargo barrier or dog grill** (above) is a great idea but gets in the way, even if it's hinged. Better to design a system and then follow a procedure where nothing deadly can fly forward when the vehicle stops suddenly or rolls over.

PACKING SYSTEMS

Heading off to drive across a continent isn't quite like taking off for a fortnight's road trip. You must organise and carry a temporary home in your vehicle for the next few months so your goal is to store everything as efficiently as possible, trying to ensure that everyday items are easily accessible, that everything is secure and protected against damage from other items and rough roads, and that the weight is kept low.

Let's assume you're starting with the cavernous interior of a standard, unadapted vehicle with no rear seats, most probably a van or 4x4 hardtop. If you've bought any sort of camper or an already modified vehicle you can skip this bit, and if you have a regular car or five-door station wagon your options are more limited. Broadly speaking you've got two options: underneath a bed platform, or mounted on the sides of the vehicle.

On the floor, underneath

'Underneath' usually means under a full-width shelf on which you can sleep, otherwise it's just 'in the back'. This sort of system usually consists of a tightly packed nest of compartmentalised plastic crates or longer drawers sliding either on the metal floor, a wooden board or, less noisily, a carpeted base. If sleeping inside the vehicle then a platform works best in taller vehicles like larger vans or a Troop Carrier which has more headroom than most.

Even if using a tent, a platform to crawl onto during the day and, more importantly, as a cargo barrier to stop the stuff from jumping around. For this reason a platform is best properly fixed to the sides, either semi-permanently or with clips and hinges. In the event of a shunt nothing more lethal than possibly your bedding ought to hurtle forward.

DIY plywood platform. On the road easily fixed.

CONVERTING A VEHICLE

The drawback can be that it's difficult to get at the stuff that's out of reach, so that's the place to put things you rarely need, be it heavy engine spares or interior tanks for fuel or water that are filled via external fillers. Alternatively, certain **rarely used, non-fragile items** like radiator hoses can be stashed right out of the way between the body panels of the rear wings. Larger items like spare shocks can be attached securely under the body to chassis rails if present, or behind bumpers. Use zip ties and wire backed up with duct tape.

A good way to get to hard-to-reach areas under the sleeping platform is to **divide the bed board into three parts**, as shown in the mattress picture on p184. The middle portion can be more permanently fixed, but both front and rear sections want to be liftable to provide access to both areas front and back, which sure beats sliding boxes out of the back just to get to that tin of beans you're craving. If you choose to do it this way, make sure you come up with a foolproof support like the stick that holds up the hood of a car, so you can rummage around with both arms without fear of getting bashed.

Crates and boxes

Plastic crates or boxes are a light, simple and cheap way of compartmentalising your gear in the back, the key to well-organised packing and storage. It should also mean that no one crate is too heavy to pick up and that, up to a point, same-sized crates can be simply swapped around as needs change. People often get crates with attached plastic **lids** but, apart from items that want to remain dust-free, the underside of the bed board should be all the lid you need; a crate lid is just another thing that gets in the way.

It doesn't hurt to colour code **label** your crates for easy identification or make a map with a list of the stuff you bury deeply, hopefully never to use. On your crate map identify the contents of distant crates so that in the stressful event of needing to retrieve your OBD II reader you can look at your treasure map and know where to start digging.

Be wary of the **under-bed crates** you might buy at somewhere like Ikea – they're not necessarily up to the beating and yanking they'll get on the road. When you just want to get at something, you don't want to come away with just a plastic handle in your hands. Better to find something chunkier that's designed to be reused. Definitely avoid crates that fold up and collapse, they're way too flimsy, or crates that stack into themselves like buckets; vertical-sided containers don't waste space and lock together better.

Cheap hardware store stackable plastic crates. Better for shorter trips.

Banana boxes may sound like a joke but I got the idea from a German veteran whose boxes were on their sixth African outing. Banana boxes are free, strong, an ideal size and rattle-proof. I still use them on shorter trips, but you couldn't expect them to last more than a few months.

Some people like tough aluminium **Zarges boxes** or plastic Pelicases designed to protect filming gear. Certainly cameras or other fragile gear are best stored in such a sealed container, but putting all your stuff into heavy alloy or plastic cases fitted with decompression valves is a bit over the top, unless you're expecting some very deep rivers.

You can put all these either directly on the vehicle floor, sliding on metal rails on the floor, or fit a half-inch sheet of plywood. Plywood adds more scope for custom fittings such as rails, partitions or lashing points without unnecessary drilling into the vehicle floor. It's unlikely that the crates you find will perfectly fill the space between the sides or wheel arches of your vehicle so, among other options, wooden or metal **rails** or taller partitions fixed to the plyboard can help keep the boxes in position, and partitions work well when lined with carpet tiles to reduce rattling.

Lashing down and preventing rattles

Unsecured items that rub against each other and **rattle** can drive you nuts – not to mention the mess that occurs when packaging splits or breaks. I once drove a Land Rover like this, and with every bump the contents of the cupboards would lift weightlessly like Chuck Yeager at the zenith of his supersonic arc… and then crash back down with a wince-inducing clatter.

Unless you're using a pickup and canopy, where you're oblivious to the din, you need to get on top of rattling at the construction stage. If you don't know how at the point of departure, then after a few weeks on the road you'll learn the hard way to pack food thoughtfully. Even tightly screwed glass jar lids can undo themselves after a day of washboard. Short of pulling a tie-down over each row of boxes, the best way I've found to seal and jam the boxes into place from the back is a big pillow or thick piece of foam against the back door

Unless you're racing, **fittings** and straps don't have to be enormously strong, just sufficient to constrain the containers. Quick-release straps make access and, more importantly, relocation effortless – often overlooked when you're packing up in the morning or in a rush. Stronger ratchet straps or tie-downs have hooks and can hold anything from a tyre to a motorbike on a trailer. Elastic bungees may not be strong but have a multitude of uses just to bundle things up or stop light things rolling about. Carry an excess of **straps, bungees and tie-downs**: long, short, thin, wide, ratchet, quick-release and something 50mm-wide and chunky for really big jobs. They're always useful but tend to get lost or wear through.

Cargo drawer systems

A **roll-out roller drawer system** works like well-made kitchen drawers. Made from steel or alloy and lined with fabric, they're often combined with vibration-proof roll-out fridge platforms and cater for well-heeled off-roaders.

Try and make a set yourself and you'll soon realise that maybe they're not so expensive after all, because anything more complex than a sheet of plywood fixed to the vehicle body needs to be designed to stay there through thick and thin. Remember, the bodies of vans and 4x4s which are rubber-mounted on a ladder chassis will flex incrementally, and when they've done so for a few weeks all your amateur fabrication may start to come apart. A friend who once drove a ratty Mercedes bus to India admitted that by the time he got there everything he'd built himself had fallen apart, and everything

CONVERTING A VEHICLE

CONVERTING A VEHICLE

Main picture: Grass-effect lockable roller drawers. © Nina Alton **Inset**: DIY sliding drawers.

from Mercedes was still intact – and that was just the main road to India, which he could have driven in an Austin Maxi with two-tone vinyl armrests. There's plenty more on self-builds starting on p219.

What you get with these cargo drawer systems ought to be something that won't fall apart on the road. Manufacturers often boast that three grown men can stand on an extended drawer, but how often will you do that? What matters is a smoothly operating system and the certainty that the frame (if not the contents) won't rattle or come apart, something's that's much more irritating with metal than plastic, wood or papier mâché.

Australian and South African desert tracks being what they are, you can be fairly sure the better manufacturers in both those countries have thought this through. Doing it well all adds weight and expense but brings with it an effortless ease of use that you'll appreciate. The bigger and longer the drawer, the more weight ends up on the rollers and so the heavier the frame. One problem I encountered with such systems are loose things inside jamming the drawer shut against a frame. It took a bit of fiddling about with a coat hanger to get the drawer open, and is something that wouldn't have happened with the more basic crate system.

Motorhome-style cabinets can make for a neater look inside and may be the answer if you have more money than time.

Small plastic crates. Inset: Drawer-free 'cubby hole' system. More suited to a separate cabin.

CONVERTING A VEHICLE

Storage on the sides

The advantage of a **wall-mounted storage system** is that it's accessible all of the time like your kitchen back home. With a smaller vehicle, if you're running a roof tent or some sort of pop-top camper body, fit cupboards to one side so there's room on the other to crouch inside the vehicle on the wheel arch on inclement days. Doing it this way involves more work than scooting around Ikea eyeing up chunky crates. Unlike crates, the system will have to carry its own weight as well as the contents and is really best left to a good craftsman who has the time or skills to do the job well. If you manage to acquire a vehicle set up in this way so much the better.

Other stowage ideas and places

You can never have enough stowage areas and your cab should have the things you need most often at hand. Inexpensive **elastic nets** are easily fitted to any vertical or overhead surface and are great for stuffing documents out of the way but in sight.

A shelf or console across the width of the car above the windscreen is another good idea. Although they've never really caught on elsewhere, in Australia they make fitted ones for all the popular 4x4s and are commonly used to house HF radios for outback comms.

ROOF RACKS AND ROOF BARS

Purists used to disapprove of roof racks as they encouraged overloading – and overloading in the worst possible place where it affects stability as well as factory designed streamlining. Be that as it may, a roof rack frees up space in the vehicle and enables bulky and messy or smelly clutter to be kept out of the way, so greatly improving interior accessibility and ambience.

Strive to use a rack only to store light, bulky and low-value items, not fuel and water or regularly used things. Remember too that the weight of a bare rack, let alone the baggage, will increase fuel consumption by at least 10%. On a LWB 4x4 or any station wagon the rack will need at least six support feet a few inches long. Whatever's loaded on the roof, try and keep the frontal profile low to minimise drag, and streamline containers where possible. Heavy loads like occasional jerricans are best fixed at the rear of a rack and away from the windscreen where the body is stronger and flexes less. In the case of fuel, it also means it's easy to get to or even siphon down to the tank filler.

Fitting a roof rack

Though heavier, roof racks have the advantage over roof bars in that they have a peripheral frame, which makes getting up as well as lashing items down less chancy. Fitting a marine plywood **baseboard** to the rack keeps the sun from heating the roof of the car and also helps spread the load (including your own when up there). The wire-mesh alternative that's now commonly used in some places is another way of multiplying your attachment points to near infinity.

Otherwise, if you fit a board yourself, take the chance to measure up and cut a few 5" circular holes where the rack floor's cross members meet. They make effective lashing points for loops of rope and for hooking tie-downs. Another option is screwing something like Slide-n-Lock bars onto the board. Usually used in pickup beds or sides, they can work well on a roof rack or even inside a hardtop.

The alloy gutters of Land Rover Defenders were well known for not being strong enough to carry a substantial load so any hefty rack must have extensions reaching down to the vehicle's steel body parts. Other vehicles' steel guttering should be up to the job provided there's no rust in there and the rack has several broad feet. However, roof gutters are a thing of the past now, so Thule and Rhino Rack, among others, manufacture a range of clamps as well

Bolting to the vehicle is better than welding, and so are solid supports and fixed ladder access.

as aerodynamic roof boxes for every car under the sun. These clamps, most often used with roof bars, can seem insecure so may need checking in the early days.

Note that cracked A pillars and windscreens are common symptoms of overloaded or inadequately supported roof racks. I once travelled in a heavily overloaded 109 and could see the whole body flexing from side to side in the front windscreen frames. On some bends the doors would fly open.

Of course not many people treat their Series IIIs like that anymore, and if you do end up carrying heavy loads on the rack, expect to have to drive much more carefully or pay the price. The owner of a lovely 40-series Toyota I travelled with on another occasion boasted he carried a tonne, much of it on the roof. Halfway through their trans-African trip the top-heavy BJ45 rolled unexpectedly on a smooth dirt road. They ended up sawing off the top half of the car, giving away their excess baggage in an impromptu roadside market and carried on south into the rainy season with a plastic sheet on their heads.

Coincidentally they also committed another mistake in the mounting of their rack that's not so commonly seen today: they attached it both to the roof gutters *and* the chassis. Land Cruisers and many other ladder chassis 4x4s have rubber-mounted bodies to permit the ladder chassis to twist independently of the body. They repeatedly broke gutter mounts without understanding why. With a rubber-mounted body, attach the rack either to the body (roof) or to the chassis, although the latter really is overkill unless you're carrying a water buffalo on the roof. This whole business of acknowledging and allowing for chassis flex is also pertinent to building your own cabin on a torsion-free mounting (more on p224).

Steel or alloy?

Racks of **galvanised steel or alloy** is what most people will be mulling over. 'Steel for strength, aluminium for lightness' is an often-quoted aphorism. **Steel** racks, as have been made by outfits like Brownchurch in the UK since the year dot, are stronger and cheaper but are heavy and rust-prone once scratched. Make sure a steel rack has holes in the tubing so the zinc can get inside. Plastic coating is nicer to handle but will eventually split or get brittle and so encourage rust underneath. Rack for rack, **aluminium alloy** will be either lighter and so less robust, or heavy and expensive.

Racks made of round tubing reduce turbulence and wind noise, as do racks like the alloy Patriots, whose primary support spars run the length of the car rather than across it. **Welded or bolted** should not be that great an issue as long as the rack is either up to overlanding standards or not so overloaded that it needs to be. Steel can be welded in any market town, alloy less easily so but it's a mistake to think a rack must be utterly rigid. The little bit of give in a bolted-together structure will mean it flexes with the vehicle and the vibration. Even steel 4x4 bodies can flex; 80 series Toyotas had a habit of breaking their 'C' pillars when loaded to African levels. The cage or basket may be welded as it's a big enough plane to flex a little but, especially with alloy, having the feet *bolted* to the tray and in turn clamped to the roof will mean the structure lasts much longer. One good thing about roof bars is that their modular arrangement allows for this.

Alloy is light and shiny, but compared to steel tends to fracture. It's one reason why suspension isn't made of alloy and why, for example, a Defender's body was built of alloy panels *bolted* to a steel frame. To make alloy as strong as steel you either have to design it cleverly or TIG weld it carefully, or more commonly, use so much it becomes as heavy as steel, but more expensive. Its real appeal is that it doesn't rust, but then neither does quality steel.

Roof bars

In Australia the trend is to fit light basket racks with a wire mesh floor on roof bars. Again, it adds up to part-time recreational use that's easily demounted. Overlanding for months on end is not the same thing.

Depending on your needs a full-length platform isn't always necessary. A couple of roof bars can carry rarely used gear such as a spare tyre or sand plates. Roof bars can be bought from car accessory shops but are designed for commercial vans, not overlanders. Make sure you get something that has the necessary rigidity and robust mounting clamps. As with all racks the key is wide feet to spread the load and secure mounting brackets. Square-section 50mm aluminium tubing makes a strong and light roof bar while the gutter brackets may be easier bought from a rack manufacturer than made by yourself. If it's a half-length rack fit it at the back where the noise if not the drag will be less prevalent and access (on a tall 4x4 at least) will be easier.

Roof access

If you're dithering about spending the extra for a rack with an **access ladder**, do it, you won't regret it. Even though you might be able to haul yourself up by standing on a bumper, rear tyre top, spare wheel or window sill, one day you'll slip and do yourself an injury. The back corners of Defenders are ideal for access ladders but vehicles with tailgates are more awkward. Ladders hanging from the upper tailgate or on full-width doors put a strain on the hinges and can only work with the door closed or tailgate lowered. But ladders on the side aren't ideal either.

A light and effective solution is to bolt a couple of **rungs** or steps onto the back corner. Many African Land Cruisers have neat Toyota access rungs (below left) bolted to their corners – you can probably buy them out there or get some made. Another is a solid fold-up clamp or I got some inch-deep alloy steps made for my old 60 which worked very well with the rear bumper.

Roof access steps are an alternative to a ladder.

Elementary electrics for overlanders

While moving you from place to place your vehicle generates electricity from the engine spinning an alternator via a belt, just like the water pump. The direct current which the **alternator** produces gets stored in the battery which, as well as powering other things like lights and instruments, enables you to start your vehicle next time by just turning the key.

This is all your vehicle's electrical system was originally designed to do. Once you decide to use your vehicle as a place to live as well as a means of getting around, the extra electrical appliances you'll run mean the standard alternator and battery may not cope. Below are some basics on the electrical system and how you might adapt things in something up to a regular 4x4 – the way most overlanders travel. Beyond that, for tips on wiring up a van or a cabin on a truck, there's more on p230.

Electrical problems

For the vehicle's entire electrical system to operate optimally the alternator must be functioning efficiently, the battery must hold its charge and the mass of wiring that link all the electrical components, in particular the **connections**, must be in good shape: not dirty, rusty, oily, melted or loose. Because having things stay like this for long is a tall order, electrical problems are not uncommon on the road, especially in damp or dusty conditions, or on roads where the vehicle gets a hammering – which pretty much sums up the overland scenario at times. Such failures are exacerbated by your own well-intentioned but possibly poorly executed alterations, or by untested demands on the system. It is these, rather than the vehicle's original wiring, which most commonly fail to perform as well as you'd hope. See p280 for advice on troubleshooting electrical problems.

As with other resources like heating, water, fuel and provisions, electrical power is not always easily accessible to the overlander or available in unlimited supply. Travelling overland rewards a more sustainable and conservation-based attitude to consumption, and never more so then when it comes to electricity because without it you're going nowhere.

ELECTRICITY – DON'T YOU JUST LOVE IT?

Electrical and electronic faults in particular can be infuriatingly inconsistent, most often due to an **intermittent physical contact** that you either painstakingly track down, or may never locate (such as in the inner windings of an alternator or any 'black box' you care to point at). Very often, simply taking something apart, looking at it and then re-assembling it is enough to appease the gods of electron. How long it takes you to get to this point is what can make or waste your day. Accessibility, good wiring practice and the possible need for future fault diagnosis is something to bear in mind when making electrical alterations.

ALTERNATORS – THE CHARGING SYSTEM

The alternator is located behind the radiator to the front and on one side of the engine, where inspection and access are fairly straightforward. In greatly simplified terms, an alternator is a device that is spun by the engine via a belt to produce electricity by means of magnets spinning over densely wound copper windings. You could say an alternator is the inverse of an electric motor, which uses electricity to create mechanical power to turn things like your wipers, windows or starter.

The alternating current produced gets separated or 'rectified' by diodes (one-way electrical 'valves') into direct current (DC) and fed via the regulator to the battery. The regulator makes sure the 12-volt battery isn't getting more than around 14.5 volts and so doesn't get cooked.

Carrying a **replacement alternator** will get you on the road quicker than a local repair. This is the best solution for all alternator problems, particularly if you've no back-up means of battery charging such as solar panels or a mains battery charger, or are driving alone.

Auxiliary and high-output alternators

Just like your engine, alternators can only put out a certain amount of power at maximum rpm. For example an alternator on a Nissan Patrol is rated at around 80 amps. Because an overland vehicle is as much a house as a means of getting around, it needs to run fridges, heaters, water pumps, lights and inverters, let alone door locking and driving lights. A standard alternator may not have the capacity to work all this and charge the batteries under the extreme conditions of maximum usage, in a wintry scenario for example.

If you're planning to run many electrical accessories in your vehicle (quite likely), you need to establish that your alternator is actually putting out the amperage it claims. The best way to do this is with a voltmeter or multimeter (a device for testing electrical circuits and levels), for more see the section on fault diagnosis in alternators, p284. If it's not, one way of optimising an alternator's output is simply to run heavier cabling from the alternator to the

---

SPARE ELECTRICAL COMPONENTS

Fitting an inexpensive **new alternator belt** at the outset is, as they say, a no-brainer. It often drives other important components like the steering- or air-con pumps and even the water pump. Keep the old one as a spare or get a second new one if the original looks cracked or is polished from slipping and age. If you can learn to fit this yourself on a quiet Sunday morning back home, you'll be better prepared when it happens in downtown Bangkok in the Friday rush hour.

As discussed in this section, having a back-up **battery** of one kind or another is a great idea, and the same might be said for taking a spare **alternator**, especially on an older vehicle. To this you can add some bat-tery clamps, lengths of electrical wire in various gauges, electrical connectors and a crimping tool, insulating tape, fuses, bulbs and your trusty multimeter. The full list of spares begins on p288.

All these items, even alternators, are fairly easy to replace by the side of the road with elementary tools, although replacement batteries are of course found wherever there are motor vehicles.

Up to a point, alternators come in a limited range of shapes and sizes and can even be repaired or built up using the good parts from your otherwise faulty item. There's more in the fault diagnosis section on p280.

battery. Just make sure that doing this doesn't exceed the rating of the alternator. Although it's possible to get a standard alternator rewound to increase its output, this is a bit like turbo-charging an aspirated engine – more power means more heat and all alternators get hot doing their job and incorporate an in-built fan. Service life may be reduced – you don't want that.

Better by far to consider an **auxiliary alternator** or replace the original with a higher-output item if your demands are great. The former obviously requires room in the engine bay, most probably on the other side of the cylinder block (often where an air-con compressor might have been) but can be quite a job with the compact design of engines these days.

A **replacement unit** with a higher output will probably be physically bigger and so, again, may cause mounting issues in the available space, and take more engine power to spin (which may affect fuel consumption), but compared to a re-wound unit, at least it's built for it. Both options are more suited to larger 4x4s or trucks, whose engines have space and torque to spare.

BATTERIES

A regular car or truck battery is known as a **starter** or SLI ('starting, lighting, ignition') battery, and is primarily designed to provide the short, powerful burst of power needed to crank an engine from cold; and once that's done, to quickly recover its charge.

Starter batteries are rated in cold cranking amps (CCA) as well as storage capacity given in amp hours (Ah). A heavy-duty 12-volt battery for an old Ford Ranger 2.5 diesel is typically rated at 830CCA and 95Ah – pretty good figures for a small diesel. What it means is the amperage a 12-volt battery can deliver for 30 seconds at 0°F (-18°C) while retaining at least 7 volts at the end of this effort. Don't ask me how I calculated that.

A battery's **reserve capacity rating** (RCR) is another value used and can be considered as significant as Ah. This is the time, given in minutes, that a battery holds a workable voltage under a 25-amp draw before recharging is necessary; 120 minutes is a typically good RCR value for a regular starter battery and is the reason why it goes flat if you leave the lights on overnight. High-CCA starting batteries are relatively inexpensive to manufacture (partly because they use less lead) and are all most drivers require. Batteries with a genuinely high RCR are more costly to make, but can also handle more full discharges before failing completely.

All these figures are unfortunately somewhat hypothetical as **an alternator can never fully charge a normal lead-acid battery**; about 70–80% is as good as it gets, though absorbent glass mat (AGM) batteries as used in electric cars are a little better. Discharging any battery below 50% too frequently will dramatically reduce its life expectancy, leisure or otherwise. And so, as accomplished overlander Stephen Stewart commented on his website (🖳 xor.org.uk): 'Imagine you bought a chocolate bar that was only 70% of the expected weight and you were told it was unsafe to eat the last 50%'.

The **true capacity of your battery** is then rather less than you might think and is what partly explains some operational inadequacies once on the road. As your electrical needs rise the answer is simple: more batteries and recharging sources, both at some considerable expense and weight.

Auxiliary batteries

Because the starter battery is such a vital component, especially with a diesel engine, which requires more effort to turn over than a petrol engine, at least one **additional battery** is a good idea and essential if you're running things like a fridge. For the cost involved, a spare battery gives peace of mind, especially if you're travelling alone or to places where you can't readily flag down

> **For overlanding, a second battery is as indispensable as a spare tyre.**

a passing car. For overlanding, a second battery should be considered as indispensable as a spare tyre.

When camping, a second battery also allows you to run electrical ancillaries without risking flattening the main starter battery. And when trying to start up on a freezing Andean morning, wired up in parallel it can provide an extra boost should the main battery not be up to the job. Unless you're on a good hill, in such an event, jumpstarting with leads from another car is usually the simple answer, as is push- or tow-starting (see Troubleshooting and Repairs, p287). For this reason a pair of jump leads and a tow strap should also be part of your equipment.

Sealed or unsealed batteries

Most of us are familiar with so-called **flooded** or **wet-cell** lead-acid batteries with six caps with gas vents. The evaporating electrolyte in these batteries needs to be monitored and topped up with distilled water once in a while to keep the lead plates submerged, especially when the battery is being charged hard.

Although up to twice the price, sealed batteries do away with this messy

---

24-VOLT SYSTEMS

There was a call to increase the regular car starter-battery standard from 12- to 16- or even 42 volts. However, as anyone who's run a 24-volt Land Cruiser will know, anything out of the ordinary can be a pain with parts, so in all likelihood we'll be driving electric cars long before the world automotive standard for diesel or petrol cars changes to 42 volts.

Like just about all trucks and diesel-engined Land Cruisers, older Range Rovers and some Patrols sold in Europe and possibly Canada have a 24-volt electrical system. With the 4x4s it's primarily to ensure reliable cold-weather starting of the big diesel engines, but it has benefits in terms of efficiency too.

European 60-series Cruisers were 24-volt throughout (including ancillaries right down to bulbs), while 80-series and later Land Cruisers feature a much more parts-friendly combination of 24-volt starting but 12-volt ancillaries. Once one of these batteries gets

tired you're in trouble and it's said that mixing batteries of different CCA and Ah is a bad idea in the long term, but only in that one battery will wear out prematurely. Again, unless you have brand new batteries, it's worthwhile having a **third battery** as a spare. As long as it's not running something demanding like a fridge, I've found a back-up starter battery works fine.

With my 24-volt Land Cruiser I ran a lead off one of the batteries to power a 12-volt socket for small items like a GPS and a stick light, but this isn't a long-term solution suited to overlanding.

Don't get bogged down in installing expensive 24-volt ancillaries just because your vehicle puts out 24 volts; **12-volt automotive or caravanning ancillaries** cost much less. Reducing 24 volts to 12 is much more efficiently done between the alternator and a set of 12-volt house batteries, rather than dropping a 24-volt house battery set-up down to 12 volts.

business while somehow managing not to explode. Use a sealed battery and you'll never have to carry distilled water, worry that acid is leaking out when the vehicle is overturned, or suffer corrosion of the battery tray due to over-filling or fumes.

Sealed batteries with the electrolyte suspended in a gel, or saturated in an **absorbent glass mat (AGM)**, are pricier still, but are much more resilient to the extreme shocks, vibrations and temperature variations that can ruin a cheap wet cell battery. **Overcharging** is more damaging than with regular wet cells so particularly if being recharged by solar panels (which can put out a lot more than 12 volts at times), make sure you fit a voltage regulator.

Leisure batteries

Auxiliary starter batteries can be fitted to run things like fridges, but for this sole purpose more costly **leisure** batteries work better. Also called 'house' batteries to distinguish them from the starter batteries, they're designed for long, slow and very occasionally complete discharging without excessive damage to the thick lead plates. Although the names are often interchanged, genuine **deep-cycle** batteries aren't the same. Deep-cycle batteries can be described as super-leisure batteries, doing everything better, but at a still higher cost.

A leisure battery usually has a higher amp-hour rating at some cost to its cold cranking ability. They're less suited to firing a sluggish 3.6-litre diesel into life and being able to do it again soon. Due to the design, starter or leisure batteries perform one function well, although it's true to say that quality AGM deep-cycle batteries have a pretty high CCA rating and are much better for jumpstarting than old-style wet lead-acid deep-cycle batteries.

As for **which brand**, you'd think you'd get what you pay for and an expensive example from a recognised brand would have superior construction to stop the case cracking or the lead plates inside breaking or shifting while bashing about off road. It doesn't seem to be the case. A no-name battery can last over a decade and expensive sealed 'space shuttle' examples can mysteriously pack up in a few months. That's why, expensive or cheap, any **back-up battery** is such a good idea.

Mounting a second starter battery

As long as there's room, a second battery is best mounted out of the way in the engine compartment. On a bigger vehicle out on the chassis is better. Either way this'll require fitting a **new battery tray** that must be tough enough to take the weight of a battery being shaken up and down on rough roads and tracks. Modern sealed types can weight up to 20kg. A solid location eliminates all movement that can lead to chafed or broken cables, shorts and possible electrical fires. On one 4x4 I used a small second battery as a back-up, but suspected the tray wasn't robust enough. Sure enough the support leg soon poked through the front wheel arch.

Second battery – don't even think about it.

Charging and managing multiple batteries

With a second battery wired in parallel to the main battery as described above, you'll want to **isolate** the two batteries if you plan to use the back-up battery at night to run lights and so on, after which it'll be partially discharged. The problem comes when starting an engine using one good and one partially discharged battery. As soon as two batteries are connected (i.e. when you turn on the ignition), they will equalise. When you turn the key 12 and 6 volts will equalise to 9 volts and you'll hear that familiar clattering from the starter.

A split-charge set-up enables a second battery wired in parallel to also get charged off the vehicle's alternator, something any bigger alternator ought to manage, depending on overnight use. Importantly, a split-charge system also isolates the two batteries when the engine is off, allowing only the auxiliary battery to be used for electrical accessories. Remember, when you charge batteries in parallel they should be similar types. Lead-acid and gel (absorbent glass mat) batteries need to be charged differently; it's not just a matter of being wired up to the alternator. Some AGM batteries can handle being charged in parallel with lead-acid types but it can shorten the life of expensive gel units.

Methods of battery isolation include: a **solenoid** (an electrically operated switch), a 'black-box' **electronic diode**, or simply a big, manually operated **switch** between the two batteries. The solenoid method is the simplest of the first two, as it can be taken apart and fixed should it fail or jam.

Solenoid-operated split charge system

With the solenoid on, both batteries are joined giving plenty of starting power, though recharging times are reduced. With the solenoid off, the batteries are isolated and ancillaries run from the second battery will only drain that unit. Wiring the solenoid to the alternator output avoids the two batteries being connected during the critical engine-starting phase when equalisation will occur. The second battery is only connected when there's output from the alternator (usually a few hundred rpm above tickover and certainly not during starting). The engine should fire even with a totally flat spare battery.

Some solenoid battery isolators **aren't suitable for vehicles with electronic engine management** (i.e. just about all modern ones) as they can cause sharp voltage surges or 'spiking' that can upset the ECU. (You may have noticed 'ECU-safe' jumpstarting cables that incorporate anti-surge protection.) For these vehicles certain diode battery isolators can be used.

Diode split charge system

Some diode battery isolators work on vehicles with internally sensed voltage regulators, but you need to be sure it's the correct type with **additional diodes** that moderate any voltage surges. Otherwise, a **diode battery isolator** can be used on any vehicle with an externally sensed voltage regulator (usually pre-ECU) and is an automatic system requiring no switches. The diode acts like an electronic one-way valve, sensing voltage drops from each battery and directing the alternator's charge towards it. The undesirable equalisation of unevenly charged batteries is avoided, keeping them **permanently isolated and independently charged**. You miss out on the advantages of paralleled batteries, and a diode takes up nearly a volt in the charging circuit, so it pays to have the alternator voltage raised to suit. Avoiding 'automatic' paralleling doesn't reduce battery life, but does have the disadvantage of being an unfixable 'black box'. Should you need two batteries to start, join them with jump leads.

Manually operated split charge

Over the years I've heard of all sorts of problems with split-charge systems, usually based around having two flat batteries one morning. For me the third option – **a hand-operated switch** – is the most foolproof. Mounted in the cab, you don't forget it's there or whether the batteries are connected or not. It requires running the second battery in parallel and in the morning disconnecting the second from the main battery prior to starting (removing the key). Once the engine has been run-

Manual battery isolation switch on the right, (left is for a back up radiator fan)

ning a few minutes, put the key in and turn the switch to get it recharged too. Their unequal states of discharge will have no negative effect once the engine is running and creating electricity from the alternator.

Battery charger

Although the idea of parking up in organised campsites (as opposed to bush camping) may not be on your adventurous agenda, you'll probably find you actually do that more often than you think. With access to mains electricity, using a **battery charger and a long extension** is an easy way of keeping your batteries in shape while allowing you to park up in cool shade and not where your solar panels require.

Managing batteries with solar power

A photovoltaic solar panel of just over half a square metre can potentially put out 40 watts, the practical minimum you want to bother with and enough to keep a single auxiliary battery in shape, even one powering a fridge. In fact it's far better for batteries to receive the small but regular 'trickle charge' from solar panels than the intermittent but heavy blast from a diesel engine's alternator.

Solar panels come in two types: the widely used mono- and distinctive multi-crystalline panels, which can be very efficient in full sunshine, and amorphous panels, which require more surface area per watt but perform better in occluded conditions. In the UK today a 12-volt 40-watt panel costs around £70, while two 100w panels (about the size of a door and as heavy as a small car battery) can be bought for £200. Prices in the US are lower.

The great advantage of running solar is that it's **independent of the engine's charging system**. A split-charging system isn't needed, though in practice it's still a very good idea. A solar panel can be connected to the house batteries (larger panels should use a regulator) that power domestic appliances while the engine is off, usually via an inverter (see p205).

A solar panel also has the added advantage of being able slowly to charge a flat starter battery **should the alternator fail**. To keep moving, solar charge

CONVERTING A VEHICLE

VOLTAGE-SENSITIVE RELAYS

We always use two-way voltage-sensitive relays (VSR), which are a solenoid controlled by a VSR controlled by a Zener diode. A Zener diode senses a given voltage and switches a solenoid or a small relay which in turn switches a bigger solenoid. As soon as it senses an increased voltage from the alternator kicking in at maybe 13.8 volts it'll parallel the batteries and then disconnect them when the engine is off at say 12.5 volts. It's wise to use an 'emergency parallel' switch with the VSR (some VSRs have them built in).

The two-way voltage-sensitive relays we use work in both directions. If your solar panels have charged the house batteries then the overflow tops up the starter batteries, perfect for when the vehicle is sitting around a while. Lately we've started using VSR-controlled motorised battery switches. They're like a normal manual battery switch but can also operate automatically most of the time. Here in Australia some of the most advanced electrical solutions for yachts and off-road vehicles come from a New Zealand company called BEP, or a very good Australian company called Rerdarc.

JOHN MARANO, All-Terrain Warriors

one while the other runs the engine until it goes flat (or just keep the engine running for as long as it takes). Driving in this manner, the battery will last even longer if you don't use any of the vehicle's electrics – even taking the brake-light bulbs out will help, but it's hard to see a modern ECU-managed engine agreeing to tolerate such treatment.

Mounting solar panels

The roof or rack of your vehicle is the obvious place to **mount panels**, but consider making them **removable** or at least possible to lift, turn and tilt in order to adopt the optimal angle when parked up. There'll be times when you may want to park up under a shady baobab tree for a day or two. By removing and positioning the panels out in the sun on an extension cable, the vehicle can stay in the shade while the sun works on your batteries.

Output and panel size

As with batteries, manufacturers' stated outputs can require some decoding. When you want to park up and rely solely on your solar panels to replace the battery power, then for the 80Ah/day example given on p205 you'll still need 100Ah/day because of the batteries' 80% charging ability. A 'day' or 24-hour period in solar-panel terms is divided into **peak sun hours** (PSH) and PSH are the number of hours that a panel will be rated to put out over a day.

An 80-watt panel makes a handy spoiler for a rack of jerries.

For example, even on a near-22-hour day in mid-summer in Fairbanks in Alaska, the PSH is only 5.9, while in winter, with potentially nearly 4 hours of daylight, it's only 2.1. Online PSH charts give you an average yearly PSH at locations based on rainfall, cloud cover and latitude. Divide the power you need to replace by the number of PSH at a given location and it'll give you a solar array size. So 100Ah/day

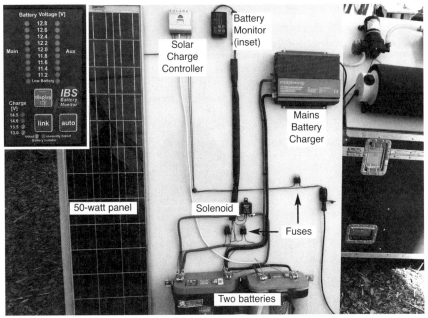

Main picture: A complete solar/mains charging set up. **Inset**: The battery monitor.

divided by a pretty good 5.5 PSH gives you 18Ah. As panels are usually rated in watts, 18 amps x 12 volts = 216 watt/hours. Therefore a 216-watt solar array might be regarded as necessary to replace the daily load given on p205, but again it's still not that simple. If you need 216 watts of solar you're going to need more than that in panels.

Panel outputs are rated at their optimum **position**, in other words when the panels are pointed directly at the sun. When lying flat on the roof of your truck they're less efficient, so you can derate them by at least 20%, depending on the sun angle and your latitude. It's said for a given latitude north or south of the equator you should angle your panel at the latitude plus 15° in mid-winter and less 15° in mid-summer. So travelling anywhere between northern Mozambique and Eritrea in June, for example, your panels laid out flat on the roof will do OK during the middle of the day.

You also need to derate them for the **temperature** because as a panel gets hotter, as it'll do in East Africa in June, performance drops. Panels vary and the most efficient types in terms of generation are the most affected by heat and sun angle. Cell temperature derating figures should be specified under each panel along with the other specifications. So, if your panels are only going to provide maybe 75% output once you factor in these losses then you're going to need 290 watts of solar panels because 216 watts divided by 0.75 = 290 watts. This is all still rather optimised as apart from the expense and complication you've nothing to lose by having substantially more solar potential. The expense isn't so great these days; the question is have you enough roof space to mount more than 200 watts of panels.

CALCULATING ELECTRICAL CONSUMPTION

Electricity can be measured in three ways: volts, amps and watts (today we won't get into ohms or 'resistance'). A good way to comprehend these values is to imagine a Sony Trinitron television being hurled from a hotel window by a Spinal Tap tribute band. Volts are the height or floor that the Sony is dropped from, amps are the speed at which it falls, and watts equal the size of the hole it makes on the coffee terrace below. In short, **volts x amps = watts**.

Another less anti-social analogy involves a garden hose: voltage is water pressure in a hose, the current expressed in amps is the speed of the flow through the pipe (much like a river's current), and the distance the water squirts out of the end of the pipe is the wattage. (Pipe diameter is resistance; greater diameter means less resistance, but we're trying to keep off ohms).

It's not too difficult to calculate the maximum possible electrical draw or consumption of your vehicle's electrical array and so get an idea of whether your alternator and indeed your batteries are up to the job. Remember, alternators only put out maximum charge with the engine running at above say 2000 rpm; at idle it'll be much less. You can of course run the engine for the several hours necessary to charge up, but it'll be pretty noisy.

Establishing electrical consumption

Each electrical appliance, be it a bulb, a fridge, speakers or an inverter, draws a wattage that'll be marked on the unit; **watts divided by volts = amps**, or electrical current, and as we know battery capacities are measured in amp hours. So a pair of 60-watt light bulbs in a Hyundai Pingu GL will draw 10 amps each because 60 watts / 12v = 5 amps each. A total of 10 amps means that, uncharged, a 100Ah battery will be flat in ten hours – as you'd expect with a Pingu left overnight with the lights on.

However, driving through a Kazakh sandstorm with the fan on full, a bank of spotlights on full beam, a fridge running flat out inside the stuffy car and ABS and traction control engaging every so often, it's possible to exceed the alternator's capacity to keep the batteries charged. Next morning, after a freezing night camped out using lights, you're in trouble. Any charging source (alternator, generator, solar or mains) needs to match the constant load plus provide enough current to replace whatever is lost while the charging source is applied. If it can't even keep up with the constant load, it will simply be inadequate.

SOME OTHER HANDY ELECTRICAL EQUATIONS

Volts x amps	= watts (consumption)
Watts/amps	= volts (power)
Watts/volts	= amps (current)
Volts/ohms	= amps (resistance)
Amps x ohms	= volts

A thicker cable (more copper) will reduce resistance at the cost of voltage. This is why a heavy-duty set of thick jumpstarting leads may not start a small car as well as a thinner set may do. They don't deliver enough volts to do the job (or, to put it another way, too many volts are 'absorbed' in the cable).

By pinching the end of the hypothetical garden hose mentioned above, you increase the resistance (measured in ohms), but with the same pressure (volts) the rate of flow (current, or amps) is reduced even though the water jet reaches further (more watts).

Along with establishing if the alternator is up to it, estimate what your **daily electrical consumption** will be on a typical day. For example, on a 12-volt system:

	Rating	Daily use in hrs	Ah/day
Water pump	5A	0.2	1Ah/day
Laptop	50w	2	8.3Ah/day
LED lights (4)	5w	4	6.6Ah/day
Bedside fans (2)	2A	1	4Ah/day
Fridge	4.5A	12	54Ah/day

Total daily drain: **73.9Ah/day**

A good benchmark figure is to have a **total battery Ah capacity** of at least twice but ideally four times the average daily draw. If you round up the above – a pretty modest estimate – to 80Ah then four 90Ah deep-cell batteries totalling 360Ah will do you nicely. After 24 hours without recharge those batteries will be 25% discharged – approaching the limit you want to push lead-acid batteries to on a regular basis. This leaves no reserve for camping wild for a couple of days unless you turn to solar or run the engine – or of course drastically reduce your electrical consumption.

The cost in the UK for four 90Ah batteries will be over £300, while the combined weight will be the weight of a passenger. An AGM battery can be discharged to 50% and so, although more expensive, you need fewer batteries, which also adds up to less weight and storage space.

The next thing to remember is that **recharging** most batteries is **only 80% efficient**, maybe a little more for gel or AGM. If you take the 80Ah/day estimate given above, you'll need to put 100Ah back in. Meanwhile, once the engine's running, a **100Ah alternator** would still take **several hours** to recharge the 80Ah debit in the batteries because they aren't designed to replace power as a bulk charge constantly. They dump bulk charge in initially then it tapers right off so the last part of the charge can take hours if it's a big bank of batteries. This is why smart regulators and alternators have been designed for charging big house battery banks on yachts. They offer true three-stage charging in the optimum time so if you need to run your engine purely to recharge your batteries, it can be in the shortest time.

INVERTERS AND GENERATORS

Inverters convert a vehicle's 12-volt DC into household voltage (usually 240 volts AC), so **enabling the use of household electrical appliances**. Just as an alternator is a reversed electric motor, an inverter might be described as an 'inverted' mains battery charger and in fact there are marine and campervan units that do just that, but at quite some cost.

It sounds like a great idea, making toast on the dashboard while hoovering the back, but making 240 volts AC out of 12 volts DC does have its limitations. The great advantage is that you can avoid buying expensive 12- or 24-volt marine/campervan appliances and simply run ordinary domestic ones fitted with a regular mains plug. Whatever vehicle you're using you're bound to find a use for an inverter to recharge low-power items like phones, laptops and camera batteries.

CONVERTING A VEHICLE

CALCULATING FRIDGE CONSUMPTION

Nearly all good fridges running efficient Danfoss compressors draw around 4.5 amps. You then need to ascertain the **duty cycle**, or how many hours the compressor runs in a 24-hour cycle. This will depend on the ambient temperature, how cold you have the fridge set, how full it is and the efficiency of the fridge's insulation.

It can be difficult to get accurate consumption figures, but **12 hours** is average. Good portable fridges have walls up to 5" (13cm) thick and only need to run for about 8 hours. A house fridge converted with a 12-volt Danfoss compressor may need to run for 20 hours in the same conditions.

JOHN MARANO

CONVERTING A VEHICLE

There are two types of inverter, both of which try to replicate the frequency or wave pattern of mains AC voltage, which is 50 or 60 hertz. Quasi- or **modified sine wave** (MSW) inverters do so crudely and cheaply. **Pure sine wave** inverters (PSW) more closely mimic the waveform of household AC and aren't that much more expensive with a 500-watt example from £50. They can run just about any appliance (power permitting).

As with any 'something-for-nothing' electrical conversion, inverters are inefficient. Most units need a cooling fan and consume a lot of battery power and should be switched off when not actually needed.

Any appliance running a **'resistive load'** such as a heating element or filament – like the aforementioned toaster, or an electric kettle – works fine on an MSW inverter, so will power tools and a fridge's compressor. But they may run less smoothly than on a pure sine wave. Appliances with an **'inductive load'**, such as microwaves or electric motors, will run much higher loads than their rating may suggest. Furthermore, appliances such as electric motors momentarily draw much higher loads on starting up before settling down. This explains some inverters' 'peak load' rating: what they can handle for a short time.

If you're building up a truck-based camper you'll want to fit it out with mains voltage and so will require a **substantial PSW inverter** rated at 2000-watts if running 12-volts (or 3000w for 24v), especially if using a microwave oven. You can now only pay £350 in the UK for a shoe box-sized unit weighing about 3kg.

To achieve such wattage you'll need a bank of house batteries charged by half a roof's-worth of solar panels. It's when looking for somewhere to carry 80kg of batteries that the extra payload of a truck pays dividends. There's more on p230 but the bottom line with inverters is this: get an inexpensive 300-watt MSW inverter for low-amperage applications like charging camera batteries or running laptops and, depending on the extent of your conversion, get a much bigger PSW inverter for running wide-screen TVs, radar or microwaves.

Generators

For the cost and bulk, let alone the noise, portable **generators** producing mains AC don't suit most overlanders as well as they do those parking up in north Arizona or south Morocco for the winter. They're supposed to *replace* your house batteries, but, if required to charge them, not all generators work well with modern electronic automotive battery chargers. If you have the desire and space to take this route, ensure the two are well matched, or use the generator as a mains power source instead of the batteries.

CAMP LIGHTING

After a few weeks of trying to hold a torch in your teeth while rummaging around in the back, you'll have learned not to underestimate the need for **good and reliable lighting** when camping. A full moon and stars can help a lot, but not when it comes to chopping just onions and not your fingers. Good lighting is an important safety consideration. Just as the home is the most accident-prone environment, so too is your nightly bush camp.

The courtesy lights in the car are of some use and most 4x4 station wagons feature a second light over the back doors. They obviously won't be bright enough for much more than groping around, so something more effective needs to be set up to undertake the evening's chores.

Fluorescent lighting

The best combination of versatility and minimal power drain is 12/24-volt **fluorescent lighting** powered by the house batteries. These consume next to nothing, have no bulb filaments to fracture and a few of them strategically fitted will provide all the light you'll need. Along with fixed fluorescent lighting, get a couple of fluorescent tubes or **light sticks** that plug into 12-volt sockets on leads five metres long. Jammed in overhead or on the end of a broomstick, you can illuminate any part of your vehicle as well as a roof tent or nearby ground tent. If doing this, add a switch at the light end (most don't have one) so you don't have to tear yourself away from your cosy nest to switch off.

Lighting attracts moths, even in the depths of the desert – very frustrating when they take a dive at your dinner. Some places are worse than others but other than occasionally turning everything off or setting up a brighter decoy light to lure them away, yellow lighting is less insect prone. If you cook around the tailgate area it's worth having the fixed light here in yellow, as well as one of the light sticks.

Cooking on the road

How you organise your cooking and eating arrangements depends primarily on your vehicle set-up, which is likely to be influenced by your destination, the season and the expected duration of your trip.

TABLES AND CHAIRS

You don't have to be Jamie Oliver in cowboy boots to know that having some sort of flat surface on which to prepare your food (as well as carry out many other tasks) is essential and, just as at home or at work, you can never have enough flat workspace. Including the ground below your feet in this category may work while hiking or on picnics, but cooking full time on your knees when overlanding will soon become tiresome.

What you need is a work surface beside the vehicle, be it the roof or bonnet of the car or 4x4, or more sensibly a fold-out table that either stands alone or hinges off the side of a van or out of the back. A small fold-out off the inside

Left: After sitting down all day it sure is nice to sit down ... because (**right**) there won't be a handy roadside picnic table in the shade every time you want it. © Rob & Ally Ford

CONVERTING A VEHICLE

of a back door can be fine for a stove, but if it's any bigger it'll interfere with access to the back of the vehicle and so can be a fire hazard. Taking into account shelter, think carefully about where you plan to use the stove and avoid any need to reach over it to get to things. It's bound to end in tears.

Even if you have a nicely set up dining area inside your truck, you don't always want to eat inside and so a **separate folding camping table** of at least a square metre is the way to go, even if it requires stashing somewhere. Unlike anything fixed, it can be positioned out of the wind, rain or sun without you having to move the vehicle. Just like at home, your table could well become a focal point for your non-driving leisure hours so put some thought into it.

There's plenty of designer campsite furniture available but, when eating, a **chair** with an upright back is best, not the slouching geodesic deckchairs complete with beer holders. Also useful, though not necessarily for meal times, is a simple folding **stool** or two. They're handy for sitting on while doing wheel repairs, for example, as well as for keeping things off the ground when you've run out of flat surfaces. A **robust design** that'll last the course is what counts. As with so much overlanding equipment, from the vehicle to a torch, it's not the lightest, fastest, cheapest, slickest or shiniest that wins the day – it's what's still working or usable when the big adventure ends.

Having said all that, there are places where you might feel rather foolish sat at your camp table with a napkin tucked under your chin. Taking a Bedouin approach to eating and relaxing on a large **carpet** or tarpaulin with **cushions** can be most agreeable, and these items don't break or rattle about. You could buy something memorable in the bazaar in Esfahan, but any old rug or piece of carpet is easily rolled up and slung on a roof. As you become more attuned to life on the road you may even choose to pull out the mattress and sleep on the ground once in a while, in which case a carpet will be nice to spread out on. If you plan to eat like this , then use a wipe-down plastic **table-cloth** on which to set food and drinks in case of spillage. A **tray** can also be useful to move stuff to and from the cooking area or for hot or grimy pots.

Bring some big firm **cushions** for support or use holdalls full of clothes or bedding. I've found that some sort of back support or a way to get your backside just a few inches off the ground (a jerrican under a cushion for example) is much more comfortable while eating. After that you can stretch out again and watch the kettle boil.

STOVES

Two people can manage with a conventional **camping stove** that has at least two burners and possibly a grill, plus a secondary portable means of cooking that doesn't entail the main stove. A portable stove – main or otherwise – enables you to cook outside if the fancy takes you. Even with a big truck, in the right weather cooking outside is far more agreeable.

Somethin' smells good! © Chris Collard

The optimal set-up is a twin-burner stove running off bottled gas with a bottle in reserve. One bottle can be attached to a fixed counter-top stove via a hose, and the portable back-up can be used occasionally for outdoors cooking by screwing a big burner head on directly. This is all backed-up by a single-burner camping stove that runs on something else should bottled gas temporarily become hard to come by. Note that shipping lines and some tunnels may **forbid the presence of bottled gas** on a vehicle. If followed to the letter this can mean arriving into a foreign country with urgent need of bottled gas.

Fire extinguishers

This is a good place to remind you of the need in any overland vehicle of a **fire extinguisher**. If you have a fixed stove in the back, an extinguisher should be mounted close at hand and, particularly if your vehicle has a separate driving cab from the living area, another one should be mounted there for possible fires in the engine bay. Some countries require a 2kg fire extinguisher.

Which fuel?

When it comes to cooking fuel, the choice is principally between **bottled gas** (available through much of the world though not always in handy-sized small bottles) and more powerful but less clean-burning **petrol** stoves.

Diesel-powered stoves might sound like a great idea and are often fitted in boats, where diesel's comparative combustible stability is warranted. The problem is diesel stoves require pre-heating in some way and as a cooker they're slow, messy or expensive. And what works at sea level and temperatures well above freezing isn't always applicable overland. Some 13,000ft up alongside Tso Pangong lake in Ladakh, a diesel stove and any other pressure-sensitive equipment (including some cassette toilets) could spell trouble.

The same limitations apply to other oily fuels such **kerosene** and **paraffin**. Although the latter is used in northern India as a stove fuel, so is yak dung, and both are more suited to external use or well-ventilated tents.

In North America, where automotive gasoline is cheap by European standards, **white gas** (naptha) is sold as a camp-stove fuel. It burns much more cleanly than automotive gasoline, works fine below freezing and is widely available, but not out in the world, where the only gasoline is what comes out of a fuel bowser pumped by a bloke with an oily satchel. Stick with a stove that'll run on automotive petrol or settle on bottled gas.

Bottled gas

If it's not wood or charcoal then **bottled gas** is the domestic cooking fuel of choice for most of the world, including many European countries which lack a mains gas network outside the cities. There, as elsewhere, every fuel station will have a rack of gas bottles to exchange for your empty.

Besides its wide availability, bottled gas has many advantages for over-landing. The flame lights instantly and burns cleanly with no soot or flaring. Simmer control is perfect (a common complaint with petrol), and the stoves are simple, light and cheap to buy. Bottles can be bought or refilled in towns (albeit the larger 15kg examples). You'll understandably be reluctant to fire up a petrol stove inside while it's lashing down outside; not so with gas.

You can simply screw a **big burner head** with a tap directly into a bottle and dispense with the whole counter-top stove. There's something to be said for that as cheaper camping stoves can shake themselves to bits. Some come with a **grill** which can extend your repertoire and is vital for toastaholics.

In cylinders and bottles you predominantly get either **propane**, which evaporates at -42°C/-44°F, or **butane**, which does so at 0°C. Butane is there-fore unsuitable in sub-zero environments, but in countries that regularly see freezing temperatures it'll likely be a seasonally varied mixture of propane and butane, like with automotive LPG or autogas, which is the same thing.

Just as with autogas, the main drawback with bottled gas is the lack of standard **threads and fittings** such as regulators around the world. But a new bottle and reg' cost peanuts, and over the months you'll acquire a range of hardware that'll only increase the value of your camper when it comes to sell-ing it. There'll always be a way to make the local fitting work, even if it means splicing a hose, so carry some spare and a couple of hose clamps. The lesser problem is bottled gas doesn't have the calorific **energy** of petrol or domestic mains gas. To be efficient it needs to be out of the wind, which is another rea-son to consider carefully your vehicle's cooking arrangements.

Refilling the gas bottle

A **4.5kg bottle** of gas about the size of a football is a handy size for a van or 4x4 station wagon and when used just for cooking could easily last two peo-ple up to two months, especially if another source is used for boiling 'day' water. Problem is these small bottles are quite hard to find compared to the larger 15kg items that suit fixed domestic use. Better then to **carry two** so as

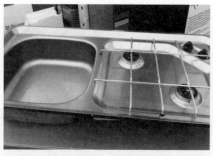 

Two ring stove-top and integral kitchen sink, or a less expensive stove with a grill, fitted in place.

one runs out you have a few weeks to track down a replacement. A 15kg household bottle may last half a year but takes up a lot of room and day to day is less portable. Just like needing to fill your vehicle's tank with the right type of fuel, refilling with gas is simply something you'll have to anticipate and is the reason why a reserve is a good idea.

It's possible to re-fill a gas bottle from a larger one manually; I've had this done in a Tunisian backstreet. Just make sure it's **not overfilled**. Overfilling gas bottles can lead to a deadly explosion, as a motor-homing couple in South America found to their cost one time. As with a jerrican, there must be an **air gap** to allow the already pressurised liquid petroleum gas some room to expand. The excess gas might find a way to leak out as ambient pressure decreases with altitude or the temperature rises. The only way to be sure is to know what a correctly filled bottle weighs (assuming the same type is used again and again), or what sort of splashing sound a correctly filled bottle makes. No splashing could mean it's full to the brim and with an old bottle that's been knocking around the veldt for ten years, that could spell trouble. A telling sign of over-pressurisation is frosting on the hard-pressed regulator managing higher-than-normal pressure. The temperature drop is similarly extreme, causing frosting (depending on ambient humidity and altitude).

Petrol stoves

Having read the above you may suddenly be attracted to petrol stoves. As long as they run reliably on **automotive petrol** (gasoline), you'll never struggle finding fuel, and the thermal energy is 30% greater than propane.

The problem will be the quality of automotive petrol you come across on your travels. Petrol stoves need to be pressurised by hand prior to lighting, at which point you're never fully sure if you'll get a clean blue flame or a flaming yellow flare that takes off your eyebrows. **Coleman's** well-known twin-burner **Dual Fuel** petrol stove runs poorly on automotive petrol even though the 'dual fuel' label means it's supposed to. The same goes for the **533** single burner which otherwise makes a great portable back up stove.

Unleaded petrol is now widespread in the developing world – very few countries in Africa don't offer unleaded at the pumps. The problem for camping stoves are the many **additives** introduced into automotive fuel to reduce wear on modern, lean-running car engines. It's probably true to say that due to more stringent emissions regulations, unleaded petrol back home will have more additives than what you find in the Overland Zone. This is a good thing as when running these stoves on unleaded, the brass generator tube where the fuel vaporises tends to clog with the residue of fuel additives and eventually needs to be replaced; cleaning it isn't so simple.

My experience with Coleman twin-burner stoves is they're powerful once hot but clanky and poorly designed. The generator/tank deployment in a Coleman is fiddly to set up when compared to the simple, turn-the-knob-and-light operation of bottled gas. And, like a 40-year-old V8, Coleman petrol stoves get through petrol pretty quickly compared to butane gas – you can get through a tank in less than two hours. It certainly pays to run these stoves on nothing less than unleaded automotive fuel, and every once in a while do a hot control burn with naptha or white fuel to clear it through.

CONVERTING A VEHICLE

OVENS, MICROWAVES AND KETTLES

Depending on how you like to cook and available space, an **oven** might sound like a great idea. The reality is that few can replicate the performance of a domestic unit and, if they get close, consume vast amounts of energy. Before you settle on an oven or microwave consider the culinary uses of a twin-burner gas stove with a **grill**. Overlanding requires some compromises and you can't expect to have all domestic mod-cons at hand. When you tire of your own cooking there'll always be roadhouses or restaurants. Taking leave of the mother ship to eat in these places is all part of the adventure.

Microwave ovens

For overlanding, 12-/24-volt microwave ovens exist, but just as at home, they're best suited to swiftly warming up leftovers rather than actual cooking. Remember that on the road it's unlikely your fridge will be brimming over with leftover meals because the reality of cooking, eating and storing fresh food means most days you'll only cook what you plan to eat right then.

Huge **power consumption** is required to enable the speedy cooking miracles achieved by microwaves; half an hour's use could flatten your batteries. Of course the whole point is that that they're only typically used for a couple of minutes and so, as with so much in this vehicle conversion section, it depends on your cooking priorities as well as budget and space. Be warned though that the rating in watts displayed on the case is the 'delivery or cooking power', typically 700 watts, but the energy the actual device could consume will be nearly twice as much, 1200 watts or more. This is the actual power consumption and will be stated on the back somewhere.

Yachting and motorhome suppliers sell hyper-expensive 12-volt examples costing ten times more than a mains microwave. You do wonder if for the same outlay and the occasional use you'll probably put it to, you couldn't simply make do with an inexpensive **mains microwave** and a 2000-watt inverter positioned close to the battery with thick cables. What you don't want is for the microwave to become a **white elephant** in your carefully designed living area where space is at a premium. Whatever oven you decide on, **test** it first.

Kettles

Don't get involved with those mini immersion-heater gadgets you dip in a cup. If you want to save gas and time get a 'cordless' **one-litre mini kettle** as often found in B&Bs or hotel rooms. Rated at around 900 watts, they'll boil a pint of water in less than three minutes, making a modest use of a rechargeable power source. See also volcano kettles, opposite.

WOOD FIRES

Don't forget it's possible to cook out in the wilds on a **wood fire**. Not only is a fire fun, it's a great way of extending your vehicle's fuel supplies (especially if you want to cook something slowly) and a great opportunity to be more than two feet away from the car.

Thick fireproof cast-iron pots called Dutch ovens or **camp ovens** are commonly used in Australia. They're designed to be buried deep into glowing **embers**, with more embers piled onto the lid, and left for as long as it takes. At the simplest level they work best for stewing.

Other types of cooking or even **baking bread** in this way require some practice or luck before you can depend on your evening meal being ready before midnight. To bake bread you don't even need a heavy Dutch oven; I've baked bread-mix in the sand under hot embers using a thin stainless steel bowl and some foil. While it's certainly a treat to enjoy freshly baked bread, it does take up most of the evening preparing it and can be a hit-and-miss affair.

You can bake delicious bread like this in a stainless steel bowl buried under hot embers.

A chunky metal **grate** from an old oven or BBQ takes up little space and can be set on some logs or rocks over embers either to cook meat directly or to support non-fireproof cookware. But before you get too excited about going bush, recognise that anything more than boiling or frying is something of an art that requires experience, as many a BBQ guest has found to their cost.

Appreciate too that in desert and high-mountain areas **wood** might be a scarce local resource that's better left for the locals. If you get into cooking on fires, collect wood where it's prolific or better still, gather waste wood. To this end a small **saw** and **axe** will be handy tools. Charcoal apart, the key is to use dry, dead and ideally hard wood, which burns hotter than pine and makes the all important bed of red-hot embers.

Volcano kettles

A volcano kettle (to give one of its many names) is a cylindrical container with an outer chamber or jacket that holds about a litre of water. Combustible material or refuse is stuffed into the central 'chimney' or cone and set alight. The large surface area inside the cone quickly heats up the water. Like a Trangia, a volcano actually works better in the wind.

Volcano kettles – hot water using combustible rubbish and wind. Work on a stove too.

Once you get the knack, a volcano will boil a litre in three to four minutes. I've found the one-piece, stainless version from Australia (pictured) more in tune with the simple ethos of the volcano than the corked, aluminium Kelly Kettle version commonly sold in the UK.

These kettles give you the satisfaction of **using combustible waste** and whatever else you come across, while at best matching the speed of a gas stove. They're more suited to desert and tropical regions as a means of saving on your main cooking fuel, or where there might be a nightly fire ready to use. They work on a gas stove too, if you cap the chimney top to retain the heat.

FRIDGE-FREEZERS

Depending on your preference, a fridge is either an unnecessary luxury or an essential accessory to your overlanding lifestyle. You could say the same for showers and toilets, ovens and 24/7 internet. For those who've never travelled overland with these things nor ever plan to, they miss nothing until the day they're invited into someone else's van and are offered a cold beer and a slice of roast chicken while they check their emails in the shower.

If you have the space and the budget, a fridge is a nice idea, but first ask yourself what you'll be putting in it once you reach the steppes or the jungle and your perishable supplies have run out? Even without air-con, the interior of a vehicle can remain remarkably cool if you keep the sunshine out and pack thoughtfully with minimal air gaps. In the desert, while unpacking the back of a car during a 30°C lunch break, I'm often surprised just how cool some buried and sealed items can remain even after a night that was far from freezing (though the desert is an optimal, low-humidity environment).

It's not so difficult to adapt to a **non-refrigerated lifestyle**, especially once you see the cost of a decent overlanding unit. For example, many sauces need refrigeration once they're opened, so buy small bottles and use them in one go. The same applies to long-life (UHT) milk, if even available. Hard cheese actually lasts very well without a fridge, indeed at the end of one six-week trip I wondered just what was in that red ball of rot-proof Edam. Butter or margarine can remain fairly solid if kept out of the sun, and well-buried vegetables can be stored in pieces of cloth to prolong their lives.

Fresh meat and fish are another matter. In arid countries **meat** is cut into strips and hung out to dry overnight on a bush; thereafter it's kept lightly wrapped in cloth on the roof, which dries it still further. On many desert trips with 4x4s or camels (admittedly in mid-winter) we had fresh **salads** right up until the day we returned to civilisation two weeks later, though, as mentioned, what lasts long in a desert soon rots deep in the tropics. With a bit of thought it can be done, but enough of this rationalising: you want a fridge!

Caravanning absorption fridges

Unlike a microwave, **household fridges** don't adapt well to overlanding, although a full-size unit might last just inside a big bus or road-based motorhome that isn't bashing round the boondocks. The next option might be a 'three-way' motorhome or **caravanning fridge** designed to run off 12/24 volts, mains electricity or the same butane as the stoves described earlier. Preceded by the word 'caravan' you'd expect the zeros to fall away from the price tag, but you'll soon find this is not the case.

These three-way models are the 'absorption' type. Einstein himself had a hand in co-patenting a design in the 1930s, and while there's no noisy compressor or indeed any moving parts, it needs to make heat which means high electrical consumption. Most caravanners or motorhomers run these fridges on bottled gas while on the road, or off a mains hook-up when in a park. For an overlander neither are practical.

The technology behind this type of fridge – ammonia evaporating out of a water solution, combining with hydrogen, dropping its pressure and so cooling and condensing before being reabsorbed back into the water tank – also requires

KEEPING COOL AND BEING DISCREET

Despite the benefits of driving an airy vehicle like the latest sedans with full glass roofs, having acres of **window glass** can create an unwanted 'greenhouse effect' inside a car. Blanked-out rear windows keep your vehicle and its contents much cooler and hidden from prying eyes.

Professional **stick-on tinting** looks good but is expensive and doing it yourself can get messy if done badly (trapped air bubbles form in the heat). Painting the windows with whitewash or cutting cardboard are simpler solutions. **Curtains**, which can be open or closed are a bit more work but add a homely feel. Whatever you choose, lighter colours are more reflective so absorb less radiated heat.

On any vehicle the cab also get hot from the engine as well as the sun, especially when you're driving towards the equator (i.e. into the sun most of the day). With their near-vertical glass angles Defenders, old kombis or big trucks are superior in this respect. A pair of angle-adjustable **blower fans** make the cab more agreeable if you don't have air-con and don't want the windows open.

You don't have to be an abandoned pet to know that a car left out of the shade on a hot day can easily reach 45°C inside.

Getting into a car like this can be very uncomfortable and also means that a fridge (if present) will be working flat out, draining your batteries. A **sun visor** stuck on across the top 10cm of the windscreen is useful when driving into low sun angles, but for overlanding a proper roll-down visor or inner screen is best. You can buy the silver padded ones, which look the part, but anything semi-rigid that'll stay in place on the inside of the windscreen will do, be it cardboard or Karrimat. Pictured is a roll-down visor of light canvas fixed on the front edge of a roof rack. It may have been a noisy wind-trap but in an HJ61 who can tell? It was quick to deploy by parting a couple of Velcro straps, and once tucked under the wipers stayed put in the wind with a bamboo stick in either end to keep it rigid.

Smooth black plastic **dashboards** are especially prone to wafting unwanted heat over the occupants. Laying or pinning a towel or piece of carpet across this area greatly helps reduce heat glare, though properly cut and moulded carpets are available for many 4x4s. Whatever you use it still needs to be a dark colour if it's not to reflect distractingly in the windscreen.

CONVERTING A VEHICLE

---

the unit to be well ventilated (even to the point of having its own small fan) and to operate within a few degrees of horizontal. This is easily achieved while cruising along the Riviera, less so when trying to transit Angola in five days. The cooling ability of an absorption fridge is also **tied to the ambient temperature** and can only drop by 25–30°C below that. If you inadvertently leave the blinds off while visiting the ruins of Merv on a May afternoon, the interior of your vehicle could easily exceed that and there goes your Brie. Long story short, avoid cheaper absorption fridges. For reliable overland refrigeration, read on.

Overlanding fridge-freezers

A domestic fridge operates with a compressor and the best overlandable fridges use the same technology optimised and downsized to make them much more efficient. Compressors use conventional refrigerant that's pumped around to vaporise and cool; and they can do this at up to 30° from vertical.

For operating efficiency fill up the air space, even if this means using beer.

CONVERTING A VEHICLE

Most importantly, the fridges listed here can legendarily take a hammering while still making ice for your sundowner. As well as build quality, efficient motors plus effective insulation to reduce motor running times are what separates an Engel from Acme's Auto Igloo DLX.

These fridges are **top-loading** because cold air being heavier than warm, when you open a conventional domestic fridge, cooled air tumbles out unseen. No such problems with top-loading fridges. Three names are well known in the trade: **Engel** from Japan, **National Luna** made in South Africa and **Waeco** from the US. The best of these use the Danish Danfoss BD35 compressor or Engel's own ingenious Sawafuji swing motor. If you'll be sleeping alongside your fridge, the noise it makes turning on and off is something to consider. In the UK Engel prices start at around £650 for a small 15-litre-capacity fridge-freezer running 12/24/240 volts, to nearly £800 for a 24-kilo **MT45**. Waeco models in the same volumes are cheaper. With an average current consumption of as little as 1.4 watts (in non-freezer-mode) the MT45 and fridges like it can last up to three days off a fully charged 12-volt battery bank, which of course can easily be extended by solar power.

Fridge and cool-box tips

- Minimise air space inside. Solids and fluids stay cold longer than air so the motor needs to run less often
- Avoid putting warm things inside
- Keep the vehicle or cabin shady and ensure the fridge is out of direct sun
- Try and ensure airflow through the vehicle when stationary
- Open the fridge as little and as briefly as possible during the heat of the day
- Use a thermal cover to insulate the fridge further,

COOKING UTENSILS

Overlanding isn't backpacking so there's no need to buy gimmicky camping equipment if what you have at home will do the job fine. Some breakable items like plates are better in plastic or stainless steel, but your favourite LRO centenary mug can be easily protected and is nicer to drink from. A vehicle has room enough to carry a few luxuries and real coffee from an espresso pot is something worth getting out of bed for.

As with everything, when packing utensils envisage a typical cooking scenario and group things together for easy access. Keep small, loose items like cutlery and tin-openers together in a small box and wrap clanking items in tea towels to stop them rattling against each other. Don't forget you may host visitors so another set or two of eating implements will be handy.

Kitchen equipment list

- Bags, plastic and zip-lock – transparent ones are useful for wrapping and identifying leakables
- Bags, cloth and shopping – cloth bags or pillow cases are good for storing vegetables
- Bin liners (in a roll) – for keeping bread fresh, and for rubbish
- Bowl, stainless steel, various sizes
- Bowl, washing up – a general purpose container
- Cafetière or espresso coffee pot
- Chopping board, wooden – doubles as a useful stove windbreak
- Cleaning fluid, all-surface
- Colander or sieve, stainless steel
- Condiment box or drawer
- Corkscrew and tin opener
- Cutlery in cutlery box
- Egg box
- Fridge, or cool box (Esky)
- Frying pan with lid
- Grater for cheese and vegetables
- Jug
- Kettle, electric or hob
- Kitchen knife – get a good-quality item
- Mugs and beakers – large ones are useful for cereal too
- Oven gloves
- Paper towels
- Pepper grinder
- Plates or large bowls, plastic – take a spare for covering things or for visitors
- Pot, cast iron for cooking in wood fires
- Saucepans, small and large with lids
- Steel grill – for wood fires
- Steel wool (Brillo) pads
- Tea towels
- Thermos flask – especially if you don't have a 'day stove'
- Tupperware boxes with clamp-edges, or deep-screw plastic jars, various sizes
- Washing-up liquid – or use sand on china and stainless steel
- Water bag – a hanging 10-litre 'day bag' avoids lugging out a heavy jerrican if no pump
- Wooden spoon

CONVERTING A VEHICLE

6

BUILDING A CABIN

This section covers **building a shell** or a **box** on a **van or truck chassis**. Many names are used for this space: shelter, living module, capsule, box and so on, but **cabin**, as opposed to the driving cab, is the term used here to define the area in the back where you spend time when not driving. Even if you're only fitting out a 4x4 or a van, it's worth scanning this section as it includes ideas that might be useful to all overland conversions.

Going step by step through the entire process of the build would take another book. Instead here's an outline of the tasks involved, particularly the more obscure ones that won't overlap with outfitting a regular motorhome. You'll soon learn that certain brands such as Eberspächer heaters (Espar in North America), Seitz windows and doors, SMEV stove and sink assemblies, Thetford toilets and SHURflo pumps are universal in the campervan outfitting world, just as a limited range of marques get used for overlanding.

The many ways of equipping the cabin as a living space for the open road are also covered in greater detail on many travellers' **websites** and particularly in the UK on the Self-Build Motor Caravanners Club website (⌨ sbmcc.co.uk), whose cheery motto is 'We Build, We Travel, We Enjoy'. Hopefully after being engaged in the first you'll experience the latter.

Grand designs for the open road

To take on a self-build and be able to leave materials and tools for half-complete jobs out overnight you'll need a secure **space**, not something that most people living in congested Europe have to spare. A big 4WD truck blocking out the sun on your suburban street could upset the neighbours so you may need to factor in the cost of renting a secure barn or warehouse, as well as calculating what opportunities you'll actually have to go there and get on with the job. Having such a place will be an incentive to take on a job that will undoubtedly last **many months**.

You need to consider everything from possibly devising a **torsion-free subframe**, fabricating a cabin shell to mount on that frame, **cladding** and weather-proofing it, **insulating** and lining it, fitting it out with **storage** compartments, worktops and furnishings, as well as installing a shower / toilet. Then you'll need to devise an autonomous **electrical** power system, organise a way of storing, delivering and disposing of **water** used for drinking and washing, and address any **heating** requirements.

This section doesn't intend to be comprehensive right down to the most suitable pattern for your fireproof curtains. Nor does it try to be definitive because your creativity, time, budget and preferences can lead you in any direction you choose. There is no single best way of building, mounting and outfitting a cabin, but there are a number of ways that are best.

DON'T BUILD, BUY

Why would you build a cabin? It'll be a monumental task that won't pay back the expenditure on materials, let alone your time. Partly because to buy a professionally outfitted vehicle can **cost** much more than your trip: from at least £50,000 ($64,000) to over ten times that for the truck-based, globe-trotting AWD penthouses produced in Germany or the US. Another reason is you like the challenge of the project and think you could do a good job.

Remember, this won't be some rat van to hang out in at summer festivals or for surfing weekends. Unless you intend to spend every other day making minor repairs, it has to be either very simple and essentially unfitted – nothing wrong with that apart from the daily inconvenience – or built to a high standard. The latter is something that not every person has the patience, skill and dedication to achieve. For others it's all part of the adventure but can take so much out of you that it's not uncommon to find near-finished vehicles for sale that have never been used. For these creative pioneers the build *was* the journey and the momentum to break away and live life on the road was lost – or perhaps never really existed.

Substantial savings can be made and months of work avoided by tracking down a **used overland camper**. The reason most people will carry on regardless is because they think it'll be satisfying to design and build something of their own. In most cases they'll be right, but just like building a house for the first time, it could be at some cost.

THINK FIRST, SPEND LATER

Long before you set to your vehicle with a chainsaw have a long think. Research thoroughly and try to visualise your living space before you make expensive purchases or irreversible alterations. You want to have a near-crystal-clear plan because, just like your journey, it's unlikely to pan out as expected. There's no optimal design, but there are pitfalls, and chances are you'll return knowing exactly how to do things much better next time.

Trawl the net of course, but if possible also try and actually see a few cabin interiors at motorhome or caravan shows. Even better are **overlanding shows**, pre-eminent being the **German** Abenteuer & Allrad show in Bad Kissingen in June (🖥 abenteuer-allrad.de), Overland Expo in **America** in May and October (🖥 overlandexpo.com), or something like the Queensland Caravan Camping & Touring Holiday Show in **Brisbane** around mid-June (although every Australian state capital stages an equivalent). Bad Kissingen is the pick of the bunch, focused on overland travel and not 4x4s, and is where you'll see just about every permutation of overland camper and may even find your dream truck for sale.

Brits might be dyed-in-the-wool caravanners and the French keen motorhomers, but these Germans really are the experts in this niche field of building overland campers. The **catalogues** (all in German) from the likes of Woick, Tourfactory, AMR, Reimo (also in English), OutdoorWelt and, not least, Ormocar will give you an idea of the equipment and fittings available, as well as the thought-provoking prices.

GETTING IT MADE

Alternatively, you could get your custom-made cabin professionally built for you – so-called **'coach building'**. As you can imagine, this isn't something you'll find in the Yellow Pages. In the UK at least campervan conversions specialise in fitting a roof and outfitting the insides for vans only. Instead, you might want to look to builders of **horseboxes**; these truck-based transporters are designed for getting show horses to multi-day events and generally incorporate basic overnight lodgings for the crew. This makes them a little more qualified than regular **commercial van** coach builders, who produce rear bodies for specialised applications only.

Better at fitting out the interior might be a **boat builder** (not least in the UK). In this application the principles of safety and rust proofing, as well as the quality and ruggedness of fittings in a compact space are well understood. Motorhome and caravan manufacturers you'd imagine have got their schedules full knocking out their own designs. The important thing to note is that only a boat builder is likely to appreciate the need for easy access in terms of maintenance and repairs on the journey, but neither will necessarily appreciate the reality of how it all holds up when bashing across the Kalahari for days. There is no oceanic equivalent of corrugations. Under-building might be expected from caravan makers, but **over-engineering** is equally flawed and adds unnecessary weight and expense.

Just as when getting the builders in at home, the safest bet is probably a place that's done a similar overlander-outfitting job before, or better still one that's been recommended by an overland traveller whose finished vehicle didn't come complete with hay bins and a loading ramp.

Be under no illusion that this work will add many thousands to the job, but if you've well-paid employment you may be better off earning and paying someone else to fabricate. Whatever your job, you may also recognise you just don't have the skills, the space, the time or the help needed to do it all, but you've sold the family jewels, the company or the house and instead have the money.

BUILDING A CABIN

Self-build strategy

Before you load up the credit card, spend at least a couple of weeks thinking it over, armed with a notepad and pencil. Indeed you may well have been thinking about it for many years. During that time you'll establish what your priorities are. Here are some things to consider, all of which are studied in more detail in this section:

- The physical size of the cabin
- Walk- or crawl-through access to the cab
- Build from scratch or acquire a shell
- Necessity for a torsion-free subframe
- Interior layout
- Electrical power supply
- Water system
- Heating and ventilation
- Toilet and shower room
- Roof hatch/access
- Storage for bulky gear like kayaks or bikes
- Security

Remote mountain tracks like this in northern India are the sorts of places you want to explore on your Trip of a Lifetime, but along with certain bridges, they impose limits on width. Just after this picture was taken a landslide meant only jeeps like the one shown could get through and reversing a lorry from that point would have been a long drive backwards.

Once that's all narrowed down you ought to assess the **cost and the time** required, even if you're bound to get it wrong. The short version is to work out both and then add 50% plus a month. Get as much information on prices as you can; it's all there on the web or in suppliers' catalogues. Quality stainless steel or brass screws, nails, catches, latches and hinges, special tools as well as Sikoflex glue can all add up to hundreds of pounds.

Up the Spiti Valley in the Himalaya it's either the river or hard rock.

THE SIZE OF THE CABIN

When looking at a fixed-roof cabin that's high enough to stand in and wide enough to sleep across, a **length of 3 metres** (118″) might be considered the absolute minimum. In this case the dining table and seats would need to convert into a bed, and a shower cubicle would need to be built into the entrance portal. Another metre in length (157″) will enable a fixed bed and fewer arguments, and about 5 metres (197″) will easily allow for separate beds and more than two people.

Anything more than 5 metres will make for a truck at least 6 metres long end to end, which might limit your ability to park easily or negotiate some backroads or tracks without damaging the bodywork or the environment. Depending on what type of trip you have in mind, you may resent the vehicle's bulk when driving, but you won't when parked up at night. You need to settle on your balance of driving mobility and camping comfort.

If you estimate on having an interior floor-to-ceiling **height** of 1.9 metres (75″), the box will be at least 2 metres high before anything goes on the roof. On a 4WD truck chassis with 14-inch rims and a torsion-free subframe that will mean an overall vehicle height of over 3 metres and **3.5 metres** (138″) is considered a practical limit to maintain a go-most-places ability.

Besides the risk of hitting overhanging trees and snagging low-slung electrical wires in some villages, you'll have to turn back at low bridges and, in Africa, won't be able to get past the gates of many of the missions that offer overlanders' accommodation. Trees and certainly wires can be deflected by running a cable from the top of the front of the cab to the cabin's front corners (allowing a little slack for chassis flex). Along with this you have to consider anything snaggable on the roof too.

With width you're obviously guided by the cab, but it's better not to exceed the width of your mirrors, which can be used as 'feelers' for squeezing through very narrow gaps. An **interior width of 2 metres** (78″) ought to enable even a six-footer to sleep OK, so with insulation, keeping within 2.2 metres (87″) outside means tight tracks won't leave their mark.

CAB-TO-CABIN ACCESS

With a panel van it's possible to have open-plan walk-through access from the cab to the cabin. Some campervans even include swivelling front seats in the cab to face back to the cabin area: all very agreeable most of the time.

With a separate truck cab on a chassis it's less easily done as the rear body needs to be allowed to flex separately from the cab and in many cases the cab needs to tilt forward to give access to the engine. In this case a **crawl-through hatch** can be arranged, most easily by fitting sliding panels or windows facing each other in the back of the cab and front of the cabin. Whether this is made big enough to crawl through or just to 'hand through' is up to you. The unease some expect to feel about being isolated from the cab while asleep is understandable but unfounded (there's

As you'll soon read, the cab and a separate cabin need to articulate independently, but two lockable hatches between each section – even just 'crawl-throughs' – will be a very welcome feature.

more on p182, from a similar roof-tent point of view). Occasions when you'd want to hop out of bed and dive directly into the driving seat at 3.30am before the shooting starts, may never occur. Much more useful is the day-to-day practicality of a crawl-through hatch if, for example, it's freezing or pouring outside. There's also something to be said for an **alternative emergency exit** from a cabin besides the door; either a big enough window that can be opened right out, a roof hatch (see p235) or access to the cab as suggested here.

ACQUIRE A SHELL OR BUILD FROM SCRATCH

Clearly, mounting a ready-made cabin – be it a caravan, an ex-military shelter or commercial freezer box – saves a lot of work and caravans have the advantage of being potentially ready to simply wire up. However, anything formerly used by the army or a delivery network will likely have a rear door (as discussed on p56) and won't necessarily be sufficiently well insulated; nor will a **commercial body** be robust enough for overlanding. A **caravan** is a fragile structure, as any number of *Top Gear* episodes have proved. At the other extreme are the tough, demountable **ex-military metal shelters** available on the continent from NATO or ex-Warsaw Pact countries (see p122).

BUILDING A CABIN

Pictured earlier but worth repeating; an ex-Telecom van shell costing a few hundred pounds fitted back-to-front on an Iveco.

A former refrigerated body cleaned out and outfitted as a camper on the back of a lorry. The point in doing this is the great insulation.

A €12,000 shell manufactured by a refrigerated truck body fabricator in Spain for the German market. Insulation was about 100mm all round and with windows and doors fitted it can actually be considered pretty good value for money.

Only your imagination can hold you back when it comes to fitting a cabin-like structure on the back. I once thought a scrapped **refrigerated body** or even a Mercedes 814 freezer van might do the job, and later saw such a cabin at Bad Kissingen. Here the insulation might be as good as a €12,000 GRP FS shell (glass-reinforced plastic foam sandwich; more on p240). As long as the smell of kippers can be erased, a well-insulated GRP fridge body is easy to cut windows into and, if the freezer-compressor assembly is still attached, you'll have air-con to die for!

Remember, **effective insulation** (more on p244) keeps the interior cool in hot weather or warm when it's cold outside, as well as minimising the energy needed to both heat and possibly cool a cabin. As you will read insulation is something that can be difficult and expensive to do well from scratch.

ADDRESSING CHASSIS TORSION

A detailed and hopefully coherent explanation follows as this is an important concept to understand when mounting a cabin. As some have found, being unaware of it at the outset, or addressing it incorrectly, can prove nearly as disastrous as building a dream house on tidal sand.

Grab a long stepladder and jam one end against the base of a wall. It's easy to apply a little 'torsion' or twist to your end of the ladder. In doing so it won't break apart in a flurry of rungs and once you release the tension it will return to shape. It can be surprising to learn that seemingly solid structures such as

Left: Despite the effect of suspension and some give in the tyres, chassis deflection is clear when one axle is on a slope and the other is on the flat. In fact truck chassis are designed to flex in this way to absorb energy – if not they'd either snap or weigh twice as much. The problem comes when you want to mount a rigid box onto a chassis which cannot cope with flex. © knutsgarage.de
Right: Work had started on the cabin floor when the Bedford's chassis twist was recognised.

bridges, oil tankers, aircraft and even skyscrapers can also deform and recover in a similar way. To make any elongated structure or vessel completely rigid is either very expensive or results in it being incredibly heavy.

On a road vehicle you'd imagine the tyres and suspension are there to cope with uneven surfaces, while the chassis and body remain utterly rigid. A short, space-framed Baja desert racer can probably achieve the engineering grail of near-total **chassis rigidity**; a mass-produced, 4-metre-long 4x4 pickup or a longer truck chassis cannot.

Flex is unavoidable but on a 4x4 station wagon the one-piece body shell is a relatively rigid three-dimensional entity that's rubber-mounted on the chassis to isolate it from largely undetectable distortion. Even then, a **body shell** can still flex, especially on a cheap hatchback car because the body shell is also the **load-bearing structure**, a weight-saving design with no separate chassis called unibody or **monocoque**. Put your fingers against the inner edge of the door-top trim where it seals against the roof-lining and you can feel door-to-roof movement along a bumpy road, especially when heavily loaded.

The two body elements of a conventional pickup – the cab and the load bed – are less of a box-shaped structure than on a van or a car, and in one piece cannot be easily, lightly and cheaply made rigid. This is why the load bed is separated from the cab enabling both to move independently on the chassis. It enables the load bed and cab to deal with their respective payloads while subject to minimised flex over a shorter length of chassis.

Recognising that flex is inevitable, it might follow that repeated deformation leads to metal fatigue and eventual failure. In fact, within limits, a **chassis** can flex and recover just as your suspension does, and the Unimog chassis is designed to twist by up to 20°, bumper to bumper. A popular misconception assumes that this movement is an extension of suspension – with a Unimog this may be true but elsewhere not really; it's just an aspect of chassis design. Similarly, it's not the case that a traditional ladder chassis will flex only when all possible movement in the tyres and suspension is taken up. Some torsional flex will always be present, even if you're not trying to tie it in knots.

BUILDING A CABIN

Central pivots or trunnions in a 4-point set up, fixed directly to the cabin floor – no subframe.

Note the pressure on the chassis to twist and conform to uneven terrain is much greater under a **high payload** which is an overlanding certainty. An unloaded vehicle will more readily simply lift a wheel. A 4WD truck built to carry payloads of several tonnes off road has a chassis designed to twist. The trucks pictured on p225 are under no load but the deformation is clear.

The problem comes when you choose to mount a cabin, with all the added interior complexities of a small apartment, on a ladder chassis that will twist. Mount the cabin directly to the chassis and, unless it's built like the *USS Monitor*, the torsional stresses will eventually ruin it. Assuming the mounts hold up, the box will either crack, buckle or split and inside cabinets and other fittings may separate from the walls or each other.

Remember, it can work both ways. A very rigid cabin mounted directly to a chassis it was not designed for can stress the ladder chassis to breaking point. The **chassis has to be allowed to bend** because it needs to relieve stress, ideally by distributing it over its full length. Concentrating those stresses behind the cab, or even on a torsion-free subframe mounted on just four points, can be more than a chassis can take. And it's worth remembering that all this only applies to torsion (twisting). There are **many other ways a chassis can break or bend**, getting airborne or crashing among them. If not isolated, chassis twist can destroy a box, but pounding can finish off any chassis, subframe or not, especially if the payload is at the limit.

Mounting methods

Rubber-mounted 4x4 body shells are low, short and light but, beyond a certain size chassis, having rubber mounting that copes with the dynamic range of chassis twist can lead to other problems. When supporting, say, a 1-tonne, 2-metre-high cabin, the whole outfit can develop a cyclic wobble that could eventually pick up enough momentum to seriously affect steering and stability, like a pillion goofing about on the back of a motorcycle. Installing a regular **suspension damper** in line with the movement can fix that.

Mercedes' Unimog gets around the problem more elegantly with an ingenious geometric solution: having a **second subframe** on top of the chassis and mounted to it at three or four points. This arrangement of perpendicular pivots, or trunnions (illustrated opposite) effectively isolates the subframe from the twisting chassis while keeping the load above it securely in position. The flat plane of the subframe remains undistorted and as it's attached directly to the floor of your cabin, the floor too is isolated from chassis twist and so won't

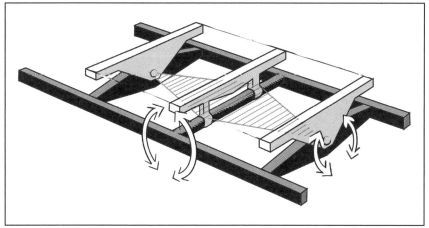

How the four points system works; allowing deflection in two planes, while keeping
any oscillation in the box under control without resorting to dampers.

blow your maple-veneer cupboards apart. A drawback with subframes is they
raise a load bed by up to 20cm (8") and so companies like Unicat in Germany
take it a step further and incorporate the subframe into the floor of their cabins. This has the important benefit of lowering the centre of gravity and so
making for a more stable platform.

The point where the relative displacement of the two parallel chassis rails is
minimal might be assumed to be midway: on a pickup it's the gap where the
back of the cab meets the front of the load bed. With cab-over pickups and trucks
commonly used in Europe and Asia, the load bed extends forward beyond this
neutral point, so making the load bed more susceptible to torsional distortion.
This is why the **four-point or 'diamond pattern' subframe** mount can work better. The two mounts in the middle are said to be closer to the neutral point.
Whether using three- or four-point mounts depends on chassis length and flexibility. Longer Unimogs use the more stable four-point system, which might be
said to be two three-points back to back across the chassis.

What does this all mean to an overlander intent on building or mounting
a cabin on a lorry chassis? If it's a European **ex-army 4WD truck**, chances are
it'll have some torsion-reducing
arrangement under the load bed, even
if it's just the rubbers pictured on the
next page. Theoretically you should be
able to mount a greenhouse on there
and drive around a motocross course
without making a mess. If it's a commercial 2WD flatbed, like the one pictured on p60 or even the **4WD Isuzu
and Fusos** described on p129, there's
no factory subframe, although some
manufacturers provide detailed guidance on how to proceed. Older Fuso

Old style rear pivot where chassis distortion
is most pronounced.

BUILDING A CABIN

Mounting methods. Top, left: Rubber mounts are the easy solution and how most cars and pick-ups deal with torsion but a heavy cabin may oscillate and require a damper (**top, right**).
Middle: Steel springs are another way of enabling a subframe to lift off a chassis in a controlled manner (**right** is from the GRP shell on p224). **Bottom**: Even bolts can give a little; **left** is the rear mount of the MAN on p238 and **right** is a U-bolt.

chassis are particularly flexible by European truck standards and don't adapt well to Unimog-style trunnion technology, which localises stresses. A subframe here must endeavour to distribute, not concentrate forces.

If in doubt, err towards vehicles with **torsion-reducing elements**, or be prepared for the complications and expense of getting it done yourself. There's more on p242 and some useful information online. Some ways round the whole business include: using a Tatra or MAN KAT truck, which are based around a **central tube** rather than a ladder chassis; devising a flex-accommodating shelter like a soft-top or a tent; or running a three-wheeler. Three points define a plane but like the apocryphal four-legged bar stool, a three-wheeler will settle evenly on any uneven surface without torsional issues. You wonder why NATO never went that way with a fleet of camo Bond Bug.

THE LAYOUT

Eating, sleeping, washing and storing: these activities sum up 'living' in a cabin. You'll certainly want to sleep, cook and sit down to eat, you may also like a toilet and a shower room. If fitting a ready-made camping cabin, most of these features are provided for you. If building from scratch you've the opportunity to lay it out exactly as you please. Take your cues from the illustration below. Designers have spent decades working out how to optimise the functions of living in a small mobile space.

Whatever you choose or build, if you plan to sleep across the width of the cabin make sure it's wide enough. Ideas like this are a possible leak point (as well as being cramped overhead).

One thing you might want to pin down is whether **sleeping** in the slot of an over-cab, or Luton extension, is suited to you. Some demountable over-cab cabins are so compact they have a rather inelegant drawer (above) that slides out of the side to make room for your feet. You'll do more in a bed than just lie prone and it may include sitting up and reading by a fan or the light of a window. Even if room is wasted, you will definitely appreciate having enough space above the mattress to sit up and breathe.

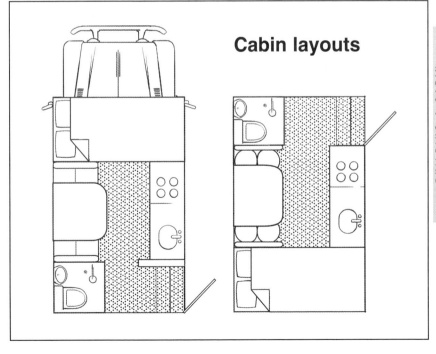

Cabin layouts

ELECTRICAL POWER SUPPLY

When it comes to running appliances the choices will be whatever your vehicle produces from the alternator, solar panels or portable external sources in 12 or 24 volts, as well as **mains voltage**. Broadly speaking, mains voltage comes in two spectrums worldwide. Over 90% of countries operate anywhere between 200 and 240 volts at 50 hertz, and half a dozen (including Brazil, Peru and South Korea) run the same range at 60 hertz. The rest, notably Japan and everywhere from Canada and the States (both 110v) down as far as Ecuador run between 100 and 127 volts/60 hertz.

This mainly has a bearing for **North American overlanders** equipping a vehicle to travel beyond the American continent. If they want to hook up to a mains supply once in a while, they'll be much better off acquiring **230-volt appliances** as used in Australasia, west, south and Southeast Asia, Europe and half of Africa; half the world in fact. The alternative means using power-consuming **transformers** or being autonomous with a 110-volt **generator**.

Be aware that in some countries the mains power supply doesn't run smoothly and predictably. India and Pakistan are perhaps the best known places where frequent power cuts and more damaging **voltage spikes** could fry your electrical gadgets.

WATER

Some form of storage as well as filtration, delivery and disposal needs to be arranged, which means frost-proof tanks, piping, filters, pumps and outlets, as well as possible storage of **'grey water'** (what goes down your plug holes as opposed to down the toilet, which is known as **'black water'**). All toilet waste ought to be disposed of responsibly and black tanks aren't really suited to overlanding, but you might consider a grey-water tank unnecessary too. Out in the bush for one night it'll be OK to have a wet patch of grey water draining under the truck, but if camped in missions, hotel car parks and proper campsites this can become messy and anti-social.

One way round it in these situations is to either place a bucket under the grey-water drain point beneath the vehicle, or run a long hose of 10 or 20 metres (up to 60ft) from the drain point into the long grass. Be aware that, as it's collected outside the cabin, a grey-water tank can be prone to freezing, so consider an alternative outlet if you intend to stay parked up in sub-zero conditions and don't want your sink to back up. Once on the move the flow of engine heat will probably free up a frozen grey-water tank.

Like fuel, gas, money and visas, filling up with water can become an obsession and is of course most easily solved with a large capacity as well as the ability to refill water from all types of sources: natural, unfiltered and domestic. There are some ideas on p172, with the rest on p247.

HEATING AND VENTILATION

If you're between the tropics and stay below about 1000 metres (3300ft), with good insulation and bedding and if you preserve the heat from cooking, you might never need additional **heating**. But it is fairly easily achieved and can provide a much greater comfort range, which one day you're bound to appreciate.

One simple way is to extend the driving cab's **heater system** into the back cabin. Although this relies on a hot, running engine, it's a great way to pre-warm a cabin prior to stopping for the night and, with good insulation and a hot dinner, might do you for the evening. Problem is your cabin will be coldest first thing in the morning, at which time small, autonomous **diesel-powered heaters** with fan blowers can quickly warm it up.

Engine-heated radiators plumbed into a Carawagon. © Toby Savage

More commonly, **condensation** will be an issue in a confined space, especially while cooking. As with any room, the answer is **ventilation**: a flow of air across the cabin, using an arrangement of windows and strategically positioned **fans**. Condensation can also form under the mattress against the bed base so you'll need some slats or a similar arrangement underneath your **mattress** to create airflow if you're to avoid mildew. To make airing, flipping, cleaning and taking outside easier, fit a mattress made of three slabs: the boxed-in rim will keep it in place.

A roof hatch (see p235) is a quick way of purging hot air from the cabin. If there's room and enough strength up there, on hot nights the **roof** will be a far more agreeable place to spend the night than inside. It's a good idea to cover all windows and other apertures with sliding or removable **mosquito screens**, including one to hang over the door and even a mosquito net to drop down over the bed on hot nights. After a summer in Siberia, you won't feel so blasé about insects. More on p252.

SHOWER AND TOILET

This might be the biggest question you face in your build, or quite possibly the reason you want to build a cabin in the first place, having formerly roughed it in a station wagon or compact campervan. A dedicated **shower room** might take up an eighth of your floor space, and add considerably to the cost and plumbing complexity, but it's not something you're likely to regret.

As always, the caveat is that you're on the road for months, not just a couple of weeks when 'roughing it' can be a laugh as you'll be home soon or can pop into a motel. On the road your van is your home and despite the complications, a permanent shower and a sit-down toilet won't be regretted, not least should you get struck down by diarrhoea while queuing patiently on the Torugart Pass.

Showers

Privacy and climate notwithstanding, a shower can be taken as agreeably, and with fewer bashed elbows, **outside the vehicle**. Van-side shower tents are commonly used by 4x4 drivers for this purpose and Trevor and Jan Rutters at ⌨ gapyear4x4.com raved about their hand-pumped, 5-litre Hozelock Portashower, which costs just £20 and features a useful trigger at the shower head. It's based on gardening hand-pumps for spraying plants; just make sure you flush out any DDT before hosing yourself down.

BUILDING A CABIN

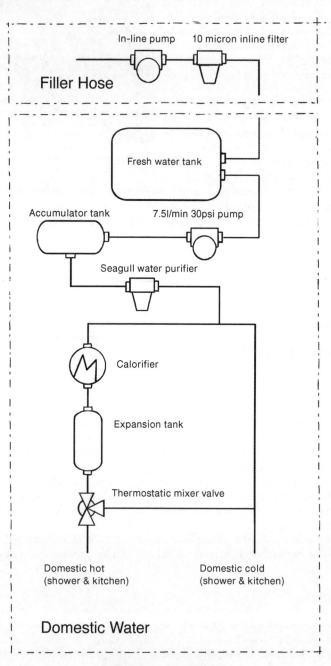

Water system

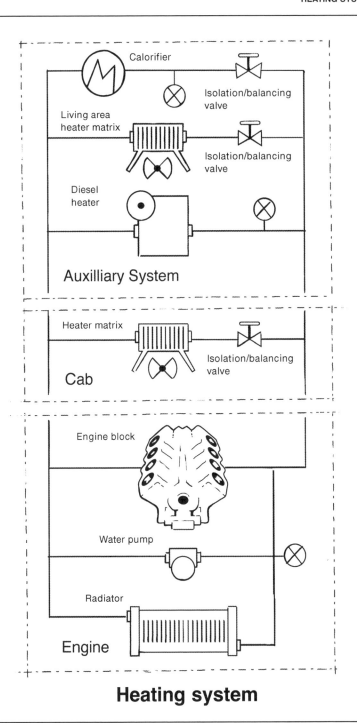

Heating system

From top. 1: Even if you have a shower in the cabin it's often easier to do it outside, if not off the side of the Lake Nasser ferry. © David Horner. **2**: So fit a hose connection outside the vehicle. **3**: With no water system to speak of, a plant sprayer does the job. **4**: Shower squeezed into the 130 Land Rover pictured on p218. Full size bed on the left, too.

BUILDING A CABIN

Even without a shower room, **inside a cabin** it's possible to rig up a **temporary means of washing** using either a bucket and pitcher or an inexpensive submersible 12-volt water pump dropped into a jerry of warm water with a handheld shower head. Both can be used inside a shower curtain hung from the ceiling with the bottom either tucked into a child's inflatable paddling pool, a plastic tray, or positioned in a stepped-down, self-draining area by the entrance door.

Making-do can work, but the prospect of just stripping off and stepping into a shower room without any faffing about is irresistible. Remember, this can also be used as a **laundry room**, a toilet, or somewhere to hose down muddy boots or hang dripping clothes while on the move. If you fit a fan vent plumbed to the engine coolant circuit (along with an extractor fan), the cubicle can even become a **drying room** that uses the engine's waste heat as you drive along.

Toilets

Fixed or portable **cassette toilets** are compact, light, easy to use, and have a waste tank that can be easily detached and emptied. You don't have to use them all the time and so the periods between emptying the tank can be extended, although four or five days seems the average for two people. It's urine combining with solids that creates bad odours, so if you can pee elsewhere, so much the better. A fixed unit can be positioned in a shower room and plumbed to a black-water tank; portable units can go in there too, though it's more common to have them slide in from a side cavity.

Toilet fluids require using special paper and are now considered a thing of the past. Overlanding, you'll eventually run out of both, anyway. These days the form is to run a **'dry' toilet** system with an extractor fan that purges smells via a charcoal filter. Plenty of fresh air is all it takes to decompose solid waste, and is partly how composting toilets work.

The **leading name** in portable cassette toilets is Thetford, while the German SOG company is the equivalent for extractor-fan assemblies made to fit Thetford's models, although something like this could be made yourself without too much difficulty. A portable Thetford costs from £300 and weighs about 7kg. An

A plughole in every corner is a clever way of ensuring a shower/toilet cubicle drains fully.

SOG unit costs about £100, but will require installation into the body shell.

ROOF AND SIDE HATCHES AND ROOF ACCESS

If you're familiar with roof tents you'll know that getting up on the roof can be fun. To be able to do so from inside the vehicle via a **roof hatch** has many benefits, in addition to greatly improving ventilation. Although a marine-grade hatch won't be cheap, it avoids the need for an external access ladder and either way the benefit is a roof terrace that's part of, but outside the cabin. This may require strengthening the roof and rearranging any gear up there, as well as possibly adding side rails, but the appeal in being on the roof as well as being able to leave stuff up there overnight, out of the way and out of sight, will all be worthwhile. Get one that opens right out back onto the roof.

The obvious place to **position** the hatch is over a fixed bed from which you can easily haul yourself up and drop back in. Once closed, water leaks shouldn't be an issue, but there is a risk of forgetting to close the hatch and ending up in soaked bedding, much worse than a wet floor. If getting on the roof is not a priority, position it where it's most convenient.

Some upmarket AWD motorhomes now have a huge **portal** of a metre square or more that opens right out. Set in a side wall, usually alongside the dining table and reaching right down to the cabin floor, it can be the next best thing to eating alfresco and will vent your cabin almost instantly.

BUILDING A CABIN

Fold out flat sunroof (also pictured on p126).

A big side hatch by the table – it's almost like having a balcony.

A typical upswept rear storage compartment. Wooden slats limit damage from loose items.

STORAGE FOR BULKY GEAR

Taking things like bikes and boats needs secure and accessible storage. A bike sat on a rear platform or rack is commonly seen, but will be vulnerable to damage, dirt and theft. The cab or cabin roof are more secure if less convenient. A surfboard or canoe can only really go on the roof.

While they may only be playthings, **ease of access** is vital, otherwise you won't bother using them. It means being able to act on the desire to cycle somewhere and afterwards re-secure it with a minimum of fuss. Stepladder-like rollers on the edge of the roof or the rack can help. Otherwise, the cabin example illustrated on p229 features a large **rear compartment** commonly used for this sort of stuff. It can be arranged or partitioned to give access both from the inside under the bed, and outside from the side or the rear, and will always have a use to store items you don't want or need in the cabin.

SECURITY

The theft of your vehicle is pretty unlikely, but petty theft will be a worry, especially when the vehicle is unattended. Try and imagine leaving it in the open or a public space for a few days. How much and what kind of attention will it attract? What exterior items might get pilfered? How might a thief get in and what things of value could they take once there?

'Out of sight, out of mind'. If there's nothing to catch the eye, it may go unnoticed. This need not mean grills and tinted windows; just remember to leave **nothing on show in the cab**. One good thing about a big truck is windows well above head height.

Most ordinary caravans and motorhomes have doors which are easily prised open. If this is a worry, fit a door with deadlocks into a solid frame as well as pins slotting up and down. Some overlanders recommend using **flimsy door handles** that'll break off before the door gives. A broken handle is easily replaced.

Along with all this comes common sense. **Big cities** rather than a dark desert highway are where your van is most at risk, and where it's worth the hassle of storing all your exterior items inside.

In the end, just as at home, you cannot stop a determined thief with a crowbar or a sledge hammer, but you can slow them down once inside. Made for the job are compact **vehicle safes** for daily use or for storing back-up documents, SD cards and cash and bolted directly to the floor of the cab. Some feature easy-to-use digital combination locks so there's no worry with keys, only amnesia. Back in the cabin it's worth bolting a larger **stout metal locker** to the floor, but, again, out of clear sight. This can be used to easily store cameras, laptops, satellite phones and other valuables while you are out shopping or sightseeing.

In the end what do you really need to be left with? As with the backpacker's 'decoy wallet' containing a bit of cash and expired credit cards to hand to muggers pressed for time, it's worth having a similar arrangement in the van if you find yourself getting cleaned out under duress: something substantial to hand over from the obvious 'treasure chest' locker. Meanwhile, have some cash, a mobile phone plus essential details (see p25) stashed in a place that would take some luck to find. Think laterally: it can't hurt that access to the cache might require unscrewing or moving something – just don't forget where that place is. You may never need it but it's good to know it's there.

Building and mounting a cabin

Even if you know your way around CAD graphics, try to mock up your intended living area in real space. Go into an empty garage or a room with tape measure and masking tape and **size out the volume** of your intended cabin. Factor in insulation of up to 6cm (2.5"), a bed at 1.4 metres (55") wide and all the overhead cabinetry. Knock up some interior walls and a stoop-free ceiling, and with a kitchen, dining area and a shower/toilet cubicle it can all look rather compact.

You don't have to build a perfectly **rectilinear box**. A bevelled edge along the top sides can reduce the **frontal profile** and makes the body less prone to tree strikes on narrow tracks. It's a design found on Soviet-era LAK cabins (right) with the bevelled walls being a good position for out-of-the-way sky-

light windows. But even though maximum headroom at the wall tops inside is rarely needed, these bevels do eat into potential cupboard space.

Cutting back the top front edge, as with the MAN pictured overleaf, has benefits in streamlining and quite probably wind noise too. You just need to calculate the fuel saved for the time and cost it takes to make that extra edge. Eventually you'll pin down a size and style that suits you, but just as you wouldn't start building a house by ordering a load of bricks, joists and tiles, so you shouldn't rush

LAK body with bevelled edges; building similar takes time and money.

into building a cabin before you can clearly visualise the finished unit. It cannot be emphasised enough that like a Coen brothers film, you need to have the whole plan figured out before the first pieces of cut steel are ordered. Sure, you can change your mind, but it'll cost you time and money and you're already spending plenty of that.

Where will the cooking-gas tank, the house batteries and the water tanks go? How will the tanks be filled, filtered and drained? How will the electrical system work and where will the wiring run? Are the windows and door in the ideal position? And not least what will this all actually **cost** you; the electrical conversion and management units, pumps and filters, piping, wire and joints, insulation and plywood lining – all the materials as well as the tools to fit them. The time it takes? That's free.

Once that's estimated, make some **plans** of the systems similar to those on p229, p233 and p251. They don't have to be engineering-style, computer-generated blueprints, just a schematic map so you know the 'hip bone is connected to the thigh bone', and so on. If nothing else, these plans will be an asset when it comes to someone else repairing or selling the vehicle.

INTERIOR LAYOUTS

Conventional motorhome and caravan layouts closely match what's used by overlanders. No surprise there. But you'll also need greater autonomy and range, may have to face more extreme climates, and will want everything to hold up a long way from home and far from support.

The graphic of a **side-entry layout** on p229 is one you'll see replicated in cabins everywhere: the bed at the back on a platform with storage underneath, kitchen to one side, dining area opposite and on a platform, and the shower room in one corner or the other. Rear doors, as found on panel vans that also may have a sliding side door and whose living space can be integral with the cab, require a different set-up, as do rear-door-only ex-military shelters that are isolated from the cab. When making your own cabin, with the bed out of the way at the front, the door is more often set to the rear with the shower room in the opposite back corner.

FABRICATING THE BOX

The traditional way of fabricating a box is with a **metal frame** or superstructure that sits directly on the chassis, a torsion-free subframe or a load bed. **Mild steel box section** is what most use; strong, inexpensive and easy to weld or get welded, but it corrodes and is much heavier than aluminium. **Stainless steel** can be heavier still, costs double and requires more skill to weld. It's also more 'brittle' against shock loads but will corrode less quickly. In the same size tubing, **aluminium** is lighter and especially in round tube can be as strong if correctly designed with the aid of high-pressure hydro-forming and then hand welded (as with better MTB frames). Such engineering marvels are unlikely to occur in your garden shed, and although it's non-ferrous, in some circumstances aluminium can rot just as badly (see opposite) and lacks the springiness of mild steel. Aluminium is a little less expensive than stainless.

The frame is then **clad** either in sheet metal, most commonly aluminium, or in combinations of GRP (glass-reinforced plastic) either side of cores that might include plywood or foam. If you're used to working with **wood**, you could simply clad the exterior in **marine ply**, skipping the weatherproofing elements of sheet metal, and the superior insulation value of GRP sandwich panels. On a 4-metre-long box you save at least 32 square metres of aluminium, weighing 125kg.

Cladding the body in ally and ply.
© theoverlander.org

None of these cladding methods add load-bearing strength to the cabin. That needs the metal frame, although as well as riveting, **gluing** the panels to the frame helps spread loads. Indeed, gluing instead of riveting may be perfectly adequate. Many cars and planes are made this way, the crux is to work with perfectly clean surfaces and the right glue, which can include a thick, elastic layer. With a lot at stake, until you know better, it's understandable to resist putting all faith in glue.

ALUMINIUM TO STEEL CORROSION

Contact between dissimilar metals like mild steel and aluminium can lead to **galvanic** and **electrolytic corrosion**. The former is exacerbated by salt-laden roads or seawater, the latter is due to stray electrical currents and can be much more harmful, as many Land Rover owners will know. Your vehicle or any mixed-metal structure becomes an immeasurably weak battery and is why oil rigs and ships are fitted with sacrificial aluminium anodes, drawing any current from the steel structure to decay harmlessly.

We're talking about a tiny current so it'll take a couple of years, but the thin aluminium sheet used for cladding would be especially prone. The simple answer, known to the aircraft industry for decades, is to separate the surfaces with an **inert coating** of paint, tape, glue, rubber or wood, while sealing the vessel against external moisture.

Therefore, don't rivet your aluminium sheet directly to an uncoated mild-steel frame (stainless will be less prone). Any coating such as zinc or paint will help but is bound to wear off, so much better to glue and press the sheet alloy onto plywood or similar and then rivet through that to the frame. This has the obvious benefit of making the soft exterior aluminium skin more resistant to knocks as well as being the first step in insulation.

Plywood

Plywood is made from several thin sheets of wood glued together under great pressure with the grains in each ply at right angles to the next. This makes it very strong and resistant to cracking, warping, bending and shrinkage. As with all wood, it's a good insulator too. 'WBP' means 'weather- and boil-proof', in other words suited to outdoor use, and it comes as inexpensive softwood commonly sourced from the Far East, or birch or other hardwoods, which can be twice the price and about 20% heavier per square metre. **Marine ply** is waterproof and treated against rot.

At 26mm (1") thick, plywood weighs about 100lb for the standard 1220 x 2440mm (4 x 8ft) sheet bought off the shelf. That's 15.3kg per square metre so a 4-metre box clad in 1" ply comes in at over half a tonne – a good example of how easily weight can multiply.

GRP panels

In self-building cabin applications, GRP (fibreglass) panels are usually two skins a couple of millimetres thick, bonded to a **core** of either plywood, open-celled foam, or a honeycomb in aluminium or polypropylene like NidaCore (Nidaplast), Airex or less expensive Hexacor. All come in an array of grades and finishes for different uses and are often used in boat building.

Panels can be used in two ways: to clad a metal frame or, using thicker more rigid panels, to make a **monoblock box** or any shape where the GRP walls are the load-bearing 'bricks and mortar', not the 'wallpaper and plaster'. Fabricating the actual box solely out of GRP panels rather than clamping it to a metal frame has many benefits, but cost and ease are not among them. It's a job best left to professionals or those confident their efforts won't unravel.

An individual might be able to master **cladding a frame**, because panels can come in sizes big enough to build the side wall, floor or roof of a very long cabin out of one piece. Successfully gluing together the six panels to make a box for overlanding, rather than delivering frozen peas to Tescos, is not for the faint-hearted. One idea is welding up a **perimeter box-frame** of 80mm (or

COLD BRIDGES

In building construction a **cold** or **thermal bridge** is a highly conductive interface or conduit along which heat is drawn from a warm interior to the cold exterior. Metal, especially steel, is a very good conductor of heat so to maintain effective insulation, bolts driven directly from the outside through any insulation to the inside should be minimised, or avoided altogether.

In building a functionally insulated cabin, you're trying to emulate the insulation mechanism of a duvet jacket or sleeping bag; the fluffy down fill separates the body-warmed inner and exposed outer surfaces, trapping a layer of warm, still air. A 'cold bridge' in this sense equates to a sewn-through seam on a cheap bag.

Cold bridges can be a problem when lining out the non-rectilinear form of a **panel van** that has bulky metal structural members directly spot-welded to the thin sheet-steel body panels to give them form. With a self-built cabin, a plywood sandwich between the outer sheet-metal skin and the frame is the first step in giving you an insulation benefit over a panel van.

more) aluminium angle, and then gluing the GRP panels into it and to each other. This way the alloy frame adds the strength that you may not be able to achieve gluing panel to panel without special machinery or years of practice.

In Europe you can buy an **overland-ready GRP FS cabin** as a shell ready for outfitting for about €12,000 with insulation to refrigeration standards and a tough plywood floor. Home-made or a shell, the huge **benefits** in GRP sandwich panels of up to 100mm thick include a hard, smooth, easy-to-clean surface that's also easy to cut into and glue on to. As an exterior skin, a typical 2–3mm thickness is also much more resilient to light knocks and scratches than aluminium, even when it's backed on ply. It's lighter than sheet steel and

FABRICATION MATERIALS: COMPARATIVE WEIGHTS AND PRICES

Some prices and weights per metre of steel, aluminium and GRP panels. It's all bound to get out of date and will vary according to the quantity bought, location and so on. The idea is to compare weights and costs to help with the budget.

Material	Price (both per metre or m²)	Weight
Sheet		
Galvanised mild steel sheet 1mm	£30	8kg/m²
Mild steel sheet 1.5mm	£33	11.7kg/m²
Galvanised mild steel sheet 1.5mm	£41	12kg/m²
Aluminium sheet 1.5mm	£31	3.9kg/m²
Tube		
Mild steel 40mm square x 2.5mm	£10	3kg/m
Alu 51mm (2") square x 3.25mm	£17	1.7kg/m
Inox 40mm square x 1.5mm	£18	1.8kg/m
Ply board		
Softwood (Far Eastern) marine 4ft x 8ft x 18mm sheet	£60	10kg/m²
Hardwood/marine 4ft x 8ft x 18mm sheet	£87	11kg/m²
Panel		
RP FS 1.5mm skins + 12mm plywood, 85mm	£110	12kg/m²
GRP FS 1.5mm skins, 85mm thick	£96	4kg/m²
NidaCore panels, 2mm skins, 25mm thick	£200	4kg/m²

Foam sandwich panels, some with GRP skin and some with plywood on one side. Six of those plus some glue and you have yourself a cabin.

The NidaCore honeycomb alternative – with each cell sealed it's less prone to water migration in the event of a crack.

even on the few occasions it doesn't come ready painted in white, it still reflects UV rays better than both metals. And best of all you get no cold bridges or rusting while gaining excellent **insulation**.

The only flaws might be that you don't get a chance to tidy away the plumbing and cabling behind inner panels and so **ducting** will need to be fitted. As this can run inside cabinets along the top or bottom of the walls, it's no great loss compared to the insulation properties you gain, and at least means it's accessible.

Take a look at this sample corner from the GRP shell pictured on p224 and ask yourself if you can do as good a job. The floor panel is a solid ply and foam construction that can probably be mounted directly onto the torsion-eliminating trunnions as pictured on p227. The floor itself has a hard wearing coating and channels for underfloor heating pipes.

SIKAFLEX AND 3M SEALANTS

Both these companies make a baffling range of adhesives and sealants that all fit into the glue gun but are intended for quite different applications. While other brands such as Tiger Seal, Geobond, Carabond, Carafax IDL 99 and Gripfill make less expensive equivalents, they're not all just a version of the silicon mastic you squirt around the edge of a bath or shower pan. As you'd expect, a same-sized tube designed for caravans can be half the price of something intended for marine applications.

Some are high-strength polyurethane adhesives for **fixing your alloy cladding** to plywood. There's nothing too technical in that other than a good, permanent bond. Other types are **designed to bond and flex** when applied to a minimum thickness with the aid of spacers. Among other uses, these are suited to interior partitions that might otherwise come away as a new cabin body settles into shape after a few rough tracks. There are also **sealing but non-setting**

agents like Carafax, which are suited to fittings you might want to remove later, such as the frame of a broken window. Use a high-strength adhesive for this and you'll destroy the surfaces either side of the frame trying to take it apart unless you can get a sharp blade in there.

You need to know your Sikaflex 221 polysulphide adhesive/sealant from your 512 'Caravan' all-purpose, polyurethane sealant, and elastic 521 UV polymer sealant, while at the same time not waste money on something that's designed to seal torpedo tubes in the Arctic. Even the Sika website is not so clear. Note too that these products have use-by dates after which they will slowly begin to harden.

As with all adhesives, **clean surfaces** are vital, especially with plastics and aluminium, which oxidises so quickly a protective coating is applied during manufacture. If you're unsure, a quick blast of something like Panel Wipe will eliminate any grease.

GRP with an open-cell foam core is susceptible to water absorption if damaged or not fully **sealed**, which can eventually rot the foam. All joins must be perfect, adding a level of skill to the task, and any subsequent cracks repaired quickly. Although only available in thinner thicknesses, the NidaCore-like honeycombs are deemed superior by some cabin builders as in the event of the GRP skin getting pierced or cracked, water ought not to spread beyond the damaged or exposed cells.

Joints or angles where panels meet will require sealing with glue or resin and fibreglass. There'll be at least twelve exterior edges and eight corners, all which need **capping**, for example with 5mm alloy or GRP angle sealed with Sikaflex or 3M 5200 (see box above). And you want to be sure that any angle trim along the lower edges is completely sealed against possible water ingress.

MOUNTING THE CABIN SHELL

Assuming the vehicle's chassis is solid and complemented with a very thick cabin floor and more than four mounts, a short and robust cabin in GRP or a steel frame could be mounted **directly** to a 4x4 pickup chassis, as is the case with the Italian Gobi pictured on p71. Very much depends on the inherent torsional rigidity of both structures. A longer chassis will flex for sure and it's something you may not be able to calculate, other than by copying previous designs and hoping for the best. A common mistake is to overbuild the cabin, adding weight and expense. As mentioned above, it goes both ways: in trying to protect a cabin from distortion you may stress the chassis to breaking point. Even on a chassis with a mounting length of only 2 metres, where flex might not be expected, simply **bolting the sides** of a subframe directly to the chassis with sheer- or fishplates will allow for a little movement, possibly enough to preserve your cabin from damage. It's the same stress-reducing principle behind bolted rather than welded roof racks, though of course an eye must be kept on these chassis bolts. Where you fit these plates is also critical as under torsion all stresses will be concentrated there; the **best-practice documents** from MAN will give you some ideas.

Even fixing with special bolts works. Fishplate on the right keeps subframe in line.

You'll see the 7.5-tonne Chinese flatbed truck pictured on p60 is arranged like this, but with a layer of hardwood between the chassis and the subframe. This hardwood – or any similar material – supports the load while enabling some movement. It also has the added effect of reducing resonance so making for a smoother, quieter driving experience.

Rubber mounting

The next easiest way is **rubber mounting** the underside of the cabin on outriggers attached to the chassis, as pictured on p228 on an Iveco. It's the simplest guarantee that the structure won't fail and may have been how an original body was mounted, which means the thinking's been done for you. Having more than four mounts will distribute stresses and limit your tall cabin's rocking movement. It's a matter of matching the rubber mounts to the expected weight and driving conditions. Apart from the above-mentioned best-practice documents, no textbooks or formulae exist as there are so many variables. There are only people who've done something similar before and by chance, or following trial and error, got it right in the end.

Coil springs

A **line of springs** also on outriggers can be as effective as rubber mounts and may be more suited to a heavy cabin. Again, a hardwood batten between the chassis and subframe would reduce creaking and steel-on-steel grinding, but as with rubber mounts, the whole point must be that the subframe (or the floor of your cabin) experiences no torsion while the springs take up any deformation in the chassis. To have the longitudinal strength to do this can mean the steel subframe 'C' beams might end up weighing almost as much as the section of the chassis they lie against, although up to a point a rigid cabin floor will work with them and can even replace them (see photo p228). Finding the correct spring rates for your set-up will be another complex calculation which may end up being an educated guess.

The good thing with the spring- and the bolted-side plate methods is that most of the time the weight of the cabin is fully supported along the entire length of the chassis, an ideal arrangement compared to having the cabin weight perched and therefore concentrated on half a dozen rubber mounts or even 3- or 4-point mounts as outlined on p226.

BUILDING A CABIN

COUNTERACTING POSSIBLE CABIN OSCILLATION

The problem with the rubber or coil spring methods is that they can't suppress possible **side-to-side swaying** of the cabin once on the move – that is, when looking from the back, the cabin swaying from left to right around the mounts as the road's irregularities, braking and acceleration magnify the momentum. It's probably worse with rubber mounts, whilst coils ought to be matched with the weight of the box, something that is difficult to calculate.

One way to reduce excessive cabin sway is to fit an automotive shock absorber – or a 'damper' to be precise. As with suspension, dampers will suppress any unwanted cyclic oscillations that could easily escalate (as mentioned on p228), while permitting full deformation in the springs/rubber and chassis when needed. Purists will claim that if the mounting arrangement is correct, such as the 3- or 4-point Unimog system, there should be no need for a damper. This is true, but just as with suspension, rubber or coil springs have little inherent damping and so may need some help.

A damper should link the chassis to the cabin subframe at around 45° and in line with the expected lateral rolling of the cabin; see the picture on p228. One chunky shock on each side ought to do it and you could experiment with a sliding, adjustable mount at one end to find the best angle; 45° is just an optimal average. Because it's a relatively easy job, there is nothing to be lost by at least making some damper mounting points. If they're not needed but the torsion-free arrangement still works then you can pat yourself on the back and patent the system.

Other mounting options

Another solution is to **bolt the subframe rails to the rear** of the chassis while retaining springs along its length, or at least at the front behind the cab. Viewed from the back the bolted end rotates to the left or right with the twisting chassis ends while, at the front of the 'free' subframe rail, ends located by springs lift away.

Freestyling like this introduces all sorts of uncalculated stresses into the chassis, which was quite probably designed for something entirely different. Within reason, a chunky European, all-terrain truck will handle something like this better than an Asian cab-over pickup. Very much depends on the mounted loads and how hard you intend to push the vehicle.

A better option to the above is a **trunnion pivoting at the rear** with bolted or sprung mounts at the front. The lifting occurs here as the trunnion moves independently off the chassis on self-aligning bearings, rather than expecting the end-bolted fixing (as suggested above) to give a little. Here you're moving towards 3- or 4-point mounts and so lifting the weight of the subframe (and the cabin sat on it) onto the mount points and off the chassis rails, so the engineering needs to be sound.

If you finally arrive at the need for a Unimog-style torsion-free solution you're much better off buying a vehicle with that set-up from the factory rather than going through the effort and expense of making your own.

INSULATION AND LINING

The value of insulation in an overlanding vehicle is commonly under-appreciated, just as it used to be in houses. An effective thermal barrier between the outside diurnal fluctuations greatly stabilises the temperature in your cabin around the domestic standard of 18°C/64°F and makes it easier to achieve the optimal 'cool in summer, warm in winter' ideal.

Before you get too carried away you need to decide what form of insulation you're going to use and also whether these cavities will be running conduits for electric cabling and water. It's a reminder that you need to look at the build as a whole and not just view it as a series of discrete tasks.

At the very least figure out how water will get from the water tank to the outlets, including the kitchen sink and shower, and then where it goes from there, as well as where you'll want lighting and electric sockets. To improve weather-proofing you want to have as few holes in the lining and cladding as possible, but you also want to avoid having to pull everything apart should you decide to add a socket or fix a light by the bed. Remember, once you've used certain Sikaflex-type glues on the lining and insulation, there's no going back. It may be less neat, but having **wires and piping boxed in** along the edges of the walls makes access, repair and modifications easier.

The good thing with cladding your own frame of box section metal tube is that, once done, there's a ready-made cavity of, say, 40mm to fill with insulation. **Panel van** converters have a harder time of it, as the factory body isn't a perfectly rectilinear box. Curved roofs and interior structural members onto which the steel shell is pop-riveted require the gluing of carefully profiled wooden battens so the insides can be made perpendicular to the floor.

Having a double-glazed-style **air gap** between the lining and the outer shell works OK, but not as well as lagging, which traps thousands of small air pockets rather than one big one. Assuming the lining is not hermetically sealed, **condensation** will form inside the body's outer steel skin and run down. Any insulation will do, even those annoying peanut-shaped polystyrene pellets you get for protective packaging. As with a duvet, it's all about limiting air convection – stilled air makes a barrier to the outside.

Don't forget that unlike in a house planted into the ground, **the floor** of your cabin needs as much insulation as the roof, if not more. Converters of 'unibody' panel vans often shy away from doing this as headroom is quickly lost, but the air flowing underneath the steel shell of a van will cool or heat the floor just as it does the walls and roof.

Condensation

By including a thermal barrier in your cabin you not only keep warm but also greatly reduce the chances of **condensation** – water vapour from cooking or breathing forming as tiny water drops on shiny, cold surfaces. As we all know, in a vehicle window glass is most prone to this, followed by sheet steel. Some condensation is inescapable but its formation can be mitigated by good ventilation and by minimising smooth interior surfaces. Of course, living in a stationary cabin or a camper rather than driving it around will exacerbate condensation. Any water in a closed vessel will tend to run down to the lowest point where, if it can't evaporate easily, it'll collect and fester over time. You don't want that. Certainly it's worthwhile integrating a **steam hood** over the cooking area or even having a top-hinged inward-opening window here to let the vapour escape (at the cost of occasionally letting some rain in).

A method used in the back of a hardtop van is simply **lining the interior sheet metal** with a felt-like material. It may not insulate much but any moisture will readily evaporate on the rough, woolly surface.

Types of insulation

Broadly speaking two methods exist. You either inject cavities or spray on expanding, quick-setting (PU) foam, or you glue on slabs of closed-cell foam panels, rolls of wool, foam-like wool or rockwool lagging.

Two-part **expanding PU spray foam** can be bought in kit form, although it can work out cheaper to have it done for you. Once you've masked off areas you don't want buried in hardened foam, and installed any ducting or conduits, dial-a-foam-man hops in and lets rip. How evenly the coat is applied will determine how much work you have to cut it back to a smooth surface.

Another way to get a complete, gap-free fill behind your panelling is to first apply a thin coat to the inner metal skin, then fit your plywood panels and finish off by **injecting** foam. Be careful how you go about this cavity-fill method as once foam expands it can push a plyboard away from the wall.

Although all insulation does this to a certain extent, a side benefit of this self-hardening 'pressure fill' is in adding some **rigidity** to the structure as well as reducing resonance and improving overnight **soundproofing**.

Laying on the lagging.
© theoverlander.org

If spraying is not for you then you can do it all yourself by installing **rolls of lagging** such as fireproof mineral-based rockwool, or 'eco-wool' loft insulation made mostly from recycled plastic bottles. Designed to lie horizontally with your old toys in a dark and dry attic for the next few decades, it's not so suited to being hung vertically on the sides of a van that's prone to condensation. Even if it's glued on or battened in place, the shaking and extreme temperature changes may see regular roof lagging break down. And the whole point of insulation is to achieve full coverage across the entire cabin, just as you're trying hard to avoid any cold bridges.

Thermafleece makes slabs from real sheep's wool, which is meant to breathe out any moisture it might absorb. Try and install insulation on a hot, dry day and then hermetically seal off cavities with a **vapour barrier** such as a plastic sheet so no moisture can ever get in there.

Depending on the shape of your cabin, **rigid foam panels** can be more difficult to fit. It's similar to the closed-cell foam used in the old Karrimat sleeping mats or those split tubes of pipe lagging. It cannot absorb water and so is waterproof so if tightly applied it eliminates the need for a vapour barrier, which some other insulation materials may require. It may be worth deciding what you plan to use and distancing the cabin's metal frame members accordingly. Kingspan make various products, as do Thermaflex, Xtratherm and Celotex. As you'll soon discover, there's a whole parallel universe of exciting insulation products waiting to line your cabin. When it's all done you can fill any gaps with the expanding foam used in car repairs and clad the whole lot in plywood. And when that's done, don't forget to turn down the thermostat a few notches.

Mission control.

ELECTRICS

The basics of **electrics** in a 4x4 are covered on pp195-216. Wiring out a cabin to the standard of a house and including mains voltage sockets is another job entirely in which the positions of batteries in relation to other components, cable thicknesses, fuse boxes, regulators and relays are all critical and better left to a professional, unless you know better. With all this done you'll doubtless end up with some sort of **control panel or board** with battery charging and other monitoring devices as pictured above, and, not least, a **battery isolator** switch should something electrical short out and threaten to start a fire.

When installing cable runs don't forget to include a few **spare wires** for things you may add later, or have a tied-off string in there with which you can pull additional wires through. Failing that, a vacuum cleaner is said to be able to suck a new wire up providing the bends aren't too severe.

PLUMBING

While electricity above 24 volts ought not to be something an amateur gets involved with, water and plumbing systems are easier to understand and less dangerous when you get them wrong.

With a storage tank set at floor level and any waste tanks positioned below that, some sort of pumping will be required to raise the water to a sink tap or a shower head. This doesn't have to be an electrically operated **pump**; you can simplify a build with a hand- or foot-pumped feed using boating or caravanning taps, although this becomes less viable if you want at least one water outlet to pass through a fine filter.

BUILDING A CABIN

Electric pumps can operate with a pressure switch: when the tap opens pressure drops and the pump activates. A downside of this is that if a leak occurs the pump will engage and steadily drain your water tank out through the leak. A pump like this can often cut in for a second overnight, as pressure seeps away to the point where the pump activates and quickly re-pressurises. For both reasons it's worth **switching the pump off** when not in regular use, as well as fitting an **isolator valve** upstream of the pump. And you also want to be careful to choose the correct **flow rate** in a pump; too much force will waste water.

A pump and filter are best **housed** close to the water tank and readily accessible. An access hatch under the dining area where the tank might usually sit works well. As Graham Jackson writes opposite, it's not necessary to **filter** all the water you use – at least not down to 1 micron – only what comes out of a dedicated drinking tap. Water used for washing or cooking need not be purified. By doing this you'll extend the life of your fine filter, although there's something to be said for pre-filtering all water down to 10 microns.

As with other appliances requiring redundancy (see box p134), you'll need a **back-up** in case the electric water pump packs up. An identical replacement is best, otherwise try to visualise how you'll access your water, possibly with some manual pump arrangement. Along the plumbing network it's worthwhile fitting cut-off valves in case a leak should develop, as well as a simple means to **drain** the whole system completely, should you have to leave your van for a few days in sub-zero conditions. Taps at the bottom of the tank work best, and you need to be sure you've pumped all the piping dry.

Pumping station. This picture and the previous page are from the 911 truck pictured on p116.

HOT WATER

Your engine sheds masses of heat into the air and through the water-cooling system, so heating water or the cabin need not require any additional energy source. As described below, fitting a **heat exchanger** will enable you to tap that engine heat into a suitably insulated tank in the cabin, giving you an evening's worth of hot water following a day's driving. A heat exchanger is basically like a radiator with two water circuits, adjacent but not connected to each other. The engine's hot coolant passes through one channel and warms the passive water alongside it, which feeds a tank or fills a jerry.

Another way of doing the same is to use a permanently installed **calorifier**, also an insulated tank but one which effectively has the heat-exchanger element mounted inside. Hot engine coolant is plumbed to run in and out of the tank (see diagram on p251), warming it from within more efficiently than an exterior heat exchanger. The calorifier has a pumped feed and outlet for your hot water but of course is also dependent on a running engine and so is only likely to last a day when you're parked up.

The most common solutions for non-engine-dependent hot water include the humble **kettle**: three litres of boiling water mixed into seven of cold is enough for a shower. A shallow **black tank sun-warmed on the roof** is another effective method for generating hot water, but only works when you're parked up in the right conditions of high radiated heat and minimal wind.

Once you've tried and tired of all these adequate but inelegant solutions (and you have around £1000 to spare), you may well turn to an independently powered water-heating source, of which the Eberspächer, Mikuni and Webasto **diesel-powered heaters** are the best known. Assuming you're running a diesel, fuel consumption pumped up from your vehicle's fuel tank is likely to be minimal in return for what they offer.

Hot and cold running water

GRAHAM JACKSON

I returned from a nine-month trans-Africa trip in our Defender determined to re-design the water system and to install hot water while I was at it. What we had worked for short trips, but on long trips we needed something better. Keeping water in jerricans and using a portable backpacking filter to clean the water was too cumbersome on a long expedition, even for basic camping. Using a **solar shower** also proved inadequate for water heating as, even under the African sun, vehicle motion cooled the shower almost as fast as the sun heated it. Had we stayed stationary for long periods the solar shower would have worked better. From other overlanders I met en route I discovered many ways to improve the set-up, and with that in mind my criteria were as follows:

- True hot water capability
- Shower with pump
- In-line filtration with a pump

- Enable water to be drawn from sources outside the vehicle
- Ability to use either filtered or unfiltered water
- Allow the tank to be filled by the onboard pump
- Provide a gravity-feed back-up tap should the pump fail
- Position the tanks low and centrally in the Land Rover
- Fit a robust and field-serviceable filter capable of eliminating all biological nasties
- Compatible fittings on all outlets
- Minimum tank capacity of 75 litres

This required putting a little thought into the design and fitting and doing some online research to select the appropriate equipment.

Tanks
Since it had proved very convenient, I decided to keep our 28-litre tank mounted on the rear quarter-panel (see picture on p171). To increase the capacity, I replaced the two jerricans I'd used in Africa with a single 57-litre tank from ⌨ plastic-mart.com and mounted it behind the rear drawer system just forward of the rear axle. The tank is only 22cm tall and so kept the weight low. Neither tank had an access port for cleaning, so the system was rinsed with chlorine.

Filter
Looking into the many filters available, I narrowed it down to Doulton's IP100SC, an under-sink-type filter housing with what Doulton refers to as a 'supercarb' candle filter. This filter has **three stages**: a 0.2-micron ceramic filter to trap particles, bacteria and cysts; a silver-ceramic matrix acting as a bactericide and viruscide; and finally an inner core of activated carbon, which removes chlorine, unfilterable organic compounds and improves taste and odour. The non-renewable or washable carbon core limits cartridge life to 3800 litres at a flow rate of 1.9 litres a minute, although the primary ceramic element is easily washed and scrubbed with a scouring pad, like a Katadyn.

Along with many other water filters, I got to forensically test my Doulton's claims as part of a review for *Overland Journal* magazine. The results supported Doulton's bold claims; no bacteria got through the filter, nor did anything else.

Heat exchanger
Hot water for washing and showers had become a high priority for us. I despise re-inventing the wheel on an overland vehicle, so the idea of using an electric water heater did not sit well. Since a running engine produces all the heat we need, I selected a Helton HW-1 heat exchanger and mounted it in the engine bay, plumbed into the engine water-cooling circuit. Of course it only draws heat from a running engine so once we stop, a shower is first on the list, while the vehicle ticks over. If we need more hot water a running engine can fill a jerry in 20 minutes, depending on the initial engine temperature.

I decided against an insulated holding tank though that may suit morning showers. Since showers use a lot of water, we draw water from a jerry rather than from the on-board water tanks to gauge water use more accurately.

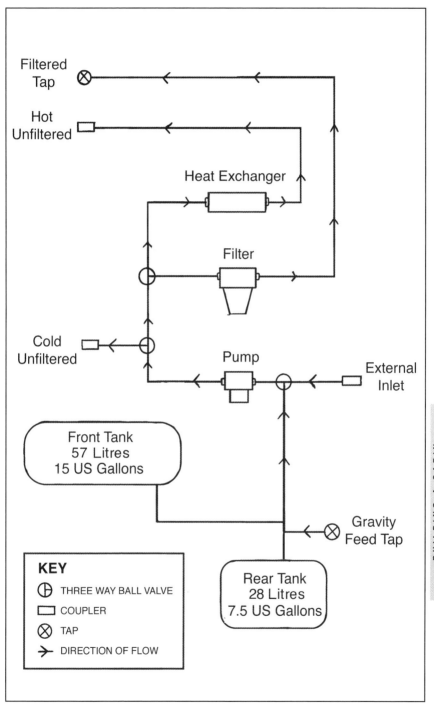

Filtered
Tap

Hot
Unfiltered

Heat Exchanger

Filter

Cold
Unfiltered

Pump

External
Inlet

Front Tank
57 Litres
15 US Gallons

Gravity
Feed Tap

KEY

⊕ THREE WAY BALL VALVE

▭ COUPLER

⊗ TAP

➤ DIRECTION OF FLOW

Rear Tank
28 Litres
7.5 US Gallons

BUILDING A CABIN

Pump and hose

A SHURflo RV 3390 pump delivers up to 10.6 litres per minute at 40psi with a pressure switch that cuts flow at 45psi and restarts at 25psi. In conjunction with a toggle switch mounted by the back door, manual activation is simple. A small, easily cleanable inlet strainer protects the pump from sediment and I adjusted the stop pressure on the pump to deliver 2 litres a minute through the filter circuit.

To link all the parts together I selected several different runs of **hosing**. For the link between the two tanks and for the pick-up lines I used clear, braid-reinforced PVC hose with a 1.25cm inner diameter. This hose also fed into and out of the pump. For the lines running to the heat exchanger I used Buna N PVC hose, like that used in vehicle cooling systems. I selected black and in future will insulate the return run from the heat exchanger to improve shower heat. For the runs from the filter I used 9.5mm polypropylene hose, which is food-grade and very convenient with press-fittings on the filter housing.

CONNECTING IT ALL TOGETHER

With components chosen, it was just a matter of becoming a plumber for an afternoon. See the diagram on p251. To select the source (hot, cold, potable) I used brass three-way ball valves. For changing from shower to tap I used couplers on all the outputs except the filtered water. I wanted to make sure no tubing that had contacted non-potable water could be connected downstream of the filter.

Using the on-board pump, the system can draw, filter and heat water from the two onboard tanks, or with a hose reaching out to an external source such as a jerrican, a well or a stream.

We now have four types of water on hand:

- Gravity feed from a tap mounted low at the rear of the Defender. It's a handy way to wash your hands after a messy job and also serves as an emergency back-up should the pump fail, as well as a drain valve for the entire system. Water from the tap is cold and unfiltered.
- Cold, unfiltered water pumped to a coupler at the rear door. This is used to fill the tanks as mentioned above.
- Hot, unfiltered water from the heat exchanger in the engine compartment and also pumped to a coupler at the rear door. We have a regular hose and a shower attachment for this one. The car can now literally wash itself!
- Finally and most importantly, potable pumped and filtered cold water dispensed from a dedicated tap at the rear door.

MAINTENANCE

The system as installed is for **temperate environments** and must be drained to prevent freezing in cold weather. It would not be too hard to add line insulation and tank heaters to allow it to operate in cold weather. The couplers use **o-rings** to ensure a good seal but, as they're positioned by the dust-prone rear door, dirt can easily get into the female fittings when they're not connected and damage the o-rings. To avoid this I fit loose male plugs in the female fittings when not in use, and wipe male ends of a hose free of dirt before connecting.

Because a fixed tank can be more difficult to fill than individual water containers, we still carry a **water jerry**, both for quickly topping up the system without a pump as well as a source for showers. A leisurely hot shower can take more water than you think but by using an external source the amount is easily gauged and the onboard supply is not affected.

Which brings up a current weakness in my system: **how much water** is on board. The plastic main tank is transparent enough to view the water level, but the quarter-panel tank is not. To get a better idea of remaining capacity I set the top of both tanks to within a centimetre of each other. The main rear tank is deeper than the plastic tank, so once the plastic tank is empty we have a reserve of 57 litres.

Cabin cooling and heating

Cooling a stationary cabin with an air-conditioner uses more energy than most overlanders have to spare. In the low-volume, glassed-in driving cab with the engine making power, air-con certainly has a place as driving with windows open is noisy and can be dusty, but there are other strategies that can keep the cabin from heating up to the same extent.

As explained already, hot or cold, good insulation keeps your cabin isolated from extreme outside temperatures, but cooling can be achieved with **shaded windows** while driving, **parking in shade**, and enabling **airflow** and using small fans when stationary. In arid climates where temperatures can exceed 45°C, hanging a **wet towel** across the doorway of your stationary vehicle will cool the through breeze as it evaporates on its way through the cabin and out a roof hatch; a convection-cooling idea developed by the ancient Persians. This trick won't work in the humid tropics where, although temperatures cannot rise above the mid-30s°C, it feels much less comfortable and so **fans** are your friend. Having a set-up that enables you to sleep outside the cabin, making the best of any breeze (but protect yourself from insects), can also make a big difference. There are more cool ideas on p215.

HEATING THE CABIN
Diesel heaters can heat water both for domestic use and, in the sealed engine-coolant circuit, pre-warm the engine on freezing mornings (not something cylinder bores or batteries are likely to complain about). With the engine part of the circuit isolated (see diagram on p233), they can also be plumbed to heat small radiators that **warm the cabin** while parked up. Small fans draw the air out of ducts positioned low in the cabin or in other strategic positions like your bed area (which can be screened off with a drape to trap more heat) or the shower room.

Talking of keeping the bed warm, don't forget the humble **hot-water bottle** or anything similar and leak-proof; I've used regular water bottles in the Himalaya. A couple left in the bed or sleeping bag can make sliding in there much less traumatic when everything else is freezing.

BUILDING A CABIN

Even simpler **air heaters** feature an in-built fan which blows out hot air that can be ducted in the same ways. With the supplied electronic controller they can be set to run at certain times and certain temperatures, just like a household central-heating system. Their only flaw is said to be at high altitude, where the lack of oxygen leads to incomplete combustion and soot formation. Some units come with a high-altitude pump setting, which reduces the fuel injection to match the lean air, but even these are said to be unsuitable for extended use above 2000 metres (6560ft), which is not so high. It's another reminder to be wary of any appliance designed for sea-level boating.

Depending on how and where you mount them, a common complaint with all diesel burners is the **noise** they make, although silencers can be fitted. The one freezing night I spent years ago inside a Toyota with an Eberspächer was periodically interrupted as the heater cut in to re-warm the interior.

Propane-powered cabin air heaters from the likes of Propex are much quieter and cost nearly half the price of some diesel equivalents, but due to the refilling and fitment issues might be best saved for cooking. For an overlander, diesel heaters will always be more commonplace.

All these compact heaters require a **fresh-air-intake** as well as an **exhaust**, usually passing through the floor of the cabin, plus pumps for the fuel and water, where used. The air-intake may present some issues when wading or fording rivers; if you envisage this consider a raised intake. The exhaust outlet ought to be less affected, assuming an air lock is created but, again, its exact position may require some thought.

Wood-burning stove

In Europe there's a certain hippy-based stigma attached to an in-van **wood-burning stove** but just as at home, a real fire is a very agreeable way of keeping warm while using a renewable fuel supply and disposing of combustible rubbish. A lightweight flat-topped stove as pictured below costs from £200 in the UK and weighs from 15kg. If you pre-warm the cabin from the engine heat while driving along (as described above) you'll get the wood burner up to speed before the cabin cools. Using waste wood, you can keep warm for no cost and with nothing whirring intermittently through the night.

Clearly the stove and outlet must be located and fixed in a fireproof position, which for filling and cleaning access is probably best by the door. It's not all heat for free with a wood burner as **fuelling the stove** will require sourcing, storing, sawing and chopping wood – itself a good way of warming up. No matter how careful you are, some smoke will always enter the cabin and

leave its aroma, but there are many worse smells. Each morning you'll also need to clear the ash, which can get messy, and unless you've prepared a new stove's worth, it's at this time you might wish you could flick your Mikini air heater into action. Using a gas stove for heating isn't really so effective as it produces as much condensation as heat.

LIFE ON
THE ROAD

7

After months and maybe years of preparation the Big Day is here and one thing's for certain: you'll be nervous. If you've had the chance to get absolutely everything sorted and packed, pat yourself on the back. Chances are, though, like most ordinary overlanders, you'll have overlooked something, or will be dealing with some last-minute mechanical or bureaucratic cock-up. This too seems to be normal, another test thrown down from the gods of the overland. Expect it.

One great way of avoiding a last-minute panic is to pack the vehicle a week or more before you leave. At this time you're not yet chewing your lip over an imminent departure, but instead have a quiet weekend to load the vehicle thoughtfully and tick off the checklist. There'll still be eleventh-hour things to do, but should the steering wheel come away in your hands there'll be enough time to get another and keep on schedule.

Pack the vehicle at least a week or more before you leave.

SHAKEDOWN TRIP

Many will have travelled abroad before setting off on a big overland journey. For others with less experience the best way of reducing the shock of hitting the road on the Big One is to hit the road on a Small One. A **test run** of a week or two to somewhere as far as you dare go will be an invaluable dress rehearsal. When the real thing comes along it won't be such a leap in the dark – it's just another trip only a bit longer than before.

On a test run you'll almost certainly have a chance to refine your packing system. Some vehicle flaw may manifest itself – oversize tyres rubbing on the suspension arms, overheating or the suspension bottoming out because you're overloaded. Better to know this now when there's still a chance to do something about it.

From Western Europe, Morocco, Turkey or even just eastern Europe give you an idea of what it's like to be in a significantly foreign country on the edge of the overland zone. From North America it's obviously going to be Mexico and Central America, while South Africans can roam far north into their continent, taking on progressively more challenging countries as they go.

A test run or short overland trip can even be used to find out if you like the very idea of a long-haul trip. You may admit that a short trip is as much as you want to take on at this stage in your life. It's nice to go camping in your well set-up van for a couple of weeks, but hauling all the way to Kathmandu or Ushuaia is a bit much. Again, it's better to find this out by wading out from the shallow end than diving in at the deep end with a full backpack.

'NO TURNING BACK'

Finally on the move, it's common to want to rush ahead to try and calm the nerves. Recognise this restlessness for what it is, part of the acclimatisation process as your life takes a whole new direction. Resist covering excessive mileages in the early days. Racing through unfamiliar countries with perplexing road signs and 'wrong-side' driving causes accidents. Three-quarters of all overlanders who end up hospitalised are there because of an accident rather than as a result of an exotic disease or a bandit attack, and in many cases this happens very early in the trip. 'No turning back' it says and is how you may feel, but turning back is exactly what you should do if things start badly and you have a chance to correct them. No one need know.

Chances are the pre-departure phase was hectic, so make a conscious effort to start slow, park up somewhere warm and sunny soon and catch your breath ... get used to being away from home, but not up to your neck yet.

To help give yourself a good chance of not needing to do that, don't make any **crazy deadlines** to quit work and catch a ferry the next morning, or pick up a visa three countries away in a couple of days. Instead, make a conscious effort to start slow, park up somewhere sunny and warm, or visit friends after a few days on the road so as to catch your breath. Chances are the pre-departure phase was hectic so spread out for a while, tinker with the vehicle and just get used to being away from home, but not up to your neck yet. If you're a bit shaky about the whole enterprise it can make a real difference to your mood. And even on your own, **managing your moods** is as important as keeping on the correct side of the road.

THE SHOCK OF THE NEW

On your first trip into the overland zone it's normal to feel self-conscious, intimidated and a little paranoid. This is because you've departed the comfort zone and are embracing the thrill of an adventure in its truest meaning, the first step of what may be months on the road.

The less glamorous aspect of all this is the **stress** involved in dealing with strange people, languages, places and food. Stress is usually what you're looking to get away from, but it's not necessarily a bad thing. Leaping into the air on the end of a bungee cord is stressful, so is standing up to give a speech or even taking a long-haul flight. To a certain extent it's an emotional response to losing control, and can also be classified as excitement. Your senses are sharpened and your imagination is stimulated, but with this comes irritability and possibly an exaggerated wariness of strange situations.

Having probably lived and worked in a secure environment for years, for better or for worse setting off overland can be just about the most stressful and exciting thing you'll have done for a long time. **Fears** of getting robbed, lost or ill, of finding yourself in trouble with the police or breaking down are all the more acute when you've everything you possess for the next few months around you. Nor is the situation improved by the way overseas news is presented in the

Did you forget something? © David French

media, as one atrocity or tragedy after another. Who would want to go to places like these?

This **tension** can lead to headaches, irritability and very often absent-mindedness. An unpleasant encounter early on when you're still emotionally vulnerable can shake you up, but rest assured that in a few weeks you'll brush off any similar event as part of the adventure. Wariness outside your habitual territory is a vital behavioural trait designed to alert you to potential danger and it'll take a couple of weeks and some high anxiety plus some small mis-judgements before you **acclimatise** to life on the road. Your understandable paranoia will slowly abate and before you know it the buzz of being a stranger in a strange land will begin to take effect.

A crucial part of the acclimatisation process is learning to see the world for what it actually is: **ordinary people** getting on with their ordinary lives rather than spending their weekends sewing up and then burning infidel flags. In fact, many experienced overlanders come to recognise that, when all is said and done, it's the good people they meet on their travels who count for more than the places they saw or the gnarly roads they drove. It's hard to think so when you've spent months and a small fortune equipping your overlander while keeping tabs on the latest terrorist outrage, but without expecting to teach the world to sing in perfect harmony, it's perhaps the single biggest lesson to learn from travelling.

One of the most frustrating scenarios is when you realise you've been rude to someone who was only trying to help or be friendly. This can be understandable when you've been pestered for days by hustlers urging 'Meester, psst, psst'. Distinguishing one from the other comes with experience. Very often the most genuine encounters occur in **rural areas**, where people are less interested in flattering their self-esteem at your expense (or simply ripping you off).

It's common to see overlanding as a series of hops from one congested, hassle-ridden city to the next, and often it's a bureaucratic requirement (city strategies are on p261). But out in the country pressures are less acute, so make the most of roadside cafés for tea breaks and rests. They're great places to mix with local people without feeling overwhelmed or like you're on stage. The owners and customers will be regulars used to passing travellers and may treat you like any other customer. Very often this is all you want.

Driving abroad

Driving along a two-lane highway might be described as a contract predicated on the risk of mutually assured destruction. It's what compels us to keep awake, concentrate, and remain on the correct side of the road in a lane that is usually only a little wider than our vehicle. One thing that distinguishes the overland zone (OLZ) is local driving standards fit to give a Danish traffic warden a heart attack. You'll learn that you must **expect the unexpected** because out here anything goes, and your life may depend on it.

In the OLZ the driving contract is skewed by the clause that **might is right**; a big bus doesn't need to be considerate to smaller road users as it can crush them, and sometimes does. Very often the **horn** is used in place of the steering wheel or brakes. There is no respect for road rules and other road users. There's also the fact that driving a car or a truck in the OLZ gives a local a higher status over common folk. Even if you're driving with all the care and alertness you can muster, the ante is upped further by a possible absence of driver training, licensing, roadworthiness, sobriety and motor insurance.

You'll be sharing roads with underpaid, overworked and amphetamine-fuelled truck drivers, and with ageing bangers which, if it weren't for stringent local import regulations, would have been melted down into cutlery many years ago. Mixing with these unroadworthy crates are the imported, blacked-out limos of local criminals, businessmen or politicians; stray, domestic and wild animals; and dozy pedestrians who were never taught to 'look left, right, and left again'. Throw in too much alcohol, some Latino/Arab/Indian machismo, donkey carts, bad roads, unlit vehicles and unsigned diversions, plus grossly overloaded vehicles, and you've arrived in the crazy world of driving in the OLZ where anything goes.

All this can require an intense period of adjustment as you say to your partner 'Did you see that?!', or shudder at some impossibly mangled wreckage being hosed off the road. You have to be ready for anything and even then you'll be caught out once in a while. Growing eyes in the back of your head helps, because what's needed is **alertness** and a moderate dose of assertiveness that doesn't extend to aggression. This can be difficult to modulate when, because of your foreign plate, you feel you're being singled out by young men who regard being overtaken by you as a slap in the face. A good way of rationalising this is to accept that among the hundreds of drivers you pass in a day you're bound to encounter a dickhead or two. Don't take tailgating personally; there's a different concept of personal space (both on the road and in daily life). What's incredible is that this doesn't result in round-the-clock carnage, especially in congested cities.

You do need to **drive defensively**. After a while this new style of driving can actually be quite liberating and makes you realise how rule-driven our road manners are back home. What counts is that all road users are on a similar wavelength, even if for you it feels off the scale.

LOCAL CUSTOMS

It's said that in Mexico, and certainly in Morocco, a vehicle in front that you wish to pass will **signal** on the off side if it's safe to pass and to the near side (the kerb) if it's not safe. This is the opposite of what's done in Europe and North America, where a slow vehicle will indicate to the near side – 'pulling over' – that it's safe to pass. Misunderstanding this could be disastrous. Although it's not helped by possibly having a driving wheel on the near side and yelping at your passenger 'Is it clear? Clear now?' while a queue of traffic fills your mirrors, it's best not to be rushed in such situations. Try to depend on your own judgement and visibility when performing such manoeuvres.

Back home, **flashing the headlights** usually means the person you're flashing can go ahead; it can also mean 'Warning, speed trap/cops ahead!' when done to oncoming vehicles. In parts of North Africa flashing seems to be used by oncoming vehicles to ask 'Have you seen me? Please respond urgently!', except that just about every oncoming vehicle whose lights work seems to require this affirmation on a flat, perfectly clear road. If you don't flash back they'll flash again urgently. It can also be a message indicating 'Hey, you've got your lights on in broad daylight!', but it's rarely pointing out something you don't know like your roof tent is still up.

Some local aspects of **driving etiquette** are mentioned in the Continental Route Outlines and should be addressed in more detail, along with other driving information, in the better travel guides for a given country or region.

THE WRONG SIDE OF THE ROAD

If you've never driven in a country where they drive on the other side it's natural to be anxious about dealing with things like roundabouts and overtaking. In fact I find the real danger comes when you're relaxed and on autopilot, rather than when leaving a foreign port in a hyper-agitated state, or cross a border where driving sides change (as with the northern borders of Pakistan, Angola or Kenya). If it's early in the trip you'll probably be very alert and driving very carefully.

In my experience you occasionally get it wrong when you've either been off-road for days with no defined roads and little traffic, or you pull off the highway in a rural area for a lazy lunch. On returning to the road, the lack of any roadside infrastructure or passing traffic sees you instinctively do what you've done all your driving years. Hopefully your partner or someone else will point this out before something terrible happens. When there's other traffic about or obvious indicators, it's easy to do the right thing; when there isn't, you can slip back into old habits. Luckily such mistakes are usually made on quiet roads.

The other time you might blow it is when you've been driving for 20 hours straight, chomping Nescafé granules straight out of the jar. In a moment of panic you don't know if right is wrong or left is right. This confusion can mess you up even if you're in a country where they drive on the side that you're used to back home. As a Brit for example, you assume anything 'abroad' must equal driving on the other side of the road. Not if it's Kenya or Thailand or crazy India, where left is right, right is wrong and anyway, might is right.

LIFE ON THE ROAD

WHY DO WE DRIVE ON THE LEFT OR RIGHT?

From earliest times mounted or wheeled traffic kept to the left side of the way, but today three quarters of the world's population drive on the right. Theories abound as to why there was a mass switchover.

Much of the original left side-ism has to do with human **right-handedness**. Today around 85% of us are right-handed, and as recently as the last century that figure was even higher because it wasn't done to admit to being left-handed. The word 'sinister' is derived from 'left' in Latin.

In days of yore, when knights were bold and bandits roamed the land, it was safer to keep oncoming wayfarers to your right, whether riding or on foot. That way, the right, **weapon-bearing**, hand could be quickly armed on the side of the stranger. With a scabbard dangling on the left, getting onto a horse was also easier from the left or 'nearside' for right-handed folk.

When carts and stagecoaches came into common use, the driver sat on the right, nearer the **crown of the road**. The centre of the road was often filled with animal muck and hoof-churned mud, so passengers on the left could more easily disembark onto the clean side of the King's Highway.

All this made sense until **revolutions** swept Europe and some of the New World colonies in the 18th century, bringing an urge also to sweep away every aspect of the old order. In France the aristocracy formerly travelled on the left side of the road and peasants on the right, all the easier to feel the lash of a passing coachman's whip. Following the revolution a proclamation was made in 1794 to keep right or risk joining the rest of the headless toffs. Subsequent

Napoleonic conquests spread right-sideism across much of Europe, including the half of Austria he occupied in 1805. The rest of that country remained leftist until 1938 when Hitler, appropriately, sent all traffic to the far right. Over the Atlantic, liberated Pennsylvania made a similar decree in 1792, followed by New York in 1804. Newfoundland in Canada held out till 1949.

The scramble for Africa in the late nineteenth century saw road rules implemented according to the coloniser's custom, while the flurry of post-WWII independence campaigns led to revolutionary-style switching in many former colonies such as Nigeria.

Only three territories have ever changed from right to left: East Timor and Okinawa in the 1970s and Samoa in 2009; in the latter case this was simply to benefit from cheap cars imported from nearby RHD Japan.

Like the waggoner's seat, the **driver's wheel** has typically been on the side nearest the crown of the road. This is convenient for disembarking passengers, helps the driver judge the position of oncoming vehicles, and improves forward visibility when overtaking – the latter being the biggest issue for overland drivers whose steering wheel is on the nearside. In the Alps today some trucks used solely there are RHD so the driver can better judge the edge of the road.

How does this affect you? None of the handful of RHD countries put restrictions on LHD vehicles, especially transitting overlanders. But some have turned on even tourists passing through in a RHD, notably **Costa Rica** and **Nicaragua** (see p443). In Nigeria some cops try it on with RHDs, but it's just a scam. Stand firm!

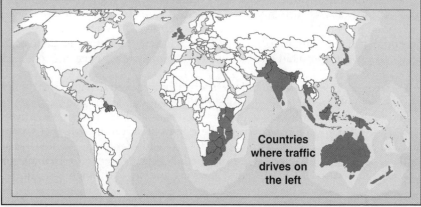

Countries where traffic drives on the left

SHARING THE DRIVING

On a good day, and if driving without long breaks, 400–500km is a reasonable distance to cover on normal roads. But even if you encounter only some of the above-listed distractions, by the end of such a long day it sure is nice to stop. With other equally competent and willing drivers aboard, spending only a couple of hours at a time at the wheel is ideal. That way no one gets too bored or worn out.

Being allowed to drive is another matter. It's common for male driver-owners to be reluctant to relinquish the controls of their pride and joy, or for others to be intimidated by the responsibility of piloting a lumbering three-tonne bus through the wilderness.

Of course it helps if everyone can drive a car but, conservative as this may sound, if it works best with Him at the wheel and Her over the maps, let it be so. The first few days on the road will be tiring for everybody, both driver and passenger(s), as all accustom themselves to the new environment. Soon everyone and everything settles into a routine and you can begin to relax and appreciate your surroundings.

In these moments of panic when you can't think straight, **slow down and pull over** to the kerb, whether it's the correct side or not, and let the oncoming traffic pass by with just a blast from the horn. Wrong-sidedness can also get to you weeks or months after you've returned home and are living a conventional life. After the period of intense overland driving abroad, when pulling out onto a quiet road – again where there is no passing traffic as a guide – it's possible to wonder again which side are you on today?

CITY STRATEGIES

Cairo, Quito, Dakar, Delhi: it's a good thing they're all so far apart, but like it or not your overland trip will be punctuated by the need to visit cities like these, where dealing with congestion, noise and pollution comes on top of security issues and the expense of staying there. You'll need to go to these places for spares or repairs, to check email, get visas and, who knows, maybe even to stroll around the national museum or admire the Old Quarter.

Try to arrange visits to big cities on your terms. Above all it helps to know where you're going as opposed to blundering around looking for a hotel. Initially it can be least stressful to stay **on the outskirts** and bus in to see the sights or do the errands, happy that you're not paying a fortune in a downtown hotel while your vehicle is secure. Some places like Islamabad and cities in East Africa have centrally located **camping parks** (sometimes guarded), which solves the issue of location and expense, and of course these are great places to meet other travellers.

Once downtown, modern Sheratons and the like are often easy to spot by their sheer size. You'll probably be paying what you would back home but at least they feature **secure parking**. Depending on your vehicle, some hotels will allow you to camp in the car park; you've nothing to lose by asking and a self-contained motorhome will be more acceptable. Elsewhere **guarded parking compounds** occupy waste ground yet to be developed and aren't necessarily good spots to sleep in the vehicle.

If you're having trouble finding a place, hire a taxi driver to lead you there, even if it risks turning into a remake of Death Race 2000. Alternatively, ask a trustworthy-looking local to accompany you; older men are usually more reliable than less worldly women or feckless young men.

LIFE ON THE ROAD

DRIVING WOMEN CRAZY

'You've driven all the way from North America?' the woman asked.

'Alone?'

Just to be sure she understood my affirmative reply, she asked several more times. The question wasn't unusual in the slightest, even if the times asked – 12 – was a little extreme. Certainly in many Middle Eastern and African countries it's almost unheard of for women to drive anywhere but within the big cities, but I thought things would be different in South America. However, I hadn't seen another woman driver in months.

One of the joys of travelling overseas in your own vehicle is the sensation that you're exempt from the rules and customs which dominate the lives of local women. And you are until you step outside your bubble. When you do, be sure not only to adjust your Western-style dress, but to tailor your mental outlook to encompass the workings of a more traditional society.

Mechanical matters

Contrary to popular belief, most **mechanics** aren't out to swindle every woman who comes along – especially in foreign countries. The fact that you've driven as far as you have alone will be such a surprise they'll instantly put you in a separate category from both their male customers and their wives and sisters, who've probably never driven at all. Men in most countries feel a certain amount of protectiveness towards women, so impress on them with a smile how important it is that the vehicle is in good working order when it leaves their garage.

With motors being far more complex today than what your family owned when you were growing up, the average man knows little if no more about the running of a vehicle than you. You don't have to be an expert.

That's the mechanic's job. But as you're the one behind your vehicle everyday, you're the best person to listen for **sounds and subtle changes** that could mean a problem. If you spent more of your childhood in the kitchen than in the garage you're bound to be intimidated by the workings of an engine. Don't be. Though most men will have you think differently, the principles of cooking and mechanics are not dissimilar. In both workshops, A has to fit snugly into B, and the correct elements need to be combined in a very specific way to get the desired results. The main differences are that more brute force is needed when dealing with vehicles (unless you're kneading bread), and engine grease is more difficult to remove than cooking oil.

While your vehicle is being serviced find out exactly what they're doing, (without being a pest) and try to be familiar with some basics. This will hold you in good standing if the same problem happens again, and give you more knowledge in the long run. Even if you know nothing, the men will assume you're interested and will want to do their task well. If you get bored, bring out your camera. This could be more assurance that the mechanic will try his best to do a good job – no one wants to be identified with bad work.

If you know you've got a **big repair** coming up, try out a mechanic on a small job to ensure his price doesn't escalate drastically from what he originally quoted, and that he finishes the work in a timely manner. Allow some leeway for miscalculations. There's not always a way to know if a job is more complicated until the faulty parts are taken to pieces. Before the mechanics get underneath the vehicle, ask if they sense anything else is wrong so it can be fixed promptly, and you're not stranded by the side of the road.

Hitching

Breakdowns are probably the number one reason more people don't take their vehicles into another country. But rest assured that some countries, like Mexico, have mechanics in marked vehicles who patrol the roads, and free towing is offered along uninhabited stretches of Chile's Atacama Desert.

If you do break down, see if a passing bus or police car might take you to the nearest mechanic. In many countries hitching is a common way for people to get from A to B and doesn't have the same stigma and fear factor as in the West. Even so, listen to your instincts. If you have any qualms about the person offering, don't get in.

Checkpoints and borders

Government officials and the military have all the power in deciding if you and your vehicle will move forward or not. A single woman travelling alone is a curiosity to stare at, even if you've hopefully thrown a more conservative article of clothing over whatever you're wearing. They're bored. You're intimidated, which is understandable considering the number of guns you'll see slung casually over the shoulders of boys who probably haven't finished the equivalent of secondary school. Though most will appear stern, remember they probably haven't had much education, and will often be disarmed by a smile. In some countries you'll sense being too friendly could lead to a sexual advance and you'll feel the need to **tread a fine line** between being disrespectful and too nice. Nod your head, say hello, answer questions politely, and move forward when you're given the signal.

Though these people, usually men, do the same job everyday, it will often seem like your form is the first one they've ever seen. If they have computers, your information will probably be entered with two fingers. Border crossing can be painfully slow. Bring a book to read, and answer the questions politely and briefly. Though small talk can ease the way forward, it can also make their task take longer. Chat nicely only if there's a problem.

In traffic

The two-lane road is three and sometimes four deep with halted rush-hour traffic. Cars are on the sidewalk and would enter the cafés if they could. Then a police siren. It's clearly impossible that the emergency vehicle will be able to manoeuvre its way through. But within minutes, the cars perform what seems like a complex group tango, and the police vehicle edges through.

In Western society, people stand at polite distances from each other and, when driving, keep to their lanes and obey a specific set of **rules**. In more social societies, the tendency to be in closer proximity while communicating verbally is mirrored in their driving – lane boundaries are more flexible, and there's far less adherence to traffic regulations. Instead of feeling frustrated by drivers who stop in front of you without using

indicators, try and flow with their system. Though initially difficult to see, there is a rhythm to their driving style. Dance with that rhythm and you'll feel much less stress.

In the rare event you sense you're **being followed**, scan the road for places where there are plenty of people, pull over and stop. If you're in an isolated area, chances are they're just curiosity seekers and want to get a closer look at a foreign woman behind the wheel. If you feel this is the case, maintain your speed and don't stop.

Camping

You're likely to have the most questions asked about why you're travelling when you stop in a village, or outside someone's farm or house (make sure you ask permission first). It won't occur to anyone you're alone, as this will be a completely foreign concept to them. So if you feel awkward about your single status, or don't want to be bothered, say your **husband** is about to return, or you're supposed to meet him shortly – just make sure you're wearing a ring if you're not already. You might also bring out a picture of your 'husband'. If you aren't married, consider staging a photo before you travel with someone who looks like Hulk Hogan. If you don't want to use the husband excuse, waiting for friends is a viable alternative.

Either scenario will also make locals feel more at ease. In traditional societies, **family** is all-important and having a single female in their midst is unsettling. If you want to stay longer than originally anticipated and the 'friends' still haven't arrived, say they've been delayed by vehicle trouble. You can also disappear gracefully by saying you've gone to help them out.

Camping in **wild places** is often completely safe, since it's more than likely no one else is out there. If you feel the need for some extra assurance, consider displaying huge, grubby work boots, or something which suggests 'Big Male Lives Here'. Though you won't want to bring a firearm, carry a few sets of fire crackers to light and toss out the window if you sense there's someone lurking around. Prowlers probably won't stick around long enough to investigate if the explosions were real gunfire or not.

LORRAINE CHITTOCK

Timing, and pinpointing a location

If you aim to arrive in a city **soon after dawn** you'll find you can actually see more around you than just a tooting wall of car- and van sides. You might even score a good parking spot right outside your preferred hotel.

In-car satnavs (see p274) may not have worthwhile mapping for all the cities in Africa and Asia and you may not be running one anyway, but a **GPS waypoint** can be nearly as useful. It takes a bit of messing around as well as internet access, but by comparing a guidebook map against **Google Maps** you can find the spot. By right clicking on either 'Directions from here', 'To here', 'What's here' or 'Go to' you'll get a waypoint like this: 0.380334, 9.451659 – the beachside Le Meridien Hotel in Libreville, Gabon. Key that into a GPS or GPS-enabled smartphone set up to read UTM and at least you'll know how far away and what direction the hotel is. This sort of preparation can save stressful hours battling through city traffic.

Borders and checkpoints

Along with shipping, border crossings will be the most predictably intimidating events on your journey. Expect to encounter crowds of locals pushing to get through, signs you can't read and instructions you can't understand, hustlers looking to make a few bucks, and officials struck down with narcolepsy at the very sight of a foreigner wanting to leave or enter their country.

On top of all this is the worry your documentation won't be up to scratch, or a search will reveal something restricted like two-way radios, a GPS, alcohol or an RPG launcher. You may not have the right type of fire extinguisher, warning triangle or fluorescent vest, or a countersigned testimonial from the Secretary General of the UN. The learning curve can get steep as your passport disappears in one direction and your vehicle documents in another.

Borders

Notorious crossings include: western Russia, mostly due to the language and forms; Egypt; the Mauritanian–Senegalese border at Rosso (getting better); and some Central American crossings, where $5 handed out here and there helps to keep things moving. If you get through any overland border in less than an hour you've done well.

Elsewhere, where an alphabet or numerals unfamiliar to you are used – notably Arabic – local 'helpers' in league with the officials may try and overcharge you on genuine mandatory expenses like insurance or other permits. The main Iran–Turkey border at Bazargan has been notable in this respect so learn your **Arabic numerals**; it's not hard – see p408.

The thing to remember is you're not the first person to have done this, and at the very worst your naivety or momentary weakness may cost you a few dollars. As with all rude or uncooperative staff you might have to deal with at embassies, look at these bottlenecks as the small price you pay for the wonder and thrill of being out on the road.

Border strategies

Over the weeks and months border procedures will get easier to decipher as you learn the drill and the right levels of assertiveness. Here are some guidelines; you'll soon develop your own strategies:

- Remain polite and smile a lot. They're stuck here day in, day out and don't get paid any more for being efficient
- Impatience is usually counter-productive. Settle in for the long haul and have food and drinks on hand
- Accept delays, queues and sudden 'lunch breaks'
- Obey all the instructions for searches, however onerous
- Resist arguing – bite your lip in the face of provocation
- But don't put up with people pushing in, outright theft, or attempts at petty extortion

Stoicism and **good humour** can defuse a tense situation. Remember that the glamorous benefits of an ill-fitting uniform and an old machine gun soon pale when living in a tin shed far from your family and you haven't been paid for four months. Recognise that if something's wrong with your paperwork it's your problem. Read the situation. If there's a need to make some **payment** to get moving, do so. The great thing about the flexible regulations in the OLZ is they work both ways. An expired visa or other irregularity need not be the inflexible 'rules-are-rules' impasse that in Europe or North America would see you on the next plane home. A small consideration and a promise to get it fixed may be all that's needed.

It's important to understand that **bribes** aren't exclusively the unceasing daylight robbery of gullible tourists, but a way of life in parts of the OLZ. You may resent this custom but that's just what it is, a custom that oils the wheels. A few dollars or euros can save hours, and these payments are usually tiny in the overall scheme of things. You'll know when you're expected to pay – accept it as part of travelling, but don't assume you have to pay your way through every border or checkpoint just because your number plate reads like a string of dollar signs. And if the guys at a lonely border have been reasonable and friendly but look like they're living on rations, don't be averse to giving them an unasked-for present; it could make their day.

Border procedures

The most common requirements are listed on the next page. Apart from visas, unless otherwise stated, all these **documents** are obtained at the relevant border or office. Some border officials may want to see vaccination certificates and in some countries there may be further procedures like the need to register with the police elsewhere within a certain number of days. It may also be a good idea not to  display any controversial or flashy gadgets like satnavs, walkie-talkies and sat phones too prominently.

- Track down and fill out an immigration card (see previous page)
- Take the card and get your passport stamped
- Complete a form to temporarily import your vehicle (your vehicle ownership document will be needed)
- ...or get your carnet stamped
- Fill out a currency declaration form, which may include 'valuables'
- Declare any restricted items or hide them well
- Show vaccination certificates
- Change money
- Rent local number plates (Egypt, China, among others)
- Buy motor insurance, if possible or necessary

Roadside checkpoints

Highway checkpoints are imposed by many countries to control or monitor locals; they also crop up near borders to catch illegal immigrants. Elsewhere, you'll be recognised as a harmless tourist and waved through, but no matter how many times this has happened so far, **always slow down** and make eye contact with someone before driving on. In countries where suicide bombers blow themselves up in cars, proper checkpoint etiquette is vital.

Some checkpoints alongside strategic installations or in disputed areas such as eastern Turkey will have arrangements of spikes, oil drums and single-lane barricades to slow you down. There will be a 'Stop' sign set up a short distance from the actual checkpoint and possibly a guy with a gun up a tower. At night these places may require you to turn off your lights. Wait at the 'Stop' sign until you're waved on – it's usually one vehicle at a time.

The people at the checkpoint may want your personal and vehicle details and you can make things easier for them by having this information to hand out on a **pre-printed form**. You can download and adapt a French–English checkpoint form in Word at 🖳 sahara-overland.com/fiche-3. These forms can also be handed over to hotel receptionists on check-in. At a checkpoint (or a hotel), resist giving your passport away to anyone other than some sort of official.

Sometimes you'll be pulled over just because they're curious or bored. This curiosity can extend to hospitality, or it can go the other way and they can try it on, making up some bogus infringement, as they often do in western Russia. As always, the old trick of playing dumb and pretending not to understand them or any shared language can help them lose interest. But as with all such encounters, it's best to look them in the eye and kick off with a polite greeting and a smile, and accede to any reasonable requests.

A working knowledge of the current composition of the **Manchester United** football team can help break the ice but unfortunately predatory types can sniff out the nervous or gullible wayfarer. A lot depends on how you respond to each other, which is why **a greeting and a smile** is a good way to start, even if it's ignored. They may assume you'll have a disrespectful attitude to foreign cops and be in need of taking down a peg or two. You may be pulled over for the nth time that day, thinking this is another scam and this time you're not going to stand for it. Learning how to slip through checkpoints like a wet eel is all part of the game.

Changing money and bargaining

As mentioned early on, the best form of money is **cash drawn from ATMs**. The best hard currencies are euros in North and West Africa and parts of the Middle East, and US dollars everywhere else, best brought from home or withdrawn from an ATM.

Once you're on the road you'll find some borders have currency-changing kiosks with posted rates, while others will have a guy walking around with a satchel full of local cash and a calculator. Otherwise, the nearest town will have a bank, ideally with a cashpoint, which is the simplest way to obtain local currency without getting diddled. If there's a good network you need withdraw only a little cash at a time.

If ATMs are unknown or they don't take your cards, it may be possible to buy the local currency in the preceding country. Otherwise, changing money officially can take hours in some banks, going from one counter to another. **Currency-exchange kiosks** in the centre of large towns won't necessarily be as dodgy as they look and might even offer a slightly better rate than a bank. And in some countries you can simply pay your hotel bills in foreign currency.

'Sorry, no change' is something you're bound to hear when paying for a local service with a high-denomination note so learn to hoard **low-denomination notes**: they're useful for tips or incentivisation.

Currency Declaration Forms

Some countries try and undermine currency black markets by using Currency Declaration Forms (CDF). On it you fill out all the currency you're bringing into a country, and possibly other sellable valuables like cameras. Any further official exchange transactions you make in that country must match receipts or entries on the CDF, so that when you leave the cash you brought in equals what you're taking out, less what you officially exchanged.

Half the time these forms aren't checked when you leave, but don't count on it. Any hard currency you don't declare on the form must obviously not be discovered, but having a **stash of undeclared money** is a good way to cover unexpected costs or do a quick black-market deal.

BLACK MARKET

Black market transactions are an accepted, if these days less common, part of travel. It's also a popular way of fleecing naive travellers and by its very nature is illegal.

Use the black market by all means (sometimes there is no choice and some banks encourage it to save work for themselves), but keep your eyes open and your wits about you. If you're a beginner, here are some guidelines:

- Establish exactly how many 'dogons' you're being offered for a dollar (for example). Repeat to them: 'So you are offering me 40 dogons for one dollar?' and if they agree then spell out the total amount you want

LIFE ON THE ROAD

to exchange: 'So you will give me 600 dogons for 15 dollars?'
- Ask to see the currency offered and check that the notes have the right number of zeros. It's helpful to learn to read the nine cardinal Arabic numerals if heading that way – see p408.
- If there's room for negotiation, go ahead. A wily black-marketeer is going to offer as little as he can for your valuable currency.
- Deal one-to-one and don't get rushed or drawn into any shady corners.

Watch out for **sleight of hand**. I was caught out near the Libyan border once. There's some ploy where they count out the money offered, then give it to you to count before taking your money. They then take it back to recount, and even though you're staring intently at their hands, something happens. They now take your money and hand over theirs which you've just counted. Only later do you realise you got done. If this 'count-then-hand-back' deal happens, switch to high alert. Black market deals can represent a major boost to your funds in some places such as Venezuela, but don't stick your neck out for a measly 10%. If you're ever unsure, trust your instincts and walk away.

BARGAINING

Whether bargaining or negotiating, the first step is to appraise the object of your desire or your service needs and ask yourself **what you are prepared to pay**. Even if it's over the odds, once you've established this in your mind you should have no reason to feel cheated once you pay that amount.

When it comes to **souvenirs**, all the time-worn tricks will be tried to make you spend more: free shipping, two for the price of one plus a free pendant, but stick to your price unless you want the object at any cost. You may be asked to 'give me your best price', but remember that if you name a price, bargaining etiquette deems you pay it, so don't let any figure pass your lips that you're not prepared to pay. Bide your time, because this – along with that wad in your pocket – is your greatest asset. If you have the chance, look around for a few days and get to know the vendors and what they have (often it's all from the same source). If you find it awkward to simply walk away, say you might come back tomorrow. Try not to allow yourself to be intimidated, however persuasive the vendor. In Islamic lands be wary of being drawn in by a carpet seller to have tea unless you're confident you can handle the extreme pressure they may put on you. In Morocco these vendors are notorious and can get aggressive to the point of virtually robbing you.

Negotiating over mechanical repairs, guides or food is less customary. There's usually a **set price** for such commodities. Despite the market scene in *The Life of Brian*, locals don't go to the souk to engage in protracted negotiations for the same bag of onions they bought last week, unless it's a seasonal commodity or the quality has varied. But if you feel you're being overcharged, most likely because of your origins, give it a go or ask the price in advance. In some cases, not to barter is seen as weak and not playing the game. It's all part of the experience, with market encounters one of the few occasions you interact with locals as normal people, not men in hats with guns. Enjoy it.

Keeping in touch

NICK TAYLOR

Assuming you have a **GSM phone** (aka: 'mobile', 'cell' or 'handy'), you'll probably be aware that they can be expensive to use outside of your home country, and that you need to be less than 40km from the nearest GSM mast in line of sight. They can be ideal for short calls or text messages to co-ordinate a rendezvous with others, and are especially useful if you get split up. In remote rural or wilderness areas there probably won't be a signal, although in an emergency getting to high ground is always worth a go.

Per capita usage of mobiles in some African and Asian countries is much higher than in the West. The market is huge, especially as a courting aid among the young, with mobile phone boutiques and advertising everywhere. In many countries investment has seen the network leapfrog a land line system that was never much good in the first place, and per-minute charges are much lower than we're used to back home, especially for calls abroad.

Providing your own handset is **unlocked** to accept alternative providers (something easily done in any phone boutique), buying a **local SIM card** is a cheap way to stay in touch. If you can't unlock your phone, the cheapest Nokia 'dumbphone' does nothing but voice and texts and costs as little as $25. With your local SIM card just make sure you're joining a network that'll cover you on your intended travels; a little research online may help. India for example has several **regional providers** who might as well be in adjacent countries; what works in one state won't work elsewhere. Otherwise, to save you buying card after card, international roaming SIM cards are available from many providers, offering a good discount over your domestic provider when calling from abroad.

For a link back home there are a number of options. GSM phones are obviously the most convenient. Even without a local SIM card, the odd text message or a brief urgent call is usually cheap or important enough to be worthwhile. Failing that, for a good natter with those back home, **international phone cards** to use from a phone box or land line may be found.

Internet access

These days we're travelling with our own laptops, tablets and smartphones, picking up a **wi-fi** signal anywhere, both secure or unencrypted. While some parts of the world seem to be connected to the internet by a frayed washing line, in terms of price per bit, getting a quick email out can't be beaten. If you get a good connection, voice and even video calling is possible through Skype or one of the other voice over internet protocol (VoIP) services. All will be far cheaper than using your GSM phone. Using internet cafés is also an ideal way to upload larger amounts of data to a website, especially imagery.

The downside of **internet cafés** is baffling keyboard layouts and who-knows-what sort of dodgy software recording your online banking password, perhaps? **Never risk such activity on public computers.**

Satellite phones

There are two principal **satellite phone networks**: Thuraya and Iridium. **Iridium** is the only company that offers truly global coverage (except North Korea), but if your travels exclude the Americas, currently Dubai-based **Thuraya** offers coverage from Norway to Australia and from Angola across to Mongolia. In other words, everywhere on land except far northern Russia, southern Africa and, as mentioned, the Americas. Charges per minute are around $1.50 with various prepaid packages giving free air time. You probably just want a scratch card for occasional use. In the UK, a used Thuraya handset goes for around £300 and is the size of a pre-smartphone mobile.

Both Iridium and Thuraya offer **data connections** of up to 60kbps (Iridium needs additional software, otherwise it's a miserable 2.4 kbps). With an enabled handset, short **emails** can be sent using the telephone keypad. Some satellite phones like Thuraya's can also accept your regular mobile's SIM card to work in ordinary GSM mode, should you be in range and the charges cheaper. This can be handy if your GSM phone packs up, but battery life is poor so in practical terms it's better to have a separate GSM phone as well as a satellite phone. Some handsets, notably Thuraya, can also pick up a GPS position after a few minutes, which can be easily forwarded as an SMS, although this feature can't really be used for anything but the most rudimentary navigation. Just like GPS or satnav, a satellite phone needs to be **out in the open** to get a signal. With Thuraya handsets, it helps to point the retractable antenna towards Somalia, above which their satellite is positioned.

Once outside the developed world, radios and other communications equipment including sat phones are generally **prohibited for civilian use**. In practice the question is rarely asked at borders, but if you're currently rotting in some awful, sub-Saharan prison – well, you should have hidden it better.

Such a situation befell a guy in northern India. Being popular with jihadis and smugglers, Thurayas were banned in India after the Mumbai attacks of 2008. Unfortunately the guy – along with the other billion people in India – knew nothing of this. A short spell in prison, followed by a few months legal procrastination and he was let off with a 1000-rupee (£10) fine. Even more than GSMs, sat phones can be precisely tracked, so unless you know better, conceal them at borders, and in dodgy countries save them for emergencies.

'I'M GOING BACK TO POSTCARDS AND POSTE RESTANTE'

That was a message I got from a guy who resurfaced in another country five days after his SPOT tracking disappeared in deeply inauspicious circumstances. In a single vehicle, he'd just crossed an unrecognised desert border where kidnappings and robberies had occurred. His last 'ping' was last thing at night, just when such events occur.

When his relatives contacted me I assumed the worst as his hitherto reliable pattern of messaging had stopped. Turns out it may have all been down to a sandstorm or the usual GPS tracking anomalies, but not before consular intervention deployed the French army to his last known position.

A similar thing happened to me trekking on a remote desert plateau while (unknown to us) jihadists attacked an oil base nearby. To block Thuraya comms the ensuing army operation scrambled the GPS signal across our area, just when those back home saw the news and wondered why our Spot map signals had stopped. Moral: a bit of tracking fun that can also cause alarm when interrupted.

GPS trackers

The simplest automated way to let others know where you are is to use a **personal tracker**, like the well-known palm-sized Spot tracker, or more discreet units wired to your vehicle and designed primarily as an after-theft tracker.

As well as sending 'All OK' or 'Help' messages to pre-determined contacts (and an all-out panic button usually of little use in the OLZ), a Spot or similar can be used to pinpoint your position every ten minutes to a public or privately configured Google map page which currently drops locations older than two weeks. That's about as long as the recommended but hard to find AAA lithium batteries last. Anti-theft trackers work off the vehicle battery and will retain your full RTW track, but 'ping' less frequently.

The problem with using these as trackers is the GPS signal is weak and your gadget's reception can be lost for days at a time without you knowing unless you check the online map. It's essential to advise those who might worry not to rely on trackers as a live locator. If you're passing through a dodgy area and need to reassure someone, a voice call is best.

Maps and route finding

Mapping these days comes in four forms: traditional inexpensive **paper** maps; the same map in **digital** form to display on a screen or print off – a raster map; scrollable and zoomable **vector maps** for satnavs like Garmin Nuvis which can be expensive, or free from OSM (see p274), as well as **online** maps like Google Maps which of course require internet, but can be cached for offline use.

PAPER MAPS

The digital revolution may have mapped the world for us using online aerial imagery and routeable street-level satnavs, but some sort of **paper mapping** is still desirable. Light, portable, robust and battery-free, just like books, there's still no better way of easily displaying and accessing a large amount of information over a large area or subject in a simple, inexpensive medium. Like all printed media, they soon get out of date but, assuming they were accurate in the first place, if a map is only a few years old it's still going to be useful.

Map scales

A paper map's scale is given as a ratio of how much smaller it is than the actual land surface: a 1:1,000,000 (1m) scale map is a million times smaller than the area it represents. This can cause some confusion: **small-scale maps** cover a larger area in less detail. Small scale = small [amount of] detail but big area; large scale = large [amount of] detail.

Small-scale maps with scales from 1:2m to 1:5m give you a big picture of an area, which makes them great for planning a trip, if not necessarily for following a precise route. A good example is the Michelin 700 series of maps covering Africa at 1:4 million. Driving in an unfamiliar country with anything above 1:5m scale becomes less detailed and so less useful, but it's handy to spread out on a table at the planning stage and get a feel for relative distances.

Medium-scale maps between 1:500,000 and 1:2m are ideal for driving. On a 1:1m map, one millimetre represents one kilometre on the ground (1 inch = 15.8 miles). If the cartographic design is good, the map will be easily interpreted and the millimetre/kilometre relationship makes distances on the map easy to visualise. A typical 1:1m map might cover between seven degrees of longitude and from five degrees of latitude, which is around 700km (440 miles) from east to west and 550km (340 miles) north to south.

Anything **large scale** below 1:500,000 (1 inch = 7.9 miles) is where terrain and landforms as much as any tracks will govern where you can drive. In other words, when things get gnarly you'll a large-scale map to work out a way through.

As you can potentially cross a 1m-scale map in a couple of easy days that can add up to a lot of maps which is why a small scale map or **driving atlas** is handy, backed up with maps in a GPS or satnav.

Know your maps

There's a lot to be said for taking an interest in your paper maps. Inspect your route or area closely before you go there, study the key and see what everything means and how **relief and road hierarchies** are depicted.

METRIC AND IMPERIAL MAP SCALES

Map scales are given in metric or imperial ratios. Most of the world uses metric, even the UK; the US and a few other places hang on to imperial. With the metric format millimetres are easily translated into kilometres. With US mapping, imperial measurements like inches and miles prevail and so it's common for map scales produced there to have some abstruse ratio like 1:633,600. This might not mean much to anyone apart from the map being 633,600 times smaller than real life, but it happens to equal an intuitive 10 miles to 1 inch. The 1:4m Michelin, for example, represents 40km to 1cm, or 63.1 miles to 1 inch.

Mapping using either scale is fine, but in the overland zone imperialists will want to try and get used to thinking metrically. As 1km is 0.621 of a mile, a quick formula is to **halve kilometres and add a quarter** to get miles: 100km / 2 + 25% = 62.5 miles. Near enough. You may even want to get your vehicle's analogue speedometer changed to a metric instrument. Some modern digital speedos can be configured to display mph or kph.

LATITUDE AND LONGITUDE

If you expect to be using GPS to calculate your position on a paper map rather than just relying on a spot on your satnav, you'll need maps with a lat–long grid. This is a printed grid that actually criss-crosses the face of the map, and not just a lat–long scale shown around the edges; not all maps have this.

Latitude and longitude is a grid system used to pinpoint a location on the spherical Earth using horizontal (latitude) and vertical (longitude) measurements. (I find the expression "in southern latitudes" helps remember which is which). The equator is the zero line of reference for latitude, dividing the globe into northern and southern hemispheres. The Greenwich or Prime Meridian is the zero line for longitude, dividing the world into Western and Eastern hemispheres.

Lines of latitude are parallel rings stacked up like cake layers. They divide the globe into bands at equal distance from each other so anywhere on the globe each degree of latitude is about 110km or 68 miles (or 60 nautical miles) apart. One minute of latitude (a 60th of a degree) equals one nautical mile or, more usefully on land, 1.85km or 1.15 miles. One second of latitude (a 60th of a minute) equals 30.8m or just over 101ft.

You'll occasionally find what's shown as a track on a map is now a two-lane highway, but most frustrating is when what's depicted on a map as a good road turns out to be a track. Assuming a perfectly good road was not dug up in some barmy prisoner rehabilitation scheme, this is incompetent map-making and, like a travel guidebook making up information, you rightly lose confidence in the data.

Along with accuracy, the best cartography offers a balanced combination of **clarity and detail** that enables you to read the terrain like a book. If you're lucky enough to live near a good map shop you can inspect over half a dozen maps of the same country. Compare scales, clarity and the quality of the paper and see which suits you best; not everyone likes the same look.

Although sat nav mapping is made by driving every road, it's just too expensive to update paper maps on the ground. All that effort and expense just gets copied (including mistakes) by other mapmakers.

In countries where the Latin alphabet is rarely used on road signs – including China, some Arab-speaking countries and Russia (see p371) – having a map with the **local alphabet** can be more useful than you think. Even if you can't read it, a local can, plus you can also compare the illegible (to you) squiggle on a road sign with the matching squiggle on the map.

Lines of longitude slice the earth into vertical segments like an orange. The width of these segments varies, being widest at the equator where, like lines of latitude, they're around 110km apart. Moving away from the equator lines of longitude converge towards the poles, where they meet.

The lat–long grid divides the globe into **360 degrees** (abbreviated as °). Each degree is divided into 60 minutes (abbreviated as ') and each minute has 60 seconds (or "); this is easily remembered as °, ', ", or zero, one, two. Positions are shown with latitude (N or S) followed by longitude (E or W).

With this system of co-ordinates it's possible to give a **grid reference** for anywhere on the planet to an accuracy of 15m using just six digits of latitude and seven digits of longitude. A grid reference in the traditional format looks like this: N35° 02' 45.44" W90° 01' 22.56" (Graceland in Memphis). However, these days seconds have been superseded by decimal fractions of minutes, so that the grid reference for the home of the undisputed King of Rock 'n' Roll would now be written as: N35° 02.757' W90° 01.376', although for navigation purposes rounding it up to N35° 02.8' W90° 01.4' is sufficient.

The default on Google Maps uses decimal degrees so Graceland is 35.045956, -90.022933. The first figure is called a northing and if it's preceded by a minus it's south of the equator. The second figure is an easting, but being preceded by a minus in the case of Graceland means it's west of the Greenwich meridian. With this system the ° symbol is not used and the + symbol is considered redundant. You can set a high-end GPS and most satnav units to show a position in any of the above formats, and probably a few more besides.

Locating your position on a map

Locating your position on a paper map can only feasibly be done with a scale of 1:2m or less; a clear plastic ruler can help.

Putting a straight edge along a line of latitude will reveal that the seemingly horizontal line actually curves upwards in the northern hemisphere and downwards in the south. Meanwhile, measuring the distance between vertical lines of longitude will show them a little closer together at the top in the northern hemisphere and vice versa in the south. Only the equator can ever be depicted as a truly horizontal line. Depending on the map's projection, lines of latitude curve along a radius from the nearest pole, while longitudes diverge from the nearest pole. This means that **trying to draw your own grid** on a map with any degree of accuracy is not as easy as it seems.

SATNAVS AND MAPPING

After centuries of paper mapping we're now accustomed to using routeable satnavs to get around ('sat navs' in this context mean Garmin Nuvi and the like, as opposed to Garmin Montanas which are called 'handheld GPSs'). We key in a destination and an on-screen map guides us all the way there, while a soothing but authoritative voice tells us which turns and junctions to take along the way. It's a graphic, map-based version of what you might get in the 'Destination' menu on Google Maps.

In a foreign country that has satnav mapping coverage it also saves struggling with paper maps and illegible road signs when you want to be concentrating on dodging the mayhem around you. The problem is that this wonder of technology has yet to cover the world adequately and it'll be many years before it reaches the levels of street-by-street mapping we're used to in Europe and North America.

But some countries are already giving it a go. Right now you can buy downloadable maps for a Garmin or TomTom satnav for South Africa and East Africa, Turkey, Chile, Brazil and Argentina, western Russia, India, Malaysia and Thailand – the total cost: several hundred pounds. Very often the detail is patchy and many interesting places – some Andean countries, Central America, much of Africa and Asia – are yet to be mapped like this.

As with computer software, certain advocates of **open sourcing** like 🖥 openstreetmap.org have taken it on themselves to try and map the world and then offer their versions for free, or for a minimal price; in places these have better detail than what Garmin and the others sell. Just remember, it can be a mistake to rely solely on satnavs as you may do back home. Above all they lack the **big picture** around you, currently something that can only be achieved with a paper map.

Maps for your satnav

For a GPS or satnav unit to be useful in a navigation sense, they're best combined with imported mapping onto a GPS unit with a **usefully sized screen**. Aim for at least a 5-inch diagonal screen or hook up a laptop to a GPS.

Digital maps

Raster maps can be bought (see above), but now any map in digital form, even a scanned paper map, can be used as long as it's been **calibrated**, something that's easily done with software like OziExplorer, Fugawi, TTQV, or MacGPS Pro, or as an image layer imported onto Google Earth and manipulated. The accuracy of your position on such a map will depend on how accurate the map was in the first place (a matter of distortion or 'projection' – the perennial cartographic quandary of displaying a spherical object like a planet in a two-dimensional plane like a sheet of paper or screen) and how well it was scanned. Scanning a map is a time-consuming task and can be an infringement of copyright. Of course it's only the former that puts people off, so have a dig around to see what's online.

Among others, the German mapping house Reise Know-How covers the whole world except far eastern Russia with over 180 maps, all of which are available as **digital pre-calibrated raster maps** for all the above-listed software except MacGPS Pro. They cost around €15.

Online maps

As long as you have internet you have access to the vast range of global mapping available online from Google or Microsoft's Bing, to name the two main players. Both offer WYSIWYG **aerial imagery** with a quick random check showing that ever evolving Google is still far superior.

As mentioned already, aerial images are very useful, especially in cities, but the plain map graphic screens can be a less cluttered way of getting a good city-centre map. Using a screen-grab feature or software like Google Map Buddy to make a bigger-than-screen-sized map, you can then calibrate it by layering it over Google Earth (as explained earlier), download it to view as an image or print it off. Doing this you then have **a paper** or **GPS raster map** of just about anywhere in the world, with Google Map back-up to help identify actual buildings from a waypoint so you know what you're looking for when you get there.

With a wi-fi or GSM signal it's possible to cut out the paper element and view such a map on a smartphone or iPad, except that with a phone you'll be paying heavily unless you use a local SIM card. Some can be bought for internet-only use costing just a euro a day.

Don't forget that in most cases, unless you're engaged in some black op, entirely adequate paper maps exist or can be found in guidebooks. Also be aware that out in the world, paper, digital and online maps will never be able to keep up with what you might actually encounter in any given place or season. At this point you'll be no better off than Lewis and Clark, Marco Polo or Bilbo Baggins and will have to pull up and **ask a local**.

FINDING YOUR WAY AROUND

Stepping back a bit from the mind-boggling possibilities of digital mapping, successful navigation anywhere basically requires keeping track of two things: where you are now and which way you want to go. To do this you can deploy any number of the navigation aids listed here.

Orientation and trip meter

Even when travelling in unfamiliar territories it's always useful to know your **orientation** (N, S, E or W), not least when trying to get out of a city. As long as you can see it, **the sun** can help. Using an analogue watch, point the hour hand at the sun; halfway between that point and 12 on your watch is south in the northern hemisphere (or north when south of the equator). This technique only works between 6am and 6pm, but anyway, after some practice a quick glance at the sun and the time will do the trick. For a **compass** rely on the one in your satnav or GPS. It can be hard to get magnetic compasses to work reliably in cars, although a pocket compass will be handy.

Get into the habit of resetting the **trip odometer** each time you fill up with fuel. It can help establish your position and is the most reliable way of gauging how far you can cover on a tank of fuel.

LIFE ON THE ROAD

Not getting lost

Blindly following roads or tracks without giving a thought to landmarks, **orientation** or maps is the most common way of getting lost. If in doubt, stop and think or settle on ending up somewhere unexpected – it's (yet again) all part of the adventure. Otherwise look around you, consult your map or ask a local. If none of this is possible and you haven't a clue, **turning back** is the most sensible action. At some point along the way you just came you were not lost.

Lost near towns

Between towns there's usually only one main road heading in one direction, but getting confused near settlements is a universal experience, especially settlements that are inland or lacking in some other helpful geographical landmark to narrow your options, be it Bogotá or a Turkish village.

The bigger the settlement the more roads converge, offering a baffling choice of routes as well as more distractions than you can handle while trying not to run over a street vendor. In the countryside, routes might connect a village to all sorts of places: the river, another village, a rubbish tip; or it might start off in your intended direction only to turn away or peter out. To-ing and fro-ing across town is more frustrating than unnerving, though it's something that, where available, good satnav mapping can minimise.

Ask the audience

Asking someone can be hit-or-miss which is why we cling so dearly to our nav gadgets. A lot depends on who and how you ask. Don't make Tony Christie's elementary error of **pre-suggestion** by asking 'Is this the way to Amarillo?'. Instead, take a tip from master navigator Dionne Warwick and enquire politely 'Do you know the way to San José?'. It won't guarantee a correct answer but hopefully won't elicit the **automatic affirmative** nod just to please or get rid of a stranger. Although you may be steaming from the ears by this point, remember to be polite and, as with all exchanges, start with greetings and handshakes.

> **Don't make Tony Christie's error of pre-suggestion by asking 'Is this the way to Amarillo?'. Instead, take a tip from Dionne Warwick and enquire 'Do you know the way to San José?' There's a big difference.**

Unless you're in a place where people might be literate, avoid suggesting that locals look at your map. In the remote corners of the OLZ it's generally only tourists who use and understand maps. However, drawing a mud map in the dirt, or in the dust on your bonnet can help.

It also helps to **ask the right person**. I've found policemen, soldiers and older men to be the most reliable, knowledgeable and straight. Women and young girls might rarely travel out of the village, will seldom be drivers, and are less likely to speak English. In some remote places they may also be embarrassed by your attention; elsewhere they'll enjoy teasing you. Groups of kids or young boys may mislead you for a laugh, to get a tip or cadge a free ride to impress their friends. Sometimes it's less hassle to just try and work it out for yourself, which eventually you always do.

Lost in the wilderness

Getting completely lost is rare, but even when you're just temporarily disorientated you can become anxious, especially if there are other worries pressing on your mind or it's getting dark. At times like this use your logic to work out where you went wrong. It's almost always your navigational mistake and not the commonly blamed map or the Pentagon messing with the GPS signal. Good navigators always recognise their own fallibility.

The most common reason for getting lost is not paying attention to your orientation, then jumping to conclusions and making the situation fit the facts.

LIFE ON THE ROAD

The most common reason for getting lost is not paying attention to your orientation, then **jumping to conclusions** and trying to make your situation fit what you think are the facts. Very often this is down to **pre-empting** or over-anticipating a landmark or turning – a natural consequence of your mild anxiety in not wanting to miss it. You feel that something doesn't add up until you can't deny it. It takes some experience, but in the city or the bush you'll soon gain a feel for whether a road or track is the one you want to be on.

Stop and have a good look around. If you're out in the wilds, **get to high ground** and scan around. Assess the 'quality' or feel of the track you're on; does it appear well travelled? Are there power lines that'll lead to a village for sure? Is a track corrugated or showing other signs of frequent vehicular use, or just littered with the bones of your predecessors? Check your position and bearing from the GPS if you have one. Look at all the facts objectively, not just the ones that confirm your preferences. Above all, rest assured there was a point, not too long ago when you weren't lost. If you can't correct your mistake, **go back**, waiting till daylight if need be.

With 4WD you may think you can go anywhere, but unless you can clearly see where you're trying to get to, taking **cross-country shortcuts** as a way of getting back to where you were can often get you in more trouble. Play it safe and go back the easiest and safest way, however galling it seems, or be prepared to face the consequences.

Wild camping

Camping wild is a big part of the overlanding adventure and luckily you've a vehicle that's equipped for it. I can guarantee you it'll be the nights spent wild camping out in the mountains or deserts that'll make up the best memories.

Even before you settle down for the night, for lunch stops and the like do yourself a favour by **parking well off the road or track**. Besides the safety factor of not getting run over or choked by dust from passing trucks, this avoids giving too much of an open invitation to chancers or the inquisitive – particularly relevant when you're close to a settlement.

It's amazing how in certain countries, even if you think you're miles from anyone, an audience emerges, seemingly from thin air. Initially you may think this is all part of the travel experience, but being stared at by 22 kids as you eat your lunch is not a normal situation.

In many poorer countries concepts of privacy and personal space aren't so valued and the idea of sleeping alone and away from others out bush is seen as deviant. Don't be surprised if, just when you've pitched the rooftent and donned your slippers, a local rocks up to see what you're about. They may even advise you this isn't such a good place to overnight on account of bandits or wild animals, and that there's a perfectly fine hotel down the road.

Choosing a spot for the night

That's why it's a good idea to try and not be seen heading for your night's camp and once there, **not to be visible to passing traffic**, or be far enough to discourage casual visits. This can be easier said than done but will make for a more relaxing night. The first night or two wild camping can be frightening, and over the months you're bound to have some unnerving encounters.

As the sun sinks it's common to keep on driving 'just over that rise' to find somewhere that feels just right, until it's too dark to see anything and you end up sleeping alongside the road. Try and pin down a good spot well **before dark**, especially if you may have trouble getting far enough off road.

If you're confident you won't disturb someone or cause a commotion – the usual problem with wild camping, rather than issues of security – the answer can be to go right up to some isolated dwelling and **ask** if you can camp nearby even if that won't be so wild. If the road or track you're following is surrounded by fields and you decide to camp among them, you can be pretty sure that in a developing country you won't get the hostile reception from a farmer that you might back home. Nevertheless, on arable land make the effort not to trample crops, or mash carefully dug irrigation ditches.

Be careful about how far and how hard you roam in your search for nocturnal seclusion; you don't want to make any manoeuvres or river crossings that may be difficult to reverse the following morning. It can also be a good idea to **switch off your lights**, to avoid attracting attention.

Once you find a spot, give yourself a few minutes to adjust to your new locale. You may have been so intent on finding a place that you haven't noticed someone's nearby shack, the awful reek of undefined roadkill, clouds of mosquitoes stirring from a stagnant pool, or a slavering pack of rabid dogs zeroing in on your camp from all directions. And almost perfectly **level ground** is also more important than you think.

Trees of course make ideal cover. It's also worth noting that sand loses the day's heat quicker than rocky places. Altitude above 1000m will also have a noticeable effect on overnight temperatures, though that may be something you want in the tropics.

It can be unnerving when you're settled in and then someone looms up out of the dark to 'say hello'. Depending on their behaviour, you never know if they're just being friendly while emboldened by drink, are on the scrounge, or have other ideas. In this situation you may prefer to **move on** to avoid the nagging fear of theft. As said earlier, it's the reason why camping far from a road and, at least initially, being discreet with your lighting are good ideas.

Vehicle maintenance and troubleshooting

Many countries in the OLZ practice a 'wait till it's broke, then fix it' vehicle-maintenance policy, presumably seen as getting the full service life out of something like brake shoes, tyres or engine oil without wasting time on inspection or servicing. You'll almost certainly recognise the value in preventative maintenance, if for no other reason than your vehicle is your lifeline.

REGULAR VEHICLE CHECKS

On older vehicles some things like **tyre pressures, oil and coolant levels** and **leaks** should be checked daily. In practice you won't do this once things settle down so consider the list below a good basis when giving your vehicle a once-over. Definitely undertake a full check before a long, remote stage, as well as after a multi-day hammering. **Home-made fittings** are especially prone to failure on the first corrugated track. So that you don't ignore anything for fear of getting dirty, put on some **overalls and latex gloves**; that way you'll get stuck right in without hesitation.

Outside and underneath
- Damage to tanks, cabin mounts, steering linkages
- Exhaust mounts and connections
- Free play in propshafts, UJs and diff pinions
- Leaks under engine or gearbox
- Spare-wheel fitting security
- Suspension and dampers
- Tyres: pressures and sidewall damage
- Wheels: rims and wheel-bearing play

Engine bay and front
- Air-filter connections
- Batteries: connections and mounts
- Belt tension and condition
- Engine-oil level
- Hydraulic-fluid levels
- Lights and grill
- Radiator coolant and hoses
- Roof-rack fittings
- Water-pump free play

Inside the vehicle
- Tanks and fittings
- Lashing points and loads

Print then laminate your own version of this checklist and keep it in the cab so you can easily work through the full list with a quick prod, pull or glance. It's easy to skip a vital check when distracted by a boiling kettle or the peal of a rogue hippo on heat.

LIFE ON THE ROAD

IMPROVISED REPAIRS

Making repairs is something that worries many overlanders, and there's often justified nervousness about getting a bad job done locally. You won't have the means to get a dealer's stamp in your service record, but often all you need is a **bodge** to keep moving and maybe fixing it for good. It's rare for a vehicle to be completely stranded and unrepairable and the more irresolvable the problem, the greater the ingenuity of you or the people around you in fixing it.

Use a systematic, logical approach to fault diagnosis and, if necessary, a lateral approach to problem solving. **Improvisation** is at the heart of many bush-mechanic solutions and is how the developing world's vehicles keep running. But with just about all the remedies listed below, it pays to initially drive slowly and check the repair frequently. Very often it won't be initially effective, especially if sensitive to vibration, and you may have to try something else. These ideas cover only vital items. Usually, if you get the engine running, however badly, you can keep moving.

All this messing around will no doubt get your hands dirty. If you're not using latex or nitrile **gloves**, wet your hands with soap, let them dry and go to work. Once the job's done you'll find with a little added soap, the muck will rinse off much more easily. Otherwise, washing your hands in a mixture of washing-up liquid and **sand or sugar** also removes oily grime. Don some **overalls** too: you probably don't have clean clothes to spare.

Binding broken leaves together can limit stresses spreading to other leaves and can even work if the main leaf is broken.

Broken springs

Broken coils or leaves, or burst dampers, need not be a show-stopper, though a snapped torsion bar is less easy to fix. With coils you may not even notice they've been broken for months and when you do, a bit of **rebar** can be welded alongside the snapped section.

With a leaf broken on the articulated 'shackle' side, you can limp along with the axle on the bump stop as the axle is still held in position by the other direct-to-chassis attachment point. Broken leaf springs are one thing that can be replaced in any sizeable town and it's always worth carrying a **spare shock** or two, though they too can be fairly easily replaced wherever other 4x4s are found.

ELEMENTARY FAULT DIAGNOSIS AND FIXES

If you don't know how engines work, try to be systematic: **will it start; will it run; will it go, steer and stop?** Engines won't start for two main reasons: a lack of electrical power or fuel. More rarely some mechanical issue like a broken starter motor may be the problem, or, more commonly these days, a relatively insignificant electronic malfunction has disabled your engine by default.

Should an **error code** appear somewhere on the dash, get on the internet to find out what it means. For cars, try 🖳 obd-codes.com. Generally, they're

LIFE ON THE ROAD

classified with prefixes which relate to 'P' (powertrain), 'B' (body), 'C' (chassis) and 'U' (network). It's not uncommon for non-terminal error codes – to do with emissions, for example – to flash up even if the vehicle seems to be running fine. You can ignore these.

Once running, **engines** perform badly or intermittently usually due to a poor air/fuel mixture, though again on modern, electronically managed engines, a loose connection, faulty battery, or some electronic sensor may also be to blame. Assuming the engine started and is running sweetly, only some element of the **transmission** can still be a show stopper – brakes and steering usually leave you something to get by with.

A **clutch** shouldn't go without warning unless it's been flogged hard. If you're lucky, it's the master or slave cylinder seals (one is opposite the clutch pedal in the engine bay, the other alongside the clutch housing under the vehicle). If you're unlucky, it's the clutch plate. On an old vehicle it's worth fitting a new clutch plate and carrying the usable spare – or just carry a new spare. It's heavy work but  two people can fit a new clutch plate by the roadside in half a day. Replacement gaskets of any type can be made from cardboard, providing the single piece is big enough, or use gasket sealant.

Gearboxes give even more warning, often thousands of miles, before they pack up entirely. If any transmission component in a 4x4 from the back propshaft to the axles fails, you can continue in front-wheel drive only at a moderate pace with four-wheel drive or any central diff-lock engaged.

Which leaves only **tyres**; the most likely cause of a breakdown and the most easily fixed; see p289.

Common battery problems

When you run into electrical problems – the vehicle is dead or won't start – before testing the alternator as described below, check the fuses and then the battery terminals. It's possible to have low-wattage items such as small lights working, but not have enough electrical power running from the battery to turn the starter motor. A quick wiggle of the cable clamps may be all that's needed. Even if they're not loose, oxidisation can make a poor contact (hence terminals covered in a grease like Vaseline). If poor contact looks like the cause, try filing the inside of the battery clamps and the lead battery terminals, to make sure each clamp is tight. Because terminals are made of soft lead, they can erode over the years so that the vehicle's original clamp can't tighten properly around it. File at the clamp jaws, or more easily jam in a spacer between clamp and terminal to enable a better contact over the greatest area. Don't forget to check where the battery's **negative lead** is earthed, usually at the vehicle's steel body or the chassis nearby. Rust can develop here too, degrading the contact. After unbolting, this is easily remedied with a file, or by rubbing the removed lead on a rock until it's shiny bare metal again.

Fault diagnosis

Here are some leads on getting to the bottom of common problems. Your vehicle repair manual will have more ideas.

Fault	Possible cause	Possible cure
Engine won't turn over; dim or no lights.	Flat battery, faulty alternator (see p284).	Find another battery or push start; in freezing conditions pre-warm the engine and battery.
Lights are fine, but starter won't engage.	Some sort of starter safety cut-out is in operation.	Is the auto gearstick in gear? If not, a switch may think it is.
Starter motor spins but won't engage.	Can still be a weak battery or a worn starter. More likely a dodgy solenoid switch or a jammed Bendix gear.	Sharply tap the starter housing with rock or hammer to release Bendix. Remove starter, check and clean the solenoid.
Engine turns over but won't start.	No spark at the plug (petrol). No fuel (diesel or petrol).	Check for spark by removing a plug and turning engine over while holding the plug against the cylinder head. Replenish fuel level or find blockage or air lock.
Engine running badly or misfiring.	Inadequate battery charge. Poor fuel mixture. Blocked fuel filters. Faulty EGR valve (diesel only). Very high altitude.	Change or replace battery. Check for air leaks in the fuel system. Check fuel pump. Check/replace fuel filters. Remove and block off EGR valve (not a roadside job).
Oil pressure light won't go out, even above 2000rpm.	Faulty oil-pressure switch (unlikely). Engine-oil level low or oil very old (thin). Badly worn engine, (usually associated with tapping or knocking noises).	Check oil level. Check oil switch. Change oil. Rebuild engine following a cylinder-compression check (easily done with a small gauge).
Overheating.	Too high engine speed for ambient conditions and load. Slipping or broken fanbelt. Lost, loose or worn radiator cap. Insufficient coolant or oil level. Radiator fins blocked with mud or grass seeds. Faulty viscous fan unit. Overloaded vehicle. Old, worn engine.	Check oil and coolant levels; check radiator and cap; leaks can evaporate almost instantly. **Slow down** if it's 42°C in the shade and reptiles are fainting. You're expecting too much and need a new or bigger engine.
Flat battery.	Discharged overnight; faulty alternator; broken or loose belt. Low fluid level in unsealed battery.	Use spare battery; recharge battery with charger or off solar; replace alternator and/or belts. Top up with distilled water, though any water will do in an emergency; see p284.

Fault	Possible cause	Possible cure
Broken brake line.	Damage, rust or perishing.	Metal or rubber, fold the brake line over on the upstream side, crimp closed and bleed the system. (There'll be no braking on that wheel.)
Auto box won't shift up.	Wrongly adjusted kick-down cable. Lack of oil in gearbox. Gearbox has overheated and is damaged.	Adjust cable. Check or change oil. Track down an auto box specialist.
Leaking radiator.	Rust, damage.	If you don't have a proprietary radiator sealant, use curry powder, egg white, or ground cork – anything that will swell or harden as it's forced through the leak. Alternatively, remove the radiator and repair with solder and a flame-heated tyre lever.
Split radiator hoses.	Old age or wear. Loose or worn engine mounts (too much movement).	Bind tightly with wire and duct tape, though replacement is better.
Broken or leaking exhaust.	Vibration, old age, rust.	A fracture mid-pipe can be splinted with a cut-open tin can and a pair of jubilee clips. Holes near the silencer require plugging with paste, or fit a sleeve loosely on the pipe end and push it into the can and then clamp down the sleeve. Vehicles can run OK without a silencer, especially old turbo diesels.
Cracked fuel tank or engine/ gearbox casing.	Rock damage, weak mounts, vibration.	A bar of soap rubbed into a cracked tank is an old bodge though the 'chemical metal' epoxy pastes made for the job are better and can be strong enough to hold a thread and bolt in other situations.
Engine cuts out in hot and slow conditions.	Vapour lock – occurs when petrol vapour blocks the passage of liquid fuel through the fuel pump. (Does not occur with fuel-injected engines or diesels.)	Let everything cool down or drape the fuel pump with a wet rag to cool it and condense the fuel vapour. Only a short-term solution.
ECU error code appears.	ECU registers a fault (there may not be one).	Establish fault or clear error code with OBD reader.

Next, if the battery isn't a sealed item, check the **electrolyte fluid**. With the battery level (in the horizontal sense), electrolyte acid should **cover the plates** of all six chambers. If it doesn't (it's common for levels to be uneven), top them up with **distilled water**; the battery may well recover, but you ought to wonder why the levels have suddenly dropped unless you've not checked them for ages. At worst, the battery is being overcharged by a faulty voltage regulator on the back of the alternator.

To top up, any water will do if you're desperate, but don't confuse boiled water (sterilised) with distilled water. Boiled water may well be *more* mineral-rich (less distilled) than normal water; it's the evaporated steam that, once condensed, can be called mineral-free or distilled. Or better still, get a sealed battery and never have this worry.

Of course this is all a comforting old-school scenario of roadside diagnostics, at which many of us have become master practitioners. These days an **error code** (more on p42) might also highlight an electrical fault. Quite possibly it's something you'd never have known about in the old days until that component or system failed. **Loose or worn connections** will still probably be the physical cause of such a malfunction, but to that must be added the array of **sensors** and other electronic components that monitor or manage a modern vehicle's functions and all of which can complicate matters, while minute by minute the beating of jungle drums gets louder and louder.

Charging system – the alternator

When, due to age, wear or possibly overuse (too much drain on the electrical system), an **alternator** starts malfunctioning (it can become only partially efficient), your vehicle may continue running as normal, but the battery won't be getting adequately charged. After a few hours, or if you suddenly increase electrical consumption by turning on headlights for example, the **red charge warning light** (usually a 'battery' icon) and maybe an error code will light up on the dash. Lights will soon dim, electric windows may not work and the vehicle may even misfire or stop.

On seeing this warning light **don't stop the engine**: chances are the battery won't have enough power to restart it. Instead turn off what electrical ancillaries you can. Open the bonnet and, while being careful of the spinning radiator fan, check that it's not just a snapped or very loose belt. The great thing with **older diesel engines** is that, once started, the engine can run without electrical power as long as there is fuel, because fuel pumping and injection was mechanical. Electricity may only be required to power the fuel cut-off solenoid to stop ignition, but if that doesn't work you can just stall the engine in gear or pull the cable between the fuel shut-off valve and the solenoid in the engine. However, petrol and modern diesel engines rely very much on electrical power, if not sensitive electronic management, and CRD engines will shut down very quickly if the system voltage drops minimally (something you might want to be aware of when winching for too long).

Back to alternator fault diagnosis. If the belt appears in good shape, the engine still runs and it's safe to continue without lights, drive on to a place where you're prepared to switch off and be stuck until you fix the problem. It could be hours or it could be days so it's at a time like this that your second or spare battery may get you out of a tight spot.

Ascertaining the voltage

Before you stop the engine make one more test. Get a **voltmeter** or multimeter (a device for testing electrical circuits and levels), set it to DC and check the voltage across the battery terminals with all lights, fans and so on turned off.

With the engine running at about 2000rpm it should read between **13.5** and **14.5 volts** – normal for a 12-volt battery. If the voltmeter reads much less than 12 volts with the engine running, the alternator is not functioning fully. You can make further checks by turning on lights and fans and revving the engine. The reading across the battery terminals should still show around 14 volts as the alternator adapts to the added load on the battery. If it reads less than 12 volts, or worse still is dropping before your eyes, it's more proof that the alternator is kaput. If it rises way over 14 volts as

This voltmeter is at least 35 years old. By now they're bound to be digital and include a bluetooth facility.

you rev the engine the **regulator** isn't regulating and may have already damaged your battery. (Incidentally, to rev an engine actuate the mechanical throttle linkage in the engine bay, rather than have someone press the pedal inside. Newer vehicles may not have a mechanical link, only unseen electronics.)

It's also worth reperforming this test on the thick wire coming from the back of the alternator to the battery. This way you can be sure it's the alternator at fault and not the thick wire or battery terminals that you may not have checked properly. At a sub-1000rpm idle an alternator won't put out much current, but **between idle and 1800rpm** the voltage should jump from 12.5 to 13.8 volts.

Alternator problems

If the **bearing** has gone on the alternator – through simple wear or possibly due to over-tightening the belt, you'll hear the noise. (Pinpoint noises in the clamour of a running engine using a long screwdriver as a stethoscope pressed against your ear, or a piece of hose to funnel sounds.)

More commonly but less obviously, one of the sets of **copper windings** inside the alternator body has broken or shorted out. They can only be repaired by a specialist so replacement is the simplest route, either with the spare alternator you're carrying (which you've tested and know is the correct fit), or hopefully at a garage in the next town. It's not always possible to see the break in the windings, but if on removal and disassembly they appear black rather than coppery, it could be a bad sign.

Alternators also have a pair of small **carbon brushes** picking up the alternating charge generated from the spinning rotor and passing it to the diodes. As with everything else electrical, good contact is critical here, but over time these brushes can get worn, dirty or broken. On older vehicles they used to be easily accessible for inspection or replacement from the outside; it's worth checking yours. Otherwise, open up the alternator to inspect them.

Dude, smell my car

It pays to develop a nose for your overlander's odours. Some, like windscreen wash, are benign and pleasant, others – like burning wire insulation or butane gas – are clearly more serious and together are an especially bad combination.

It's possible to become over-paranoid in all senses when you're in a desolate area, or to be alarmed by ambient or less urgent smells. The fridge might have been off for days; that burning oil or clutch smell is the old banger you just passed. Temporary foul smells could be festering roadkill or a roadside factory. Trust your nose, but use your brain.

Smell	Possible cause
Fuel.	Spilt or leaking fuel from cans or tank.
Steam.	Overflowing or leaking coolant circuit, including radiator.
Sweet sickly smell.	Glycol in anti-freeze fluid, usually green and not to be confused with screen wash, usually blue.
Sweet-scented smell.	Windscreen wash, usually just after spraying.
Burning fibre or resin	Dragging brakes (handbrake on?). Slipping clutch.
Burning rubber/plastic.	Electric wiring on fire or plastic touching the exhaust manifold.
Butane gas.	Leaking gas bottle or fittings.
Burning rubber.	A jammed or slipping belt. Tyre rubbing on bodywork. Very hard cornering (see 'screeching') or emergency braking.
Mildew smell with air-con.	Fungus in the air-con evaporator, the radiator-like unit. Check it's draining away condensation correctly.

Smell	Possible cause
Rotten eggs.	Assuming it's not actually rotting eggs, it could be a faulty catalytic converter not burning off the sulphur in petrol, or a very rich fuel mixture (blocked air filter?), or very high-sulphur diesel (see p49).
Setting epoxy resin (Araldite).	Possibly the glue on some component getting warm; probably not important. I often smell this one in cars.
Burning oil.	Thick white smoke from tail pipe, especially when cold, means a worn engine – either piston rings or valve guides. Engine oil dripping onto the exhaust manifold. Overheating ATF in an auto gearbox.
Bubbling lasagne.	Dinner's ready.

Tracking down worrying noises

Diagnosing errant sounds takes experience and is another good reason to take a test run for a few days. The added weight could reconfigure the harmonics. Obviously noises requiring action include scraping along the road or an everlouder **tapping or knocking from the engine**. In my experience it takes less than 50 miles from such a noise first being audible to a destroyed engine. In one case a mechanic said all was fine and advised me to get the valve clearances checked, on another occasion I knew it was terminal but had no choice.

If you're not used to them, old diesels in perfect condition can sound like bags of nails, and low-octane petrol or high temperatures can also make an engine sound noisier. After driving off road it's not uncommon for a stone to get caught in a brake disc cowling or under a bash plate and rattle annoyingly. Don't beat yourself up about over-reacting to noises; that's why evolution gave you senses. It's quite easy to isolate and so diagnose a noise while driving along by following these actions:

Noise	Possible cause
Only at a certain speed or increases with speed?	It could be something loose on the bodywork/exterior or speed-related resonating.
Only in a certain gear?	If yes then it's probably a faulty gearbox, which could be manifested by stiff gear changes. While driving along press the clutch in and let the revs drop. If the noise is still present it's not associated with the engine and is coming from the transmission, wheels or body.
Noise drops off as the revs drop, with the clutch in.	It's the engine or clutch. Stop soon and investigate.
Engage neutral and rev the engine.	If the noise increases with revs it's coming from the engine.
Engage neutral and coast.	Does noise match the vehicle's speed as it slows down? It could be propshafts, UJs, axles or wheels.
If you have part-time 4WD and manual FWH it's possible to further narrow down the source. Does the noise only occur at full steering lock?	Suspension or front CV joints (clicking).
Screeching tyres at normal cornering speeds.	Tyres too soft or speed too high for the load. Very hot tarmac.
Sirens.	Pull over.

Jumper cables and tow or push starts

It's said that modern cars aren't suited to jump starting and some leads come with built-in 'surge protection' devices to stop the ECU from getting a jolt. Note that thicker, heavy-duty cables may not be better for regular vehicles as they draw too much power before it reaches a flat battery. Long cables are more useful. The donor car may need to rev their engine to get a charge up.

Tow starts work best in a higher gear. Start in neutral and, once moving clutch in and engage third; first gear may merely lock the wheels, especially on dirt. If neither a tow strap or a downhill are available, a car can be **push started** by another car as long as the bumpers can come to an agreement.

Welding repairs

It's possible to arc weld off two (or better still three) 12-volt batteries attached in series, making 24v or 36v and plenty of amps (home arc-welding machines produce about 30–40v). A jump lead attached to a pair of mole grips can hold a welding rod, and bits of thick cable or wire can join the batteries if necessary. This isn't going to do your batteries a power of good in the long term so is best used for emergencies, but I've seen a broken chassis repaired like this.

Remove **batteries** from the vehicles and, if unsealed, protect them from sparks. Prepare the welding area well and wear all the sunglasses you can get your hands on assuming you don't have a glass.

Steel arc welders are easily found in towns and are always busy. **Welding rods** and a glass can be in short supply so bring your own; they're tradeable commodities.

Alloy welding is less common so making repairs with glue, rivets or drilling and bolts are your roadside options. Alloy is rarely a structural element in cars, though auxiliary fuel or water tanks made of aluminium can cause problems if they come adrift and crack.

VEHICLE MAINTENANCE KIT LIST

This is a basic list; consider it a start. Tools and spares for any special features that your vehicle has, not least the electrical and plumbing fittings in the cabin, are not covered here but will be as essential. Other suggested lists appear under their related subjects: first aid (p333), documents (p25), tyre repair (p290), recovery (p306) and so on.

Tools

Allen keys
Bottle jack, hydraulic or screw
Bow saw, small
Brushes: tooth (for cleaning), paint (dusting), hand (sweeping), wire (cleaning)
Drill, rechargeable, and bits
File, half round
Grease gun
Hacksaws, large and small, and blades
Hammer-axe
Inner tube (emergency use)
Multimeter, electric
Multi-tool or penknife
Oil filter removing tool
Pliers, adjustable (Mole)/grips
Pliers, circlip (for UJs), electrical, regular
Rivet gun and rivets
Sandpaper
Screwdrivers, selection
Shovel
Socket set and ratchets to suit your vehicle
Spanners, adjustable (large and small)
Tyre levers
Tyre-pressure gauge
Tyre puncture-repair kit (for tubeless or tubes)
Wheel brace and same-size socket

Vehicle spares

Alternator
Battery (used as back-up)
Bolts, nuts, washers and self-tapping screws (selection)
Brake-cylinder repair kits
Brake pads (shoes generally last longer)
Bulbs
Caps: fuel filler and radiator
Chain and padlock
Clutch-cylinder repair kits
Clutch friction plate
Damper, front and rear
Electrical connections, clamps, fuses, wire
Fanbelts
Filters: fuel, oil and air
Head gasket
Jump-starter cables

Keys, spare
Pipes: fuel (rubber), siphoning (clear plastic), brake (metal)
Propshaft UJs
Radiator hoses
Spark plugs, caps, leads, distributor
Water pump and gasket
Wheel nuts
Windscreen wiper blades

Oils, protective wear and sundries

Not all of these items will last you months on the road, but it's a start.
Cable (zip) ties, twine, wire, coat-hangers
Carpet or tarp (for lying on the ground)
Degreasant (fuel can do)
Distilled water
Fluid, hydraulic
Gearbox or ATF (some manuals run ATF)
Gloves: latex (disposable), thick rubber and fabric/leather
Goggles or protective eyewear
Grease, regular and copper (for non-locking threads)
Jubilee (hose) clips
Motor oil
Overalls and rags
Radiator sealant
Screen wash
Sealant for exhaust plus epoxy glue; metal repair and gaskets
Tape: packing, duct, electrical and cloth
Thread-locking cement
Torches: head torches and handheld
Warning triangle, high-visibility jacket(s), fire extinguisher (all three can be demanded at fine-seeking checkpoints)
WD40 or similar
Welding rods
Work boots

Coat hanger, hose clips, plain gas bottle valve, jerrican seal, battery clamps.

Tyre repairs

Out in the world, most towns that have shops and fuel will have a tyre-repair place, even if it is just a hole in the wall with a trolley jack by a pile of scrap tyres. Where possible this is the best way to get a flat fixed, very often while you wait, and for small change.

However, because flat tyres are the most common cause of immobility, particularly if you don't run **sealant fluid** inside, it can help to be able to perform your own tyre repairs and not just wheel changes as a repair can be safely put off if you have a **second spare**. For repairing tubeless tyres with a plug – a very easy repair that some claim is only temporary – see the box on p151.

Wheel changing: step by step

These days more than ever it's possible some drivers will never have done this and the correct sequence is important.

1. Park on firm, flat ground in gear (in 4WD) and with the handbrake on.
2. Chock front and rear wheels.
3. Remove the spare tyre and jack.
4. Loosen the wheel nuts.
5. Jack up the car.
6. Check wheel chocks.
7. Finish undoing the wheel nuts and remove the wheel.
8. Fit the spare and refit nuts loosely.
9. Lower the vehicle off the jack.
10. Tighten the wheel nuts fully.
11. Try and ascertain the cause of the puncture.
12. If not repairing immediately, re-stow the flat tyre and jack.
13. Check all tools are replaced and that the pressure in the newly fitted tyre matches the others.
14. Remove chocks and drive on.

Removing tyres on one-piece rims

If you've never changed a car tyre before, let alone a chunky 4x4 tyre, practice at home, not somewhere like the Gobi desert; it can be heavy work. Why would you want to remove a tyre? Possibly because you're running tubes on split rims (see below). Or you need to repair your last tyre properly from the inside, not with an external ram plug.

In an emergency **split tyre sidewalls** and even inner tubes can be sewn up but will need a big patch, but don't enter the Monte Carlo Rally with tyres in this shape. If you can get a professional to do it, so much the better. Some tyres come off like old slippers, others leave you traumatised for hours.

If buying new tyres for your trip, try mounting at least one or even all five – then you really will be an expert. Observe the **jacking** precautions given above. If jacking on soft ground, use a rock or some jerricans for added security. Work on a sheet in the shade with stout footwear and gloves.

LIFE ON THE ROAD

The tools you will need to remove a tyre are:

- **Jack**. Hi-lift or air-bag jacks are easiest to use (see p308), but you'll need the vehicle's standard bottle jack as a back-up.
- **Wheel brace**.
- **Tyre levers**. Two, about 60cm long and 25mm wide are ideal. A third short lever can hold the bead up as you lever the next portion.
- Puncture-repair kit plus a **solvent** like alcohol or petrol (not diesel), and talcum powder or chalk.
- Spare inner tubes. They often get ruined in a puncture; carry up to four.
- **Compressor** (more on p154) or manual pump.
- A **bead-breaking tool** like Tyrepliers, though other methods work.

Breaking the bead

Removing a tyre presents two challenges: breaking the bead or edge of the tyre from a groove in a rim; and then levering it off a one-piece rim. With a good technique and the right tools there should be no huge effort involved.

Take your time. Some are harder to separate than others: new tyres can fit too snugly and old tyres can rust onto steel rims. A **hot** or recently punctured tyre is more malleable, but if you've left it a while, warm it in the sun.

1. Stand on the tyre sidewall to try and push the tyre off the rim into the well; this rarely works unless the tyre is a loose fit or you weigh 450lb. Instead, lacking a set of Tyrepliers or similar, drag the tyre under a front bumper, put the base of a jack on the sidewall alongside the rim and jack the car down onto it. This can be tough on the sidewalls but the rounded corners of a hi-lift base shouldn't do any damage. As a last resort you can try the African method of driving over the tyre to break the bead. With either method, squirting some soapy water into the rim can help, as it can when remounting the tyre.

2. With the bead off one side you're ready to lever the tyre off. The important thing is to make sure the part of the tyre bead opposite to where you're levering is pushed deep into the well of the tyre. In this position it gives the bead the necessary slack to be levered over the rim without you giving yourself a hernia. Excessively hard levering can damage the tyre's bead. Kick the tyre repeatedly into the well as you lever round. Once you get about 20cm of the bead over the rim, the rest is easy. Repeat for the other side of the tyre and remove it from the rim.

Breaking the bead with a hi-lift and some Tyrepliers.

Changing an inner tube

1. Remove the valve cap and unscrew the valve core with a valve tool, taking care that the valve core doesn't shoot off as the air escapes.
2. Push the tyre bead off the rim as outlined earlier. On offset wheels with unequal rim widths, the narrower rim is usually easier to break.
3. Lever off the tyre.
4. It may now be possible to drag out the tube, but it's sometimes easier to completely remove the tyre from the rim.
5. Carefully inspect the tyre tread and sidewalls for damage. Then pass a hand across the inside of the carcass to find any possible protuberances. In thorny acacia country you may find several thorns in the tread. Rocks then tend to push them in deeper so they must all be removed with tweezers to avoid the possibility of more punctures for days on end.
6. Either replace the tube or repair it (see below).
7. If not already powdered, some talc sprinkled inside the tyre helps a fresh tube align itself in the tyre without creases.
8. Refit the valve core and fit the partially inflated tube back into the tyre, trying to avoid twisting and keeping the valve straight.
9. With the tyre upright, fit the narrower rim into the tyre, seat the tube in the tyre and push the valve through the rim. If the valve stem is short you may want to screw on the valve tool to stop it slipping into the rim during fitment.
10. Back on a sheet, begin levering the narrower rim (if off-set) into the tyre. Working round make sure the bead opposite the levers is fully in the well, giving the much-needed slack for the final push over the rim. Soapy lubricant, WD40 or just water reduces the effort.
11. Check the valve is perpendicular to the rim. Inflate the tyre.
12. Complete all the wheel-changing steps described in points 8 to 14.

Repairing inner tubes: step by step

It's best to **replace** a tube rather than repair it, but a time will come when you have no choice. Locals in old bangers often try to scrounge **patches** and even tubes. You may have spare patches, but think twice about giving away tubes. Patches are sold in every town by the roll.

1. Inflate the tube to locate the puncture. Pass in front of your eyes or wet lips to sense the air jet from a hole, or dip the tube in a pool or trough and look for bubbles. Otherwise, spit on possible puncture holes and watch for bubbles. **Don't assume there's only one hole**, especially in thorny country or if the wheel travelled for some distance while flat.
2. With holes located, deflate and roughen the hole area with sandpaper.
3. Clean off loose sand and rubber grit with solvent.
4. Apply a thin film of glue to suit the patch and wait till it's touch dry.
5. Unpeel the patch (usually the foil or clear side sticks down). Using a roller or a screwdriver handle, press the patch firmly to the tube, making sure the edges are stuck down. Now sprinkle talc on the patch.
6. With wheel refitted and everything put away, check the nuts after a few miles or at the first stop.

LIFE ON THE ROAD

Two things not to forget: find what caused the puncture if possible (it won't always be this obvious), and chock the wheels as well as putting the vehicle in gear.

Remounting tubeless tyres

A situation may occur when you need to remove or just remount a tubeless tyre back onto the rim. The difficulty is getting the bead of the tyre over the small lip of a tubeless rim without an inner tube to push it out. Normally a quick blast of high-pressure air mounts the tyre. Without it the tyre won't 'catch' and air escapes before any 'mounting' pressure builds up.

This sort of high-pressure air is something you usually only find in a tyre shop or get by using the Icelandic technique: squirting lighter fuel through the valve housing and igniting a small explosion, which usually mounts the tyre and possibly demounts your eyebrows. I've never tried this as the bicycle-tube technique below worked fine but I'm told:

> The fuel I always use is Butane cigarette lighter gas. First jack up the problem wheel, then arrange the tyre with the biggest gap between tyre and rim at the top, spray in the Butane (a stock 205x16 RR tyre usually requires about a 4-second burst of butane gas). Stand back and throw a match at the gap. With a loud pop the tyre is back in place ready to be reinflated to working pressure.

The **bicycle-tube technique** seals one side of an unmounted tubeless tyre and enables a build-up of pressure to mount the tyre onto the wheel rim. You need a bike tube that matches the size of your rim, more or less. With the loose tyre fitted inside the rim, put the wheel on something like an oil drum or a jerrican. This ensures that the full weight of the tyre is resting – and so sealing – the lower tyre edge against the rim. If you try to do it on the flat ground the weight will be on the tyre not the rim which will cause air to escape below.

1. Inflate the bicycle tube, cover with **soapy water** and tuck it around the upper rim so the tube seals between the tyre and rim. Try not to overinflate the bike tube because a bike tube tends to stretch unevenly around the valve which may impede the seal.

2. Now remove the valve core from your tubeless rim to greatly speed up inflation, and inflate the tyre. You'll need a compressor with engine running and may need to jiggle the tyre around and push or pull the bike tube to ensure a constant seal, but as soon as you get it right the tyre suddenly seals and inflates quickly. A soapy bike tube should come away even with the tyre nearly in place. To finish, refit the valve core and pump the tyre up to the required pressure.

Dirt-road driving

Getting off a sealed road and onto a track is a big part of the adventure in vehicle-dependent overlanding. You head away from built-up areas into the countryside or wilderness where the driving becomes more engaging, but usually in a good way. Partly due to the poorer surface and less predictable conditions, and because of less traffic rushing you along, on a track you tend to slow down too – and that is something many overlanders can benefit from.

You also tend to be more observant as you dawdle along, and can find it easier to stop on a whim for a look around or a photo. Villages off the highway also live life at a **slower pace** and may rarely see tourists, which can mean a warmer or more genuine welcome. Tracks are also great for finding a quiet place for a wild camp without trucks rumbling past all night.

It's said that 80% of the world's roads are unsealed **tracks**. Depending on the drainage and level of maintenance, they're all vulnerable to damage from heavy rains, and in that unconsolidated state, get ruined by passing trucks. Not all countries in the overland zone can afford to maintain their back roads and so once you leave the tarmac you must be ready for anything. In Angola, Baluchistan or Chile it's not uncommon to have a tarmac road turn into dirt, very often when you cross from one provincial jurisdiction to another. Across very high mountain passes, even the best tarmac surface has a hard time surviving the winters and subsequent spring thaw. In most countries they don't bother as such roads are usually closed for six months anyway so don't expect too much asphalt above 4500 metres (14,760ft).

Don't assume you need a 4x4 with a hi-lift jack and a snorkel to leave the tarmac; most local vehicles you encounter will be regular 2WD load-carriers and transporters. What you do need is a robust rig matched with a thoughtful driving style. It's possible to bite off a little more than you can chew, especially if the weather turns on you and you can't go back.

One of the keys to dirt driving is **being ready for anything**, which means slowing down, looking out and being prepared to get out and have a closer look if things seem marginal. Before you drive in, think about how you'd recover your vehicle stuck in a river, a ditch, soft sand or mud. The techniques here are for all kinds of vehicles. Obviously some will work better with 4WD.

TRACTION

Wherever you are, maintaining **traction** – better understood as 'grip' – is what it's all about, whether cruising, accelerating or braking. Even on a bad surface, when cruising steadily the torque applied to the ground surface is negligible and two-wheel drive is sufficient. Once you accelerate, four-wheel drive spreads power over all four wheels, increasing the traction and making wheelspin – loss of traction – less likely. As mentioned elsewhere, it's the difference between running up a very steep hill (eventually your feet will slip) or crawling steadily up on all fours. Losing traction when **braking** or simply entering a bend too fast can happen as easily in a car, a van or a 4x4, except in a full time 4x4 skidding or sliding may be easier to control.

Traction, and therefore control, is reduced or lost when one or more powered wheels begins to spin or when any wheel is locked up and skidding. Besides accelerating or braking too hard, wheels most commonly lose traction for four reasons:
- The surface is too loose, wet or fluid.
- Tyre pressures are too high for the type of terrain.
- The vehicle's weight is resting on its undercarriage, not the wheels.
- One powered wheel is in the air (usually over very uneven ground).

Any of the above situations will lead to you either losing control or getting stuck – possibly one soon followed by the other. The reaction times needed to deal with this is why keeping the speed down is advisable on tracks. The slower you go the more time you have to deal with the unexpected.

TYRE PRESSURES

Tyres run at insufficient pressures for a given vehicle weight or speed will **overheat**, and their performance and life expectancy will be reduced. If you've just filled up with a week's worth of fuel and water, your vehicle weight can increase by 15% so you must increase tyre pressures on a highway (or leave them unchanged for a good dirt track, where you'll drive slower). Remember this can occur on a baking day while speeding along an Argentinian highway just as much as trundling along a sandy desert piste in winter.

What this means is that you need to **check pressures** frequently and **modify them** to suit terrain, speeds and payloads. It's something most people overlook and is why the combination of using quality tyres and a powerful compressor, as recommended on p154, is so worthwhile.

The dynamics of deflated tyres

Whether driving a Mercedes Unimog, a G-Wagen, a Sprinter van or a 230D sedan, reducing tyre pressures off road can make a big difference to control and forward progress. A softer tyre makes for a **smoother ride** on rough tracks too, just as a soft pillow is comfier than a jerrican.

When deflated, a tyre's **contact area** with the track surface increases, which greatly improves traction and reduces ground pressure: the snow-shoe principle. On mud or wet sand a clawing tread works better, but has

Exaggerated for clarity, contact area gets longer not wider at low pressure, but tyre gets hotter too.

negative consequences in tread life, weight ratings and maximum speeds.

Note that it's a tyre's **diameter** or height that counts when deflated not, as many imagine, width. The reason is that, contrary to popular perception, when you deflate a tyre its contact area with the ground *lengthens* much more than it broadens. For this reason tyres with a **tall profile**, like the popular 235/85 R16 size used on European and Australian 4x4s, or a 7.00x16 light-van tyre, achieve a longer footprint than a wide 15" tyre at the same pressure. This is why tall tyres are a good idea for 2WDs too and why, as mentioned earlier, traditional rear-wheel-drive farm tractors have back wheels as tall as a car.

In a **2WD** reduced pressures can mean you don't need to blast across a sandy creek on momentum and risk mashing the radiator on the opposite bank. Tall tyres work well in sand because, unlike in mud, tread is less important than the long, caterpillar-track-like contact area as pictured. And on any vehicle, tall sidewalls maintain ground clearance even when deflated.

Why tyres get hot

On each wheel rotation a tyre sidewall is squashed as it meets the ground and springs back half a turn later, a bit like a tennis ball being repeatedly squashed in your hand. At 60kph (37mph) this is happening 10 times a second. As with any flexible material, including human muscle tissue, this flexing creates internal friction which manifests itself as heat. Overheated tyres can lead to all sorts of problems, not least punctures, delamination (blistering in the sidewall) and accelerated tread wear. This is why you must **keep tyre pressures as high as possible but as low as necessary** – see the guidelines over the page.

An easy way of checking if your tyres are getting hot is to touch them. If the sidewalls feel too hot you should slow down or increase the pressure. On- or off-road, this can all be down to your payload, speed or the ambient temperature. All three must be considered. So if your tyres are at the correct pressure, you simply have to slow down.

At the **extreme low pressure** of 1 bar or less which is needed briefly for an emergency recovery, don't exceed 30kph (18mph) for long periods; up to a point, however, driving in snow or mud and water will cool a tyre more than running the same pressures across desert dunes.

Tyre pressures on different surfaces

Below are guidelines for tyre pressures given as percentages of normal highway pressures. Actual pressures will vary according to your vehicle's weight and tyre size; a Mercedes 230D runs lower pressures than a Unimog.

Normal load and speeds	100%
Maximum payload, fast highway	120% (see vehicle's guidelines)
Good dirt track, max load	100%
Corrugated dirt track	80–90%
Occasional sand, mud or snow	70%
Sandy creeks, dunes, deep mud	50–60%
Emergency recovery	25–30%

FOUR-WHEEL DRIVING

The agility and indestructibility of 4x4s is frequently overestimated by first-time users, something not helped by adverts depicting SUVs scaling dam walls and mountain peaks. It's vital to have an understanding of just what your 4x4 can or cannot do before you tackle the north face of Cerro Gringo.

Your fully loaded four-wheeler is now a lifeline, just as a camel is to a nomad. Inexperienced tourists have perished in North Africa, the Outback and Namibia because they didn't take actions as basic as locking a diff, reducing tyre pressures or even putting the car in four-wheel drive.

You can't just turn a dial and drive anywhere: skill, judgement are still needed. Like any new skill it has a steep learning curve and satisfaction in its mastery. **Sympathetic, defensive driving** protects the vehicle as well as its occupants from damage.

When the text below advises to 'engage four-wheel drive' this corresponds to 'engage central diff-lock' on full-time 4x4s with a manually operated control. There's more on all that on p305.

DRIVING A 2WD ON TRACKS

As the wartime Long Range Desert Group and many overlanders have proved, a well-driven 2WD can manage much more than you think. **Ground clearance** is key but in a 2WD you're also missing a low-range gearbox. What this means is that at times you only have **momentum** to get you through. Maintaining momentum, knowing when and how much to accelerate and when to back off, is crucial to avoid getting stuck while not damaging your vehicle. With 2WDs at times it can be one or the other and because you're bound to get it wrong once in a while, this is where underbody protection is worthwhile.

As you have read, **reducing tyre pressures** gives you a bit more traction. This is at the cost of ground clearance and possible damage to tyres, but will be essential in the short term. As with 4x4s, go down to 1 bar or 14psi (including the axle without drive) when you're really stuck.

When driving through **deep ruts**, either sandy, stony or muddy, which a higher 4x4 could manage, a low-slung road car has to drive with one wheel on the centre ridge and the others off the track to avoid getting dragged to a halt. Up to a point the smooth underbelly (assisted by a large bash plate on which to slide) plus independent suspension enables the driven wheels to reach down into the ruts and maintain drive. But independent suspension (as opposed to a 4x4's solid beam axle) is less effective over rocks because when one wheel rolls over a rock or a hump, the body stays level, so compromising ground clearance (see diagram p40), something that a 2WD doesn't have to spare.

Get 4x4 trained

Wherever this book is sold there'll be outfits to train you in using your 4x4 safely and effectively. The Land Rover Experience and other marques offer their own **training programmes**, while independent training schools will be less expensive. Just make sure you establish exactly how much time you'll be spending behind the wheel on a typical one-day course. Out of curiosity I once took such a course, but three of us ended up sharing the centre's Defender with the trainer and drove less than an hour each.

The sort of obstacles you'll tackle and techniques you'll learn on these courses – terrifying 45° slopes and axle-twisting terrain – will rarely be attempted on the overland road, but especially with traction-defying marvels such as ETC and ABS (see p78), it's good to learn what your vehicle could do. It makes sense to be able to get the most out of your 4x4 when you need it.

These off-roading courses rarely include the messy and sometimes dangerous business of **winch-free recovery**, either when high-centred or extracting yourself from mud or sand. For that there are several good clips on YouTube or my *Desert Driving* DVD. It's something you want to be comfortable with beforehand rather than learning on the road. There's more below.

Understanding four-wheel drive

Because of the undesirable effects of differentials (see p305), 4x4s aren't truly all-wheel drive in all situations. Even with centre diffs locked on a full-time four-wheeler, it only takes two wheels – the diagonally opposite ones on each axle – to lose traction and deprive you of drive. Getting **cross-axled** like this over rough ground, with diagonally opposed wheels spinning or in the air, is a lot easier than most off-roading novices imagine. The effect of diagonally spinning wheels can be mitigated by:

- Axle diff-locks.
- Good axle articulation (flexible suspension).
- Reducing tyre pressures (to optimise traction).

Reducing tyre pressures and good axle articulation have already been covered; the latter helped by removing or disconnecting anti-roll or sway bars. Axle diff locks and ETC are other ways of overcoming getting cross-axled.

Diff-locks and traction control

Locking an axle differential forces the wheels on that axle to be turned by the engine at the same rate. Manually operated rear diff-locks are often standard equipment or options on proper 4x4s as well as Unimogs, old Syncros and the like (Defenders were a notable exception). Front-axle diff-locks are less common and are regarded as a hardcore, off-roading feature. Axle diff-locks were also a commonly fitted after-market accessory in the pre ETC era but because your vehicle is heavily loaded and far from home, you're rarely seeking to push the outer limits of traction for fun; you simply don't want to get stuck crossing a flooded track.

A diff lock is operated by a cable, compressed air or electronically. Any 4x4 with front and rear axles locked (and central diff, where present) will have **true four-wheel drive** but turning becomes very difficult with good grip. Fully locked up like this, you can grind resolutely forward or back – or can dig yourself deeper into a mire if you've not cleared the wheels, for example.

Dropping tyre pressures can be nearly as effective as engaging axle diff-locks, but of course means re-inflation later on. In my experience, stuck in dunes and another time in a flooded creek with my car filling with water, pulling all three diff-lock levers made no difference. On both occasions I had to be towed or winched out.

Axle diff-locks can still damage the transmission if used injudiciously on hard surfaces or on a steep, boulder-strewn climb. If the airborne spinning wheel suddenly drops onto grippy bare rock, it can send a fatal jolt straight into the transmission. This is why manufacturers prefer fool-proof ETC.

Low range: when and how to use it

A low-range gearbox is what separates a true 4x4 from fashionable SUVs. Usually a lever close to the main gearbox, low range gives you the same number of gears, but at a much lower ratio and also more closely spaced. Typically, in a five-speed 4x4, low-range third is the same as high-range first and low fifth the same as high second or third.

On a part-time 4x4 engaging low range automatically selects four-wheel drive but, if present, manual freewheeling hubs (realistically, a thing of the past) must also be turned on. Low range gives much greater control on inclines as well as the ability to pull away in power-sapping conditions like soft sand that would otherwise strain the clutch or overheat an auto box.

Pulling away in low second or third means less chance of wheelspin on a loose surface too. And because the ratios of low-range gears are close together, the step up from say second to third low is smaller than it is in high range. This means upward changes are less likely to bog the engine so you keep moving – essential in dunes.

It's best to **select low range at a standstill**. Usually the fact that you're bogged or are about to try something tricky means you've come to a stop anyway. Make sure the transfer lever is fully engaged. Once moving, you can change up to high range – useful in dunes – although achieving this without undue clunks takes some practice.

Be aware of the **additional torque** or leverage that low-range imposes on transmission components: be extra smooth with the clutch, throttle and gear changes, especially on hard surfaces or with powerful engines. Also, avoid driving for long periods in low-range top. The higher engine revs combined with the low ground speed means less air through the radiator, which can overheat the engine.

OFF-ROAD DRIVING

The typical situations you'll encounter on tracks will only occasionally end up with effortful recoveries – and this occurs less and less as experience teaches you to scout first or try somewhere else. Dust, corrugations and potholes are the more commonly encountered threats to visibility, traction and the undercarriage.

There can be a tendency to chill out when off a busy highway, which can include not using **seatbelts**. The only time this might be a good idea is in a slow river crossing when you want to be sure you can get out of a flooding or capsized vehicle fast. Elsewhere, not least on white-knuckle climbs and descents, always wear a belt.

Dust

Dust can dominate your experience in hot or arid regions and despite your best efforts it soon finds its way into the vehicle. Centrally operated **locks** on rear doors can stop working; cover dust-prone locks with tape.

Bull dust is sand ground down into a fine powder that can get so thick your own dust cloud can envelope you. A bigger problem can be the dust raised by oncoming vehicles on narrow tracks. **Visibility** may well be lost

Explosive bull dust. © M Soffiantini

for a few seconds so the only answer is to slow down lest you stray onto roadside boulders or into a ditch. This gets even more perilous when trying to pass a truck that's trailing its own tornado. Even getting close enough can be a gamble, let alone diving into the cloud and hoping for the best; overall, it's better not to. Better truck drivers will slow down and pull over to let you pass.

Corrugations

Also known as washboard, these maddening formations of **parallel ridges** are caused either by the braking and acceleration of passing vehicles (they get worse either side of a bend) or by the unyielding suspension of heavy trucks (corrugations appear on the most-used tracks). Wherever a track allows vehicles to speed up and the ground conditions are right, corrugations will form.

Driving over four-inch high corrugations is brutal as vehicle, contents and occupants experience a jack-hammer pulverisation. Fractured exhaust mounts are common, as is damage to brackets that hold any component that can get some inertia going, even the rubber-mounted engine and gearbox. The only good thing to say about them is if you're lost and you come across a corrugated track, you can be sure it leads somewhere significant.

Driving on corrugations

It's said that accelerating up to 80kph (50mph) the vehicle skims over the tops of each ridge to give a smoother ride. However, your vehicle isn't really in touch with the surface and can spin out on washboard bends. It's a matter of seeking out the 'optimum harmonic velocity', something that's different from vehicle to vehicle or may not even exist. At times you must resign yourself to

juddering along in second although **deflating tyres** help soften the ride.

The good thing is, really agonising stretches last only a short while but following a hard day's washboard check battery, exhaust, fuel tank and rack mounts and wheel nuts. In fact anything that's attached to anything else. If nothing's fractured after the first really bad session, chances are it'll survive more of the same.

Crossing a ditch or a creek bank

Getting **bellied-out** or hung up on either bumper usually happens when trying to get over a ditch or a creek that's cut across a track. On frequently used tracks any water-carved edges soon get worn down by passing traffic unless you're the first person on the scene, say following a storm.

There are two ways of dealing with such an obstacle. As long as you feel you won't jeopardise the vehicle's stability and tip over, consider traversing the ditch, step or ridge **at an angle of 45°**, not straight on. This technique is more suited to 4x4s with better-than-average clearance, so engage low range for control, and let each of the four wheels individually do their thing. By crossing at an angle you effectively shorten the wheelbase by up to 50%, so greatly improving the ramp breakover angle, or belly clearance. A low back end can still hang up a 4x4 so traction control or axle diff-locks will help here, as will having someone watch the vehicle's clearance to guide the driver.

The other technique is to **transform a step into a ramp** by:
- Piling rocks or soil, or placing a spare tyre against the step.
- Kicking or digging away the lip of the step.
- Using logs, supported sand plates or bridging ladders (ultra rigid sand plates) to make a ramp.

In normal overlanding such a situation is rare and is usually a consequence of recent rains or roaming far off the beaten track. The crux is to **keep the undercarriage off the deck** to maintain traction. As with digging out in sand (see later), don't skimp on the effort; that way you can be sure you'll get over in one go. And have a plan for if it doesn't work out first time. Gentle acceleration and lowered tyre pressures can avoid traction-robbing wheelspin.

Rocky ascents

When gradients get severe – as little as 1:3 – a track's surface can become gouged by spinning wheels and then exacerbated by run-off. At times, a less frequented track can also pass over bare rock whose sharp edges can damage tyres and dent rims. In all situations where you can't see the end of the obstacle, **walk first** to plan a route, moving rocks and filling holes as necessary.

Although it doesn't feel right, once moving let a tyre slowly roll right over a sharp rock rather than try and avoid it and risk damaging the sidewall. Any tyre's tread is much thicker and tougher than its sidewalls. Leaning out of the window may not be enough. If tyres need to be positioned accurately or there is a risk of grounding the undercarriage, get someone to **guide** you. This is a time to engage low range if you have it, crawling forward slowly but surely. Assuming the traction is very good on dry rock, keep the central diff unlocked to avoid inter-axle wind-up. Part-time 4x4s in low range will just have to deal with possible wind-up while ETC makes it all effortless.

Hand-throttle ascents

Sometimes a very rough ascent will rock your vehicle from side to side and, together with the need to steer away from a precipice, this makes smooth progress hard to maintain. As you're thrown around, your foot jabs the accelerator, causing the vehicle to lurch forward and back (bracing your foot against the footwell helps), possibly spinning a wheel and losing traction. This loss of traction can see you slide backwards. Not good.

Hand throttles were standard on most diesel 4x4s twenty years ago, or you can make a hand throttle using a choke cable, assuming of course there is an actual throttle cable there. Nowadays you might have Hill Ascent Control doing all the thinking for you. Crawling forward like this you'll still roll around, but the engine will rev evenly at whatever rpm you set it. With feet off the pedals, control is much improved, enabling you to concentrate on picking the smoothest path around the rocks, loose stones and ditches and away from any edge. This technique also smooths progress on very stony, walking-pace creek crossings, sparing the transmission. A dab with your foot to the pre-loaded accelerator pedal can be given if some extra oomph is needed.

Stalling during a steep ascent

Should you **stall** on a steep ascent the technique outlined below is worth practising beforehand on a less severe gradient. It assumes that once stalled you don't start sliding backwards with all wheels locked up. If this does happen you need to act very quickly to get it in reverse gear. Tackle steep hills **without changing gear** – a gear that's as high as possible but as low as necessary.

- Once stalled, above all, do not depress the clutch.
- Stamp on the brakes.
- Leave the stalled vehicle in gear.
- Engage the handbrake and turn off the ignition.
- With the brakes still on, depress the clutch, engage reverse (in low range if you have it) and release the clutch.
- Look out of the window and make sure that the front wheels are still pointing straight ahead.
- Release the brakes slowly. Being in gear the vehicle will creep or lurch back a bit and be held in place by the engine compression.
- Without touching the accelerator or clutch, start the engine in reverse gear. The vehicle will lurch backwards and slowly descend the slope, with you looking back and steering a straight line.
- Dab the brakes if you feel the need, but in low-range reverse you should be going extremely slowly, much less than walking pace.
- If possible, have someone guide you down.

Steep descents

Descents can look worse than they are and this sequence applies to clambering down a steep creek bank or descending a long stony hillside or a dune.

- If the descent is severe walk down first to plan your route, marking points to place wheels and clearing rocks or filling holes as you go.
- Consider lowering tyre pressures for better traction.
- Get someone to guide you around the worst obstacles.
- Engage four-wheel drive and low-range second, if you have it.
- Move off, keeping both feet on the floor and away from the brake and accelerator pedals. Resist the urge to brake unless absolutely necessary – you'll probably skid, which will quickly get worse. If you're in low second you should be doing much less than walking pace.

If the vehicle **slides**, don't brake – turn into the slide and accelerate gently to let the wheels to catch up with ground speed. Then back off and hope the vehicle slows down with you. If it doesn't, point straight down and ride it out.

Sand

Sand is not like any other surface and certain techniques and practices will keep you moving or recover your vehicle when it's buried up to the axles. You may have read of keen desert expeditions practising on coastal sands in temperate lands. It may look the same but real desert sand is much drier and looser.

Driving on soft sand and salt pans

Driving on something like the flat, trackless Selima Sand Sheet on the Sudan–Egypt border, you can enjoy some serene, easy driving. But even on sand sheets you'll come across **soft patches** when the engine drones as power is sucked away. If it's just a patch the vehicle will pick up speed. If not, **change down fast and accelerate** smoothly – your vehicle's **momentum** aided by the tyres' flotation is what keeps you moving. Engage 4WD if you feel you need the extra traction. If you start losing speed keep changing down until there's nothing left. Avoid any sharp turns or sudden ascents which kill speed. Keep in high range (if you have the power), using lower revs as wheelspin is less likely and so traction is maintained. If you know you're going to get stuck, **admit defeat early** and clutch in before forward progress stops. Acknowledging defeat now saves digging later.

One technique I've seen is **swerving the steering wheel** from side to side as you push through soft sand. Although it appears contrary to the advice about minimising wheel drag, the theory is that sand building up ahead of the front wheels flows away to either side as the steering wheel is turned, rather like a snow plough. Pushing away the build-up, front wheels have less sand to push through or over and are less likely to sink. It may be worth trying once you get some speed up with less powerful cars or 2WDs that need every trick in the book, but I suspect it makes little difference in a 4x4. If you anticipate lots of soft sand ahead, consider lowering your tyre pressures.

Salt pans can have the same trackless appeal of a sand sheet but can be as lethal as driving on a tidal beach. The Makgadikgadi Pans of the Kalahari, the Salar de Uyuni in Bolivia, the Chott el Djerid in Tunisia and Lac Iriki in Morocco are well-known examples. Just remember, any run-off from distant ranges may be percolating up from *beneath* a seemingly solid, dry crust. Having your wagon break through into the **saline slush** underneath is one of the nastiest recoveries in off-roading. I once looked down from the causeway alongside the Chott to a set of deepening tracks that led to a mess of footprints and disturbed sludge which told its own story. Once you get out, many hours later, **hose the vehicle down** with fresh water, otherwise the salt will steadily eat at the metal and electrical contacts, causing problems for months to come.

Caught in a wet patch of sand on the Beach Route in Mauritania. This is a messy recovery, especially alone when it's all the more critical not to take risks on terrain like this.
© Roger Shuttleworth.

If you're driving on salt or a similar clay surface and you feel the vehicle **sinking**, stop quickly and reverse out. If you're going too fast and have ploughed in, as long as you're moving there's nothing for it but to power on to one side or the other. Otherwise stay off them unless they're clearly in regular use, as they are in Botswana and Bolivia.

Reading sand

Depending on the type of sand, driving in existing **ruts** can be better, but not always. In dense sand where a deep, steep-sided trench is formed by a passing wheel, the ruts can drag on your wheels and slow you down, so you're better off pushing your own way through. At other times the pre-compressed sand can be easier going. There's no firm rule. You have to experiment and learn from experience. Generally the **lighter the colour**

A tricky recovery.

of the sand, the softer it is. One theory suggests darker sand is younger and less leached out, with larger, angular grains, which interlock and give better support to a passing wheel.

Grey-surfaced sand is called *feche-feche* in the Sahara, though in my experience this term is widely over-used for any soft sand or bulldust. Real fiche-fiche is in a class of its own: a flour-like powder very often capped by a crust that can only rarely be driven over. Hit a patch or break through this crust suddenly and clouds of the yellow powder explode around you. If you fall into real fiche-fiche you'll know it. I've only encountered it in Libya and Algeria, and both times it was almost like hitting a landmine. Trying to maintain momentum while steering back to firmer ground is your only option. Recovery from fiche-fiche is hard work – backing out is best.

Tyres in sand

The first-time sand driver quickly recognises the huge difference **very low tyre pressures** make to driving in soft sand. Because we're reminded by safety experts to keep tyre pressures at correct levels, letting them down seems contrary to good sense. Equally off-putting is the thought of having to laboriously pump them up again in just a few hundred metres. For that at least, get a powerful compressor.

In all situations err towards higher pressures but recognise that if the conditions demand 1 bar, 1 bar it's got to be. Pressures increase as tyres warm up through the day and tyres on the sunny side get hotter still. Take this into account when you're checking tyre temperatures with your hand and when taking readings. Expect one side to be at least 10% higher if it's been in the sun. Assuming the tyres were all equal to start with, reduce pressures by seconds rather than with a tyre gauge. Consider bleeding some extra air out in the course of a long day through dunes. There's more on advanced dune driving in the *Desert Driving* DVD which may go online one of these years. Sand recovery techniques are on p313.

LIFE ON THE ROAD

Crossing rivers

Many people have paid with their lives by underestimating the power of a tor-rent flowing across a road or track. It's possible to wade across a slow-flowing river up to your hips and even drive through that sort of depth if your air intake is high enough. It's also possible to get pushed downstream by faster water that's barely up to the wheel tops.

Some tracks develop **crossing points** that move around with the seasons or erosion. Elsewhere a concrete ford may mark a regular crossing point, but these can get undermined or ripped out. If there's a queue of vehicles bigger than yours waiting, sit it out unless your Unimog towers over all present.

Before you drive in, be sure you can see or know the point where you'll **drive out**. If you're not alone and there's a chance of a towed recovery if it goes wrong, **prepare tow straps** on the front or rear before you enter the river. Drape them over the bonnet or roof in readiness; it may be too dangerous to try and do so mid-stream.

Petrol-engined vehicles will of course be prone to the **electrics** getting wet and packing up, but then so will many modern vehicles heavily reliant on electronics. If the ECU gets wet it could be an expensive repair. Lash down a tarp over the grill and consider going as far as removing the fanbelt to stop it spraying water all over the place.

A first-class bow wave. © Capt. J. Stephenson

You'll read a lot in about crossing rivers at a speed that maintains a **bow wave** in front of the vehicle; the idea is that immediately behind the wave the water level is lower. Maybe in the per-fect speed-and-depth scenario it is, but don't count on it. Certainly you shouldn't be going so fast as to spray water in all directions unless the water is a few inches deep. It takes steady nerves to keep moving forward as water starts lapping at the base of the windscreen.

Flash floods

Flash floods can develop in no time and block a road, after which time the flow recedes just as quickly. **Waiting** just a few hours, or overnight, can see a vio-lent, impassable torrent drop to a trickle of mud and debris. If it's raining or you're not sure about the flow, put a stick or stone by the flow's edge. If they end up washed away you could be in for a long wait.

All flowing fords or faster flash floods should be given at least a moment's thought before charging in. It only takes a flow **a foot deep** to build up on the side of a van and push it off any concrete surface onto some unseen rubble or the **undercut downstream edge**. If the undercut edge is a big drop, your vehi-cle will tip sideways or roll over. That's how many drown.

Pick your spot. Generally where the flow is wider it's less deep and the current less strong; it may look a long way across but it'll be shallower. If in doubt and there's no one around, the simplest answer is to **walk across** if it's

READ THIS FIRST: 4X4 TRANSMISSION WIND-UP

As explained on p75, the characteristics of axle differentials are undesirable in some off-road situations, but on powered axles no differential effect (or a locked diff) is even less desirable for 4WD transmission. Pay attention as this applies to your trick ETC 4x4 too.

Just as wheels on a driven axle cover varying distances (and so need a differential mechanism), **front and rear axles** linked to give 'four-wheel drive' will also turn at slightly different speeds. Even a small variation is enough to cause tension in the drive train: **transmission wind-up**, binding or 'crow hop'.

Imagine having each limb twisted in a different direction. That's what's happening to your axle half-shafts when you use locked-out four-wheel drive on a hard surface

On a loose or **slippery surface** like mud, sand or snow this tension dissipates as undetectable wheelspin and staying locked-out in 4WD is fine. But on a surface with good traction such as bare rock, wind-up soon becomes apparent. The steering stiffens, your transmission clicks and groans, and then suddenly a wheel unloads the tension with a hop – or a half shaft snaps.

Obviously you wouldn't use locked-out four-wheel drive on a dry tarmac road, but particularly on rocky hairpins you should avoid driving a selectable 4x4 continually in 4WD or the more common full-time 4x4s with the central diff locked for long periods.

To release the tension in the system only requires momentarily unlocking a central diff (or releasing freewheeling diffs or hubs). If there's a lot of tension, disengagement may take a few bends and a minute or two.

Only engage selectable (or 'part-time') four-wheel drive, or lock the central diff on loose surfaces where you think you'll need the extra traction.

If you're now wringing your hands wondering if you can use your fabulous 4x4 safely on the dirt, don't worry about it too much. Whatever system your vehicle runs, most of the time you can simply leave the road and follow a track without doing anything until the going gets tricky. **Lock in the 4WD with the central diff or engage the front axle when you must, unlock it all when you can**. After a while you'll get the feel for what's needed and will soon know exactly when to bring locked-in four-wheel drive into action.

This must be understood clearly. Full-time 4WD with the central diff locked provides near-optimum traction but could also wind up and damage the transmission. Therefore the same limitations to driving on hard surfaces must be observed: lock the central diff only when you really need to and never engage it with the power on and wheels possibly spinning; it won't like it.

safe, using some sort of stick to support you as you lean upstream. By walking you can pick a good line, get a feel for the riverbed, which can include rocks, holes or broken concrete waiting to snare your wheels. If it can be easily walked it can probably be driven, but not every time.

If it's too dangerous to walk then driving across in a light, low vehicle can be marginal. While water may flow around your knees fairly harmlessly, it can build up on the side of a

Morning after a flash flood in Namibia. Note the protruding wheels of another Rover in the background. © Mike Page

car. One way to reduce this force is to ferry across; that is, **drive slightly upstream**. kayakers will know the drill. By driving at an angle upstream the flow propels the vehicle forward and the pushing effect of the current is reduced. All you need to be sure is that the angled route you follow is entirely driveable, which is why in some parts of outback Siberia, tracked flatbed trucks act as wheeled ferries to carry small cars.

If for some reason the vehicle stalls or **cuts out mid-stream**, you better hope there's someone around to pull you out and that the water is not rising. If all hope is lost, water rises above the air intake and the vehicle starts to splutter, you can **save the engine** by switching off before any water gets sucked into the cylinders. Once injected, water cannot be compressed – instead the con-rods or crankshaft snap or bend.

Even without suffering an hydraulic lock, a vehicle that's spent a couple of hours or even a day submerged may have more value as scrap. Give it your best shot by painstakingly **draining everything** and drying the electrics, purging the fuel system and draining the motor oil, which will have mixed with water and emulsified. If you can get the engine running then it's a cue to change all the rest of the emulsified oils and hope for the best. Even then, the vehicle may have been permanently damaged.

Off-road recovery: equipment and techniques

It's possible to drive a long way around this planet and never get stuck at all. But one day it may happen: you'll be stuck in a roadside ditch, a mud hole, a riverbed or on a dune. First up, you want to be confident your vehicle has **secure recovery and towing points** front and rear, while appreciating that being pulled out of deep sand or mud will involve much greater forces than merely being towed along a road by a water buffalo. Many of the techniques and much of the gear described below will be demonstrated online on YouTube and the like.

A **shovel** has many uses, not least for digging away sand or mud to clear wheels prior to a recovery. Not taking the time to do this properly is a common cause of failed recoveries and fried clutches. I find a full-size pointy-ended spade with a hand-wide 'D' handle works better than a flat-bladed spade or a 'T' handle. Folding 'trench tools' are handy and compact but are only fit for toilet duties or gardening. Get a proper shovel or use a plate.

Recovery equipment kit list
- Jack: bottle plus hi-lift or airbag
- Jack pad
- Gloves
- KERR rope
- Sand plates or mats
- Shovel: with D-handle
- Tow straps or 3-core nylon ropes: 20m and 6m

ROPES, STRAPS AND ATTACHMENT POINTS

Whatever you're driving, a **tow strap** and **solid towing points** front and rear will (along with a sand mat and a shovel) one day get you out of a fix. You don't have to be stuck yourself: a rope can be used to help others. Straps can be as strong as ropes and roll up to be more compact. Both straps and ropes can be **joined easily** with nothing more than a tightly rolled-up magazine or a stick, as pictured.

Depending on where you're going and what you're doing, a 20-metre strap rated at at least twice the weight of your vehicle is very useful for recovery when deeply bogged. A shorter 6-metre strap is handy for highway towing. Ropes made from synthetic as opposed to natural materials are best, 3-core nylon being strongest and with a bit of give. Keep them in a bag away from UV sunlight.

Joining two loops with a rolled up magazine or a stick. © Rob & Ally Ford

Snatch ropes (KERR)

For deep boggings in mud or sand your long strap (or series of joined straps) enables the recovery vehicle to work from firm ground. Otherwise, snatch ropes or kinetic energy recovery ropes (**KERR**) are long, elastic ropes which stretch and build up energy until the stuck vehicle suddenly lunges free.

Assuming any necessary digging has been done to clear the stranded vehicle's wheels, you just hook up with a few bends of slack on the ground then with an agreed signal, the **recovering vehicle reverses away quickly**. Nothing will appear to happen as the rope elongates until suddenly the bogged vehicle lurches forward out of the hole. See the *Desert Driving* DVD.

Though immense, the strain on the vehicles is linear and smooth and the lunge is not hard to control. As mentioned, towing points must be especially strong with snatch-rope recoveries due to the much greater forces involved. Never use a snatch rope if you think the towing point isn't up to it; KERRS are not suited to all vehicles.

Towing points

Bumpers like on a Defender are a rare thing these days, although off-road vehicles will usually have something solid mounted directly to the chassis at both ends, ideally an **open hook** rather than a ring, which can take a tow strap loop without the need for a shackle. Shackle (giant karabiners) are best avoided for normal overlanding but a local vehicle helping you out may not have a nice hook in which case a tow hitch will do.

The rings you have on the front of a regular car may not be for towing, but approved towing rings may be available to bolt on. Other cars have a towing eye stored somewhere near the spare tyre that screw on manually behind a discreet panel on the plastic bumper. Whatever vehicle you have, check how it can tow or be towed securely, though if desperate attaching to any stout element on the chassis or axles will have to do.

Balancing jacks and flip flops.
Only for the brave.

JACKS

Make sure your vehicle's **tyre-changing jack** is up to the job. Whether it's a scissor, pillar or hydraulic jack, you'll also need a metal plate or a **wooden board** when lifting on soft ground. A spare tyre will do, unless of course you happen to be changing the wheel.

Overall, with a road car you may want to supplement lightly built pillar or scissor jacks with an extra-long **hydraulic bottle jack**; there may be times when two jacks are useful.

Remember, wherever you're jacking up and by whatever means, make sure it's lifting in the **correct place**, or a point that can take the vehicle's weight, otherwise all you'll do is damage something. Secondly, **never get under a vehicle resting solely on any jack** for more than a few seconds. If you're getting under the car, immediately back the jack up with a rock, jerrican or spare tyre. Sometimes there's no need to even use a jack to look underneath; just drive one side up a slope or a ledge where the vehicle is stable.

Hi-lift jacks

Commonly used by off-roaders, **hi-lift jacks** come in various lengths. The 48-inch version will do for a 4x4 but weighs 13kg. A hi-lift has a mechanism that climbs up the jack's notched stem, lifting the vehicle as you crank the handle. Flick a lever *with the handle in the upright position* and it steadily clicks back down the stem until the weight is released. It's essential to read and understand the **instructions** that come with these devices – being American, the original Hi-Lift's handle and booklet are plastered with warning labels.

The lifting point for the hi-lift foot must be capable of taking a vehicle's weight – ideally the chassis or a flat-bottomed bumper bolted directly to the chassis as on the front of a Defender and 70-series Toyotas. But bumpers are now rounded pedestrian-friendly items not suited to hi-lifting without an adapter. Lacking one of these, you want to avoid the chance of the jack sliding sideways under load. Fix something on so the jack's foot locates securely.

Hey ho, it's a jack pad with locating pins!

Lifting the rear of a fully loaded 4x4 can be hard; try it at home before finding out you need someone sitting on your shoulders. If you can't, get an air bag. Lifting even both front wheels is quite easy as it's a shorter pivot, but in this situation a jack is very unstable and can fall sideways. This is actually a quick way of lifting the front out of ruts and letting the vehicle fall sideways onto higher ground, but comes with stern health warnings.

Air-bag jacks

Air-bag jacks are tough **vinyl balloons** the size of a dustbin which use the vehicle's exhaust pressure to effortlessly lift one side of a 4x4 in a minute (as long as your engine is running). Air-bag jacks don't look as purposeful as a hi-lift bolted by the back door, and are more expensive too, but they're much lighter and can work with any vehicle; special jacking points are not needed, just a flat area to take the weight. An air bag also requires less physical effort than a hi-lift and won't knock your head off if your hand slips off the handle.

For a regular car or light 4x4, a cheap air-bag jack rated at two tonnes may do the trick; for a heavier 4x4 a higher-rated item is better. The bag needs less than one bar to lift a car, so no engine damage can occur from back pressure, although the **exhaust system** must be sound if it's to survive – and also have one outlet or the others blocked for lifting. I found on my old Land Cruiser that after some air-jacking it started blowing through the braided section between the engine down pipe and the exhaust.

For **sand recoveries** or even **righting an overturned vehicle**, an air jack is ideal as, unlike other jacks, it spreads the weight over a large area, but whatever you're doing you must think carefully where to position it on the ground *and* under the vehicle. You may need something to spread the load, because half the vehicle's weight will be resting on this point, as well as a thick piece of carpet or similar on the ground if thorns or sharp rocks are present.

Before filling, you need to get the deflated bag **correctly positioned** and levelled up or else, as the bag fills, it'll squirm out to the side, especially in a muddy situation. Here a hessian bag or sand plates thrown over the mud may improve grip. The bag will also lose air slowly and so if used for tyre changing, you'd want the spare tyre ready alongside to fit quickly before the vehicle sags too far.

Air bags will slowly deflate, so for prolonged repairs plan ahead with a jerry or rocks.

Recovery with a hi-lift jack or air bag

This method requires no grovelling under the car with a shovel and, especially if you have the appropriate mounting points, is the quickest and most effective option. Both techniques are demonstrated in the *Desert Driving* DVD.

Using a **hi-lift**, you can jack up both front wheels off a solid Defender-like bumper or, with the aid of a sling or adaptor, lift each wheel individually. In this situation there should be no need to chock the other wheels, which are all well entrenched. Once the wheels are clear of the deck and you're sure the jack will stand alone, push sand or brush into the hole or trench below the wheel, or lay down a sand plate. When you lower both wheels the axle should be clear of the ground. Repeat the same for the other axle if necessary. Reduce tyre pressures if appropriate and drive out in low gear.

With **air bags** it's the same procedure, but you place the bag under the side, lifting and clearing first one side then the next. A wobbly air bag can't securely lift the front or rear of a vehicle without it rolling off the bag to one side. It can take some experience to position the air bag so it doesn't squirm out or melt on the pipe. Once you have the knack of sealing the air bag hose's nozzle over the tail pipe, it's great to watch the wheels rising effortlessly as the bag quickly fills.

SAND PLATES AND MATS

Going under many names, the **sand plate** was probably developed once cavemen progressed onto mammoth-drawn carts. On an unconsolidated surface a plate, mat, towel, plank or roll of chicken wire provides a patch of secure **traction** and so the **momentum** to free a vehicle from a light bogging. The good thing with sand plates and the like is that, as long as you haven't gone too far, you can quickly recover yourself with no help.

Rigid or flexible, plate or mat, dayglo or camo – sand plates become less necessary as your experience in reading terrain grows in response to the learned tedium of getting stuck. In choosing one for your needs, balance the likelihood of use in either mud, sand or both, with the price, weight, the ease of mounting and deployment (including possible damage to your vehicle) as well as any possible secondary utility. Rigid plates can make a bench between two boxes; mats as something to stand on.

PSP and alloy plates

The term '**sand ladders**' dates from the early years of motoring, although in my experience actual ladders, not surprisingly, tend to sink into the sand or mud before much traction and momentum is gained. **PSP** stands for 'pierced-steel plank' and is much more effective. A WWII artefact, the interlocking sections were once used to make temporary roadways and even landing strips in the US-led Pacific War. Like hi-lift jacks, PSP became adapted for off-road driving use, and is still cheap to buy from military surplus outlets. But at around 10 kilos a metre and edged with jagged interlocking teeth, it's wider than it needs to be for anything except a Unimog.

PSP was much copied and became part of the 4x4 'expedition look' in smoother, lighter and shinier **aluminium alloy**. The pierced holes enable easy mounting and handling and more crucially grip as the plate is pressed down

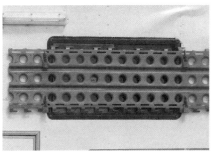

Secondary use of PSP padlocked across a
window. Nasty edges are an added deterrent.

For lighter vehicles like this Hilux-engined
VW, half-width plates will do.

into the ground. (Anything with too smooth an underside can be spat out by
the torque of the turning wheel.) Longitudinal creases give rigidity, but alloy
plates can still easily bend so choose thicker versions or use **steel** for heavier
vehicles and trucks. A small bend is no drama (drive back over the arched
plate to flatten it out), but can make re-mounting onto fixed points awkward.

A **plate** is typically 1–1.5m (40–60″) long and 30–47cm (12–18″) wide. A
light car or van can manage on a single alloy plate cut down the middle into
two 23cm-wide pieces. Rigid plates should be shorter than your wheelbase
because the plate tends to lift as a wheel rolls onto or off it, before ideally dropping back to the ground as the next wheel rolls on. A too-long plate may get
jammed into the approaching wheel arch – nasty. Rigid plates ejected by spinning back tyres are also something those pushing at the back bumper should
watch out for, and is one reason less shin-slashing mats are preferred. Having
a plate with one **pointed end** helps jam it in under a tyre; some of the excessively wide plates could benefit from this modification.

Flexible and roll-up mats

Smooth metal plates can get flicked out and when wet, tyres will spin before
any momentum has been gained. Anything works to temporarily gain traction: grass, wood planks, a thick canvas sheet, the floor mats in your car, but
in my experience unless you pull away gently, **roll-up mats** like South African
bakkie mats tend to scrunch up.

Just about the cheapest and lightest recovery mats I know are French-
made **Soltracks**, a robust, pliable mat
with a knobbly surface like a giant
ping-pong bat. A 1.2m x 45cm mat
weighs just 1.4kg and costs £70 a pair.
They don't sink like waffles or ladders, nor ruck up like bakkie mats,
and they can't stab your shins or your
car's sills like PSP. For a **2WD campervan** they'd give peace of mind while
having a minimal impact on space and
payload. In the UK Matt Savage sells
them as 'Wild Mats'.

Soltracks; a light, inexpensive and effective
traction aid for light vehicles including 2WDs.

Waffles used as ramps to level out a camper.

Much copied Maxtrax work well in sand and can bridge a ditch. They weigh 4 kilos each.

GRP waffles and plates

A while ago cut-offs of industrial GRP grating nick-named **waffles** became in vogue for off-roading, at least in the UK. Normally used as high-grip decking on exposed, all-weather walkways, prices dropped to a reasonable £40 for a 1.2m x 35cm slab. The 38–50mm (1.5–2″) thick ones will suit a heavy 4x4 but **weigh a back-breaking 14kg (31lb)** each for a 1.5-m section. Think about that when grovelling under your fourbie, trudging back across a dune to recover them, or shaking them free of caked mud after an exhausting and messy recovery. The other problem is waffles tend to sink into fine sand or soft mud.

The main advantage is that short, thick waffles are strong enough to double as **bridging ramps** to get across narrow ditches and up rock steps. Such a situation may occur while driving around looking for somewhere to get really stuck on a Sunday afternoon, but overlanders rarely encounter genuine bridging situations. A quick shovel or moving rocks around will do.

Mounting sand plates

A light mat can be slung anywhere in the back and plates don't have to be ready for action 24/7. But once you leave a highway you want the plates **mounted where you can get to them** without fuss or using any tools. Having to climb onto the roof rack to unstrap them every time you get stuck is very tiresome; should you find yourself in dunes you may be using them every half hour. The same applies for your **shovel** and **tow strap**. Keep them handy.

	Mud	Wet grass	Snow	Sand	Bridge	Weight	Ease	Cost
WHICH PLATE OR MAT?								
Steel PSP	O	O	O	✔	O	✘	✘	✔
Alloy PAP	O	O	O	✔	✘	O	O	O/✘
Waffles	✔	✔	✔	O	✔	✘	✘	O
Flexy GRP	O	O	O	✔	✘	✔	✔	O/✘
Maxtrax	O	✘	✔	✔	O	O	✔	✘
Bakkie	✘	O	O	✘	✘	✘	O	O
Soltracks	✘	✔	✔	✔	✘	✔	✔	✔

✔ Good   O OK, but depends on surface and/or design.   ✘ Not so good

On a hardtop 4x4 a rigid plate mounts readily on the flank of the vehicle and can double as a security grill or shade device over windows. Kits with a small round plate held down with a butterfly nut are common but are too fussy. Ideal mounts use quick-release clips that bolt onto the car's side or roof rack, or a big clamp that screws on by hand as pictured on the right.

It's something that's easy to operate when tired and is less easy to lose than a tiny butterfly nut.

Hooks take the weight while bolts and a nut welded to a bent metal clamp secures.

Alternatively, a pair of hooks can take the weight through the holes or from below, with a quick-release strap or clip to secure and release the plate.

Assuming you have the clearance and the plates are short enough, another option is slipping them into **'C' channels** between a roof rack and the roof, although this works best with GRP plates, which can't bend out of shape. A simple strap or elastic is all that's then needed to keep them from slipping out.

Recovery with PSP or mats

This is the traditional if rather effortful recovery method: getting down and **scooping or digging** the mud or sand from under the vehicle and around the wheels faster than it flows back. A shovel is useful for the axles, but even short ones are hard to use under a vehicle where hands are easier.

Once you've cleared the wheels, **push your plates or mats just under the tyre** so that it can drive onto the plate easily without a step; pointy-ended plates work well for this. Shove them right against the tyre in whichever direction you're driving off – if you're reversing put them under the back wheels so once they've passed over them, the front wheels can use them too, to get some momentum going. Reduce tyre pressures if you haven't already done so and have a look at the best way out if it's not obvious.

RECOVERY IN SAND

Despite all the above advice you'll probably get stuck in the first soft sand you encounter. If you stopped early, you should be able to reverse out without any digging or pushing. Once back on firm ground, have another go, **accelerating** through the soft patch or taking another route.

The biggest mistake made by novice or stubborn sand drivers is **not stopping soon enough**. You plough on ever more slowly until you're revving the engine but are moving downwards not forward. You try and reverse, but it's too late and deeper in you go. You try going forward again, this time in low first and the torque spins you down into the sand a little more. Finally you admit that your 4x4 is not so all-terrain after all and you're embedded in the landscape, but not like an Antony Gormley sculpture. Depending on how dogged you were, or how soft the sand suddenly became, all the tyres will be buried up to the bottom of the wheel rim.

Clearly this Land Rover was not engaged in any radical manoeuvres on big dunes, but in certain desert light conditions it's possible to drive onto an unseen slope which tips you over. This is where packing with a low centre of gravity can make a difference. © thisfabtrek.com

Bogged down

First decide whether it's best to go **forward or back**: if you're on a slope, aim to descend the gradient. If you can't go back, walk forward and stamp on sandy ground with your foot: a firm print means drivable sand, an oval blur means it's probably too soft to support a vehicle. Checking that there's still air between the undercarriage and the ground, **scoop or shovel the sand** away from the sides of the tyres. A pair of hands work as well as a shovel. Clear the sand away right down to the bottom of the tyre and dig away a **smooth ramp** for the tyre in whichever direction you're going. There must be no lip for the tyres to roll over if you're to have a chance of a first-time recovery. Depending on tyre pressures and the terrain ahead, consider **letting some air out**.

Once this is done to all four wheels, drive out in low second or reverse and **keep going** until you're back on firm ground. If there are a couple of people around to **push**, this can make the difference between staying stuck or getting free. There should be no need for sand plates and the whole business should take no more then five or ten minutes. With a long section of soft sand, the pushers should run with the car and push again if the car hits another soft patch or until they can't keep up. If driving forward it's possible for a pusher to hop onto the back bumper as the car picks up speed and jump off to push again if necessary. Don't try this on bumpy or hummocky ground though as if the driver is going flat out to get clear it's impossible to hold on at the back.

A clear track means the sand is solid. The same goes for a footprint when scouting ahead. Blurry footprint: still soft.

Sunk down to the axles

This situation becomes less frequent as you learn to read the sand and to stop early. It need never happen at all but at some time, especially in dunes, even the most experienced driver can plough into an indistinguishable soft patch and sink before they know it. Usually the dragging axles stop the car going too deep, but that's plenty.

Sand must be cleared right to the bottom of the tyre, making a ramp to drive out on.

Recovery from this situation is going to take two people at least half an hour. There are three methods of getting out: using a hi-lift **jack** or an air bag, digging with a **shovel and sand ladders**, or the quickest; **tow out**.

Be aware of the risk of **sunburn and dehydration**. Wear a shirt and a hat while you're working and take a good swig of water when it's done. If it goes on like this in stops and starts for hours, expect to need a rehydration drink.

RECOVERY FROM MUD AND SNOW

Getting stuck in sand is not so bad; it's usually sunny and warm and sand drops away from the hands. Mud is not like that. As often as not, you can get stuck in a puddle where there's no way out without making a mess of yourself. Some routes in the Congo basin are notorious as trucks grind down ever deeper holes just as iron-rimmed wagons carved 'holloways' in medieval times. Regular vehicles with less clearance than a truck can't manage the ruts and so people try and drive around the sides, the mess spreads, some slide back in and a jungle track can become blocked for hours.

Cameroon. Note the bucket – sometimes a shovel is just not enough. © Frederik & Josephine

In a single vehicle a **winch** can be useful, and solid attachment points on any vehicle will be essential to getting towed out rather than having your bumper ripped off. Rugged tyres can literally give you an edge, or they can dig you in deeper, depending on the type of mud. In the end it's all down to clearance: keeping the undercarriage off the mud and the tyres driving you forward. Across the Congo it all becomes part of the adventure, pulling people out of the way so you at least can get through.

If your 2WD has merely strayed too far from a good surface – onto mud, wet grass or snow – and got one wheel spinning, one trick that can work is what's called **left-foot braking**. Accelerating gently with the right foot while pressing on the foot brake can act almost like a foot-operated diff-lock, slowing a spinning wheel enough to get the other wheel turning and inching the vehicle forward. The other option is to use a sand mat or plate of some kind.

Snow and ice are conditions you'll either be prepared for or it's a situation that takes you by surprise, usually at high altitude. In the mountains of Asia the highest drivable passes re-open as late as July but can get briefly snowed over at any time until winter closes them again. In India, between certain dates the army is obliged to recover travellers stranded by unexpected snow, though most probably it won't be the snow that stops you, but a long queue of stationary traffic. Without snow chains or 4WD there's nothing for it but to sit it out and either wait for the machines to clear the pass or turn back.

If you wake up to find a foot of **snow fallen overnight** and no clear markers or snow poles marking the course of the road, to continue or even return is a lottery. Once passing vehicles compress fresh snow, the surface becomes slick and, until it's salted, the slightest gradient can immobilise a vehicle.

Should you **slide off the road** it's the same deal as mud or sand: you need to get the weight back onto the tyres. The easiest way is to get **pushed or towed back onto the road**, otherwise a **shovel** or a plate can help shift large volumes of snow; or lift your vehicle with an airbag. The left-foot braking trick can work here too, as will getting twigs, floor mats under the wheels – the Soltracks mentioned earlier work as well in snow as they do on sand.

Stuck in snow there's no escaping a lot of shovelling. © Wayne Mitchleson

Single-vehicle shipping

DOUG HACKNEY

Setting off on a long overland journey can require crossing an ocean or two, especially for those based in North America or Australasia. That means you need to confront and slay the Overseas Shipping Dragon. After reading this section you may consider revising your itinerary because you can drive between the farthest corners of Europe, Africa and Asia without needing to go anywhere near a container port. The aggravations associated with freighting an individual vehicle by sea may even make you consider renting or buying and equipping it overseas. Otherwise **sea freight** is the only option – air cargo is just too prohibitive.

THE PROCESS

It's important to maintain a sense of perspective about the shipping process. To you, your vehicle is everything. In some cases, it may be the sum total of your worldly possessions. Naturally, you're extremely concerned about it and consider it worthy of the highest levels of care and attention during shipping. To the shipping industry, however, your vehicle is an abnormal type of cargo which requires inordinate amounts of handholding, additional paperwork and, worst of all, interacting with you, someone who knows nothing about shipping, its terms, requirements, processes, players or realities.

The latest containers come with cute tiled roofs. © Rob & Ally Ford

Consider that in the shipping world your vehicle is one 20-ft container, a unit known as a **TEU** ('twenty foot equivalent'). In 2016 over 145 million TEUs shipped around the globe and your precious vehicle is just one of them. Most sea cargo moves between outfits that ship tens of thousands of containers weekly – bulky, low-value items – the very opposite of fast-moving air cargo. During your travels you're likely to ship a couple of TEUs a year. Is it any wonder that just about everyone you interact with in the shipping industry considers your vehicle a pain and worthy of extra costs? Keep this in mind when you ship your vehicle.

The **general process flow of sea freight** is explained below. That **chart** may flow as smoothly as warm rum, but:

- You'll probably be lied to repeatedly throughout the process.
- The ship's schedule will change often.
- The ship will almost certainly be late.
- Your vehicle will take much longer to process through Customs than you think, or are led to believe.
- There will be extra and unanticipated costs that will almost certainly need to be paid in cash.

Due to these all-too-frequent circumstances, it's important to remain patient, steady and even-keeled through the shipping experience, just as you do at protracted border crossings. Remember, the goal is to begin or resume your adventure. It's worth losing a battle or two with listless bureaucrats or untrustworthy shipping people in order to win the overall war of overlanding.

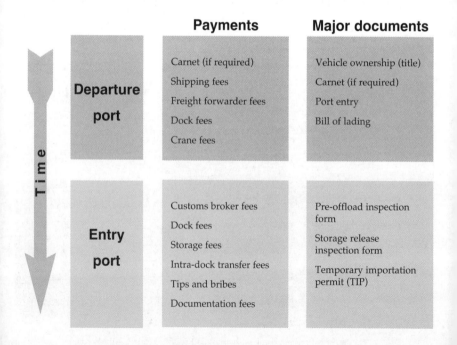

Time		**Payments**	**Major documents**
	Departure port	Carnet (if required) Shipping fees Freight forwarder fees Dock fees Crane fees	Vehicle ownership (title) Carnet (if required) Port entry Bill of lading
	Entry port	Customs broker fees Dock fees Storage fees Intra-dock transfer fees Tips and bribes Documentation fees	Pre-offload inspection form Storage release inspection form Temporary importation permit (TIP)

TYPES OF SHIPPING

There are several types of shipment available for vehicles:

Container

The vehicle goes into a secure shipping container, which is lifted by crane on and off a ship. Container services are available on all global shipping routes.

Roll-on/Roll-off (RoRo)

The vehicle is driven on and off the ship by the crew. RoRo is not available on most shipping routes.

Flat rack

A vehicle that is too big for a container is securely attached to an open platform and craned aboard. Empty flat racks aren't available in many ports and may require significant additional waiting time and costs.

Cradle lift

The exposed vehicle is lifted by crane via a cradle placed under the axles. Cradles may not be available in all ports.

Less than container load (LCL)

The vehicle shares a container with other freight on a space-available basis.

Trailer

On some shipping routes it's possible to ship a complete truck with the vehicle(s) inside the trailer. This method could allow vehicle packaging other than a container or flat rack.

Interface	Entities	
Freight forwarder	Shipping company i.e. KLine, Seaboard, etc	Storage subcontractor company
		Loading subcontractor company
		Other subcontractor companies
Customs broker	Wharf service management company	Unloading subcontractor company
	Port management company	Storage subcontractor company
	Customs	Other subcontractor companies

If at all possible, **use a container**. The sea-freight industry is optimised to move, store, track, transport and deliver standard-sized shipping containers either 20ft or 40ft long (see p41 for exact dimensions). If your vehicle is too tall, use the taller 'high-cube' version, but note that high-cube containers can be more expensive and range from being more challenging to impossible to obtain, especially in minor ports. Over-width vehicles are usually consigned to flat racks, although if your vehicle won't fit into a container and a genuine, guaranteed **RoRo** service is available, choose RoRo. **LCL** will likely delay your vehicle, so avoid it. It's far preferable to **pay for your own container** than have your vehicle sit for weeks on a dock waiting for space in a shared container.

Unscrupulous freight forwarders will often sell you RoRo services, and charge you premium rates, then allow your vehicle to be cradle lifted onto and off the ship instead, thus exposing it to potential damage. It's up to you to independently confirm that RoRo service is available on the shipping route you require and on the shipping line your freight forwarder plans to use.

Where RoRo is not available, put your vehicle on a **flat rack** and ship it via a container ship. Lock your vehicle to the flat rack to prevent the dock crew from using a cradle to lift it off the ship separate from the rack.

DOCUMENTS

Countries often take a dim view of bringing a vehicle for personal use into their ports. Even though crossing a land border may take up to a day, it is a relatively common occurrence. In contrast, bringing a used vehicle into a port is an uncommon occurrence, and the people who work in the Customs and inspection offices may never have seen their government's required documentation for the process, much less know how to fill it out.

SHIPPING BRIBES

Bribes are a popular topic of debate among overlanders. When, where, who, how, how often and how much are the usual questions, especially related to shipping. I've met overlanders who've been around the world and claimed never to have paid a single bribe. Conversely, I've shipped into most areas of the world and paid bribes when and where required to do so. You'll need to establish your own policy when you experience the shipping process. For non-shipping related bribes, see p205.

Shipping involves so many entities that it's difficult to discern where a service charge ends and a bribe begins. Typical shipping bribes are to **dock crews** or to gatekeepers of the shipping process such as **Customs** officials. It has been my view that a few extra dollars to ensure good handling or rapid paperwork-processing has been well spent. My preferred method is to have our freight forwarder or Customs broker handle all **the distribution of funds** related to the shipment. I'd rather pay the additional 'handling charges', which can include bribe distribution, than be personally doling out cash on the dockside. Putting the local freight forwarder or Customs broker between me and the transaction also gives me some plausible deniability in case things get ugly. Again, you'll need to determine what exactly your approach will be to bribes, should you find yourself in a position where they're required.

You must also be very conscious of your situation and the **local culture**. In many developed countries, an attempted bribe could land you in trouble. On the other hand, in some countries, without a small bribe your vehicle could rust clean away before you get the single stamp you need. As in all things overland, be aware of your surroundings, local cultural mores and local expectations.

   This lack of familiarity with the process and incomplete knowledge of the required documents often leads to a complex kabuki dance of bureaucrats attempting to save face with their peers, while simultaneously maintaining their official haughty bureaucratic demeanour. Consequently, at all costs, avoid embarrassing the bureaucrats, especially in front of their peers. If you know where a signature or stamp is required on your carnet and the clerk across the counter is looking at it like it's Einstein's notebook, point subtly rather than shout it out. You could save yourself hours or days of delay.

   When you're shipping a vehicle into a country, your final goal is either a **stamped carnet** or a **Temporary Import Permit (TIP)**. For many of the bureaucrats you meet crossing their particular 't' is one of the few sources of power and respect in their lives. Try to avoid getting caught up in minor conflicts along the way; keep your eyes on the ultimate goal: getting back on the road.

Documents to ship out of a country

- **Vehicle ownership document**. In the UK it's called a V5, in the US and possibly elsewhere, this adds up to two documents: the title and the vehicle registration. The title must be unencumbered (meaning no liens), or must come with a notarised letter from your lien holder authorising you to take the vehicle out of the country. The registration needs to be current and include the licence plate details. Use a two-sided colour copier in developing countries.
- **Carnet de passages**
- A **passport** that matches the identity on the vehicle's documents.

Documents to ship into a country

- The original **Bill of Lading** (B/L). This is prepared by your freight forwarder and created by the shipping company. Once your freight forwarder receives the B/L from the shipper they send it and the original titles and carnet (if required) via courier to your Customs broker. Even in non-obscure countries it can take four to six days for this delivery to arrive and clear Customs.
- **Passport** (for vehicle import). In countries that don't require a carnet, your vehicle will be brought in on your passport. Your Customs broker will need your passport and your entry visa for at least one day to process this transaction. Tip: Don't get involved in any bar fights or complex espionage while your Customs broker has your passport.
- **Temporary Importation Permit**. This will be issued by the Customs inspection office at the port of entry. They'll sometimes physically inspect the VIN of your vehicle before issuing this certificate. If you have motorcycles stored inside your vehicle it'll help to put an easily visible sticker on the bike stating: VIN ### and Engine: ####.
- **Proof of insurance**. Some countries will require basic third-party liability motor insurance before you leave the port. Buy locally or with a global policy, provide copies of your policy documents. Always provide copies, not the originals.
- **International Driving Permit**. Very rarely you may be required to show your IDP (more on p23) as part of the import process. Always provide copies, not the original.

The Copy Shop run

It's common for bureaucrats to demand multiple copies of your personal and vehicle documents for the exit and entry process. In many cases, they'll direct you to a local copy shop which happens to be operated by a close relative. If you have the space, a combined colour scanner/printer can nudge you ahead a few places. Whatever your vehicle, have plenty of **two-sided colour copies** of your **vehicle documents, the photo page of your passport and your IDP**.

When entering a country some documents need to be stamped, signed and inspected by multiple agencies. Those departments may be located all over the port city, or even in another city altogether. Be prepared for long, hot rides through packed streets from one dreary office to another. A good Customs broker, interpreter and fixer can be invaluable here.

THE PLAYERS

When shipping out of a country you'll employ a **freight forwarder**. They prepare the necessary paperwork, book the shipping line, get your vehicle processed through Customs, prepare the Bill of Lading, get you and the vehicle onto the docks and so on.

Once at your destination you'll need to hire a **Customs broker**. They coordinate getting your vehicle off the ship, into storage, out of storage and into and out of inspections and Customs. They facilitate getting all the paperwork submitted, stamped, completed, delivered and filed.

The Customs broker will probably speak a different language than you. If you don't have business-level language skills in their language you'll need to hire a **local interpreter**. In most places, personal relationships are very important so it's best if you can hire an interpreter familiar with the area, the Customs broker and the individual vehicle import process.

The entire process involves many different companies, people, departments and agencies. You'll often be amazed at how many documents, departments and people are required in this process and how many hand-stamps are used. The ultimate goal of the Customs broker is to get your vehicle past the Customs inspector and through the exit gate of the port. Depending on the country you're in, that may require cash incentives.

PREPARING FOR CONTAINER SHIPMENT

Get in you bast@*d!
© doubledutchworldsafari.com

To ship your vehicle via a container you must be prepared to load and secure it inside the container yourself. The shipping container won't be flush with the ground, so you may need **ramps**. Most shippers don't provide **retaining straps** or **wheel chocks** for shipping; these too will be down to you. Dockside handling involves high G forces and rapid motion – you will need ratchet straps and chocks to ensure your vehicle stays in position.

Most shippers don't provide **locks**

for containers either. Many high-security locks won't fit, so test any non-standard lock you plan to use on a similar shipping container prior to arrival at the loading location.

These days more than ever, gaining **access** to docks and container-loading facilities can be complex. Bring everything you need with you because chances are you won't have the opportunity to leave and then return to the site, or to purchase things on site.

You may need to **load the vehicle** in an insecure area, so having someone along to watch the vehicle while you fill out forms is helpful. Prior to loading, **take photos** of all sides of the vehicle to document its condition prior to loading and shipment. Once your vehicle is loaded and all inspections are complete, the container will be closed. You'll then be able to attach your lock. The container is often also closed with a **Customs seal**. Photograph and write down the Customs seal number and keep it with your important documents.

Make a copy of all Bills of Lading and documents. Take photos of all shipping stickers, tracking number stickers and the serial number of the container painted on its side. Photograph the entire process.

PREPARING FOR NON-CONTAINER SHIPMENT

When you ship RoRo you hand over your ignition key – not an easy thing to do. Strip your cab and vehicle exterior of everything of value. If you have a pass-through to the cabin, **lock it up** tight. You may even want to screen all windows on the inside of your cabin, empty any exterior lockers and fit additional security or cladding to the cabin door. The more deterrents the better.

If you're shipping a light truck or 4x4, install a **cargo barrier** between the front seat and the rest of the vehicle. Keep all items in the back covered and don't let anything of value be seen through any window or from the front seat. Again, blocking the rear windows to discourage passing interest will help.

- Strip the cab of all items of value; provide only an ignition key.
- Remove all electronics, including the in-dash radio.
- Remove all accessories, including remote controls.
- Lock your spare wheel in place.
- Remove all external mirrors, auxiliary lights and accessories.
- Lock, empty or remove all external fuel and storage containers. Secure any externally attached equipment such as rooftop tents and racks.
- Do all this before arriving at the docks.
- Take photos of the vehicle to document its condition prior to shipment.

For **flat-rack shipment**, take photos of the serial number of the rack painted on its side as well as any Bill of Lading stickers and tracking number stickers. With non-container shipping, anything you don't remove from your vehicle that's not bolted down or locked away will almost certainly be stolen. Vehicle **break-ins** are common in some ports, especially in **West Africa**. Note that your vehicle's route may include stops in high-crime ports: some routes from Europe to South America, for example, include stops in West Africa. Anything you do leave in the cab must be considered expendable or as **gifts** to the loading drivers in the hope they'll treat your vehicle with care. These can include a packet of cigarettes, DVDs or whisky, whatever you think might do the trick.

WAITING FOR THE SHIP TO ARRIVE

The time between stepping off the plane in the destination port city and when your ship arrives can be highly stressful. Instead of stewing away make use of your time. First, contact and **meet your local Customs broker**. Personal relationships are important in most of the interesting places in the world, so venture down to the office and meet your Customs broker in person.

Ask your Customs broker to recommend a **guide** for a tour of the town, especially the docks neighbourhood and the relevant government offices required for your transaction. If possible, **meet all the officials**, bureaucrats, shipping company and dock managers who'll be involved. A prior relationship can ease tensions and frustrations once your vehicle arrives.

Ask your Customs broker about any fees or charges that will need to be paid and start **stockpiling cash** to meet those requirements. On the day of your vehicle's arrival you don't want to hit your daily ATM limit when you're so close. Locate multiple ATMs so you'll be ready to gather together the cash payments that are often required.

Familiarise yourself with the area where your vehicle will be processed and with the rules required for to and from those areas. With a ship's name there are various websites or apps which **live track** the position of commercial shipping, so relax and enjoy the port city or take a tour up country while unburdened by your vehicle.

A 101 and a Beach Buggy arrive in Singapore.
© G.Kelley

When your ship comes in

Expect several days between your ship berthing and driving away to continue your journey. And even then you may need a day or so to restore your rig to full overlanding configuration.

When your vehicle arrives you'll be unable to access it until it passes through Customs and other inspections. It's common for unexpected, **last-minute charges and fees** to be imposed at this time, just when your bargaining position is weak. It doesn't hurt to put up a fight but in the end you either argue, pay or wait. A good local Customs broker is invaluable in this situation and can save you considerable time, grief, worry and money.

If you have locking compartments, you may be required to participate in the **Customs inspection** by opening them. In other ports the Customs inspection is after the vehicle is turned over to you but prior to exiting the docks. Reunited with your vehicle, inspect it for damage and for **missing contents**. If anything is amiss, take photos to document the evidence and immediately contact your Customs broker and local insurance representative.

COSTS

Costs for shipping vary widely depending on method and destination. If you're shipping between Asia or North America and Europe, shipping volume will be high, options will be many and rates competitive, regardless of the method.

Shipping by **container** typically has the lowest costs. The exception is a port on a **regular RoRo route**, usually for delivering new cars into or out of the country. In those special cases, RoRo rates can be lower than container.

In general, shipping between two popular ports on two continents with a lot of trade has low shipping costs. Examples include **between Europe and North America** and **between east Asia and North America or Europe**. Examples of high-cost routes include between the **west coast of South America** and just about anywhere, or to/from a low-volume port. Avoid low-volume ports. You can save money and time using **a high-traffic, high-volume port**, even if it's on the other side of a country or continent. For example, between low-volume Valparaiso, Chile and high-volume Buenos Aires.

THE ROUTES

Selecting a shipping route is usually driven by your primary destination and itinerary, although as mentioned at the start of this article, it may be better to plan it the other way around. Additional factors can be local conditions or requirements at a port of entry as well as closed borders.

For example, to ship **from Europe to North America** choose Canada to avoid the stringent process of temporarily importing vehicles via a US sea port. These days very few routes are served by shipping companies that provide **passenger transportation**, enabling you to travel with your vehicle, but the Grimaldi service from Europe to Montevideo and back is one, and takes about a month with stop-offs in West Africa.

A major concern for overlanders is whether to go for a direct route or trans-shipment. **Trans-shipment** means your container is loaded from one ship to another and there may be multiple trans-shipments. Each trans-shipment introduces the possibility of delay, damage or pilfering so avoid them when possible.

An ideal **direct route** runs straight from the port of departure to the port of arrival. In reality only when shipping between say Rotterdam and Busan is direct shipment likely. In or out of a minor port, trans-shipment is certain so your best bet for a direct shipment is to stick to **high-volume trade routes** (see the table: 'Busiest ports' on p329). Armed with this knowledge you may wish to modify your itinerary.

There are over **400 shipping companies** servicing the world's trade routes. Most shipping lines run weekly services on these routes. Remember: the key to a quick and direct shipment is shipping between high-volume ports.

MAJOR OVERLANDING SHIPPING ROUTES

Europe to North America
Canada is typically a low-hassle destination and departure port.

Europe to South America
High-volume ports offer the most flexibility on dates and the lowest rates.

South America to Australia or North America
This route may actually be less expensive via Caribbean or Atlantic ports than from Pacific ports due to low volumes on the direct routes between the west coast of South America and Australasia.

North America west coast to East Asia

The most popular destination ports in east Asia giving access to Russia are South Korea and Japan. If you visit Japan along the way there are high-volume ports between Japan and South Korea and lower-volume traffic between Japan and Russia, but Japan can be a complex and expensive place to temporarily import a vehicle; South Korea is a more conventional choice. The highest-volume port on the Pacific coast of North America is Los Angeles/Long Beach in California. Excepting China, in east Asia it's Busan, South Korea.

North America west coast to Southeast and East Asia

There are very high-volume shipping routes from Los Angeles/Long Beach to the major shipping ports in Southeast Asia, including Singapore, Kuala Lumpur (Malaysia) and China. Alternative west-coast departure ports include Seattle and Vancouver.

Central America to South America

You need to ship between Panama and Colombia (see p445). The most popular routes are from Panama to the Caribbean coast of Colombia. Costa Rica is also a popular port in Central America for this route. There are additional costs for passage through the Panama Canal, so it's best to match your port cities to either Pacific to Pacific, or Caribbean to Caribbean.

South Africa to Europe

There are RoRo services on this route, depending on your port in Europe.

South Africa to South America or Australia

Routes are low volume, so choices may be limited and costs higher.

East Africa to India

A low-volume route that's expensive as well as traumatising once in India.

India to Southeast Asia

Better to take an escorted transit 'tours' via Myanmar and Thailand.

India to Europe

A long-established trade route; choose high-volume ports at either end. There's something to be said for not shipping directly back to your home country, such as a Brit returning to Rotterdam and then driving home. Authorities may take less interest in a non-local vehicle, handy when it features the imperfect standards of roadworthiness you may be accustomed to after months on the road.

SHIPPING INSURANCE

Purchase international shipping insurance from your shipping agent. Costs vary dramatically and rates begin at less than 1% of declared value, upwards. Standard sea-shipping insurance covers only **total loss** and unless your vehicle falls off a ship or the ship sinks in a typhoon, it's not a total loss. Anything else: falling off the crane, crushed or accidentally burned is not a 'total' loss in the shipping world. For comprehensive coverage it's best to purchase **supplemental insurance**.

A sample set of shipping insurance terms and conditions is here: 🖳 hackneys.com/mitsu/docs/maritime-insurance-terms-and-conditions.pdf.

PAYMENT TERMS

Pay your freight forwarder anytime you want as long as it's **in advance**. The amount will be for all their fees, all the domestic port fees and all the shipping costs. Yes, you read those terms correctly. You pay a huge amount of money in advance for a service that may or may not deliver your vehicle and may or may not destroy it along the way. But wait, there's more. When your vehicle arrives in the foreign country, you'll pay your Customs broker with cash. Lots of cash that you get to carry around the docks neighbourhood to their office. And you know how comforting these dock neighbourhoods can be.

WHAT CAN GO WRONG

By some freak the actual list manages to be shorter than infinity, but it's daunting nonetheless. Common mishaps include:

- Vehicle or contents damage or theft
- Shipment delay
- Temporary or total shipment loss
- Embarkation and disembarkation port extortion
- Customs and inspection delays
- Unexpected additional costs
- Language difficulties
- Large cash payment requirements in foreign ports

WHAT CAN GO RIGHT

Shipping can also be a painless affair when dealing with competent professionals in the private and public sectors. After all, the shipping industry manages to move more than 145 million containers around the planet every year. Be prepared to experience:

- No hidden fees or charges
- No vehicle damage
- On-schedule arrival
- Timely Customs processing
- Courteous and efficient service

I've experienced every 'what can go wrong' and 'what can go right'. Shipping involves a long series of challenges and frustrations, interminable hours sitting in sweaty offices waiting for a comatose bureaucrat to lift his hand, take aim and slap a single stamp on a document. It can include terrifying trips to the docks with your pockets stuffed with wads of local cash. It can include vehicle damage and delay. It can include serious doubts if your journey will ever begin or resume.

But when the Overseas Shipping Dragon has been slain and boiled down to glue, there will come a day when you turn that key and drive out of the docks, punching the air like the guy at the end of *Midnight Express*. Only then can you can look back over your shoulder and say, 'Boy, it feels so good when the beating stops!'

... interminable hours in sweaty offices waiting for a comatose bureaucrat to lift his hand, take aim and slap a single stamp on a document

LIFE ON THE ROAD

SHIPPING GLOSSARY

The shipping industry, like all industries, has its own set of obscure terms and cryptic acronyms. Some key terms and initialisms you're likely to encounter when shipping a vehicle by sea freight include:

BAF (Bunker Adjustment Factor) An adjustment in shipping charges to offset price fluctuations in the cost of fuel. Also known as a **Bunker Surcharge (B/S)**.

Bill of Lading (B/L) A document issued by a common carrier to a shipper that serves as: 1) A receipt for the goods delivered to the carrier for shipment; 2) A definition of the contract of carriage of the goods; 3) A Document of Title to the goods described therein. This document is generally not negotiable unless consigned 'to order'.

Bonded warehouse A warehouse authorised by Customs for storage of goods on which payment of duties is deferred until the goods are removed.

Break-bulk vessel A vessel designed to handle large or oversized cargo; generally cargo unsuitable for container stowage.

Cargo insurance Insurance to protect the financial interest of the owner of the cargo in the event of a loss during transportation.

Carnet See p24.

CFS (container freight station) At the loading port CFS means the location designated by carriers for the receiving of cargo to be loaded into containers by the carrier. At discharge or destination ports, CFS means the bonded location designated by carriers for de-vanning containerised cargo.

Consignee The individual or company to whom a seller or shipper sends merchandise and who, upon presentation of necessary documents, is recognised as the receiver for the purpose of declaring and paying Customs duties.

Demurrage A penalty for exceeding free time allowed for picking up cargo.

Dim weight (dimensional weight) An air-freight term describing the results of computing the chargeable weight from the measurement of a shipment.

FCL Full container load, full car load.

FEU (40-ft equivalent unit) Term for a 40ft (12m) sea container.

Force majeure The title of a standard clause found in marine contracts for carriage exempting the parties from fulfilment of their obligations by reasons of occurrences beyond their control, such as earthquakes, floods or war.

Forwarder, freight forwarder, foreign freight forwarder An independent business that arranges transport for exporters. The firm may ship by land, air or sea, or it may specialise in one of these. Usually it handles all the services connected with an export shipment, including preparation of documents, booking of space, warehousing, pier delivery, and export clearance. The firm may also handle banking and insurance services on behalf of the exporter.

Gross weight (GR Wt./GW) The full weight of a shipment, including cartons and packaging materials.

Hi/high cube Any container exceeding 259cm (102") in height.

In-bond A term used to describe the movement of cargo from the first US port of unloading to another Customs port for clearance and entry purposes.

Inspection Certificate Document certifying merchandise was in good condition, or in accordance with certain specifications prior to shipment.

LCL Less than container load.

SOME OF THE WORLD'S BUSIEST CONTAINER PORTS

Port	Country	TEUs*
Shanghai	China	35.2m
Singapore	Singapore	33.9m
Shenzhen	China	24m
Hong Kong	China	22.2m
Busan	South Korea	18.6m
Dubai Ports	UAE	15.2m
Rotterdam	Netherlands	12.3m
Port Klang	Malaysia	10.9m
Hamburg	Germany	9.7m
Antwerp	Belgium	9.0m
Los Angeles	US, west	8.3m
Long Beach	US, west	6.7m
New York/N. Jersey	US, east	5.8m
Algeciras	Spain	4.6m
Valencia	Spain	3.6m
Felixstowe	UK	4.1m
Santos	Brazil	3.7m
Port Said	Egypt	3.5m
Seattle	Canada	3.4m
Balboa	Panama west	3.1m
Tangier	Morocco	3.1m
Colon	Panama east	2.7m
Cartagena	Colombia	2.6m
Durban	South Africa	2.6m
Vancouver	Canada, west	2.5m

Source: worldshipping.org

* See TEU p330

LIFE ON THE ROAD

M/T or Metric Ton 1000kg or 2204lb.

Net weight (actual net weight) The weight of the goods alone without any shipping cartons or packages.

Pilferage As used in marine-insurance policies, the term denotes petty thievery of small parts of a shipment as opposed to outright theft. This coverage must be added to ordinary marine-insurance policies.

Port of discharge The port where cargo is discharged from the vessel.

Port of entry A port at which foreign goods are entered into the commerce and admitted into the receiving country.

Port of loading A port where cargo is loaded aboard the vessel or aircraft.

Proof of delivery (POD) The delivery-receipt copy of a freight bill or Bill of Lading indicating the name of the person who signed for a shipment with the date and time of delivery.

RoRo (Roll-on/Roll-Off) Vessel A ship designed for cargo that's driven on or off. Many RoRos can also accommodate containers and break-bulk cargo.

Shipment Freight tendered to a carrier by a shipper for delivery to a consignee as designated in the Bill of Lading or airwaybill.

Shipper Term used to describe the person or firm who contracts with the carrier for movement of goods (usually the seller).

Steamship line A company who owns (or leases) its own vessels and engages in the movement of goods by sea.

Stowage The loading of cargo in a vessel in such a manner as to provide the utmost safety and efficiency for the ship and the goods it carries.

Strikes, Riots and Civil Commotions (SR & CC) An insurance clause referring to loss or damage directly caused by strikers, locked-out workmen, labour disturbances, and riots of various kinds. Coverage against it must be added to an ordinary marine-insurance policy.

Tare weight The weight of containers without the goods.

TEU (20-ft equivalent unit) A unit of measure for certain sea containers (20ft, or 6.1m). A standard 40ft (12m) container (FEU) equals two TEUs.

THC (terminal handling charge) A charge for handling services performed at terminals, either at origin or destination.

Trans-shipment The transfer of a shipment from one carrier to another, most frequently from one ship to another. Because reloading may cause damage, trans-shipments should be avoided.

Volume weight International air-freight term describing the results of computing the chargeable weight from the cubic measurement of a shipment.

Warehouse receipt A receipt of commodities deposited in a warehouse identifying the goods deposited. It's non-negotiable, permitting delivery only to a specified person or firm, but it's negotiable if made out to the order of a person or firm or to a bearer.

Weight, tonne A metric tonne equals 1000kg or 2204lb, also known as a long ton (the measurement that is also used in this book). A short ton is 2000lb.

W/M Weight and/or measurement.

Health for overlanders

CLAIRE DAVIES

Most people stay healthy on trips overseas apart from minor stomach ailments. It's rare to come back with a textbook collection of parasite infections. The most common problems other than stomach complaints arise from injuries sustained in traffic accidents or around the camp while cooking or working on the vehicle.

Because of this think seriously about taking a **first-aid course** before you leave; reading this health section is no substitute and the practical knowledge could benefit others as well as your own party. Make sure your vehicle is well maintained and follow the safety procedures mentioned elsewhere, chief among which is **not to drive at night** on unlit rural roads if you can help it.

The following information is meant as a guide to aid you in decision making when help is far away. It's impossible to condense medical training into a few pages, so where available it's always essential to **get professional medical advice**. Many people are mistrustful of health facilities in developing countries but it's here that you'll find the most dedicated practitioners lacking only the resources to do their job well.

PRE-DEPARTURE

You wouldn't leave your vehicle preparations until the week before, so don't leave health checks until the last minute. Travel health advice can be obtained from specialist travel clinics and some surgeries. Book your consultation at least **six weeks in advance** to allow time for all the shots as well as starting a course of anti-malarials if necessary (see p332).

Although having your name followed by 'O+' stencilled 'rally style' on the car door may be going a bit far, establish your **blood group**; it will speed things up if you require a blood transfusion abroad.

Vaccinations

You'll need to be up to date with your primary immunisations (including boosters for tetanus, diphtheria and polio if you need them). Which vaccinations depend on your destination but they will probably include:

Typhoid
Caught from infected food or water. One vaccination. Boosters every three years.

Hepatitis A
An infection of the liver caught from contaminated food and water. One dose gives protection up to one year; get a booster jab after six months to a year for 20 years' protection.

Meningococcal meningitis
Common in sub-Saharan Africa, especially in the dry season. One injection of the ACWY vaccine lasts five years.

Hepatitis B
Another liver infection caught through unprotected sex, unscreened blood transfusions or contaminated needles. Recommended for long trips or travel to remote regions. First course is given as three jabs over 12 weeks.

Rabies
Caught from the saliva of infected animals in the final stages of rabies – usually dogs (see p358) but can include other mammals such as bats or foxes. Given as a course of three injections over three weeks. If you're bitten and haven't been immunised then you'll need treatment with rabies immunoglobulin, which is very hard to obtain.

Yellow fever
Found only in the tropical regions of West and Central Africa and South America, this is a special case as far as your paperwork goes. Border officials from countries which harbour it (as well as those in adjacent countries) will probably insist on your showing an up-to-date vaccination certificate.

A yellow fever stamp (valid for 10 years) should appear alongside others on an **International Certificate of Vaccination** (ICV), which you'll get when you acquire the immunisations listed above, or your old ICV will be updated if you already have one. This document comes in a set format in English, French and Arabic and lists the dates and updates of all key immunisations alongside the health centre's stamp. Officials at many borders will want to check the yellow fever element of your ICV.

Other possibilities requiring immunisation include **tick-borne encephalitis** for campers in Eastern Europe and Russia (particularly Siberia in early summer) and **Japanese B encephalitis** for long stays in rural Asia.

Cholera vaccinations used to have the same border requirements as yellow fever mentioned above, but while outbreaks do periodically occur they're quickly contained and vaccination certificates are no longer essential for overland travel.

Malaria prevention

Malaria is a serious parasitic infection occurring mainly in sub-Saharan Africa, parts of south Asia and South America. Transmitted by **mosquitoes**, the falciparum type of malaria kills more than one million people annually; up to 40% of the world's population are at risk of the disease. The good news is the vast majority of infections are avoidable by following the 'A-B-C-D' **rules of prevention** listed below:

Awareness of the risk. Find out if it's in your area and act accordingly.

Bite prevention. Malaria-carrying mosquitoes bite from dusk until dawn so cover up, use insect repellent (50% Deet is most effective), spray your room and sleep under a mosquito net treated with permethrin.

Chemoprophylaxis (anti-malarials). Used alone they can give 90% protection or above; used with the bite-prevention measures above protection is increased to 95% or more. Contracting malaria while on anti-malarials is usually due to missing doses or not bothering with bite prevention.

Diagnosis saves lives and prevents early infections developing to lethal levels. See p340, for further guidelines.

The travel-health advice about malaria and patterns of drug resistance is **continually changing**. Travel clinics will have the latest information on which particular anti-malarials are recommended for your region. Some anti-malarials are costly, others are cheaper but no less effective. If you're travelling far off the beaten track for long periods or you're still determined not to take **anti-malarials**, then you might want to consider taking a course of standby treatment (see p340).

Travelling with pre-existing conditions

You wouldn't set off in a high-mileage car without a full service so it makes sense to approach your health in the same way. If you have a long-term health condition, consult your doctor or a specialist travel clinic well in advance – three months ahead is not too soon. These are some of the questions you and your doctor will need to address:

- Is your condition stable and well controlled?
- Will travel make your problem better or worse? Psoriasis gets better in sunlight but diabetes will become out of control when long days of driving lead to irregular meals.
- Can you get travel health insurance cover?
- Do you have enough medication to last the entire trip (plus a reserve). If not, can you get hold of it overseas?
- Do you have enough knowledge to know what to do if something goes wrong? It's important to realise that evacuation from remote regions can be a lengthy process, often taking days rather than hours.

The Traveller's Good Health Guide has excellent sections on individual health conditions and travel.

Eyes and teeth

Make sure you're up to date with any **optical and dental** checks. If you use **spectacles**, take a spare pair or two and a copy of your prescription. Dust and strong sunlight are harmful for eyes so splash out on some good **sunglasses**.

First-aid kit

Store your first-aid kit accessibly and make sure everyone is familiar with its location and contents. The following list of items is a good starting point but is by no means exhaustive:

- Antidiarrhoeal drugs or 'blockers' such as Loperamide, Lomotil or Imodium
- Antifungal cream or dusting powder for sweaty feet
- Antihistamines for allergic reactions
- Antiseptic cream or ointment
- Bandages and gauze
- Diarrhoea emergency treatment kit such as ciprofloxacin and/or tinidazole (both are prescriptions)
- Dressings for burns
- Hydrocortisone cream 1% for skin inflammations
- Laxatives (useful due to dietary changes)
- Needles and syringes, sterile
- Oral rehydration salts (ORS) such as Rehydrat or Dioralyte (in sachets)
- Painkillers: paracetamol or Ibuprofen
- Plasters, waterproof
- Safety pins and tape
- Scissors and tweezers
- Thermometer, clinical
- Water purification tablets or iodine tincture

Travel health insurance

Travel health insurance is essential. Your policy should include a **24-hour emergency helpline** and **evacuation by air ambulance** if needed and where possible (see p346). Keep your policy somewhere accessible as well as a copy in another place and make sure all party members can locate it.

If you're driving through Europe, a **European Health Insurance Card** (EHIC) allows EU citizens treatment abroad at reduced cost within these countries. Application forms are available online or from post offices.

ON THE ROAD

Think about your body in the same way as your vehicle: regular attention and checks will pay dividends in keeping you going.

Acclimatisation

If you're used to a temperate climate or air-conditioned living, your body needs up to three weeks to adjust to hotter conditions. During this time don't overexert yourself in the middle of the day and make sure you're drinking plenty of water – enough so that your urine maintains its usual colour. Your body usually requires around **two litres of water per day** (just under two quarts), but this can shoot up to **12 litres** in the hottest environments, while still leaving you exhausted. In such conditions do as the locals do and leave non-essential heavy work for the relative cool of the evening. If you need to change a wheel in the middle of a hot day try to **find some shade** or position the vehicle so it's shading you and, no matter how hot it is, **cover up**, especially your head. Shade is not so easy to manage when digging a car out of sand, but when it's all done, have a good swig of water and if it's been an especially long, hard and hot day of sand recoveries, knock back a sachet or two of rehydration salts come the evening; you'll almost certainly be dehydrated.

Diet

Some places will have an amazing variety of fresh fruit and vegetables; elsewhere will seem to have nothing on sale except bottles of vegetable oil and sacks of rice. Stock up on **fresh fruit and vegetables** while you can – they'll keep for several days if you store them in a cool place or an Esky. Eggs, beans and lentils are good sources of protein if meat isn't available. Nuts and dried fruit are healthy, high-energy snacks useful for long days on the road. Drinking plenty of water is another good way to boost your metabolism.

Exercise

It takes a certain amount of commitment to find ways of exercising during an overland trip: shifting a gear stick to and fro or putting up a roof tent are not among them. All too soon you'll feel sluggish, find yourself piling on the pounds and be prone to minor ailments. Where there are no concerns about leaving your vehicle or possibly your partner unattended, taking a **half-hour walk** in the evening can help maintain a minimum level of fitness. Most capital cities have hotels with a swimming pool you can use for a small fee and when in these places awaiting visas or dealing with other matters, walk where you can. In many cases the local traffic conditions will make this a less stressful option anyway. Packing a **bicycle** (more on this and other 'toys' on the website) is also a great way of keeping fit and of course provides you with a useful secondary source of mobility. Ten minutes at the end of each day will give your muscles a much-needed stretch, while proficient yoga practitioners will be familiar with the additional mental benefits.

Alcohol

There's nothing like a cold beer at the end of a long day's drive, but overdoing it night after night will leave you run down. Stick to one or two beers per night and have a break from alcohol two or three days a week. If you've had a very late night, then it's likely you'll still have alcohol in your system, so have a rest day before you start driving again. Remember that drink-driving laws vary from country to country – some forbid driving with any alcohol in your system at all.

Water

Contaminated food and water can harbour many diseases: diarrhoea, dysentery, hepatitis A and typhoid to mention a few. Depending on its source, consider **treating your water** in developing countries – particularly in the tropics – using at least one of the following methods:
  • Simply sieving water through a cloth or letting it drip slowly through a canvas Millbanks bag removes suspended particles like silt and organic matter. Used alone the benefits are merely 'psychological' – cleaner-looking water; any microscopic bugs will skip through six abreast. However, when resorting to heavily occluded water sources, sieving is still worth-

while as a pre-treatment to the steps listed below. If nothing else it saves prematurely clogging up water-filter pump cores.
- Boiling for two minutes kills all germs but does not remove impurities (see above).
- Pump-operated water filters (manual or electric) that use combinations of ceramic, silver or charcoal cores need no fuel, work instantly and when maintained correctly are as effective as sieving and boiling.
- Iodine drops or tablets (such as Potable Aqua) are inexpensive and very effective but leave a metallic taste, take half an hour to take effect and are poisonous in high quantities. Get the kits that now come with a neutralising powder to eliminate the taste and smell. Although it's no longer available in the European Union, it's still an effective method of water purification if you can get hold of it. Iodine should not be used continuously for more than a month; it's best kept for emergencies.
- Water purification tablets. These kill bacteria but not the cysts of giardia or amoeba. Katadyn Micropur are known to leave no aftertaste compared to chlorine- or iodine-based versions.
- Bottled mineral water should be safe to drink as long as the seal hasn't been tampered with.

Of course you may well have built a water-filtration unit into your water system; if you haven't, see p250 for some ideas.

Food hygiene
Hot, freshly cooked food, all the better from a street corner where you can see it being cooked, is likely to be safe, as is packaged and tinned food. Fresh fruit is fine as long as you wash it in clean water and peel it. The following foods can be contaminated and depending on their source carry the risk of sickness:
- Salads, unless you've prepared and disinfected the vegetables yourself. Add a triple dose of tincture of iodine to some water and leave the salads to soak for 30 minutes.
- Ice in drinks.
- Locally made ice cream (packaged brands are fine).
- Food left sitting around on a buffet for a couple of hours – a great way to attract bacteria.
- Undercooked meat.

A small mouthful of something that subsequently turns out to be suspect is unlikely to do any harm. If a local offers you something you don't like the look of, refusal is often thought to offend but taking only a small quantity brings minimal risk.

ACCESSING HEALTHCARE OVERSEAS
Availability of healthcare in developing countries is patchy, adding up to one of the adventurous elements of overland travel. Occasionally standards may be of a better quality than you're used to at home; more usually, facilities are worse or non-existent, though medical staff should be no less dedicated than their peers back home. If represented locally, your embassy can provide a list of reputable doctors in-country although in practice you may find this list is confined to the capital.
If you find yourself needing **medical help** then consider the following issues:
- How far do you need to travel to reach a decent medical facility? If your condition is serious think about initiating some standby treatment if you have some.
- Public hospitals in many developing countries can be poorly maintained. Mission hospitals or private facilities can be a better bet.
- Healthcare workers in some places are demoralised and underpaid. Be polite and don't make criticisms openly. Clarify issues about payment up front.
- Check the expiry date on any medicines prescribed and what the ingredients are.
- If you're seriously ill and in need of hospitalisation, contact your insurance company straight away. Remember this is exactly what it's for and failure to do so may invalidate your cover. If necessary they may organise evacuation by air.

TRAFFIC ACCIDENTS AND OTHER SEVERE TRAUMAS

The media may be preoccupied with reporting violent crime and natural and man-made disasters, particularly in developing continents, but in reality **accidents** are your most likely cause of injury, most probably while driving, undertaking vehicle maintenance or repairs, or while camping.

Preventing accidents

Although it's largely the same story back at home or in the office, on the road the lack of routine and the number of unfamiliarly stressful situations can lead to **thoughtlessness**. Dealing with a puncture with the car hastily balanced on a hi-lift jack while rushing to a border post; boiling a pan of water in the half-darkness; pretty much **doing anything when you're dog tired** at the end of a tough day. These are occasions when you should make a conscious decision to **slow down** and take five.

Undertake **vehicle repairs** slowly and systematically, particularly anything involving jacking up the car on soft or uneven ground, where a single jack should never be relied on for any but the briefest wheel changes.

Around the camp, always **cook** in daylight or in well-lit conditions and make sure stoves and pots are stable. Never use a gas canister near a nylon tent. Make sure ladders or steps leading up to roof tents are securely attached.

It can't be said enough times: **take care while driving**. Road accident fatality figures in most developing nations are astronomical and are set to rise to near the top of the 'premature cause of death' table as global car ownership increases without the commensurate enforcement of seatbelts, vehicle roadworthiness or driver training and licensing that we all take for granted. There's more on defensive driving on p258.

Dealing with accidents and trauma

A knowledge of **first aid** is by far the best preparation for dealing with a serious injury such as a road accident; remember, it may not be just yourself you're able to help.

If a vehicle is involved in an accident check first that it's **safe to approach** anyone who is injured: is fuel being spilt and has the ignition been turned off?

Ascertain **whether the victim is conscious** by talking to them or tapping them on the chest. If there's no response try to get someone to summon help.

Meanwhile, establish or implement the three vital signs summarised as A-B-C: **Airway, Breathing, Circulation**.

Check that the **airway is clear of any obstruction** and that the victim is still **breathing** (by feeling for breath on your cheek, for example).

If they're not breathing or not breathing normally, you'll need to start **cardio-pulmonary resuscitation** or **CPR**, which generates artificial circulation and lung ventilation by compressing on the heart rapidly and breathing into the victim's mouth with the nose closed. The latest guidelines (for all ages) are **thirty compressions followed by two breaths** while not wasting too much time on correctly diagnosing a pulse. CPR is unlikely to restart a heart, all it can do is maintain a flow of oxygenated blood through the heart to the brain, to reduce the possibility of permanent brain damage, until the victim begins breathing spontaneously or proper help arrives.

In the case of **severe bleeding**, use a piece of cloth, clothing or a dressing to apply direct pressure onto the wound and hold it there. If it's a limb, raise the body end above the head to reduce the blood flow. Consider carrying an emergency haemostatic agent such as Celox in your first-aid kit, which stops life-threatening arterial bleeding from gaping wounds.

Major road accidents carry a risk of **spinal injury**. If this is a possibility only move the casualty if it's for their own safety.

For more on **local procedures** at the site of a traffic accident, see p346.

DIARRHOEA AND SIMILAR AILMENTS
Fifty per cent of travellers are likely to experience problems with some sort of diarrhoea during their trip. Following the precautions set out in the sections on food-hygiene and water will help minimise the chances of it happening but it's still quite common. Fortunately, most cases are no more than a nuisance.

Travellers' diarrhoea
Travellers' diarrhoea causes watery stools five to six times a day as well as abdominal cramps. Most cases are self-limiting and resolve within 48 hours. The principal treatment is to **maintain hydration** (see below) **and eat less** – failure to do the former will leave you feeling miserable and lethargic, while ignoring the latter may prolong the symptoms.

It's better to spend a day or two resting if you've got diarrhoea; you'll probably prefer to be close to that all-important toilet anyway. If you must travel, then it's OK to take a **blocker** such as Imodium to reduce the frequency of the diarrhoea. Avoid taking blockers like Imodium if there is blood in the diarrhoea.

Seek medical advice if the diarrhoea persists for longer than a few days, especially if you have bloody stools, a high fever or if it's accompanied with persistent vomiting leaving you unable to keep fluids down. If you have standby **antibiotics**, 250mg of ciprofloxacin twice daily for three days is the correct treatment.

Rehydration
Plain water isn't enough for adequate rehydration as it can't replace the vital body salts lost in the diarrhoea. You can make your own rehydrating solution by mixing **eight teaspoons of sugar and half a teaspoon of salt in a litre (a quart) of water**, but proper rehydration powders such as Dioralyte or Oral Rehydration Sachets (ORS) are much better. These contain the full range of mineral salts the body requires (not just regular table salt), and in the correct proportions. Observing the speedy recovery of a dehydrated person after swigging down a Dioralyte is quite gratifying.

If you're **vomiting**, small, frequent sips are more likely to stay down than knocking back a litre of water at a time – and anything too salty will guarantee another heave (in case you don't know, salt tablets are a thing of the past).

As for **energy**, initially a clear soup such as Japanese miso is best, but **eat** when you feel like it: start with light, easily digestible things such as rice, dry biscuits or bananas.

Giardia

A parasite infection caught from contaminated food or water, giardia leads to a feeling of malaise, moderate diarrhoea, bulky stools and excess wind and gas, the latter often referred to as 'eggy burps'. Get a stool test done if you can, otherwise treat with 400mg of metronidazole twice daily for a week, or a single 2g dose of tinidazole, avoiding alcohol.

Dysentery

Dysentery comes in two varieties: bacillary (sometimes called shigellosis) and the amoebic form. **Bacillary** dysentery manifests itself as chills and high fever accompanied by severe diarrhoea, which may be mixed with blood. The **amoebic** form also causes diarrhoea but is relatively less severe, although blood may still be present in the stool. Fever occurs with amoebic dysentery too, but is usually mild. Bacillary dysentery will make you unwell within hours, whereas amoebic dysentery's onset is slower, lingers around and leaves you with almost constant abdominal cramps.

Both forms of dysentery are serious and should not be mistaken for bad diarrhoea. You should arrange to consult a doctor for a stool test. If medical help is a long way away then consider using your standby **antibiotics**, if you have some. Ciprofloxacin at 500mg, twice daily for five days is the usual treatment for bacillary dysentery. Amoebic dysentery can be treated with 800mg of metronidazole twice daily for five days while avoiding all alcohol. If you've had amoebic dysentery then you'll need a course of diloxanide later to clear any remaining amoebic cysts.

With both forms of dysentery following the actions for **rehydration** outlined below are vital. If you've been in a malarial area, then you should also be aware that malaria can sometimes cause a fever and diarrhoea (particularly of the bloody variety), so it's important not to misdiagnose your symptoms if you're unwell. See the malaria section on p340 for more details.

HEAT-RELATED ILLNESS

Along with dehydration there are two types of more severe heat-related illness: heat exhaustion and life-threatening heatstroke.

Heat exhaustion

Heat exhaustion is caused by prolonged dehydration and salt loss through sweating (possibly unnoticed in very hot and arid conditions). Symptoms include headaches, fatigue, dizziness and muscle cramps. **Temperature** may be slightly above normal, which is **37°C** or **98.8°F**. Move into the shade, rest, and sponge the skin with tepid water. Fluids are best replaced by drinking a combination of water, oral rehydration solutions (see p337) and something salty (packet soups are good). Prompt action is needed to stop heat exhaustion developing into heatstroke.

Heatstroke

The result of untreated heat exhaustion or prolonged and extreme exertion in high temperatures, heatstroke is a **medical emergency** that is fatal if not treated immediately. The body's thirst impulse cannot keep up (or is being ignored) and what is so shocking and potentially deadly is how quickly heatstroke can develop once your body fluid drops below a critical level. As this happens the sweating mechanism collapses, triggering the onset of heat-stroke as body **temperatures** begin to climb. Once the body's core rises to 41°C (106°F) or more, the victim will lose consciousness and soon die or have a seizure.

Symptoms include red, hot but dry skin, a racing heart and the sufferer becoming confused, drowsy and even irritable or aggressive. Heatstroke is a very high risk when overdoing it in mid-summer desert environments with ambient temperatures well above 40°C. But it can also occur in exceedingly humid environments that inhibit the cooling effect of evaporating sweat, even though the ambient temperature rarely exceeds body temperature.

Treatment includes moving the victim into the shade or a cooler environment, sponging them with cold water while fanning to cool the skin. Offer oral rehydration solution (see p337) if the victim is conscious, although by this late stage fluids are best replaced by an intravenous drip so arrange for urgent medical attention.

BITES AND STINGS

Irritating insect bites are usually part of the trip and are internationally recognised as the scourge of the Siberian summer. Resist the temptation to scratch as this only inflames the bite even more and may introduce infection. Very itchy bites will settle with hydrocortisone cream or an **antihistamine** tablet. The latest antihistamines are much less likely to make you feel drowsy but if they do affect you, let someone else do the driving.

Ticks

Ticks are experiencing a renaissance thanks to global warming. Wear long trousers tucked into your boots when walking through long grass and inspect yourself at the end of the day. If you do find one (they look like small nodules attached to the skin), remove it gently with tweezers. Most tick bites don't lead to illness but watch for any symptoms of fever or rash in the following weeks.

Scorpions, snakes and spiders

These creatures don't like being disturbed under their favourite rock, nor do they take kindly to being trampled on by your bare feet as you stagger around the campsite in the dark. Snakes are usually shy but like scorpions they're attracted to warmth so **keep your tent zipped up** and take care when **rolling up bedding or ground tents** in the morning. Scorpion bites are very painful but are not usually dangerous. The same applies to spiders; there are only a few deadly varieties so if you're bitten check locally what the situation is and note that most locals would have no hesitation in killing anything nasty-looking found crawling around their camp. Remember that despite the phobia many of us have about these creatures, they have little to gain in taking an unprovoked bite and wasting venom on you. They will only do so if surprised or as a last measure. If someone is **bitten by a snake** act as follows:

- Keep calm and reassure the victim.
- Keep the bitten part of the body (usually a limb) as still as possible and preferably below the level of the heart.
- Splint the limb straight across its full length.
- Wrap a bandage gently but firmly around the limb, beginning at the affected part. The aim

is to minimise blood flow and the consequent spread of the poison into the system.
- Do not apply a tourniquet and, even if it looks good in the movies, do not attempt to suck out the venom, either with a kit or your own lips.
- Use paracetamol for pain (not aspirin).
- Get medical help. A description of the snake is helpful but avoid any unnecessary heroics involving catching it or clubbing it over the head with the jack. Let it get away.

MALARIA

Malaria can occur any time seven days after entering a malarial area and for up to a year later. Classic **symptoms** are rather like a bad dose of the flu and include very high temperatures along with shivering. Malaria, however, is the great mimic and can cause a whole variety of other symptoms: vomiting and diarrhoea, mild fever, headaches or just feeling unusually tired. People feeling under the weather can be diagnosed with malaria up to a year after leaving a malarial zone.

More serious malarial infections can cause severe headaches, neck stiffness and reduced consciousness (cerebral malaria) or extremely dark urine ('black-water fever'). Equally, symptoms may be mild even with a dangerously high level of parasites in the blood. Any sign of malaria should be taken seriously and prompt you to seek medical attention.

Malaria is **diagnosed** by a microscopic search of a blood slide. A minimum of three slide scans on three consecutive days are recommended if you have ongoing symptoms. Unfortunately, there is a trend in some countries to either over- or under-diagnose malaria, so it pays to get to the most reliable medical facility. If you are told your film is positive then you should take a course of treatment. Equally, if the film is negative then you should arrange for a repeat test the next day if you're still unwell.

If you suspect you have malaria and are far from medical help, take your standby treatment including Malarone, Riamet or quinine together with doxycycline, although it's still essential that you arrange for a blood test to check that the parasite level in your blood is coming down. Deterioration can occur even after starting treatment so it's important to get yourself checked out.

OTHER COMMON HEALTH PROBLEMS

Unfamiliar climate, a change of routine and additional responsibilities can take their toll on your mental as well as physical well-being.

Cuts and grazes

Cuts and grazes can quickly become infected in hot, humid environments, particularly in conditions of poor hygiene. Clean cuts under running water if available and apply antiseptic or iodine. Cover the wound with a dressing to keep it clean and change the dressing regularly.

Burns and scalds

Following a burn from a flame or an extremely hot object the first action is to **pour cool water over the wound for at least 10 minutes** – catch the water and reuse it if necessary. Remove clothing from the affected area unless it has stuck to the skin. Burns should be covered with something clean and non-fluffy. If you don't have a burns dressing such as Melonin, Primapore or a cooling, gel-based dressing like Water-Jel, then a plastic bag or cling film will do. Scalds where the skin has not broken can be expected to blister – the body's own way of cooling the wound – but a burn bigger than the size of a postage stamp requires medical attention.

Back pain

The long-suffering backs of *Homo sapiens* have not yet evolved to a point where they like to sit hunched over a steering wheel while being repeatedly hammered by heavy-duty suspension and potholes. Nor do they take kindly to performing Unimog wheel-changes single-handedly or lugging full jerricans around. To avoid lower-back pain always lift heavy equipment by bending at the knees. Keeping fit or doing regular **exercise and stretches** will help strengthen your lower-back muscles and help prevent problems.

If you have an attack of **lower-back pain**, bed rest is not advisable, instead keep moving. Take painkillers and avoid lifting any heavy objects until your pain has settled. Lying face down on the floor for 20 minutes twice a day may help to relieve the pain. If you experience weakness or pins and needles in your legs, or if you notice trouble passing urine or opening your bowels, these are signs of more serious problems such as a slipped disc. See a doctor right away.

Stress and anxiety

Overlanding can induce no shortage of stressful times, be it culture shock, not getting on with your companions, missing home or the ever-present anxieties over the state of your vehicle, documentation and the next border. Look at stress as the flipside of excitement; at least you're alive and out there!

Most difficulties are transient and most challenges must be dealt with somehow, but occasionally it can all feel too much. That low afternoon has suddenly turned into days on end of wondering how you ended up here and, worse still, why?

Minor **mood swings** can improve with regular exercise so make sure you're doing some kind of physical activity every day. Caffeine and nicotine can both increase your anxiety levels so keep the use of these to a minimum or at least recognise their influence on your moods. It's also best to keep alcohol intake to a minimum. Getting drunk might give momentary relief but will disrupt your sleep and make you even more miserable the next day. It's better to let your fellow travellers know that you're feeling like this rather than keeping it bottled up. At the same time, if you're a verbose type who lets it all hang out, remember your companions may not be enthused by an endless litany of complaints or xenophobic rants.

Coughs, colds and chest infections

Overland travel can leave you run down and prone to **colds**. If you're susceptible it's probably a good idea to take any favourite remedies as you're unlikely to find them en route. Some people swear by vitamin C or several daily cloves of garlic as both cure and prevention; others find them ineffective. **Coughing** up green or yellow phlegm doesn't necessarily mean you need antibiotics unless it's persistent for more than 10 days or you feel more unwell than you would expect with a normal cold.

Conjunctivitis (irritated and red eyes with a mild, sticky discharge along the eyelids) is a common accompaniment to a cold. Left alone, it may clear itself with regular cleaning of the discharge. Severe or persistent cases need antibiotic drops.

Urinary infections

Symptoms of an infection include pain when passing urine, discomfort in the lower back or abdomen and having to empty your bladder more often. If caught in the early stages, there's a good chance of clearing the infection by drinking plenty of water and passing urine regularly. If this is ineffective then a course of antibiotics such as 250mg of ciprofloxacin twice daily for five days will clear it up.

Protecting your skin

Protect your skin from **sunburn**. When outdoors, use headwear, apply a high-factor sun cream and cover up in bright sunshine, even if it's not actually baking hot such as at high altitude, in sub-arctic regions or when it's windy. Bald heads and exposed shoulders are most vulnerable.

Other **skin ailments** include:

Fungal infections in humid environments. These resemble red, scaly patches with an irregular edge. Prevent them by bathing regularly and wearing loose cotton clothing that lets your skin breathe. Treat with an antifungal cream such as miconazole.

Skin ulcers that fail to heal may mean an infection by leishmaniasis (a parasite carried by sandflies). Any non-healing skin ulcer should prompt you to seek medical attention. Prevent sandfly bites by sleeping under a mosquito net and raising your bed off the ground.

Hypothermia

Hypothermia is the cold equivalent of heatstroke: a dangerous condition that if not treated can quickly develop into a life-threatening situation. Unlike with heat, the human body has no way of dealing with extreme cold so the best measure is **prevention and protection**. If you expect to be travelling at high altitude or maybe even in the sub-arctic winter, it's presumed your vehicle and your personal equipment are ready for the extreme, sub-freezing conditions you'll surely encounter.

In a less extreme and more common scenario you may have gotten wet during a river crossing, somehow have become separated from your vehicle and the weather has turned, bringing sub-zero temperatures. Chances are as long as there's a vehicle that's running you'll have mobility, a source of warmth or at the very least protection from the elements. Only when there is no vehicle or the last vehicle's heater packs up are you potentially in trouble. In such conditions:

- Take suitable clothing and equipment. When outdoors, wearing several layers of clothing will trap warm pockets of air. Outer layers should be wind- and if necessary waterproof.
- Wear a hat and a hood. Most body heat is lost through the bare head.
- You must eat large amounts regularly to enable your body to generate heat via metabolism.
- Along with this comes the need to drink adequately.
- Set up a buddy system to monitor signs of hypothermia in each other. These include a feeling of intense cold and uncontrollable shivering, which progresses to lethargy, mental confusion and irritability.

First aid for hypothermia is as follows:
- Exchange wet clothing for dry as soon as possible.
- Place the victim in a sleeping bag.
- If you can, get in the vehicle and put the heater on full.
- Give hot, sugary drinks. Alcohol should be avoided.
- If necessary zip your sleeping bags together and warm up your companion with your own body heat.
- If normal body temperatures do not return soon get the victim to medical help as soon as it is safe to do so.

Altitude sickness

Altitude sickness occurs most commonly above 3000 metres (9850ft). Experienced and fit mountaineers making fast ascents can run into problems but it's more likely to happen if you're overweight or older.

At 3600 metres (11,800ft) the barometric pressure is only about 40% of what it is at sea level, which adds up to as many fewer oxygen molecules per breath. The body must adjust to this deficit of oxygen; among other ways, it achieves this over a couple of days by producing more oxygen-carrying red-blood cells and increasing pressure in pulmonary capillaries to force blood deeper into the lungs to take on oxygen.

With altitude sickness it's not so much the height you reach as the speed at which you do so. The key to prevention is a **slow ascent** to allow your body to acclimatise and engage the processes described above. Slow ascents are something that can be a tall order when driving in parts of the Himalaya or particularly the Andes, but if you're feeling poorly above 3000 metres (9850ft) endeavour to sleep **no more than 300–600 metres (1000–2000ft) higher than the previous day** and incorporate a rest day for every 1000 metres (3280ft) you ascend. Early **symptoms** include:
- Mild headaches.
- Nausea and dizziness.
- Loss of appetite.
- Breathlessness.
- Disrupted sleep patterns.
- Fatigue and a general feeling of malaise.

All these usually settle within a couple of days as long as you don't keep going higher. If your driving route forces you to ascend more rapidly than is ideal or you have a splitting headache then the drug **acetazolamide** (Diamox) may help you acclimatise; it's often sold in high-altitude tourist areas such as Ladakh. It's easy to drive up to 4000 metres or more without any hardship and then find yourself helpless at the slightest effort.

Many people will experience vivid dreams and disrupted sleep above 3000 metres. When **sleeping** above this height most people are unable to sleep deeply and may experience a medical phenomenon known as **periodic breathing** (PB), when low carbon-dioxide levels in the blood inhibit the breathing impulse. Cycles of PB can last all night and begin with a few

5000 metres (16,400ft) by lunchtime.

shallow breaths followed by deep sighing respirations that drop off rapidly and even stop entirely for a few seconds (an alarming condition known as apnoea), after which shallow breathing returns. During an apnoea you may wake yourself up, gasping, after a sudden feeling of suffocation. Too many nights of disturbed sleep will eventually wear you out, but PB is not considered abnormal at high altitudes. Diamox is helpful in relieving periodic breathing.

More deadly altitude sickness affects the lungs and the brain as **high-altitude pulmonary oedema** (HAPE), where fluid in the lungs restricts breathing capacity; or **high-altitude cerebral oedema** (HACE), where fluid causes the brain to swell up. Both are medical emergencies but are unlikely at the momentarily extreme elevations of around 5000 metres (16,400ft) you'll reach in a vehicle. The immediate cure for both these dangerous conditions, as well as lesser discomfort, is to **return immediately to lower elevations**.

Bilharzia

Also known as **schistosomiasis**, this parasitic blood fluke is present in fresh water in sub-Saharan Africa as well as parts of South America (particularly eastern Brazil) and Southeast Asia. Its lifecycle revolves around moving between two hosts: freshwater snails and humans. Larvae penetrate your skin when you're in fresh water inhabited by the infected snails, and during a four-to-six-week incubation the eggs migrate to your liver where they mature into male and female adults. Here they migrate to the veins in the lower abdomen where they mate continuously; it's the blockages caused by the hundreds of eggs produced daily and not excreted in urine or faeces that make you ill, but different types of flukes migrate to different areas of the body which helps explain the global variety of symptoms.

Most people infected (up to 300 million worldwide) don't know they have bilharzia, others may find blood in the urine, become anaemic or just feel unusually tired. Avoid the risk by not swimming or paddling in fresh water or at least do so wearing footwear. If you have been in infected water then get a blood test as soon as possible but note it can take three months after possible infection to guarantee accurate results. Most infections are quickly cured by a course of praziquantel.

Sexually-transmitted infections and HIV

Sexually-transmitted diseases (STDs) and HIV are widespread in many parts of the world. It's not just the locals who might put you at risk. Being away from home lowers many people's inhibitions and casual sex is part of the trip for some travellers. Abstinence is the best protection, but if not, **condoms** keep the risk to a minimum. Locally bought condoms may be of poor quality so take some from home.

HIV can be contracted through unprotected sex, unscreened blood transfusion or injections with unsterile needles. If you've been inadvertently exposed to HIV, there is a post-exposure treatment available. It works best if started as soon as possible after exposure (within an hour) but there is still some benefit in starting the treatment up to 72 hours later. Side effects can be unpleasant, so better to avoid risky activities in the first place.

BACK AT HOME

It's a good idea to have a **medical check-up** when you get back home, especially if you've been in the tropics or have been ill. This might include a stool test and a blood count to check for parasite infections, plus a blood test for bilharzia if you think you've been exposed. Malaria can occur up to a year after you've left a malarial zone so seek medical advice if you have flu-like symptoms and let the doctor know where you've been.

Reverse culture shock

Coming home after a long trip can feel like a huge letdown. Suddenly you're not an exotic traveller hailed in every village, just another anonymous drone returning to the well-worn treadmill of the familiar day-to-day life, perhaps even back in that same job that you swore you'd never return to. Most of your friends and family seem more interested in updating you on the TV soaps than hearing about your trip.

It's common to also find yourself repelled by the materialism back home. This revulsion is often accompanied by rose-tinted views about events that were actually miserable at the time. It helps to meet up or communicate with other travellers who have done similar trips, maybe people you met on the road or someone you can share your experiences with.

Feeling fed up is normal so let life take its course. If things aren't brightening up after a few months, if you're not sleeping, or if you're feeling extremely low, then it's worth having a chat with your doctor just to check you're not clinically depressed. For most people, however, these are just normal feelings of readjustment for which the only solution is hitting the road again, emigration or a complete change of lifestyle.

When things go wrong

Not every day in the overland zone will go as you'd wish. If you're very unlucky you might find yourself in a nightmare situation, made more stressful because you're abroad. The most common misfortunes on the overland trail are serious illness or injury, road accidents, getting into trouble with the law, and theft. Much less common dangers include rape and assault, armed robbery, the total loss of your vehicle, and being abducted or imprisoned.

Travelling in foreign cultures has its potential perils, and if you find yourself in one of the above scenarios it's as well to remember that the rules, laws and customs of your home country may not apply. Getting out of a legal tangle could be as simple as paying the right person. With any other show-stopping catastrophe, your best option may be to get back home with the aid of travel insurance and **your government's representative** abroad.

Before you leave it's worth apprising yourself of exactly what your government can do for you when things go wrong abroad; this should be set out on their foreign office or travel advice website. It may not be as much as you'd hope, because they're bound by the laws of the nation that hosts their diplomatic mission. One further caveat: if an insurance provider can find a reason for not paying out on a claim, expect them to try to do so. See p21 for more on buying the most **appropriate travel insurance**.

SERIOUS ILLNESS OR INJURY

When you or one of your party is afflicted by a serious illness or injury, or has been in a road accident (for more on which, see below), it's time to make use of your **travel insurance**. This is what you're paying for, and the person on the end of the all-important helpline will be practiced in dealing with your predicament even, in my experience, up to the point of offering basic medical advice to keep a person alive. It's worth finding this **helpline number** on the policy document and recording it in a few other places, including on your mobile phone. There's basic advice on **first aid** for trauma victims on p336.

However, don't expect travel insurance costing a pound or two a day to get you the sort of emergency support that expensive sporting events or rallies can muster. Once you make the call they won't mobilise International Rescue to despatch a Chinook full of nurses to your location by nightfall. Instead, in most cases the patient must be brought to a town or city with a hospital, a journey which, depending on the condition of the patient and access to painkillers, can become agonising. Getting to a hospital will be the priority, and better still, to **a hospital in a city with an international airport**. See 'Accessing healthcare overseas' on p335 for some guidelines. You may want to **contact your embassy** at this time, especially if you've been injured in a criminal attack. If nothing else, embassy staff should be able to advise on local medical facilities, legal help, money transfers and so on.

Once the patient is stable, the travel insurance provider will almost certainly organise **repatriation**, but this is unlikely to be a Lear jet from MSF. If the patient is able to go on a scheduled flight, even in a wheelchair with a drip, that's what they'll use, although transportation to and from the airport and at any stopovers should be covered. If any payments for medical services have to be made, make sure you get receipts or guidance from the insurers on how to proceed.

If you **don't have travel insurance** you'll be on your own of course, though this need not mean financial ruin. Getting out of a fix can cost no more than the price of a visit to a hospital and then, if necessary, the next flight home.

ROAD ACCIDENTS

A 2010 report by the FIA (🖳 fiafoundation.org) estimated that of the 1.24 million people killed in road crashes each year, some 25,000 were tourists, and when others are involved, be they drivers, pedestrians or even livestock the situation can become extremely intimidating. The familiar procedure of the speedy arrival of police, ambulances and the exchanging of insurance details could be muddied by the forming of a curious and possibly hostile crowd.

Small inter-vehicle shunts with minimal damage usually don't need to result in the police being called, and can either be shrugged off or **settled on the spot**; if all are in agreement, it's the best way to solve the situation. A local in the wrong might well offer to get your vehicle repaired; you may want to do the same if you feel you were at fault.

Single-vehicle rollover; a common type of accident in Namibia. © pindoriapost.blogspot.com

If you've seriously **hurt or even killed someone**, most likely a pedestrian, then you're just going to have to ride out the events and hope for the best. This must be understood though: in the poor countries through which you'll be travelling it's a mistake to think a **pedestrian** should not have been wandering along the road in the first place. Even if it's a motorway of some kind, in most countries the road is also the pedestrian's right of way. In countries like India it's the right of way of a good few animals too, many of them extremely valuable.

Following an accident, it's best not to admit any liability, even though you may get locked up for a short while until things are sorted out. This is the time to get in touch with **your government's representative**, if there is one. If the details are not to hand (check the city listings in a guidebook), it may be simpler to call someone at home and ask them to track down the **contact details** online.

Motor insurance bought locally ought to cover you for such events, but it's not uncommon to regard it as having little actual value save being something to present at checkpoints. While having it may not greatly improve the situation, not having it will certainly make it worse.

If you're thought to be in the wrong, local mobs can gang up on you and, in some places, victims who are probably desperately poor can see the chance to make a quick buck. I read of some overlanders in Ethiopia being charged several hundred dollars for running down a cow. In some such situations, overlanders have been advised by well-meaning policemen to swiftly leave the scene. At other times the policeman or other authority figure may insist or suggest some sort of **on-the-spot compensation**. It's up to you to judge whether it's required, fair, or extortionate, but as a foreigner in a flashy vehicle, you won't have too many cards in your hand. Many travellers are so freaked out and indeed outnumbered that they'll happily pay anything to get out of there.

THEFT AND ROBBERY

As long as travellers have travelled, brigands and swindlers have preyed on them. The perils of travel are much less great than they were five hundred or two thousand years ago, although the need for vigilance both on the road and in foreign settlements has always been the same.

Accept that on the road it's possible that you may lose something or even everything, through carelessness, bad luck, theft or outright robbery. Much has been said about the need to keep your valuables safe, but in the end it's all just stuff that can be replaced, albeit at a price and great inconvenience. This is just a simple fact, the not-so-glamorous side of adventure travel.

Theft is just a pain, from your person or your vehicle; the perpetrator is long gone before you noticed anything is missing. **Robbery or mugging** is another matter. During the months preceding your departure, it's likely at least one person – an individual who watches a lot of tabloid television and doesn't travel much – will have expressed alarm at your adventurous itinerary. 'Africa/Iran/Colombia, are you crazy?' You might knock back some bluff reply, but underneath you can't help thinking they might have a point.

City strategies

Cities anywhere are the lairs of thieves who prey on conspicuous and gullible tourists. Markets and crowded travel termini are favourite haunts for pickpockets. As you wander into these places check that everything is zipped up, and be alert. Try to keep the evidence of your wealth or your confusion under wraps. **Wallets** should always be zipped into inside jacket pockets or kept in money belts, not bulging in a rear trouser pocket, and cameras should not dangle temptingly around your neck. If you're walking around with a day pack on your back, don't put valuables in there; use a **shoulder bag** that can swing round to the front of you where you can see it.

Avoid gazing in befuddlement at town plans on street corners. In dodgy cities like some African and Latin American capitals, **plan your route** before you walk out of your accommodation and when you do walk, imitate the advice given to women walking alone at night: march with a single-minded purpose that emits the signal loud and clear: 'Don't even think about it, punk!'. Beware of pats on the shoulder, newspapers, flowers or babies being shoved in your face, people claiming to be wiping bird droppings off your

---

TRAVELWISE MANIFESTO

- Trust your instincts – if a situation or a place does not feel good, move on or be prepared to leave quickly.
- Wild camp out of sight of the road or stay in the security of settlements.
- Don't drive yourself ragged; rest often.
- Don't drive at night unless unavoidable.
- Keep a low profile in hostile areas or just avoid them altogether.
- Leave M16s, mace and machetes at home.

- Keep your valuables on you at all times, but have a back-up stash.
- In towns and cities park off the street overnight where possible. Many hotels let you park round the back even if you don't stay there.
- Avoid exposing cash or valuables in crowded places.
- Learn and use the local language – you'll be amazed at the positive response.

finely ironed lapel, and any number of other distractions which are **set-ups** for snatches or pickpockets. If you expect to be coming back drunk from a bar in the early hours, carry only things you can afford to lose. At other times, whether valuables are with you or locked in the vehicle safe, you'll know which feels most secure.

Guidebooks advise leaving your valuables in the hotel's safe or at reception, but not all **hotels** you'll stay in will inspire such a feeling of security, so some travellers prefer to keep valuables on their person at all times. Never leave valuables in your hotel room.

Getting robbed

While theft is usually an urban problem, robbery, or what's quaintly know as banditry, usually occurs in rural or remote regions, and is as likely in the US or outback Australia as anywhere else. Again, be wary of set-ups like a **feigned breakdown**, which can be a set-up for a robbery. Generally, a family group sat at the roadside by a steaming car will be what it seems, but a couple of shifty-looking young men may have other plans. If you're unsure in a situation like this, **keep moving**. Someone else will help them soon enough.

If the game is up the important thing to remember is that they've nothing much to gain by harming you as that could result in a whole lot more trouble. Acting as a submissive tourist is the best strategy; I've heard of tourists getting shot trying to get away. Valuables and occasionally 4x4s are what the robbers are after. Galling though it may be, **let them have it all.**

In the very unlikely event that you ride into an **ambush** or are set upon by armed bandits, again, the common advice is to let them take what they want and be happy to live to tell the tale. If they don't take your vehicle and you're smart, you'll have a stash, as described earlier.

Overland vehicles are rarely stolen though 4x4s in parts of the Sahara are an exception. Canny items like hidden **fuel-cut-out switches** have been shown to be of little use, merely earning a rifle butt in the face when they come back to where they left you after your vehicle staggers to a halt. Fuel-cut-out switches are more useful as additional anti-theft devices.

Carrying weapons for self defence

Many overlanders wonder whether they should carry a weapon as a means of self defence and, if so, what kind. You might imagine situations where it could be reassuring to have some mace close to hand in the cab, thinking that pepper-spraying or clubbing an assailant would be an effective deterrent but less dramatic than using a knife or a gun. The fact is, you'll almost certainly never need to act like this, and possibly won't even have the aggressive instinct to do so when you should. Your best weapon is the common sense to **avoid or flee** from such situations, although you never know what you might manage on the day. One overlander I know of disarmed a drunk and threatening soldier of his AK-47 then knocked him down. He later bent the AK's barrel sideways in a tree in his bid for world peace.

Most of us have never seen a handgun and would consider the idea of carrying one abroad absurd, but for overlanders from societies where gun ownership is widespread, the prospect of travelling with a gun may not be so far-fetched, even if they know it's bound to be illegal. Using a handgun or even a knife to protect yourself might be advisable if you happen to know how to use one, are prepared to use one and are then prepared to face the consequences of doing so, including getting it wrong. For anyone else, it's just a bad idea.

When you're feeling a bit insecure it can be fun to fantasise about wasting some dirtbag who tried to rob you, but it's hard to think of an overlanding scenario where being able to get to your gun will do anything more than escalate the situation. Most people appreciate that real-life armed struggles and fights aren't beautifully choreographed stunts from a Bourne movie, but messy, clumsy and sometimes sickeningly brutal. In the unlikely event of a hold-up, will you have the gun to hand and know how to deal with a bunch of thieves who may be armed too?

Mace or **pepper spray** sounds like a more innocuous and compact alternative, recommended in some ursine habitats and sold elsewhere as an urban self-protection agent. But, again, ask yourself: how often are you likely to come up against a sole assailant who can be dispersed with a quick squirt? The reality is that if you are indeed under attack and unable to flee, you'll be either petrified or just very frustrated that it's happened to you.

POLICE TROUBLE

It pays to be on your best behaviour abroad, if for no other reason than you can land yourself in trouble for any number of unknown and **unexpected transgressions**. These can include immigration or visa infractions, a road-traffic offence or accident, entering or 'spying' in a restricted area (including some border areas), possessing illegal drugs or bootleg DVDs, smuggling (including antiquities or prehistoric artefacts), not fully declaring something (including certain foods and satellite phones), talking with the wrong people or being in the wrong place at the wrong time, political or religious insensitivity including insulting behaviour, or being disrespectful about the head of state.

Once they have you they'll be in no rush to admit a possible mistake and release you. You don't have to be in a North Korea-style police state to recognise that **human rights** in many of the countries you plan to visit are woeful; falling foul of the system and having to undergo even a short spell in prison could be traumatising. Whatever you think of the quality of policing back home, it'll be heavenly compared to the pitiless contempt for citizens' rights you might encounter abroad. You can also be **set up** by corrupt police or vengeful locals who you may have annoyed.

If you're **arrested**, the first step is to **get in touch with a friend or family member** and then your **local embassy**, high commission or consulate, or an embassy or honorary consul that might represent your country. This is vital if you're not to disappear because you'll be helpless and need people on the outside to fight your case.

Drugs

Drug offences probably get more young overseas travellers in trouble with the law than anything else. Not a few of them have been set up by dealers or guest-house owners working with the police. The best advice must be to just say no while you're on the road, unless you're clearly in a comfortable situation. Otherwise, along with any number of other traps you can fall into, there's too much at stake.

SURVIVAL DOS AND DON'TS

- **Don't go alone** in remote areas or bad weather.
- **Know your limits.** There's no rescue service.
- **Avoid known danger areas** where there are bandits, terrorists, wars or mines.
- **Don't travel in desert regions in summer or high mountains in winter.** Summer is when most desert travellers die because survival margins shrivel.
- **Know where you're going.** Keep on the track and avoid cross-country short-cuts. Carry adequate route information, navigational tools and communications devices.
- **Never carry on when lost.** Stop before you go too far, accept that you've made a mistake, and if necessary retrace your steps.
- **Carry enough fuel and water** for your entire planned stage, including a reserve. Difficult terrain and physical activity will greatly increase consumption of fuel and water.

- In remote areas and extreme, sub-zero conditions, **it may be better not to turn the engine off** for several days. As long as you have the fuel, it won't do it any harm.
- Even before things go wrong, **avoid wasting water**. Get into the habit of being miserly with your washing and cleaning needs.
- **Carry essential spares and tools and know how to use them.** You should at least be familiar with tyre removal and repair, and fault diagnosis (see pp279-288).
- If travelling in convoy **keep your companions in sight** at all times. Or tell them what you're doing and where you're going, both when driving and when going for something like an evening stroll.
- **Avoid driving at night.** Even on the tarmac roads there's a danger of unlit vehicles and stray animals.

SURVIVAL SITUATIONS

Very occasionally an overlander might find themselves in what is called a survival situation, a scenario that more commonly befalls hikers in the wilderness. An overlander has the big advantage of a fabulously equipped vehicle with which it would take quite an effort to get in trouble, but that could happen, most probably due to bad weather, a fire, getting lost or breaking down in a wilderness area. It's much more likely to happen to foolhardy travellers or day-trippers who go out unprepared, bite off more than they can chew in an ill-equipped vehicle, and then get scuppered by a stroke of bad luck. Being stranded need not escalate into a desperate situation if you have a **GPS, a map and a compass, a sat phone and sufficient supplies of fuel and water**.

Should you be stranded, unless you're certain help can be found nearby, it's best to **stay by your vehicle**. Unless it's burned to a crisp it contains many of the elements you need to maintain or improve your situation. If you're immobilised far from habitation and help, the situation is more serious.

Try to see if there's a way that you can fix your problem, which is most probably **regaining mobility** (see p282 for advice on troubleshooting common problems). It's a well-established fact that people underestimate their ingenuity as well as their strength until faced with a crisis. For example, as long as the terrain allows it, a car can drive on three wheel rims with broken suspension and just one low gear if necessary. Make repairs or improvisations calmly, methodically and, if it's very hot, work in the shade and in the cool part of the day. Don't be hasty and risk an injury. Conserve your energy.

If you're **in a group** and have another working car the situation is of course far less serious. Send some or all of the people on to get help or arrange the retrieval of the abandoned vehicle, while being prepared for the vehicle to be looted in your absence if you leave it unattended.

Honey let's take the kids

John Higham

The Higham family did not travel the world in their own vehicle, but the lessons and experiences John Higham describes are valid to any family on the road long term.

So, you're thinking that someday you'll settle down, get married, and have children. Or maybe you've been there, done that. Does this mean that you'll sit on the couch, comatose, in front of the TV late at night, longing for the days when you were free and adventurous? Do you see that goal of travelling around the world fading into oblivion?

No way! Travelling around the world with children is not only possible, it's even more fun than re-runs of Gilligan's Island. During our family of four's 52-week, round-the-world trip, not only did we experience the wonders of the world, from the stunning Angkor Wat in Cambodia to the amazing Amazon rainforest, we discovered sites and had adventures that we never would have dreamed of had we not had children in tow. Did you know that the United Arab Emirates has the galaxy's best water park? Or that Carnaval in Latin America is much more family-oriented than you might expect after

If this is school then what can holidays be like?
For our website and book, see 360degreeslongitude.com. © John Higham

watching Blame it on Rio? Can anything compare to seeing children of different cultures and colours enthusiastically hunting chameleons together in the mountains of East Africa?

Before we had children, my wife September and I discovered how travelling can shape one's thinking. We wanted to give this experience to our children. From that early concept the idea of a year-long round-the-world trip with our children emerged. Jordan, our youngest, was just learning to talk when he heard of the trip. When referring to it, the words 'world-the-round trip' came tumbling out of his mouth; the name stuck. Katrina, three years older than Jordan, hadn't yet been to kindergarten when she cycled down the Pacific Coast Highway on the back of a tandem. As the children grew older we backpacked and camped in far-flung corners of the world to learn what worked and what to expect. Saving and planning became family activities. To unite us in our goal we would consider even modest expenditures as a family and say, 'Do we really need this, or would we rather save the money for our big trip?'

Finally the time came and we quit our jobs and packed up our home. Over the next 52 weeks we visited 28 countries on five continents, crossing 24 time zones. Along the way we saw the beauty of the Swiss Alps, the grandeur of the Great Wall of China and the ugliness of the Cambodian Killing Fields. We stayed in the humblest of inns on the Bolivian altiplano and witnessed the dazzling lights of Hong Kong.

Think you might want to do something like this? You've come to the right place. Be confident that the most difficult part will be to step on that first plane, full of anticipation and anxiety.

What is the magic age for children to travel?

We've known families who have taken babies and toddlers out on extended trips, and as long as both parents have the energy to attend to the constant physical needs of a child this young, there's no reason to rule out travelling with very young children. But if you want your children to remember much of where they've been, it's probably best to wait until they are a bit older.

One criterion in our family was that our youngest child had to be able and willing to read long books – there's lots of down-time on the road. I couldn't even imagine tackling a trip of this magnitude with children who couldn't keep themselves entertained with a good book. At the other end of the age window, we wanted to leave before our oldest was in high school, as we felt that missing a year of high school might stunt them both academically and socially. We ended up leaving when our children were eight and eleven – old enough to understand what was going on, but young enough that they weren't embarrassed to be hanging out with their parents.

Of course, now that we've been there and done that, and we're thinking of our next extended adventure, we're wondering if having our oldest child miss a semester or two of high school could really be that big a deal!

Set reasonable expectations

If you're thinking of striking out on the road with your children, keep in mind that your itinerary is not going to be exactly the same as if you were travelling with only adults. Many children will declare that museums are b-o-o-o-ring,

LIFE ON THE ROAD

Kids insist on only one rule: a massive
plate of chips every day!
© John Higham

and if you've seen more than a couple of castles in Europe, you've probably seen enough. Rather than try to see every last temple and shrine in Tokyo, why not find Thunder Dolphin, one of the world's coolest roller-coasters, conveniently located in downtown Tokyo? Or play paintball in Panama City. Make a point to discover the best chocolate (Bariloche, Argentina) and the worst ice cream (Turkey).

You'll meet a whole different set of people than you would meet if you stayed on the typical guidebook's museum/nightclub/shopping circuit. And these interactions with real people – people who have nothing to do with the travel industry – will be some of your most cherished memories.

Take it slow

Ever had a day where you took a ferry ride at 7 o'clock in the morning, visited an archaeological site at 10am, took a tour of an ancient church at 1pm, went on a cycle tour at 3pm, and took in a concert in the evening? Your kids won't put up with it, and if they're miserable, everyone in the family suffers. We found it best to commit to **two rules**:

1. One significant activity per day That means one hike, or one visit to a museum, or one trip to a historical site. After that, spend the rest of the day in unstructured activities, perhaps at the park tossing around a frisbee. And yes, you will need to pack that frisbee, baseball and origami paper, or whatever your children are passionate about.

You can probably get away with leaving the trombone at home, but just because you're taking a year off from your normal lives doesn't mean that your child's every interest will be suspended. We hauled half a ream of paper on our tandem bicycles throughout Europe so that our eight-year-old son could continue to design superheroes and work on his self-authored 100-plus-page comic books.

2. Weekly P-Day (Preparation Day) About once a week make a plan for a **no-travel day**; spend the day simply relaxing and preparing for the upcoming week. That means hanging out at the hostel doing laundry, writing emails home and trying to figure out where you will even be the next week.

Won't the children be permanently scarred by missing school?

Disregard that school propaganda! Your kids will be fine. The experience of seeing the world will be an education in itself, though it won't help them to learn how to factor a polynomial. After considering the school curriculum our children would miss for a year, we concluded there was one subject that would significantly affect their opportunities for academic advancement for years to come if they fell behind in it: mathematics.

Before we left on our trip we purchased several **maths workbooks** for the kids' grade (year) levels and signed up for online homework help. While we travelled we spent an hour every morning working on maths with our kids. In that one hour per day for a year the kids went through two full years' worth of maths books. When they returned to their schools the next year, they were ahead of many of their classmates.

Reading or dozing in class?
We're not so sure.
© John Higham

School is, of course, more than mathematics. Before we left, September ordered age-appropriate **books** for the kids that covered some aspects of the places we were to visit. Grandma then Fedexed a box of books to us wherever we happened to be. Shipping books around the world isn't cheap, but Red Scarf Girl, about the Chinese Cultural Revolution, had a much greater influence on them when read in Beijing than it would have done if read at home.

Lastly, the kids wrote in **journals** every night. Between formal maths lessons, lots of reading, plenty of journal writing, and the learning that naturally comes from experiencing other cultures, any kid will receive a fine education.

When we returned home, the kids simply moved on to the following grade with their peers as if nothing were amiss. Indeed, nothing was.

Won't it cost a fortune?

In global terms, yes, it will. In local terms, you'd be surprised at the numbers. Travelling abroad for a year costs less than supporting a family for a year in many US coastal cities. Unfortunately, the pay isn't as good. So, unless you rode the stock-options wave of the late 1990s and cashed in at the peak, you'll need to make some lifestyle adjustments in order to save.

Depending on how you travel, you should budget about $50 per person per day, not including airfares, even if that person is only eight years old. That was our actual cash outlay, averaged over one year, for everything from hostels, to ice cream on the beach, to long-distance train fares. As they say, your mileage may vary. This number can be reduced by perhaps as much as half by spending less time in locations like London or Tokyo, and more time in budget havens like Bangkok or Mumbai.

But why do extended travel with kids?

Well, first of all, it's hard to get a babysitter for a whole year. If you want to continue your adventurous lifestyle, you're just going to have to bring 'em with you! And really, what's more important than spending time together as a family? Because as anyone with school-aged children knows, between work, school, soccer, piano lessons, cub scouts and gymnastics, it can become impossible to find enough time to spend together. But traveller beware! After only a few days of travelling together, I remember sleeping in a tent with a rather small elbow in my back all night thinking 'What have I done?' It's true, all that togetherness was a bit overwhelming at first. Yet it was only a few weeks later that our family had mastered the art of communicating by quoting lines from favourite sitcoms. By the time we returned we had spent 365 solid days within two feet of one another, and our modest-sized house seemed so unnaturally large that we couldn't bear to be in separate rooms.

Won't we miss our stuff?

There are far more reasons to plan a bout of extended travel than getting to know your spouse, children and even yourself better than you ever thought possible. Our society puts a very high value on material possessions. So high, in fact, that in getting caught in the chase of acquiring more, many people are unaware of what they have. Travelling to a developing country is the best way to demonstrate to the younger generation that as long as you have something to eat, something to wear, and somewhere to sleep, you are among the world's elite. The iPhone is, like, *totally* optional.

Won't I be putting my children in harm's way?

The world is a small place, and it's getting smaller. It's tempting to try and understand that world through the lens of mass media, which would lead us to believe that around every corner lurks a terrorist who is bent on annihilating every Westerner he sees. After spending a year travelling with our kids, we learned that our world is a much more complicated and wonderful place than what you might believe from watching the *Six O'Clock News*. We felt welcome everywhere we went, from Oman to Beijing. We even felt welcome in France! Our children were a magnet for friendly strangers, and we were showered with goodwill wherever we went.

How should children shape the itinerary?

There are two ways to answer this question. We have a huge map of the world on a wall in our home. Before we left on our trip, we put sticky notes on our map for all the places we wanted to visit, and why. This was a process to which everyone in the family contributed. Jordan, after studying China in school, wanted to visit the Great Wall. After watching a few too many National Geographic documentaries, Katrina had romantic notions about the

'From Kathmandu to Machu Picchu.'
© John Higham

Serengeti. These destinations and more made our itinerary's final cut. The other half of that question is, are there countries to which you shouldn't take the kids?

September and I honeymooned in Mexico. While we were checking in at a small roadside inn near the Yucatan Peninsula's Chichen Itza, we observed an American family with a high-school-aged daughter who was absolutely hysterical because she had just seen the largest spider of her life. 'I won't go in there!' she screamed, pointing to the hotel room. 'You can't make me go in there!' Between frantic sobs, the girl swore she wasn't going to get out of the rental car for the next two weeks. Perhaps she and Ron Weasley share an unnatural phobia for spiders. But her parents' rather coddling reaction to this scene suggested that perhaps she had simply spent too many years on the greener side of that white-picket fence.

Kids are much more **flexible and adaptable** than adults; they'll adapt to those cold-water showers and that 23-hour bus ride much better than you will. After a few weeks on the road, 'home' will simply be where your stuff is.

Don't shun **the developing world** because you believe the conditions are too harsh for kids. Remember, kids live there. Focusing just on the industrialised nations of the world during your travels will give you and your kids a skewed version of reality. Plus, it'll be mighty hard on your budget! The world is both a beautiful and ugly place. You should have the intestinal fortitude to see it – all of it – for what it is. Be sure to include the full spectrum of what the world has to offer, from the grandeur of the Alps to the stunning poverty off the beaten path in Africa. Visit historical sites from Cambodia's Killing Fields to the birthplace of Gutenberg's printing press. Revel in the contradictions that make us all human.

Health concerns

Reasonably healthy people have nothing to fear. There is impressive medical care all over the world that is cheaper and more accessible than what you will find in the US.

When travelling in developing countries there are two mantras to live by, or suffer the indignity of diarrhoea. First, stick to bottled water for everything, including ice in drinks and brushing teeth.

Second, before you put anything in your mouth, **wash it, cook it, peel it or forget it**. Even when being careful, some pathogen will find a way to sneak through your defences. While in Poland, someone's bio-terrorism experiment disguised as a cheeseburger found its way onto my plate. This could happen to you, so bring along some Cipro or Imodium (see p337).

Be prepared

We spent many sleepless nights before leaving on our year-long journey worrying about all of the things that could go wrong. We needn't have worried because it didn't help; nearly everything that we imagined could go wrong, did. You will face **challenges** that you couldn't fathom. Six weeks into an 18-week bicycling trip across Europe, Katrina was rock climbing and her rope broke. She tumbled to the ground and shattered her tibia. Rising to the challenge of coping with a broken leg pulled us together as a family in ways that wouldn't have been possible otherwise. While we were grateful the accident wasn't much worse, the sudden change in plans taught us survival skills we would appreciate over and over again.

There will be other types of challenges as well. For example, most kids from Western cultures are used to **strangers** keeping their distance. As we proceeded further south in Europe, we warned our kids that their personal force fields would be invaded, but we had no idea what a culture shock Turkey would be to our eight-year-old son. The first time a stranger swooped down and grabbed Jordan, exclaiming 'You're mine now!', was a bit of a shock for all of us. Turks not only love children, they also put a high value on male children and do not have the same cultural requirement of keeping an arm's length away. Mix that with the novelty of blond hair and blue eyes, and Jordan got way more attention than he bargained for. This pattern of overly abundant affection from strangers continued throughout Asia, in Africa, and well into Latin America. Things will happen that you can't control. **Be prepared and be flexible**, and you'll come to enjoy the craziness that makes our planet spin.

In summary

Taking your family to the edge of the world and back takes some planning, and unless you win the lottery it will probably take some serious sacrifices, but for most people it's an opportunity that only comes around once. Do the maths: one backyard landscaping + one new minivan = many months on the road. The minivan will get old, and weeds will eventually take over the backyard, but you'll remember the experiences you had on the road with your children forever. Take your children backpacking in Thailand and have them paddle a canoe in the Amazon. Experience the grandeur of Istanbul's Hagia Sophia. They'll understand that the inhabitants of this planet are much more complicated and interesting than what they've seen on CNN. You will too.

Taking the dog

LORRAINE CHITTOCK

You wake up in the morning to the cries of monkeys and exotic birds. Before you have a chance to get out of bed you wonder, 'Should we take our morning stroll on the beach or through the little village?' You fling open the door of your vehicle. With infinite abandon, Toto bounds out to sniff some smells that appeared in the night. 'Thank goodness he's here with me and not stuck in a kennel,' you think gratefully. For anyone devoted to their dog, taking it along on your foreign travels is a dream come true. However, as with any Garden of Eden, there are serpents to contend with in the jungle.

Before embarking on a grand expedition with your canine companion, it's worthwhile for you both to have done some travels previously. Pack your dog's food bowl, another one for yourself and hit the road. You'll learn, for example, how your mutt handles the experience; whether it's better to break up a long drive or push straight through. If a trial run of at least a week doesn't leave claw marks all over the interior, below are some additional considerations before setting off on a long overland adventure.

Pre-departure

These are some things to do before you get on the road with your pet.
- See a vet
- Get identity discs fitted with a microchip
- Vaccination against rabies
- Blood test

- Treatment against tapeworm and ticks, issued with an official certificate of treatment
- Official PETS certificate (UK)

Borders and quarantine

Most pet-owning travellers are concerned about border crossings as well as possibly lengthy periods in quarantine, either on the road or on returning. In fact, as far as the dog goes, most borders in developing countries are straightforward. Besides your own immigration formalities, you may also need to visit the agricultural office to show a **vaccination certificate** for rabies and distemper. On rare occasions you may be asked for a note from a veterinarian in the country you're exiting stating the animal is in good health. Costs to import your pet range from nothing to $50.

Once in the country it's doubtful anyone will check your pet's paperwork and on leaving you won't be required to show paperwork for the animal. Requirements for **shipping an animal by air** are drastically different and you'll need to check each country for their import and quarantine regulations. You can expect them to be strictest in the few places where rabies is not found, which include Britain, Australia, New Zealand, Scandinavia and Hawaii.

On the road

Like most of us, pets thrive on stability and yet the overland scenario of continual movement and change is far from stable. Just as you can expect to experience **stress** dealing with the multiple and mundane challenges of life on the road, your dog may also feel the strain. The way many owners communicate with their dogs is by prior knowledge of its needs and by intuition. Add some tension to your relationship and this interaction becomes strained and the link between you weakens.

In constantly changing and unfamiliar environments make sure you spend quiet time with your dog and give **ample attention** to make it feel at ease. You'll find it will calm your nerves too, which is part of the reason for taking your dog along for the ride. Moving too fast may also stress your animal so (in a parallel with travelling with children, see p352) plan a **relaxed schedule** with plenty of non-travel days.

Make sure your **vehicle** is pet-friendly too. Your animal needs to have a place to call his own in there, away from the stresses of life on the road. Create a den-like space for your pet, filled with familiar items.

Dog food

Even in places like Africa where pets are uncommon, dried pet food can be found in the capital cities, and some brands you may recognise. Canned food is less common. However, food from markets and restaurants could be less expensive so consider learning which foods are best for your animal before you travel. Note that the presence of local dogs can put your own pet off eating, so give it some space. This way while you're enjoying experimenting with different flavours your pooch will be having a healthy diet too. In Latin America *menudo* or tripe soup is served everywhere but always ask if there's onion in the dishes as this is toxic to dogs.

Pee and poo

In congested urban environments there won't always be handy places to pull over for doggie pee breaks so stop while you have the chance, before getting stuck into somewhere like Cairo's traffic battle zone. And don't forget, after being cooped up in the car, a dog needs extra time to adjust to new smells. Dogs especially can't poop unless they're relaxed or if other dogs are around.

Heat

Leaving your animal unattended in a vehicle in Arizona can get you a $2000 fine. Overland, it's solely your responsibility to make sure your animal has adequate ventilation and is comfortable. In one country I met a couple who opted to abandon the coastal regions for higher, cooler altitudes to avoid worrying about their vehicle-bound mutt while running errands.

If faced with hot weather and a need to secure your vehicle, it's best if one person stays with the animal. If you're solo, take your dog with you, otherwise park in the shade and do errands first thing in the morning when it's cooler. And if you're a sun lover, make sure your animal enjoys these temperatures as well. Remember, your dog needs to acclimatise and drink too, but on the move a bowl is impractical. At every stop make sure you put down a bowlful of water for Muttley.

Health

Where they exist, **vets** in rural environments will be generally more knowledgeable about livestock than pets. If you need the best care, head for a big city. Plenty of information is available on the **internet**. University veterinary schools are usually located in capital cities. For vets in specific cities, post a question on 💻 craigslist.org under 'pets', or check 💻 worldanimal.net to see if there's an animal organisation in that country that might be able to direct you. Cities with Western companies often have expatriates with pets who may know of local vets.

If your animal has health issues before departure that aren't too serious, be sure to take a good supply of medicine. It's likely to be available overseas but may be under a different name (something worth investigating before you leave).

Transmitted by infected mosquitoes, **heartworm** is prevalent globally, as is the risk of **tick fever**. In low-lying areas of Africa, particularly in the south and east, you'll encounter tsetse flies which, if infected with the parasite, can cause **sleeping sickness**; this affects dogs particularly badly (as well as tens of thousands of humans). Local vets will know what works best in their region as insects become resistant to specific insecticides. Try giving your animal plenty of **raw garlic** as a cheap and effective alternative. Other external **parasites** such as fleas and lice, and internal parasites (roundworms, hookworms, tapeworms and whipworms) can also be contracted. Keep your dog on a preventative such as Revolution, which protects against all of these, or buy medicines over the counter from veterinarian supply stores.

Your animal would need a high degree of physical contact with another dog to contract a case of **mange**. If it does, there are effective ointments you can bring with you or you can buy them from veterinarian supply stores. And remember to wash your own hands after touching other animals.

Transmissible venereal tumours, or **TVTs**, are a real danger. Almost eradicated in America, they are common in street dogs whose immune system is low, and can be passed from one dog to the next not only from mating, but by friendly nose contact of the afflicted area. These tumours appear grotesque when on the genitalia, but can afflict internal organs too. They're usually curable by chemotherapy and surgery, but be very careful with your dog in areas where you see this disease.

An encounter with the natives
© Lorraine Chittock

Native dogs

Some cities put down **poisoned bait** to kill street dogs. Keep your dog on a leash in cities where this might be a problem and don't let him eat anything off those streets. If you suspect your dog has eaten something poisonous, take him immediately to a vet.

In countries where guard dogs are common, to compensate for the lack of police services, people can have a pronounced **fear of dogs**. The most common question you'll hear in Latin America is 'Bravo? Morder?' ('Aggressive? Does it bite?'). While walking casually with your dog you may feel these attitudes are extreme. They're not. In places like China poor vaccination rates and increasing pet ownership has made **rabies** the country's second deadliest pathogen after tuberculosis, killing up to 3000 humans a year. Each new epidemic results in the culling of tens of thousands of dogs so when confronted by a look of terror, smile and assure the person your animal is friendly – unless of course it's not!

Some dogs you encounter might appear like **street dogs**, but are actually fed by the community. Others are strictly scavengers and shun people. Both often exhibit different behaviour from dogs raised in a household. Since they don't have someone regularly feeding and caring for them, they sometimes run in a pack to protect each other. This doesn't mean they're aggressive. If you allow your dog to mix with them, you might be privileged to discover a different aspect of your dog's personality around these less domesticated canines.

If you and your dog are on **another dog's territory**, whether they be street dogs or owned, your dog might need to assert his role in the hierarchy, or put on a show of submissiveness. This usually lasts anywhere from a few seconds to a few minutes. If you think the interchange is getting out of hand, dogs in other countries are often used to having rocks thrown at them. Just bending down to pick up a rock is often enough to disperse the crowd. Street dogs specifically are used to being treated as pariahs and will usually be wary of humans. If you have more than one dog, street dogs will perceive you and yours as a solid pack and keep away.

Restaurants, stores and hotels

In big cities you can't expect your pet to be welcomed with open arms every-where you go. In rural communities it's much more common for animals to accompany their owners, and rules are usually more lax about permitting them in places where there's food. You'll often see dogs trailing behind women on their way to the market. However, their dogs sometimes wait out-side the **store**. If you're unsure whether your pet is welcome, ask first. In trop-ical environments many **restaurants** are without doors and windows and both owned and community cats and dogs often roam in and out to scrounge.

Small dogs are often welcome in **hotels**, though generally there will be concern about barking and making a mess. Larger dogs are a tougher sell. In general, the cuter the dog the easier it's going to be to obtain lodging. If you have a dog that doesn't fall into the small/cute category, try selling the recep-tionist on the idea while your animal is still in the vehicle. And keep in mind that though hotels are a nice break, it's yet another new place for the animal to adjust to. Consider this when stopping anywhere unless it's for more than one night.

Dog rules

In **cities**, you might see lots of owned dogs not on leads. Leash rules might be flexible depending on where you travel. Just as back home, it's good practice to bring plastic bags to pick up the poo, and in more developed cities you'll see signs to that effect.

In rural areas where people usually earn their livelihood from farm ani-mals, having your dog chase anything bigger than a chicken will be frowned upon. If your animal kills any **livestock**, apologise and don't hesitate to com-pensate the owner financially for what the animal would be worth at its most marketable.

Camping and wildlife

National parks might not allow pets, and **game parks** certainly won't. Consider camping just outside the boundaries of the park; natural beauty often extends to both sides. Less-populated countries are renowned for having plenty of wide-open space where you can camp for free in beautiful places where there are no leash restrictions for your animal.

If your dog is from the city, it will have little experience of **wildlife**. Chances are it will either react aggressively or, in the case of predators like big cats, their scent alone could terrify it. All animals sense when there's a real threat around and will want a safe place to hide. Never leave your pet alone, even for five minutes, while you're in the bush.

If you're planning on bush camping you might want to bring **a second dog**. The dynamics change totally and, instead of being prey, the dogs will act as a united pack. If you don't want to commit to a second dog, consider ask-ing tribe members from that area if you can rent one of their animals. Your dog will have canine companionship and be safer, and the native dog might bene-fit from your additional food or medicine. Certainly you will have an amazing story to tell.

Military and men

Dogs generally don't like people in uniforms, though it's possible your animal could be responding to the man inside the uniform and high levels of testosterone. While overlanding you'll encounter no shortage of roadblocks and checkpoints and in these situations it's quite possible your dog will act aggressively and bark, which can be stressful for all parties. Keep smiling while talking to the official, and try to speak soothingly to your animal at the same time.

Cultural differences

Though locals may well have pets, seeing travellers with a dog is unusual and can attract crowds: stressful for both you and your animal. While driving around, some will laugh or look incredulously on seeing a dog's head hanging out of the passenger window. Others, usually men and boys, find themselves compelled to bark.

Cultural differences apply to animals as well as humans. An animal whose ribs are pronounced might not necessarily be starving, it could just be a healthy, lean animal. Over time you'll learn to see the difference between a genuinely healthy native dog and one which is diseased.

You'll almost certainly encounter **treatment of animals** that will go against your values. Some of these instances will be downright cruel, but consider that there might actually be a logical reason behind what you observe. In other situations, what you consider lack of care could just mean lack of knowledge or financial means. Just because a family has an animal they don't treat the way you see fit doesn't mean there isn't love. People in other countries don't always show the affection to their animals like we do in the West, though many are just as devoted.

For a family earning a local wage, an imported flea treatment, even if available, could cost a week's salary. Consider buying a supply of dewormer or other **medicine** like eye drops to distribute to those who might not be able to afford it (or administer directly to needy street animals, while being sure of your own safety first). Always make sure to talk to the owners before stepping in and righting what you think is a wrong. You risk being seen as an interfering foreigner and hurting, rather than helping the animal in need.

On your journey, you might become attached to a local animal. Before **adopting**, be very sure the animal doesn't already have an owner. Most animals do not wear collars. Ask extensively before assuming an animal is lost or abandoned. It may just have a very large route it travels on a daily basis.

A two-way bond

Though your dog will certainly alert you to approaching strangers, and provide a degree of security, travelling with an animal is little different than doing so with anyone dependent and you'll sometimes be called upon to forfeit some of your plans. Instead of being resentful, remember this journey was your idea, not your animal's. If there's ever a time when the bond between you and your furry companion gets stressed to its limit, travelling overseas will be it. You may not have the freedom to visit all the places you'd like, but because of your dog, you may be privileged to see and enjoy other experiences. Don't forget, if you take care of your dog, your dog will take care of you.

8

ASIA
ROUTE OUTLINES

From Istanbul or the Urals to a stone's throw from Alaska – and from above the Arctic Circle to below the equator close to Australia, **Asia**, the world's biggest landmass, just about has it all. And for an overland driver it's all getting easier, with new overland routes and visa-free regimes. Asia offers sealed highways from the Bosphorus to Singapore and right across Russia to Vladivostok.

Part of the appeal of driving in Asia is its rich and diverse historical and architectural heritage, a range of fabulous cuisines as well as the **low cost of living** in the south of the continent (potentially much less than in Africa or Latin America). In places fuel prices can be among the lowest in the world too, though they're finding other ways of making you pay.

HOT SPOTS

Apart from North Korea which won't be opening to overlanders any time soon, hot spots remain. **Syria** as well as all but the Kurdish part of **Iraq**, **Yemen** and **Afghanistan** away from the Wakhan Corridor are very risky, less so parts of the **Russian Caucasus**.

Saudi, **China** and **Vietnam** severely restrict or complicate independent travel with motor vehicles, and importing a car into Japan gets difficult and expensive. **Pakistan** has laid on border-to-border transit escorts for years, but that is more down to security. The great news is **Myanmar** is now open between India and Thailand and maybe China too, even if Thailand and adjacent countries may have taken a backward step (more on p401).

VISAS FOR ASIA

Visas will have a major impact on your route because getting them for Russia, Iran, Pakistan, India and some of the Central Asian 'stans' can't always be done in a neighbouring country in a day or two, let alone at a border. Assuming this may ease up for Brits, if not Americans as things stand, Iran will still take weeks to acquire, something that's best done before you leave. In Turkmenistan you might find yourself racing across, simply because a quick transit visa means you don't have to pay out for the 'escorted tour' that's required with the longer tourist visa. Russia offers an easy solution: one long duration visa. More details follow.

PRINCIPAL ROUTES: TAÏGA, HIGH ASIA OR TROPICS

Unless you're a family of Yakut herders bound for a snorkelling holiday in Sri Lanka, Asia overland is primarily a lateral transit and broadly speaking there are **three routes** between the east and west:

- The Trans-Siberian route and its adventuresome offshoots runs across Russia to Vladivostok from where ferries run to South Korea.
- The 'Silk Route' links the Caucasus with the mountains of Central Asia, to join eastern Russia with Mongolia, or western China for India.
- Finally, the 'Road to Singapore' runs through Turkey and Iran to India then across Myanmar for the rest of Southeast Asia.

Coming from Europe, around Turkey and Iran the high and low routes interweave with the middle route, but as you move east the mass of China divides your options. On this eastern side the mainland termini of all routes are more specific: possibly Magadan but more likely the conurbation of freighting sea terminals around **Vladivostok** in Far Eastern Russia with ferry links to South Korea and on to the port of **Busan**. Or **Singapore/Kuala Lumpur** (Port Klang) on the equatorial tip of Southeast Asia. These are the key ports you'll want to ship to if you're approaching Asia from the east.

Mile for mile, culturally, historically and scenically **Central Asia** offers the diversity that Russia lacks while also being **carnet-free**. It was through this region that the fabled Silk Roads developed two millennia ago; a network of trade routes along which not only silk, but paper, gunpowder and, of course, ideas shuttled west to Europe via places like Samarkand, before trade passed into the hands of Western Europe's 17th-century seafaring empires.

For the time being **China** sticks to its historic isolationism, at least behind a wheel – on foot or with a bicycle you're freer to roam. Otherwise you'll need to organise the expensive escort and permits months in advance.

Borders in the far west and east of **Mongolia** mean this distinctive and undeveloped country can now be transited in full via Ulaanbaatar, or you can use the route to the north from Ulan Ude in Russia. The only entry point into China is south of UB on a track that becomes a road to Beijing.

Turkey

Traditionally, coming from the Balkans, **Asia** begins once you cross the Bosphorus from Istanbul into Asia Minor. As a taste of what lies ahead, rather like Morocco, **Turkey** offers just enough challenges to curb complacence. Although too far from Western Europe to be treated as a test run for the big trip, it's a destination in its own right, full of fascinating sites that you wouldn't want to rush, even if you could. The east and northeast regularly feature as highlights among overlanders, although in the ethnically Kurdish areas along the Syrian, Iranian and Iraqi borders, watchtowers and checkpoints are a common sight and tensions occasionally escalate.

Most travellers get an e-**visa** at ⌨ evisa.gov.tr/en – border visas are being phased out. Buy **motor insurance** for up to three months and that's it. The downside is the **high price of fuel** which may well dictate how many miles you cover here. But whichever way you go, it's hard to choose a bad route. At the far end of Turkey the party could be about to end so brace yourself. Excluding going back home, you have five options: (cont'd on p368)

ASIA – ROUTE OUTLINES

CARNET COUNTRIES IN ASIA

Bahrain, Bangladesh, Cambodia, India, Indonesia, Iran, Japan, Kuwait, Malaysia* Nepal, Pakistan, Qatar, Singapore, Sri Lanka.

* If arriving by ship as opposed to visiting from Thailand overland.

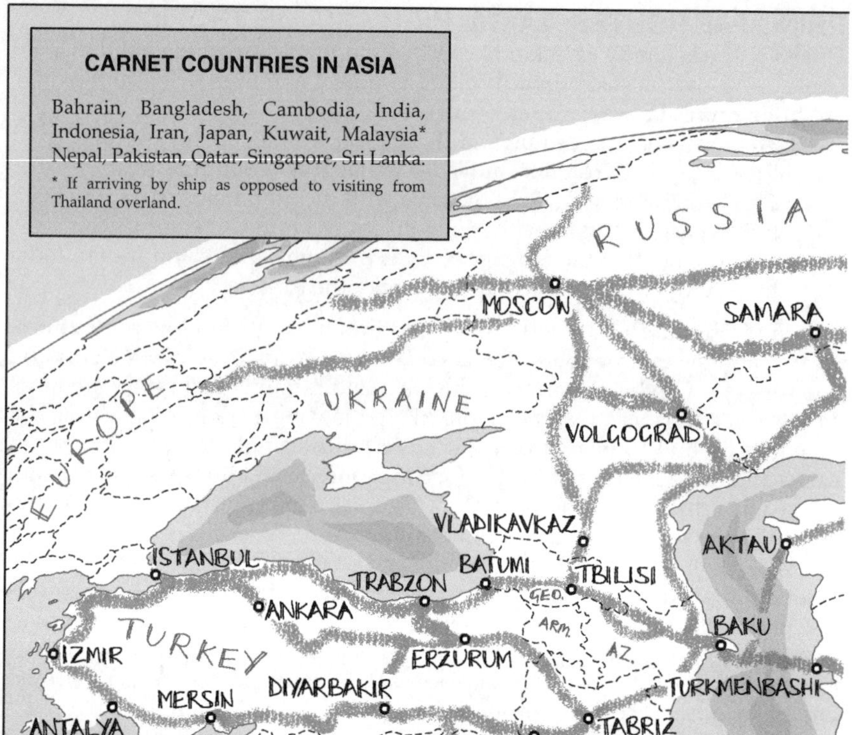

RUSSIA

MOSCOW

SAMARA

UKRAINE

VOLGOGRAD

EUROPE

VLADIKAVKAZ

AKTAU

ISTANBUL

BATUMI

TBILISI

TRABZON

GEO.

ANKARA

BAKU

ARM.

TURKEY

IZMIR

ERZURUM

AZ.

TURKMENBASHI

ANTALYA

MERSIN

DIYARBAKIR

TABRIZ

DOHUK

ORUMIYEH

TEHRAN

ERBIL

DAMASCUS

SYRIA

SULAYMANYAH

HAMADAN

HAIFA

PORT SAID

IRAQ

ESFAHAN

IRAN

AQABA

SHIRAZ

THE ASIAN CLIMATE

For trouble-free travel across Asia there are two things you want to avoid: the tropical **monsoon** on western coasts from June to October, and, more importantly, **winter** anywhere north of the Himalayas.

For Asia-bound riders starting from either Europe or the east, if you're heading towards India, leave in summer and ride into the autumn. If Central Asia or even just eastern Turkey is your destination, plan to arrive in the spring or early autumn – winters in the Asian interior are extreme. Further north, eastern Siberia will only be rideable in the late summer (see p377).

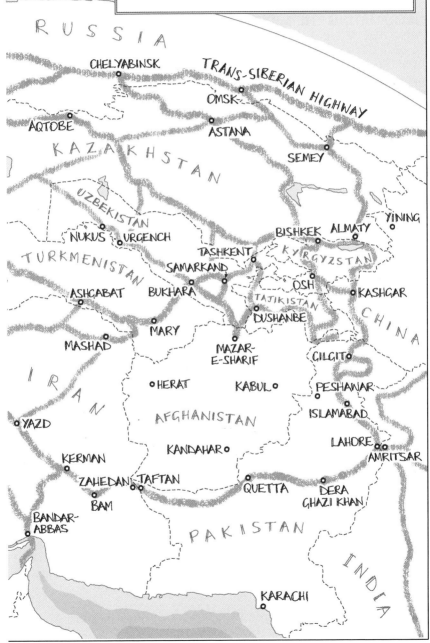

Main overland routes across West Asia

- Ferry Trabzon to Sochi (Ru). Irregular and redundant as Georgia is easy
- Into the north Caucasus and over into Russia for Kazakhstan
- Cross the Caspian Sea to Turkmenistan or Kazakhstan
- Southeast into Iran, either direct or via Kurdish northern Iraq
- A ferry to Israel for Jordan, Egypt and the rest of Africa

NEGOTIATING THE MIDDLE EAST

At the time of writing (you'll be hearing this phrase often...) the war in **Syria** shows little sign of ending. The conflict has greatly disrupted overland traffic from Turkey to Africa, but Asia remains relatively immune. Currently the options are the **ferry** to Israel then overland to Jordan. With access to northern Sinai restricted, the daily ferry between Aqaba down the eastern arm of the Red Sea to Nuweiba in the Egyptian Sinai (🖳 abmaritime.com.jo) has become the only way of getting into Egypt. Coming north, don't even think about crossing Yemen, even if there are boats from Djibouti. And if you somehow find yourself in Dubai, there's a ferry to Bandar Abbas in Iran.

Be aware that even though **Israel** can stamp you in and out on a piece of loose paper, rather than in your passport, countries like North Sudan and definitely Iran, have been known to closely scrutinise the dates and places on passport entry and exit stamps. If they find the point of entry was at an Israeli border, they may well turn you away, especially if they're having a bad day or don't like the look of you. In fact, you rarely hear of such problems in Sudan.

THROUGH THE CAUCASUS AND ACROSS THE CASPIAN

For many the Caucasus represents the jumping off point – the sudden transition from the home comforts of Europe to the rigours of Asia – although over the past few years **Azerbaijan** and **Armenia** have become more tourist-friendly and overlanders may feel that they're still in eastern Europe.

Entry points from Turkey are at **Batumi** and **Vale** and once in Georgia there's no rush as you **won't need a visa** and can stay for up to a year. Make the most of it because the next two countries eastwards aren't so accommodating. Be sure to hang out in the capital Tbilisi, as well as Kakheti, Georgia's wine region and home to a number of impressive monasteries. In Azerbaijan the unspoilt and mountainous northern regions are also worth a look – Kifl and Lahıc being two of the area's highlights.

Most find the *Lonely Planet* guide for Georgia, Armenia and Azerbaijan a decent travel companion and for Azerbaijan, Trailblazer's guide is worth a look. As these are all former Soviet republics, **Russian** will be the most useful **language** here, though English will be understood too. It's unlikely you'll get your head around Georgia's ancient, curly Kartvelian script.

Fuel, money and internet

Fuel is around two-thirds cheaper than Europe. **ATMs** are widely found in all major cities and many regional towns. Some fuel stations in Georgia and Azerbaijan take credit cards, as do many hotels in major towns, but as always, it's **safer to pay in cash**.

You'll find plenty of inexpensive **internet cafés** in all major cities as well as free wi-fi in hotels, smarter cafés and restaurants, especially in the capitals.

Caucasus

As for local driving standards, the Georgians are the most aggressive and impatient, although outside the major cities there's little traffic. Road manners in Armenia are good, whilst Azeri truck drivers should be passed with caution. For some reason driving standards in **Baku** are far more chaotic than the rest of Azerbaijan, so polish your mirrors and be prepared.

Apart from Azerbaijan, **traffic police corruption** is much less worse than it used to be, so if you're stopped for speeding and have picked up bad habits in either Russia or Central Asia, offering to pay your way out may not be the right thing to do.

Motor insurance is only compulsory in Azerbaijan where it should be issued to you at the border for around $30. You'll be unlikely to obtain motor insurance at any Georgian or Armenian borders, although it's possible to buy it in the major cities, if you can be bothered. In Georgia, **Imedi** provide local and Green Card insurance (useful if you're transiting Georgia on the way home). They have offices in Tbilisi (20 Chavchavadze Avenue) and in Batumi on the Black Sea. Note, if you are entering Turkey from Georgia it'll cost you far less to obtain your Green Card in Georgia than it will from a European company or at the Turkish border.

North Caucasus and the road to Russia

Once you've explored Georgia you have three options: **north to Russia** from Georgia, or via Abkhazia or Azerbaijan; south to Armenia; or east to Azerbaijan. Versions of the first option have become preferable as Azerbaijan's transit visa and uncertain ferry schedules put overlanders in a pickle. All this has come to pass as the brutal secessionist war in Chechnya seems to have run its course, though in 2008 Russia was provoked to complete its 'annexation' of the contested Georgian province of **Abkhazia** in the northeast. With a transit visa from $5 for 12 hours, you can enter Russia this way, but it can get a little edgy here and coming from Russia via Abkhazia into Georgia can't be done as you'll have insulted Georgian territorial integrity.

A much less contentious border into North Ossetia (Russia) exists at **Kazbegi/Verkhny Lars** on the road from Tbilisi to Vladikavkaz ('Kavkaz'; 200km). Buy **Russian insurance** at the border; it's about €30 for three months.

Turkey and Armenia's borders remain firmly closed, whilst crossing from Turkey to the Azeri enclave of Naxçivan limits you to exiting either into Iran via Culfa-Jolfa or returning to Turkey. Note that you also can't cross from Armenia to Azerbaijan and if coming from Georgia, Azeri officials may quibble over an Armenian visa stamp if you've come direct rather than hanging out in Georgia for a bit. Conversely, there's no problem entering Armenia with an Azeri visa stamp. Read that again looking at a map and it makes sense.

Whichever way you do it, crossing into **Armenia** is relatively expensive: visas are available online and at the border they may offer to skip the stamp if you ask, but you'll have to pay various taxes to bring your car in for up to 15 days; a 30-day vehicle permit is available. Have photocopies of everything.

It's only possible to exit Armenia via Georgia or Iran – you can't get back into Turkey from here. If crossing to Iran be sure you have your visa and note, otherwise you'll have to pay another spurious departure tax.

Azerbaijan and the Caspian
Coming from Georgia with your Azeri visa, crossing into **Azerbaijan** is straight-forward. The northern crossing at **Lagodekhi** is more foreigner-friendly than Krasny Most. Visas can be arranged in Batumi on the Black Sea or in Tbilisi; a 30-day **tourist visa** takes three days to get and costs around $100 but with a vehicle Azerbaijan insists on a temporary importation deposit up to its full value which of course is a non-starter unless you're related to the president. Most go for the a **5-day transit visa** for $20, or $40 double-entry and valid for 30 days from the date of issue.

The problem is the welcome from the men in hats in Azerbaijan is not always so warm and the associated driving permit is usually valid for only 72 hours. Assuming the ferry game will take longer than that to unravel, you'll be stuck. You can leave the car in Baku, or Alat's port's customs area, and hope it'll be secure there – and if you need to get the 70km from one port to the other – the customs guy should stamp and sign off your permit. As it is, it's said that fines for overstaying the driving permit a few days aren't huge, though don't try that with the visa.

Exiting from Azerbaijan to **Iran** at Astara on the coast is possible, but not many travellers go this way, and of course Iranian visas don't grow on trees. You can also cross from Baku up into Dagestan, **Russia**. It's an 800km drive to the Kazakh border near Astrakhan via the ancient Silk Road city of Derbent on the Caspian. These may be good escape routes if your plans to catch either ferry go awry, but depending on your experience, few overlanders willingly throw themselves through Azerbaijan's burning hoops just to drive out the easy way overland. Most are intent on ferrying over the Caspian Sea.

Across the Caspian Sea for Turkmenistan or Kazakhstan
The idea of crossing the Caspian Sea on a boat from **Baku** to **Turkmenbashi** in Turkmenistan – or now from **Alat** south of Baku to **Aktau** in Kazakhstan – has a romantic ring about it, especially to former CS Lewis readers. But with no fixed schedules and baffling delays once at sea, the frustration and run-around in getting you and your car onto and then off either boat puts travellers off, especially now the Russian north Caucasus is safe.

The hassle adds up to grumpy and corrupt officials, the uncertainty in securing a place, and more bribes, especially at the Turkmenistan end where you're faced with an other five-day rat run. The vessels are primarily rail freighters with a few spare cabins, a long way from a P&O pleasure cruise with a karaoke happy hour. Once heading for either Turkmenbashi or Aktau, the boats seem to float motionless for days on the 200- or 400-km crossing.

If leaving from Baku enquire at the ticket office at the port (N40° 22.47′ E49° 51.94′; the Lonely Planet Baku map marks the ticket office, customs and the loading point) about the next departure and get on a list. Tickets aren't sold until the departure is imminent and once that's decided, loading can happen very quickly so don't stray too far. Passenger tickets for both crossings are still around $110 per person for a basic en-suite cabin with a window, and at least as much again for your vehicle, plus another $20 for clean sheets and toilet paper. There's a café on board, but that can run out on longer crossings so bring extra food and water for up to two days.

For Turmenistan see p379, for Kazakhstan see p381.

Russia

Unless you detach yourself from the trans-Siberian tramline, scenically, mile for mile Russia can lack diversity, but it sure is a great way of sweeping across the continent on one fat visa. At 17 million square kilometres (6.6m square miles) the half of this land mass above 60°N probably has the lowest population density on earth and geographically, 'Europe' ends rather too neatly at the **Ural mountain** chain running from the Arctic Ocean down through the Kazakh border and into the Caspian.

Away from the southerly network of the **Trans-Siberian** railway and nearby highway, land-based travel can be arduous. In winter major rivers such as the Ob, Yenisey, Lena and Kolyma become navigable ice roads or *zimniks*. In the short northern summer melted snow saturates the top soil and any attempt at building and maintaining a highway becomes literally undermined as an annual temperatures swing 40°C either side of freezing point. Roads expand, crumble, freeze and then get washed away by floods. Hopefully you're not driving along it when any of this happens.

Above all, do yourself a favour and learn the **Cyrillic alphabet** (see below) so you don't end up in Xandyga when you wanted to get to Huevos Rancheros; it's not totally alien to the Roman alphabet and the numbers are the same. English or German may get you by in the West, but not east of Irkutsk. Learning a few phrases greatly enhances your trip, so get on it.

ASIA – ROUTE OUTLINES

CYRILLIC ALPHABET

Cyrillic letter	Roman equivalent	Pronunciation*	Cyrillic letter	Roman equiv	Pronunciation*
А а	a	father	П п	p	Peter
Б б	b	bet	Р р	r	Russia
В в	v	vodka	С с	s	Samarkand
Г г	g	get	Т т	t	time
Д д	d	dog	У у	u, oo	fool
Е е	ye	yet (unstressed: year)	Ф ф	f, ph	fast
Ё ё	yo	yoghurt	Х х	kh	loch
Ж ж	zh	treasure	Ц ц	ts	lots
З з	z	zebra	Ч ч	ch	chilly
И и	i, ee	seek, year	Ш ш	sh	show
Й й	y	boy	Щ щ	shch	fresh chips
К к	k	kit	Ы ы	y, i	did
Л л	l	last	ь		(softens preceding letter)
М м	m	Moscow	Э э	e	let
Н н	n	never	Ю ю	yu	union
О о	o	tore (unstressed: top)	Я я	ya	yard (unstressed: yearn)

* pronunciation shown by underlined letter/s

BORDERS

Borders will be one of the prime places to judiciously demonstrate your mastery of Russian. They'll appreciate it and the arduous processes will take less time and be more fun. Forms are normally in Russian. Try and find a female officer – who are ever more frequent at border posts these days – as they'll always be the first to help you and may even fill out your forms for you.

Assuming all your paperwork is in order, there's no need to pay out any bribes. You'll get through, just as others have done before you, but without help expect it all to take several hours. Consider yourself lucky that you're not a truck driver at the wrong end of a 50-kilometre queue and a three-day wait. Unfortunately, there's a need to **re-register** and renew permits continues once you're in Russia.

VISAS AND REGISTRATION

There was once talk of easing regulations with the EU and allowing a reciprocal 30-day visa to be issued at a border, but then the war in Ukraine kicked off, Crimea was annexed, sanctions were imposed by the EU and relationships have all gone a bit *zimnik*. The innocent traveller is caught in the middle.

As with Iran and the Central Asian 'stans', a felicitous alliance with certain visa agencies has developed. You have to use them and apply in your home country – they do all the work for you, including obtaining the so-called letters of introduction ('LOIs'). You'll be hearing a lot about them from now on.

The most basic is a **single-entry tourist visa** which lasts 30 days and costs around £130 through an agency in the UK, less for other EU nationals and – for the moment – from $250 in the US. A **double-entry** visa allowing a second 30-day visit within a year costs about 20% more, and both take about a week to issue. You must have confirmed accommodation or transit information for every night of your stay in the country, but the small fee for a 'visa support letter' can get round this requirement. Brits (as well as Danes) now have to submit to a full fingerprint scan which will require a visit to the visa agency. A month-long double-entry visa will easily be enough to get you across the country with a drop down into Central Kazakhstan or Mongolia.

Anything of longer duration or with multiple entries is classified as a **business visa**, although you don't actually have to be involved in any kind of commerce. Costs for a double-entry 90-day business visa start at over £200 for Brits (15% less for most EU citizens) and take at least two weeks to issue; to get it within a week costs half as much again. Prices and delivery times **for multiple-entry business visas** lasting six months are nearly double for Brits (a lot less for others) and take two weeks. Visas need to be used within a year, which is longer than most.

With a visa like this you could just about fill up the driving season to-ing and fro-ing between the Baltic and the Pacific, while visiting Central Asia, Ukraine, Mongolia and, if you're quick, the North Pole. However, technically the consulate can refuse to issue a multiple-entry visa if you don't have a previous Russian visa in your passport, although as with all things Russian, this rule is not enforced consistently. Unless you're sure you'll be in Russia for only a couple of weeks, always go for the **longer lasting business visa**; Russia is a big country and your plans may change.

This is the former USSR so getting a visa is just the start. Within **seven days** of entering the country (excluding weekends and holidays) you must **register** your visa with the Office of Visas and Registration (OVIR, aka UFMS, Federal Migration Service Organisation). Your passport or the immigration card you filled out at the border is stamped, and you obtain a **registration slip** showing the period you're registered to stay in any one place. In addition to the dates, it'll also include details of where you're staying. Very often the **hotel** you're staying in immediately after crossing the border will do this for you for a minimal charge. However, this applies more to the popular tourist cities of Moscow and St Petersburg in the west. In many provincial cities some hotels will register your visa for a fee, even if you're not lodging there.

If you're not passing through the west or are camping, a **Registration Support Letter** will help you register yourself at the nearest OVIR. You'll be asked to complete a **Notification of Arrival** form; it's in Russian so you may need help; see the image on 💻 realrussia.co.uk. Give the top part back and possibly get another stamp on your immigration card or passport.

It's not over yet. In theory once on the road you need to register in any sizeable town within three working days but, if you're not staying there for three working days or more, technically there's no need to register. However, on the road it's worth doing so once in a while and getting another **registration slip** to avoid any potential problems with 'gaps' in your registration. And don't forget to de-register your visa with the OVIR every time you leave Russia if you're on a multiple-entry visa, or it's the salt mines for you, comrade.

There are obviously plenty to choose from, but the realrussia.co.uk website is well designed, up to date with prices and shows graphics (including translations) of immigration documents. It also has a useful list of **restricted provincial cities** with details of where and how to register if not staying in a hotel. They include Barnaul or Novosibirsk if coming out of northeastern Kazakhstan, Gorno-Altaysk if coming out of northwestern Mongolia, Irkutsk north of Ulaanbaatar, plus Vladivostok and Khabarovsk. They even run a forum to discuss Russian topics. Pay it a visit because this could all change.

Vehicle documents

A translation of your vehicle ownership document will be useful if stopped, although the temporary importation permit (see below) issued at the border ought to suffice. Get an IDP too (see p23). **Motor insurance** (*strahavanie*) you buy at the border and pay in roubles at around about €30 for three months.

No carnet is required; instead you get a three-month **temporary importation permit**. It can be extended for up to a year if your visa is that long but if you leave Russia for the 'stans or wherever, the permit expires so if you come back you have to start again. Get the triplicate barcoded **customs declaration form** (sometimes available in several European languages) and indicate on it that you're temporarily importing a vehicle. Insist on a stamped copy that includes a description, otherwise there'll be problems getting out of Russia, Belarus and Kazakhstan which are all joined in a customs union.

As you drive away from a border after what may have been several hours bouncing around chasing documents and stamps and doing that leg-kicking Cossack dance, resist the urge to gun it; just down the road radar speed traps or more document checks are quite likely.

ON THE ROAD

Fuel prices in Russia start at around 35 roubles a litre for diesel. Generally fuel costs more in the far east and in western cities. If you're visiting Kazahkstan, fuel costs about 30% more; in Mongolia and Ukraine it's about 35% more. To stop runaways, at most fuel stations you pay first, then they turn it on. On the trans-Sib east of Chita there are **roadhouses** every 150km or so, but in the sticks you know the drill: fill up or run out.

For **mobile internet**, you may need to show your passport to buy a SIM card. Buy the **countrywide** tariffs from the country's three main operators: Beeline; Megafon or MTS because by European standards they're amazingly cheap for the mass of monthly data you get. You can top up in ATM-like terminals in most shops. Don't bother looking for **free wifi** out in the sticks; get a dongle or SIM and rely on the cheap mobile internet.

Driving standards in Russia are poor; a combination of uncarworthy roads, unroadworthy cars, **drunkenness** and a healthy dose of machismo, evoking Putin in one of his raunchy vids. Once you factor in dealing with the *militzia*, in big cities it may be easier to park up and get around by taxi or even on foot. **Radar traps** and checkpoints are found on the edge of every town as well as places in between, and you'll almost certainly be stopped for speeding or crossing solid white lines whether you did so or not. **Speed limits** are 60kph in town, 110kmh on motorways or as signposted. Maximum fines for moderate speeding are only around 300 roubles; but just 5kph over the limit will get you a ticket unless you settle on the spot and negotiate the fine.

They'll want your passport, immigration documents, registration slip, IDP, TIP and anything else you got ending with P, to copy into their ledgers. If they don't ask for these immediately it's probably a prompt for a bribe (*straf*) of 300 roubles or less, or maybe just a friendly chat about your cool rig. Carry photocopies of everything, as losing one item to them puts you in a fix and can mean having to cough up a bribe.

There are a couple of Russian road atlases or, as they call them, auto-atlases. They cover just about all of the driveable parts of the country at scales from 1:200,000 in the west to 1:3 million in the east, and are occasionally available from specialist map shops in Europe or North America, but at three times the price. Once in Russia these atlases may take some tracking down outside the big cities. However, unless you're roaming off the beaten track, a regular folding road map, either European or Russian produced, will do you. You'll find Russian editions for sale in fuel stations.

Of the proprietary digital maps to import into your GPS from the likes of Garmin, their current Russia download is hopeless in the east, just where things begin to get interesting. The best available will be on OSM 🖥 open streetmap.org. And although it's all in Russian, web browsers can translate 🖥 roads.ru/forum to get up-to-date news on the state of the roads.

Dodging the police – the other 'Great Game'

Thanks to the struggling rouble, **bribery and corruption** are a way of life in Russia and Central Asia. The first thing to know is it's easier for them not to stop you if you don't make eye contact, so remember: sunvisors down, tunnel vision on whenever you see the cops. Learn the rules of the road, though admittedly this is trial and error. Here are some pointers to get you started:

- Speed limits are 90kph (56mph) on highways and 60kph (37mph) in towns. As in Europe, town limits start at a sign and end at the same sign with a red line through it. Except that in Russia these signs can be **miles after the last house** to give the radar cops a chance.
- Never cross a solid white central line. Cross on dashed lines only, or use designated U-turn areas. Following speeding, this is a common trap.
- Signs often tend to tell you what you can do, rather than what you can't. In most cities like St Petersburg, Moscow as well as Almaty, Bishkek, Tashkent or Ashgabat, if there's no turn left sign then you can't.
- Slow down if you see a police car, even if you're under the speed limit.
- If an oncoming car flashes you, it's probably because there's a police radar check up ahead.

At checkpoints make sure you closely observe the painfully slow speed limits. If there's a 'Stop' sign, wait there until you're waved on, even if it's just 10m to another one. This 'double stop' combination is a nice little earner for the rozzers; don't give them the satisfaction!

When you're **stopped**, first find out why. They may just be interested in where you're from. If they request your documents, again, politely ask: *'prabliem?'* ('Is there a problem?') and add that you're a simple tourist. Be reluctant to hand over essential documents if you suspect the policeman may be difficult and will need inducement to give them back, but definitely don't refuse to hand them over.

If you're stopped for **speeding** ask to check their radar read-out if they don't show it first. For a minor offence that's 10–30kph over the limit, a smile, chat and a postcard of Kate Middleton at Ascot may be enough; if not then pay a 'fine' or *straf* of no more than a few hundred roubles. For that amount don't push your luck and ask for a receipt, and bear in mind they'll often initially ask for something like $50. Negotiate down by showing them the sorry contents of your wallet, which at all times contains no more than 300–400 roubles. It's even worth having a special 'cop' wallet for such encounters.

If, however, they're claiming you were doing 140kph when you were actually doing 57, then ask to see the radar, the speed sign and argue for as long as it takes. When they ask to see your passport, show them a copy of the photo page; same with your visa and other documents.

It's illegal to pay traffic fines in dollars so if they ask for dollars deny that you have any (*U menya niet*; 'I have none'). It's a form of bargaining though don't treat it as such. Usually they'll then ask for a hefty sum in local currency which will be more than is in your cop wallet. You should end up paying no more than $8 unless you were more than 40kph over the limit, or have jumped a red light, both of which are much bigger fines. You may find yourself in their sweaty, nicotine-tinged Lada whilst negotiating the *straf*. Don't let this put you off, it's all part of the experience and who knows, you may have never seen the inside of a Lada up close before.

If you speak Russian then above all don't waste this god-given talent on the cops. Make their job as tedious as possible by smiling a lot, repeating 'tourist' and feigning subterranean IQ. If you're lucky, they might give up on you as a bad job; their next victim will be along shortly.

WESTERN RUSSIA

Western Russia feels like Eastern Europe, and if you're from Europe and are no stranger to centuries-old buildings, aggressive driving or a bored cop with a radar gun, you may not be so impressed with heartland Russia compared to what lies ahead – or indeed to the south via Turkey and the Caucasus. Many people find a **much warmer welcome** along with a more adventurous frontier ambience in the distant outposts, even in the huge cities of Far Eastern Russia. If you're Pacific-bound, you may want to dodge west Russia via the Caucasus to Kazakhstan as it's another country out east.

Heading east of the Urals the adventure approaches, but not until you've traversed the thousand-mile basin of the Siberian Plain and reached Novosibirsk. The principal overlanding route now closely parallels the Trans-Siberian Railway, the only route that traverses the entire country. Even then, it only goes as far as Vladivostok, 10,000km from Moscow but still 2500km short of the easternmost extreme at Cape Deshneva on the Bering Strait.

To the southeast of Novosibirsk lie the **Altai mountains** and a sealed road right up to the western entry into Mongolia at Tsagannuur (see p402). Even if you're not heading for Mongolia, the wild Altai region and the border track to Tuva to the east are well worth exploring (permits required; check the HUBB). You now leave the Siberian plain and ascend imperceptibly onto the like-named plateau towards Krasnoyarsk on the Yenisey River, the natural boundary which separates western Siberia from the more interesting eastern side.

NORTH OF THE TRANS SIBERIAN

Looking at a map you'd think there's only one major highway to Far Eastern Russia, and you'd be right. That road parallels the Trans-Siberian Railway and is now sealed right through to Vladivostok. While the surface lasts, it's easy driving in most weathers. But there's another, less well-known railway reaching to Far Eastern Russian's Pacific ports; the 4400km 'Baikal-Amur Mainline' or **BAM** which runs around the north side of Lake Baikal to meet the Pacific at the port of **Vanino**, opposite Sakhalin Island. Where there is a railway there's a service road. Or so you'd hope.

Now as well known as the Kolyma Highway among hardcore overlanders, the BAM was a failed Stalin-era project similarly built over the bones of tens of thousands of Russians or WWII prisoners of war. Work was suspended on Stalin's death, but revived in the 1970s in the face of cooling Soviet-Sino relations because the vulnerable Trans-Sib ran too close to the Chinese border.

Completed at huge cost, the line recovered from being a Cold War white elephant and now, instead of supplying secret bases and gulags, trains run along it day and night, transporting goods from the Pacific ports, serving mines and sustaining the depressed communities strung out alongside it.

The BAM track traverses just a fraction of Russia's vast eastern wilderness, buried in turn by winter snows then flushed by the thaw before a brief, hot, insect-ridden summer – the only time to consider driving the BAM.

Nearly ten per cent of the line is made up of **rail bridges**, well over 4000 span the rivers and swamps. You may think that as long as the locos keep running, these rail bridges could be used. Sadly that'll be a *niet*. Armed guards man them and even just walking across to ask permission to drive across can earn a hostile: *zapresheni!* (forbidden). Where guards are present, tread gently.

EAST OF IRKUTSK

A thousand kilometres from Krasnoyarsk, **Irkutsk** is a city with a distinctive European feel. Founded in the mid-17th century, a few years after Yakutsk, unlike the former it retains a largely Russian rather than native Yakutian population. A beautiful road leads around the edge of Lake Baikal to Ulan Ude and the start of the Wild East.

Ulan Ude is the capital of the vodka-loving Buryat Siberians and where you can turn south for the main route into **Mongolia** (more on p402). From **Chita**, another old Russian outpost, the **Amur Highway** runs all the way to Vladivostok. A short distance after Skovorodino the **Amur-Yakutsk Highway** leads up to the city of that name and the Kolyma Highway to Magadan, the easternmost point on the Russian mainland accessible in summer.

North to Yakutsk

Soon after Skovorodino, depending on recent weather the promisingly named **Amur-Yakutsk Highway** can be 1150km of either recently graded fast dirt, or all-out mud wrestling carnage. It crosses the BAM route at **Tynda** and is interspersed with sections of asphalt, crossing two mountain ranges before dropping into the Lena basin. With a northbound railway ending about halfway at

---

YAKUTSK AND THE KOLYMA HIGHWAY TO MAGADAN

On a slightly lower parallel than Fairbanks in Alaska, **Yakutsk** is just 400km south of the Arctic Circle. If the road is in good shape Yakutsk could be worth the return 2300km ride from Skovo', even if you're not planning to continue to Madagan. As various private interests tear their way into the region's mineral deposits, the city is one of the few in Siberia that seems to be prospering and possesses a notable proportion of native Yakut (aka: Sakha) and Evenk inhabitants.

Most likely though, you'll only find yourself in sunny Yakutsk if you're heading to, or have come from Magadan. And for the eastbound, Magadan really is the end of the road in Russia.

'The Road of Bones'

The Old Summer Route (OSR) part of the Kolyma Highway has became an adventure traveller's rite of passage, rather like crossing the Sahara. And like the Sahara, it can be over before you know it, or it can turn into an epic. These days there are organised tours as well as an easy way round to Magadan.

Built in the 1930s at great human cost to enable access to the region's rich mineral resources, like the BAM track, the section between Kyubeme and the ghost town of Kadykchan was falling into disuse before its rediscovery. Countless bridges had col-

lapsed, the track has subsided and maintenance fell to the last party to pass by, these days mostly local hunters in AWD trucks or 4x4- and moto adventurists.

From Yakutsk via Khandyga to the turn off (fuel) for **Kyubeme** and the OSR is 700km of good or dusty gravel involving summer-only **ferries** across the Lena and then the Aldan rivers. At this point the official way arcs 650km north via the mining outposts surrounding **Ust Nera**, before bending south to meet the original route at Kadykchan.

The gnarly bit lies in the **240-km section** of the OSR between the outpost of **Tomtor-Oymyakon** (155km east of Kyubeme and hitting a record -70°C in winter) and the end at **Kadykchan**. This can take a couple of days or over a fortnight. Besides the obvious suitability of your vehicle, much depends on the **weather** in July, the optimal month. Hit the OSR in a dry spell and it's only dust you're eating. Hit it wet and the OSR kicks back.

Some 60km south of Kadykchan is the settlement of **Susuman**. At the junction here you can follow the more scenic and less truck-clogged alternative route – the so-called **Tenkinskaya Track** – via Ust Omchug (food, fuel) to rejoin the main road at Palatka, just 80km from Magadan where you either turn back or ship out – usually to Vladivostok or thereabouts.

Aldan, there's more traffic than you'd expect and along the way there are plenty of roadhouses and towns. Getting into Yakutsk itself requires ferrying across the Lena River, now 4km wide, about 80km upstream from Yakutsk.

THE AMUR HIGHWAY TO VLADIVOSTOK

Beyond Skovorodino is the Amur Highway to Khabarovsk. How this highway will survive the road-wrecking 80°C temperature variations of the Siberian seasons remains to be seen. They say sometime around 2012 the length of the new highway was intact, before frost heave, pounding trucks and floods began to break it up, along with the money to do anything about it.

Roadhouses with **food and fuel** are plentiful, although secluded wild camping isn't so easy as the road is built up over the swamps and Armco may stop you getting off the road to good spots. **Khabarovsk** is a relative late developer, but along with Vladivostok is now among the biggest cities in Far Eastern Russia, with up to three-quarters of a million inhabitants. You'll see many Japanese and South Koreans establishing businesses here, and with a **Chinese consulate** at the Lenin Stadium (N48° 28.8' E135° 02.8') on the west side of town just north of the city beach, there's a chance to nip over the Amur for a day trip to China (without the car, of course).

Vladivostok and the end of this particular road are just 850km away, through the wooded hills where the huge Amur Tiger once harried the railroad builders of the late 19th century before its private parts got ground down into aphrodisiacs. Perennially miserable weather doesn't make it the most inspiring place to end your trans-continental trek. But chin up, you're here!

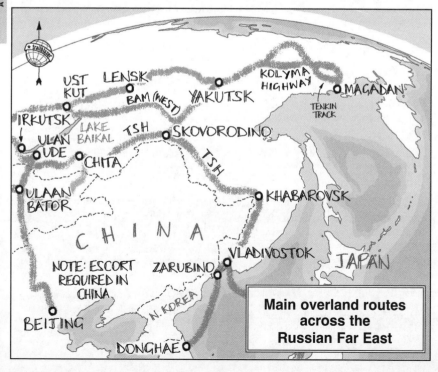

Main overland routes across the Russian Far East

GETTING OUT OF VLADIVOSTOK

Arriving at Vladivostok most will put their vehicle on a ferry to South Korea. Conventional cargo shipping out of Vladivostok is possible, but costs and bureaucracy issues make it a less than attractive option. DBS Cruise Ferry (🖳 dbsferry.com/eng) operates between Vladivostok, Donghae (South Korea), and Sakaiminato (Japan). Offices are in room 239 of Vladivostok ferry terminal, right behind the Trans-Siberian Railway terminal. If going on to Japan after visiting South Korea, you can take DBS again or the less expensive Korea Ferry (🖳 en.koreaferry.kr) from Busan to Hakata. Even leaving the country, customs procedures in Vladivostok can be difficult; it may help to get in contact with Yuri Melnikov at Links, Ltd. (🖳 links-ltd.com). You'll almost certainly need help with customs getting into the country.

Korea doesn't accept **carnets**, but you may be required to make a refundable deposit. Japan does require a carnet in most cases. If you do your research into the laws and procedures, and have the time and patience to work with the bureaucrats, you may get into Japan without one. If you decide to take the less stressful route and use a carnet, you still need to have it validated by Japan Automobile Federation (JAF). Information is available in English on the JAF website (🖳 jaf.or.jp/e). Procedures will go faster if you fax a copy of your document in advance. There are JAF offices near Sakaiminato and Hakata ports, and the ferry company personnel should be able to direct you to them (or even give you a lift if you ask nicely). My website 🖳 www2.gol.com/users/chrisl/japan has plenty of details on the temporary import scene.

From Korea or Japan, most of the major shipping companies provide services to help you get on to your next destination. Shipping agent Wendy Choi in Korea (🖳 wendy-choi2@gmail.com) may be able to help you get your vehicle on a ship to someplace.

Chris Lockwood

Central Asia

Assuming you're wanting to get round the north side of Afghanistan, the four smaller 'stans' of Central Asia offer a much more satisfying alternative to hauling along the Trans-Siberian Highway or the interminable steppe of Kazakhstan away from its eastern corner. The highlights here are the yurt-dappled pastures of **Kyrgyzstan** and the stunning Pamirs of **Tajikistan**. The fiery deserts of Turkmenistan and Silk Route cities of Uzbekistan cap off a rich cultural experience. As in much of this part of the world, central Asian people – be they Kazakh or Kyrgyz, Turkmen, Uzbek or Tajik – are amongst the most hospitable you'll meet, making the irritations just about worth the effort.

Language, maps and money

Although **Uzbekistan** and **Turkmenistan** are slowly moving to modified Roman alphabets, learn the **Cyrillic alphabet** (see p371) so you can read the road signs. **Russian** is still the lingua franca throughout the 'stans although the universal '*Salaam aleikum*' of Islamic lands goes down well.

Gizi Central Asia and Kazakhstan **maps** (1:3,000,000) cover the entire region effectively and the German *Reise Know-How* (1:1.7m) provides better detail and information on smaller routes. As for **guidebooks**, Lonely Planet is the major player for Central Asia.

ATMs are found in all cities but very rarely anywhere in between. Fuel stations will generally only accept **cash** – although in an emergency you'll probably be able to pay in US dollars at a terrible rate. After US dollars, euros will be the most useful **hard currency**. Uzbekistan is the only 'stan where a thriving currency black market prevails. Changing dollars is not difficult here. **Credit cards** are really accepted only in expensive hotels in large cities, and the occasional Western supermarket aimed at ex-pats in places like Almaty and Bishkek.

BORDERS
Most Central Asian borders are open daily in daylight hours. Chinese road borders with Kyrgyzstan are at the 3672-metre **Torugurt Pass** 180km north of Kashgar and the 3005-metre **Irkeshtam Pass** 240km east of Osh, 80km from Sary Tash and about 250km west of Kashgar. It has a slightly better reputation for formalities but it's a long, rough track up from Sary Tash. Expect both to be closed at weekends and on public holidays on either side.

Turkmenistan's borders require mind-boggling paperwork. Here, a pre-arranged **guide** is mandatory to drive through the country on anything other than a five-day transit visa and despite the exorbitant expense – about $100 a day or about half of what you'll pay for the whole crossing – a guide certainly helps at the border. Caravanistan (⌨ caravanistan.com) or DN Tours (⌨ dntours.com) are experts in arranging self-drive logistics and guides. Getting into **Kyrgyzstan, Uzbekistan** and **Tajikistan** is much less complicated. The general rule with border paperwork is, if you need it, someone will ensure you have it before you're allowed to leave the border area. Your carnet is not recognised here; keep it stashed.

Customs declaration form
As in Russia, a **customs declaration form** must be completed in duplicate, sometimes triplicate. The form is normally in Russian (sometimes you might get an English one) and it's essential it's filled in correctly, so if in doubt get an official to help you. Both copies are signed and stamped and one or more is retained by you until you leave the country.

Due to the currency black market, Uzbekistan is the only country where you must accurately declare the amount of dollars you're officially importing. What you don't declare can of course be used on the black market, just make sure that stash isn't found on departure.

Vehicle importation or transit certificate
This varies from country to country and some charge a fee, for example $20 in Tajikistan or 500 som in Kyrgyzstan (they may ask for more). Most countries will give you fifteen days on your certificate, or as long as you ask for, though **Uzbekistan** may insist you can have only three days to transit the country; make sure you ask for more; there's a lot to see there.

Vehicle tax or transit fee and motor insurance
A transit fee is seemingly only necessary for Tajikistan and Turkmenistan, and costs $20 in the former, with another dose on the way out. A dollar amount is calculated on your pre-approved route mileage in Turkmenistan. Turkmen fees are complex and expensive: expect to pay around $150–250 in transit fees,

comprising the mileage-based fuel price differential, mandatory third party liability and numerous documentation fees.

Insurance is required in Kyrgyzstan, and theoretically a legal requirement elsewhere, but only Tajikistan and Turkmenistan demand it at the border. Elsewhere it's sometimes available at the borders and buying it is up to you.

Vehicle documents

Throughout the 'stans a multi-lingual translation of your vehicle ownership documents (in the UK known as an International Certificate for Motor Vehicles) may be useful if stopped, if for no other reason than to add to the 'document surge' with which you can bore and confuse your tormentor.

Obviously, you'll need your domestic driving licence; an International Driving Permit (IDP) to back it up helps. Theoretically, none of the CIS countries now requires your vehicle to be declared in LOIs, visas or passports so you're not 'attached' to your machine and may be able to nip home for a break.

VISAS AND REGISTRATION

The entire visa system throughout the 'stans' is in a constant state of flux and the degree of time, paperwork, difficulty and cost involved varies considerably. Use what follows as a guide only and see what's new at the excellent 💻 caravanistan.com, an invaluable resource for cutting your way through the Gordian complexities of the 'stans. Note that LOI (or letter of introduction) has become rebranded as 'visa support', but amounts to the same thing.

Kazakhstan leads the way with **no visa** required for many nationalities if you spend less than fifteen days in the country – an experiment running until the end of 2017 but that will hopefully become permanent. Even given that it's about 3000 kilometres wide, with that sort of inducement you'd be encouraged to get your skates on and anyway, you can nip into a neighbouring country and re-enter Kazakhstan (ideally the next day) at which point the no-visa metre is reset.

If for some reason you take a fancy to the place, one- or two-month single- or double-entry visas are obtainable in Kazakh embassies in Bishkek, Tashkent and Dushanbe and take a week to process. No LOI needed. The only hassle is that all overland arrivals must register with the OVIR within five days of entering, unless they get a second stamp on their white entry card. It seems that most overland entry points now give you this second stamp. Without it you face a fine when you leave the country. See the caravanistan website for recommended OVIR addresses.

There is no visa needed for **Kyrgyzstan** for nationals of 44 countries for stays of up to sixty days and no requirement to register once in the country. **Tajikistan** nearly followed the above examples but for the moment sticks with visas in advance; no LOI needed. You'll also need a permit for **GBAO** (Gorno-Badakhshan Autonomous Oblast – essentially eastern Tajikistan) to ride the **Pamir Highway**, obtainable from numerous travel agencies or embassies when you apply for your visa for around $75. Gorno-Badakhshan is Tajikistan in the raw, Central Asia's off-roading filet mignon.

The Tajik embassy in London issues same-day 30- or 45-day, entry/exit date specific single- or double entry visas for £140; about as high as it gets. It's said not to bother in Washington, so currently recommended places in the region include Istanbul ($50 while you wait or $25 in a couple of days); Bishkek (same day $75 plus GBAO too; Ashgabat (while you wait if they're in the mood) and Almaty (two days, $110 with GBAO). Expect prices to change.

For **Uzbekistan** an LOI is not required with visa applications for most Western Europeans and Americans, although they'll take at least a week. You'll need an LOI if getting a visa from a consulate in a neighbouring country, obtainable from numerous travel agencies, but with it your visa application is processed more quickly, therefore many choose the regional LOI route. The visa cost varies from $70 to $110 depending on where you're from and where you obtain it as well as sun spot activity on the day. The Uzbek consulate in Bishkek is said to be one to avoid, while Ashgabat again gets good reports.

And finally there is the police state of **Turkmenistan**, the most difficult 'stan for visas. A tourist visa requires booking an expensive 'tour' at around $200 a day all inclusive. Most don't want to do that so go for a **transit visa** costing around $85 allowing three to seven days (usually five) to typically cover the 1200 kilometres between Turkmenbashi and Turkmenabat.

Among the many permutations applying in say Ankara, and collecting in Baku works (don't apply in Baku), or from the other end, apply and collect in Dushanbe a week later. Others report the refusal of transit visas from various other regional consulates. As much as any other country, securing a Turkmen visa is prone to violent consular mood swings but at least with a five-day transit you don't have to get involved with OVIR registration.

If you're transiting **Turkmenistan** westwards for the Caspian ferry, you'll probably need a tourist visa with all that comes with the deal. The authorities are fully aware of the ferry delays so won't issue transit visas .

If you're entering Turkmenistan on a pre-arranged transit visa, your visa dates are fixed. Should you be delayed for four days getting into the country, you'll only have one day to leave Turkmenistan. As it's over 1200 kilometres along the rough M37 main road to the Uzbekistan border post, this isn't a realistic prospect which is why visa-free Kazakhstan looks so much better.

ON THE ROAD IN CENTRAL ASIA

Coming off the Caspian ferry at Turkmenbashi, there's a raft of entry fees, taxes and fuel taxes to pay before you can clear customs. A fixer will help. You should get a **receipt** (*polichenie*) for everything – ask for one before you hand over any money. Unless you're on a transit visa your most important document will be a green A4 sized 'map' certificate, detailing your approved route through Turkmenistan. Without a guide, the customs process can take up to eight hours so note the parking charges in the port.

Heading westwards, aim for the customs office at Turkmenbashi port (N40° 00.37' E53° 00.89') and put yourself on a list for the next sailing. There will be a $20 departure tax and other small fees, but you pay the passenger cost to the crew and for the vehicle once you disembark at Baku.

In Kazakhstan, Kyrgyzstan and Tajikistan, away from the principal cities there's a lack of traffic, though like Russia, beware of **drunk drivers**, especially in Kyrgyzstan. As in most Asian countries, drivers pull out of side roads without paying too much attention, and in rural areas goats, sheep and cattle are a common sight on the roads. Big cities tend to be more aggressive.

By far and away your biggest headache whilst driving in the 'stans will be the *militzia*'s dedication to self-enrichment – or could that be topping up an inadequate wage. **Checkpoints** entering and leaving major towns are a favourite cash-cow, as are cunningly hidden radar speed traps. However clever you are, always play the imbecile, as explained earlier.

Speed limits tend not to be clearly demarcated. Work on 90–100kph on rural highways (though in many places the road condition will make these speeds unachievable) and 50–60kph in towns. Many towns have signposted 40kph and even 20kph zones around schools. Drooling police tend to congregate round these areas (for the fines, that is).

In Tajikistan routes between Khorog and Dushanbe are prone to landslides, floods, earthquakes plus civil unrest around Khorog. It's all part of the adventure, not least the 400-km **Bartang valley** between Khorog and Murghab. There will be rivers. For an excursion into **Afghanistan's Wakhan Corridor** get a visa and permit in Khorog (about $100 each), and cross at Eshkashim but expect it to be hard yakka. A geopolitical relic of the 19th-century Great Game, forget crossing into Pakistan without yaks and a disguise worthy of Younghusband.

Fuel prices average around 50% less than Western Europe, a bit higher than that in Tajikistan and Uzbekistan, and a bit lower in Kyrgyzstan, Kazakhstan and Azerbaijan.

Parts of southern Kyrgyzstan and the Pamir region of Tajikistan experience regular **fuel shortages** which lead to dramatic price spikes at which time you can beware of water and other contaminants. It's the same story or worse in **Uzbekistan** where fuel shortages seem endemic the further you get from Tashkent, so fill up whenever you can and consider added fuel capacity for the odd chance you get the good stuff. It'll help in desolate western Kazakhstan too. Otherwise you can easily buy over-priced watered-down stuff by the roadside, so having a water-separating **fuel filter**, such as the Mr Funnel or similar, is a good idea out here. Petrol in **Turkmenistan** is among the cheapest in the world but as a foreigner they get you with a **fuel tax** or some such at the border.

ACCOMMODATION

Expect to pay between $50 and $70 for **guesthouses** in the capitals and other major cities (lock the vehicle securely). Outside the cities, roadside *gostinitzias* or *chai-khanas* (teahouses) are good, inexpensive alternatives. It should be possible to avoid the decaying and overpriced Soviet bunker-hotels, although for the experience you should consider staying in at least one.

If **wild camping** try to attach yourself to a local roadside café, yurt or farmhouse to legitimise your presence and provide some extra security for the night. If this isn't possible, make sure you're well out of sight of the road thought you're only ever likely to get hassle from a passing drunk or the cops. As it is, camping with a local family will doubtless provide memorable hospitality for which many of the Central Asian peoples are famed.

Elsewhere, Kyrgyzstan and the Pamir region of Tajikistan have extensive **homestay** networks which are cheap, convenient and delightful experiences. They cost around $25 per person half board.The flat deserts of Uzbekistan and Turkmenistan don't lend themselves so well to wild camping. There are many **B&Bs** in the touristy cities of Bukhara, Khiva and Samarkand.

Iran

For many overlanders Iran is an unexpected highlight of their journey across southern Asia, with some of the most cultured and welcoming people you'll meet. Iran is more developed than many expect, except they've taken their own route. Absent here are all the familiar brands of Western consumer culture – Pepsi, iPod, Burger King – that pervade the rest of the planet, although many exist under local names.

The roads are in great shape and the range of landscapes from mountain, lakesides, coasts and desert are especially striking. Human rights for Iranians may not be so rosy, but regionally Iran is far from unique in this regard. Providing you behave respectfully – which out of the car includes women wearing a head covering and an enveloping *chador* – you'll not be harassed by officials for your nationality, despite the high profile posturing of politicians on the international stage. Foreigners' movements within the country aren't tracked too closely, though Iranian friends might be checked up on, so as in many countries like this, beware of putting locals in compromising situations and avoid **political discussions** unless you know better.

VISAS AND GUIDES

This remains the main stumbling block. Getting a visa depends on your nationality and the diplomatic ambience at the time. That got rather turbulent in relation to the economic sanctions imposed due to Iran's nuclear programme. A deal was agreed but the new administration in the US may have its own views on seeing it through. As a result Brits and Canadians join Americans in requiring an **escort** or an outright tour, not a great incentive even if it's said some slip the border without picking up an escort. Americans are unlikely to get in overland, but for Brits a thaw occurred with the reopening of their Tehran Embassy in 2015 and its counterpart in London a year later. It's quite possible that the escort/tour requirement for Brits may get dropped and there's even talk of a visa-free regime for many countries, which will really open the tourist flood gates on Iran. For the moment everyone has to do the visa dance, and for that to succeed you don't want any evidence of having visited Israel in your passport.

As with Russia, using an approved **travel agency** is the only way to go. This can cost up to £200 for Brits or more like €50 for many Europeans. What you actually get is a **visa authorisation number** from Tehran. When applying don't mention travelling by car – that's officially 'not allowed' but you may get through the border fine. With the number, visit the consulate you nominated to get the actual visa. In Turkey they're in Istanbul, Ankara, Trabzon and Erzurum, or quite possibly **on arrival** at the border. Iranian visas are valid for **three months** with the usual 30 days which can be easily extended twice. Women: cover your hair for passport photos. Lots more up to date tips to be found at ⌨ caravanistan.com.

LANGUAGE, MONEY AND INTERNET

Farsi is the language, but the alphabet is Arabic (for numerals see p408) and many young people speak English. The **currency** is the rial, currently about 34,000 to the euro. Iranians commonly quote prices in **toman**: one toman equals ten rials so that's 3400 toman to a euro. You can get by on about 80,000 toman (€25) a day. Bring euros or dollars in cash – foreign credit cards won't work in Iran and getting extra money officially is difficult.

Don't be too irked if you discover you're paying ten times what locals do to get into museums and the like. It's official policy, the same in many neighbouring countries and anyway, it's still pennies. Less officially sanctioned overcharging goes on in some hotels so be prepared to bargain (although hotels do pay higher taxes for foreign guests).

Internet and **mobile phone** access gets restricted by the state at times, but **cyber cafés** with slow connections are everywhere. Reception for foreign mobile phone service providers is patchy; local SIM cards are easily bought and much cheaper, but even they can be hit and miss.

MAIN BORDER CROSSINGS

Iran has borders with seven countries, but most overlanders are transiting between Turkey and Pakistan, or possibly to or from those two countries via Turkmenistan. A **carnet** is needed, though it's said that a local version is available at the border but as you'll need one for Pakistan and definitely India, you may as well include Iran.

There are two border crossings with Turkey. **Dogubajazit–Bazargan** is used by most, a busy commercial border that's open all year but can be slow and a little corrupt. Southeast of Van in the midst of a similarly militarised zone of Turkish Kurdistan, is the **Esendere–Sero** crossing. Less used by travellers, foreigners can be treated like VIPs on both sides of the border, though in midwinter this crossing may be snowed in.

Show your passport to any official that makes eye contact and they'll either wave you in the right direction or stamp it and fling it back at you. On the Iranian side expect a cup of tea and officials speaking good English. They'll guide you through the entrance process which involves a thorough search and triple check of your documents and your car's VIN. There is no fuel tax in Iran (despite what some might try on) and the fuel card rationing system – Iran's way of trying to curb smuggling – has been dropped.

ON THE ROAD IN IRAN

It's at least 2400km from Turkey to Taftan just inside Pakistan, but as always and visa duration notwithstanding, if you can get off the direct trans-national highways so much the better. Along with the wide open desert and distant ranges, the **architecture and bazaars** in cities like **Esfahan**, **Yazd** and **Shiraz** as well as the ruins of **Persepolis** and what's left of **Bam** are what you've come here to see. As a guest in Iran, you'll be waved through toll booths and, as with fuel, attempts to pay will be met with a confusing look to the sky and tut, the Iranian equivalent of shaking your head.

Petrol used to be among the most subsidised in the world, but the impact of Western sanctions and soaring inflation forced Iran to raise the price to around 1000 toman a litre, still the cheapest around.

Highway madness

Highway niceness. © Lois Pryce

Iranian road users are demented so driving through cities can become a contact sport until you get a feel for the rules. To save you some time: there aren't any. A motorway may have three marked lanes following the international convention; actual lane capacity depends on how many vehicles can fit abreast without the outside ones falling off the edge or having a head-on. In Tehran it's often less stressful to arrive or leave in the dead of night.

Steady, predictable driving and keeping the pace if not the style of the local traffic is the key to avoid being shunted. Keep an eye out for cars reversing fast or driving in the wrong direction on the motorways. Usually they're thoughtful enough to confine themselves to the hard shoulder, but it's not uncommon to find traffic coming straight at you in the fast lane.

Roadside recoveries

When you need a break the better roadside fuel stations will often have restaurants and resthouses, as well as mechanics. As for **food**, the only complaint might be that the ubiquitous **kebab and rice** gets pretty repetitive in Iran, but try *dizzy*, lamb stew and pitta – you'll need to ask the waiter to show you how to eat it and so provide some all-round entertainment.

Eating out isn't cheap in Iran, so to save funds be prepared to cook. At the same time the generous Iranians make it hard to pay for anything out of your own pocket, part of a social custom called *tarof*, but make sure to put up a fight to pay if your host is clearly being generous beyond their means.

To Pakistan

On the east side of the country, the nearer you get to the **Pakistani border** at Taftan, the greater the chance of an Iranian police escort scooping you up to make sure you get there. As with so many of these escorts, it's a largely futile exercise intended to protect you from the bandit hordes. If they pick you up a long way from the border progress will be slow as you'll have to stop at checkpoints along the way for escort changeovers and refreshments.

Fill your tank with cheap Iranian fuel well before the border as Pakistani truck drivers and Baluchi smugglers can run the final filling stations dry. As a last resort you can get cheap smuggled fuel in Pakistan.

Entering Pakistan you'll be competing with local lorry drivers for the attentions of those little rubber stamps and their uniformed keepers. The Iranian side involves visiting an unfathomably high number of counters with hand-written ledgers, something that must be tackled in a specific order which you'll eventually divine.

Once you've patiently endured watching Iranian officials valiantly trying to make sense of your unfamiliar documents, there's a tough initiative test to find the actual exit for Pakistan.

(cont'd after Asia Trip Reports colour section)

* * * * T R I P R E P O R T * * * *

London-China-Mumbai – Range Rover

Name, Year of birth, Job Emile Waite-Taylor, 1968, Director
Where and when London–China–Mumbai, 2013
Duration, distance, cost Eight weeks, 17,000km, LR paid
Vehicle model and year Range Rover Hybrid Prototype, 2013
Modifications Winch, roof rack
Vehicle's strong point Diesel-electric amazing at < 5000m
Vehicle problems None
Biggest headache A few punctures in remote locations
Biggest surprise People hospitable and friendly everywhere
Favourite places Kyrgyzstan, China, Himalayas
Next trip USA coast to coast; Cairo to Cape Town

Photo Tong La (5150m), Tibet, © Nick Dimbleby

* * * * T R I P   R E P O R T * * * *

RTW – Land Rover Defender

Name, Year of birth, Job Roy Rudnick, 1974, writer;
Michelle Weiss, 1984, photographer
Where and when Second RTW, started in 2014
Duration, distance, cost So far 900 days, 109,000km @ $65/day
Vehicle model and year Land Rover Defender 130, 2004
Modifications Cabin, susp, winch, air lockers, tanks, heaters
Vehicle's strong point Small outside, big inside
Vehicle problems Diff, susp, pumps, brakes, rocker shaft, engine fire
Biggest headache Robbed twice
Biggest surprise Very kind people in Wakhan Valley, Afghanistan
Favourite places Bolivia, Russian Far East, Mongolia, Tajikistan, Afghanistan
Next trip Ushuaia with '48 Series One

Photo Mangystau, Kazakhstan © Roy Rudnick & Michelle Weiss

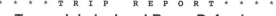

Trans global – Land Rover Defender

Name, Year of birth, Job Haydon Bend, 1985, British Paratrooper
Where and when Trans global, departed June 2016
Duration, distance, cost 2 years, 50,000km so far, £30,000 est
Vehicle model and year Land Rover Defender, 2011
Modifications Winch, long range fuel tank, wheels and tyres, snorkel, spots, compressor, shower, roof tent, 60L water tank
Vehicle's strong point Off-road capability – which we often use
Vehicle problems Roof stressed from the extra weight; standard bushes and ball joints needed replacing after 50,000km
Biggest headache Thailand changed vehicle entry regulations
Biggest surprise How easy it is to travel with a vehicle
Favourite places Tibet
Next trip Africa and India

Photo Kyrgyzstan © Haydon Bend

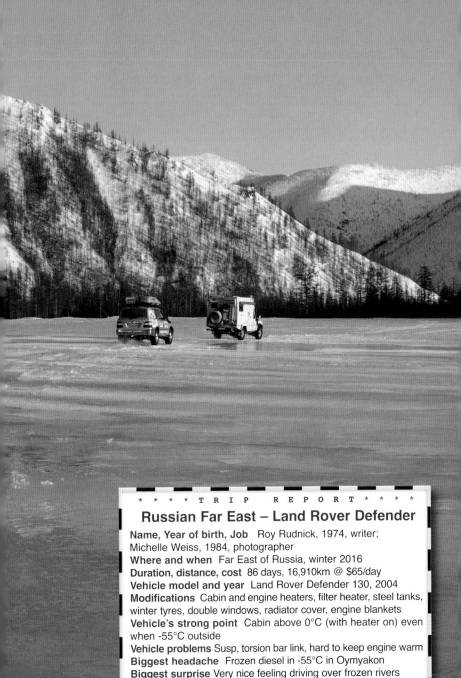

Russian Far East – Land Rover Defender

Name, Year of birth, Job Roy Rudnick, 1974, writer; Michelle Weiss, 1984, photographer

Where and when Far East of Russia, winter 2016

Duration, distance, cost 86 days, 16,910km @ $65/day

Vehicle model and year Land Rover Defender 130, 2004

Modifications Cabin and engine heaters, filter heater, steel tanks, winter tyres, double windows, radiator cover, engine blankets

Vehicle's strong point Cabin above 0°C (with heater on) even when -55°C outside

Vehicle problems Susp, torsion bar link, hard to keep engine warm

Biggest headache Frozen diesel in -55°C in Oymyakon

Biggest surprise Very nice feeling driving over frozen rivers

Favourite places Yakutsk, Magadan, Oymyakon, winter road to Ust-Kuyga (Latitude 70)

Photo Almost 900km over frozen rivers and lakes © Roy Rudnick & Michelle Weiss

Pakistan

Perhaps it's because, coming from the west, it's the first place **English** is widely spoken for a while, many overlanders find Pakistan an unexpected highlight on the drive to India. This despite the fact that the security situation has deteriorated to the point where convoys of siren-wailing **police escorts** herd overlanders swiftly the 1500km between Taftan and Lahore, close to the Indian border near Amritsar. Unless you manage to evade these escorts, before you know it Pakistan has slipped by which will be a great shame.

From Lahore you're allowed to continue unescorted to the border, which also means you can slip off and head north to Islamabad and continue up the fabled Karakoram Highway right through to the Chinese border.

VISAS
Get them in your home country (several regional consulates in the UK) as they can be valid for up to six months. In adjacent countries it's harder. You'll need an LOI from an agency like ⌨ snowland.com.pk, along with a basic itinerary. Long extensions are easily obtainable. If coming from China on the KKH, they won't let you leave Tashkurgan without a visa.

BORDERS, FUEL AND RISKY AREAS
Coming from Iran, if you clear formalities at Taftan after 2pm, expect to be told to spend the night there before joining a free and compulsory armed escort across the badlands of Baluchistan to Quetta, and then right across Pakistan to Lahore. The customs compound is a safe haven for overnight camping. Travellers have long been warned of bandits in **Baluchistan** and in Sind Province (Karachi and Hyderabad), as well as to avoid travelling at night in remote areas; a precaution that's become more widespread in recent years.

Pakistani frontier officials are friendly, straightforward and fast by Asian standards. A **carnet** is necessary, though some have been allowed in without them in the past (an apocryphal story you'll hear from many carnet lands). There's one official border crossing to Iran at Taftan, one to India at Lahore and the seasonal one with China at the 4700-metre Khunjerab Pass, the highest border crossing in the world. As for the Khyber Pass crossing into Afghanistan, it's unlikely you'll want to go there just yet, and forget about nipping over the slender Wakhan corridor to Tajikistan too – the 19th-century Brits made it impassable for a reason. Elsewhere it's sealed roads and the usual mayhem between Iran and India with **fuel** going for around the regional average of $0.70 a litre.

The 630km between the border and the first big town of **Quetta** can all seem a bit close to Afghanistan's Helmand province for some people's liking. Expect a rough, hot, dusty **escorted drive** east of Dalbandin, either belting

Opposite – Asia Trip Reports colour section – Top: Crossing the Russian Far East in winter – see trip report on preceding pages. **Bottom:** The Northern Lights, Latitude 70. (Photos © Roy Rudnick & Michelle Weiss).

along flat out at 110, or dawdling at 50kph. You can drive between the border and Quetta in about ten hours, but two days is considered normal. There's a rest house at Dalbandin halfway; in Quetta you'll be confined to one of three tourist hotels charging tourist rates but negotiable down to $20. At some point you'll need to get a **No Objection Certificate** (NOC) needed to pass through **Baluchistan**, but heading east, Quetta will be your first chance by which time it's nearly over.

What's known as **Waziristan**, the region bordering Afghanistan, more or less between Quetta and Peshawar was never under state control and is now the main front line with – or is it of – the Taliban? Even in the good times overlanders had difficulty in visiting this region and these days it's unlikely you'll get anywhere near it. Peshawar has also become too dangerous to be visited for too long by conspicuous foreigners.

NORTHERN PAKISTAN AND THE KARAKORAM HIGHWAY

The way things are at the moment, Pakistan can be a hard nut to crack, but one highlight that many agree is worth the effort is following the **Karakoram Highway** (KKH) and its offshoots up towards the Chinese, Indian and Afghan borders.

All of northern Pakistan is designated tribal territory that never really came under state control, although that can be said for much of the country. However, it's the significant cultural difference between what used to be called the Northern Areas, now Gilgit-Baltistan through which the upper KKH passes – and the legendarily notorious region once known as North West Frontier Province alongside Afghanistan, which will impact on your experience. It could be summed up on the one hand by the proud, xenophobic and ethnically Afghani Pashtun who occupy the former NWFP (and who make up the core of the Taliban) – and the much more tolerant and approachable Balti followers of the Ismaili Muslim sect living in the north of Gilgit-Baltistan. Here women and girls are more conspicuous and unveiled, social attitudes are more progressive and even Ramadan is not so strictly observed. 'For us, every month is holy' a guy once told me in Karimabad with a grin.

With mountaineers still drawn to several of the world's highest peaks, and the less ambitious attracted to the 'Shangri-La' reputation of the Hunza valley, tourism in the area collapsed following 9/11, then slipped further following the Taliban killing of ten foreign climbers at Nanga Parbat base camp in 2013 in response to US drone strikes. And yet the few who make the effort to get up here admit it's one of the continental highlights.

The free **map** of the KKH still at ⌨ johnthemap.co.uk gives you a feel for the area. Otherwise the two-sided Nelles 1.5m map of Pakistan was the best, as was the better-than-average Lonely Planet **guidebook**. I also used Trailblazer's *Himalaya by Bike* with a detailed and well-mapped account of the KKH, along with 10,000 kilometres of other high mountain routes in this part of the world, including the Indian Himalaya (see p394).

The Karakoram Highway

The Karakoram Highway runs for 1300km (800 miles) from Islamabad over the 4693m Khunjerab Pass on the Chinese border and on to Kashgar in Xinjiang. Built in the 1970s and regarded as one of the engineering wonders of the world, it's become one of the world's great drives, tracing a former branch of the Silk Route along the Indus valley which in places is lined with thousands of petroglyphs dating back 5000 years. It also passes through the densest concentration of 7000-metre peaks in the world, and it's this dramatic contrast with the surrounding peaks towering over the Indus and, later, Hunza valleys far below which makes the KKH so special, especially compared to the higher roads of Ladakh and Spiti in India (see p394).

Part of the reason for all this mountain drama is that the Karakoram is one of the most **seismically active** areas in the world, where the Indian continental plate pushes under the Asian plate, lifting the Himalaya and the adjacent ranges as it goes. Because of the steep, loose slopes, at any point along the mountainous stages of the KKH **landslides** frequently block the road after a downpour or one of the frequent tremors. Diggers move in fast to clear the blockage and rebuild a road, but as you'll read below, bigger landslides can disrupt travel on the KKH for years.

Altitude and lodgings

Sat in a car, the effects of high altitude can easily be overlooked as you cruise up a series of impressive and daunting switchbacks. That is until you need to do something like get out and stand up. Acclimatising takes time: **drink lots of water** and once above 3500 metres or so, aim not to sleep more than a couple of hundred metres higher each night. If you feel bad **descend immediately**; even a few hundred metres helps (there's more on p343).

Lodgings along the way are plentiful and a **fuel range** of 250–300km will cover you. Hotels can get pretty grotty in the villages. If you want a change from camping, look out for the PTDC motels (💻 tourism.gov.pk) dotted around the north. Half board is inexpensive and they're often set in great locations. The *Madina Guest House* in Gilgit is a travellers' institution.

The lower KKH

Leaving Islamabad, an **alternative summer route** to the KKH towards Chilas runs up into the hills at Murree, on towards Muzaffarabad and over the 4170m Babusar Pass. In doing so it avoids the lower reaches of the KKH in **Indus Kohistan** where the welcome from the Pashtun villagers isn't always so warm; wild camping is a bad idea in the KKH between Abbotabad and Chilas. Even before the Taliban came on the scene, police periodically escorted travellers to beyond Chilas – not a town to linger in. After Chilas, you pass the bulk of Nanga Parbat mountain whose 8126m summit is just 40km away, but towers nearly 4½ miles above you.

From Chilas towards the Chinese border there's a lot of **road-widening** construction going on, with frequent detours and long sections of gravel. Pakistan is trying to make sure the port of Karachi gets its share of China's 'New Silk Road' programme.

Excursion to Skardu

Even if you're not planning to cross into China, northern Pakistan still has a lot to offer, with two or three obvious excursions off the KKH. Late spring and early autumn are the best times to travel, but the KKH itself is open all year as far as **Gilgit**, situated at only 1500m and some 600km (370 miles) from Islamabad.

A short distance before Gilgit, the Indus river barrels off eastwards towards **Skardu**, at times a precipitous and narrow road you'll find challenging in a cumbersome truck. Over the churning Indus far below, the occasional quake-proof suspension bridge straddles the tectonic front line, leading to isolated villages and their surrounding terraced plots.

Skardu (2500m, 8203ft) is set in a vast desert-like basin with roads leading to the area's famous peaks and the disputed Line of Control with Indian Kashmir. The route to Askole and K2 is constantly being rebuilt with some very rough sections and daunting hairpins high above the river. East from Skardu to Khapalu is sealed, beyond to Hushe is rough or blocked, but offers astonishing scenery below the 7800m peak of Masherbrum.

Gilgit and the high road to Chitral

Back on the KKH, **Gilgit** is a sprawling administrative centre set in a basin and hosting occasionally violent altercations between the Shia and Sunni. In the bazaar you'll wonder just how many mobile phone boutiques a town needs. From here there's an easy route west that lacks the exposure of the Skardu road, around 360km to **Chitral** over the 3720m **Shandur Pass**, of polo field fame, and with a couple of fuel stops on the way. Ask first if Chitral is safe to visit. It's a spectacular drive up to the broad, yak-dotted plateau where the Pass is situated; a great place to camp or even spend a day or two.

Continuing west, you pass into the Hindu Kush and the NWFP, or Khyber Pakhtunkhwa as the province is now known. The road deteriorates as you drop down past Mastuj and Buni, leading to Chitral, just 30km from the Afghan border. Over the domes of the town's Mogul-era mosque the distant peak of Tirich Mir is visible to the north. Chitral is a congested, one-street town lined with bazaars. Continuing over the 3118m Lowari Pass towards Peshawar is thought to be too risky, so the only way out is to return to Gilgit.

Hunza and the road to Kashgar

Continuing on up the KKH beyond Gilgit, the ascent begins in earnest and soon you arrive at the fabled **Hunza Valley** where people were thought to live to over a hundred on a diet of dried apricots, sunshine and wacky backy. With the 7788-metre mass of Rakaposhi to the southwest, most hotels are based in the town of **Karimabad** (Hunza), although Altit is friendly and cheap.

In January 2010 a huge landslide blocked the entire Hunza valley at the village of Attabad 14km up the road. Soon a **lake** backed up, submerging four villages and over 30km of the KKH. In the intervening years the highway got re-aligned and new tunnels were dug, so that now you no longer have to perch your car on two planks across a skiff to cross the lake.

Passu is a small village where the Batura glacier nearly reaches the highway and where a famously photogenic cluster of spire-like peaks rise above the valley. Some 84km short of the Khunjerab Pass, **Sost** (2790m) is a rough and ready border post where the Pakistani border formalities are done. Without a **Chinese visa** and all the escort arrangements, Sost is where you'll need to deposit your passports to make the two-hour excursion up to the Pass as the valley tightens in around the frost-mangled KKH. Jammed in an ever-narrowing cleft, scree slopes teeter just a tremor or a downpour away from the next tumultuous landslide.

Xinjiang transit, western China

As you top out at **Khunjerab** (closed December–March) the land opens right out into broad valleys dotted with grazing Bactrian camels. Just below the pass is the Chinese immigration post at **Pirali** – expect a chilly reception and heavy searches. Asphalt rolls down 125km to the ethnically Tajik town of **Tashkurgan** (3115m).

It's another 275km along elevated sections of the KKH to **Kashgar**, over the 3995m **Ulugrabat Pass** where Karakul Lake spreads out beneath the snowy mass of Mustagh Ata peak. From the lake you drop down through the Ghez river canyon, pass a checkpoint and head on through Tajik farming villages and past the hazy Pamirs to **Kashgar** from where you're probably heading for the Kyrgyzstan border posts via the Torugurt or Irkeshtam passes. See the box on p398.

The cost of this short transit isn't wasted because, as a way of linking the 'stans of Central Asia with the Indian sub-continent, the **Xinjiang transit** allows a journey among some of the world's greatest mountain ranges and is well worth the weeks and two thousand-odd dollars it may cost to organise. Coming from Europe and Russia via Central Asia, picking up the KKH to Pakistan, visiting India and then heading back via Iran and Turkey is one of the great overland journeys.

ASIA – ROUTE OUTLINES

India

You'd think if you've driven all the way overland across Iran and Pakistan, India would be just another crazy south Asian country. But within a short distance of the border you'll see that yes, there is an 'eleven' on the scale after all. This land of over a billion, the world's biggest democracy (for what that's worth) can still take your breath away: the pollution and filth alongside beauty and ancient splendour, the anarchic road manners and the scoffing at safety or even common sense despite a suffocating bureaucracy, and of course the emerging wealthy elite amid a mass of the world's poorest people. Over 3000km from tip to toe and almost as wide, you can't expect to see it all, but if you give it a try you'll come back with some tales to tell.

... within a short distance of the border you'll see that yes, there is an 'eleven' on the scale after all!

Driving here you'll be fighting for your place on the road with every mode of land transport since they invented the packsaddle and the wheel. Horn-steered Tata trucks and buses trail a wake of carcinogenic soot past Victorian three-wheeled contraptions, slick Bajaj scooters and blacked-out Range Rovers (owned by Tata), while among them humble farmers lead cows to market.

It sounds daunting but once you catch on and recognise that the Highway Code is just an unpublished Dan Brown prequel, India becomes a whole new adventure. By turn terrifying, exhausting and frustrating, above all it's an unforgettable sensory feast to which it's hard to be indifferent. All you have to do is learn fast then keep up. Heading west, many get on their knees in thanks on crossing into Pakistan, knowing that India is behind them. And Pakistan is thought to be so dangerous that, if you give them a chance, the police escort you right across at high speed.

VISAS AND BORDERS

Visas are available in Islamabad in three days with a Letter of Introduction (LOI). Try to get the longer, **six-month** visa, even though it starts on the date of issue. An LOI is not required for a visa issued in your home country. In the UK the job is now outsourced and costs about £82 for a single-entry three-month tourist visa, with six months on discretion. Otherwise, go for the 30-day online visa for half that cost; you'll need to upload documents.

The only land border with **Pakistan** is at **Wagah–Atari**, 20km from Lahore and 40km from Amritsar, open daily 10am–4pm. Arrive early and bring lunch as the immigration process on the Indian side can take hours (the Pakistani side, by contrast, is relatively efficient). Vehicles are often searched. You must have a **carnet** and you should try to buy **third party motor insurance** at the border, although you might have to wait until Amritsar for this.

There are several crossings into **Nepal** (see p397) which include Sunauli in Uttar Pradesh to Bhairawa (south of Pokhara) and Raxaul in Bihar to Birganj (south of Kathmandu). For **Bangladesh** the most straightforward is **Benapole**, 75km northeast of Calcutta. The Indian side is shabby, but the Bangladeshi side is highly efficient, especially for foreigners. They'll want a carnet, but bear in mind that even after India you may find the Dhaka–Chittagong Highway a recurring finale of *Scrapheap Challenge* on crack. The only overland route into **China** is via Nepal, and for **Myanmar** it's Moreh in Manipur; more on p401.

PRACTICALITIES

Part of the fun is that **English** is widely spoken, even to a limited extent in the smallest villages. **ATMs** can be found in major cities and tourist areas. Otherwise the black market or licensed **money changers** might offer a slightly better exchange rate and will be much less tedious than major banks. Bureaucracy for anything from buying a train ticket to extending a visa is truly mind-boggling. It's often easier for a travel agent to organise tickets for you. If you're heading away from big towns, have a stash of pounds, dollars or euros and make sure you hoard small denomination rupees.

There's something to be said for not using the ubiquitous Lonely Planet **guidebook** if you want to avoid the tourist tramlines and ghettos; break out and try the *Footprint India Handbook* in conjunction with Nelles or LP maps. The *Rough Guide to India* is also very comprehensive.

A great Indian road trip website with a lot of knowledgeable local content, as well as routes to places you've never heard of is 🖳 indiamike.com. Local SIM or phone cards or even phones are easily bought and much cheaper than your own and **internet cafés** are widespread.

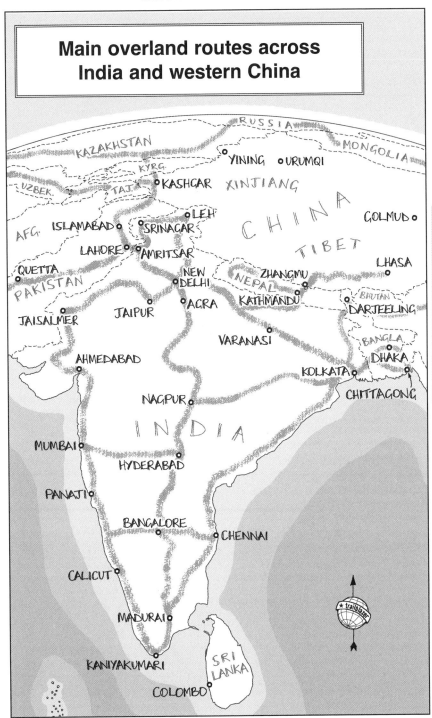

Main overland routes across India and western China

KASHMIR AND LADAKH:

Driving from Srinagar east then south to Manali via Leh is the overlander's equivalent of the Haute Route across the Alps from Chamonix to Zermatt – although much, much higher. If you've made it up to Kashmir, rest up for a few days and take in the beauty of Lake Nagin (far quieter than the heavily touristed Lake Dal) before setting out again; these mountain roads will need you to be on good form.

Set aside at least ten days for the trip as you'll want to spend a few days exploring the monasteries of Ladakh and probably a few days acclimatising in Leh (3560m, 11,678ft). It takes at least two days to cover the Leh–Manali highway. Note that **Srinagar** periodically erupts in anti-government protests led by the Islamic population at which time, most recently in 2016, curfews descend on the town and it's probably a good time to move on or avoid the place.

We set off from Srinagar on a sunny, late August day and drove through the lush Gund valley towards the grassy, high plateaus of Sonamarg. Beyond here National Highway 1D deteriorated as we began to climb through cliff-hugging, vertigo-inducing switchbacks that have been carved out of the fragile rock-face approaching the 3528-metre (11,575ft) Zoji La Pass, the first of the major passes on the way to Leh.

After the pass the road flattens out; there's not much traffic up here except for the endless convoys of very slow moving Indian Army trucks, belching out black fumes as they creep up the hills at 10mph. This whole part of Kashmir is one of the most militarised regions of India, as the country faces down what are thought to be its encroaching foes in Pakistan and China. Within an hour, we had lost count of how many trucks we'd passed. The ceasefire **Line of Control** with Pakistan was close to the north, although the relaxed faces of the soldiers we passed at the few checkpoints indicated relations were at that time much better.

We stopped for the night at **Kargil** – not an inspiring town by any means but the only logical stopover. India's northernmost city lies just three kilometres from Pakistani territory and the town reminds us, to a degree, of Gilgit and Karimabad (Skardu is less than 100 kilometres away) – although ironically the people here are far more traditionally Islamic. We stayed in a hotel just off the main street but got little sleep, thanks to the town's mosques ringing out reminders to pray and eat every two hours through the night – it was the middle of Ramadan.

Bleary-eyed next morning, we missed the bridge leaving Kargil and instead drove two hours southeast into the Suru valley in beautiful **Zanskar**, an interesting side trip but not one we were planning this time around. By 10am we were back in Kargil and this time took the correct road northeast out of town. A couple of hours later the scenery and the culture started to change, first imperceptibly, then dramatically. The jagged peaks, precipitous valleys and poplar-lined avenues around the villages now gave way to a more rounded, barren plateau – a sweeping high-altitude landscape of rocks, sands and undulating, snow-capped peaks. Soon we spotted our first stupa, a decaying white mound beside the road, next to a Buddhist prayer wheel. At the tiny village of Mulbek suddenly Islam was behind us and Tibetan-style Buddhism was all around. It was an extraordinary transition, like crossing a border, but without the usual four hours of paperwork and sixteen stamps. This is **Ladakh**, culturally more akin to Tibet than India – in fact some say it's more like Tibet than Tibet itself now that the Chinese have interfered so much with the traditions there.

We pushed on, snaking up the gravelly, desolate Namika La Pass (3700m, 12,198ft) before freewheeling down the far side, gasping at the myriad colours that the mountain's mineral deposits have left in the rocks.

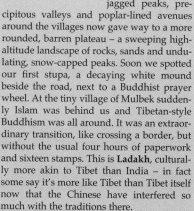

THE WORLD'S HIGHEST ROADS

Shortly afterwards we reached the highest point on the road to Leh, the 4108m (13,479ft) **Fotu La Pass**, then wound our way down to **Lamaryuru** (pictured left), one of Ladakh's most remote monasteries, determinedly perched on a jagged rocky outcrop hundreds of metres below us in the valley. It was hard to imagine that this morning we were in conservative, Islamic Kargil.

We overnighted in peaceful Alchi, some 40km short of Leh, hidden up a winding track across the Indus from the main road. We were at nearly 3000 metres and the evening air was cool as we enjoyed well-earned cold beers. There was little to disturb the peace except the prayer flags fluttering in the breeze and the occasional yak shuffling through the back-streets near the monastery.

Leh was a real shock. Unarguably beautifully located, it's the most easily accessible town in Ladakh thanks to its airport, and the tour groups and backpackers, both Indian and foreign, were here in their droves. Having not seen a tourist for weeks, we took shelter in a quiet hotel and decided to spend the afternoon driving up and down the **Khardung La Pass** – at 5359 metres (17,582ft) one of the world's highest drivable passes. You theoretically need a permit from the town's mayor to get past a checkpoint on the way up (beyond the pass is sensitive territory thanks to the disputed border with China up ahead) – we didn't have one, so after a little pleading and negotiating with the checkpoint guards we managed to leave our passports with them as collateral.

The road to the top was surprisingly good, and not as steep as we'd expected. Thanks to the huge military presence, these strategic roads are kept in good shape by the Border Roads Organisation (BRO), who surely have the toughest road maintenance mandate in the world. At the top I felt pretty sick due to the altitude so we turned tail and headed back to Leh, at a relatively low-lying

CAUTION!
YOU ARE AT 17586 FT (5360 M)
✓Do not exert
✓Try not to spend more than 20 minutes here
✓Refrain from smoking
✓In case of breathlessness and/ or chest pain, seek medical attention immediately
✓Protect your eyes from sunlight by wearing goggles

3500–3600 metres (11,560ft). After spending a day or two exploring the fabulously remote **monasteries** dotted in the Indus valley around Leh, we set off south along the **Leh–Manali Highway** where we drove over what are claimed to be the world's second and third highest paved mountain passes, at 5325 metres (17,470ft) and 5059 metres (16,598ft) respectively. The scenery changed dramatically as we headed south, from the barren steppe of the **More Plains** to the extraordinary sandstone formations of the Sumkhel Lungpa canyon, the grassy plateaus around **Sarchu** and the vertigo-inducing valleys beyond Keylong.

The final stretch to Manali, over the 3978m (13,051ft) **Rohtang Pass**, is the most treacherous of all of the Manali–Leh passes. This is the south-facing flank of the Himalaya which catches all the north-bound monsoonal rains and is usually the first to get snowed up in winter. At any other time the road is muddy, narrow and congested with endless Indian Oil trucks crawling up to Leh to re-fuel the military camps. Every now and then a truck or car gets stuck, causing massive delays. Unless you're on a bike there is no way round.

Finally, we descended through a densely wooded, alpine valley to **Manali**, where it started to rain. It rained all night, and all the next day. It was only early September but the following day we learned that the rain had fallen as snow on the far side of Rohtang, trapping 70 locals and tourists for 24 hours on the blocked mountain roads.

The Leh–Manali Highway is officially open until September 15th, but this is only the cut-off date the BRO are obliged to send out rescue operations in the event of early snow. Don't think for a moment that Mother Nature obeys these dates!

CHARLIE WEATHERILL

Accommodation in India is cheap and plentiful but you get what you pay for. A budget of around £10-15 per night will usually find you in a decent mid-range hotel, outside of Delhi and Mumbai. Excepting the Himalaya, **wild camping** in a country of over a billion is not so easy. Expect visitors.

As for the **best seasons**, the hyper-humid build-up (late March and April) as well as the subsequent **monsoon** (May–late September) are well worth avoiding, even with air-con. Driving into the cool post-monsoon season makes more sense, unless you're heading up to Kashmir and Ladakh where the cool Himalayan season runs from the clearing of the high passes in June until September. After mid-September it's said the road crews of the Border Roads Organisation (BRO) stop clearing the bigger landslides or early snowfall until the following summer, although it's possible to keep driving up there well into October; there's more on the previous page.

ON THE ROAD IN INDIA

Driving in India is about as chaotic and unpredictable as it gets and the driving rule 'Might is Right' is the only law both here and in Bangladesh. Bus drivers are particularly deranged and seem to be chasing impossible schedules. Don't get carried away; **keeping pace with the local flow** works best. Even on a 250-horsepower all-terrain limo you're still at mid-foodchain level. Rear view mirrors are merely for hanging tassles or judging squeeze-through width which is why a **loud horn** is vital.

Locals have no faith in the traffic police (who are virtually non-existent anyway) or the judicial system, so if you're involved in an **accident** the usual advice is to disappear as quickly as possible, irrespective of whose fault it is. With the countless hazards that Indian roads throw at you, **driving at night** is a bad idea. If you must do so, drive with full beam (like everyone else), cover the brakes and expect the worst.

Aside from the ceaseless widescreen chaos and carnage, there are a few other tricks to master in India. The **police**, whilst certainly corrupt, are generally insipid and if you're ever stopped and asked for 'baksheesh' then hold your ground, be firm and rude if necessary, and don't give in. Hard and fast traffic laws are unheard of in India.

Fuel works out around $1 a litre. **Motor insurance** takes a bit of effort. Try to get it at the Pakistani border or the first big town.

Where to go

Alan Whicker wasn't joking when he described India as a vast country packed with geographical, cultural and ethnic diversity. From the snowbound Himalayan expanses of Ladakh to the deserts of Rajasthan; the lush alpine valleys of Himachal Pradesh to the steamy tropics of Kerala and the cosmopolitan frenzy of Mumbai to the mist-clad plantations of Assam and the far northeast. In India there is just **too much to take in** in a single trip before your nervous system begins to twitch.

Your entry point and ultimate destination may dictate your itinerary. If **shipping** onwards towards Southeast Asia, chances are you'll finish up in Mumbai, Chennai or Kolkata, except that now transiting Myanmar (see p401) is possible for about the same cost and infinitely less hassle.

Head for the hills

Aside from some of the classic high mountain road trips (see box on p394), there are a handful of must-sees down on the plains, if you can put up with the fellow tourists. A drive encompassing **Delhi, Agra, Varanasi** and not least **Rajasthan** would leave few people disappointed and includes many of India's cultural highlights, although you're very much on the beaten track.

Possibilities for exploring India's vast centre will give you a memorable taste of more remote, local life. Consider setting out across the **Deccan Plateau** and visiting the beautiful hill station of **Pachmarhi**, the caves at **Ellora** and **Ajanta**, the erotic 10th-century temples at **Khajuraho**, and then ending up in either **Mumbai, Goa** or if time permits, tropical **Kerala** in the deep south.

Driving east of **Kolkata** will be rewarding – the remote and intriguing states of **Sikkim, Nagaland, Manipur** and **Arunachal Pradesh** all require permits. This area is far removed from the rest of India, both culturally and geographically. Far-east India isn't without its problems and ongoing insurgencies, but it's now the way to Myanmar (see p401), so make sure you have a good look around.

In the end does it really matter where you go or what you see? Much of the fun of India is simply the day-to-day driving, observing and surviving – hair-raising and exhausting, though it is. Get used to it and it becomes an experience that you actually might miss one day.

NEPAL AND EXCURSION INTO TIBET

For once getting a **visa** for Nepal couldn't be easier, and after India some travellers experience a kind of reversed PTSD which can lead to dizziness and euphoria. Simply rock up at the border and pay for 15, 30 or 90 days at around $10 a week. You can stay for up to five months per calendar year on a tourist visa, and it takes no time to renew the visa once inside the country.

Coming from India and despite the devastation following the 2015 earthquake, you'll be pleasantly surprised: lodging, meals and **fuel** are as cheap. What's missing is the sound of truck horns and oncoming vehicles trying to rush you on the path to reincarnation. As an **overlanders' hangout** Kathmandu with a vehicle doesn't have a lot going for it. **Pokhara** is nicer and there's a free campsite in the tourist Lakeside part of town, as well as a more secluded spot at Palme, five kilometres up the lake track.

The Tibetan capital of **Lhasa** is just 1000km from Kathmandu along the **Friendship Highway**. With a Chinese visa and Tibetan travel permit, a bus tour via Everest Base Camp (Tibetan side) is fairly easy to arrange at the cost of around $100 per day. Driving up there in your own vehicle is not something you can organise on the hoof in Kathmandu. Special group visas as well as permits must be applied for months in advance – see next page.

Note that the G219 road across the **Tibetan plateau** to Kashgar stays well above 4000m and frequently crosses 5000-metre-plus passes between Lhasa and the G315 Khotan road southeast of Kashgar. Whichever direction you do this, it may be better to grab a week's acclimatisation at around 4000m in a neighbouring country rather than suffering in China at over $100 a day. Once on the plateau there's no quick way down if altitude sickness strikes, bar an emergency flight out of Shiquanhe (aka: Ngari or Gar) airport, near the Indian Kashmiri border.

ASIA – ROUTE OUTLINES

China

Under current policy, it is very complicated to have a self-driving trip for ... tourists, including going through public securities and customs. The complex procedure makes foreigners' self-driving hardly possible in China.

Secretary-General Wei Xiao'an
China Tourism Leisure Association; August 2015

For years driving your own vehicle in China has been restricted to being escorted on expensive 'tours' that took months to set up with approved local agents who demonstrated varying levels of professionalism and avarice as well as eye-watering costs. As always, tales flit around of travellers who waltzed through or hoodwinked officials, very often with either a discreet local vehicle, an 'extra-full' Chinese driving licence or some other inscrutable combination. As things stand most give China a miss or limit it to the transit between Pakistan and Kyrgyzstan (see below).

If you're still tempted, to drive in China you need:
- Customs, national and regional permits for every province visited
- Chinese driving licence
- Temporary Chinese registration plates
- Motor insurance
- Government approved escort; you cover their food and lodging

Then it emerged that China had changed a law in 2013 to permit unescorted transits, but for obvious reasons tour agencies had been slow to pass this on, or less cynically, didn't want to risk being the first to put it to the test. In 2015 an edict was issued: 'China's tourism is going global and becoming more open, aiming to link to the world'. Effective October 2015 all the complex, time consuming paperwork was being ditched to encourage self-driving foreign tourists – but the escort requirement remained.

Part of the problem is that overlanders typically arrive via the remote western provinces of Xinjiang and Tibet where China's been battling civil unrest for years. If it's like other autocratic countries, you can imagine that adversaries within the ruling elite – military versus tourism, for example – are trying to protect their hegemony. The HUBB is a good place to hook up with other intrepid Chinese overlanders looking the share the cost and experience.

XINJIANG TRANSIT

A 3- to 5-day Xinjiang transit organised through an agency can cost **about $2100** and will take a few weeks to organise. Both the Khunjerab (from Pakistan) and Torugurt (to Kyrgyzstan) passes are closed on weekends but you'll need to be in Kashgar on a weekday to get a temporary Chinese licence and number plate.

Chinese visas can be straightforward to arrange in Kathmandu and Islamabad, less so in Delhi.

Entering at the Pirali borderpost on the Chinese side, expect them to be pedantic, or, as they might call it, thorough.

Southeast Asia

Cheap living, good roads in places, a great climate in season, **food** and scenery and amazing beaches and islands all combine to make Southeast Asia one of the world's **most popular tourist destinations**. And now, after nearly sixty years, you can drive there overland on a road built from northeast India across Myanmar – that is until **Thailand** decided to move the goalposts (see below). Again, it's all here, from the isolated Angkorean temples deep in Cambodia's jungle; the western and northern ranges of Thailand and Laos, Malaysia's rugged and unspoilt east coast and the gilded shrines of Myanmar.

Some countries have been well and truly discovered, and the thought of slugging it out with hordes of frizzy-haired backpackers and package tourists might not sound too appealing. But once you get in, having your own wheels opens up the beaten track in Southeast Asia. You'll have no difficulty avoiding Thailand's heaving beaches and the tourist tramlines of Chiang Mai, or skirting the tourist trails of Cambodia as well as picking and choosing your remote jungle destinations in Laos. Myanmar requires an escorted tour and it could be that Thailand's heading that way too.

Southeast Asia comprises six mainland countries and three island nations. **Vietnam** still forbids entry to foreign vehicles, unless they're from Cambodia, Laos or China (buying a bike in all but the latter is possible). And congested **Singapore** gets complicated and expensive when burdened with a car. Of the island nations, **Indonesia** is the easiest to reach, although the numerous ferry rides can become tiresome. Consequently this section focuses primarily on the five easy overlanding countries: **Thailand**, **Cambodia**, **Malaysia** and **Laos**, plus **Myanmar** in the box on p401. Like Japan, you may find Singapore and the other countries more easily visited without a car.

PRACTICALITIES

Visiting this region can be a bit of a holiday if you've come from India, Indonesia or even China. **English** is widely spoken, as is French in much of Indochina. **ATMs** are everywhere in Singapore, Malaysia and Thailand, and **credit cards** are widely accepted at major fuel stations. In Laos and Cambodia ATMs can only be found in cities and tourist destinations and fuel stations want cash. In these two countries it's possible to pay in US dollars saving endless trips to ATMs which often don't dish out large amounts. There are no currency black markets save for a slight discrepancy in Cambodia.

Maps and online info

Besides **OSM** options for your sat-nav, *GeoCenter* have several **maps** covering the entirety of Southeast Asia (1:2m). In Laos and Cambodia, *Gecko Maps* (1:750,000) have excellent local detail and the *GT Rider Touring Map of Laos* (1:1m) is waterproof, and GT also has smaller maps covering parts of Chiang Mai in northern Thailand. Though bike oriented, 💻 gt-rider.com is an online goldmine of information for the roads of northern Thailand and Laos.

ASIA – ROUTE OUTLINES

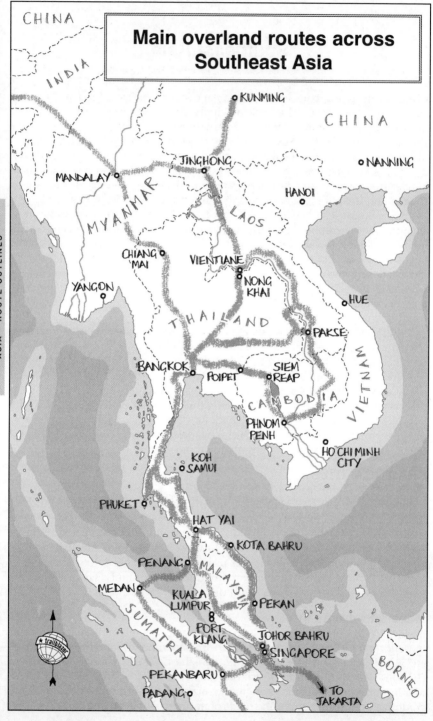

Main overland routes across Southeast Asia

BORDERS

Throughout Southeast Asia you'll need your vehicle ownership documents, your domestic driving licence and an IDP. Your vehicle isn't stamped into your passport in any Southeast Asian country, but some issue TVIPs. **Singapore** is often considered more hassle than it's worth with a foreign car; for more information visit 💻 lta.gov.sg. You need an **International Circulation Permit** (ICP; S$10 in Singapore) in both Malaysia and Singapore – a blue tax disc without which you can't buy insurance.

In an attempt to control issues resulting from a surge of uninsured Chinese RVers in Chiang Mai, in 2016 **Thailand's** Department of Land Transportation introduced much stricter rules for foreign vehicle entry, and in 2017 they became stricter still. Initially, special permits combined with motor insurance costing some 7000 baht ($200) were required and having a carnet helped greatly. It seemed that Laos was also making similar demands, and although Chinese RV visits (which must come via Laos) collapsed, in 2017 the rules were extended to require tour **agency escorts**, as in neighbouring Myanmar. A couple of tour agencies were assigned to issue these permits and escorts, but as this situation is still evolving, keep up with what's happening on the HUBB's Asia page: 💻 horizonsunlimited.com/hubb/southern-asia and the Facebook group linked from there. It's possible it may all get revoked once it's recognised as an over-reaction.

Crossing to **Cambodia** from any of its neighbours is refreshingly efficient and corruption free (Thai customs officials aren't averse to conning tourists out of a few dollars for 'form fees', so have lots of £1 bills to spare). A **carnet** is optional (there's no TVIP here) and so is motor insurance. Hunt around for a Lao-Viet Insurance Company kiosk or get it when you can – no one seems too strict on this, but as you can see, such relaxed attitudes ended badly in Thailand.

Shipping from Singapore to **Indonesia** can be easy with companies such as Samudera (💻 samudera.com) who regularly ship containers to Batam, Palembang and Jakarta in addition to numerous other smaller Indonesian

---

MYANMAR: THE ROAD TO MANDALAY

Another hue to Asia's diverse cultural palate awaits overlanders in Myanmar which, as predicted, now allows **escorted drives** between India and Thailand.

You can get in from Thailand without a tour, but due to the sensitive border area alongside India's Manipur province, an escorted transit (with a bit of sightseeing) is required to secure the border permit. It's up to you to contact agencies like 💻 burma senses.com and finding other overlanders crossing at the same time will reduce costs.

Border crossings are **Mae Sot** (Myawaddy) in Thailand and Tamu/**Moreh** on the Indian side, about 1400km apart, via a direct route. The above agency quoted

$1200-1400 per vehicle for a mixed group of bikes and a Land Rover for the 12-day crossing. This includes B&B accommodation and all other fees except other meals, your visa and fuel which goes for about $0.90 a litre.

E-visas for Myanmar are only valid for fly-ins, not transiting overlanders, so you'll need to apply at an embassy for around $25. Validity is one to three months with 28 days in the country. Nearby consulates include Dhaka, Bangkok, Kunming, New Delhi, Kuala Lumpur, Kathmandu and Bangkok where they can do it in a day for 810 bhat.

It's said there's no overland crossing to Bangladesh for foreigners but a border crossing with Laos may be on the cards.

MONGOLIA: YOU ARE THE ROAD

Mongolia is one of Asia's great destinations; your 'golf course' fantasy made real and on an epic scale too. Food can be rough and accommodation grotty or overpriced in the few tourist areas, so autonomy is a must – it's how most countryfolk live. **ATMs** work in modern Ulaan-Baatar (UB), elsewhere they're rare so carry dollars or local tugriks.

Besides English, Russian is useful and the ring-bound 1:1m *Monsudar Mongolian Road Atlas* has the best **map** detail, though don't assume a bold red line adds up to any sort of a road as you understand it. Otherwise, get a GPS and foster a good sense of direction. **Fuel** quality drops right off in the sticks. The same goes for **drinking water** so fill up regularly or plan to filter.

Visas and borders

At present four land borders are open to foreigners: **Altanbulag–Kyakhta** south of Ulan Ude; **Tsaagannuur–Tashanta** in the far west, 600km southeast of Barnaul in Russia, and **Ereentsav–Solovyesk** 900km east of UB and some 250km south of the Trans-Sib – handy for Vladivostok or if coming from there, visa in hand. Turning up at the **Zamyn Uud–Eren Hot border** for China requires months of preparation (see p398).

Considering where you are, formalities are simple; allow a couple of hours and a couple of dollars to maybe get your tyres disinfected plus $30 for motor vehicle insurance. Carnets out here are nothing more than a type of Cornish ice cream. Americans get a three-month visa at any border, most others get it in advance and it's valid for 90 days.

Mongolian consulates in Siberia

Irkutsk
11 Lapina ul.
N52° 16.8' E104° 17.1'

Ulan Ude
Near corner of Prostsoyuzaya and Lenina ul; look for a large domed roof.
N51° 49.9' E107° 35.0'

Both do 30-day tourist visa for $100 same day, or $55 next day (pay in roubles).

Planned stays longer than a month require registering within a week of arrival at the Aliens and Naturalisation Office at the Ministry of Transport off Genghis Khan Ave, in UB (N47° 54.6' E106° 54.8'). Get thoroughly deregistered there before departure.

If not driving there, consider putting your vehicle on the **Trans-Siberian railway** in Moscow. Direct trains to UB leave weekly, take five days but cost at least $2000.

Driving

'Extreme continental' is how they classify the Mongolian **climate**, which means two out of three days are sunny and rain is rare. UB's average annual temperature is actually a couple of degrees *below* freezing so don't expect to break out in a sweat, even in mid-summer in the Gobi, while elsewhere or at other times, be ready for snowy sub-zero episodes even if the aridity makes deep snowfall rare. Up in the Mongolian Altai it can be freezing at any time.

There are about three paved roads in Mongolia, all emanating from UB: up to Altanbulag; west to the touristy Kubla Khan capital at Arvaiheer and east 550km to Baruun-Urt, with another 350km to the Russian border. Elsewhere is common land with no fences, few signs and indistinct tracks. Once you get your head around the fact that you are the road, it's an easy country to get around compared to the bug-ridden waterlogged taïga to the north. Pick a spot on the map and as long as the steppes are dry and mountains, deep rivers and lakes permit, you can drive straight there.

Therefore, unless you have the instincts of an Alaskan salmon, a GPS and a map (free TPCs 🖳 lib.utexas.edu/maps/tpc) is useful. As in Russia, watch out for **drunks** and drunk drivers at all times of the day, and as usual, avoid driving at night.

Checkpoints are rarely troublesome and Mongolians are generally honest and friendly, but it's not unknown for things to disappear overnight so when camping make sure everything is put away and locked up.

Cheeky Mongol © Tom Bierma

destinations. You'll need an IDP and motor insurance to drive in Indonesia as well as a carnet and a report or a list of documents and vehicle data sent to 💻 imi.co.id (search the HUBB for 'Indonesian Vehicle Report'). Driving standards here are amongst the worst in Southeast Asia. **Ro-Ro** ferries operate between Bandar Lampung and Jakarta (crossing about one hour) and between almost all of Indonesia's islands.

VISAS
With the region being so open to tourists, many countries don't require visas, or issue them at land borders. Those who need them generally pay in US dollars. For **Malaysia** no visa is required for British, US, Australian or EU nationals for stays of 1-3 months; same with **Singapore** which issues 'Social visit passes'. For **Thailand** a free 15-day visa waiver is issued on arrival. This can be extended by 30 days at the Thai Immigration Department in Bangkok, or by exiting and re-entering the country at any land border, but with the new vehicle rules, that's the least of your problems. **Cambodia** issues E-visas online, otherwise get a 30-day tourist visa on arrival from $30, dependent on nationality. **Laos** also does a 30-day visa at land borders from $35. Most foreign visitors can visit **Indonesia** visa-free for 30 days.

POLICE AND FUEL
Outside of Singapore and Malaysia, police in all Southeast Asian countries are not averse to a bit of petty bribery. If you're stopped by the police, don't attempt to speak the language, be polite and firm. Spurious accusations of petty offences should be strongly denied; if it's speeding ask to see the radar reading (Thai police are especially fond of estimating your speed). Continued harassment is unlikely and with a little patience the police will usually let you carry on because it's far easier for them to pick on the poor locals.

Unless you're in a restricted area (in Long Chen in Laos, for example, or near some sensitive parts of the northeastern Thai–Cambodia border) checkpoints are unlikely to give you any hassle.

9

AFRICA
ROUTE OUTLINES

Of the three continents covered in this book, Africa presents the biggest challenge, or at least that's how some perceive it. Many overlanders have travelled the world and the seven seas, but have never set foot in Africa. As always, it's not as bad as you hear – the hotspots are well known and easily avoided. Moreover, the Chinese 'roads-for-resources' programme has sealed the gaps on the main routes through Congo, north Sudan and northern Kenya, now making the trip viable in a regular 2WD. Of course it remains to be seen how these rapidly built roads will themselves handle a few monsoons or Saharan summers under the wheels of the typically overloaded local transportation.

The headaches of crossing Africa include regional conflicts, road conditions, the climate (in the wrong season) and petty corruption, but above all getting a **visa** (a **yellow fever** certificate is often required). Some countries only issue visas easily in your home country; on the road consulates will present hurdles, delays and eye-watering tariffs while as elsewhere, former border visas are becoming online **e-visas**. This all depends on your nationality, where you apply and where you cross a border, and not least, the cut of your jib or their mood on the day (things often change when consular staff move on). What works for one overlander with a Colgate smile gets you nowhere, and all your advance planning can unravel. Yes it's part of the adventure, but what can't be sorted can lead to unplanned expenses. Having a **second passport** can definitely help when making visa applications, as well as having enough **paperwork** (relevant, kosher or otherwise) to choke a full-grown hippo.

© Rob & Ally Ford

And yet behind all this aggro is the iconic lure of the landscapes and, less expected by overlanders, the generosity and warmth of the ordinary people you'll encounter who struggle to survive under some of the most mismanaged kleptocracies on earth.

GOING REGIONAL

As much as any other continent, overlanders feel compelled to take on a **trans-African crossing** from Casablanca or Cairo down to Cape Town, not least because it's one of the great overland routes. When starting from Europe, once you're south of the Sahara you may as well keep going, although crossing the Sahara these days can be just a two-day road drive. Even then, getting to Senegal from Morocco, and especially Sudan from Egypt, is quite a trek and once in these countries your regional roaming options are still limited by topography, climate and politics. So, unless you're an old hand, initially most will see Africa as somewhere to cross rather than a place to explore.

One exception is **Morocco** (see p408). With enough of an edge to keep you on your toes, it offers the perfect introduction to Africa and makes a great place for a shake-down trip in advance of longer travels in Africa or elsewhere. Another is **southern and eastern Africa**. Relatively stable, sharing time zones with Europe, and with winter coinciding with the northern summer vacation period, many tour operators offer **fly and drive tours** here. From South Africa itself, visits to half a dozen nearby countries can be ticked off as far north as Uganda and Kenya, and on tour you can have the drive of your life, even if – or is it because? – it's all organised for you.

In between lie the feral republics of **central Africa**; principally the Democratic Republic of Congo (DRC). No one heads here for kicks as they do in the places mentioned above, as complications with Angolan visas can mean an onerous 2400km run through southern DRC to or from Zambia (see p418). Probably more than anywhere else in Africa this is a place to test yourself and as such, along with the former central Saharan crossing (see p407) it's the bit you dread most but remember best.

MAPS AND GUIDEBOOKS

The three 1:4m-scale **Michelin maps** (# 741, 745 and 746) are the best paper maps for planning a trans-Africa trip, though in central Africa they're not keeping up – no paper map is. For the GPS Garmin's **North Africa Topo Light** is well worth a look as it's inexpensive and produced in collaboration with OSM (see the detailed review and comparison on ⌨ sahara-overland/maps).

Lonely Planet, Rough Guide and Bradt produce regional guidebooks in paper or e-book form with useful titles for parts of North, southern and East Africa, but don't keep up with the less visited countries. For that you have the internet: LP's **Thorn Tree** (⌨ lonelyplanet.com/thorntree) or of course the **HUBB** ⌨ horizonsunlimited.com/hubb.

FUEL PRICES, MOTOR INSURANCE AND CARNET

While in Algeria **diesel** costs $0.12 a litre and in Egypt it's just over twice that, in Sudan, Ethiopia, as well as Nigeria and Mozambique you pay around $0.60 cents a litre and overall **$0.80 cents** a litre is the norm for diesel (85c in Morocco, less in Western Sahara). In Namibia it's also 80 cents, in South Africa 90, but at this time in DRC, Zimbabwe and Zambia fuel cost nearly the same as Europe. **Petrol** (probably low octane) is cheaper in Nigeria and Mozambique, but overall budget on around **$1 a litre**. Unleaded is virtually ubiquitous and new laws intend to have high-sulphur diesel (imported from Europe, not just produced locally) banned or restricted in East and West Africa.

AFRICA – ROUTE OUTLINES

For non-UK EU nationals your domestic **insurance** can cover Mediterranean countries. Elsewhere, buy as you go. Countries in a given region often band together in common markets (sometimes sharing a currency too) with one policy covering all participants. In West Africa the ECOWAS agreement (⌨ ecowas.int) is one; on the east side COMESA (see p425) does the same from Sudan to Zimbabwe, and ECCAS supposedly covers Central African states from Chad to Angola. Certainly in the ECOWAS zone motor insurance – known as a *carte brune* (⌨ brown-card.ecowas.int or ⌨ cima-afrique.org) will be valid from Senegal to Chad, so it's safe to buy months of motor insurance for the time you expect to spend in that region.

As for **carnets**, you'll need one in Egypt, elsewhere they can sure make borders easier until you get to Angola or Tanzania.

Trans-Africa routes

Typically a drive across Africa clocks up some **11,000km/7500 miles** and takes two months. Today, overland access in North Africa and the Middle East is still reeling from the consequences of 2011's Arab Spring. As a rule, political instability develops quickly and subsides very slowly, while lawless regions in an ostensibly stable country are another where overlanders can blunder in. Once in a while someone manages to cross a region long thought off limits. The word gets around and others follow as such a route tries to circumvent logistical and bureaucratic visas contortions. And these days news spreads very quickly online. All you have to divine is whether the new route is here to stay, an aberration and above all, whether they've even heard the news at the border posts you'll pass through. The key thing is: **once you're in** a country, you're in and ought to be able to stay there for the duration of your visa.

EAST OR WEST SIDE?

Negotiating Africa overland is like a game of snakes and ladders and right now there are only two ladders across the Sahara: the **Nile Route** down to Khartoum then east into Ethiopia for Kenya where the driving eases through Tanzania and southwards via Zambia, Malawi or Mozambique to South Africa. Or the **Atlantic Route** for Senegal or Mali which converges on Nigeria before slipping down the equatorial west coast for Namibia or Zambia.

East is easier and offers more classic African icons: pyramids; Nile; Kilimanjaro; Serengeti and Victoria Falls. The **western route** (via Cameroon and the Congos) needs a cunning visas strategy and an appetite for adventure.

The way things have been in recent years, once you start down one ladder it's fairly dangerous or unpredictable to get across to the other until you get down to Zambia where the neck of the 'Y' joins up. The enduringly ungoverned mass of eastern DRC as well as the Central Africa Republic (CAR) and southwestern Sudan see to that. If you're thinking of driving **there and back**, depending on your nationality visas and other challenges fall into place better if you go down the west side and up the east.

North Africa and across the Sahara

North Africa can provide a taste of the continent which is distinctly different from sub-Saharan Africa and it was the Dakar Rally of the 1980s which helped establish the popularity of exploring the desert in your 4WD. The problem is the best countries for true desert travel: Libya, Algeria and parts of Niger and Egypt either require an expensive **escort** or are not places you'd want to visit unless you're good mates with Andy McNabb.

The **Sahara** has for centuries been an ungoverned barrier separating what lay to the south from the Arab-influenced Mediterranean. In the 1980s the classic crossing ran from Morocco or Tunisia through Algeria down to Mali or Niger. Then in the 1990s political troubles beset northern Algeria and a desert-wide rebellion in the south cut off northern Mali and Niger. With that region closed the **Atlantic Route** opened up with the waning of the unconnected Polisario war. A few years later Libya opened its borders with Tunisia and Egypt for overlanders. Then in the Noughties desert tourists became targets for kidnappings by Islamist groups, and now post-Arab Spring, much of the central Sahara has reverted to its lawless roots.

WHERE CAN I SEE THE REAL SAHARA?

The Sahara stretches from the Atlantic to the Red Sea, but rolling along a highway past either you don't exactly feel like Lawrence of Arabia. To experience the full exhilaration of the desert you have to get onto the sands and pistes, but in recent years the security implications brought about by groups like AQIM make this risky.

Libya is clearly a basket case and will remain so for a while. It's the same with the adjacent Ténéré of northern **Niger** and even in the Western Desert of **Egypt** where, in 2015, a dozen tourists were mistakenly shot up by Egyptian gunships hunting smugglers.

Algeria (pictured) is the greatest desert driving destination of all, and actually safe enough away from borders, but past kidnappings followed by mandatory **escorts**, closed borders and an oil-based economy that puts little value on desert tourism have greatly restricted overland tourism there.

The Tubu of northern **Chad** never had any truck with AQIM-types and the spectacle there equals anything in the Sahara. The problem is getting there through West Africa, let alone the expensive escorts.

Tunisia may have a corner of the Grand Erg sand sea, but has also proved to have weak security and is a pricey ferry crossing just to drive some dunes. In northern **Sudan** you might try to traverse the Nubian desert east of the Nile, but most here are intent on simply getting stuck into the east coast transit.

The **Malian** Sahara has long been off limits which leaves **southern Morocco** (see p408) including its part of Western Sahara, as well as **Mauritania**, which is most interesting in the Adrar region. We were there in early 2017 so see what's new at ⌨ sahara-overland .com.

ARABIC NUMERALS										
0	1	2	3	4	5	6	7	8	9	10
·	١	٢	٣	٤	٥	٦	٧	٨	٩	١٠

MOROCCO TO MAURITANIA

Coming from Europe, **Morocco** offers ancient Moorish cities on a par with western Asia, as well as tracks over the High Atlas to the fringes of the Sahara.

Ferries leave the Spanish ports round the clock and take as little as 30 minutes. There's no need for a carnet or in most cases, a **visa**, making entry and paperwork relatively undemanding. Even then, if it's your first time out of Europe, Morocco can be intimidating: cross to Tangier Med, a modern port with few hassles. Elsewhere, stick with someone who knows the ropes.

Imperial cities excepted, northern Morocco isn't so interesting. The fun begins in the **Atlas** which, along with the desert beyond, is best in the **intermediate seasons** when it's neither baking in the desert or freezing on the High Atlas. At any time after summer you can get massive disruption from floods. **Fuel** costs about 20% less than in Europe, while food and lodging can be less than halfway off the tourist 'tramlines'. All these qualities make Morocco an ideal place for a test run as well as a great destination in its own right. Garmin's North Africa **map** is inexpensive and detailed; for the long version see my *Morocco Overland* book or 🖳 sahara-overland.com/morocco.

Mauritania

Even before they sealed the Mauritanian section, the **Atlantic Route** to Mauritania was a rather dull way of crossing the Sahara. Inland routes to Moroccan Western Sahara aren't so inviting, so most bomb down the coastal highway to the Mauritanian border where a few kilometres of sandy piste lead across No Man's Land. On the link above you'll find a **blank form** to fill and print with your passport and entry details – it speeds up the checkpoints in Western Sahara and Mauritania. In 2017 visa prices at the border dropped to €40 but fixers now demand a bite; a taste of things to come.

Morocco was all very well, but many travellers feel needlessly intimidated by the many checkpoints on the highway south to Nouakchott where they can get a **Mali visa** (N18° 06.5′ W15° 58.7′; 6500UM; same day) or head for Senegal. In fact, security wise Mauritania is on the case, while as yet not insisting on border-to-border escorts. This means you can roam the southwestern corner of the country – anywhere to the far north or east is less interesting, may be restricted and is potentially less safe too.

So for a taste of the Sahara take the sandy, 520km piste east paralleling the railway towards **Atar** (rest up at *Bab Sahara*, on the west edge of town at N20° 31.2′ W13° 03.7′). Then explore the sandy canyons and rugged tablelands of the Adrar plateau as far as Chinguetti or Ouadane, as well as excursions to the south. Or consider the more demanding crossing south towards Tidjikja, ideally not alone (they're slowly improving this road, but it'll be a few years). From Tidjikja head for Kiffa and then Mali (with a visa). As it is few try this option – a memorable fortnight in an under-rated African highlight.

West Africa

West Africa covers the sub-Saharan region from Senegal as far east as Cameroon and Chad. Much of it was once under French colonial rule and today **French**, and to a lesser extent English (in the Gambia, Sierra Leone, Liberia, Ghana and Nigeria) will be the **languages** you'll use the most. A romantic notion is to drive right along the **Atlantic coast**; the problem is that between Dakar and the Ivory Coast border, there is no road and some countries in this corner of West Africa can be hard work. Coming from the north and still wet behind the ears, most Cape-bound drivers make it easy on themselves by reducing borders and so visas to save their energy for central Africa where there'll be less choice. As it is, since the Arab Spring, right across West Africa anti-government protests and coups (or coup plots) have become more numerous, and with key countries like Mali and Nigeria under attack and the ebola epidemic of 2014, overland travel dwindled on this side. Southern Mali and Burkina remain safe to cross, despite a bloodless coup in the latter, and at this time the scourge of Boko Haram is either being contained in northeast Nigeria, or is being trounced by more newsworthy atrocities.

Local currencies in West and Central Africa

Travel in this region is eased by the **CFA currency** which is shared by Senegal, Guinea Bissau, Mali, Ivory Coast, Burkina Faso, Benin and Niger. It's abbreviated on currency websites as CFA XOF. The other CFA currency zone (CFA XAF) covers six Central African countries: Chad, CAR, Cameroon, Congo, Gabon and Equatorial Guinea.

You can't use one in the other zone, except possibly near borders between the zones but the international rate of exchange is the same for both and pretty stable at 655 to a euro.

WEATHER IN AFRICA

Two climactic factors govern your departure and route: summer in the Sahara and the equatorial monsoon. The Sahara crossing in Mauritania and Sudan is a road, but when things go wrong you need to act decisively when it's 45°C (113°F) in the shade.

More commonly though, the **Saharan summer** is a time of sandstorms when night time temperatures stay over 30°C for weeks at a time. This round-the-clock heat drains your body and stresses old engines, and travel becomes endurance rather than enjoyment. It's not a time to be exploring desert pistes alone.

In central Africa the **rains** fall for up to ten months a year, certainly from June to September alongside the equator, and to a lesser extent from February to April. South of the equator the sealed road network makes the rains in eastern and southern Africa less of an issue from November to April, although your ability to explore off the beaten track will be greatly reduced.

If heading across the continent from Europe and wanting an easy time of it, **set off around October or November**, driving into the Saharan winter and the central African dry season.

WEST AFRICAN VISAS

Burkina Faso visa in Bamako
Off rue de Guinee, just east of the US embassy. N12° 37.9′ W08° 00.9′

Three photos and 24,000CFA for a 3-day transit visa issued same day, or 94,000CFA at the border.

Nigerian visa in Bamako
South of the bridge, close to the *Sleeping Camel* on the RN7 to the airport. N12° 37.0′ W07° 58.6′. Displays a visa price list for each country. 40,000CFA. Recommended.

Ghana visa in Ouaga', Burkina Faso
Ave d'Oubritenga. N12° 22.7′ W01° 30.6′ Four photos and 15,000CFA. 1-3 days.

Nigerian visa in Accra, Ghana
Akasombo Road, Airport Residential Area. N05° 36.7′ W00° 10.8′

Photos, copies of passport, form, Ghana visa plus itinerary, insurance, vehicle ownership papers, carnet and at least $100. At the border you may need Yellow fever certificate.

Benin visa in Accra, Ghana
Switchback Lane, Cantonments N05° 35.2′ W00° 10.8′
Two forms, photos, 10,000CFA, same day. Also in **Ouagadougou** somewhere on Ave Prof. Joseph Ki-Zerbo. Cost 40,000CFA and issued on the same day.

SENEGAL, MALI AND BURKINA FASO

Leaving Mauritania, the border on the Senegal River at **Rosso** long had a reputation for intimidation on both sides. Many avoid the ferry and head 50km downstream to the **Diama** dam bridge (via a 'national park'; fee required). In Mauritania police and customs will each try for a €10 fee – or just stick to your guns. Crossing the bridge might cost a few thousand CFA but on the Senegal side **visas have been ditched** for most. Here you pay an *official* 2500CFA for a **two-day laisser-passe**r (aka: passe-avant) to get you to Dakar port, Gate 8 where Douane (customs) extend it for free, or stamp your carnet.

Leaving the border, several **checkpoints** on the road to St Louis might also be angling for fines for minor or invented transgressions. Regional **Carte Brune insurance** is sold at the border for up to six months, or you could have bought it in Nouakchott (though it's not valid for Mauritania).

Like many African capitals, **Dakar** can be a grind (Mali visa, 25,000CFA, same day; Burkina 48,000CFA, next day) although the former colonial capital of **St Louis** just down from the border is worth a stop. Some 18km south of St Louis the ever helpful *Zebrabar* (N15° 51.9′ W16° 30.7′) is a popular hangout were it not for the rush to visit Dakar port customs.

With the reputation of Senegalese borders, many head directly into Mali and with a visa from home, Nouakchott or Dakar you're in. The road is sealed from Kiffa to Nioro and on to **Bamako**, and there's a sealed route coming in from Tambacounda in Senegal via Kayes too. In southeast Mauritania stay clear of Nema for the moment.

Bamako can be a little crazy and even risky after dark, but it's a useful place to obtain visas, especially Nigeria (see box above) which is getting harder and may be an e-visa by now. South of the main bridge *The Sleeping Camel* (N12° 37.5′ W07° 59.2′) is a good place to meet travellers.

Located a thousand kilometres northeast of Bamako, **Timbuktu** was briefly over-run by jihadists, and tourists kidnapped in 2011 are still in captivity. It may be under state control but along with Gao, is right on the front line with the north. Travel further south in Mali is fine bar the pricey fuel.

EAST FOR CHAD OR NIGERIA
From Bamako, sealed roads run via Burkina Faso to English-speaking Ghana, or Benin. From Niger there's little chance of getting into Algeria, and beyond Zinder the bitumen breaks up and disappears altogether around Lake Chad. This was always a tough bush track of at least two days to **Chad**'s expensive capital, N'Djamena, but these days it passes through Boko Haram territory, so no one's done it for years. As it is, Chad's only viable exit is south into Cameroon. On the east side around Abeche they get jumpy and if you do get into Sudan (one guy managed it in 2015), you'll need to join escorted convoys from Al Junaynah through Darfur to Khartoum.

© Rob & Ally Ford

Nigeria
Despite **cheap fuel** (often watered down just over adjacent borders) and a chance to commune in English, **Nigeria** didn't have a great reputation even before the wave of atrocities carried out by Boko Haram. But this is a country of 100 million people so as long as you keep your wits about you, a transit ought to pass without incident. Unless you know better, simplify things by taking a low transit across the country, perhaps swooping past Abuja for some key visas.

Abuja to Cameroon
In Abuja many camp free round the back of the Sheraton Hotel (N09° 03.8′ E7° 29.1′). Pull up to reception, ask nicely and they'll show you where to go and where to shower by the squash courts. They may refer to you as a 'tourist', as virtually none of the other foreigners in the hotel will be. Down on the southeast coast, **Calabar** remains your best chance for an easy Cameroon visa, then, as long as it's dry, head up to Ikom and into Cameroon at **Ekok**.

SOUTHBOUND VISAS IN WEST AFRICA

Angola visa in Accra, Ghana
Liberation Road, just west of airport. N05° 36.60′ W00° 10.62′
Bank statements plus copies of everything; 30-day tourist visa €140. From two days.

DRC visa Cotonou or Lome
Carré 221 Ayélawadjè, Cotonou. 8-day transit, same day; €22. In **Lome** (Togo) N06° 08.77′ E01° 12.7′, One month, CFA40,000. May need to become a temp resident.

Cameroon in Abuja, Nigeria
469/470 Lobito Crescent, Wuse 11 (near Hilton Hotel). N09° 04.24′ E07° 29.4′
I month; 90-day validity. Two days, 50,000CFA or N17,500. Or try Calabar.

Congo-Brazzaville (Abuja)
Same road as Cameroon embassy. Same day N13,000–18,000, next day N10,000–12,000. Price varies. Valid 90 days from issue for a single-entry 30-day visa. Or try Doussala border with Gabon: 15 days for 20,000CFA.

DRC (Abuja)
Azores St. N09° 04.9′ E07° 28.1′
N17,000, similar documents to Angola – better off in Cotonou.

Cameroon visa in Calabar
Off Spring Road. N04°59.8′ E08°19.44′
Two photos and forms. While you wait from 51,000CFA.

Western Route via DRC

Once you've made it to Cameroon you should be getting into the swing of things. On the forecast may be days of churned up mud tracks, heat, humidity, over-friendly insects, opportunistic cops and obnoxious consular staff until, slightly stunned, you pop out of Angola, or DRC's southern frontier, into southern Africa. Enjoy any new tarmac roads while they last. Chances are the climate, pounding cargo and lack of maintenance will see them only last a few years. This western route could be experiencing a golden age of all-weather accessibility before the jungle reclaims all.

With the various **visa hassles** on this route, it's often a case of simply getting to the next country rather than cruising around looking for cool stuff, as you can on the east coast. Many will be out of their comfort zone, locked in the charm offensive to get visas, or driving dawn-to-dusk before others expire. All this can sour the rhythm of your trip and even on the easiest routes this'll be the toughest stage of your trip, so it's common to **team up** with others.

It's also worth noting that **maps** are hit and miss in this part of Africa. Place names won't match up and you'll pass through villages that don't exist or miss villages that do. It's all part of the fun, but having Tracks4Africa (tracks4africa.co.za) and other pre-researched **waypoints** comes into its own here, allowing you to explore with some vague idea of where you are some of the time. Along with that, knowing some **French** (though not always letting on) and having a good stash of cash is a big advantage. It's a jungle out here, but usable ATMs don't grow on trees.

GABON TO ANGOLA

On the new road from the Nigerian border, most have an easy time in Cameroon, despite having to hang out for days in Yaounde getting what may be the final batch of visas. And despite the extra visa, most head for **Gabon** on their way to Congo-Brazzaville because, as you'll read in the box opposite, it's a whole lot easier. Forget visiting **Equatorial Guinea** – for some reason they severely discourage overland access.

GETTING SOUTHBOUND VISAS IN YAOUNDE, CAMEROON

Most of the embassies you want are in the Quartier Bastos at the north end of town.

Gabon
Rue 1816, Bastos. N03° 53.7′ E11° 31.2′
Photo and form, 35,000CFA. Pick up next day express, or three days. Smarten up and learn some French or don't expect a warm welcome. Also said to be available at the border.

DRC
Blvd de l'URSS, Bastos. N03° 53.6′ E11° 30.9′
Photos, form, copy of passport, 100,000-150,000CFA, or **get it in your home country**.

Congo
Rue 1815, Bastos. N03° 53.7′ E11° 31.2′
Photos, vaccinations and bargain for 60,000CFA. 9.30am–noon. Four days.

CAMEROON TO CONGO DIRECT

If a Gabon visa proves to be a pain in Yaounde fear not, it's possible to drive directly into the Republic of **Congo** (or 'Congo-Brazzaville' as it's known to distinguish it from the river or the DRC). What you save on acquiring one less visa you may pay back tenfold hacking along overgrown, waterlogged tracks until you get to Ouesso.

Ouesso via Socambo

Opposite the southeast corner of Cameroon, the key town to aim for is **Ouesso** on the Sangha river in Congo-Brazza, about 800 clicks from Brazzaville.

The feral option runs east from Yaounde along the N1 via Bertoua to Yokadouma then south another 300km to **Socambo** (N01° 41.6′ E16° 07.8′), a few kilometres – but over the river and border – from Ouesso. Bush meat poaching, gun-running and border disputes abound in this forgotten corner of Cameroon

where the heart of darkness is lit by a 10-watt bulb. Last heard, the tarmac ends some 350km east of Yaounde, at Mandjou.

From Socambo logging ferries come and go from the mills at **Pokola**, about 60km downstream, but on the wrong side of the Sangha for Ouesso.

Ouesso via Mbalam

An hour south of Yaounde, turn east at Mbalmayo onto the N9 and follow logging tracks 430km southeast to the border at **Mbalam**. On the Congolese side little used tracks lead through Mpé and Souanké to Sembe from where in the dry it's an easier 200km to Ouesso. Expect a couple of days of tough conditions until you're east of Sembe.

South of Ouesso the tracks improve greatly as the tarmac creeps northward from Oyo. Next stop, Brazzaville on the Congo river, opposite the border with DRC.

After Cameroon, Gabon is expensive, the fuel isn't and the roads feel empty. Along the equator there are **no seasons** to speak of; it rains pretty much all year so it's a matter of luck whether you hit a bad road during a wet spell. Rain is a mixed blessing though, it cools everything off for a while and allows a decent night's sleep. Around here you'll appreciate an airy tent which can be pitched with the inner only like a mossie net, but under a shelter.

It's only about 270km from Yaounde via unnervingly named Ebolowa to the border with Gabon. Immigration is done at the police station in Bitam opposite the *Shell*, but expect the Gabonese side to be unhelpful, even though some travellers have reported getting visas here on arrival. At least it's tarmac from the border for 400km as far as the **junction** just after the equator at S00° 04.6′ E10° 57.5′, and just before Alembé, which leads east for the Lopé National Park.

Here you have **three options** to get yourself into DRC and lined up for Zambia or Angola. Neither adds up to a precise itinerary and there are other routes; instead it's merely a trio of possibilities which between them juggle bad roads, awkward visas and tricky borders. Whatever weather you get on the way, that comes free.

● Head east on the N3 for Franceville (470km), then follow a new road to Oyo in Congo (another 350km) and down to Brazzaville (450km). This might become the main all-weather road to Brazza once the Chinese have finished with Congo.
● Head south through Gabon any way you like and once you get to Dolisie in Congo, turn east for Brazzaville (360km) initially along a very rough road adjacent to a railway.
● With a double-entry Angolan visa, at Dolisie head west on for Pointe Noire on the coast, then enter the Angolan enclave of **Cabinda** (220km). Once in DRC, head inland from Muanda (60km from Cabinda) to Boma – a tough drive in the rains. Cross the Congo river bridge into Matadi (220km) right on the Angolan border.

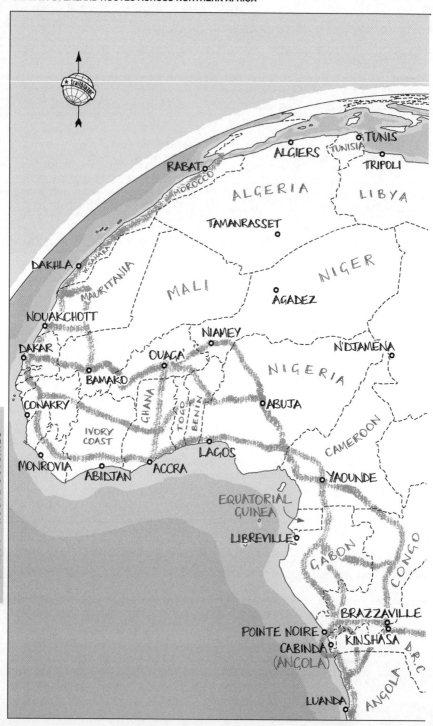

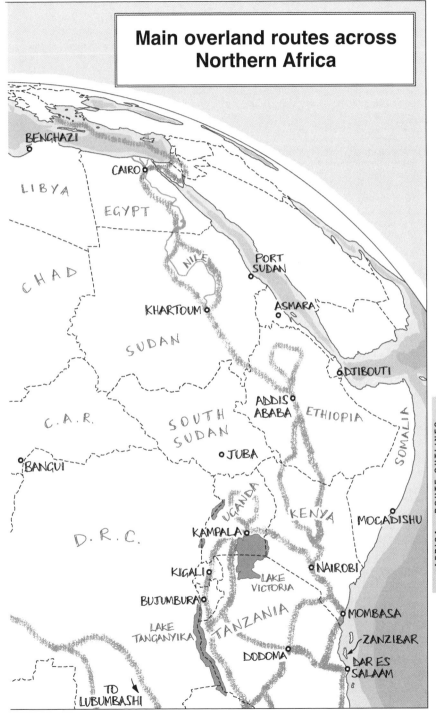

Main overland routes across Northern Africa

ASKING DIRECTIONS IN AFRICA

On stopping to buy water, a snack or confirm directions at times young men were 'in my face' and the attention could be intimidating. One time a local farmer among the group seemed especially aggressive. I didn't take it personally and it was interesting to note that when I addressed him directly, answering his questions genuinely and asking some myself, he seemed to come around – indeed warning off a couple of other young smart asses who were suggesting exacting a 'toll' from me.

I had a similar experience in Cameroon. Stopping for directions at a fork, I chose someone whose appearance suggested some 'worldliness'. He was a teacher who instantly took responsibility for the situation but as

the inevitable crowd gathered the usual argument broke out and things became quite heated. I was to experience this further into central Africa and knew it was a cultural trait that didn't necessarily mean what it would back home in Ireland.

Remaining unperturbed was the best strategy. My defender had a stand off with one chap, accusing him of saying 'silly things' about me. The other guy backed off, things calmed down and the teacher would not let me go before I knew exactly where I was, the name of every village and even the hills all the way to Bamenda, my destination.

HUGH BERGIN
⌨ kilkennytocapetown.com

Southeast for Ojo (Congo)

Roadwise, the rot may well set in south from Mevang in Gabon, and as far as Lambarene and the Congo border at Doussala is the usual central African scenario. So take the road east out via Lopé National Park to Lastourville (probably sealed by now), after which it's tar to **Franceville** all the way to the border at Lekoni. **Border formalities** are said to be easy enough; maybe a little trickier if heading west into Gabon from Congo. Few maps show this yet, but once in Congo it's 200 kilometres of newly sealed road over grass-covered high plains via Okoyo to Oyo, 450km from Brazzaville.

In **Congo** the people are friendly again and, for a central African capital, **Brazzaville** manages to be an agreeable city – until you get too close to the ferry port, that is. Many overlanders camp for free at *Hippocampe Hotel* (S04° 16.4' E15° 16.7') where great Vietnamese food is served. If heading north and in need of Gabonese or Cameroonian visas, see the box on p419.

Southwest for Pointe Noire and Cabinda

Backing up to Mevang in Gabon, most pass on expensive Libreville and once over the bridge at Lambarene, 160km down the road, head southwest 700 kilometres to Pointe Noire on the coast of Congo-Brazza. From here you'll be crossing the Angolan enclave of Cabinda for DRC so make sure you have an Angolan visa strategy in place. Once in Congo, immigration is done 50km after the border at Nyanga, where there's also a Catholic mission.

An alternative route to Congo turns off at Moanda, and takes a little-used route south via Bakoumbe to the border and Mbinda for immigration. **Mila Mila** (S03° 42.9' E12° 27.1') is a junction that doesn't appear on most maps and where a corner-cutting track leads through the hills 150km to Pointe Noire. Otherwise continue south to Dolisie junction and the railway and turn west. At Pointe Noire camp at the Yacht Club (S04° 47.3' E11° 50.9') and hope they'll give you an **Angolan transit visa** (S04° 47.5' E11° 51.6') to get you across Cabinda. You don't want to waste your 30-day tourist visa from Accra here.

Cabinda (Angola) and southwest DRC

Like a lot of the cities on this coast, **Cabinda** isn't cheap. Oil, imports and expats see to that, and for many travellers the place doesn't encourage extended stays, especially with visa fuses fizzling away. Cross into DRC and head inland on a graded dirt towards Boma and Matadi. This track can be perfect or it can be a mire when the heavens open.

Once at Boma you rejoin tarmac and head north through the hills to come back down to the Congo River for the **toll bridge** into scenic Matadi, 120km from Boma. In dry conditions you can do Cabinda to the Matadi in a day. Among other places, there are **missions** to stay at in Muanda (S05° 55.9' E12° 20.5'), Boma (S05° 51.2' E13° 03.4') and Matadi (S05° 49.9' E13° 27.7'). If heading for Angola, at Matadi there's a pricey and demanding Angolan consulate at S05° 49.7' E13° 27.7' as well as a **border crossing** to Noqui – or it's 80km to the **Songololo** border; see next page.

Dolisie to Brazzaville, or slipping quietly over the Congo

On and off **Dolisie** was one of the few places to get an **Angolan visa** en route, but in late 2016 Angola introduced a new computerised system which might not make it here before sea levels rise. Until that day, head for Pointe Noire.

East from Dolisie, the 360km to Brazzaville was once plagued by Ninja separatists until they disbanded to pursue solo careers. Today the road remains well and truly rooted to Mindouli, 140km from the capital. When dry and dusty it can take two days to cover those 220km; when waterlogged and blocked by trucks it's polite not to ask. Expect roadblocks with set tolls.

South of this road there are recommended **alternative crossings** to the main Brazzaville-Kinshasa ferry over the Congo. Both involve tracing little used tracks on either side of the river. At **Mindouli** turn right and cross into DRC then follow a gnarly track south 100km to **Luozi** where a pontoon drops you on the far bank at **Banza Sanda**. This is the crossing you must use if you got your DRC visa unusually easily in Benin or Togo (see p411). These visas (as well as others) won't wash on the Kinshasa crossing The track continues south to the road near **Kimpese** not far from the Angolan border at Songololo.

Or, coming from Brazzaville, turn southwest at Kinkala for Boko where the tarmac ends. A track leads to Manyanga and DRC border where the track deteriorates to Luozi. In off-road miles the distance is about the same for both approaches to Luozi, but **if it's wet** you're better off throwing yourself at the mercy of the Brazza-Kinshasa ferry. Think twice about the ferry at Pioka, 25km directly east of Luozi. It's said the track on the south side to Gombe Matadi has holes deeper than you are tall. Allow two days for either route.

DRC: THE CONGO FERRY TO KINSHASA

Brazzaville might be an easy-going place by regional standards, but it's time to board the **ferry** to Kinshasa in the Democratic Republic of Congo (DRC). Start by scouting out the costs and timings. The Brazzaville side is easy enough with a semi-fixed tariff of inflated prices of around 40,000CFA; the crossing takes 20 minutes to an hour. Arriving on the Kinshasa side the costly whipping can take several hours. Lately they've been **denying entry** on visas not issued in your country of residency. All negotiable no doubt, but all the more reason to slip in via quiet **Luozi** (see above) or get your DRC visa at home.

Kinshasa

After all that, is it any surprise not everyone finds **Kinshasa** a relaxing place to spend time? The situation fluctuates, but this is one country where hanging around too long can get costly or unpleasant. Kinshasa hotels are expensive so most end up camping for free at the Procure Sainte Anne Catholic **mission** (S04° 18.0′ E15° 18.9′) next to the cathedral, a short distance from the ferry terminal, and opposite the US embassy (with other embassies close by).

The track to Lubumbashi and Zambia

Even with its visa difficulties, most travellers would still choose to continue to Angola and so Namibia for the Cape, but to do that you need that visa, and as things stand you won't be getting it here unless it flies in courtesy of DHL.

The alternative means heading east some 2400km to Zambia via Kikwit and Tshikapa, then Kananga, Mbuji-Mayi, Kamina and Kolwezi for Lubumbashi and on to the Zambian frontier at **Kasumbalesa**. In the 1960s this was the N1 highway with an adjacent railway and trams running in the towns. Fast forward half a century and the neglect and wars have seen the sort of dehumanising collapse of society for which DRC is infamous.

It's good tar for the 530km to Kikwit, and at the other end from Kolwezi to Lubumbashi and Kasumbalesa, but that still leaves well over 1500km along the atrophied remains of the former N1. Whatever geniality you've experienced so far dries up as incessant and aggressive demands for hand-outs, as well as village 'registration' fees and other bogus taxes add to the sustained assault on what has undoubtedly become the toughest 'main' overland route in Africa. Some days in the rain you'll barely manage to cover 50km. If you and your vehicle are up for it, allow up to **two weeks** to get across. For a preview of what lies ahead, look up the Al Jazeera documentary on youtube ('Risking it all – DRC').

Or, until the day the Chinese hose it all down with bitumen and bridges, consider what's emerged as a **less difficult option** (including fewer venal cops). About 145km after Tshikapa, in Mutombo, turn south onto the **N29** and follow it south via Kazumba, Luiza and Musumba Kekese. About 30km before Musumba, at S08° 16.2′ E22° 35.7′, hope there's a way across the 100-metre wide **Lulua river**. Then at Sanduwa on the same river, cut east and south on the R607 to rejoin the N29 and later the tarmac (and N1 route) at Kolwezi.

ANGOLA

It's 270km of good tar from Kinshasa to the most used **Songololo-Luvo** crossing which leads to initially good roads in Angola. Even then it can still take half a day to get on the road to Luanda, and at the mercy of a five- or maybe a seven-day **transit visa**, every hour counts. Coming north you might have got a 30-day tourist visa from the Angolans in Cape Town (S33° 55.2′ E18° 25.4′), but these require persistence and magic beans. All of which is a great shame as, despite the ruined roads and very high prices, like Nigeria or Sudan, the ordinary people of Angola make it a favourite amongst overlanders. Encountering delays on a five-day pass adds to the pressure, but **over-staying** by a few days won't mean transportation to the local Ilha do Diabo. If it's just a couple of days they may let you go, or argue over the fine, but it's best not to get caught living it large in Luanda with an expired visa.

(cont'd after Africa Trip Reports colour section)

***** TRIP REPORT *****

Trans-Africa – Toyota Land Cruiser HJ47

Name, Year of birth, Job Fabian Plock, 1989, Jasmine Kempe, 1990, Students   **Where and when** Africa, 2013-14
Duration, distance, cost 11 months, 29,684km, €17,676 or €52/day
Vehicle model and year Toyota Land Cruiser HJ47 1984
Modifications Aux tank, roof top tent, mud tyres and 16" steel rims, snorkel, awning, solar panel, aux battery, camper build
Vehicle's strong points Reliable, sturdy, no electronics
Vehicle problems Noisy, no power steering, easy to break into
Biggest headache Getting visas; time pressure due to expiring visas
Biggest surprise Overall friendliness and just how safe we felt
Favourite places   All of Angola and Morocco, beaches of Sierra Leone, Bjagos Islands of Guinea-Bissau **Next trip** Eastern Europe
Photo Atlantic coast, Western Sahara © Fabian Plock & Jasmine Kempe

```
*  *  *  *  T R I P     R E P O R T  *  *  *  *
```
Morocco – Steyr 12M18

Name, Year of birth, Job Marc Heinzelmann, 1968, IT
Where and when Morocco, 2016
Duration, distance, cost 2 months, 10,000km, €3000
Vehicle model and year Steyr 12M18, 1991
Modifications Michelin XZL 14.00R20 on split rims, custom cabin, motorcycle on platform
Vehicle's strong point Robust 4x4, goes nearly everywhere
Vehicle problems 3.5m height and 2.5m width
Biggest headache Customs formalities for car and bike
Biggest surprise No issues with the Steyr
Favourite places Oued Rheris, Erg Chegaga, Tafraout
Next trip Tassili N'Ajjer, Algeria

Photo Oued Rheris, Morocco © Marc Heinzelmann

****TRIP REPORT****
Morocco – Mercedes 508d

Name, Year of birth, Job Tom Flynn, 1983, roofer; Natasa Dupalo, 1979, social worker
Where and when Morocco, 2015-16
Duration etc 2 months, 5000km, £2000
Vehicle Mercedes 508d, 1987
Modifications 7cm lift, oil sump bash guard, front bumper modified to carry two jerrycans
Vehicle's strong points Reliability, durability, simplicity
Problems Leaking brake cylinders
Biggest headache Splits in the tyre side walls
Biggest surprise Vastness and emptiness of the landscape
Favourite places Tizi-n-Ouano Pass, Anti-Atlas canyons, Tamassint to Tagounite desert route
Next trip Central Asia

Photo View towards Zguilma after Agoult
© Tom Flynn

****TRIP REPORT****
Around Africa
Jeep Wrangler

Name Dan Grec, 1982, engineer
Where and when Around Africa, counter-clockwise, 2016-18
Duration etc 2 years, 80,000 miles, est $40,000
Vehicle model Jeep Wrangler Unlimited Rubicon, 2011
Modifications Camper, water system, fridge, solar, bumpers, winch, lights, compressor, etc
Vehicle's strong points Excellent sleeping, interior space
Problems Too heavy (6000lbs)
Biggest headache Nothing so far
Biggest surprise Guinea – friendly, and amazing mountains
Favourite places Fouta Djallon mountains, Guinea
Next trip Europe to SE Asia

Photo Fouta Djallon, Guinea © Dan Grec

```
*  *  *  *  T  R  I  P    R  E  P  O  R  T  *  *  *  *
```

Chad to Sudan – Toyota Land Cruiser HJ60

Name, Year of birth, Job   Gerbert van der Aa, 1968, journalist
Where and when   Chad to Sudan (Africa in stages), 2014
Duration, distance, cost   One month, 2400km, €2000
Vehicle model and year   Land Cruiser HJ60, 1986
Modifications   None
Vehicle's strong points   Very reliable engine
Vehicle problems   Broken leaf springs
Biggest headache   Getting Sudan visa
Biggest surprise   Crossing war-torn Darfur went smoothly
Favourite places   Hospitable people everywhere
Next trip   Mauritania

Photo West of El Obied, Kordofan, Sudan © Gerbert van der Aa

* * * * T R I P   R E P O R T * * * *

Around Africa – Land Rover Defender 110

Name, Year of birth, Job Gee CM Hurkmans, 1952, teacher
Where and when Around Africa solo with my dog Thimba, 2014
Duration, distance, cost One year, 65,000km, €15,000
Vehicle model and year Land Rover Defender 110 Tdi, 1991
Modifications Roofrack, awning, fridge, water filter, compressor etc
Vehicle's strong point A bush mechanic can fix anything!
Vehicle problems Lost fifth gear, broken transfer box
Biggest headache Would my wife still be waiting for me when I got home after a year? **Biggest surprise** Yes, she was!
Favourite places Guinea, Liberia, Sierra Leone (West African Ebola countries). They deserve so much better.
Next trip Morocco again (5th time)

Photo Desert wild camp in the Sudan near Meroe pyramids © Gee CM Hurkmans

Make sure you have enough fuel when you enter from the north to get 300km to N'zeto where the first reliable fuel supplies start. **Land mines** are still thought to be a problem in rural Angola and because of this **bush camping** takes some effort or risk, but as always there's a network of missions.

Trans Angola

If not trying Matadi–Noqui, at Songololo turn south to **Luvo**. Change your dollars on the Angolan side. No carnet needed, the TIP lasts up to a year and it should be cheaper fuel and a good road to M'banza-Kongo and another 250km to **N'zeto on** the coast. From here the 200km down the coast to Caxito could be brand spanking new tar, or crumbling at the edges.

From Caxito it's tar to **Luanda** where the few have benefited greatly from Angola's recent boom. A Via Expresso **ring road** speeds up your transit: from the north stay on the good sealed road that descends into a potholed mess within the city limits until you see a motorway overpass (S08° 46.2′ E13° 23.2′) and roundabout. This is your ticket around Luanda if that's what you want. Otherwise, see if they still let you **camp for free** in the secure car park at the *Clube Nautico* (Yacht Club) down in the marina (S08° 48.1′ E13° 13.4′).

Leaving Luanda

South of Luanda follow the coast 540km to **Benguela** on mainly good tar. The humidity finally begins to drop off, the land turns to savannah and at night you can enjoy the cool again. The checkpoints, desperate scams and general hassle of the equatorial countries drops off too. Maybe it is the climate after all.

From Benguela head inland towards Lubango, rising up to a cool 1500m, or continue along the coast via the impressive **Leba Pass**. Lubango to the border can be done in a day if you leave early. The main border crossing is at **Oshikango** (Namibian side), but if it's not too wet, try the track from Xangongo down to Ruacana in Namibia.

Crossing the border the strain of the previous weeks lifts. Some find the adjustment quite a shock and in a perverse way miss the struggle that gave each day a purpose. Ahead lie the fabulous desert landscapes of **Namibia** so don't be in a rush just because the pressure's off. Just make sure you **drive on the left**. The finale down to Cape Town is a piece of cake, as long as you're vigilant in Namibian cities. South Africa's on p434.

AFRICA – ROUTE OUTLINES

NORTHBOUND VISAS IN LUANDA AND BRAZZAVILLE

LUANDA

DRC visa
Largo de Joao Seca, just south of the South African embassy and near the hospital.
S08° 49.52′ E13° 13.74′

Congo visa
Rua de Joao de Barros, by Meridian Hotel.
S08° 48.22′ E13° 14.55′

Gabon visa
Near the Miramar Park and just east of the Congo embassy. S08° 48.51′ E13° 15.0′

BRAZZAVILLE
Both just south of the Meridian Hotel and a ten-minute walk north of the Hippocampe Hotel.

Gabon visa
Boulevard du Maréchal Lyautey.
S04° 16.12′ E15° 16.65′
Possibly same day and 45,000CFA.

Cameroon visa
Rue Gouverneur Général Bayardelle.
S04° 16.17′ E15° 16.54′
Two days and from 51,000CFA.

The Nile route

'Cairo to Cape', the long-established run down the east side of Africa is the classic route and much less of a challenge in terms of terrain and visas. Composed largely of former British colonies, **English** is widely spoken and as few as **seven** English-speaking borders separate Egypt from South Africa, though fees at some borders add up. On this side of the continent a Visa card and the **US dollar** is the hard currency of choice; further south the **South African rand** is acceptable in the countries which border RSA.

South of the equator those with Commonwealth nationalities can usually get **visas** at the border, although Brits pay much higher prices. Coming north from Kenya, your Ethiopia and Sudan visas don't fall into place anywhere near as well. And now with the main routes in northern Sudan and northern Kenya **sealed**, for the moment you can drive all the way on tarmac – make the most of it as the good surface may not last. It does mean the right **season** is less critical, though as you near the equator the increase in **elevation** creates a more equable climate, with a lushness that makes places like Uganda well worth the diversion. Away from expensive game parks, mile-for-mile the lowland plains or *veldt* of Tanzania and Botswana can get dull.

Hotspots and highlights

Places to **avoid** (or where they won't let you go) include northern Sinai and the Western Desert in Egypt, the easily avoided border regions with South Sudan as well as western Sudan, eastern Ethiopia and Somalia. Very few have ventured in the Central African Republic or eastern DRC for a while, either the South African AA has a good website; of particular value on the more commonly travelled east side: Crossborder Information 🖥 aa.co.za/services/travel-services/into-africa/cross-border-information.html.

Highlights include the monuments of pharaonic Egypt, the desert of northern Sudan, Ethiopia's highlands and Coptic culture, Uganda and the White Nile, game parks galore or chilling on the Indian Ocean coast. As you near Zambia or Botswana, Namibia's worth a detour before wrapping it up.

EGYPT

Egypt's failed revolution and the western spread of ISIS has seen a collapse in mainstream tourism on which the country was heavily reliant. What hasn't changed is the mind-numbingly protracted **paperwork** required when entering with a vehicle – you'd think they might connect the two as China claims to have done. Visas may no longer be issued for overlanders at borders – an **e-visa** system may now be in place. Although some claim to manage without one, you'll need a **carnet** (as do most countries on this eastern route) even if Egypt issues you with their own TIP. Add to that a temporary driving licence, rented Arabic number plates (for which your deposit is supposedly refunded on departure), plus vehicle registrations (which might only be valid for a month, unlike your visa or TIP), x-rays, permits and on-the-spot fees which

---

SOUTHBOUND VISAS IN CAIRO

Sudanese embassy in Cairo
8 El Sherbiny St
Dokki (2 photos, $100)
N30° 02.4' E31° 12.7'

Ethiopian embassy in Cairo
21 Mohammed El Ghazali St
Dokki (near Dokki metro station)
N30° 02.5' E31° 12.3'

---

you'll lose track of. **Insurance** is about LE70 a month bought in monthly segments. With costs being arbitrary (even when posted blatantly on a wall), it all fees like a well-oiled system of informal taxation – there's rarely an outright demand for *baksheesh*. In or out, it will all run to some $200 or more and take half a day. Just remember, it's not only you who pays and it's really only pocket money. The latest details will on the HUBB's North Africa Forum.

A greater difficulty is **getting to Egypt overland**. The situations in Syria and certainly Libya won't improve soon. A **Ro-Ro** service between Lavrio near Piraeus in Greece to Haifa, **Israel** (weekly, 60 hours; via Cyprus which is accessible from Tasucu in Turkey; 7 hours) is the only way short of shipping to an Egyptian port. As you read from p317, combining 'shipping' with 'Egypt' can lead to the gnashing of teeth. The Israeli–Egypt land border at Eilat–Taba on the Gulf of Aqaba may be off limits depending on who's got the upper hand in north Sinai, so proceed to Jordan for the regular **ferry from Aqaba to Nuweiba** (allow half a day at each port) in the Sinai and skirt round the southern edge up to Suez.

Once in Egypt **fuel** is cheap, so are the half-empty lodgings and the monumental splendours are well known and not to be rushed. You're likely to need to stop in **Cairo** for onward visas – brace yourself for your first immersion in the madness that is urban African **traffic mayhem**.

The **Western Oases** of Bahariya, Farafra and Dakhl'a make a rewarding excursion, but right now you need an escort and can't camp out in the desert safely. And even before the current troubles you couldn't roam west of that road towards the Great Sand Sea and the fabulous Gilf Kebir without a guide, all sorts of permits and armed guards which took months to organise.

Crossing to Sudan

For years crossing into Sudan required negotiating a place on a disorganised ferry from **Aswan** across the world's biggest artificial lake, even though perfectly good overland routes existed. In 2014 a land border finally opened with Sudan on the 22nd parallel east of the lake. But getting there still requires joining a **convoy to Abu Simbel** on the west side, where a ferry (50LE) crosses Lake Nasser just 10km to Qustul on the Egyptian east bank and 55km north of Wadi Halfa in Sudan, with the border post halfway.

There's also a less well-known road on the west side, running down from Abu Simbel to Argeen on the border and on to Dongola. There's talk that this may become the main crossing, avoiding ferries and Wadi Halfa altogether. Some have managed to use it, but the charges paid to the Egyptian army (who seem to run the whole deal down here) are huge.

So for the moment Abu Simbel to Wadi Halfa it is. You might think that's an improvement but this is Egypt so the costs manage to match the old Aswan ferry – only the delays and unpredictability have been reduced. Taking the pre-dawn convoy out of Aswan, you can be in Wadi Halfa by nightfall. Here, an entrepreneurial guy called Mazar Mahir has long been the 'clearance facil-itator', charging ten dollars to stamp his stamp. Some pedantic types resent this; others find his services helpful and his fee is really quite negligible in the scheme of things.

Northbound from Wadi you can take a ferry direct to Abu Simbel or reverse the land border route; the direct ferry must be quicker and the total to get out of Sudan and into Egypt will run to about $250, most of that for Egypt. The Wadi–Abu Simbel ferry officially costs less than a dollar. Whether you actually pay that is a matter of luck or who you meet.

SUDAN

Even if you weren't expecting Las Vegas on stilts, **Wadi Halfa** is still no oasis. The original settlement is submerged beneath Lake Nasser, but there's every-thing here including a bank and any number of permit-issuing government offices – including the mandatory Alien Registration Office (do it here or in Khartoum) all helping to turn dollars into documents. Keep a stash for the **black market**, you'll get around a fifty per cent better rate, otherwise Sudan can get pricey; **ATMs won't work** for you. Get **insurance** (you can't get the Comesa yellow card extension until Addis – see opposite).

From Wadi Halfa two routes lead south, each tracking one side of the 1000-kilometre tall 'S' bend of the Nile between the border and the capital, Khartoum. The more-commonly driven western route is now **sealed**. It meets the east bank of the Nile about a third of the way to Dongola. Here you can take the west bank and join a sealed road all the way to Khartoum, or stick to the east bank and head southeast through the desert to the Meröe ferry in the middle of the 'S' bend.

The more isolated **eastern route** from Wadi follows the **railway** and tele-graph line across the Nubian Desert to Abu Hamed on the Nile and subse-quently Atbara at the Port Sudan junction, for Khartoum. If it's the cool sea-son, on the initial stages of this route you can wander into the desert away from the sandy rail-side track. Depending on the duration of your visa, make the most of it; you'll miss the open desert later on.

Southbound travellers should have done it at Wadi Halfa, but if **coming from Ethiopia** you need to park your spaceship and **register as an Alien** with-in three days of entering Sudan. In **Khartoum** the Alien Registration Office is at the airport (less busy) or in a city market at N15° 36.0' E32° 31.1'. You'll need photocopies of your passport and Sudanese visa and possibly a letter from your lodgings. You may also need a Permit to Travel to get up to Wadi Halfa from the ministry about a mile southeast at N15° 35.4' E32° 31.82'. Plus a pho-tography permit from the Ministry of Tourism, though you can dodge this as long as you're not caught shooting a controversial, feature-length documen-tary about a telegraph pole. If you stay at the *German Guesthouse* near the air-port (N15° 34.1' E32° 33.8') they'll help you get the first two permits. And it's said that the once-popular *Blue Nile Sailing Club* by the main bridge (N15° 36.7' E32° 32.1') is getting a long overdue makeover.

If you need a **visa for Egypt** in Khartoum (consulate: N15° 36.2' E32° 31.4'), it costs SDG160 and can be valid for a month from issue and is issued the same day. Heading south, get an **Ethiopian visa** often on the same day for $20 by applying in the morning at: Plot No. 04, Block 384BC, just west of the Farouq cemetery (N15° 34.9' E32° 32.06'), or consider getting it in your home country. In London a six-month multiple-entry tourist visa costs £54.

With the exception of Meröe, a couple of hours north of Khartoum on the Atbara road, Sudan doesn't match the ancient historical grandeur of Egypt or Ethiopia. However, despite the tedious bureaucracy many travellers report it's all done with a wily smile, much less *baksheesh* than Egypt and the people are among the most hospitable on this route.

South Sudan looks no more accessible than since it was formed and the old route across **Chad** through Darfur doesn't look too promising either.

ETHIOPIA

From Khartoum most head straight down the sealed road to Gedaret and Doka and the border at Gallabat for **Metema** in northwest Ethiopia. On a good day Ethiopian immigration and customs formalities are said to be among the quickest in Africa, with **insurance** down the road in Gonder. They're happy to stamp your **carnet**, but Ethiopia isn't in the carnet zone (it ought to be excluded from the list on the back of the document). So many travellers have their carnets blithely stamped here that getting a TIP can take some persuasion. Note that **ATMs** are only found in larger towns and cities.

Get the **visa** in Khartoum or your home country. Coming up from the south, you'll be very lucky to get an **Ethiopian visa** in Nairobi, or a Sudanese visa is Addis. For Ethiopia try **Harare** back down in Zimbabwe, or call in DHL. A Sudanese visa can take three days in Nairobi. As always, your nationality has much to do with it.

After the arid plains of Sudan, **Ethiopia** is an exceptional-looking country. The classic northern tour into the Simien Mountains for Axum, Debre Damos monastery and the climb up to the carved rock churches of Lalibela is not to be missed, even if the roads can hammer the stuffing out of you. With bad roads and steep mountain tracks, picking the right **season** in Ethiopia is important. The months building up to June get very hot in the lowlands of the south and east, while from then to September the rains can disrupt travel anywhere. You'll also be driving as high as 3350m (11,000ft), so around January bring a hat.

Unfortunately the welcome from the locals isn't always much warmer and the language barrier doesn't help. You may get worn down by the petty aggression and incessant yells of 'you, you, you!'. It's clear from the tone that they're not cheerfully recalling Alvin Stardust's chart-topping 1974 hit. Showers of sticks and stones can also make you wonder what you're doing here, although as always, some travellers managed to draw more flack than others. Strategies range from waving in appeasement to driving straight at them, but at least the police aren't too demanding.

This primary axis through Ethiopia is relatively stable, but in the far east the Danakil and more especially the Somali borders remain places to avoid. As African capitals go, **Addis Ababa** isn't what you've ridden thousands of miles to see, but is the first place to buy your **COMESA Yellow Card** from the Ethiopian Insurance Corp. for the drive south. To meet up with the gang, stay at *Wim's Holland House* (N09° 00.6' E38° 45.3').

INTO KENYA VIA MARSABIT

This once-notorious track is now sealed – all the more reason to try the Omo valley route (see below). There are no more border **visas for Kenya**; get them online for $51 at ⌨ ecitizen.go.ke with 90 days' validity and duration.

From Moyale it's 500km to Isiolo. Many overlanders choose to stay in **Marsabit,** halfway down, at the renowned *Henry's Camp* on the west side of town (N02° 20.75' E37° 58.0'). At **Isiolo** you can legitimately beat your chest and make Tarzan noises: you've arrived in East Africa.

East and Southern Africa

Coming from the north, most trans-African overlanders customarily take a breather and get repairs done in **Kenya**, sub-Saharan Africa's most visited and touristy country after South Africa. Along with a dramatic improvement in the road and tourist infrastructure, you also start **driving on the left** from here all the way down to the Cape, **English** is spoken and, depending on your nationality, the worst of the itinerary-restricting **visa hassles** should be over.

But the human psyche being what it is, it can all become a bit of a parade or extended *safari* (the Swahili word for 'journey') as you hop from one divine waterside lodge to the next, while dodging rowdy backpacker haunts or overland truck groups. Suddenly, it's like Southeast Asia with endless choices and a cold beer always in the fridge. After too much of this, some profess a nostalgia for the rough travelling in Ethiopia and Sudan, places which may have been rushed through early in your African experience.

In East Africa most **carry on camping** from around $10 per person as, along with national park entry fees, fuel prices and tempting supermarkets, things can get **expensive**. A few lodging recommendations are given in the text, but **online** is clearly the place to see where's cool or new – start looking on LP's Thorn Tree or Trip Advisor.

ETHIOPIA TO KENYA VIA LAKE TURKANA

To string out your adventure head down to the **Omo Valley**, among other things the home of Mursi tribeswomen famed for their wooden lip plates, as well as the odd, trigger-happy herdsman. Note this hyper-arid corner of Kenya around Lake Turkana is a hot, stony stage and barely borders the lake.

From the Rastafarian enclave of Shashemene, 220km south of Addis, head for Jinka or Abra Minch and Konso. Here it's another 190km to Turmi (last fuel, if they have any). You pass the turn-off for the Kenyan border before **Omorate** (aka: Kelem) where you stamp out your carnet. Back at the

turn-off, cross into Kenya and at **Ileret** sign in with the police. You'll need to complete your immigration in Nairobi.

Head inland through the Sibiloi National Park coughing up a $20/day fee as you pass by. Loyangalani, about 220km from Ileret, may have the first expensive fuel. Continue another 230km to Maralal (ATM, fuel, shops) and on to Baragoi for Archers Post on the main road to Nairobi.

Now back on the highway, after a thousand kilometres there's the small matter of crossing the equator and remembering to drive on the **left**.

INTO KENYA

With a South African registered vehicle, Kenya is the first country that may
be a headache, requiring vehicles from
outside the East African Community
(EAC) to have a **carnet** as well as a
licence disc for a 'Foreign Private
Vehicle' (FPV) costing $40 a month at
the border, or $100 for three months
from the immigration office at Nyayo
House in Nairobi (S01° 17.2' E36°
49.1'). From the north and heading for
Uganda and Rwanda, ask about a **visa**
to cover all three countries for $100.

Slow traffic in East Africa.
© duksjourney.net

Wherever you're coming from, armed with your FPV, a carnet, your
Yellow Card (or local insurance) and some ripe Swahili jokes, you'll be ready
for any bribe-extorting policeman. The **COMESA Yellow Card** programme
(🖳 programmes.comesa.int) is similar to the Green Card issued in the EU and
provides **extension** to your already obtained third party motor insurance in
supposedly every country on the east side up to Sudan. Like a Green Card it
isn't valid in the issuing country and coming from the south, Zambia is the
first place to buy it; expect to pay about $100 for six months.

Police road blocks in Kenya concentrate around major towns and usually
wave foreigners through, unless you're speeding. As elsewhere in sub-
Saharan Africa, you'll find the occasional officer stationed at a roadblock looking for an 'ATM' to come rolling by. Get into the habit of having all your
paperwork handy and always ask for a receipt for all on the spot 'fines'
because that'll usually put off anyone who's up to no good, or reduce an official fine. Another good counter-scam is to claim your embassy insists that you
photograph and report all fine/receipt incidents immediately, to counter any
possibility of corruption which has been known to occur in these parts.

Towards Nairobi

From **Isiolo** you'll no doubt want to pull up at **Nanyuki**, made famous in a
thousand snaps because it straddles the **equator**. In town you'll also find guys
demonstrating the water-down-a-plughole trick, plus a big supermarket,
pharmacy and a few banks. The road to Nairobi passes west of Mt Kenya with
an excellent campsite at *Naro Moro River Lodge*, one of the base camps for those
who want to have a crack at reaching the 5199-metre summit. From here it's a
straight 200km run to Nairobi.

Nairobi

As you near Nairobi the road deteriorates, as does the quality of the driving.
Hey ho, it's another crazy African capital. Passing Thika you'll be entering the
city from the northeast so be prepared for several large, chaotic, roundabouts.
If you brought your 'Ben Hur' wheel spikes, now's the time to fit them. One
roundabout is where the A2 road filters down to Forrest Road; another is at
the junction of Forrest and Ngara roads. Try to avoid the rush hours, especially on the Uhuru and Mombasa roads.

Dealing with Nairobi

The risk of crime in 'Nai-robbery' is overrated, especially if you're driving a battered machine (can it be anything else by now?). But as with any big city, keep your wits about you and have a destination in mind before you get there.

If entering Nairobi from the northeast and heading towards the western side of the city where many **overlanders hang out**, when you hit the Museum Hill roundabout, get on the Waiyaki Highway (an extension of Uhuru to Mombasa Road) and head back out of town. Just after the ABC Plaza turn left and take a short cut along James Gicheru Road. This will take you to either the famous *Jungle Junction* (S01° 17.3' E36° 45.6') or *Upper Hill Campsite* (S01° 17.2' E36° 46.4'), a couple of kilometres east of the Junction.

East to the coast

By the time most southbound overlanders reach Kenya, the idea of laying up on an **Indian Ocean beach** while a local mechanic tends lovingly to your rig is an agreeable scenario. Mombasa, Lamu or any of the other small resorts up and down the Indian Ocean coast are perfect places to recuperate before heading south to Tanzania. Just make sure you survive the drive to **Mombasa**.

KENYA TO TANZANIA

As the travel hardships ease beyond Kenya, suitably refreshed and with your car now running like the Swiss watch it once was, you can now entertain all sorts of ways of complicating things again. Going south into **Tanzania**, world-class game parks and natural spectacles abound, including Kilimanjaro, the Ngorongoro Crater and the Serengeti, as well as Dar es Salaam and Zanzibar on the Indian Ocean. From Nairobi there are **two main ways** to get south: either the well-trodden route through Namanga, Moshi, Same and Korogwe – or from Mombasa south along the coast through the Lunga Lunga–Hora Hora border post and all sealed road to Tanga in Tanzania.

Kenya–Tanzania border

Whichever you decide, at the Tanzanian **border** get a one-month tourist visa from $50 to $100 depending on your nationality. A two-week transit visa costs from $30, though you'll need a full tourist visa to visit Zanzibar. The **Temporary Import Permit** (TIP) is another 50 bucks. The choice is yours as to whether you use your carnet or not, but a TIP requires using a customs' agent to clear the vehicle. No bond is required, but it takes an extra hour and of course the agent charges for the service. There is also a fuel levy of $25.

Exiting Kenya via the Namanga border post, 170km south of Nairobi, is a relatively painless business, the only irritation may be the many Maasai women who throng around, pressing their colourful wares on you.

Kenya may well have caught up by now, but in Tanzania and in many countries south of here, watch out for radar gun slinging **speed traps** with the choice of an on-the-spot fine, reduced 'receipt-free' rates, or your day in court. Note they've copied the Russian trick of ending the '50kph' town speed limit zone miles down the road where your guard is down. Quite often they're just looking for a 'kitu kidogo' ('a little something'); always check their speed guns are working. Despite, or perhaps because of their powder blue uniforms, you'll learn to love or loathe the Tanzanian Police department.

Main overland routes across Southern Africa

WEST TO UGANDA AND THE RWENZORI MOUNTAINS

Depending on the season, the lush highlands and cool lakes of Uganda can be a tonic after Sudan and Ethiopia. Many travellers are startled by this verdant upland region because there's no shortage of arid savannah and desert further north or south.

As yet many find that Uganda lacks Kenya's commercialism or the prices found further south. Gorilla spotting in the rainforests is an exception, but there's rafting on the Nile at Jinja or you could just chill by a lake. With the relatively inexpensive fuel, for overlanders Uganda is an East African favourite. **Visas** at the border for Brits and Western Europeans are no hassle ($50 or $100 for one that covers Kenya and Rwanda too), but make sure you have your carnet and the Yellow Card, or buy it at the border. You'll also pay a vehicle tax adding up to at least $20.

The road out of Nairobi passes through the **Rift Valley** with inexpensive camping at *Fisherman's Camp* on the south side of Lake Naivasha at a cool 1890m, and *Kembu Cottages* 25km west of Lake Nakuru. Crossing the **equator**, there are more lakes before reaching **Eldoret** and *Naiberi River Campsite*, 16km southeast of Eldoret.

In **Uganda**, the main road takes a turn towards Lake Victoria and Jinja, a popular place for white water rafting which may well have the same colouring effect on your hair.

If you decide to raft with them, *Nile River Explorers* at Bujagali Falls are recommended as well as offering inexpensive camping.

If coming up from the south, not least Kenya, travellers find **Kampala** a relaxed and inexpensive capital. The established *Red Chilli Hideaway* is 5km east of the city centre (N00° 19.21', E32° 37.8'); the Red Chilli folk also have a rest house at Murchison's Falls, 250km north of Kampala; a good base for Murchison Falls National Park.

Along with the vast **Lake Victoria**, Uganda shares several smaller lakes with its neighbours, including Lake Albert and Lake Edward. Along the south shore of Lake Albert visit the Kibale Forest National Park and the Kibale Forest Primate Reserve. Here the *Lake Nkuruba Community Campsite* offers camping on a manicured lawn right next to the best of the crater lakes.

West of Kibale is Lake Bunyonyi between Kisoro and Kabale, and close to the Rwandan border. East of town you'll find the camping *Lake Bunyonyi Overland Resort* to be another idyllic place.

The road from Kibale to Kisoro looks due for asphalting, and as you progress southwest you're now heading towards the **Rwenzori Mountains**, Bwindi National Park, the Virunga Mountains, Rwanda's Parc des Volcans and of course, Dian Fossey's famous troop of silverback gorillas.

Kenya to Tanzania via Namanga

Once through the border you'll find Tanzania's main highways are well maintained, although they deteriorate quickly out bush (as does the use of English, Swahili's the lingua franca here more than in Kenya). Expect a band of unsigned and especially acute **speed bumps** at the beginning of any village.

Heading south to **Arusha**, Tanzania's safari hub, there are lots of places to stay, from 1970s-style hotels in town, to camping out of town at places like *Meserani Snake Park*, about 25km west of Arusha on the Dodoma Road. This is also the way to Lake Manyara, the Ngorongoro Crater and the Serengeti.

East leads to Moshi, the tourist hub for Kilimanjaro, and again full of places to stay, most geared up to accommodate tourists and overlanders with bars, food and secure parking.

There are also **campsites** just out of town, such as *Maasai Camp* in Arusha (noisy at weekends), or the nicer and cheaper *Marungu Campsite* on the way to the 5900-metre mass of Kilimanjaro. If you're cabin feverish and serious about climbing Kili, Trailblazer has the *Kilimanjaro* guidebook for you, or check out the author's informative website: ⌨ climbmountkilimanjaro.com.

The road to Dar es Salaam
Heading for Dar, if you fancy visiting historic Bagamoyo on the way – once the end of the trail for slaves heading to Arabia – then head south from Segera where, 37km north of Chalinze at Msata (S06° 20.0' E38° 23.4'), there's a 60km long track running east to a former trading post. From Bagamoyo to Dar is another 70 clicks down along the coast. Alternatively, if heading northward, 44km east at Chalinze on the road to Dar, at Mlandizi (S06° 43.0' E38° 44.3') you'll find a gravel track leading north to Bagamoyo.

Dar es Salaam is another of those places whose romance is these days more a sepia-tinted memory than reality, but it's a lot more agreeable than many African cities. Primarily it's the jumping-off point for Zanzibar or the Pemba islands. Traditionally overlanders stay north of Dar at *Silversands*, however there are many more campsites on the coast to the southeast via a ferry over the harbour mouth. They include *Kipepeo Beach Village* which lives up to its name with chalets or camping plus secure parking while you visit the islands. Or the nearby *Makadi Beach Resort*. The *YMCA* in town can also look after your car for a small fee.

SOUTH OF TANZANIA
Whether you've taken the road to Arusha, past Kilimanjaro, or down the coast, both roads meet at Segera before continuing south to **Chalinze** where you can either turn east for Dar es Salaam or west on to Morogoro. For most overlanders it's a choice between keeping inland for Malawi and Zambia, or east for Mozambique and the coast. The latter can lead you directly to the eastern border with South Africa, from where Cape Town is less than 2000km away. As with many such crossroads, much will depend on the state of you, your wallet and your vehicle, as well as your capacity for more adventure and border queues.

RWANDA AND BURUNDI

Entering from Uganda near the Parc des Volcans, **Rwanda** doesn't require visas for UK citizens, they'll just stamp your passport. This is a beautiful country too, but some travellers find it quite 'hard' by regional standards as the locals aren't really interested in travellers or tourism; they have their hands full serving aid workers and the UN.

Camping doesn't exist as elsewhere in East Africa, so Presbyterian missions are your best bet. Add **fuel** that's up to 25 per cent more than Kenya or Uganda, as well as national parks fees and it all becomes an expensive proposition. Furthermore, currently Rwandan **ATMs** only accept local bank cards so arrive with plenty of dollars to exchange, though some banks will advance cash on Visa cards.

To the south, **Burundi** may no longer issue **visas** at the border so pick them up on Boulevard de l'Umuganda, Kigali west (S01° 56.5' E30° 05.2'). With that you can take a loop via Makebuko to Bujumbura, then down the east shore of Lake Tanganyika to Mabanda to cross into Tanzania for Kigoma.

If you don't want to visit Burundi you can leave Rwanda via the border post either side of the bridge at Kagera River, however the route south alongside Lake Tanganyika is rough. Instead, you can head east to Mwanza at the southern end of Lake Victoria and on eastwards to the Serengeti, adjacent to Kenya's Masai Mara and where the wildebeest are stamping their hooves and calling your name. Or, head south for Mbeya and so to Zambia via the Tunduma border post.

Tanzania to Zambia

If you skipped Dar and pushed on to **Morogoro** there's plenty of accommodation on the way, and in the Mikumi National Park there's a chance to see giraffe, zebras and elephants if you've not seen any yet – as well as warnings about hippos.

Coming down from Morogoro, the next major town is **Iringa** (*Iringa Farm* has great camping), with access to the Ruaha National Park. From Iringa, heading on south and west it's a long trek to Mbeya. The Tunduma border post with Zambia is now 100km down the road where again, all visas and other papers can be bought at the border.

Zambia

Like Uganda, Zambia delivers a surprisingly verdant country that's the home of the two Luangwa national parks. Brits pay $50 for a visa at the border where you might also be asked to cough up for a carbon emissions tax, $30 road access fee plus motor insurance sold for one or three months ($20), if you don't have a Yellow Card (see p425). If heading south check you don't require reflective stickers too. **Climate**-wise, you're south of the equator with the cool dry season from May to August; the build-up sets in and the rains let loose from December until April when tracks become impassable.

Taking a short cut by **crossing DRC** via Sakania is said to be OK but it's another visa; the western border crossing with Angola is very rarely used by travellers. Elsewhere the main roads are in good condition; you can shoot across Zambia in three days if the pipes are calling, or you can spend time and a whole lot of money in the national parks; even waterfalls can cost $15 for a quick look-see. As often in sub-Saharan Africa, the capital **Lusaka** is a place to be wary after dark with tourist resorts like **Livingstone** near Victoria Falls also attracting nocturnal thieves and muggers.

In Zambia

The road from Tanzania enters Zambia at the Tunduma–Nakonde border post which can be particularly overwhelming due to the sheer number of trucks, money-changers and touts offering to expedite your paperwork for a fee. Park up outside immigration, roll your sleeves up and get stuck in. Once you've cleared customs, got your carnet stamped and paid all the rest, they open the barrier and let you run free.

This road is known as the 'TanZam Highway' and passes the North and South Luangwa national parks to its south and Kapishya Hot Springs to the north. There are lots of places to stay in Lusaka itself, otherwise 50km before you enter the city, see if *Fringilla Lodge* takes your fancy.

Your choice now is either to continue southeast and enter Zimbabwe through Chirundu, or head west to Kaufe National Park 200km west of Lusaka. Otherwise, head past Choma to Livingstone and the **Victoria Falls,** close to where Namibia, Botswana and Zimbabwe meet Zambia.

Tanzania to Malawi

Backing up a bit, the other main route from Tanzania runs south to **Malawi**. About 10km east of Mbeya at Uyole, turn south on the B345 and enter Malawi at the Songwe–Kasumulu border post alongside Lake Malawi. Show your yellow card or buy **insurance** and a TIP for 1200 Malawi kwatcha if you think your carnet needs a rest. Most Europeans don't need an advance visa.

The road starts close to the shore and, passing Karonga, it climbs towards Mzuzu and the Viphya mountains on the way to the capital, **Lilongwe**. You can also take the lakeside road which passes through Nkhata Bay and Senga. Both this road and the main road from Lilongwe carry on to the southern end of the lake where you'll find Monkey Bay on **Cape Maclear**, an overlanders' favourite.

There are other border posts in the south of Malawi, but most are now heading for South Luangwa National Park in Zambia and so need to retrace their steps back to Lilongwe, before heading 110km west for the Mchinji crossing to Chipata in Zambia.

In Malawi
Malawi can be a nice place to rest up, but it can also get **expensive**, with pricey fuel and 8% charged on Visa card transactions. Be aware too of the **national speed limit** of 80kph out of towns. For a place to camp in the capital, Lilongwe, the central *Sanctuary Lodge* on Youth Drive (S13° 58.1' E33° 47.2') has been recommended in preference to the better known *Golf Course* a couple of kilometres to the south.

ZAMBIA TO BOTSWANA
From Kazungula you can catch the ferry across the Zambezi to **Botswana**. As you approach the crossing, drive past the long line of trucks at the side of the road to the passenger vehicle queue.

Once there you need to pay around 20 pula for a Road Fund (about $2) which is valid till the end of the year, as well as a Road Permit of P50 for a single transit. There's no Yellow Card here, so insurance is about P50 for 90 days.

Considered a sub-Saharan success story, Botswana has taken the 'high quality, low impact' tourism route and if you're not yet 'gamed-out', a number of reserves and national parks fill nearly a fifth of the country, including Chobe close to the above border post, as well as Moremi Wildlife Reserve in the Okavango Delta, the Central Kalahari Game Reserve and the incredible Makgadikgadi Salt Pans. If you've chosen to string out the impending end of the road, the only entry into **Namibia** outside the Caprivi Strip is at Mamuno, west of the Central Kalahari Game Reserve.

ZIMBABWE
The US dollar is now the *de facto* currency in Zimbabwe and unlike white farmers and members of the MDC, **security** for visitors has never been a problem. However, there are a lot of poor people and beggars on the streets of Harare or Victoria Falls. They aren't dangerous, just the product of Mugabe's disastrous Land Reform Programme.

Police, driving and currency
The **police** in their khaki uniforms are usually educated, polite and speak English; the paramilitary police in dark blue outfits with ZRP flashes may not be as genial but despite what you might think, you won't be robbed blind by the authorities. **Roadblocks** are plentiful and you may occasionally be asked for a little food or drink, but the outright solicitation of bribes is rare.

Take care though, **speed traps** abound and Zimbabwe has instituted a system of road tolls – usually with a police-manned toll gate just outside most towns. As a foreigner you'll be waved through most of these.

Although the US dollar is now the currency, you can also use the South African rand or Botswanan pula, especially in the west and south. US dollars come from ATMs in all major cities. You'll need lots of **small denomination** notes for the toll roads you can't dodge – usually one dollar.

Zambia to Zimbabwe via Victoria Falls

Leaving Lusaka it's a 500km drive to **Livingstone** which has picked up on the 'adrenaline' activities offered over the border at the tourist resort of Victoria Falls. Accommodation for backpackers and overlanders can be found at places like *Fawlty Towers, Jollyboys Backpackers* behind the Livingstone Museum, or *Maramba River Lodge*, out of town, quiet and safe.

Victoria Falls can be an easy border. After checking out of Zambia you cross the bridge over the Zambezi from which bungee tourists can be seen hurling themselves into the abyss below. Once on the Zimbabwean side, park up and enter the little office to get your visa. Be prepared to pay $55 for that; $55 for your TIP (carnets aren't valid but give it a go); more for insurance if you don't have a Yellow Card, a Road Access fee, possibly a Carbon Tax and whatever else they've dreamt up since.

Victoria Falls, Hwange and Bulawayo

Victoria Falls is the name of both the waterfall and the small Zimbabwean resort. Accommodation ranges from five-star hotels to basic camping at the municipal campsite (S17° 55.5' E25° 50.2') or national park lodges. There are a few fast-food joints in town, but consider a meal at *The Boma* to get a taste of the wildlife you couldn't eat at home without getting raided by the RSPCA.

Food and fuel are plentiful at the Falls, although for spare parts or mechanics Hwange, 100km south, is a better bet and lends its name to Zimbabwe's largest national park. They say there's only one place to stay in **Hwange** town and that's the *Baobab Hotel* (S18° 20.65' E26° 30.2') on top of the hill to the north of the main road to Bulawayo.

Carrying on east from Hwange leads to Lake Kariba and the small resort of Mlibizi, the lake's southwestern terminal for the ferry. Passing by Mlibizi is the road to Binga where you'll find another little piece of waterside paradise called *Masumu River Lodge* (S17° 35.4' E27° 25.3') right by the lake.

Bulawayo is a lovely quiet city with wide open streets and a relaxed, friendly atmosphere. There's a municipal **campsite** (S20° 09.5' E28° 35.6'), but a better choice might be some of the small lodges in the southeastern suburbs, such as *Burkes' Paradise*. Having refreshed yourself in Bulawayo, you're ready for quite possibly your last African border crossing into South Africa.

Zambia to Zimbabwe via Chirundu

Chirundu border post is about 150km southeast of Lusaka and after passing the turn-off for Livingstone, you start your descent towards the Zambezi River and the border. Being the main trade route between Lusaka and Harare, it can be blocked for days by overturned or trapped lorries. If you look over the edge you'll see the wrecks of trucks that didn't make the bends.

Entering Zimbabwe at Chirundu finds you close to various safari and hunting areas that bound the western edge of Mana Pools National Park. This is a truly amazing wilderness area for walks or canoe safaris. The park charges at least $20 per person for campsites that really are in a wilderness, so the wildlife can be a concern. You'll need to pay in Marangora before heading back into the park along the 70km of dirt to Nyamepi Parks Office. From Makuti drive down to Kariba where the **ferry** (from $470 for two full board with car; 22 hours; 🖥 karibaferries.com) leaves at 9am for Mlibizi – a pleasant way to dodge 1200km of driving. Otherwise, carry on for Harare.

Harare is a bland city laid out in a grid fashion, rather like Bulawayo. The Rufaro Stadium is where Bob Marley and Paul Simon played during Zimbabwe's 1980 independence celebrations; there hasn't been a lot to celebrate since. From Harare you can drive southeast and enter Mozambique at Nyamapanda or go directly east to visit Mutare, Mount Nyangani and the beautiful Vumba Mountains before crossing into Mozambique.

MOZAMBIQUE

One of Africa's oldest former colonies, **Mozambique** was never the jewel in Portugal's crown and ended up more exploited and less developed than most. As elsewhere, independence led to a ruinous civil war (stirred by neighbouring countries) from which Mozambique is still recovering.

The country's sole attraction is its comparatively undeveloped **coastline**. Along with a visit to Ilha de Mozambique, if you've not had your statutory week off by the Indian Ocean yet, the resorts opposite the Bazaruto Islands near **Vilanculos** in the far south could be what you're after.

Inland you'll find not much more than a hot arid plain until you rise up into the mountains bordering the east side of Lake Nyasa (Lake Malawi). Few people venture here so it's bound to be an adventure.

Like much of the region, the **police** in Mozambique have a reputation for being a little overzealous, so observe the speed limits or pay the price. If pulled over they may want to see all the usual papers.

The infrastructure in Mozambique may not have got quite as trashed as Angola's, but both of these countries share the menace of **landmines**. It's why most overlanders still view Mozambique as a short transit rather than a place to explore.

If time, money or will are drying up, **cross into South Africa** at Ressano-Garcia (95km northwest of Maputo) for Lemombo (Kotmatipoort) south of the famous Kruger Park. Coming into Mozambique, visas are expensive; they're cheaper via Swaziland.

Some 250km upriver from the coast, between Mtambatswala village in Tanzania and Negomano in Mozambique, the **Unity Bridge** across the Rovuma River was inaugurated by the respective presidents. All-weather roads to the crossing may not be complete, but the fact that there's a bridge is half the battle won.

There's another route further inland towards Lake Malawi. Head south from Makambako to Songea, then another 100km south to cross the bridge over the Rovuma (S11° 34.7' E35° 25.7'). **Border formalities** can be rather informal on both sides, but you continue south to Lupilchi (aka: Segunda Congresso or Olivença) for Cobue on Lake Nyasa (Lake Malawi), Metangula and so Lichinga, back on the main road network. You can now strike out for Malawi at Mandimba by Lake Nyasa, or cross at Milange further south, for Zimbabwe via the once infamous Tete Corridor (the road from Zimbabwe to Malawi via the Zambezi bridge at Tete). Or head for the coast at Inhambane to meet the backpackers.

Moz' visa in Lilongwe, Malawi

You can get a 30-day visa at some non-Tanzanian land borders for $90 or in advance in Dar es Salaam or most easily Lilongwe, Malawi (S13° 57.7' E33° 47.3'). Bring two photos, one form, 5700MK (under $40). Issued same day.

For a great up-to-date source of information on overland travel in Mozambique, check out 🖥 mozguide.com.

Zimbabwe to South Africa via Beitbridge

Both routes south from Harare and Bulawayo end at the hot, dusty town of **Beitbridge**, the major crossing between Zimbabwe and **South Africa**. It's well known for its crippling summer heat and the huge volume of traffic that passes through during the holiday seasons, so knowing this you may want to use a less busy border. The process is relatively simple but can still take hours.

On the South African side show your carnet if you've come from Zimbabwe or Mozambique (no need to show it or get it stamped if you've come from Botswana or Namibia). Basic **third party insurance** is included in the price of fuel. If staying for a while comprehensive insurance is available.

Once clear of Beitbridge or any other border with the adjacent countries, you'll be on some of the best roads in Africa and suddenly find yourself the slowest thing on the road whilst still being the target for every speed cop with a twitchy finger. But try as they might, they can't touch you now. The journey is over and the end (or turning point) is in sight.

SOUTHERN AFRICA ONLINE

What some grandly call overlanding is simply recreation to many South Africans. They also benefit from minimal carnet or visa issues across southern Africa right up to DRC and Kenya. As in Australia, a huge off-road scene exists with books, DVDs, tours, detailed GPS routes and of course forums.

Aimed at 4x4s, the **South African Overland Forum** covers six country categories plus the South African former homelands, medical and GPS chat. 🖳 overland.co.za.

SELLING VEHICLES IN OR FROM SOUTH AFRICA

Selling a foreign-registered vehicle in South Africa will attract approximately 65% tax. This doesn't apply to SA residents returning home after more than a year with a vehicle in their name for that time, unless it was registered before 2000. There are also restrictions on selling it on again within two years. For the full story see 🖳 sars.gov.za.

Coming the other way, selling a South African-registered vehicle in the UK for example, will be subject to VAT of 20% plus 10% import tax, along with various conformity certifications and a not-too-stringent test of roadworthiness.

LATIN AMERICA ROUTE OUTLINES

10

Of the three continents covered in this book, the countries south of the US border offer the easiest destination in terms of language and documentation, along with about as much geographical diversity as one planet can offer. For Americans in particular, Latin America also conjures up images of banditry and corrupt police. Living standards and the state of security vary greatly from country to country or even regionally, but as usual, once you actually go there the reality is far more benign.

Above all, compared to parts of Africa and Asia, the lack of requirements for carnets and for most, visas in advance, greatly **simplifies border crossings**, particularly in South America (Central America still likes to make a meal of it). Instead, right across the region a temporary vehicle import permit (**TIP**) is readily issued and usually lasts three months. Just remember to cancel it before leaving a country; it's not always demanded but if you come back your vehicle will still be registered and you may have problems. The absence of an expensive carnet also makes **buying a vehicle** possible, either locally or more easily, from another foreigner, enabling a fly-in trip which time or budget might otherwise forbid. Check the tips on the Horizons Unlimited South America forum, the best resource for travelling down here. And whatever its value, a **yellow fever certificate** may be required at some borders.

The cost of living isn't always so modest and compared to the US, in most places **fuel** will be more expensive. But whatever the season (see p450), there's a decent network of sealed roads so a 4x4 isn't necessary (though there's as much off-road action as you can cram in). Most will find the crazy local driving standards adventure enough, particularly in Peru.

No surprise that the **US dollar** is the most useful hard currency and is the *actual* currency in El Salvador, Panama and Ecuador. Elsewhere, wait until you're in the country and then change just enough to get you to an ATM where you'll get the regular exchange rate, except in Venezuela (see p464), where a currency black market thrives. Above all, outside Brazil and the Guianas, knowing or **learning some Spanish** will transform your experience and reduce 'gringo' taxes. Early on, consider parking up for a month and attending a school. It's an easy language to learn.

Mexico and Central America

Parts of Mexico have had a bad time these last few years and while problems still exist, they're mainly in the north in places like Juarez, so plan to get clear of the border zone on day one. Note also that **right-hand drive** (RHD) vehicles are no longer permitted in Costa Rica or Nicaragua. The latter may let you in by mistake, the former – less likely. Ship from Houston or Miami.

South of the border

Mexico immigration issues a **tourist card** (FMT; *forma migratoria para tourista, transmigrante*; or FM3 for multiple entry) valid for 180 days. It can also be acquired in advance from Mexican consulates. Once in the country it's rare to show your FMT and, unlike elsewhere in the world, the police may be more interested in seeing a driving licence (*licencia* – a de facto ID) than a passport.

Unless making an excursion to Baja, around Sonora, or staying within the 'Free Zone' close to the border, you'll need to buy a **temporary import permit** sticker by showing proof of ownership (original US title), vehicle registration (not the same as title in the US), your passport, driver's licence and proof of Mexican vehicle insurance. The TIP (*Declaración de Ingreso de Vehiculo Automotivo*) costs around $50 with a $400 bond (less for pre-2007 vehicles) deposited with the *Banjercito* bank (🖳 banjercito.com.mx) with a credit card. On leaving Mexico make sure you cancel the TIP and get a refund from the *Banjercito* (not present at smaller borders), otherwise you may run into trouble returning into Mexico which has computerised the TIP process.

Vehicle insurance (*seguro de vehiculo*) is required and unlike further south, needs to be taken seriously; you're looking at around $130 a month or not much more for six months. Following an accident everyone's considered guilty until proven innocent, and having insurance can be the difference between having your vehicle impounded, or moving on. Insurance from a Mexican provider is easily obtained at the border or in advance over the web from places like 🖳 mexinsure.com, 🖳 mexpro.com or 🖳 mexadventure.com.

If you have an accident in Mexico, immediately contact your insurance provider who usually has a legal advisor that can help you in negotiations with the police. Don't sign anything before involving your insurance company, especially settlement agreements with other parties, as they could invalidate your insurance. These companies, and many more in North America, can also sell residents **vehicle recovery insurance** valid throughout Central America. A relay of local providers shuttle you back to the border, so although it won't be a seamless transit as in the States, you will be recovered. Without it you can of course organise an informal recovery, as you would elsewhere.

On the road in Mexico

Driving in Mexico is reasonably sane, though chaos can reign in urban areas plus there are the usual livestock and night-driving hazards. Roads often have no hard shoulder and asphalt can stop suddenly. Truck drivers also have a

AN AMERICAN IN MEXICO

I lived in Mexico for a year and found it to be safe. Yes petty theft occurs, and yes drug smugglers get killed in horrible ways, but the average tourist will feel safe and welcomed. You won't be shot at while driving your vehicle in Mexico. Has it ever happened? Sure; same can be said for the US.

Now the important stuff! Smiles, *holas, buenos dias, buenas tardes, buenas noches, por favors* and *gracias* go a long way. Get a **Mexican Spanish phrasebook** and practise the basics. If nothing else say *hola*, smile and look people in the eye. Mexico is a slower paced society too, so it's rude to rush or be too direct. Start a question with salutations or pleasantries then fire away, you'll get a better response.

If you're lost, asking for the next location is best. Mexicans think it rude to not have an answer, even if it's the wrong one, plus many haven't travelled more than a village or two away. In cities I ask for the next biggest city and often ask someone again just to verify. For **GPS** I use routeable bicimaps (🖥 bicimapas.com.mx), plus the Guia Roji paper atlas (see p440).

Mexico is a cash society. If businesses accept cards they're probably over-priced tourist joints. The easiest and safest way to get cash is from an ATM; let your bank know you'll be in Mexico. You might pay a transaction fee so get the maximum each time.

If you offer a gift to a Mexican they'll say no, then expect you to offer it again when they will accept. Works the same if receiving.

© thedarienplan.com

Almost anything can be haggled over except at stores, fuel and tolls. At a market it's expected. For a cheap hotel, ask for *habatacion mas barato* or *economico*.

Expect to pay for a public toilet and bring your own tissues or use a restaurant toilet when you can. Fuel station attendants are paid with tips; they'll let you pump but give them a few pesos or stop shy of a round figure and let them keep the change. Food store baggers also survive on tips and as in the US, 15% is normal at restaurants.

Accept that the boundaries of personal space are smaller than in the US, so when lines form be assertive or they'll pass you by.

Photocopy your important papers and show them to the cops if stopped. After that give a copy of your driving licence. By law they can't keep your passport so never even show it. If you've done nothing wrong wait it out; insist they write a ticket or let you go. They're waiting for a bribe. I resisted a transit cop in Puerto Vallarta for ten minutes, then he gave up and only transit cops tend to give tickets. On the road Mexican drivers are fast but alert and compared to the US traffic rules are less rigid which can be liberating once you get in the swing. And try as many types of **foods** as possible. The variety will blow you away. The best meals and prices come from street vendors.

BILL EAKINS 🖥 butlermaps.com

habit of signalling left to indicate that it's safe for you to pass – or do they plan to move out or turn left? Engage your telepathic sensors before attempting to pass. Roads through towns have speed bumps (*topes*) that are often unmarked and can hammer the suspension if taken too fast.

In rural areas here and in Central America, delays can occur when militant locals set up **road blocks** in response to some injustice or complaint; a frequent Latino way of expressing grudges with authorities. Handle it right and as a foreigner you might slip through, but don't count on it. Just because the protestors aren't state officials doesn't mean they're inconsequential.

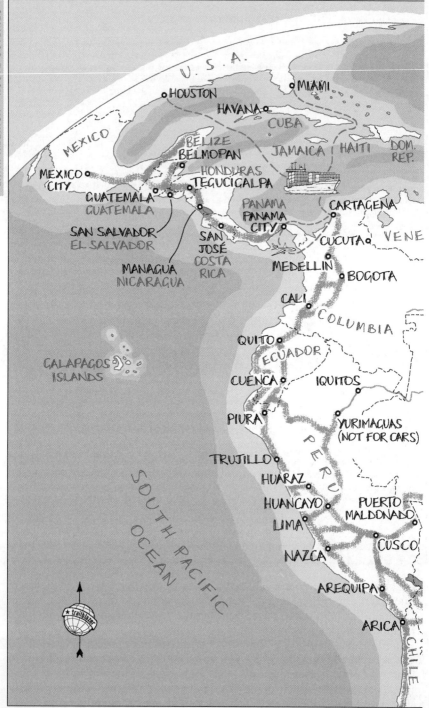

Main overland routes across Central & South America

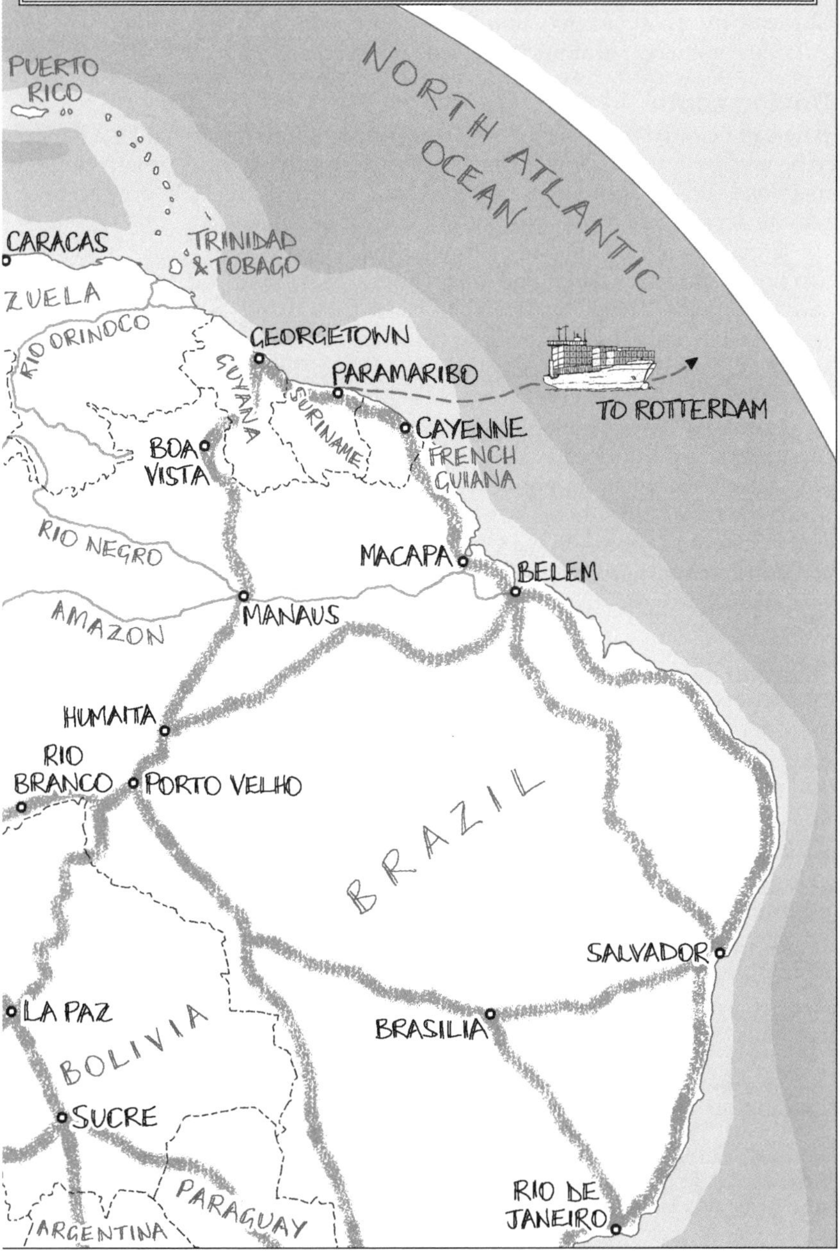

Fuel is dispensed from the state-run Pemex stations. Nationwide, **ATMs** take most credit cards but it's also possible to pay in dollars and get change in pesos at the normal rate for most services, including fuel.

In Mexico **police checkpoints** are more of a problem than the military equivalent. Heading north towards the US, they're looking for drugs, so a sniffer dog may make the rounds. Police are less professional, especially around Mexico City. To avoid that area get the national road atlas, the **Guia Roji** (🖥 guiaroji.com.mx) at around $15. It gets updated annually.

Driving south

Baja can be regarded a recreational extension of California that also happens to be an easy introduction to Mexico, with ferries from the southern tip to the mainland. Bush camping is easy and safe, beaches are easily accessible and remote deserts and mountains make for great adventures.

Crossings are less hassle at smaller border posts like Tecate, Mexicali or San Luis in the east, rather than busy Tijuana. Make sure you do the full tourist card/insurance/TIP deal as detailed earlier; it's easier than at La Paz where **ferries** leave daily to the mainland from the Pichilingue terminal. One docks at Mazatlan after a 12-hour crossing; the other at Topolobampo (six hours). For route planning 🖥 discoverbaja.com is a great website.

Mainland Mexico is not like Baja. While remote areas can certainly still be found, it's harder to locate discreet **bush camps** as towns and private fenced land becomes more common. Picturesque beaches can be found all the way down the mainland side of the Gulf of California which also allows exploring of the Sonoran Desert. On the Caribbean coast Mayan ruins in the south offer some of the finest archaeological sites in North America. Palenque is considered one of the best, but travelling into the **Yucatán** you'll have no end of great choices.

Tolls and more checkpoints

On the way south another big mainland feature are the **toll roads**. Main highways have toll booths and can end up being pretty expensive. Again, watch your change from the toll attendants as you do at fuel stations.

There are **military checkpoints** all over mainland Mexico, but especially along the coast directly west of Mexico City and in the state of Chiapas on the Pacific border with Guatemala. Just as in Baja, the main reason for these posts is to limit the traffic in illegal drugs and immigrants. The soldiers are often pleasant and may want to see your paperwork as well as to perform a cursory search, but asking for *mordidas* (bribes) is extremely unusual. The police aren't quite the same.

MEXICO & CENTRAL AMERICA: RELATIVE FUEL PRICES

Apart from Mexico, distances are modest in Central America, but everywhere except Panama (10% less) fuel is either the same (El Salvador and Guatemala) or more expensive than the US. In Mexico fuel costs 10% more; in Nicaragua, Honduras and Costa Rica gasoline is 50% more while diesel's 15%. In Belize it's nearly double. Once in Colombia, fuel costs a little more the US. Of course, one currency crash or a fuel crisis will mess up these figures, but it's a start.

BELIZE

Crossing from Mexico to Belize you pass from a Latino to a Caribbean culture which itself has diverse origins and influences. As the former colony of British Honduras, **English** is the official language here which can make things easier except when you need to act dumb. There's great **diving** and kayaking on the coast, and inland the jungle offers more Mayan ruins.

Bringing a vehicle into Belize involves nothing more than showing proof of vehicle ownership along with passport and your driving licence. Your domestic licence will be accepted for visits under three months; for longer stays an IDP (see p23) is required, but on any big trip an inexpensive IDP is handy anyway. They'll also require three copies of all your documents (title, registration, passport and licence) as well local **insurance** which costs about $50 for three months; you'll get an ICB insurance sticker. As with much of Latin America, the **temporary import permit** is valid for 90 days. On leaving the country you may be charged a departure tax, though this is more usual at airports.

Belize isn't heavily populated, with only 20,000 in the capital, **Belmopan**. Roads between the few cities aren't busy, but few are paved. **Driving standards** are consistent with developing countries and vehicles are often in bad shape – the two seem to go hand in hand. In the **rainy season** from June to November downpours transform the top layer into a greasy, tread-clogging mire. For **fuel,** fill up in Mexico and before Guatemala and you'll save a lot.

Travel is easy until you close in on the Guatemalan border. **Police** tend to keep a low profile and in rural areas are virtually non-existent, although Belize City has a bad reputation.

Bush camping is difficult in Belize mainly due to the amount of private land or the density of the jungle. When on jungle tracks it can be hard to find enough space to camp, though traffic is sparse in many areas, so camping by the road itself may be possible.

GUATEMALA

Guatemala gets a bad rap and the border experience can support this. Mexico and Belize are all very well, but in poorer Guatemala border officials can be surly and make heavy demands on your paperwork.

As elsewhere, you'll need proof of vehicle ownership along with passport and driving licence. Three copies of each document are required and can be made at the main border posts. Things might start with a **fumigation** for a few quetzals, and if entering from Mexico you may be asked to show the receipt for cancelling your Mexican TIP. A passport stamp comes next and may cost a few pesos or quetzals, but no motor **insurance** is required. Show a US driving licence or an IDP and buy a tourist permit for some 40 quetzals.

Temporary vehicle importation permits ('SAT') are issued for 160

Out of the frying pan ... © Nick Taylor

quetzals and last for 90 days with extensions available. Since Guatemala is part of the Central America Four Border Control Agreement (CA4) with Honduras, El Salvador and Nicaragua, you should be covered for 90 days for all these countries on immigration, but in practice there seems to be no reciprocity on vehicle imports, at least for foreigners, so you'll have to repeat the procedure in each country. Just like in Mexico you'll be issued a sticker which needs to be surrendered on export.

On the road

The CA13 highway heading north to south is in good shape, and the Western Highway from Belize may be the same. **Guatemala City** is the largest city in Central America and the traffic is horrendous. To add to the torment, just as in Mexico, large and often unmarked **speed bumps** (*topes* or *tumulos*) are ready to catch the unwary. Guatemalan drivers in the capital are aggressive, but elsewhere driving is no worse than usual.

Once away from the border and Guatemala City, **police** tend to keep a low profile and checkpoints aren't too common. **Fuel** is easy to come by with branded stations from Shell and Texaco providing most of the service.

Attractions in Guatemala centre on the **Mayan ruins** and ancient sites, Tikal being best known. There's camping here in a non-fenced site with a night watchman. North of Tikal, Uaxactun can prove a challenge to reach, but offers entry into the Mayan Biosphere Reserve as well as the ruins of Peten. Finca Ixobel, just south of Poptún near the Belize border, offers nice camping, good food, wi-fi and tour services.

HONDURAS

Entry is the same story except they might want four copies of each of your documents, as well as four copies of each of the import permit documents issued at the border and the stamps in your passport. Facilities for money changing and copies are available at the borders, as are pushy fixers. No proof of **insurance** is required to leave the border and the 90-day vehicle *temporal* costs some 250 lempira.

Some report bribes being demanded at Honduran borders, especially El Florido east of Guatemala City where you may also pay a foreign licence plate fee of L435 and a few more to the customs. Membership of CA-4 makes little odds and the usual vehicle import hoops still have to be cleared with space-consuming stamps in your passport on entering and leaving the country. Total border costs are around $45 for vehicle import fees.

There'll often be a police checkpoint shortly after the border, watching for infractions and demanding a copy of your TIP. Making extra copies at the border can alleviate hassle here. Leaving the country, some travellers end up paying a couple of dollars for a passport stamp and a few dollars more to fill out a customs form, others pay nothing which you assume is the norm.

Honduras is very mountainous in the west where roads are narrow and the going slow, especially behind heavy trucks. Overland travel is more difficult in the lowlands to the east of the country as there are few roads.

Police checkpoints are frequent along the Pan-American highway approaching borders. Usually you'll just be asked for your papers, but some officers will go further or just be a pain. On the CA-3 highway from Choluteca to the Nicaraguan border at Guasaule some get stopped half-a-dozen times.

Because of these well-known hassles in Honduras, some travellers cross from Guatemala into El Salvador and from there try to nip across Honduras to Nicaragua in a couple of hours. It's less than 200km but El Amatillo border is notorious and the Honduran police know your game; a lot of shakedowns occur on this section. Use any other border to get into Honduras.

In the pine forests in Honduras **bush camping** spots can easily be found, but near towns it gets difficult and security can be a concern.

EL SALVADOR

With well-paved roads for the main arteries, El Salvador can be crossed quickly and navigated easily. Along with many familiar US fast-food franchises and the US dollar currency, **beaches** are the major draw here, with every beach running six-foot plus surf between March and October.

At the border it's the same story as before, but with only two copies of everything required. No one asks for **insurance**, but it is a good idea, as is an IDP. Entry permits last 90 days and extensions are possible. Fumigation costs a couple of bucks but only happens at some crossings. Otherwise, there may be a $5 road use fee. Fixers or *tramitadores* inhabit all borders and can be helpful, especially if you don't speak Spanish. **Police** do set up checkpoints, but dodgy dealings are less common than neighbouring countries.

El Salvador is the most densely populated country in Central America so **bush camping** can be quite a challenge. Beach camping is possible in certain areas, but check with the locals. Since the beaches are the main tourist attraction, there are many hotels along the coast.

NICARAGUA

At the border it's another Xerox hoedown with three copies of everything. Buy **insurance** for around $12 a month and a 90-day TIP once you've shown your *boleta de revision turismo* or **tourist card** that's surrendered on exit. **Fuel** is at familiar stations like Shell and, as in El Salvador and Panama, you'll find the familiar American fast-food joints and a much more developed feel than in Honduras or Guatemala. Brits take note: a driver in a **proscribed RHD vehicle** (see p260) was let in from the north but not into Costa Rica, nor back into Nicaragua. Two weeks later and a bit thinner, he got transported out of No Man's Land and shipped out. You have been warned.

In a bid to stem the flow of narcotics, roadside police checks are becoming much more common and experiences vary greatly from polite hellos to full shakedowns. Nicaragua seems to be split down the middle; the west is mainly Spanish-speaking with a well-maintained infrastructure and some charming colonial towns, while the English-speaking east is a wild and remote jungle, once the stronghold of the Sandinistas and with less-intact infrastructure. With fewer ancient ruins in Nicaragua, the interesting historical sites are old cities like León and Grenada. Both are well worth exploring, with a wonderful colonial ambience as well as great restaurants and charming (if expensive) hotels. **Volcanoes** dominate the skyline especially between lakes Managua and Nicaragua.

Even on a good day Managua itself can be difficult to get around. Protests are frequent and as mentioned, roads get closed by the police.

COSTA RICA

By Central American standards Costa Rica is a mainstream tourist destination, and as such might offer a bit of a respite if you're still finding the going hard. North Americans and backpackers fly here to take regular vacations they wouldn't dream of taking in most of the neighbouring countries. There's lots to see here, but with the usual tourist-related issues which includes the relatively higher cost of living. There are several biosphere reserves, zip line canopy tours, volcano hikes and fabulous sandy beaches, but unless they rescind the law, you **won't get in with an RHD** vehicle and would have been better off shipping direct to South America.

Without one of those it's the usual procedure: they want to see vehicle ownership (original US title) and registration along with passport, driving licence and your mother-in-law's embroidered marriage certificate; three copies of each. **Insurance** costs around $20 a month. Where it's required, fumigation costs $2 so if there were any bugs stowing away when you left Mexico, by now they're well and truly extinct. Borders teem with fixers and as elsewhere, before you hire anyone, agree on a price, set some conditions under which they won't be paid (if extra costs are incurred, for instance) and don't pay until the border dance is complete. Also don't hand over any of your documentation; often they'll try to get things going in a second line while you're waiting in the first. A little patience here can be invaluable and avoid situations where your documents are held to ransom. On leaving fill in a form to cancel your vehicle import permit.

PANAMA

For much of the last century the US controlled the **Panama Canal**, and these days Panama feels like a state of the USA. The local currency is tied 1:1 to the **US dollar**, highways abound and ex-pats roam the streets.

Vehicle import, you know the drill by now: **insurance** at the border for $15 a month; temporary vehicle importation permits (TIP) are good for 30 days, but can be extended at customs. If you're shipping out of Panama it's vital that this document is completed correctly and that they know the difference between your licence plate (registration number) and your VIN (chassis ID plate). As mentioned at the start of the book, it helps to highlight the long VIN on your vehicle ownership documents (or copies) with a marker pen so it's clearly distinguishable from your licence plate. Fumigation costs at least a dollar and individuals buy a $10 tourist card plus a $1 sticker for the passport. These stickers are sometimes offered by bystanders, probably looking for a tip.

Once on the way, checkpoints tend to be staged closer to the border with Costa Rica so watch your speed in the first few miles. It's possible to store vehicles at Panama customs in both David and Panama City, though some have had mixed results with the security in Panama City. The famous canal is the main attraction here, offering impressive views of huge ships gliding past.

Panama City itself has modern high-rises with the feel of Dubai in some places, but in the old town squatters live in bombed-out buildings while the Pan-American highway is in pretty good condition. Road signs aren't common though and finding your way can mean asking the locals. The drive from David north to Boquete is well worth the scenic views and visiting Parque Nacional Volcán Barú makes a great end to that section.

Shipping around the Darien

For a few months around 2015 the Ferry Xpress service ran between Panama and Colombia but, like previous such operations, it did not prove viable when air fares dropped. Bikers hitch a ride on a sail boat or use air freight – you unfortunately must get involved in the costly and tedious world of shipping. The cost of a 40ft container that will take two regular vehicles to Cartagena works out around $2500 but, even for this short crossing, a container (more on p319) is most secure than the Ro-Ro services

Colón. With centimetres to spare, a world-weary Iveco is secured inside a container and the doors slam shut. © philflanagan.net

(mandatory for vehicles more than 2.7m high). When your vehicle is your home, the effort required to outwit the risks of a Ro-Ro service (see p319) may be too great. If all this has come as a bit of a shock, consider shipping direct from North America. **Miami** is the best port from which to organise shipping to Cartagena, Rio, Buenos Aires (BA), or even Santiago, and if you live there at least you can get the process underway while still at home.

Otherwise, container ships depart for Cartagena weekly, the 500-km transit takes a day or two, unless there are delays or re-routings. In Panama City the whole process can all be pinned down in a couple of days, using a shipping agent like Fernie, Rozo or Barwil Agencia, based in the business park at the former Howard Airforce Base, south of the city (N08° 55.67' W79° 35.57') and who work with Wilhelmsen. Many choose to deal direct with a shipping company, with good experiences reported with **Seaboard** (🖳 seaboard marinepanama.com) located on Ave. Miguel Brostella in the El Dorado district on the west side of town (N09° 00.4' W79° 32.29').

DARIEN GAP – THE END OF THE ROAD

The Panamericana comes to a stop at Yaviza on the Rio Chucunaque alongside the so-called Darien Gap. The next nearest town is Turbo in Colombia, 300km north of Medellín. It may seem absurd that 48,000 kilometres of Pan-Am are broken by just 80km of jungle and swamp, when nearby, over a century ago a canal nearly as long was built to link two oceans. Recent politics in northern Colombia, which also happens to be the world's biggest cocaine producer, is why in turn the world's biggest consumer of that drug – the US – is happy for the gap to remain intact.

Since a Land Rover and a Jeep took nearly six months to be the first to drive across the Darien in 1960, a handful of other 4x4s have repeated their achievement over the years. Often resorting to rafts, one mid-1980s attempt using CJ-5s progressed at an average of a mile a week to complete an all-land route over a period of nearly two years.

'Two days' can of course become two weeks, with all the associated expenses. Unfortunately, these sorts of delays, as well as plain old overcharging, are all par for the course in the wretched world of single-vehicle shipping.

See what's new on the usual forums but in Panama City you need to visit the places below where, as in any city away from the central tourist or business district, you want to be sure your vehicle is secure or better still, someone with a scowl is sitting in it. As you might have guessed, you'll also want several copies of all your paperwork and documents. The receipt or proof that you paid for the shipment may help in retrieving your BoL at Cartagena port where they don't know you from Adam.

- Having made contact, secured a date and paid the fees, get a **Bill of Lading** (BoL) from the shipping agent or company in Panama.
- When you're ready to go, **dress formally** (no shorts) and visit the Policia Tecnica Judicial (N08° 57.9′ W79° 32.68′) who'll inspect your vehicle and issue a **report** affirming the VIN on your TIP matches that shown on your ownership documents and the actual VIN plate on the vehicle.
- Visit the Secretaria General right across the busy road from the PTJ who'll have forwarded your report to them. Once here, get permission to export the vehicle from the *control de vehiculos* office. You now have eight days to get the vehicle shipped out.
- When the time comes, drive up to Cristobal harbour (N09° 20.57′ W79° 54.54′ – small entrance fee) in the port city of Colón, 60km from Panama City. Get the *aduana* to cancel the *entrada con vehiculo* stamp in your passport and have the vehicle inspected. Then arrange the loading paperwork with the shipping office also located here.

It can all feel a little disorganised at Cristobal because what you're doing isn't a common procedure at any commercial port. If going to the expense and security of using a **container** rather than Ro-Ro or Lo-Lo, politely resist offers to drive and load your vehicle for you. You know what's at stake and so do they. The whole point of using a container is to eliminate your vehicle's exposure to pilfering, as well as the need to spend time taking measures against that. It's most reassuring to attend the slamming, clamping and sealing of a container door, including adding your own padlock, rather than dropping the keys of your pride and joy into the hands of a troop of drooling wharfies.

VEHICLE RELEASE IN CARTAGENA

Once in **Cartagena**, again it's possible to be out of the port in a day at a cost of around $200, while remembering that from around 11.30am to 2pm all activity ceases. Better to set aside two days. Employing a local agent can expedite things and may well end up costing a little less.

There are various ports in Cartagena, but chances are you'll use the centrally located Muelle Del Bosque with the harbour office to be found, rather inauspiciously, on Isla Diablo, at N10° 23.9′ W75° 31.63′. If doing it all yourself the procedure is as follows:

- Retrieve the original BoL from the shipping company's office.
- Take that to the office for *Formulario de Importación Temporal de Vehiculos* at the Customs office (DIAN) a couple of km round the harbour

(N10° 24.53' W75° 32.03') along with photocopies of your Colombia passport entry stamp and all the usuals. A Customs inspection will be arranged back at Muelle Del Bosque, but probably not the same day.

- Escorted by port staff, locate and unlock your container, 'unstuff' the vehicle (wharfies may do this), get it inspected and pay any port fees.
- Go back to the DIAN where you'll be issued with your TIP.
- With a TIP you can now buy your third-party insurance or SOAT (*Seguro Obligatorio contra Accidentes de Tránsito*). Expect to pay around $20 for a month's cover from Previsora (🖥 previsora.gov.co) on Calle de Arsenal (N10° 25.1' W75° 32.8'), number 10-25. It's less than a kilometre from the DIAN and there are several hotels in this district.
- With your SOAT you can return to the port and get your *salida permiso* (exit permit), after another inspection and a weighbridge.

Getting yourself to Cartagena

You can **fly** from Panama to Cartagena in a little over an hour for about $350, but a more interesting alternative is to spend a few days **sailing or cruising** across the Bay of Darien, passing along the San Blas Islands. The Panamanian archipelago is home to the protected Kuna Indians, but most of the 340 or more islands are uninhabited. The tiniest can be just a cluster of a dozen palms on a white sand platform and the area is ideal for snorkeling.

There are several scheduled cruises that will cost at least twice as much as flying, and although once you leave the archipelago the crossing of the Bay can get rough, few overlanders regret taking this option. When they're based there, the 100-year-old German-run Stahlratte sailing ship (🖥 stahlratte.org) allows you to get involved in the crewing on the passage to Cartagena.

For smaller craft, visit the marinas like 🖥 shelterbaymarina.com to see if anyone wants help crewing over to Colombia.

From Panama you can catch a plane to Cartagena or you can join a cruise on a variety of craft passing the San Blas archipelago on the way. © thedarienplan.com

Main overland routes across South America

South America

WITH MARK HARFENIST

Driving around Central America isn't so difficult if you're based in North America, and it's a great way of dipping your toe into the overland experience. But in South America you're overlanding for real, if for no other reason than you can't nip home inexpensively. Still, when you add it all up South America might well be the best overlanding destination on the planet. An extreme range of environments await you from barely penetrable jungle to hyper-arid deserts, wildlife-rich wetlands and fern-clad mesas, the shimmering volcano-dotted altiplano and the snowbound passes across the Andes. Did I miss anything? Yes, a rich pre-Conquest heritage, nearly a single language, fewer border games than Central America and visa issues only for Americanos.

That leaves only **crazy drivers**, shaky infrastructure in the poorer Andean countries, and the **fear of crime** in some cities, all of which can either be avoided or taken on with your wits firmly strapped about you.

Routes in South America

There are thirteen countries in South America, but most overlanders are satisfied visiting about half (especially with the current closure of the Colombia–Venezuela border to vehicles (see p464). They follow the **Pan-American Highway** along the Andean-Pacific axis where Colombia leads to Ecuador, Peru, and Bolivia where you criss-cross the Chile–Argentine border for Ushuaia and **Tierra del Fuego**. That done, many head for **Buenos Aires** and ship out.

In taking that drive of 16,000 kilometres or more, it's not impossible to rise 13,000ft or four kilometres in a single day which can mess you up, but mile-for-mile this route delivers uninterrupted spectacle and if time, funds or will are limited, you'll certainly see the best of South America this way.

From the **inland borders** of Colombia, Ecuador and Peru no reliable roads lead into the Amazon basin. Linked by an hour's drive, Nauta and **Iquitos** are in the heart of this area in eastern Peru, but both are only accessible by boat or air.

COLOMBIA

Despite its once notorious reputation, Colombia is a hit with overlanders. The idyllic beaches, jagged mountains and verdant jungles were always an attraction and the people welcoming. Roads are sometimes superb, not least when twisting through the Andean sub-ranges,. Main roads will be paved and may include tolls unless you go out of your way to look for gravel or dirt. There are also travel-friendly hostels, relatively easy availability of vehicle parts and an upbeat air in a country emerging from a long civil war. Plan on spending longer and having more fun in Colombia than you may have expected.

LATIN AMERICA – ROUTE OUTLINES

SOUTH AMERICA: CLIMATE AND SEASONS

The immense size of the continent, along with its extreme variations in landforms and altitude make generalisations difficult. The only certainty is that you'll experience a certain amount of uncomfortable weather.

During the **southern summer** (November to March) thunderstorms roll through southern Brazil, northern Argentina and the altiplano of Bolivia, Peru and Chile. In places they may temporarily disrupt travel, but they're localised; you'll often spy black clouds stalking the altiplano without experiencing a drop.

Summer temperatures in the **altiplano** often slip below freezing at night but during winter (May to September) it gets brutally cold, although this is also **dry season**, and the sun quickly warms the thin air. Take this into account if camping.

At lower elevations throughout southern Brazil, Paraguay, Uruguay and northern Argentina summers tend to be hot and humid. This area is more comfortably visited during March and April. During winter it gets surprisingly chilly and a damp 10°C/50°F is not uncommon.

Down in Patagonia moisture-laden air runs up along the Pacific side of the Andes from Tierra del Fuego through the ice fields and rain forests to the Lakes District of Chile and Argentina before petering out completely around the latitude of Santiago. This produces gorgeous weather in the Chilean Lakes District during summer, after which winter storms roll in. At the same time, areas on the western side of the range south of 45 degrees latitude tend to have damp, chilly summers until the storm track shifts northward. Shielded by the heights of the southern Andes, Patagonia is generally dry, if famously **windy**. Note the abrupt change as you transit from steppes to mountains just before reaching Ushuaia; the winds die, you're suddenly surrounded by forest, and almost instantly it begins to rain and snow, even during summer.

North of the equator, you'll find that there's no real dry season in the Amazon, although there are 'less wet' periods. December to March is generally rainiest; April to November slightly cooler, June to August a bit drier. In Colombia the dry season is most pronounced from January to March; in Andean regions of Ecuador it's June to September, while the rest of the year can be cloudy and cool, obscuring views of the volcanoes. In the Guianas and Venezuela, two rainy seasons prevail: one from October to February with a peak from December onwards, the other April to July. However, with August to October even hotter than the rest of the year, the best travel window is February and March.

These guidelines should be taken with a grain of salt and the influence of altitude; while Cartagena boils, Bogotá can be chilly. No one's managed to come up with an itinerary that visits everywhere in the best season. Crossing the Guianas might be ideal in March, but Angel Falls in neighbouring Venezuela are best in June when the falls are at full tilt. Similarly, no single trip can see the best conditions in Colombia, Ecuador and the Peruvian altiplano. MARK HARFENIST

SOUTH AMERICA: RELATIVE FUEL PRICES

Taking US fuel prices at 70 cents a litre, *as things stand now* in Colombia and Suriname gas is the same as the US, in Ecuador diesel is less than half with gas two-thirds, and in Bolivia both fuels are 75% of US prices (at local rates, see p457). In Guyana it's 20% more, so is diesel; in Chile, Peru and Brazil gas is 50% more, as it is in Argentina (diesel too) and Peru. It's double or more in Uruguay and in French Guiana. Or just visit ⌨ globalpetrolprices.com.

In Brazil most light vehicles run on E25 'gasohol', composed of 25% cane-based anhydrous ethanol; pure gasoline costs nearly as much as in Guiana. Fuel pumps in Brazil are marked: A for alcohol; D for diesel; and G for gasoline. 'Gas' refers to CNG, also widely used. Running a car on E25 ought not to ruin it, but E100 (100% hydrated ethanol) costing around 60% of E25 won't go down so well at the spark plug.

As mentioned elsewhere, fuel prices in remote states like Amazonas (the far west) can be double those of heavily agricultural or urban states like Mato Grosso, Panara or Sao Paulo.

Latin America Trip Reports colour section – Opposite: The Road of Death, Bolivia – see trip report on following pages. (Photo © Dan Grec).

Alaska to Argentina – Jeep Wrangler TJ

Name, Year of birth, Job Dan Grec, 1982, engineer
Where and when Alaska to Argentina, 2009-2011
Duration, distance, cost 22 months, 40,000 miles, $27,300
Vehicle model and year Jeep Wrangler TJ, 2000
Modifications None
Vehicle's strong points Lightweight
Vehicle problems Zero problems
Biggest headache Selling the Jeep in Argentina
Biggest surprise Bolivia – friendly and supremely beautiful
Favourite places Bolivian Altiplano, Uyuni Salt Flats, Patagonia
Next trip Around Africa (see Trip Reports, Part 9)

Photo Huascarán, Peru © Dan Grec

* * * T R I P R E P O R T * * *

Argentina to Alaska – Land Rover Defender

Name, Year of birth, Job Keelan Bell, 1999, Jack of all Trades
Where and when Argentina to Alaska, 2012 to date
Duration, distance, cost 4 years so far, almost 125,000kms, $126,400 or $60 a day for 4 people or a dollar a mile
Vehicle model and year Land Rover Defender 130 TD5, 2003
Modifications Winch, snorkel, drawer system, canopy with RTT
Vehicle's strong points Engine and the driver (my dad)
Vehicle problems Wheel bearings, uncomfortable seats
Biggest headache Failed wheel bearings late at night in Brazil
Biggest surprise That I've actually to start travelling extensively
Favourite places Impossible to answer
Next trip Currently Europe to Asia and then Australia, Africa

Photos Top: Northern Brazil. **Bottom, left**: La Mano del Desierto, Pan-Am Hwy, Chile; **Bottom, right**: In French Guiana. All © Lulu Bell

★ ★ ★ ★ T R I P   R E P O R T ★ ★ ★ ★

RTW – Mitsubishi L300

Name, Year of birth, Job Pablo Rey, 1966, writer; Anna Callau, 1972, editor and artisan

Where and when RTW, from 2000 and still in progress

Duration, distance, cost 17 years, 450,000 km, €1000/month

Vehicle model and year 4WD Mitsubishi L300/Delica, 1991

Modifications It's quite standard. It has extra fuel tank, custom Baja Rack, Espar Hydronic D5, 3 gel batteries, solar panel

Vehicle's strong points Compact 4WD van, comfortable to drive

Vehicle problems Tyres only 15"; difficult to find spares in Africa

Biggest headaches Stranded for 70 days in Atacama Desert, Chile after visiting the worst mechanic in the world

Biggest surprise The people, always

Favourite places Atacama, Sudan, Baja California, Zimbabwe

Next trip Back to South America or over to Siberia

Photo Trans Labrador Road, Canada © Pablo Rey

Although most areas in Colombia are considered safe, there's always an element of street crime in the cities, so it's still a good idea to ask locally before venturing off the main highways to some of the standard tourist destinations. In some cities the front line between safe and unsafe *barrios* may not be apparent to outsiders. Certain rural routes are still known for banditry which may or may not relate to FARC remnants – particularly in the south.

After Central America, Colombia is a big country but unless you're an amphibious tapir, you can write off the eastern Amazonian provinces. That leaves the two lofty eastern and western cordilleras which converge to the point of a 'V' at the Ecuadorian border. How you get there is up to you.

Insurance is mandatory in Colombia, and chances are you'll be checked at some point, so buy a month's worth. In theory this compulsory traffic accident insurance (Seguro Obligatorio de Accidentes Tráfico' or 'SOAT') can be bought in fuel stations and shopping malls, but usually for a minimum of a year. In Cartagena the Sura seguros office may still be doing three months insurance for around $100. It's located on the crossroads of Calle 25 and Carrera 17 or 17A (blue and white sign; aim for N10° 24.94' W75° 32.51'), a ten-minute walk north of the Manga Marina on the Calle 24 esplanade where you may have arrived from Panama by sail. After Central America, it can feel pleasantly reassuring to be insured again. For routeable **GPS maps** for your satnav look up 🖳 mygisco.com or of course 🖳 garmin.openstreetmap.nl.

Around Colombia

For many, **Cartagena** is their first sight of South America which is a good start as it's said to be one of the continent's most beautiful colonial cities. Not so inspiring is the humid climate and relatively drab hinterland. Just up the road from Manga marina, past the Texaco and over the bridge, is the old walled town of Getsamani where most of the lodgings, bars and cafés are to be found.

Formerly the home of vicious narcos, **Medellín** is a common stopover on the way down from the Caribbean coast. The surrounding area is rugged, with ranches and coffee plantations scattered between small villages and colonial towns so the driving is rewarding no matter which way you go.

From **Bogotá** routes go north toward Bucaramanga and northwest 450km to Medellín, while the same distance over the mountains towards Cali is obvious but clogged with trucks. Ask around first before taking the even more scenic but less direct route southwest through the Neiva valley.

Cali is another stop for many. If the roof tent is a bit rank, the popular *Casablanca Hostel* (🖳 casablancahostel.com, N03° 28.14' W76° 31.79') manages to combine repair services, long-term parking and even a micro-brewery into one well-run operation. The owner can also give reliable advice about local roads and routes. South from Cali, most make a 140-km beeline to beautiful **Popoyán** from where rough roads loop through the mountains to San Agustín and Tierradentro. Enquire locally about safety, and allow at least a couple of days of exploring. The day's drive towards the Ecuadorian border passes huge mountains, and deep canyons with roiling rivers far below, as well as grassy hillsides which glow an unearthly green. A left off the Pan-Am just before the border at Ipiales takes you to Santuario Del Las Lajas, a worthwhile side trip.

Latin America Trip Reports colour section – Opposite: Death Valley, California (**top**); being unloaded from a cargo ship in Colón, Panama, (**bottom**) – see trip report on preceding pages. (Photos © Pablo Rey & Anna Callau).

ECUADOR, PERU AND BOLIVIA

Between them, these three countries boast some of the most spectacular mountain driving and highest passes in the continent, unfortunately shared with the craziest drivers and treacherous conditions.

In between grand colonial cities like Quito and Sucre, Inca ruins and puffing volcanoes, you get a well-developed tourist infrastructure which adds up to easy travelling and a rich experience through the cordilleras.

Colombia–Ecuador border

Assuming there's still **no way into Venezuela**, you'll be heading for the main Colombia–Ecuador crossing at Ipiales–Tulcán which is open daily from early till 9pm. It may be your first internal border in South America so, compared to what went on in Central America, you'll be thrilled by the speed and efficiency. Only single copies of the usual documents are required: passport, vehicle ownership and driving licence.

On leaving Colombia, in Ecuador you need to get your vehicle **TIP** which includes basic **insurance** (a great idea you'll wish was adopted elsewhere). Next, fill out a *Tarjeta Andina de Migraciones* (TAM) immigration card, making sure not to lose the half they return so you can to re-present it on leaving the country. You can stay for 90 days in any 12-month period, though you may get only a month on arrival. If they ask, say you want *noventa días, por favor*.

Ecuador

For such a relatively small country Ecuador has a lot going on; beach and mangrove coastlines, glaciated volcanoes, pristine island ecosystems, rainforest jungles and cities with more colonial splendour than Carmen Miranda jet-skiing through Venice during the Biennale. Border formalities are relaxed, services are cheap, and as the **American dollar** is the currency you can stock up on cash for the weeks or months ahead at any ATM.

Coming from Colombia, the scenery in northern Ecuador resembles what you just left behind: looming volcanoes probe the clouds between pretty upland farms and villages. A 100km from the border, Ibarra and Otavalo (another 25km) have services, and another 100km down the Pan-Am takes you over **the equator** just south of Cayambe on the road to **Quito** (2800m/9300ft) where you can reasonably expect to get completely lost and – if you're very careless or unlucky – robbed too. The streets are clogged with traffic, but there's a bypass through the hills to the west. Otherwise, we're assured exploring Quito's old town will have been worth the effort.

Having fought your way back out of Quito like an ambushed conquistador, the Parque Nacional Cotopaxi has a deteriorating road which ends at a parking area at about 4800m/15,800ft. From here try and stagger another kilometre to the refuge from where, on a clear day, the views over the ash and snowscapes can be impressive indeed.

Often described as one of Ecuador's highlights, at Latacunga, some 30km south of the Cotopaxi turn-off, you'll find the beginning of the famous **Quilatoa Loop** to the west, a day's dirt roading at around 4000m through small highland towns alongside a crater lake. The scenery is otherworldly and there are ample places to eat and sleep should you decide to spend more than a day up here. Be prepared for cold and the thin air (guidelines on p343).

That said, the scenery on the Pan-Am down to Cuenca won't see you head-butting the dashboard in boredom. A couple of hours from Quito, a left in Ambato leads to **Baños**, deep canyon at the foot of the 5000m Tungurahua volcano which has lately lived up to its name – 'Throat of Fire'. The surrounding area is well worth exploring, despite the subsequent closure of some back roads, and the town itself is attractive, cheap and friendly.

An interesting alternative to returning to the Pan-Am for Cuenca heads downhill through the canyon and past waterfalls, then takes a right in Puyo onto the E45, a paved road to Macas and a little beyond. Even here in the lowlands you're at 600m, so it gets warm but not blindingly hot. From **Macas** a splendid road winds back up through the Sangay NP over to Guamote, where you rejoin the Pan-Am. Otherwise, continue south on the E45 for 100km to Limon and turn west through deep, jungle-clad valleys over a high pass to Cuenca. As long as it's not raining cats and dogs the route's not difficult.

Back north on the Pan-Am, most will stop in **Cuenca** to admire the picturesque cobblestone and whitewash Old Town before dropping down to **Loja** and deciding on meeting the Peru border at Macará (180km), up on the coast at Huaquillas (210km), or the less-reported dirt route southeast to **San Ignatio** down in the jungle. The tar resumes at Jaen so in good weather allow a couple of days and enough fuel for that one.

Ecuador–Peru border

Depending on when you arrive, the coastal border crossing at Huaquillas/ Aguas Verdes near **Tumbez**, Peru can be a little chaotic and intimidating, with the *aduana* done a few miles before at Chacras. Low-level smuggling goes on here and, with the 'gringo' element, on a bad day there can be a fair amount of scammery going down with the local entrepreneurs as you make your way to the bridge over the frontier creek (S03° 28.88' W80° 14.59'). The **Peruvian formalities** are done a couple of kilometres down the road.

Knowing all this and depending on your destination and the weather, you may find the inland border crossing at **Macara** more relaxed. It's said to be open round the clock and involves crossing the Puente International bridge at S04° 23.58' W79° 57.83', a couple of kilometres southwest of town. The first Peruvian town of Suyo is 16km on. In most cases you'll be given 90 days on entry to Peru and even if you don't visit the well-known sites at Machu Picchu and Nazca, it's easily possible to spend a month exploring this country.

Wherever you cross, fill out the usual forms and get a SUNAT (*Superintendencia Nacional de Administración Tributaria*) temporary import permit and a two-part form; hand your section back on leaving Peru. You'll need SOAT **insurance** in Peru from a Mapfre office (⌨ mapfreperu.com, or try ⌨ soat.com.pe). A month can cost you $50. Coming from Ecuador, La Positiva Seguros in Piura has been recommended – it's on Lima #544, east of the main cathedral and towards the river (aim for S05° 11.82' W80° 37.52'). Otherwise, you may want to avoid Trujillo. If starting out from Buenos Aires and looking for multi-country insurance cover, see p461.

The best paper **maps** are a set of three sold by the Touring y Automóvil Club del Peru – ⌨ touringperu.com.pe. They have offices in major cities, including Piura on Ave. Sánchez Cerro #1237, the Pan-Am main road in the town centre. For your routeable satnavs ⌨ perut.org gets the nod.

LATIN AMERICA – ROUTE OUTLINES

Viva La Panamericana.
© thedarienplan.com

Peru

Improbable though it seems, Peru has it all but in greater quantities: the deepest canyons; the tallest peaks; uncounted miles of desolate coastal deserts alongside a substantial chunk of Amazon jungle; fantastic roads and moderate prices.

It's over 1000km to Lima, and from the north initially at least, it's tempting to follow the arid Pan-Am across the coastal desert before cutting east over to Cusco by whichever route you fancy. Don't make the mistake of proceeding directly into northern Chile, unless you're on some sort of high-speed, record-breaking caper. Do the right thing and pay your respects to Machu Picchu before carrying on from Cusco into Bolivia, or maybe over into southern Brazil (see p468). A glance at a Peru map will show roads resembling artfully arranged ribbons of tagiatelle; if you have a Dynamic Cornering Response button on the console, press it now.

Tyres and many other **parts** are cheap in Peru; postponing repairs until Bolivia may be tempting fate and Chile, Argentina or Brazil may cost you double. Lima has the best selection, but parts are also found in Cusco or even Ica, because avoiding Lima's notorious traffic is another one of Peru's must-dos.

Entering Peru from Ecuador, there may be no apparent lodging along the Pan-Am for a couple of hours, so time things with that in mind. Having temporarily forsaken the scenic Andean plateau it's likely you'll be in a mild state of over-oxygenated under-stimulation, surfing arrow-straight highways over barren, trash-strewn scrub. Furthermore, the instant you cross into Peru **driving standards** collapse. Pedestrians don't stroll across the roads here; they get their heads down and sprint. Other hazards lie down this coast too: ferocious crosswinds and drifting sand that's more dangerous than it looks when hit at speed.

So stay alert or better still, get off the Pan-Am; it's the Andes roads you want, from smooth *pavimento* to dirt tracks through boulder fields with stream crossings and gaping washouts. Just remember, passes reach well above 4500m or 15,000ft so swift climbs from near sea level may give you a headache if rushed.

Perusing Peru

From the north the first obvious side trip leads into the peaks of the **Cordilleras Blanca and Huayhuash** rising to over 6500m/21,500ft. At only 3000m **Huaráz**, 430km north of Lima, is a favourite base. There are various approaches, including from Santa on the coast (just before Chimbote) into the **Cañon de Pato** for Carza on Ruta 3 north of Huaráz. The road follows a former rail grade through countless tunnels (which may exclude tall trucks) as well as a few airy bridges over the churning Rio Santa below. Another is the 14A leaving the Pan-Am at Casma, ascending more precipitous slopes before dropping directly into Huaráz. For more check out Trailblazer's cycling route guide to this mind-blowing region at ⌨ blancahuayhuash.com.

THE WAY TO MACHU PICCHU

Machu Picchu can be done as a long daytrip from Cusco or by overnighting in Aguas Calientes (now aka: Machu Picchu Pueblo) below the ruins. But you're in a car so can leave the herd and head into the Sacred Valley to spend some time exploring the numerous ruins in the area.

Ollantaytambo is a good base; catch the train to Machu Picchu from here – buy your train and entry tickets online in Cusco .

The back way into Machu Picchu, which climbs on pavement to a high pass past Ollantaytambo, then turns to dirt and descends to river level, has become increasingly travelled since big floods washed out the railroad. It's still not possible to actually drive all the way to Aguas Calientes, but

© Bingham Thomas

you might get to a town called Hydroelectrica, where you can park by the police station and walk along the seldom-used railroad tracks to Aguas. A small tip will ensure continued access.

However, if the latest landslide hasn't been cleared you may get only as far as Santa Theresa, 10km from Aguas. Walking is still an option, as is the train.

You'll find basic lodgings in Santa Theresa, which is also a base for exploring the tracks into the highland jungles beyond. It should go without saying that inquiries should be made locally before pinning your hopes on any of these roads; all are prone to landslides as recently as 2016.

MARK HARFENIST

Cruising the cordillera to Cusco

The roads from Huaráz through the cordillera are world class and the possibilities numerous, including following Ruta 3 south then west onto 14 for a superbly twisting descent to Paramonga on the coast. Or take any number of single lane dirt tracks up into the Cordillera Blanca for glaciers, lakes and ancient ruins. Careful study of maps, blogs and forums will reveal one- to three-day loops past remote villages, high passes and through deep canyons. By now you're understanding why you left the Panamericana to the crows, but inquire locally before venturing too far afield, as security can be a concern.

Heading inland, at Ruta 3 junction south of Huaráz continue down to Huánuco over the vast and infinitely variable altiplano ringed by spectacular mountain views and lined with hardscrabble Quechua villages. It can be a rough 330km so allow a full day, if not two. Pushing on from Huánuco, keep going to Huancayo. You can make no bad choices here: the two routes reaching southeast from Cerro de Pasco are equally stunning. Down in Huancayo more superb roads extend to Ayacucho where you can bail onto the paved Ruta 24 to the coast at Pisco.

Ayacucho is a splendid colonial-era town set deep in the Andes and well off the popular routes to Cusco, yet easily accessed by the paved highway from Pisco on the coast. This was a prime battleground during the *Sendero Luminoso* (Shining Path) years, and there's a moving museum and memorial to all victims of that struggle. The road over to Abancay is another knockout; allow a full day from Ayacucho, joining the main route from Nazca to Cusco.

Back on the coast, **Lima** is one of the largest cities on the continent, but transiting on the main highway is actually surprisingly painless. With composure and a degree of blind faith you'll be through almost before you notice. To the south the desert tightens its grip and brings you to Nazca, passing the huge dunes in Huacachina just out of **Ica**.

Nazca itself is pleasant enough; the job here is to cough up for a flight over the enigmatic Nazca Lines. The shrewd overlander will skip breakfast and be airborne over Nazca early in the day to avoid the afternoon breezes and the consequent risk of hurling over the back of the pilot's head once jammed in the turbulent confines of the cabin. Aside from the lines themselves, Nazca has ruins, mummies, graveyards and Cerro Blanco: five hours up, two minutes down on a sandboard which arrives hot enough to light a cigarette.

Leaving Nazca, some strike out southeast to Arequipa before backtracking north to Cusco. **Arequipa** is a spectacular town in a spectacular setting, flanked as it is by picture-perfect volcanoes and surrounded by wild high country cut by a canyon twice as deep as that one in Arizona. Although it's possible to continue to Chile, most follow a winding road north to Cusco.

An alternative route to Cusco is the paved Ruta 26 from Nazca through Puquio to Abancay. You may be getting blasé about Peru but listen up; this is a stellar route with two highland sections teeming with comely vicuñas and split by a deep river valley awash in the shifting light and colours of the afternoon. Allow at least twelve hours, so start early or take a break in Abancay. Don't underestimate the distance; temperatures drop quicker than your keys over a drain and sudden summer storms will flush you back to the Pacific quicker than a cream cheese and salmon bagel.

Cusco

Cusco may be touristy and therefore pricey, but it was the former capital of the Inca empire so have a heart, even without the nearby splendours of Machu Picchu. To **camp** head for *La Quintalala* north of town at S13° 30.35′ W71° 59.1′. In town the *Casa Grande* (S13° 31.01′ W71° 58.58′) is just east of the Plaza de Armas, or try the *Hostal Estrellita*, on Avenida Tullumayo 445 (S13° 31.12′ W71° 58.44′). Once they've had their fill, like Cassidy and Sundance, the overland gang lights out towards Bolivia down Ruta 3, perhaps stopping in Puno on Lake Titicaca (400km) before the border (150km) for Copacabana or La Paz.

Others might choose to leave the Cusco–Puno highway before Urcos and head over the passes and down to **Puerto Maldonado** (430km) and so to Brazil. Bearing the grand name of the **Carretera Interoceanica**, this road has been upgraded in the hope of living up to its name by linking Lima with Santos near Rio, over 5000km away on the Atlantic (although your shares in the Panama Canal are probably secure for a few years yet). If you're hardcore, it's also the way through the Amazon basin north towards Guyana (more on p465). Cusco to Cayenne, how hard can it be?

Over the border into Bolivia

Whichever way you get into Bolivia from the five bordering countries, Canadian and most EU nationals can enter without a **visa**, getting from 30 to 90 days. South Africans need a visa and US citizens can buy one at the border for a hefty $160 with a passport photo. On top of that you'll need to fill out a tourist card, possibly show an international **vaccination certificate**, get a TIP for the car and a coffee from the café.

It's said foreigners don't need motor **insurance** (SOAT) for stays of less than a month, because like Peru you can only buy a policy for a year. Other overlanders just try and pass off their IDP or similar document, manage to buy an international policy covering Bolivia, or have a document which says as much. If **coming from Chile** ⌨ pentagenerales.cl may be able to cover you for Argentina, Brazil, Paraguay, Uruguay, Bolivia and Peru for a couple of hundred dollars for six months. In Bolivia you might get local cover which also includes Argentina, Chile, Brazil, Paraguay and Uruguay from ⌨ fortalezaseguros.com.bo.

At the moment **fuel** works out about 50 cents a litre but those on foreign plates must pay up to three times more. This isn't intended as a tourist-gouging measure, more a way of stopping those from neighbouring countries taking advantage. On major highways the stations sell at the high rate or aren't allowed to sell to foreigners. In smaller towns fuel goes for local price.

In Bolivia

Most sources list Bolivia as South America's poorest country and as having the highest percentage of indigenous inhabitants. For you it's one of the richest experiences on the continent, the least expensive and where the thin air gives the sky a deep cerulean hue matched by brightly dressed locals, impressive colonial-era cities and dense jungle lowlands. Oh, and don't forget those refreshing munching leaves sold in local markets right across the land.

Roads in Bolivia are undergoing upgrades which means being braced for gruelling sections of mud, gravel and sand before slithering onto steaming fresh asphalt. You might try and catch up with the state of play on the official **map** at ⌨ abc.gob.bo, while Geogroup (⌨ geogroup-online.com) produces a Garmin satnav-compatible routeable **GPS map**, as does ⌨ viajerosmapas.com which also cover Chile and Argentina. Don't forget that like Peru, rural Bolivians will mount roadblocks at a moment's notice in the name of political self-expression. As a consequence nowhere in South America are you more likely to be trapped by resultant fuel and commodity shortages or complete shutdowns of major highways. However, these evaporate as fast as they arrive so park up and meet the locals.

At 3700m **La Paz** is by far the highest capital in the world with most of the main sights and lodgings in the central district within panting distance of the Plaza San Francisco. The main thoroughfare, which follows the canyon bottom, has various names but is generally referred to as The Prado. Streets in La Paz are steep, and with the altitude's effects you'll find yourself gasping a bit. If arriving during the summer, watch out for torrential afternoon storms which briefly turn the steep streets into white-knuckle kayak chutes.

The Road of Death and other fun excursions

A popular day trip from La Paz is along the North Yungas Road or 'Road of Death' which over 70km takes a stomach-lightening 3500m drop to the torrid lowland town of Coroico and Bolivia's steamy **Yungas** region where the anacondas grow thicker than a redwood pine. It's not just a nickname. Before they built the less-dangerous bypass, the mist-shrouded Carretera de la Muerte annually saw off hundreds when it served as one of the main access roads to the capital. It now attracts thrill-seeking mountain bikers as well as

Afeitado apurado con la muerte. © John Higham

a smattering of overlanders and even quad riders – some of whom continue to feed La Muerte's deadly appetite. But as you have brakes, hands and eyes, the Road of Death needn't be a fatal excursion. As elsewhere in Bolivia, local custom dictates the driver's side of a vehicle hugs the **outside edge** alongside the abyss, all the better to judge what space remains when squeezing past oncoming vehicles. This may mean they drive on the wrong side so be prepared, though the main hazard is more likely a panic-stricken mountain biker with smoking brakes. The best photos are near the top where the drop-offs are most impressive. And don't overlook the new highway to La Paz which is spectacular in itself, cresting at 4700m/15,400ft.

Elsewhere in Bolivia

How about leaving La Paz across the altiplano to Oruro then **Potosi**, before deciding whether to head for Uyuni or turn east towards Sucre, Santa Cruz and beyond. Another option is to access Sucre directly from Oruro via Ruta 6, which mixes pavement with gravel and dirt. All routes in this area traverse the lonely altiplano, with towns and cities located at 3000–4000m (10,000–13,200ft) either side of higher passes. In summer be prepared for sudden storms which dissipate after clobbering you with cold rain, hail or snow.

Each of the cities in this part of Bolivia has its own character – Potosi with its gritty remnants of colonial wealth and jarring mine tours; **Sucre** more conventionally pretty, surrounded by indigenous towns and endless back road adventures; tropical Santa Cruz, staging point for tours into sweaty lowland jungles. From Sucre few continue to **Santa Cruz**, and fewer still continue all the way into the Brazilian Pantanal on the paved road via Quijarro to **Corumbá**. Most prefer to double back towards the mind-bending shapes and colours surrounding the fabulous **Salar de Uyuni**.

The Salar salt flat often floods during the winter rains by just a few inches. While this is undeniably photogenic, the corrosive spray will eat your vehicle's electrics quicker than a shoal of piranhas, possibly causing problems for months to come. During the dry season, it's easy enough to shoot straight across to Chile or as an excursion from town. Either way, driving the glaring pan is surreal and exhilarating.

Descent into Chile

Two routes head from Uyuni to Chile along the southern edge of the Salar. One can be completed in a long day on actual roads to the border at **Ollagüe**, then on to Calama, through valleys rimmed with psychedelic shades, perfectly formed volcanoes and smaller salars choked with flamingos on diamox.

The tougher route takes a series of roads and tracks, passing Laguna Colorado and Laguna Verde before intersecting the Paso de Jama road and dropping to San Pedro de Atacama. Travellers manage with neither GPS or a guide, but most will prefer to obtain a GPS track online or hire a 4x4 guide.

In all cases it's easier to have **passports** stamped out of Bolivia at the *migración* in Uyuni, since remote border posts can be unmanned. Aduana offices remain at, or near, border crossings. Bolivian fuel is cheaper than in Chile so smuggling is rife and as a result fuel is scarce. You'd want a range of 500km, otherwise ask in Ollagüe.

Surreal Salar. © thedarienplan.com

Other roads in Bolivia include the spectacular drive from Oruro off the altiplano down to Arica in Chile; the mostly unsurfaced routes south from Uyuni to Tupiza, Oruro to Tarija and Sucre to Yacuiba for Argentina, as well as the routes east and north from Oruro or La Paz which descend to the Yungas jungles of the Amazonas.

CHILE

Chile! Twenty times longer than it is wide, it slices through climates, seasons, expectations and landforms like lava through a glacier, and appropriately throws everything at you from temperate rainforests, tidewater glaciers, hyper-arid deserts and a chain of active volcanoes with some of the world's highest peaks looming over lakes and forests. Check the radiator and kick the tyres; the party's not over yet!

On the list are more eye-popping landscapes surrounding San Pedro de Atacama, the novelty of modern, Europeanised cities like Santiago or Valparaiso, but above all it's the picturesque Lakes District around Puerto Montt, the relatively untravelled Carretera Austral south of there, and way down in the southern latitudes, the incomparable Torres del Paine that are calling you. After weeks or months in the tropics, you're back in temperate lands where good roads and summer days last longer.

Yes, infrastructure in Chile is of a high standard and a map will correspond to a well-constructed and maintained highway. Such a **map** is Copec's *Rutas de Chile* and the atlases produced by Telefonica CTC Chile, or 🖳 viajeros mapas.com and 🖳 proyectomapear.com.ar for the satnav or smartphone.

At the bordillera

You're unlikely to need a **visa** in advance or at the border. Instead, fill out an immigration form, or *tarjeta*, of which you keep a copy to get stamped when you leave the country or indeed to show to Argentinian immigration. Next, a *temporal* for the car and maybe an SAG (Agriculture and Livestock Service) form declaring any foodstuffs you're bringing in. Chile has strict laws on this so declare everything and dump or eat any fresh produce or meat. They might then inspect your car and once that's done, you pay the immigration fee of a few dollars and move on. If you're planning on crossing the border with Argentina a few times you'll have to go through this all again each time. Unlike in Central America 'helpers' (*tramitadores*) are absent and blatant scams are rare. And as an overlander you're not required to pay the fees paid by international air arrivals – US$160 for Americans arriving in either country.

Insurance is said not to be required for non-residents. The driving is at least recognisably saner than up north, but with perseverance SOAPEX cover for foreign vehicles can be acquired. Try 💻 hdi.cl and under 'Seguros' select 'SOAPEX'. If you want it they may even sell you a **regional policy** for all neighbouring countries for a few months – if not then try 💻 svs.cl, 💻 bcise guros.cl or 💻 pentagenerales.cl.

Hitting the road

San Pedro de Atacama is an easy jaunt from the copper mines at Calama and is worth a look if you somehow missed out on Uyuni in Bolivia. You could spend a day to a full week exploring this area. And where the Pan-Am ducks inland away from the coast there are alternative unpaved routes, mainly along the seaside through parks and small towns.

North of Santiago a dozen or so roads, mostly gravel, penetrate the Andes to Argentina via high, arid passes skirting brooding 6000m volcanoes. The easiest is certainly the southernmost on the main route to **Mendoza**, which features high-speed switchbacks, heavy traffic, glimpses of Aconcagua (6962m, 22,841ft) and a notoriously busy border crossing. In the far north, Paso de Jama is also paved but don't overlook exit formalities at the customs on the outskirts of San Pedro de Atacama or you'll be refused entry to Argentina, two or three hours down the road. Between these two stretches of pavement are a series of 4500-5000m passes transected by gravel roads. Even further north, a few passes lead into Bolivia: one paved road from Arica to Oruro, plus a couple of high, sand and washboard routes to Uyuni.

Southbounders had better have a pretty good excuse to cross into Argentina at **Santiago** or sooner – most probably the icy onset of winter. From Santiago highways lead south through fertile valleys full of farms or vineyards. Then multiple routes diverge to the mountains or the coast and the terrain gets wilder as you enter the Lakes District – here, as in adjacent Argentina, a region of lakes, mountains and statuesque volcanoes. From Puerto Montt a right turn leads to pretty Chiloé island, while a left takes you onto the **Carretera Austral** which ends at **Cochrane**.

The Carretera, Chile's Ruta 7, links formerly isolated towns, parks and wilderness areas over 1200km south from Puerto Montt. In good weather it makes for a fabulous drive, but in 2008 a volcano eruption buried the town of Chaitén. The road from the north was re-opened, or you can **ferry** from Puerto Montt or from Quellón on Chiloé. Semi-destroyed and half reoccupied, Chaitén is definitely worth a stop. The volcano remains active but there are several houses renting rooms, as well as a hotel plus a few restaurants and bars. There's also beach camping north of the ferry terminal.

South of Chaitén, the Carretera consists of a mix of pavement and gravel – generally of a higher standard than the Argentine alternative, Ruta 40 (p462) and with fewer lashing gales. Services are available in Coyhoique and to a lesser extent in Cochrane. Small hotels and campgrounds are widely scattered and wild camping is easy. The route is spectacular in its own right, but there are even more impressive side roads to explore, including toward the coast at Puerto Aisén and Puerto Cisnes. The easiest exit to Argentina hereabouts is via Chile Chico after driving around Lago General Carrera (or ferrying across to shorten the journey).

Those heading north will exit via Futaleufú or carry on to Chaiten. Once at Quellón or Puerto Montt, you can explore Chile's Lake Country up to Santiago and Valparaiso, or cut back into Argentina near Bariloche and make the long trek over to Buenos Aires on back roads. One more option bears a mention; Navimag (🖥 navimag.com) cruises down the 'inside passage' from Puerto Montt over three nights to Punta Natales, just down the road from the Torres and some 750km from Ushuaia. Expect to pay US$340 for a 4x4 plus berths from $550pp.

ARGENTINA

Like Brazil, Argentina can be a bit too big for its own good, but if you pick your spots you'll find still more eye-popping natural spectacle and driving adventures, plus cosmopolitan Buenos Aires and the best beef steaks or *asado* on the planet. Those interminable grass-covered Pampas do have their uses.

Despite its economic woes Argentina has the highest per capita income in South America with **prices** now almost equivalent to Chile, and the remote south can be downright expensive. No need for **visas** for up to 90-day stays for all Westerners except Canadians ($75) and Australians ($100) who must pay reciprocity fees online in advance. You may not get past a border without **insurance** either, particularly if coming from Bolivia. It's available at border posts or adjacent towns to cover Argentina, Bolivia, Brazil, Chile, Ecuador, Paraguay, Peru and Uruguay. Look up where the nearest 🖥 sag.org.ar agency is or try 🖥 speiserseguros.com.ar.

To those making the 5600km round trip to Ushuaia from Buenos Aires, Argentina will feel unnecessarily vast. Days will pass with little change in terrain which was pretty boring to begin with. Instead, head west for some Andean action along the Chilean border. In the north are volcanic peaks and desert; the central regions have vineyards, lakes and forests; further south, glaciers and ice fields are pierced by jagged peaks. You may find 🖥 ruta0.com useful; for the satnav it's 🖥 proyectomapear.com.ar.

North to Brazil

The falls at **Iguazú** on the Argentinian border are one of the continent's premier attractions – worth seeing even if you think you've seen enough waterfalls elsewhere in the world. The most direct routes between BA and Iguazú follow Argentina's Rutas 14 or 12 where the cops had a habit of flagging down foreigners and issuing tickets for offences real or imagined. That seems to have passed, but watch your speed and make sure your papers are tidy.

Iguazú is a decision point: east leads to the Brazilian coast's sandy beaches, north goes to the vast inland wetlands of the Pantanal. Otherwise hop over into Paraguay on your way to northwestern Argentina and the Andes, or take the Trans-Chaco highway north to Bolivia (p463).

Coming from the altiplano

Swooping over from Chile like Condorman, you'll enter by one of the couple of dozen passes through the Andes. These vary greatly in character, scenery and difficulty: in the far north the Paso de Jama is the easiest Andes crossing north of Mendoza, paved all the way from **San Pedro de Atacama** (SAG agency) to **Salta**. Just to the south of Jama is the more remote, unpaved Paso de Sico winding past multi-coloured lakes and soaring volcanoes. Between

Jama and Ruta 7 near Mendoza, half a dozen less used passes of varying difficulty. Paso de San Francisco is a favourite, requiring a 500-km fuel range and frequent stops to record the epic landscapes. Others are harder still, and all top out around 4000 or 5000 metres (13,100-16,500ft). Always enquire about food and fuel because for the most part there isn't much of either. The 360km route between Santiago and **Mendoza** (Argentina Ruta 7/Chile Ruta 60) is a nice drive but be aware that the border is renowned for lengthy queues.

South of Mendoza another dozen roads cross lower passes, like the Osorno to Bariloche (240km). Others include the crossing near Futaleufú and another outside Los Antiguos. Southbound overlanders also enter Argentina directly from Bolivia, usually via La Quiaca or Aguas Blancas. These border roads are scenic, but forgo the distinct appeal of the arid Andean crossings from Chile.

Ruta 40 – the road south

Argentina's **Ruta 40** has long held iconic stature among overlanders. Other great drives in this area include the twisty 190km of Ruta 68 between Cafayate and **Salta**, the mix of *ripio* (see below) and tar on Ruta 33 from Cachi to Salta (160km), and Ruta 9 north from Salta. This is just the tip of the ripio iceberg.

Mendoza is a popular stopping place for those hankering after spares, repairs and winery tours. If heading south, this is the last place to feature whole blocks crammed with mechanics, so get ahead of the maintenance curve while you can.

West of Mendoza, Ruta 7 crosses into Chile with stunning views of Aconcagua on cloud-free days, the highest mountain in the Americas. Conversely, eastwards Ruta 7 traverses nothing much at all for the twelve hours or more to Buenos Aires. Knowing this, most discerning adventurists continue on Ruta 40 or parallel roads south toward the Lakes District. This section of 40 is paved and the driving not so thrilling; hugging the Andes on parallel routes is more like it, if long hours on gravel roads are your cup of *mate*.

The Lakes District comes with snow-capped mountains framing pretty lakes, cosy cabins, forests and cute towns brimming with adventure tourism activities. Hereabouts your satnav is trying to show you the 200km Ruta de Siete Lagos following Ruta 234 from San Martín de los Andes to **Bariloche**.

During the summer season, streets in the major Lakes towns are full of brightly befleeced tourists so lodgings can get lean, though most towns have campgrounds. Just don't expect privacy and quiet – as in Spain, camping for the Argentines is a gregarious affair.

After a day or two wandering south through the lakes and forests, subtle changes are noticed. Yes, it's **windy**; Patagonian windy. Somewhere south of El Bolsón the famed *ventarrón del diablo* manifests itself, usually blowing out of the south or off the peaks. Expect gales clocking a steady 100kph/60mph with gusts up to 160kph, and once out in the steppes your car is your only shelter.

The round stones or *ripio* with which Patagonian roads are often surfaced don't help, and may well be named after the effect they have on plastic bodywork. Tracks often consist of half-metre wide ruts with high berms to either side and when it all gets muddy more ripio is simply tipped on with compaction duties left to the passing traffic.

If you've had enough, the sealed Ruta 3 runs from BA to Tierra del Fuego with several links to Ruta 40. The problem with dodging 40 is that much of Patagonia's epic scenery lies close by: El Chaltén and the Fitzroy range, the Perito Moreno glacier, plus Torres del Paine. You don't want to miss them.

You probably know this already but **Tierra del Fuego** is actually an island divided between Chile and Argentina. To get there you take one of the two **ferries** back in Chile: either from **Punta Arenas** (2½

The Delgada ferry surfs ashore. © ihana.com

hours) or further east from **Punta Delgada** off the end of Ruta 3 (20 mins). Keep your receipt as you might get a discount on boat trips out of Ushuaia. From either ferry it's still 100km of gravel to the Argentine border with no fuel stations, so fill up in Punta or Rio Gallegos, or at Rio Grande 230km north of Ushuaia. In Argentina the road is sealed and it's about three hours over the mountains to Ushuaia. At this latitude expect snow and rain, even in high summer.

Ushuaia has a lively pub scene and a surfeit of penguin-themed souvenirage. The Campground Rio Pipio or the Rugby Club, on the western edge of town (S54° 49.90' W68° 21.56') are popular, the latter with a bar and internet.

Your obligatory end-of-the-road shot by that famous wooden sign board is another ten kilometres to the west, at the end of Ruta 3 and within the Parque Nacional Tierra del Fuego. You'll have to pay a park entrance fee to get there, but few begrudge that after all those hard-won miles. Wherever you've come from, it's been a long old drive and it's not over yet.

WHAT ABOUT URUGUAY AND PARAGUAY?

Although both are undoubtably great places to live, most travellers' closest contact with Uruguay is gazing across the River Plate estuary from BA – or Paraguay from Iguazú Falls. You could say these two countries are the opposite of the equally obscure Guianas (see p464) which are harder to get to but, by and large, reward the effort.

Paraguay's Ciudad del Este lies just across the bridge from Foz do Iguaçu (Brazil), a decrepit border town with corrupt officials surviving off contraband. Americans cough up $140 for a visa.

Paraguay's long been a smugglers' haven and a wide variety of grey- or black-market goods, including car parts, can be found in Ciudad del Este or Asunción, 330km to the west. A foreigner can easily **buy a vehicle** here too. It's not legal, but then neither is smuggling so ask around.

The remainder of Paraguay is not entirely without interest. **Asunción** has attractive colonial barrios, more shopping plus car dealers and parts. Elsewhere there are the remains of Jesuit monasteries and prosperous Mennonite towns adrift in the Chaco which fills the barely populated north.

Across this prairie stretches Ruta 9, El Transchaco, running 1400km from Asunción to **Sucre** in Bolivia on rapidly deteriorating pavement. Get here in late September and you have a chance of being shunted by the Transchaco Rally.

If that makes **Uruguay** sound all the more tempting then a ferry (🖥 buquebus .com) crosses the estuary to Colonia, 160km west of Montevideo and takes about two hours. You can freight-cruise to Europe from Montevideo too: see p470.

Venezuela, the Guianas and Brazil

At the top of the continent most overlanders stayed west for the high roads and cooler temperatures through the Andean countries, partly because eastward to Venezuela and the three countries known collectively as **Guianas** had a reputation for high prices and an uninspiring coastline. From Georgetown in Guyana to Macapa in Brazil you're stuck on a single transit route which still isn't entirely sealed and is prone to weather-induced delays. Add the low elevation and it's **hot and muggy**, year-round. Plus even with a 4x4, **inland exploration** in the Guianas takes some commitment, and anyway there's no way into Brazil east of Venezuela.

The incentive to transit this area was further reduced in 2016 by which time **Venezuela**'s simmering economic crisis had boiled over. As a distraction to the ongoing strife, in 2015 all Venezuelan borders were closed, supposedly in an attempt to combat criminals smuggling of Venezuela's subsided commodities. Around the same time the currency was devalued to undermine the thriving black market. The border from Brazil may be open, but at present Colombia can only be entered on foot. As there is no road to Guyana, coming up from Boa Vista in Brazil, you may end up trapped as the country's economy unravels with resultant civil unrest. Shipping via Caracas was never recommended, even in the less bad times.

This doesn't mean Venezuela is a bad country to visit, but your **security** requires attention here (as it does in parts of Colombia). **Caracas** in particular has been famously corrupt and sometimes violent; even before it all blew up overlanders avoided the capital.

All of which is a great shame as Venezuela has plenty to offer: great scenery and still pretty cheap fuel. Even by South America's elevated standards you'll find unique landscapes among the tepui mesas, Caribbean beaches and islands, lowland jungles where cocoa evolved, serrated peaks draped with remnant glaciers, and inland wetlands teeming with bizarre wildlife which, if you've come from Peru, may well include yourself.

While the Colombia–Venezuela border remains blocked, the only through

The other Road to Oxiana. © ihana.com

route here runs between Manaus up the BR-174 to Boa Vista for Guyana and the Guianas, then down to Macapa, back on the Amazon estuary. But as you'll read on p469, getting in or out of Manaus *overland* is a hefty proposition, which means that – unless **shipping** via Paramaribo – this 3000-km arc to Macapa isn't the best way to fill your passport pages, when you think of all the wonders to be seen elsewhere.

THE GUIANAS

Like Belize, Guyana, Suriname and French Guiana – the **Guianas** – have a Caribbean rather than Latino culture, and like Belize, few made the diversion even before the Venezuelan situation, so there's a sense of trailblazing rather than following the hordes. The route is obvious; in fact from one end to the other there's no choice.

The colonial history of the Guianas saw the rice and sugar plantations develop with the help of immigrants from the former British and Dutch territories in India and Indonesia as well as Hmong refugees from Laos and Maroons; descendants of African slaves. The less accessible inland regions not suited to cattle ranching remain largely pristine, unlogged jungle populated by protected Amerindian tribes.

Rain and muddy roads will be much more significant impediments to travel. August to November is the main **dry season**, with a dry pause in February, although downpours can hit at any time you forget your brolly.

Guyana

There's **no road link** between Venezuela. Access from the west is via the road from **Boa Vista** in Brazil, some 200km south of the Venezuelan border, for what it's worth. At Boa Vista head northwest 140km to **Lethem** on the Guyanese border over the bridge on the Takutu River. Coming from Guyana, Brazilian immigration can be slow.

As you cross the bridge start driving **on the left** and speaking **English**. An IDP may not be accepted, so along with **insurance** you may need to acquire a local driving permit if you're here (as well as in Suriname) for more than a month. Note that if coming from Suriname to Guyana at Moleson Creek (see below), you'll have to get insurance at Corriverton, 12km up the road.

Still known as 'The Trail', the once-notorious dirt road 460km to **Georgetown** is OK even during the rainy season, with a couple of mudholes on the northern section. Note that **maps** of this route are inaccurate – not least Google. Realistically, it's a two-day drive so plan to take a break halfway.

Guyana's government runs more red tape than a Marxist Morris dancer; legacy of those pedantic Brits. In **Georgetown** ordinary folks are friendly, though at night a cautious person might not stagger around drunk with pocketfuls of cash. Scotia Bank's offices have possibly the only international **ATM** in the land. Food, lodging and services are a notch or two below Suriname, but so are prices. The *Melbourne Hotel* on Sheriff Street is in a good neighbourhood and has secure parking. To get there set course for N06° 48.95' W58° 8.15'.

Suriname

Suriname has an odd mixture of British and Dutch place names befitting its colonial past. Towns called Glasgow or Manchester are a few kilometres from Europlodder, while Bombay is just down the road and Hindu temples dot the countryside. It's also one of the few South American countries where you'll probably need a **visa or 'tourist card' in advance** (check 🖥 surinameembassy .org). They're available back in Georgetown (near Anira St and New Garden St; N06 48.88' W58 08.9'; look for the red and green flag) same day for around $25. In Cayenne (French Guiana) it's €40, from the consulate at 3 Avenue Leopold Helder (near N04° 56.39', W52° 20.06').

There's a daily **ferry** late morning from **Moleson Creek** (N05° 46.75′ W57° 10.21′), some 12km south of Corriverton over the Corentyne River to South Drain (N05° 44.56′ W57° 08.18′). This brings you in 40km south of **Nieuw Nickerie** where you'll need to buy **insurance** (🖥 assuria.sr).

Oddly, driving is still **on the left** and it's a rough road from Nieuw Nickerie 230km to the **Paramaribo** which is said to be less edgy after dark than Georgetown or Cayenne. Suriname does have a few roads which penetrate the interior, offering glimpses of primeval forest without resorting to river or air travel. Try the Brownsberg Nature Reserve, 130km south of the capital.

There's an option to **ship to the Netherlands**. Track down N.V. Global Expedition in Paramaribo just south of the bridge (aim for N05° 47.85′ W55° 10.45′; 🖥 nvglobalexpedition.com/en). Otherwise, from Paramaribo the road cuts through jungle some 140km to Albina on the Maroni River to St Laurent with several daily ferry runs to French Guiana.

French Guiana

French Guiana is a former penal colony that's an overseas province of France, just like Hawaii is a US state. As such EU nationals can scoot right on in as if they were driving off a ferry at Calais; others have to do the usual trampolining between police and customs. And just as in *la belle France* you **drive on the right**, the currency is the **euro**, the food ought to be to your liking, but the **prices** may not be. French is the dominant language, Portuguese may see you through but Spanish is rarely spoken. Customs may hint at **insurance** (if from the EU, your home policy is valid) but coming from Brazil you can't buy it until **Cayenne** anyway; in Paramaribo buy from Assuria at a hefty €180 a month. Often enough, insurance papers aren't checked until you leave, but at that point they seem to be essential. **Fuel** is among the most expensive in South America, though at 450km border to border, you won't need more than a tank's worth and some of this expense is reflected in roads you could happily take home to meet the godparents.

With 5.5 million square kilometres of jungle in the Amazon basin, most take more notice of Guiana's man-made attractions, namely the **space centre** at Kourou, located here not just because the labour's cheap, but gravity is a little less clingy near the equator and (as with Cape Canaveral in Florida) an aborted launch can fall harmlessly into the sea. The other attraction is Devil's Island, a former prison made famous in the book and film, *Papillon*.

On to northeast Brazil

The good road continues to the border with Brazil at Saint Georges. Here, the suspension bridge was completed in 2011, but remains unused for the forseeable future. Until common sense makes a come back, there's a ferry a few kilometres upstream for **Oiapoque** right by the neglected bridge.

Once that's done, get stamped at the police station, then get your TIP at the *aduana* (customs) at the northern end of town (N03° 51.0′ W51° 49.9′). From here to Macapá is 590km along the BR-156, but an hour out of town the tarmac deserts you again, leaving around 150km of dirt or mud to Calcoene, 360km from Macapá. If it's been pouring and you're in a Mustang lowrider, it's best to wait a day or two, and whatever you're driving, fill up before you leave; fuel stations get stretched out in the middle.

Located on the 400km-wide Amazon estuary and strung across the equator, expect to perspire somewhat in **Macapá**. To get the pontoon ferry to Belém, track down Sanave (⌨ gruposanave.com.br) by the river in Porto Santana, west of Macapá (S00° 00.88′ W51° 12.17′). Expect a tug and **barge** plus a bill of a few hundred dollars for the 36-hour trip.

BRAZIL

Spreading across nearly half the continent and accounting for over half of its population, Brazil borders every other South American country except Ecuador and Chile. You'd think you can't avoid it, but as the Pan-Am slips down the west side, many skim this huge country, citing language and visa issues, vast distances and the surprising fact that, mile for mile, Brazil is scenically less diverse than some of its neighbours to the west. In the south, sugar cane plantations stretch for hours and days and arrow-straight highways are clogged with trucks. The northern interior is a semi-arid scrub broken by occasional mesas where again the hours turn to days without appreciable changes in scenery. The vast Amazon basin is fascinating to see up close, but driveable roadways are few and surrounding jungles have often been levelled for timber then farming.

Having said that, there are a few worthwhile destinations: for **wildlife** there are the famous Pantanal wetlands in the south; Rio de Janeiro for all the well-known reasons; the pretty colonial towns of Minas Gerais 500km northeast of Rio; the Afro-Brazilian vibe in Salvador and the adjacent beaches of Bahia; the epic Foz do Iguaçu waterfalls (see the next page) and of course the Amazon Basin. If only they were more geographically condensed.

There are mountains too – notably around Curitiba in the south, between Sao Paulo and Rio along the coast, throughout Minas Gerais province and in the Chapada Diamantina further north. These highlands are full of winding roads, ranging from tiny dirt tracks to smooth ribbons of *asfalto*. There are also stately colonial towns and Brazil features thousands of miles of stunning coastline lapped by perfectly formed waves from the southern border to the Amazon delta. Driving Brazilian back roads can be confusing, but you're never far from somewhere and most small towns will have some form of lodging, food and mechanical services.

Most fortunate of all, wherever you go Brazilians are friendly and welcoming. This spirit is the country's core appeal and because overlanders are less common here, every gas or food stop will attract interest and invitations, and it'll be difficult to spend any length of time here without making friends.

Not only is Brazil huge but it's comparatively expensive. Tyres, for example, are more pricey than elsewhere, despite the fact that they invented rubber here. Expect to pay more for lodging and **fuel** too. EU nationals get **visas** on arrival for up to 90 days; Americans need a $150 visa in advance; for Australians it's $35. The consulate in Puerto Iguazú (Argentina) is said to do a next-day service. Motor **insurance** isn't asked for.

Unlike elsewhere down here, they speak **Portuguese** and English speakers are few. Most Brazilians see no reason to speak Spanish (not as similar to Portuguese as you might think) so learn a few words. Of course it's possible to eat, drink, take a leak and buy fuel without speaking Portuguese, but where's the fun in that?

Brazil routes

Having shipped into Buenos Aires or Montevideo (see p470), travellers usually enter on the coastal route from Uruguay where roads are good but the driving and scenery uninspired until the mountains near **Florianópolis**. At 1800m they offer some relief from the heat as well as colonial-era towns in various states of decay. **Parque Nacional de Aparados da Serra** and **Canela** are recommended.

Continuing along the coast the mountains get more rugged, the colonial towns more beautiful and the beaches more sandy between São Paulo and Rio and onwards into Espirito Santo and Minas Gerais. Note that neither Rio or São Paulo are relaxing destinations for foreigners in cars – straying innocently into the wrong *barrio* can get you shot. Smaller cities like Petrópolis, Buzios and Paraty might be more amenable.

Rio aside, the biggest tourist draw in southern Brazil is **Foz do Iguaçu** on the borders of Paraguay and Argentina. Quite a few make their way here from Buenos Aires along Ruta 14 for the ease with which Brazilian visas are issued in Puerto Iguazú. Although this inland route misses some nice beaches and winding roads through the hills, you'll get your fill of all that further north.

A solid day's drive north from Iguaçu is the **Pantanal**, the world's largest savannah wetland. Reports differ on the best season for visits; some say rainy season floods concentrate the animals on high ground; others that the dry concentrates them at the shrinking water holes and you don't need a boat to get around. Contrary to what some maps show, the Trans-Pantanal highway doesn't connect the northern and southern sections and probably never will.

From the Pantanal, one paved route stretches northwest. At Ariquemes turn west for **Guajará-Mirim** (310km) and a crossing for Bolivia. Otherwise carry on for **Porto Velho**, with a sealed road to Humaitá from where river

Taxi to Humaita? © Silviu Stanescu

TRANS-AMAZON NORTH TO SOUTH

The Andes offer spectacular and lively mountain roads, but the Amazon basin is the other definitive South American habitat; a humid, partially depleted rainforest that spreads across at least half a dozen countries creating an untameable obstacle to overland travel. New roads are boldly carved so as to snatch resources, but once a few overloaded trucks churn up a mire, it gets reclaimed by the jungle as soon as you turn your back.

The only way to Manaus from the east is on a **river boat** – and with a car you won't get upstream and into Peru. Formal ferries are few, it's more of a freight barge scene, especially over longer distances; see what Sanave (⌨ gruposanave.com.br) are offering.

Top down though, you can drive across Amazonia. With Venezuela out of the picture, starting from the Guyana–Brazil border, most bar Americans get into Brazil without an advance visa and the 780km from Boa Vista to Manaus is all sealed.

At **Manaus** the Amazon is already three kilometres wide; either pay up to ferry the lion's share of the route to Humaita, just 200km from Porto Velho, or sharpen the shovels and the ferry 12km to **Careiro a Varzea** for the start of the **BR319**.

Improvements have been undertaken on this once notorious route, with the most dilapidated of the 200-plus bridges repaired. The first couple of hundred kilometres are paved and include short ferry crossings. Thereafter, it's broken tarmac with short stretches of mud and wooden bridges which may be reaching their cross-by date. The next two days will be a tough crawl at 15–20kph, and some 650km from the Amazon you get to a point just north of Humaita where Brazil's network of sealed roads resumes. You may stop and kiss the tar. Be aware that this isn't a happy-clappy tourist area but an isolated beef and logging region with drugs smuggled in from Peru and Bolivia, so in places like **Porto Velho**, be alert.

From Porto Velho you can stay in Brazil and fight it out with the truck traffic southeast towards the Mato Grosso, the Pantanal wetlands, eastern Bolivia and Iguazu Falls on the Argentina–Paraguay border, some 1400km from Buenos Aires.

Or in the dry season from April to November head for Peru via **Rio Branco**, 540km from Porto Velho with a one-hour time change on the way. Another 220km gets you to Brasileia (check out with the police) and a final 100km or so to Assis Brazil opposite the Peruvian **border** at a corner with Bolivia. A bridge crosses the river to Inapari; immigration and customs are on the left.

It's said to be sealed from here at least halfway to **Puerto Maldonado**, 240km to the south. At a lowly 200m, once you ferry over the Rio Madre de Dios you're in the hot, humid epicentre of Peru's Amazonian tourism scene with plenty of places to stay, eat, rest and get healed at the hands of shamen with their mind-expanding potions.

With that done, straighten your tie and brush down your hair; it's 430km along nothing less than the **Inter-oceanic highway** to

© Phil Flanagan

Cusco up in the Andes at a cool 3500m (11,600ft), with the 4950m (16,000ft) Hualla Hualla pass on the way and Machu Picchu nearby (see p455). They're working on making the road live up to its name, but until that happy day, expect it to take a couple of days to Cusco.

boats head down the Rio Madeira to **Manaus**. Expect to pay a few hundred dollars for the three-day trip. Or you can set off along the still infamous BR319 track – see above – or head west for the route to Peru or Bolivia, or from Humaitá spend days on the choking red dirt of the BR230 Trans-Amazonian Highway all the way back west. Driving in this area, your view will include acres of deforestation you've been hearing about all these years.

North of Rio, beaches stretch for thousands of kilometres and larger cities like **Recife** (Olinda), **Salvador da Bahia**, São Luís and **Belém** all throb with energy, while Itacaré, Porto Seguro, Arraial d'Adjuda, Jericoacoara and others offer smaller-scale charms and all the relaxation you can handle. Throughout Bahia the ethnic and cultural connections with West Africa are notable.

Although everyone owes themselves at least a quick look at Salvador and the Bahia coast, inland roads from Rio are the quicker way to Belém. A half-day's drive west of Salvador, the Chapada Diamantina offers a bit of highland relief and tracks diverge from Lençóis out to mesas, waterfalls and swimming holes. These and other inland parks offer relief in the midst of thousands of square miles of dreary, semi-arid *sertão* (but don't tell BMW Motorrad that).

Belém is a hustling waterfront city with a picturesque old town, but like many big South American cities, has a reputation for skullduggery. Ferry yourself over the huge Amazon delta to Macapá for the Guianas (see p464), or boat upstream to Manaus (3 to 5 days). Head to the marine terminal; brokers will find you and offer to secure whatever tickets you need. Prices are negotiable; you'll pay separately for car and passengers, with a reasonable surcharge if you want a cabin.

All these trips are on riverboats or even more basic **barges**, not lavish ferries equipped with casinos and karaoke, so come prepared for crowds, noise, unsanitary conditions and limited food. Loading, unloading and stowage are subject to the tides and the whims of baggage handlers who'll demand tips.

Manaus is a city of a million inhabitants in the midst of the jungle, and teems with decaying grandeur from its 19th-century rubber boom. Or you may just find it grimy, sweaty and depressing. The city is the focal point for tours into the Amazon hinterland, but scammers are on the prowl so exercise caution. For your next step see the box on the previous page.

FREIGHT CRUISING THE ATLANTIC: EUROPE TO URUGUAY

With Grimaldi (🖳 grimaldi-freightercruises .com) you and your vehicle can drive on and get shipped between Antwerp or Hamburg and **Montevideo** in Uruguay. It's about four weeks southbound, including days in Dakar, Rio and Santos. Northbound is three weeks.

Departure dates are fortnightly but can vary and sailing times are also estimates.

On arrival in Uruguay a Grimaldi agent helps with formalities and there'll be port fees to pay. A berth is €1800pp full board; a vehicle's from €1100. With a month to spare that's much less than shipping and flying.

Roads – a short history

A road is a way, a cleared navigable trail between one place and another that avoids impediments to movement. You probably knew that, but it's interesting to note that roads are among the oldest traceable links in the development of human society and civilisation.

Large terrestrial animals have had to deal with varied land forms, surfaces, and vegetation to which avian and certainly aquatic animals are immune, and whether animal or early human, the need to drink, gather, hunt or even migrate saw corridors form along **natural lines of least resistance**. Such game trails can still be found in wilderness areas today. Clearing obstructions from a viable trail or using stones or trees to ford a river would have been the earliest **human intervention** along animal trails, so making the first roads.

By the end of the last Ice Age mankind had already occupied much of the world's land mass and as early as 12,000 years ago the Neolithic Revolution – the transition from the nomadic to a settled, agrarian way of life – eventually saw **civilisation** develop in Mesopotamia (Iraq). It was some five thousand years later in the Sumerian city-state of Ur that **the wheel** was combined with a load-bearing axle to form the cart. Within a millennium it was here too that the earliest examples of road building in the form of **paving** were found. Although much of Europe was still in the Stone Age at the time of Sumer, 'corduroy roads' of parallel logs dating from 4000BC have been excavated in the marshes surrounding Glastonbury in southwest England.

Then as now, some form of paving is the vital component to all-weather wheeled transportation; capping a loose, earthen surface to bear the weight of laden cart wheels or ox

hooves. It's something that has only reached the remoter or less developed parts of the globe in the last century, and where it hasn't, in times of rain the effort required to travel on unsealed roads will account for many of your overland adventures.

Although use of the wheel was well established 3000 years ago, until the advent of mechanical power (the piston engine), **seafaring vessels** were far more technologically sophisticated and played a more significant role in the development of human history. Be it dug-out canoe, papyrus raft, longboat or galleon; in terms of payload all can be easily propelled or even borne by a current or the wind, requiring much less energy than land transport which consequentially stagnated. The humble cart or wagon took thousands of years to gain spoked wheels, iron tyres, steering and suspension.

As Mesopotamian civilisations evolved, the need for manufactured, marked and maintained roads grew from local needs to feed and administer growing populations. Although informal trade had existed between tribal groups for millennia, as parallel cultures sprang up in the Indus and Nile valleys, Turkey and China, a web of **trade routes** grew between them, exchanging not only commodities but ideas, technologies and philosophies.

Overland trade, conquest and pilgrimage

The **Silk Route** is the best-known trade route, actually a network of routes linking present-day west China with the Mediterranean. Along its byways products would be shuttled, traded and occasionally raided; no merchant actually set off to cover the whole distance from Aleppo to Turfan. Less celebrated is the Darb el Arbain ('Road of 40 Days') linking Sudan with the slave markets of southern Egypt, while in central Australia inter-tribal trails traded ochre and mother of pearl for use in ceremonial rites. By 1500BC in Bronze Age Europe the so-called Amber Trail was a similar network of routes along which salt from Austria, tin and lead from the 'Tin Isles' (Britain), flints from Denmark and amber from the south Baltic coast were all traded.

These trade routes could also become axes of **military conquest** and subsequent dominion, and even in contemporary times a war or threat of war sees roads built or improved at phenomenal pace. Examples including northern Australia's Stuart Highway, the Alcan Highway to Alaska, the Burma, or Stilwell, Road or the BAM railway.

With the advent of organised religion, **pilgrimage routes** also became established, particularly to Mecca (a shrine even in the pre-Islamic era). Late-medieval European examples include the Camino de Santiago to the city of that name in Spain and the Pilgrims' Way to Canterbury Cathedral in southeast England.

Settlement developed along these established routes until the need for new areas saw pioneers create their own recognised roads such as the Oregon and Santa Fe trails in the US. The latter-day Route 66 was built to employ and deliver depression-era migrants from Chicago to California. The Trans-Siberian railway enabled the expansion of Russia into Asia and today the highway paralleling the railway is being reinvented as a means of tapping into the steady stream of used automobiles discarded in Japan.

Road building

The many historic routes listed above would have been recognised ways, but remained largely unimproved, well-worn trails. It was of course the Romans who introduced modern **road-building technology** and indeed **regulations** such as weight limits to help preserve their work. The 50,000-mile network of Roman roads is the basis of modern Europe's transport infrastructure, but that engineering know-how sank into the mud of the Dark Ages, waiting nearly 2000 years to be rediscovered.

In fact the Romans merely developed techniques and skills acquired from their conquered neighbours or adjacent states including Carthage, Crete and Greece. It was the scale with which they deployed this technology that was staggering, taking it far beyond the city walls. They recognised that a reliable road system using a soundly engineered foundation was the key to conquering and administering distant provinces.

The Via Appia was the earliest and among their greatest achievements, eventually covering 560 kilometres from Rome to modern-day Brindisi on the heel of Italy. It drew together the key features of a thick, load-bearing **foundation**, **drainage** channels and a **raised crown** to help shed surface water and debris as well as a **kerb** lining the roadway, and all **capped** with tight-fitting cobbles. This ended up being a worked layer up to six feet deep which was fine as long as you had a ready supply of slaves to build and maintain it.

After the Roman Empire collapsed, away from Byzantium and Moorish Spain, Europe stagnated with little road-building. In England the Roman-built Watling Street (today's A5 to north Wales) survived only to demarcate a frontier between the Danelaw ('Viking') regions to the east and Alfred's Anglo-Saxon lands to the southwest. By the 12th century in England and parts of Europe the origins of Roman roads were so obscure they were ascribed to distant mythical monarchs from the Dark Ages.

At that time 'streets' implied 'constructions', from the Latin 'strata', but in the post-medieval era when horse-riding became more widespread as people became more affluent, the word was superseded by 'roads', designating a major arterial route or highway. So it is that nowadays in urban settings 'streets' identify non-arterial thoroughfares, although in London and probably many other cities you can find any number of exceptions to this rule.

In Asia the Silk Route was at its medieval apogee, soon to be undermined by the military conquests along its path, as well as the discoveries of Dutch and Portuguese mariners. Meanwhile most of the world's land-borne commodities proceeded to move around as they'd done since the dawn of trade and commerce; on carts, wagons and pack animals or on foot. At this time as a means of personal travel, **horses and carriages** were only for the rich elite.

Rights of Way

As the early medieval period ended in Europe power began to centralise, trade and manufacture were encouraged and populations agglomerated from hamlets to villages and even towns. It coincided with a revival of markets and fairs, forgotten since Roman times, as well as a new Christian fervour which led to the building of the first cathedrals. With that came the need to transport heavy stone from distant quarries and a revival in masonic trades. Crusades were also launched to the Middle East to reclaim Jerusalem from the Saracens. All these new activities, along with the perennial cycles of invasion and conquest, put new demands on the aged Roman road system.

In England land was dished out to the barons following the Norman Conquest and the idea of Right of Way was ratified by early parliament. The concept of the 'king's highway' was established and could be considered a key to a united kingdom, enabling unhindered access to all corners. Highways belonged to the king and obstructions and encroachments or 'purpresture' by adjacent landowners were offences against the realm. (In a contemporary suburban sense such encroachment is still a source of antagonism against 'neighbours from hell'.) Where a king had a right to pass, so fortunately did his humble subjects and the king's highway came to mean any public road or right of way 'for all men', linking major cities, towns and ports.

Of course it fell to local landowners to maintain these roads for the king, which they did with the practice of corvée: their serfs' annual obligation of a few days free labour to the manor. Barons and lords imposed this commitment unevenly so there was little consistency in the quality of the road network, but the notion of a public right of way became pre-eminent and survives so today. In the UK 'custom' or regular use are considered evidence of the right of public access, and such understandings have been adopted through much of the world.

Along with a right of way came a **right to diverge** if an obstruction blocked the path and was not dealt with promptly by the landowner, even if it meant trampling their sown fields. Contrary to the functionally direct Roman road, this is thought to be an explanation of the origin of Britain's winding back roads and GK Chesterton's famous poem:

Before the Roman came to Rye or out to Severn strode,
The rolling English drunkard made the rolling English road.
A reeling road, a rolling road, that rambles round the shire,
And after him the parson ran, the sexton and the squire;
A merry road, a mazy road, and such as we did tread
The night we went to Birmingham by way of Beachy Head.

The obligation to maintain these winding roads became divided, with primary highways or trunk roads being administered by the state, often classified as 'national' routes ('A roads' in the UK, 'Route nationales' in France and 'US highways') while other rural or local roads fell under the jurisdiction of local authorities.

Modern roads

As the European feudal era turned to the Renaissance, mobility was forced upon the poor who took to the roads. English peasants were ejected from manorial lands as landlords walled off their property to rear low-maintenance sheep for their valuable wool, just as their Scottish equivalents were to suffer more brutally in the waves of Clearances in the mid 19th century. Up to that point most people lived and died within a few miles of their birthplace, indebted to the lord of their manor in return for his protection.

As populations recovered from the devastating 14th-century plagues, modern European

empires evolved and early industrial production gathered pace. Inter-urban traffic increased and the Roman roads of Britain, neglected for 1500 years, quickly turned into mush under the unsuspended, unsteerable iron tyre-clad wagon wheels of the time which differed little from those used in Ur. This new mobility and increasing urbanisation all came to a crisis point in the mid 18th century.

The wheel had been around for millennia, but most portage took place on foot or with trains of pack animals. For those who could afford it, wheeled transport was only a little faster. In 1670 a coach took two days to get from Oxford to London in summer, and two weeks to Edinburgh, little more than walking pace.

Doctor Foster went to Gloucester
In a shower of rain.
He stepped in a puddle
Right up to his middle,
And never went there again.

This well-known English childhood rhyme is said to have its origins in the 13th century when King Edward I ('Dr Foster') fell from his horse and made a mess of himself on the way to Gloucester during his Welsh campaign. Even the Pope himself got bogged down on the way to an important Council in 1414. Drowning in potholes was not uncommon, nor was fatal injury from an overturned stagecoach and car-swallowing tracks like this still exist in equatorial regions.

Then as now, a wheel must balance the load it bears with the load it exerts on the ground and the drag it creates. Bigger wheels carry more but take much effort to turn on all but the smoothest hard surface.

In medieval times it was customary to undertake long deliveries during times of hard frost, a situation still analogous in Far Eastern Russia and northern Canada today when land access with heavy transporters is only effective along hard frozen ice roads in the depth of winter.

Maintenance and improvements by local landowners or parishes fell behind and the 15th century saw Acts of Parliament introduce **tolls** or 'turnpikes' in an effort to fund improvements. Although there'd been sporadic attempts in previous centuries, including fees to enter some cities (records stretch back to India in the 3rd century BC) these were merely taxes. Under the Acts power passed from local justices to trustees, an early example of privatisation to help fund public services. Well-off locals were able to band together as trusts and then as now often merely succeeded in further enriching themselves while making minimal improvements. At the same time canny merchants and porters simply deviated to routes not controlled by turnpike trusts, so further spreading the network of unmaintained mires. It's worth recognising that roads at this time were also trails of muck dropped by the animals which travelled along them, making the way all the more disagreeable despite being a great source of manure.

In 1770 a traveller noted that the Oxford to Witney toll road was 'called by a vile prostitution of the language a turnpike', while of the Newcastle Turnpike it was said '…a more dreadful road cannot be imagined'. Riots ensued, turnpikes were trashed and in response to this civil disobedience the death penalty was introduced. In an effort to reduce damage, regulations were introduced on wheel width (reduced tolls for wider roller wheels), axle width and gross weight. All met with little success as people found ways to bend the rules.

This dire situation of either terrible roads or expensive toll roads was partly why the English canal network was developed by provincial entrepreneurs in the 18th century. A barge could carry 25 times more than a cart, so reducing the cost of transporting the ever-increasing quantities of raw and manufactured commodities round the country as feudal agrarianism turned into the industrial revolution. So unreliable were public roads at this time that the mining practice of employing horse-drawn wagons on short tramways was developed to link canals, presaging the advent of railways.

The first modern road engineers

It was at this time that road engineers like John Metcalfe (1717-1810), Pierre-Marie Trésaguet (1716-1796), the bridge builder Thomas Telford (1757-1834) and John MacAdam (1756-1836) made great advances, or rediscoveries, in road-building techniques. Despite being blind from birth, it was Metcalfe who recognised the need for a strong foundation with good drainage as well as a water-shedding ability enhanced by a convex surface, something later made well-known by MacAdam. He'd hit upon the central secrets of road-making: drainage and a compacted, uniform-sized and sharp-edged aggregate which, unlike gravel, locked together to make a stable surface. Add asphalt or tar across a kerbed, compacted, well-drained foundation and you have tarmac[adam] – a 'sealed' road and the constituent of today's blacktop.

In the 17th century Britain's energy needs grew with industrialisation. With the depletion of England's woodlands and surface coal deposits quickly exploited, the earliest **steam-powered pumps** were used to drain ever-deeper coal mines. It was the early 19th century application of steam power in the form of locomotives to replace those horse-drawn trams that eclipsed the canal system. This was the biggest leap in speed and payloads since the invention of the wheel. Railways laid their own 'single track roads' quickly and therefore inexpensively. In the western US railways were the first roads and trains proceeded to move goods with similar economic benefits until WWI when, in Europe and other developed regions, the era of the car and truck finally took hold.

Roads today

Because railroads had been so successful, when cars first came to be widely used the road network was still some way behind. The early 20th century saw a lot of catching up as all weather super-highways spanned North America and Europe. By the end of the 20th century the road network had saturated most rich countries, but in less affluent regions modern engineering still has a job to do. You may think the job is complete where you live, but many primary transcontinental roads are very recent. A sealed road link around Australia was only completed in the 1980s and the Karakoram Highway linking Pakistan with western China was completed only in 1986 following 20 years' work and at a cost of nearly a thousand lives. Soon after the millennium the first sealed road spanned the Sahara from north to south and Chinese engineers are finishing the job across Sudan and equatorial Africa. An all-weather road finally linked Ethiopia to Kenya in 2016.

Globally a complete network may take another generation, but unlike railways, waterways or the open skies, roads have to be built within the fairly limited tolerances of the vehicles which use them. The nature of this planet's climate and geography means they'll always require maintenance so the job is unlikely ever to be completed.

SOME OLH2 CONTRIBUTORS

NINA ALTON AND CHARLIE WEATHERILL, fledgling off-roaders and novice overlanders, jumped into the deep end by driving from London to Singapore and back in 13 months; they also got engaged ten months in.

We are HAYDON AND ME-AN BEND, newly weds after ten years together, driving around the world for our honeymoon on, we hope a full trans-global trip. We both quit our jobs, mine as a paratrooper after three tours of Afghanistan, and Me-an as a chartered accountant in a large accountancy company. 🖳 oplongdrive.com

LORRAINE CHITTOCK explores the world's unique bond with animals. Her latest jaunt was for seven years, through sixteen countries with two dogs. 🖳 lorrainechittock.com

DAN GREC discovered overlanding during a two-year, 40,000-mile drive from Alaska to Argentina in a basic Jeep Wrangler. In 2016 he set out on a two-year journey through Africa in his modified Jeep Rubicon. Dan helps maintain wikioverland.org and records his own adventures in various publications and on 🖳 theroadchoseme.com.

PHIL FLANAGAN decided his career in the supply chain was futile and left to travel. Started with Africa in 2004 and inspired, bought an Iveco 4x4 and set off for Mongolia. Funds are tight, vehicle is basic but still moving. Last heard of in Brazil with 140 countries left.

THOMAS FLYNN and NATASA DUPALO were always drawn to a nomadic existence. With time they fell in love with the quiet vastness of nature away from civilisation. Their goal is to escape the rat race and explore the wilderness that remains. Next journey: Central Africa!

DOUGLAS HACKNEY is an award-winning author, photographer, traveller, public speaker, entrepreneur and management consultant.

After over a decade of planning, JOHN HIGHAM and his wife, and two children packed up their suburban lives and travelled around the world for a year. Upon returning, the voices in John's head needed an outlet and writing seemed the safest method. You can listen to those voices in his book *360 Degrees Longitude*.

GRAHAM JACKSON was born in Lesotho in southern Africa and has a lifelong obsession with deserts. Graham has guided expeditions in Africa, the American West, Mexico and Central America and trains US Special Forces on desert operations with a focus on North Africa. Graham is co-owner of 7P International; 🖳 www.7p.io.

German FABIAN PLOCK and Swede JASMINE KEMPE spent eight years working and travelling in different places with their trusty 40 series Landcruiser. They crossed 25 countries in African, spent two fantastic years in Australia and three winters in Norway and Switzerland. They are now based in Berlin experiencing 'normal life'. 🖳 www.norbertsadventures.com

JAN AND TREVOR RUTTERS chose the adventure of driving a Land Rover Defender 110 through Europe, the Middle East and East Africa as their shared mid-life crisis instead of a Mercedes SL55 and a young, nubile red-head with flashing green eyes. 🖳 gapyear4x4.com

Right out of the cradle MATT SAVAGE had to deploy innovative and unconventional techniques to keep his ageing vehicles running. This was to be a great education and now he's one of the best people to have on the end of a sat phone when you need 'real' mechanical advice.

TOBY SAVAGE is a photographer based in Leicester and a regular contributor to 4x4 magazines, but most winters heads south in pursuit of desert adventure. He's been involved with trips to Libya, Western Sahara, Egypt and Algeria, and co-presented *Desert Driving* with Chris Scott.

Like many things in life, JAMES STEPHENSON discovered the pleasures and pitfalls of overlanding by accident. He's since managed to clock up quite a few trips with his Land Rover including Algeria with Chris Scott, Timbuktu, Russia and Croatia. 🖳 JamesUK.net

NICK TAYLOR
I love the desert.
Dusty, sandy, Land Rover!
Perfect solitude.

For Brazilians ROY RUDNICK and MICHELLE WEISS, life changed when they left for their first three-year, 160,000-km overland trip. From businessman and architect they became photographers, speakers and successful writers. They hit the road again in 2014 with other adventures in mind, as they won't stop exploring. 🖳 www.mundoporterra.com.br

Index

2WD 52-61
and 4WD 71
CV joints 54
dirt road driving 296
ground clearance 71, 159
modifications 158-160
transmission 54
wheels 71
4WD systems 76-78
diff locks 297
permanent 76
low-range 71, 298
wind-up 297, 303, 305
4x4 choice factors 80
crossing a ditch 300
cross rivers 304-306
mountain tracks 300
pickups 81
recovery gear 306
recovery 306-316
salt pans 302
sand 302
steep descents 301
training 297

AA of South Africa, 24
ABS 107
Abu Hamed, Sd 422
Abu Simbel, Eg 421
Abuja, Ng 411
accidents 26
dealing with 336
in India 396
jacking 289, 308
split rims 156
what to do 345
ADAC, Germany 24
Addis Ababa, Et 423
Aguas Verdes, Pr 454
air compressors 154
air filter 137
air-bag jacks 309
Aktau, Kz 370
Alchi, In 395
Algeria 407
Altai mtns, Ru 376
alternator 196
problems 284
altitude sickness 343
Amritsar, In 392
Amur Highway, Ru 378
Angola 418
anti-lock braking, see
ABS
anxiety 256, 341
Aqaba, Jd 368
Arabic numerals 408
Argentina 461-463
Armenia 369
Arusha, Tn 428

Ashgabat, Tm 488
Asia, main routes 365
Astara, Ir 486
Aswan, Eg 421
Atar, Mr 408
Atari, In 392
ATF 36
Atlantic Route, Mk 407
Attabad lake, Pk 390
autogas 48-50
AWD trucks 116–132
awnings 185
Azerbaijan 368

Babusar Pass, Pk 389
Baja, Mx 440
Bakoumbe, Gb 416
Baku, Az 370
Baluchistan, Pk 387
Bam, Ir 386
BAM, Ru 376
Banza Sanda, DRC 417
bargaining 268
Bariloche, Ar 462
bashplate 141
batteries 197-199
problems 281
welding 287
Bazargan, Ir 385
Beitbridge, Zi 434
Belize 441
Benapole, In 392
Benin 411
Bhairawa, Np 392
Birganj, Np 392
Bitam, Gb 413
bites and stings 339
black market 267
Uz, 380
Boa Vista, Bz 464
Bokhara, Uz 383
Bolivia 457
Boma, DRC 417
border
Angola-Namibia 419
Arg-Brazil 461
Arg-Chile 461, 462
Benin-Nigeria 411
Bolivia-Chile 459
Brazil-Guyana 465
Brazil-Peru 469
Cameroon-Congo 413
Chile-Argentina 459
Col-Ecuador 452
Col-Venezuela 464
Costa Rica 444
DRC-Angola 418
Ecuador-Peru 453
Egypt (Sinai) 368
Egypt-Sudan 421
Ethiopia-Kenya 424

border (cont'd)
Gabon-Congo 413
Guatemala 441
Guyana-Suriname 466
Honduras 442
India-Bangaldesh 392
India-Nepal 392
India-Pakistan 392
Iran 385
Iran–Pakistan 386
Kenya-Tan 426, 428
Mauritania-Sen 408
Mexico-Belize 441
Mongolia-Russia 402
Morocco-Maur 408
Moz-RSA 433
Moz-Tanzania 433
Nepal-China 397
Nigeria-Cam 411
Pakistan-China 387
Russia 372
South Korea 379
Tanzania-Malawi 430
Tanzania-Zambia 430
Turkey–Iran 385
US-Mexico 436, 440
Zambia-Botswana 431
Zambia-Zim 432
Zimbabwe-RSA 434
borders 264-266
Caucasus 369, 370
Central Asia, 380
Latin America 435
Southeast Asia 401
with dog 359
brakes, air 60
Brazil 467-470
Brazzaville, Cn 413
Bremach 121
bribes 23
at borders 264
Caspian ferry 370
Central Asia 383
Honduras 442
Russia 375
Bucher Duro 121
budget 14
Buenos Aires, Ar 463
Bulawayo, Zi 432
Burkina Faso 410
Burma 401
burns and scalds 340
Busan, SK 365, 379
butane 210

cabin, building 237-246
cassette toilet 234
condensation 231, 239, 240, 245
demountable 69
electrical power 230

cabin (cont'd)
  fabricating 237
    materials 238-241
  Grand Erg Gobi 71
  GRP 224
  heating and ventilation
    230, 232, 254, 254
  hot and cold water
    232, 249-253
  insulation 246
  layout 229
  mounting, 242-244
  roof hatch 235
  security 236
  shower and toilet 230
  to cab access 222
  water, 230
Cabinda (An) 413
cab-over flatbed
  pickups 59
Cairo, Eg 421
Calabar, Ng 411
Cambodia 399
Cameroon 412
campervan 56, 66-68
camping 277
  tables and chairs 207
  wild 163, 182, 277
  wild Central Asia 383
  wild, solo women 263
  with dog 362
CAN BUS 42
Cape Maclear, Mw 431
caravans 63
Carawagon 72
carnet 24
  Africa 406
  Iran 385
  Latin America 435
Carretera Austral, Cl
  460
Cartagena, Cm 446
cash 26
Caspian Sea 370
Caucasus 368–370
Cayenne, FG 466
CdP see 'carnet'
cell phones 269
Central Asia 379–383
Chad 407, 408
Chaiten, Cl 460
chassis number 23
  torsion 224-228
Chevrolet van 55, 68
Chilas, Pk 389
children, overlanding
  with 352-358
Chile 459
China 392
Chirundu, Za 432
Chitral, Pk 390
Chobe, Bt 431
Citroen Berlingo 59
city strategies, driving,
  261

climate, Asia 366
  South America 450
clutch, testing 141
  wear 281
Cochrane, Cl 460
Colombia 449-451, 464
Colon, Pn 444
common-rail diesel
  injection 45
communications
  269-271
compass 275
compressors (tyres) 154
condensation 231, 239,
  240, 245
container dimensions 41
cooking and eating 207-
  217
  equipment list 217
  ovens 212
  stoves 209-212
  wood fire 212
cool box (Esky) 216
corrosion, aluminium to
  steel 239
Costa Rica 444
crawl-through hatch 223
CRD 45
culture shock 256, 345
currency 26
Cusco, Pr 455, 456, 469
customs declaration
  form, Uz 380
CV joints 41
Cyrillic alphabet 371

Dalbandin, Pk 387
dampers 146
Dar es Salaam, Tn 429
Darien Gap 445
Death, road of, Bv 457
DFAG cab-over 60
diarrhoea 337
diesel 44–50
  heater 72
  injection 44
  quality 47-50
  bio 50
  fuel-injection pumps
    45
  sulphur in 47-50
  particulate filter 47
  water separator 45
  -powered heaters 253
differential (4WD) 75, 77
  limited-slip 77
directions, asking 276
documents 13
  back-up 25
  currency declaration
    forms 267
  travel 18-22
  vaccination (ICV) 331
  vehicle 22–26
Dodge Ram 70

dogs, overlanding with
  358-363
Dogubajazit, Tk 385
Dolosie 413
Donghae, SK, 379
Dongola, Sd 422
downplating (GVW) 69
DRC 417, 430
driving abroad 258-264
  dirt roads 293-316
  licence 23
  4WD 296-316
  city strategies 261
  crossing a ditch 300
  crossing rivers 304-306
  flash flood 305
  lights 142
  local customs 259
  recovery 306-316
  road accident 346
  sharing 261
  solo women 262
  why left or right 260
DTC 43
dual-wheel rear axles 61
Dushanbe, Tm 383
dust 139, 299
dysentery 338

EarthRoamer 123
ECU 42-43, 59, 101
  error codes 280
Ecuador 452
EGR valve 47
Egypt 420
Ekok, Cm 411
El Salvador 443
Eldoret, Kn 427
electrical power 195-207
  motorhome 67
  24-volt systems 198
  alternator 196
  batteries 197-199
  battery charger 201
  battery isolator 247
  calculating
    consumption 204
  generators 205
  inverters 205
  problems, 195
  solar panels 201-203
  split-charge systems
    200
  useful equations 205
  voltage sensitive
    relays 202
  water pumps 248
electronic sensors 78
  traction control, see ETC
embassies 15
emergencies 345
  communications 270
  survival 351
engine oil 137
  air compressors 155

engine oil *(cont'd)*
  air filters 137
  assessing 136
  bashplate 141
  cooling system 136
  Cummins 60, 121
  extra cooling fan 136
  OM352 Mercedes 126
  OM617 Mercedes 56
  raised air-intake 139
equator, Brazil 467
  Gabon, 413
  Kenya 425, 427
Esendere, Tk 385
ETC 78, 102
Ethiopia 423
fault diagnosis 280
  table 282-3
  by smell 286
  by sound 286
ferries, Amazon 468, 469
ferry, Baja-mainland Mx
    440
  Brazza-Kinshasa
    (DRC) 417
  Caspian Sea 370
  French Guiana-Bz 466
  Guyana-Suriname 466
  Israel 421
  Jordan Egypt 368
  Lake Kariba, Zi 433
  Luozi-Banza (DRC)
    417
  Macapa-Belem (Bz)
    467
  Morocco 408
  Punta Arenas, Ar 463
  Punta Delgada Ar 463
  Punta Natales, Cl 461
  Rovuma river, Mz 433
  Russia-Korea 379
  Russia-South Korea,
    379
  Suriname-Fr Gui 466
Zambezi river 431
fiche 266
fire extinguisher 209
first-aid kit 333
food, hygiene 335
Ford Frieda 68
Ranger 68
Transit Connect 59
forward-control flatbed
  pickups 59
Fotu La pass, In 395
four-wheel drive, *see*
  4WD
Franceville, Gb 413, 416
fridge-freezers 214-216
fuel 44–50
  Caucasus 368
  India 396
  sedimentor 140
  Africa 405

fuel *(cont'd)*
  Angola 418
  autogas 48-50
  bio-diesel 50
  Bolivia 457
  Central America 440
  Central Asia 383
  CNG 48-50
  cooking oil 50
  custom tanks 169
  diesel or petrol 48-59
  Egypt 421
  filters 140
  French Guiana 466
  gasoline 48-50
  interior tanks 168
  Iran 385
  jerricans 165–167
  Latin America 440
  long range 164–175
  lorry tanks 168
  LPG 48-50
  Malawi, 431
  Mexico and CA 440
  Morocco 408
  oil drum 168
  petrol 48-50
  plastic tanks 170
  range/capacity 164
  Russia 374
  Rwanda 429
  South America 450
  Southeast Asia 403
  southern Africa 434
  Uganda 428
  underbody tanks 171
  waste oil 50
  world prices 14

gas, bottled 67, 210
gasoline 48-50
gearbox 36
  wear 141, 281
generators 206
Georgetown, Gy 465
Georgia 368
giardia 338
Gilgit, Pk 389
GMC G20 van 68
Google Maps 264
gov't overseas depts 15
GPS devices 271, 274
ground clearance 145
graphic 40
GRP cabin 70, 224
  panels 239-241
  waffles 312
GSM phones 269
Guatemala 441
guidebooks 18
Guyana 465
GVW 33-35, 69
  and licensing 69
  trucks 118

Harare, Zi 433
hassle 256
health 330-345
heat-related illness 338
hi-lift jack 290, 308
Honda Element 68
Honduras 442
HSD 47-50
Huaquillas, Ec 453
Humaita, Bz 468, 469
Hunza valley, Pk 390
Hwange, Zi 432
Hymer motorhome 67
hypothermia 342

ICMV 24
ICV 331
IDP 23
Illeret, Kn 424
India 391-397
Indonesia 403
insulation, cabin 224
insurance
  Africa 406
  Argentina 461
  Belize, 441
  Bolivia 457
  Botswana 431
  Caucasus 369
  Central Asia 381
  Chile 459, 460
  Colombia 446, 451
  Costa Rica 444
  Ecuador 452
  French Guiana 466
  Guyana 465
  Honduras 442
  Kenya 425
  Malawi 431
  medical 21
  Mexico 436, 440
  motor 346
  Mozambique 433
  Nicaragua 443
  Peru, 453
  Russia 373
  Senegal 410
  South Africa 434
  South America 457, 461
  Southeast Asia 401
  Suriname 466
  travel 21, 333, 345
  Uganda 428
int'l cert of motor vehicles 24
int'l driving permit 23
intercoolers 46
internet, on the road 269
inverters 205
Iran 384-386
Iridium 270
Irkeshtam Pass, Ch 380
Irkutsk, Ru 377
Israel 368
Isuzu N-series 59, 131

Japan 379
jerricans 165–167

Kadykchan, Ru 377
Kakheti, Gg 368
Kampala, Ug 428
Karachi, Pk 387
Karakoram Highway
  388-391, 398
Kargil, In 394
Karimabad, Pk 390
Kashgar, Ch 391, 398
Kathmandu, Np 397
Kazakhstan 380
Kazungula, Za 431
Kelem, Et 424
Kenya 107, 425
KERR recovery 307
Keylong, In 395
Khabarovsk, Ru 378
Khandyga, Ru 377
Khardung La, In 395
Khartoum, Sd 422
Khiva, Uz 383
Khunjerab Pass, Ch 387
kids, taking 352-358
Kifl, Az 368
Kikwit, DRC 418
Kilimanjaro, Tn 428
Kinkala, Cn 417
Kinshasa, DRC 418
kitchen, equip't list 217
Kolwezi, DRC 418
Kolyma hwy, Ru 377
Korea, 379
Kyrgyzstan 380
Kyubueme, Ru 377

La Cumbre pass, Bv 457
La Paz, Bv 457
Ladakh, In 394
Lagodekhi, Az 370
Lahic, Az 368
LAK cabin 237
Lake Victoria, Ug 428
Land Rover 37, 72,
  93-108
  in US 99
  roof racks 192
  Discovery 109-111
  Puma, Africa 104-108
  TdV6 111
  vs Toyota 106
  Puma engines 104
  Td5 101-103, 110
  Tdi 97-101, 110
  underbody tanks 171
Laos 399
Leh, In 395
Lekoni, Gb 416
Lemombo, RSA 433
Lethem, Gy 465
Lexus LX470 92
Leyland DAF 120

Lhasa, Ch 397
lighting, in vehicle 207
Lilongwe, Mw 431
Lima, Pr 454
lost, not getting 276
LPG 48-50
Luanda, An 419
Lulumbashi, DRC 418
Luobomo, Cn 417
Luozi 417
Lusaka, Za 430
LWB 80

Macapa, Bz, 466, 470
Macara, Ec 454
Machu Piccu, Pr 455
Magadan, Ru 377
malaria 332, 340
Malaysia 399
Mali 410
MAN 118, 238
  8.136 126
  KAT 118
  LE 10 220 120, 122
Manali, In 395
Manaus, Bz 464, 468,
  469, 470
map: Overland Zone 11
  world languages 12
  Latin America 438
  far eastern Asia 378
  India and China 393
  north Africa 414
  South America 448
  southeast Asia 400
  southern Africa 427
  west Asia 366
  LHD countries 260
maps 271-275
  Argentina 461
  Central Asia, 379
  Bolivia 457
  Chile 459
  Colombia 451
  India 393
  locating position 273
  Mexico 440
  Pakistan 388
  Russia 374
  Southeast Asia 399
Marsabit, Kn 425
Matadi, DRC 417
mats, recovery 311
Mauritania 408
Mazda B2500 58, 68
Mbalam, Cm 413
Mbinda, Cn 416
Mendoza, Ar 461, 462
Mercedes 37
  1017 117, 120
  190 53
  814 224
  911 116
  MG-Wagen 112

Mercedes (cont'd)
  Sprinter 67, 68, 123
  Unimog 67, 124-126
  vans 56
  Vario 59
Mexico 436-440
microwave ovens 212
MIL 43
Mila-Mila, Cn 416
Mindouli, Cn 417
minibuses 58
Mitsubishi Fuso 120,
  129-131
Mlibizi, Zi 433
mobile phones 269
Mombasa, Kn 426
money 14, 26–28
  ATMs 267
  black market 267
  changing 267
Mongolia 402
Montevideo, Ur 463
Morocco 408
motor insurance 26
motor oil 137
motoring orgs 18
motorhomes 65
Moyale, Kn 425
Mozambique 433
MPV 58
Myanmar 401

Nairobi, Kn 425
Namanga, Tn 428
Namibia 419
navigation 275-277
Nazca, Pr 456
Nepal 392, 397
Nicaragua 443
Nigeria 411
Nissan Cabstar 59
  Elgrand 68
  Kubistar 59
  Patrol 114
Nouakchott, Mr 408

OBD ll reader 42
Oiapoque, Bz 466
oil cooler, ATF 36
Omo valley, Et 424
Omorate, Et 424
on-board diagnostics 42
Oshikango, Nm 419
Ouesso, Cn 412
ovens 212
overlanding shows, 220
overloading 134
Oymyakon, Ru 377
Oyo, Cn 413, 416

packing 186-194
Pakistan 387-391
Pamir Highway, Tj 381
Panama 444

Paraguay 463
Paramaribo, Sr 466
paranoia 256
Passu, Pk 390
Patagonia, Ar 462
payload 33-35
  and licensing 69
  chassis flex 224
people carriers 58
Peru 454
Peshawar, Pk 388
petrol 48-50
Peugeot Partner 59
pickups, double-cab 115
Pinzgauer 121
Pirali, Ch 391, 398
planning 10–14
  graphic 13
  test run 255
Pointe-Noire, Cn 416
Pokhara, Np 397
Pokola, Cn 413
police, trouble 350
Port Klang (KL) My 365
Port Vostochny, Ru 377
portal axle 40
Pt Maldonado, Pr 469
Porto Velho, Bz 469, 469
Potosi, Bv 458
privacy 277
propane 210
powered heaters 253
PSP 310
P'to Montt, Cl 460, 461
Punta Arenas, Ar 463
Punta Delgada Ar 463
Punta Natales, Cl 461

Quetta, Pk 387
Quito, Ec 452
Qustul, Eg 421

rabies 331
Range Rover 105
Raxaul, In 392
rear doors 56
rec' vehicles 64-71
redundancy 134
rehydration 337
Renault Kangoo 59
repairs, battery welding 287
  inner tube 291
  improvised 280
  tyre 289-292
repatriation 21, 345
Ressano-Garcia, Mz, 433
road cars 52
roads, short history 471
robbery 348
Rohtang La pass 395
roof access 194
  bars 194
  racks 192-194
  tents (RTTs) 179-181

ropes, snatch (recovery) 307
ro-ro shipping 319
Russia 371-379
Russian alphabet 371
rust, Mercedes vans 56
Ruta 40, Ar 462
RVs 64-71
Rwanda Burundi 429

safety, in cities 348
Sahara 407
sailing, Panama-
  Cartagena 447
Salar de Uyuni, Bv 458
Samarkand, Uz 383
San Pedro de Atacama,
  Cl 458, 460, 461
Sanata Cruz, Bv 458
sand plates and mats 310-313
Sangha river, Cn 413
satellite phones 270
satnavs 274
seasons 11
security 277
  wild camping 182
sedimentor 45, 140
Senegal 410
Shandur Pass, Pk 390
shipping 317-330
  container size 41, 320
  documents 321
  best ports 329
  Europe-South Am 470
  flat rack 323
  glossary 328-330
  insurance 326
  main routes 325
  Panama-Col 445-447
  Paramaribo, Sr 466
  Southeast Asia 401
  Montevideo, Ur 470
  Vladivostok, Ru 379
Shiraz, Ir 385
shock absorbers 146
Sikaflex and 3M
  sealants 242
SIM card 269
Singapore 365, 399
Skardu, Pk 389
sleeping, beds 184
  roof tents 179-181
  in vehicle 176
snorkel 139
SOAPEX insurance 460
SOAT, 446
Socambo, Cn 413
solar panels 201-203
Songololo, An 417
Sost, Pk 390
South Africa selling
  vehicle 434
South Korea 379
sponsorship 27
Sportsmobile 66, 123

Spot tracker 271
Srinagar, In 394
station wagon 64, 80
storage 186-194
stoves 209-212
stress 256, 341
Sucre, Bv 421, 458, 463
Sudan 422
Sunauli, In 392
survival situations 351
suspension 41, 143-147
  broken 280
  2WD 159
  SUVs 79
Suyo, Pr 453
SWB 80
synthetic oil 137

Taftan, Pk 387
Tajikistan 380
tanks (fuel,water) 170
Tashkent, Uz 383
Tashkurgan, Ch 391, 398
Tatra 117
Tbilisi, Gg 368, 369
Teheran, Ir 386
temp vehicle
  importation permit 24
Thailand 399, 401
Thuraya 270
Tibet 397
toolkit list 288
torsion-free subframe,
  trucks 123
Torugurt Pass, Ch 380
tow ropes 307
towing points 307
trailers 62-64
Toyota 37
  40 series 83
  60 series 84
  75 series 87
  80 series 85
  100/200 series 87
  Dyna 59
  Granvia 68
  Hi-Ace 58
  Hilux 70, 92
  HZJ78/79 90
  HZJ79 69
  Land Cruiser 82-92
  Prado 91, 92
  Regius 68
  Tacoma 92
  Troop Carrier 68, 181, 183
  vs Land Rover 106
Trabzon, Tk 368
trackers, GPS 271
Tracks4Africa 412
traction 78, 294, 297
trailers 62-64
transmission 36
  assessing 141
  wear 281

truck, Iveco 60
  MAN KAT 228
  Mercedes Unimog 226
  Saviem flatbed 60
  AWD 116–132
tubeless tyres 292
Tumbez, Pr 454
Tunduma, Za 429
turbo diesels 45
Turkey 365
Turkmenbashi, Tm 370
Turkmenistan, escort 380
TVIP 24
  Belize 441
  Ecuador 452
  Ethiopia 423
  Guatemala 441
  Latin America 435
  Malawi, 431
  Mexico 436, 440
  Russia 373
  Tanzania 426
two-wheel drive *see* 2WD
tyre aspect ratio 148
  and wheels 147-154
  changing 290
  deflating 154, 295
  dimensions 148, 152
  dual, rear 61
  in sand 303
  inner tube repair 291
  load speed ratings 149
  oversize 153
  pliers 290
  pressures 294
  pumps 154
  repairs 151, 289-292
  size, 2WD 159
  taller 2WD, 159
  tread pattern 153
  truck 119
  tubeless or tubed 151

Uganda 428
Ulan Ude, Ru 377
ULSD 47-50
Ulugrabat Pass, Ch 391
Unimog 67
Uruguay 463
Ust Nera, Ru 377
Uyuni, Bv 458
Uzbekistan 380

vaccinations 331
Vanino, Ru 376
vans 55-59
  light commercial 59
vehicle, A-class
  motorhomes 65
  access and storage 163
  factors 32-41
  clearance 39-41
  repairs 280
  jacks 308-310

vehicle, A-class *(cont'd)*
  lighting 142
  maintenance kit 288
  maintenance log 135
  minibus 68
  MPV 68
  ownership doc 23
  packing 186-194
  parts number list 135
  payload 33-36
  push starts 287
  recovery, 313-315
  recreational 64-71
  regional differences 37
  regular checks 279
  selling in RSA 434
  spare parts 135
  spares list 288
  title 23
  transmission type 36
  troubleshooting
    279-288
  where to sleep 176-184
  workshop manual 135
Venezuela 464
  via, Chile 459
Victoria Falls, Zi 432
Vietnam 399
VIN 23
visas, Angola 411, 418
  Argentina 461
  Azerbaijan 370
  Benin 410
  Bolivia 456
  Brazil 467
  Burkina Faso 410
  Burundi 429
  Cameroon 411, 419
  China 391, 398
  Congo 411, 419
  d'entente (West
    Africa) 410
  DRC 412, 419
  Ethiopia 421, 423
  Gabon 412, 419
  Ghana 410
  India 392
  Kenya 424
  Malawi 431
  Mali 408
  Mauritania 408
  Mexico 436, 440
  Mongolia 402
  Nepal 397
  Nigeria 410
  Russia 372
  Sudan 421
  Suriname 464
  Turkey 365
  Uganda 428
  Cambodia 403
  general 19–21
  Indonesia 403
  Iran 384

visas *(cont'd)*
  Kazakhstan 381, 488
  Kyrgyzstan 381
  Laos 403
  Malaysia 403
  Pakistan 387
  Singapore 403
  Tajikistan 381
  Thailand 401, 403
  Turkmenistan 381, 488
  Uzbekistan 381
Vladivostok, Ru 377
volcano kettle 213
voltmeter 285
VW Kombi 67
  pop-top 183
  T-series 57

Wadi Halfa, Sd 421
Wagah, Pk 392
water crossings 139
filter 250
water storage 172–175
water tanks 250
tanks, built in 175
  drinking 334
  flexible and bags 174
  heat exchanger 250
  plastic 173
weapons, self defence
  349
Webasto diesel heater 72
websites, ex-NATO
    trucks 119
  Mozambique 433
  planning 15
  southern Africa 434
  travel 15
welding repairs 287
Western Oases, Eg 421
Western Sahara 408
wheel changing 289-291
  rims 156
  2WD 159
  dual, rear 61
  spare 157
  split rims 156
  steel or alloy 156
wild camping 277
winch 316
Winnebago 65

Yakutsk, Ru 377
Yaounde, Cm 412
Yekaterinburg, Ru 376
Yellow fever 331

Zanskar, In 394
Zarubino, Ru, 379
Zimbabwe 431
Zoji La pass, In 394

TRAILBLAZER

Adventure Cycle-Touring Handbook
Adventure Motorcycling Handbook
Australia by Rail
Azerbaijan
Cleveland Way (British Walking Guide) – due 2018
Coast to Coast (British Walking Guide)
Cornwall Coast Path (British Walking Guide)
Cotswold Way (British Walking Guide)
The Cyclist's Anthology
Dales Way (British Walking Guide)
Dorset & Sth Devon Coast Path (British Walking Gde)
Exmoor & Nth Devon Coast Path (British Walking Gde)
Great Glen Way (British Walking Guide)
Hadrian's Wall Path (British Walking Guide)
Himalaya by Bike – a route and planning guide
Inca Trail, Cusco & Machu Picchu
Japan by Rail
Kilimanjaro – the trekking guide (includes Mt Meru)
Moroccan Atlas – The Trekking Guide
Morocco Overland (4WD/motorcycle/mountainbike)
Nepal Trekking & The Great Himalaya Trail
New Zealand – The Great Walks
North Downs Way (British Walking Guide) – due 2018
Offa's Dyke Path (British Walking Guide)
Overlanders' Handbook – worldwide driving guide
Peddars Way & Norfolk Coast Path (British Walking Gde)
Pembrokeshire Coast Path (British Walking Guide)
Pennine Way (British Walking Guide)
Peru's Cordilleras Blanca & Huayhuash – Hiking/Biking
The Railway Anthology
The Ridgeway (British Walking Guide)
Sahara Overland – a route and planning guide
Scottish Highlands – Hillwalking Guide
Siberian BAM Guide – rail, rivers & road
The Silk Roads – a route and planning guide
Sinai – the trekking guide
South Downs Way (British Walking Guide)
Thames Path (British Walking Guide)
Tour du Mont Blanc
Trans-Canada Rail Guide
Trans-Siberian Handbook
Trekking in the Everest Region
The Walker's Anthology
The Walker's Anthology – further tales
The Walker's Haute Route – Mont Blanc to Matterhorn
West Highland Way (British Walking Guide)

www.trailblazer-guides.com
ROUTE GUIDES FOR THE ADVENTUROUS TRAVELLER

ROUTES ACROSS
AFRICA

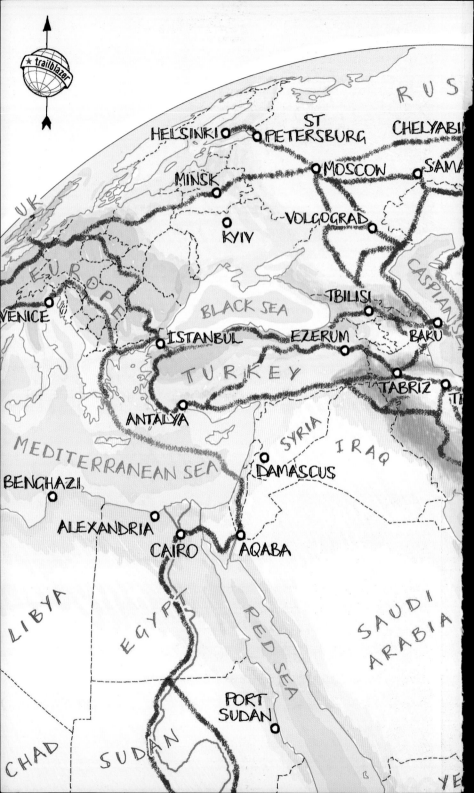